A HISTORY OF CALIFORNIA LITERATURE

EDITED BY
BLAKE ALLMENDINGER
UCLA

CAMBRIDGE
UNIVERSITY PRESS

32 Avenue of the Americas, New York, NY 10013-2473, USA

Cambridge University Press is part of the University of Cambridge.

It furthers the University's mission by disseminating knowledge in the pursuit of education, learning, and research at the highest international levels of excellence.

www.cambridge.org
Information on this title: www.cambridge.org/9781107052093

© Blake Allmendinger 2015

This publication is in copyright. Subject to statutory exception and to the provisions of relevant collective licensing agreements, no reproduction of any part may take place without the written permission of Cambridge University Press.

First published 2015

Printed in the United States of America

A catalog record for this publication is available from the British Library.

Library of Congress Cataloging in Publication Data
A history of California literature / edited by Blake Allmendinger.
pages cm
Includes bibliographical references and index.
ISBN 978-1-107-05209-3 (hardback)
1. American literature – California – History and criticism.   2. Literature and society – California.   3. California – Intellectual life.   4. California – In literature.   I. Allmendinger, Blake, editor.
PS283.C2H57   2015
810.9′9794–dc23   2015004549

ISBN 978-1-107-05209-3 Hardback

Cambridge University Press has no responsibility for the persistence or accuracy of URLs for external or third-party Internet Web sites referred to in this publication and does not guarantee that any content on such Web sites is, or will remain, accurate or appropriate.

A HISTORY OF CALIFORNIA LITERATURE

Blake Allmendinger's *A History of California Literature* surveys the paradoxical image of the Golden State as a site of dreams and disenchantment, formidable beginnings, and ruinous ends. This history encompasses the prismatic nature of California by exploring a variety of historical periods, literary genres, and cultural movements affecting the state's development, from the colonial era to the twenty-first century. Written by a host of leading historians and literary critics, this book offers readers insight into the tensions and contradictions that have shaped the literary landscape of California and also American literature generally.

BLAKE ALLMENDINGER is Professor of American Literature at the University of California, Los Angeles, where he specializes in literature of the American West. He is the author of *The Cowboy: Representations of Labor in an American Work Culture*, *Ten Most Wanted: The New Western Literature*, *Imagining the African American West*, and *The Melon Capital of the World: A Memoir*. He is also the coeditor of *Over the Edge: Remapping the American West* and has received fellowships from the American Council of Learned Societies and the National Endowment for the Humanities.

Contents

List of contributors   *page* ix

Introduction   1
Blake Allmendinger

PART I: BEGINNINGS

1 Tales of Native California   17
  Paul Apodaca

2 Indigenous Peoples under Colonial Rule   30
  Lisbeth Haas

3 Spanish and Mexican Literature   43
  Vincent Pérez

PART II: THE AMERICAN PRESENCE

4 White Explorers and Travelers   61
  David Wyatt

5 The Gold Rush   75
  Nicolas S. Witschi

6 California Nature Writers   88
  Steven Pavlos Holmes

PART III: CONTESTED SPACES

7 The Black Frontier   105
  Aparajita Nanda

8   California as Political Topography: Asian American Literature
    before 1980   123
    Catherine Fung

9   Mexican American Literature   139
    Manuel M. Martin-Rodriguez

PART IV: SOCIAL CHANGE AND LITERARY EXPERIMENTATION

10 The Protest Fiction of Frank Norris, Upton Sinclair,
    Jack London, and John Steinbeck   157
    Susan Shillinglaw

11 Dreams, Denial, and Depression-Era Fiction   171
    Jan Goggans

12 Modernism in the Early Twentieth Century   182
    Geneva M. Gano

13 The Hard-Boiled California Novel   199
    William Marling

PART V: ALTERNATIVE VOICES

14 Writing the Hidden California   215
    Phillip H. Round

15 The Beats   231
    Kurt Hemmer

16 Bay Area Poetics, 1944–1981   246
    Kaplan Page Harris

17 Los Angeles Poetry from the McCarthy to the Punk Eras   260
    Brian Stefans

PART VI: CREATING COMMUNITIES

18 African American Uprising   283
    Charles Toombs

19 Of Carnales and Coyotes: Chicana/o Literature of California   295
    Anne Goldman

20 Interracial Encounters: Face and Place in Post-1980
    Asian American Literature   309
    King-Kok Cheung

PART VII: THE SEARCH FOR UTOPIA

21 California and the Queer Utopian Imagination: 1981–2014   327
    Cael Keegan

22 Modern California Nature Writing   343
    Michael Kowalewski

23 Making California's Towns and Small Cities Visible in the
    Twenty-First Century   358
    Nancy S. Cook

24 Science Fiction and Mysterious Worlds   371
    Lynn Mie Itagaki

    Conclusion   385
    Blake Allmendinger

Bibliography   391
Index   413

Contributors

BLAKE ALLMENDINGER is a professor in the English Department at the University of California, Los Angeles. He is the author of *The Cowboy* (1992), *Ten Most Wanted* (1998), *Imagining the African American West* (2005), and *The Melon Capital of the World: A Memoir* (2014). He also coedited *Over the Edge: Remapping the American West* (1998).

PAUL APODACA is an associate professor in Sociology and American Studies at Chapman University. He has published numerous articles on Native American literature.

KING-KOK CHEUNG is a professor in the English Department at the University of California, Los Angeles. She is the author of *Articulate Silences* (1993). She has also edited *Asian American Literature: An Annotated Bibliography* (1988), *Seventeen Syllables* (1994), *An Interethnic Companion to Asian American Literature* (1996), and *Words Matter: Conversations with Asian American Writers* (2000).

NANCY S. COOK is an associate professor in the English Department at the University of Montana. She is co-president of the Western Literature Association and has published articles in numerous journals and critical anthologies.

CATHERINE FUNG is an assistant professor in English and Media Studies at Bentley University. She is working on a book entitled *The Complicit Refugee: Memory, Citizenship, and the Vietnam War*.

GENEVA M. GANO is an assistant professor of Literature at Antioch College. She has published numerous articles on modernism and the American West.

JAN GOGGANS is an associate professor in Social Sciences, Humanities, and Arts at the University of California, Merced. She is the author of *California on the Breadlines: Dorothea Lange, Paul Taylor, and the Making of a New Deal Narrative* (2010) and the coeditor of *The Pacific*

Region: The Greenwood Encyclopedia of American Regional Cultures (2004).

ANNE GOLDMAN is a professor in the English Department at Sonoma State University. She is the author of *Take My Word: Autobiographical Innovations of Ethnic American Working Women* (1996) and *Continental Divides: Revisioning American Literature* (2000). She also coedited *Maria Amparo Ruiz de Burton: Critical and Pedagogical Perspectives* (2004).

LISBETH HAAS is a professor in the History Department and chair of Feminist Studies at the University of California, Santa Cruz. She is the author of *Conquests and Historical Identities in California, 1769–1936* (1995); *Pablo Tac, Indigenous Scholar: Writing on Luiseño Language and Colonial History* (2011); and *Saints and Citizens: Indigenous Histories of Colonial Missions and Mexican California* (2014).

KAPLAN PAGE HARRIS is an associate professor in the English Department at St. Bonaventure University. He is the coeditor of *The Selected Letters of Robert Creeley* (2014) and the author of numerous articles on American poetry.

KURT HEMMER teaches in the English Department at Harper College. He is the editor of *The Encyclopedia of Beat Literature* (2007).

STEVEN PAVLOS HOLMES is an independent scholar whose books include *Young John Muir: An Environmental Biography* (1999) and *Facing the Change: Personal Encounters with Global Warming* (2013).

LYNN MIE ITAGAKI is as assistant professor in the Departments of English and Women's, Gender, and Sexuality Studies and the Program of Asian American Studies at Ohio State University. She is completing a book that examines the post–civil rights era in terms of the 1992 Los Angeles crisis.

CAEL KEEGAN is an assistant professor of Women and Gender Studies at Grand Valley State University. He is working on a book about Lana Wachowski and has published articles on LGBTQ history and literature.

MICHAEL KOWALEWSKI is the Lloyd McBride Professor of English and Environmental Studies at Carleton College. He is the author of *Deadly Musings: Violence and Verbal Form in American Fiction* (1993) and *Gold*

List of contributors xi

Rush: A Literary Exploration (1997). He also edited *Reading the West: New Essays on the Literature of the American West* (1996).

WILLIAM MARLING is a professor in the English Department at Case Western Reserve University. He is the author of *Dashiell Hammett* (1983), *Raymond Chandler* (1986), *The American Roman Noir* (2000), and books on William Carlos Williams, world literature, and globalization.

MANUEL M. MARTIN-RODRIGUEZ is a professor of Social Sciences, Humanities, and Arts at the University of California, Merced. He is the author of *Life in Search of Readers: Reading (in) Chicano/a Literature* (2003) and has edited the works of Gaspar de Villagrá and other Spanish-language writers.

APARAJITA NANDA is a lecturer at Santa Clara University. She edited *Black California: A Literary Anthology* (2011) and *Ethnic Literatures and Transnationalisim* (2014).

VINCENT PÉREZ is an associate professor in the English Department at the University of Nevada, Las Vegas. He is the author of *Remembering the Hacienda: History and Memory in the Mexican American Southwest* (2006).

PHILLIP H. ROUND is a professor in the English Department at the University of Iowa. He is the author of *By Nature and by Custom Cursed* (1999), *The Impossible Land* (2008), and *Removable Type* (2010).

SUSAN SHILLINGLAW is a professor in the English Department at San Jose State University. She is the author of *Carol and John Steinbeck: Portrait of a Marriage* (2013) and *On Reading* The Grapes of Wrath (2014). She has also coauthored *A Journey into Steinbeck's California* (2011).

BRIAN STEFANS is an assistant professor in the English Department at the University of California, Los Angeles. He has published numerous volumes of poetry, as well as essays on electronic literature.

CHARLES TOOMBS is an associate professor in Africana Studies at San Diego State University. He has published numerous articles and reviews on twentieth-century African American writers.

NICOLAS S. WITSCHI is a professor in the English Department at Western Michigan University. He is the author of *Traces of Gold* (2002) and

Alonzo "Old Block" Delano (2006). He also edited *A Companion to the Literature and Culture of the American West* (2011).

DAVID WYATT is a professor in the English Department at the University of Maryland. He is the author of *The Fall into Eden: Landscape and Imagination in California* (1990); *Five Fires: Race, Catastrophe, and the Shaping of California* (1999); *Secret Histories: Reading Twentieth-Century American Literature* (2010); and *Why America Turned: Reckoning with 1968* (2013).

Introduction

Blake Allmendinger

When I taught my first course on California literature in the early 1990s, I was an assistant professor in the English Department at the University of California, Los Angeles. At the time, it was one of the few such classes offered in the United States.

Today similar courses are taught at colleges and universities across the country. A front-page article published in the *Los Angeles Times* on January 2, 2012, claimed that the surging interest in California literature was due to "a new generation of students eager to explore the state's confluence of luxury and despair; of exploitation and reinvention."

People are fascinated by California because it represents the best and worst of America. Los Angeles is a hedonistic city. But it is also an example of well-regulated capitalism, a corporate town filled with employees who work in "the industry." San Francisco is one of the nation's most popular tourist destinations, even though gay residents recently led a movement supporting public nudity. California attracts celebrities, refugees, minorities, faddists, religious fanatics, surf bums, environmental activists, and visionary entrepreneurs. It is the land of fruits and nuts, but also the home of Silicon Valley; a blue state with a large number of conservative voters; a prelapsarian Eden with apocalyptic weather conditions. A character in Don DeLillo's *White Noise* (1985) explains why he hates California: "Mud slides, brush fires, coastal erosion, earthquakes, mass killings, et cetera. We can relax and enjoy these disasters because in our hearts we feel that California deserves what it gets. Californians invented the concept of life-style. This alone warrants their doom."

This comment illustrates the love–hate relationship people have with the state. The only thing the speaker enjoys more than anticipating California's destruction is imagining how he would feel while watching it happen. The region has always been a blank slate for projecting other groups' frustrations and fantasies. In the sixteenth and seventeenth centuries, European novelists and cartographers envisioned California as an island off the Pacific Coast, populated by a race of female Amazonian warriors. Others romanticized the region, believing that California's indigenous tribes lived together in harmony prior to the arrival of the white man. In fact, California was neither a violent kingdom nor the terrestrial paradise of popular lore.

Unlike much of the nineteenth-century American West, which was characterized as the Great American Desert, California was believed to be blessed with untold natural resources and an ideal climate. Chinese miners referred to California as Gold Mountain. Tourists and invalids considered it an alternative to the Mediterranean. They ventured there seeking relaxation and better health. Mexican immigrants call it El Norte, "The North." For them, it represented better living conditions and job opportunities.

The film industry moved from the East Coast to California in the early twentieth century. The state's geographic diversity – its spectacular deserts, mountains, and beaches – provided directors with a greater variety of outdoor settings. Once a blank slate, California now became a giant projection screen, a fictional substitute for other places.

California is a place of contradictions. It is the endpoint of Manifest Destiny, the land of eternal sunshine and youth. At times, the entire state seems like a gated community inhabited by wealthy celebrities. However, California is also associated with boom–bust economies and nightmarish dystopias. Its various geographical districts and diverse constituents are perpetually at odds with each other. Hardly a day goes by without the northern part of the state threatening to break away from the south, or the San Fernando Valley threatening to secede from Los Angeles. For every success story there are a hundred cautionary tales of disaster, thousands of "actors" waiting tables in Beverly Hills. It's surprising that the state remains the number one destination for immigrants from around the world, considering the race riots and urban unrest, the high cost of living, and lack of good jobs in the post-recession economy.

The literature does nothing to burnish the state's reputation. Nathanael West once proclaimed that "people came to California to die." Most narratives about the region aren't as dire as *The Day of the Locust* (1939), though they often portray California in an unflattering light. The Mexican ranching elite lead a privileged existence in Helen Hunt Jackson's *Ramona* (1884). But they are supported by the labor of indigenous slaves. In T. C. Boyle's *The Tortilla Curtain* (1995), a white upper-middle-class couple and their poor Mexican counterparts come to California to realize their dreams. But a series of natural and man-made catastrophes leave their fortunes in doubt at the end of the novel.

Americans are known for their optimism. Yet, our national literature seldom reflects this aspect of our character. A student once asked me why there are no happy endings in American literature. Perhaps it's our New England heritage. The Puritans were known for their work ethic, not their cheerful dispositions. In "The Significance of the Frontier in American History" (1893), Frederick Jackson Turner anxiously wondered what would happen once the frontier disappeared and pioneers had no more horizons to conquer. Turner portrayed westward expansion as a laborious endeavor, but also as a sign of God's providential design.

In reality, most Americans who went West weren't seeking religious affirmation. They were looking for adventure or a chance to strike it rich. California was originally occupied by non-Christian natives, and later by Catholic Spaniards and Mexicans. In American literature, there is a sense that the region is resistant to Puritan values and Protestant notions of progressive reform.

The Puritan fear of Native Americans was reflected in Indian captivity narratives. The natives on the West Coast were peaceful. They had been subdued by earlier colonial powers before whites arrived in the region. Visitors worried about succumbing to idleness in a land where it was possible to thrive without expending much physical energy. In *Two Years before the Mast* (1840), Richard Henry Dana noted the indolence of locals, as well as the enervating weather. Dana's lament was echoed by twentieth-century European and English expatriates and by American writers who came to Hollywood, lured by the promise of a fat payday. Many of them drank themselves to death or frittered their talents away.

If history is written by the winners, perhaps literature is written by the losers – by people who have no other way to protest the official narrative sanctioned by society. Many regional writers challenge the notion that California is a metaphorical pot of gold at the end of the rainbow. It is an exceptional place, but one where people seem predestined to fail. The literature of the Gold Rush era is filled with depictions of unlucky miners. Naturalist writers such as Frank Norris, Jack London, and Upton Sinclair are haunted by a sense of fatality. Literary noir is synonymous with cynicism and existential angst. Most hard-boiled detective novels are set in California, the fashionable dwelling place of despair.

Because California produces a vast percentage of the world's popular culture, it is often considered an intellectual wasteland. Hollywood blockbusters, amateur singing competitions, the manufactured fame of the Kardashian family – the reasons to loathe California are endless. But

California's writers are a more serious lot, concerned with the devastating effects of European and North American colonization, the cost of capitalism and the impact of industrialization, the misuse of the land and its resources, and the constant tension among the state's people and interest groups.

For some minorities and countercultural movements, like the Beats, regional modernists, and gay and lesbian writers, California is a place where personal fulfillment and artistic self-expression are possible. But as the essays in this anthology suggest, most writers portray California as a land of contestation and strife.

***

Wallace Stegner once claimed that California bears the same relation to the West as Florida does to the South – which is to say none at all. It is a state without a "regional" identity. There are very few westerns set in the California, for the same reason that there aren't any Indian captivity narratives. The formula western highlights the tension between opposing interest groups who struggle to control the early frontier. Indians versus whites. Ranchers versus sheepherders. Townspeople versus the railroad. The players vary from novel to novel, but the essential plot remains the same. California was tamed long before it was annexed as a United States territory. Its future as a state was in jeopardy for a mere two years, during the Mexican-American War (1846–48). Its acquisition seemed almost inevitable, a final sign of God's will, the last stage in the transcontinental journey of conquest and settlement.

California's reputation as the Golden State didn't become tarnished until the twentieth century. Industrialization, a continuing influx of immigrants, and increasing competition for the region's diminishing resources are among the many problems that have bedeviled the region. Instead of the western, which celebrates pioneer virtues and the triumph of white civilization, the genre most closely associated with California is noir. It features gritty depictions of urban life and a fatalistic view of human behavior. The state has also attracted science fiction writers, ranging from L. Ron Hubbard, the founder of Scientology, to African American novelists, and MacArthur Foundation Grant-winner Octavia Butler. All of their works comment on present-day California in an unflattering way. Their futuristic settings either reflect the contemporary ills of society or offer a hopeful alternative: an imaginary place where racism, class inequality, environmental pollution, and the exploitation of industrial workers no longer exist.

At a time when there is growing interest in global relations, comparative literatures, and diaspora studies, it might seem quaint to devote a volume of criticism to the literature of a particular state. The concept of a "state," with universally respected and theoretically controllable borders, is increasingly under siege in the twenty-first century. However, whether it is a mythical isle, part of a European or Mexican empire, a frontier territory, or the thirty-first state in the Union, California is a place uniquely worthy of study. It has the region's most culturally diverse population and a heterogeneous body of literature.

The History of California Literature offers a chronological survey of writers, cultures, literary genres, and regional movements that have flourished from the Native American period through the early twenty-first century. Part I, "Beginnings," features a selection of indigenous folktales from northern, central, and southern California. It includes the oral memoirs and writings of Indians and Mexicans living under European colonial rule, and concludes with a study of the Mexican era, ending in 1848.

The pre-contact period in native California lasted approximately 12,000 years. It ended with the arrival of Spanish explorers in 1509. Catholic priests collected stories from hundreds of tribes that lived in the area, starting in the late eighteenth century. Later enthnographers discovered that different indigenous peoples had their own folkloric histories. Tribes in northern California produced "earth diver" myths about animals that dove into a primordial sea to retrieve mud with which to build the earth. Those in the central region believed the trickster figure Coyote played a pivotal role in California's creation. The Three Brothers myth was popular among tribes in the south and posited the notion that twin divinities brought the world to fruition. Paul Apodaca analyzes a selection of these narratives in English translation.

Native Americans also produced oral memoirs and wrote autobiographies describing their lives under colonial rule. Pablo Tac, a member of the Luiseño tribe, was educated by Franciscan friars during the Mission era. He wrote a critical account of the Spanish entitled *Indian Life and Customs at Mission San Luis Rey* (1835). Other members of the Luiseño, Chumash, and Ohlone tribes told similar tales of oppression. Lisbeth Haas shows how these subjects asserted their humanity by contesting the European notion of Indians as ungodly savages.

Vincent Pérez considers literature from the Spanish and Mexican periods, beginning in 1796 when the Catholic Church established its first mission in California, and ending in 1848 with the conclusion of the

Mexican-American War. The literature from this period includes Francisco Paluo's biography, *The Life and Apostolic Labors of the Venerable Junipero Serra* and his *Historical Memoirs of New California*; the diaries of the Spanish explorer Juan Bautista de Anza and Francisco Garces; the autobiography of Mexican rancher Mariano Guadalupe Vallejo; and the novels of Maria Amparo Ruiz de Burton. The essay ends with an examination of Helen Hunt Jackson's *Ramona*, published in 1884, which retrospectively romanticized the Mission era.

Part II, "The American Presence," focuses on early nineteenth-century tourists, mountain men, and military officials who visited or lived in the region; on miners who came to California between the late 1840s and mid-1870s; and on environmental writers who later celebrated the state's varied landscapes and argued for the creation of national parks. As David Wyatt notes, whites who arrived here in the early nineteenth century were uninspired by the landscape and contemptuous of the region's inhabitants. In *Two Years before the Mast* (1840), Richard Henry Dana found the tropical coast disagreeable, and characterized the natives as sluggards who scarcely earned their keep. Mountain man Zenas Leonard dismissed Yosemite Valley and referred to the Spanish as stupid in his autobiography published in 1839. James Ohio Pattie expressed similar sentiments in his *Personal Narrative* (1831), written by Timothy Flint. So did mountain man James Clyman and Monterey's *alcade* Walter Colton, in their respective memoirs and diaries. Eventually, however, these men came to appreciate the California frontier.

Immigrants from all over the world flooded into the region after the discovery of gold at Sutter's Mill in 1848. Those who failed to strike it rich wrote about their misadventures, their encounters with people of other races, and their observations of camp life. Nicholas Witschi sifts through letters, poems, diaries, newspaper articles, magazines, and books published during the Gold Rush, from the late 1840s to the mid-1870s. Among the collected gems are Louise Clappe's *The Shirley Letters* (1851–52), John Rollin Ridge's *The Life and Adventures of Joaquín Murieta* (1854), Bret Harte's *The Luck of Roaring Camp and Other Tales* (1868), and Mark Twain's *Roughing It* (1872).

Decades of intensive mining triggered a movement to preserve the state's natural resources in the late nineteenth century. Geologist Clarence King published *Mountaineering in the Sierra Nevada* in 1872. John Muir, the first president of the Sierra Club, argued that the state's varied landscapes were crucial to California's identity in a series of books written between 1874 and 1916. According to Steven Pavlos Holmes, Muir also worked with

Theodore Roosevelt to oppose the damming of the Hetch Hetchy River in Yosemite National Park. Although Mary Austin didn't seek publicity for her environmental causes, her classic *The Land of Little Rain* (1903) offers a nuanced depiction of drylands ecology. Robinson Jeffers shunned the limelight as well. Yet, he attracted national attention by writing poems about nature in the 1920s and 1930s.

Part III, "Contested Spaces," chronicles the struggles of African Americans, Chicana/os, and Asian Americans from the frontier era through the mid-twentieth century. During this time, discriminatory acts of legislation were passed against minorities, including the Chinese Exclusion Act (1882) and the Alien Land Law (1913). However, it was also a period of literary innovation and political rebellion, as witnessed by the growth of the West Coast branch of the Harlem Renaissance and the 1965 Watts Riot.

African Americans viewed California as a land of opportunity. Emancipated slaves worked as cowboys, miners, and trappers in the middle and late nineteenth century. Thousands migrated to the West Coast during World War II, seeking employment in the aerospace and shipbuilding industries. Believing that the state was free from the racism prevalent in others parts of the country, they discovered that many cities were unofficially segregated and that minorities had limited economic and social mobility. The rising discontent among California's black population led to urban protests during the Civil Rights era. Aparajita Nanda traces the evolution and politicization of the African American West, examining works by long forgotten contributors to the state's cultural heritage.

Asian Americans encountered similar obstacles when they came to California. Chinese laborers were confined to ethnic ghettos. Immigrants at Angel Island were held indefinitely or returned to their homelands after the passage of the Chinese Exclusion Act in 1882. Asian Americans were prevented from purchasing farms starting in 1913, while Japanese Americans were placed in internment camps during World War II. Minorities claimed a space for themselves in the 1960s and 1970s, according to Catherine Fung, who chronicles the quest for racial solidarity and political freedom in early Asian American literature.

Frederick Jackson Turner claimed that the U.S. frontier ended in 1890, when the census determined that the nation had settled most of the land in the region. The same year marked the publication of Adolfo R. Carrillo's memoir, which represents the beginning of Mexican American literature in California. Carrillo, an exiled Mexican journalist, wrote about the northern migration of his people and their adaptation to the region. Some descendants of the nineteenth-century Californios reflected nostalgically on their illustrious past, while others rejected the pastoral romanticism associated with the Spanish missions and Mexican ranchos. Political refugees entered the state during the Mexican Revolution (1910–20) and focused on the cultural differences between recent arrivals and "*pochos*" or assimilated Mexican immigrants. They also defended the urban working class in their proletarian literature. Manuel M. Martin-Rodriguez argues that Emanuel J. Camarena's *Pancho* (1958) represents the end of the Mexican American period. The novel appeared on the eve of the agricultural strikes that would lead to the rise of the Chicana/o movement in the following decade.

Part IV, "Social Change and Literary Experimentation," deals with a time of economic upheaval and artistic rebellion. Advances in technology and rapid industrialization caused modernist writers to rethink their relationship to the material world in the early decades of the twentieth century. Social protest novels written by Jack London, Frank Norris, and Upton Sinclair began to appear during this time. The "crisis of modernity" came to a head in the 1920s and 1930s. John Steinbeck, a popular writer, and emerging modernist poets critiqued capitalism and wove socialist themes into their works. Hard-boiled detective writers offered the harshest assessment of modern society, depicting California as the cataclysmic endpoint of Manifest Destiny.

Ramona condemned California's treatment of Native Americans, but its love story encouraged readers to view it as a sentimental romance. Later authors, writing in a naturalistic vein, offered a bleaker portrait of the region in the early twentieth century, as Susan Shillinglaw indicates. Norris criticized railroad oligarchies in *The Octopus* (1901). London's dystopian novel, *The Iron Heel* (1908), examined the rise of a tyrannical government. Much of the action takes place in the Bay Area and Sonoma County. *Oil!* (1927), by Sinclair, focuses on the exploitation of the region's resources. Most famously, Steinbeck's *The Grapes of Wrath* (1939) called attention to the exploitation of farm workers, big business, technology, and the destructive environmental practices that led to the Dust Bowl.

Although the New York stock market crashed in 1929, it took some time for the aftershock to reach California. Yet, it was here that many writers, photographers, and social historians ultimately found inspiration. Jan Goggans reveals that the Depression produced two types of narratives, one dealing with agricultural laborers who came to the state, seeking work in the fields; the other, with dreamers who failed to find success in

Hollywood. Alongside *The Grapes of Wrath*, Dorothea Lange and Paul Taylor's *An American Exodus: A Record of Human Erosion* and Carey McWilliams' *Factories in the Field* were also published in 1939. In addition, a new genre known as the Hollywood novel appeared in the 1930s, attracting writers such as Nathanael West, Horace McCoy, and F. Scott Fitzgerald.

The state provided new subject matter for some writers, while offering others a unique place within existing traditions in the early decades of the twentieth century. A group of artists whom Geneva Gano calls "sub-urban modernists" were associated not with the state's rural areas or with cosmopolitan centers such as Los Angeles, but with bohemian communities in Edendale, Palm Springs, Pasadena, and Carmel-by-the-Sea. They were united by their interest in the avant-garde and by their passion for radical political causes.

Popular pulp fiction writers were often as likely to critique society as their modernist counterparts. Dashiell Hammett, Raymond Chandler, and James M. Cain wrote during the Depression, the Prohibition era, and World War II. They depicted Los Angeles and San Francisco as violent urban locales filled with characters who were driven by base emotions and animal instincts. William Marling identifies the hard-boiled private eye as someone living in a world where crime was the norm, and who was nearly as flawed as his enemies. Ironically, these authors set their works in "the Golden State," a place where they uncovered social hypocrisy, economic desperation, and moral depravity.

Part V, "Alternative Voices," concentrates on the period after the war. Paradoxically, it was a time of prosperity and increasing discontent. Those who were geographically and politically marginalized wrote about the "other" California in the 1940s. Countercultural movements in the 1950s and 1960s attacked the conservative center from a variety of peripheral vantage points, condemning homophobia, western religion, sexism, and the nation's involvement in the Vietnam War.

Phillip Round writes about the "other" California, including the coastal forest region, the Central Valley, and the Modoc Plateau. These locales didn't benefit from the post-World War II economic boom that helped the rest of the state. The establishment of the *bracero* program in 1942 reinforced cultural differences between long-time residents and Mexican immigrants. Japanese Americans maintained an uncomfortable relationship with the state's desert areas, which housed internment camps during the war. The rise of corporate farming and the completion of California's major water projects resulted in the consolidation of land holdings and the marginalization of laborers, small farmers, and loggers in these transitioning regions.

The following decade was a period of political conservatism and social conformity. As Kurt Hemmer notes, the Beats represented an alternative voice – not another place, but an "other" state of mind. They were part of a countercultural movement that challenged conventional views on religion, morality, society's relationship to nature, and national and foreign affairs. These poets promoted an aesthetic based on personal revelation and experimentation with drugs. They were attracted to Buddhism, advocated pacifism, and opposed the Vietnam War. The Beats had as many followers as they had unpopular causes. They established communities in northern and southern California; affiliated with the African American and Black Mountain poets; and shared an affinity with other dissident writers such as Richard Brautigan, Hunter S. Thompson, and Charles Bukowski.

Many of the poets who thrived during this period were located in San Francisco. In addition to the Berkeley Renaissance poets, the Language poets, and the members of Second Wave Feminism and the New Narrative movement, there were DIY magazines and non-institutional reading series allied with anarchists, labor organizers, conscientious objectors, ecological coalitions, and supporters of gay liberation. Kaplan Page Harris notes that the last group was especially influential during this era because the Bay Area had a large LGBT population and numerous homophile organizations.

Brian Stefans writes about artists who critiqued California, starting in the McCarthy era and ending with the arrival of punk in the late 1970s. They included Thomas Mann, Bertolt Brecht, and other Germans living in exile; transplanted American poets; and nihilistic singer/songwriters. In a postwar consumer society, these people felt they had no agency; no voice in a place like Los Angeles, a city known for its inauthenticity of communication, inhabited by actors and dramatists. They rejected bourgeois norms of decorum, conventional morality, the commercial entertainment industry, and even language itself.

Instead of concentrating on writers who attempted to influence the culture by exerting what Stefans calls "*negative* power," Part VI, "Creating Communities," examines artists who changed the dominant discourse by raising their minority voices in solidarity. The 1960s and 1970s saw the rise of the Civil Rights movement, feminism, gay liberation, and ecological writing. The 1965 Watts Riot and the 1992 Los Angeles Uprising motivated African Americans to speak out against racial injustice, while the Chicana/o resistance movement, the Asian American identity movement, and the

Native American Renaissance led to the publication of more minority writers, a trend that continues today.

The decades since the Watts Riots have been a time of social crisis and literary renewal. The protests in 1965 led to the creation of the Watts Writers Workshop, an organization that gave minority and low-income residents a forum for expressing their frustrations about race relations and socioeconomic inequalities in Los Angeles. Many of these problems weren't addressed by the city in the following years. The 1992 Uprising presented artists with another opportunity to reexamine issues that remained unresolved locally and throughout the rest of the state. Charles Toombs surveys African American writers and artists who have educated readers and residents in the post-Civil Rights era, examining the works of actress and activist Anna Deveare Smith, postmodern satirist Ishmael Reed, science fiction writer Octavia Butler, and others.

Chicana/o literature has flourished since the late 1950s, though many writers demonstrate conflicting regional loyalties. Some focus on the relationship between Mexico and California, chronicling the hazards of immigration and depicting characters with opposing allegiances to their newfound communities and the loved ones they left behind. Others highlight the process of assimilation, punctuated by the periodic return to their family's country of origin. Anne Goldman untangles the connections between land and livelihood, family and culture, and regional and national identity.

King-Kok Cheung writes about interracial relations in Asian American literature. She begins in the 1980s, when curricular reforms led to the study of more multicultural writers. Recent Asian American authors have reflected this awareness of other minority cultures by setting stories of an individual character's quest against the broader canvass of historical trauma. They examine multiracial political movements; interethnic alliances; the separate yet intertwined histories of Chinese, Filipino, and Japanese people; tensions that have led to outbreaks of violence in California; and the healing that can sometimes occur in the aftermath of urban unrest.

Cael Keegan refers to California's place in the queer imaginary, calling it a paradise "found and lost," associated with gay liberation as well as the AIDS crisis. He considers how notions of a queer utopia have been influenced by the Civil Rights era, Stonewall, the HIV epidemic, and social and political gains made by the LGBT community in the twenty-first century. Some works are celebratory, while others express anxieties about sexual responsibility, medical means of treating the virus, the Reagan administration's politicization of sexual orientation, and the recent fight for marriage equality. In addition to being demonized by the conservative right, the LGBT community has been riven by internal dissent. Feminists of color have mourned the decimation of the land and its native inhabitants, though other writers have heralded the state's growing importance in the national body.

Perhaps nothing symbolizes the beauty of California more than nature itself. Modern nature writing differs from its earlier counterpart in its concern with the hypergrowth, exploitation, and overdevelopment of the nation's most populous state. Poets and essayists, as well as environmental activists and novelists, share a range of concerns, dealing with the effects of urbanization and industrial agriculture, viticulture, the park system, and outdoor sports such as hunting and fishing. Michael Kowalewski notes that most works have a personal emphasis, stressing the individual's interaction with the physical world. For these writers, "nature" is another word for "community," a collective comprised of humanity and other life forms with which we share the earth.

In recent decades, California residents, searching for an ideal living environment, have moved from cities to small towns, which are more affordable, less stressful, and theoretically safer. Some writers question these assumptions by documenting the problems facing rural towns in particular: the lack of government funding for farmers; tensions among locals, urban refugees, and city dwellers looking for vacation retreats; and a conservative small-town mentality that punishes those who are "different." Nancy Cook explores our need to escape from reality by retreating into a world that seems detached from the ills of modern society.

By contrast, Lynn Mie Itagaki considers the future as an alternative to the present. Science fiction writers and certain postmodern novelists imagine California as the site of political rebellion, social Armageddon, or environmental apocalypse. The state has always been an experimental laboratory, an inspiration for religious visionaries and paranoid conspiracy theorists. More optimistically, recent minority writers, noting the region's resistance to ethnic immigrants, have depicted a fictional realm in which racism and class inequalities no longer exist.

This anthology is the first collection of critical essays devoted to the entirety of California literature, from the early Native American period through the twenty-first century. It is a survey of important (though sometimes little-known) works, not an encyclopedic catalog. It may omit certain writers, or give their works less attention than they deserve, due to the selective nature of such an enterprise, even one this expansive in scope.

It is also important to note that this is a history of California literature, not a history of California. Both history books and literature are driven by narratives. They offer numerous, sometimes conflicting, highly selective ways of recounting and processing human experience. Historians have an obligation to tell the "truth," as naive and problematic as that might sound. But artists operate under no such constraints. Most of the works cited in this anthology are novels and other products of the imagination. During the Gold Rush, even many autobiographies, journals, and letters were written by writers using pseudonyms, such as Mark Twain, Dame Shirley, and John Rollin Ridge (aka "Yellow Bird"). The American West was a place where many people sought to reinvent themselves – by restoring their health; reviving their careers; cross-dressing as members of the opposite sex; or, in the case of James Beckwourth's autobiography, passing as white.

California has attracted more pilgrims and dissidents than any other place in our nation's history. Perhaps literature is the medium in which it finds its most apt expression. California is a fanciful conceit, an elusive dream, a celluloid confection – a land where the greatest dreams and darkest disasters come true.

PART I

Beginnings

CHAPTER I

Tales of Native California

Paul Apodaca

The folktales of indigenous California illustrate the diversity of its native people. Seven indigenous language families exist in California, each one subdivided into hundreds of languages and thousands of dialects and idioms. Each language family is associated with a particular region with its own unique topography, extending from the Pacific Coast to the volcanic mountain ranges of the state's eastern border; from the Central Valley to the deserts of Southern California.

The language family within each region is divided into different cultures or ethnicities. Each one has a body of folktales related to those told by other groups within the same region or family. The folktales of California are a rich tapestry illustrating the diversity of indigenous cultures.

Folktales serve as a type of library for preliterate cultures. They convey the values and philosophies of ordinary people. They also provide the foundations for the development of religion, art, home life, and society by describing what is seen in moral terms. Folk heroes personify elements of morality and philosophy and serve as role models within a culture.

Folktales appear as myths, legends, fables, fairytales, and sayings. Most tales were sung as a part of a ceremony. A song unites the singer and audience with their past and becomes a timeless performance or cultural act. The song version of a folktale is different than its narrative form. It is often shortened to a few repeated phrases. The audience has heard the tales many times, and only needs these representative phrases to kindle its memory.

Ethnographers tend to privilege narrative folktales when documenting native groups. As a result, many tales remain uncollected that were once performed as songs by California tribes.

The Cupeño people of Southern California live in the Coastal Mountains. The Cahuilla are located in the Coachella Valley. Both groups are members of the same language family (the Takic or Shoshonean division) and share certain folktales in common. The Cupeño story of creation is almost identical to the Cahuilla version. This excerpt gathered by William Wallace illustrates the rhythmic breaks and repetition of the song structure[1]:

> Desolate it was
> Desolate it was
> Desolate the Earth
> First they appeared
> First they came out
> First Mokat
> First Tamayowit
> These the chiefs
> These the ancients

An excerpt of the Cahuilla narrative version was recorded by Alejo Patencio and translated by Julian Nortes in 1925.[2]

> Then again all the lights whirled together, joined, and produced. This time the embryos grew fully – the children inside talked to one another. They asked each other, "What are we? ..." for at the time they did know themselves. While they were in this sack they rolled back and forth; they stretched their arms and knees to make a hole so they could get out. Then they named themselves Mukat and Tamaiyauit.

The Cahuilla perform this as a funeral song, the highest form of sacred music, and as a narrative told to family or community members.

The Yurok Indians of Northern California are part of the same culture and language family as the Karok and Hupa. A song common in this cultural complex is the Chickenhawk song. The song is a Conflict or Revenge song used for protection from an enemy and energizing weapons to be used in a fight.

> Chickenhawk[3] is ... a girl who always remained a child and who never menstruated. She told her brother that a group of men were coming to fight, and then she made medicine to kill them. She had her brother throw a bundle of twigs at her, pulling away the knot that bound them so that none struck her. Then, she used her song, which she sang morning and night, and she entered the battle wearing a skirt of black oak bark (in strips). Thus, she killed a hundred men and was not struck herself, for she made herself invincible. Chickenhawk [then tells] the men to use her song and to put twigs and strips of black oak bark in their hair before they fight.

The linkage between tale, song, and ritual practice is made explicit in this story. The tale describes singing as an act of power. It instructs the men to use their power as well as ceremonial objects as a ritual prelude to a fight with another group.

The heroine controls her menstruation, remaining a child forever. An idealized form of feminine power is thus associated with the pre-sexualized personality of the woman. The child/woman is a common character in folktales around the world and is part of a trilogy of feminine power often referenced as the nymph/maiden/crone. Each expression of female power in this triad can call on the other two forms. Chickenhawk appears to conform to this pattern.

There is historical as well as folkloric evidence that California Indians occasionally fought with each other but there were no large-scale wars. Conflicts were limited to small incursions into areas shared by different culture groups. Indians who engaged in these battles were seeking to protect food-gathering areas or settle border disputes.

Chickenhawk prepares the medicine for killing a hundred men, a relatively large number of Indians. The number is meant to speak to the quality of feminine power demonstrated by Chickenhawk. Men are enlisted to assist the feminine principle, and are victimized or protected by it.

Creation tales are among the most popular myths, but there are different types of myths just as there are different types of folktales. A creation myth explains how the world was made or how people were formed while an etiological myth explains how particular things have come to be.

Fables convey a lesson or moral while fairytales discuss personal relationships and motivations. All of these tales can be found in song as well as in narrative form. Reviewing a few folktales from across California illustrates the diversity of visions and voices among the region's indigenous people.

Each tale presented here is paraphrased and summarized from ethnographic accounts but allows for an appreciation of the elements that form the heritage of California native literature.

Southern California Cahuilla Creation Tale[4]

Amnaha was the greatness of things and filled the universe. He joined with Tukmiat, the night, and flashes of lightning heralded their creation of all things. From their joining, a sack formed with life within but it failed and died. Amnaha and Tukmiat again joined and the flashes of power radiated and again a sack formed but again it died. For the third time Amnaha and Tukmiat came together and their actions produced a sack with two living beings inside who struggled and birthed themselves as they emerged.

"Look younger brother, I have a head and shoulders," said Mukat.

"Look younger brother, I have arms and hands," said Tamaiyaowit.

"Look younger brother, I have legs and feet," cried Mukat.

"Look younger brother, I have a back and can move," said Tamaiyaowit.

In this manner, they emerged from their birth sack, each one claiming to be older and therefore wiser. The two brothers decided to demonstrate who was wiser by creating the things of the Earth, each claiming their creations were proof of who was truly older.

After creating all things, the brothers were still not satisfied with their competition and decided to create people. Tamaiyaowit went to work and brought out his creations.

"Look younger brother, my people are the best. They have eyes in the back of their heads so they can see anyone approaching. They have hands and feet that face back so they can catch anything coming up behind them."

Mukat revealed his creations and said, "Look younger brother, my creations are much better than yours, they face forward so they do not stumble, their hands and feet reach in front of them where they can see them and use them to travel and make things. My creatures are much better looking and can do all things needed to have a good life."

Tamaiyaowit recognized that Mukat and his people represented a wiser way and took his creations and descended under the Earth, leaving Mukat to live with those who could speak with each other.

An analysis of this tale reveals the worldview and aesthetics of the Cahuilla tribe. The concept of monotheism is evident in the reference to a male divine force that fills the universe. A feminine force that can be seen as a creation of Amnaha in the form of Tukmiat is introduced. The association of light with the male element and night with the feminine is in keeping with the sun as a male element and the moon as female. This paradigm is further developed in a more elaborate version of the tale in which the sister of Mukat is named as the moon goddess Menyil.

The contest between the brothers demonstrates wisdom through creation and practicality. The act of creation is sanctified as divine or sacred activity but needs to be useful. Basketmaking and other creative acts reflect wisdom, divine inspiration, and practicality.

The retreat of Tamaiyaowit settles the question of elder status and prepares the way for the description of culture that is divinely organized and interactive. The Cahuilla word for speech is *Iviat* and those who can speak are called *Iviatem*. This is the way Cahuilla signify each other, as *Iviatem*, or people with whom they can speak.

Northern California Kato Creation Myth[5]

Before this world was formed, there was another. The sky was sandstone and the two gods, Thunder and *Nagaicho*, decided to keep the sky from falling apart from the sound of thunder by stretching it in four directions and holding it there with a great rock.

They then made all the things that would make life good. They made flowers in the South and a large opening in the East so clouds could come through. They made an opening in the West so that fog from the ocean could come through. They built a fire to make the clouds that would protect people from headaches from too much sunshine.

Then, Thunder and *Nagaicho* made a man out of earth and put bundles of grass into him to form his stomach and heart. They placed round clay inside of him to form his liver and kidneys and a reed for a windpipe. They mixed red stone with water and made his blood. They split the leg of the man and made woman. They made the sun to travel by day and the moon for the night.

This summarized tale conveys another twist on the two brothers form of creation myth. Time is defined, clearly marking this as a myth, and a concept of multiple creations begins the tale. Reality is shown to not be apparent, as the world in which men live is not the first one created.

The sky is substance, sandstone. This is a profound statement as the divine world organizes the material in this tale. Sound is described as a force and directionality establishes reasoned thought. Life and the universe is not random but has directions. The actions of the brothers are not to be seen as a contest as much as teamwork whose goal is a common good.

The regional realities of the world within which this culture lives are described within the organized world of directions producing wind and rain in the form of clouds from the East and the ocean and its moisture from the West. Fire is introduced as a medicinal element. Cleansing by fire is an obvious extension of this element and establishes an aesthetic value. The sun is created to shine but is too powerful for men and that establishes a hierarchy that places man beneath natural forces.

The creation of man is a joint effort that emphasizes group activity and the association of man with earth is one seen in many creation tales around the world and in California. The abundance of life seen in the myriad blades of grass on a landscape provide a metaphor for the complex systems of muscles, tendons, arteries, and veins found within humans and their conveyance of energy.

Clay as a basis for the internal organs of man alludes to a refined form of earth. The essence of the earth is reflected in our essential organs. Red stone mixed with water defines our blood as visible proof of our relationship to the world around us. The formation of woman from the split leg of a man establishes a patriarchal aspect of the culture while the sun and moon again define the union of fertility.

Central California Maidu Creation Myth[6]

All the Earth was covered by water. There was no sun, no moon, no stars. One day a raft appeared floating on the water. Turtle was on the raft. A being who shone like the sun descended down a rope of feathers. He was Earth Initiate and he tied the rope to the end of the raft. His face was covered and no one has ever seen his face. Turtle asked for dry land so he could rest from the water and for a place for people to be created.

Earth Initiate tied his rope to Turtle who then descended into the water and was gone for six years. When he came up he was covered in green slime but with a little earth beneath his nails. This earth was scraped off and rolled into a ball the size of a pebble and left it on the back of the raft. Earth Initiate returned to look at it three times.

The fourth time he looked, it was as big as the world and the raft was on dry ground. Turtle asked for light and Earth Initiate pointed to the East where his sister came up and the sun shone and brought light to the land. The sun traveled and went down and Earth Initiate told his brother to come up and the moon rose. He then called the stars to come out.

Earth Initiate called on a tree to rise with twelve types of acorns. Turtle could not keep up as Earth Initiate moved like a ball of fire under the ground and the water as he looked at the world he had made. Trees, birds, and animals were called to appear.

Earth Initiate then took dark red earth and mixed it with water to make a man and a woman whom he placed on his right and left side and lay down. The woman tickled him but he did not laugh. The first man and woman were white with pink eyes and black hair. Their teeth shone brightly and they were very handsome.

This shortened form of a Maidu creation tale describes the Earth and the water covering it. Many folktales use water as a feminine and earth as a masculine element. Here, the male element is engulfed by the female, leading to a fertile union.

Time exists though there is no sun or moon or stars. A raft appears as Turtle demonstrates that construction, patterning, and intent are products of the animal world, not the human domain. The Earth Initiate is an intriguing figure who is neither messianic nor solely responsible for creation. Nevertheless, it is crucial to the creation of the world known to man.

The feathered rope is a sign of sacredness, as is the light. Turtle forms the world by dredging up the male earth and female water elements, and serves as a symbol of divine inspiration. Humanity cannot see, understand, or control this power, witnessed by the fact that the face of Earth Initiate is covered.

In this variation on the sun and moon as fertility symbols, the sun is associated with the feminine and the moon with the masculine element. The creation of humanity once again involves the use of earth and water. Men and women are placed equally at the side of Earth Initiate. The woman's sexuality is described as tickling, though it does not disturb the divinity. This is not a rejection or denigration of her power, but a recognition of the woman. The active principle in fertility is the feminine element – the water that moves over and encases the male element at the beginning of the tale.

Southern California Chemehuevi Creation Myth – How Ocean Woman Made the Land[7]

> Ocean Woman, in the form of a worm, dropped from the sky onto the water. There was no land anywhere. She crumbled a little earth and dropped it onto the water, where it floated. Then Ocean Woman, being a Worm, went onto it. She spread it out with her hands. When it was getting wide, she spread it out with her feet.
>
> Then she made Coyote out of the oil, sweat, and skin from her crotch. Coyote went to look at the Earth, to see how wide it was getting. He went to look in all directions. When it took all day to go and return upon the Earth, he told Ocean Woman that it was big enough.
>
> Then Ocean Woman made Wolf also and Mountain Lion. Those three were brothers. Wolf, being sensible, became the oldest, so it is said, because Coyote has no sense.

This shortened version of a Chemehuevi Earth Diver tale emphasizes the feminine element. The worm is a male element, but it is controlled by the feminine. Sky and water are the domain of this feminine principle. The earth floats in the water, sustained by the female element.

Coyote is used for many purposes in California Native American literature. His sexual function is illustrated here. Coyote decides when the Earth is fertile.

Creation stories are often the most commonly appreciated and the most dramatic forms of mythic tales. Etiological myths can explain the things we see and experience. These tales include the Fighting or Robbery myth. Hero figures often appear in such tales and have dualistic natures and roles. Chief among these is Coyote.

Northern California Shasta Myth – How Coyote Stole Fire[8]

> Long ago there was no fire and the people wanted it very badly so they went to Coyote and told him, "Where Pain lives there is fire. He and his people

catch their game by starting fires that cause animals to flee and run down the paths where these people kill as many as they want."

When Coyote heard this he told Chicken Hawk, Eagle, Grouse, and Quail to stand at different places on the path to Pain's house. He would obtain the fire and pass it to Chicken Hawk who would then pass it Eagle who would run it to Grouse who would take it to Quail who would bring it to safety and the people.

Coyote wrapped himself in a blanket and entered the camp of Pain's people but only the children were there as the others were hunting using their fire. "I think you are Coyote," one of the children said. "Our parents told us if anyone came it would be Coyote."

"I am not Coyote, look, far off is the land of Coyote." He sat down and stretched his legs toward the fire. "You smell like Coyote," said the children. "No, I do not," he answered and as he spoke the blanket wrapped around him began to burn.

Coyote got up and ran as fast as he could and Pain's children ran after him. He handed over the fire to Chicken Hawk who gave it to Eagle who gave it to Grouse, who in turn, gave it to Quail.

"Coyote has stolen fire," cried Pain's children and chased after Quail who found Turtle walking along. "I'll give you the fire," said Quail as the Pain's children ran up. Turtle put the fire in his armpit and dove into the water. The children shot him in the rear and that formed into a tail.

The Pains waited for him to come up and Coyote joined them. The children gave up and went away. Turtle arose and Coyote demanded to know where had the fire gone. "You keep quiet," replied Turtle, "I will throw the fire about." He did so and the people came and got some. Coyote was the first to steal fire.

The theft of fire by Coyote is one of the most common American Indian folktales. This shortened Robbery Myth of the Shasta people contains many elements seen in other Coyote-steals-fire tales, but has its own ethnic stamp. Coyote unites contradictions, which are the basis for humor. He denies who he is and begins to catch fire. He uses trickery and deception to produce goodness and warmth, and to empower nature with fire. Coyote's contradictory nature is represented in virtually every American Indian culture.

Central California Yokuts Myth – The Lizard Hand[9]

It was Coyote who brought it about that people die. He made it thus because our hands are not closed like his. He wanted our hands to be like his, but a lizard said to him, "No, they must have my hand." He had five fingers and Coyote only had a fist. So now we have an open hand with five fingers. But then Coyote said, "Well, then they will have to die."

Death is often introduced by dualistic characters like Coyote. This tale demonstrates the force of the natural world. Myths such as this reveal the power of language. Speaking reality into existence is a form of performance that emphasizes the value of speaking and singing.

Variations of certain tales appear in different language families. Consider this variant of the Lizard Hand tale.

Northern California Miwok Myth – The Coyote and the Lizard[10]

> The Coyote-man and the little Lizard-man made the world and everything in it. After they had done this, little Lizard-man wanted to turn into the Moon but Coyote-man and Meadowlark-man would not allow him to do so.

This short tale involves Lizard and Coyote in the act of creation. Coyote's contradictory nature causes him to negate proposals or introduce negative elements that are paradoxically acts of creation that form the world we know.

The Miwok, Yokuts, and Nissenan are members of a common language family known as the Penutian. The three tales presented here depict variations on the relationship between Coyote and Lizard. Coyote is linked to creation in all three tales, where he appears as an authority figure. Contradiction is synonymous with randomness, a powerful force of nature. Coyote has many personalities and character traits. He is a loner and an important member of a community. The five-fingered Lizard is a metaphor for man.

Northern California Southern Nissenan Myth – The Coyote and the Lizard[11]

> In the beginning, the Moon-man, the Coyote-man, and the Lizard-man decided to make people but differed as to what the first man should be like. Each of the three wanted man to be like himself.
>
> After they argued for a long time they finally agreed that man should have a round face like the Moon-man but they could not agree on his hands. Coyote-man insisted that he should have paws like his own, but Lizard-man said that paws would be of no use – that man should have five fingers as he could hold of things.
>
> Finally, Lizard-man carried his point and gave man five long fingers like his own. Coyote-man never forgave him and to this day the Coyote hunts the lizard and kills him when he can.

Coyote loses his contest in this variation of the tale, and man develops the five-finger advantage. Coyote reminds us that there are other powers in the world.

He is both wise and foolish, generous and crafty, creative and destructive. Coyote's dual nature is demonstrated in his ability to die and to become resurrected in another tale.

Central California Mono Fable – Coyote and the Rabbit[12]

Jackrabbit had a pretty younger sister named Cottontail whom Coyote wanted to marry. He grew angry when he was refused and threatened to kill all rabbits and make blankets of their skins. The rabbits were unafraid and told him to be quiet. Coyote thought of a plan to kill the rabbits.

He told the rabbits it would be great fun to swing up and down from a sapling and they all agreed and began looking for a suitable young tree. Jackrabbit secretly went out that night and walked around the world and encountered Prairie Falcon. "What are you seeking?" asked Prairie Falcon and Jackrabbit told him he was looking for a young sapling for swinging on with Coyote.

"Coyote is trying to kill you because you will not let him marry your sister," advised Prairie Falcon who agreed to have a suitable sapling placed near the home of Jackrabbit. "Come in the morning and swing on the tree. I shall watch you."

The next morning Coyote came upon Jackrabbit who was swinging up and down from the sapling, crying out he had found a good tree for their fun. Coyote swung Jackrabbit up and down, intending to let go suddenly and cause Jackrabbit to fly up and come falling down so hard he would be killed. Before Coyote had a chance to let go, Prairie Falcon arrived and told Jackrabbit to let him ride the sapling.

Coyote swung Prairie Falcon up and down and suddenly let him go so he flew into the air and fell down so hard he died. He did not stay dead. He revived himself and invited Coyote to ride the sapling. "It is great fun, you will see all kinds of stars and animals," said Prairie Falcon.

Coyote mounted the sapling and Prairie Falcon bent the pole all the way to the ground. He quickly let go and Coyote sailed high into the air and came down hard, striking the ground with a thud and died. The rabbits were now rid of Coyote.

This folktale is full of fun and excitement. Coyote is challenged by the rabbits, who are equally voracious in their appetites. The sexual symbolism of riding the sapling is good-natured, rather than obscene. The tale introduces another contradictory theme: the small and weak versus the cunning and powerful. Prairie Falcon is a sky element who governs the contest and prevents Coyote from winning. However, the audience understands that Coyote's death isn't permanent.

His dualistic nature allows him to be both strong and weak. In certain tales he appears chastised by the spiritual element (the Prairie Falcon) who controls the earthy nature of Coyote's lust.

Southern California Chemehuevi Animal Fable – How Chipmunk Killed the Ogres[13]

Chipmunk and his brother were living, and as the younger brother, [Chipmunk] went out to hunt Cottontail rabbits. He followed one who entered into his hole and Chipmunk dug a hole and made a fire in it to smoke out the Cottontail.

The Chief of the Ogres was about hunting and saw the smoke and came upon Chipmunk bent over and digging. He snapped the testicles of Chipmunk who did not turn around but brushed the earth thinking a pebble had struck him. The Ogre again struck his testicles and Chipmunk spun around.

"Let us wrestle, let us cut off your testicles," said the Ogre. "All right," said Chipmunk who grappled with the Ogre who was thrown again and again. They came together again but this time Ogre threw Chipmunk and cut off his testicles before he hit the ground. He killed him and cut him up and took him home to the other Ogres who boiled him and ate him.

The Older Brother Chipmunk went looking for his brother and found where he had been smoking out a rabbit and saw what had been done to him. He then lit a fire and again poured smoke into the air. The Ogre saw the smoke and went back to the same place to see what he would find.

He found the Older Brother Chipmunk bent over and digging just as his younger brother had done and, again, snapped his testicles.

Chipmunk spun around and Ogre said, "Let us wrestle, let us cut off your testicles," and Chipmunk said, "All right, let us do it."

They wrestled and Chipmunk threw Ogre into the air and cut off his testicles and cut up his body, making strips of meat to dry in the sun. He put on the sandals of Ogre and blotted out his own tracks and went looking for his brother.

He found bits of flesh and bone and brought them home and restored his brother to life. They slept through the night. The next day the Ogres went looking for their brother and followed the tracks of his sandals and found dried meat strips laid out on rocks made hot by the sun. They stopped and ate their fill and then laid down to sleep in the daytime.

When they awoke, each complained of having bad dreams. "I dreamed we ate our brother," said one of the Ogres. They started out to track the Chipmunk who was now wearing their brother's sandals. As the Ogres followed the sandal tracks, the Chipmunk brothers were watching and had disguised the door to their hole.

When the Ogre brothers got near, the Chipmunks threw a rock down into the valley. The Ogres followed it, thinking it to be a person. Then it began to snow and the Ogres became very cold. They turned back but while going they all died of cold.

Folktales often describe heroes who rid the world of monsters. Some tales are classified as legends because they involve geographically recognizable places and are part of an area's history. Others are fairytales that illustrate psychological situations and relationships. These tales may also use animal characters as heroes, establish a value for the history of the species, and legitimize its use in ritual or ceremony.

In this tale the Chipmunk represents the small and weak who overcome the large and powerful. Here, the Chipmunk replaces Coyote as the central figure in the narrative.

Coastal California Salinan Animal Fairytale – Pelican the Murderer[14]

Long ago Raven and Prairie Falcon heard of a murderer, Pelican. He would stand by his door and when a man came by he would invite him in to pass the night in his house. When his guest went to sleep, he would go over to him and three times ask him, "Are you asleep?"

If he got no reply, he would drive his long bill into his guest's heart and in that way kill him. This is how he murdered all of his victims.

Raven and Prairie Falcon decided to rid the world of this and set out for the place where they knew Pelican lived and carried out his wicked practice. Pelican greeted them and asked them what they wished.

"We wish shelter for the night," they replied and Pelican told them, "You may both sleep here." They remained and when they got into bed they slept only a little. They got up and put in their places two logs of wood and hid nearby and pretended to snore.

When Pelican heard the snoring, he arose and said, "I will go and kill them."

He came up close to the bed and asked, "Are you asleep?" He asked this three times and, when he received no answer, was certain the two guests were sound asleep. He raised his bill and with a mighty stroke, dug into what he thought to be his guests. But he hit the logs and split his head all to pieces. He fell dead.

Raven and Prairie Falcon jumped up and said, "That is the way in which he always killed people." The world was now rid of Pelican the murderer.

The folktales of native California are catalogued in ethnographic reports. Folklorists and anthropologists use these to analyze indigenous cultures. The examples presented here contain all of the elements of literature – philosophical musings, stories about the relationship between nature and humankind, and tales about individuals embarking on heroic quests; even murder mysteries with surprise endings.

These works represent the enormous cultural diversity of early native California. For students exploring the region's rich heritage, they serve as a wonderful place to begin.

Notes

1. The tale fragment is excerpted from William J. Wallace, "Comparative Literature" in *Handbook of North American Indians*, vol. 8, ed. William C. Sturtevant (Washington: Smithsonian Institution, 1978), 658–661.
2. A complete version of the tale can be found in William Duncan Strong, *Aboriginal Society in Southern California* (Berkeley: University of California Press, 1929).
3. The song is discussed in a more complete form in Richard Keeling, *Cry for Luck – Sacred Song and Speech among the Yurok, Hupa, and Karok Indians of Northwestern California* (Berkeley: University of California Press, 1992).
4. Paraphrased and shortened by author from Strong, *Aboriginal Society*.
5. Paraphrased and shortened by author from Stith Thompson, *Folk Tales of the North American Indians* (North Dighton, MA: JG Press, 1995).
6. Paraphrased and shortened by author from Thompson, *Folk Tales*.
7. Paraphrased and shortened by author from Carobeth Laird, *Mirror and Pattern: George Laird's World of Chemehuevi Mythology* (Banning: Malki Museum Press, 1984).
8. Paraphrased and shortened by author from Edward W. Gifford and Gwendoline Harris Block, eds., *California Indian Nights* (1930; Lincoln: University of Nebraska Press, 1990).
9. Paraphrased and shortened by author from Thompson, *Folk Tales*.
10. Paraphrased and shortened by author from C. Hart Merriam, *The Dawn of the World: Myths and Tales of the Miwok Indians of California* (1910; Lincoln: University of Nebraska Press, 1993).
11. Paraphrased and shortened by author from Merriam, *The Dawn of the World*. Hart includes this Nissenan tale after presenting a Miwok version. Hart uses the spelling of *Mewuk* in his original text.
12. Paraphrased and shortened by author from Gifford and Block, *California Indian Nights*.
13. Paraphrased and shortened by author from Laird, *Mirror and Pattern*.
14. Paraphrased and shortened by author from Gifford and Block, *California Indian Nights*.

CHAPTER 2

Indigenous Peoples under Colonial Rule
Lisbeth Haas

Though the Spanish destroyed too many elements of pre-Columbian society, *sixteenth-century* monasteries trained substantial numbers of native scholars drawn from the indigenous elite. Pre-Columbian societies often had "alternative literacies" or systems of pictorial writing, as in Mexico; hieroglyphic writing among the Maya; the Inca system of the quipu; and storing knowledge, an elaborate system of working with cotton or wool cord. These systems of literacies have made scholars working on the translations and writing of indigenous text ask particular questions. They seek to *hear* particular verbal arts in indigenous writing, for example, and to understand how indigenous writers of the codices have *voiced* the painted image in their work.

The biggest literary work from colonial (1769) and Mexican (1821–48) California was written by Pablo Tac in the late 1830s. Tac acted as had many native scholars. He spoke from the position of identity with his land, family and tribe, and he represented Luiseño language and culture at the mission. He spoke of the power and visions of the older and newer indigenous leadership, and wrote about alternative forms of knowledge production at Mission San Luis Rey in the early nineteenth century along the colonial coast.

For the Spanish, images were as important as words in the conquest and settlement of the Americas. The printed image introduced into California the most abundant source of a shared colonial literary imagination. Painting also played a very big role in narrating a new reality and giving a certain vocabulary to express its meanings. The Spanish introduced a visual lexicon and brought together technologies of writing and painting. They attempted to establish a new narrative of the present and past for the community who shared the experience of viewing. They created a visual universe of shared stories about saints, virgins, and biblical scenes. The politics of the image were meant to reframe the world and produce new systems of significance.

Indigenous scholars translated new ideas and images, and incorporated their aesthetic practices, forms of knowledge production, and politics into manuscripts and images that necessarily conformed to Spanish and Mexican genres. Yet they left traces of their own meanings. Indigenous literature, visual narratives, and alternative forms of knowledge production suggest how native societies along the coast addressed colonial dilemmas. They better situate indigenous thought in California within the context of the Americas.[1]

Pablo Tac, Luiseño Writer

Spanish law favored the education of the indigenous elite to augment the numbers of subjects and administrators with the ability to write and speak in Spanish. The emphasis on education expanded with liberal reform in the late eighteenth century. By the 1790s, crown officials directed the missions, four *presidios* (forts), and three towns of California to form schools. Despite the directives received, rarely did an instructor or school last for any length of time. Though the missionaries encouraged reading and writing among some of the indigenous population, they restricted access to pens and paper. To write in a military-mission society with its scrutiny and confinement and the constant fear of and preparation against Indian revolt could be subversive. At least one man received a severe sentence – one that called for his exile from his mission to another mission in a military district far from his home – for stealing a pen.

It became common that some Indian people at each mission could read and write. During the 1824 Chumash war, when Chumash people from Santa Inés, La Purísima, and Santa Bárbara rose up against the soldiers and military and occupied Mission La Purísima for a month, Fray Blas Ordaz warned authorities not to write to Fray Rodríguez who was then held at Mission La Purísima. Fray Ordaz warned that the rebels would intercept and read any message sent. The Mexican government encouraged education in the early national era. Officials mandated that a primary school be established in every mission in California.

In 1829, eleven schools existed in California, seven of them at missions. Pablo Tac, who wrote the greatest literary piece of this era, was among the thirty-five Luiseño boys and young men who studied at Mission San Luis Rey. Both men and women received instruction in Catholic doctrine and became familiar with printed images and writing, but only males attended the mission schools. Though a school existed in virtually every mission, *presidio*, and town of California at some point between 1821 and 1845,

California lacked instructors to expand and sustain schools. Tutors and missionaries provided the most consistent formal education.[2]

Literacy and formal writing became more common for indigenous people in the second and third generations. They left written records in the Mexican archives. Indigenous petitions for emancipation began in 1826 in California. They are preserved in archives, as are indigenous petitions for land allotments written by people emancipated from the missions after 1834. Pablo Tac's manuscript is the only literary piece among these writings.

The Spanish had been in Tac's territory for almost twenty-four years before his birth, sometime in 1821. The spread of literacy during that decade enabled Pablo Tac to study and write more freely and fully than had previous generations. Tac speaks of life at Mission San Luis Rey during his youth, when more than 2,663 Christian Luiseños lived within their tribal territories and at the mission. Born and raised at the mission until 1832, he left at the age of ten, about the time boys entered manhood in Luiseño society. Having served as an assistant to Father Peyri for a number of years, the missionary selected Pablo Tac and another Luiseño assistant, Agapito Amamix, to travel with him to Mexico where he thought the boys would study to become priests and missionaries. It was intended that they would return to Luiseño territory as the first California Indian missionaries, and as scholars who could teach and write in a number of languages.

They spent two years in Mexico City at the Iglesia y Colegio de San Fernando (1775), built near the Alameda, a large park that had a foundational history in Mexico City. The Colegio de San Fernando prepared and launched missionaries like Fray Junípero Serra into the missions of northern Mexico and the Californias. This return to certain origins for Peyri and, perhaps fictively for Tac, occurred at an intense political moment. However, the connections with indigenous ideas and political sympathies in the era remained strong. From San Fernando, Tac would have been close to the Iglesia y Monesterio de San Francisco (c. 1521), where an open-air church served an Indian parish near the Zócalo, and Franciscan Fray Pedro de Gante founded San José de los Naturales (1529), the first monastic school for indigenous scholars in the Americas. The school had long ceased to serve that function when Pablo Tac was in Mexico City between 1832 and 1834.

Arriving at a time when indigenous communities in Mexico were presenting their own demands in the federal district concerning their new status as citizens of the nation, Tac must have developed a passion for politics and indigenous rights while living in Mexico City. Liberal governments held the wealth of the Church under scrutiny during this period of political battles between the Church and state, conservatives and liberals. The instability made it untenable for Pablo Tac and Agapito Amamix to remain behind in Mexico when Peyri left. The three left for Barcelona in Catalonia, Spain.

From Spain they went to Rome where Tac and Amamix began to study in the fall of 1834 at the Collegium Urbanum de Propaganda Fide. After four years of Latin grammar and a year of rhetoric, Pablo Tac devised a way to write Luiseño.[3] In so doing, he wrote the first history of Luiseños during the colonial era, and produced a grammar and partial dictionary of Luiseño-Spanish (from A–Cu). Having grown up during the initial decade of Mexican Independence, when indigenous people became full citizens under Mexican law, Pablo Tac spoke from a position of indigenous equality. He was the first to write a grammar and dictionary of Luiseño, and the first California Indian to put a tribal history in writing.

Called *Prose Lingua Californeses* and subtitled "Studi grammaticali sulla lingua della California," it can be read alongside and in conversation with mission records and ethnographic writing from the era.[4] Fray Geronimo Boscana lived at Missions San Buenaventura and San Luis Rey prior to writing his ethnographic piece on the indigenous population at Mission San Juan Capistrano during the 1820s. Fray Peyri at Mission San Luis Rey also left records and correspondence that intersected with information that Tac included. However, Tac's manuscript demonstrates his unique knowledge of language, an excellent use of literary genres, and an agility with humor and words.

Tac wrote the grammar/dictionary and history for Cardinal Giuseppe Mezzofanti, the Vatican Librarian, and an archivist and linguist who collected the grammars of many previously unwritten languages and dialects. Mezzofanti fostered cultural exchanges in multilingual poetry readings and in the archival records he constructed. He had information on indigenous translations of Catholic words for god and the saints compiled, and a Mexican manuscripts transcribed for future study. He had students write down plays, poems, and verbal orations and stories to varying degrees. Most frequently his students generated partial grammars, dictionaries, and certain historical notes or artifacts. Mezzofanti knew many languages and worked in the enlightenment spirit that favored knowledge acquisition to create a fairer society. He gathered languages from around the world, including Italian and eastern European dialects, and indigenous grammars written in translation between French or Spanish. The large archive consisted of work by students and his many assistants.

Tac's writing was unique from within that archive. It consisted of a grammar, which united it with the rest of the collection. Within that grammar he wrote a history, which he started three times, left and returned to among grammatical examples. The repetition of stories, such as that of the encounter between prominent Luiseño leaders and the Spanish missionary with his soldiers, is a technique often used in Luiseño oral storytelling. Each time the texture gets richer and more elaborate. Tac began the grammar translating between Latin and Luiseño. He soon found that too much of a "bend" and switched to Luiseño-Spanish, revealing the translations he had heard during his entire childhood. Tac continued to use a Latin grammatical structure for writing Luiseño, and many of the constructs did not apply. However, his description of the language remained relevant to the Luiseño grammatical structures found later, except for words that had fallen out of use.[5]

None of the other archives had the same depth of character and close relationship to language that Tac's writings evinced. His carefully constructed dictionary, divided into three separate booklets, led with Luiseño words and gave Spanish translations. Many of the translations would have needed cultural interpretation to be understood in Spanish. Others he left blank, seemingly because Spanish had no way to express the action, thing, or meaning.

Twenty-nine other young men entered the college in 1834. Some arrived in pairs, like Tac and Amamix, from places defined by political conflict. Tac identified himself as "*Cheegnajuisci* in California" or "people from Quechla in Californina." Quechla referred to his ancestral territory and to the land on which the mission settled. In his writing, Tac expressed a tribal and a Christian identity, that of an Indian (*indio*) and a San Luiseño. He used specific names for different indigenous groups, and called Apaches "a *casta* of people," referring to yet another kind of identity. *Casta* categories emerged over time in each place, largely through court rulings. They derived from a large array of social and historical factors that had to do with intersecting hierarchies. Tac's sense of identities might have been sharpened by studying with young men from so many places and historical situations.

Tac wrote the grammar and dictionary in Luiseño-Spanish and the history in Spanish. Read together, they present a bilingual world in which translation does not simply render one word to another. It often marks the incommensurate nature of meaning between concepts in the two cultures due to their systems of thought. The meaning and conception of God, for example, seems to be expressed in two different ways. When writing in Spanish, Tac used the Spanish word *Dios* to refer to God. When writing in Luiseño, he used *"Chanichñich."* The terms reference distinct histories and figures. *Chanichñich* is related to a much older linguistic variant on an angry being. Unlike *Dios*, *Chanichñich* conveyed the laws and established rites and ceremonies for the preservation of life through dance.

A blind Luiseño prayer leader first taught Catholic ideas to those who joined the mission in 1798. Tac's Luiseño-Spanish dictionary contains many words related to Luiseño thought and practices distinct from those in Spanish Catholicism. In the dictionary the word *caquis*, for example, meant "mimicking the caw of the raven," a sacred bird in Luiseño religion connected to *Chinichñich* ritual. Tac included nine verbs related to the raven, including the "person who ordered [the caw of a raven] be mimicked" and "the person who made the caw of the raven many times."

Many of Pablo Tac's dictionary words are about movement related to dance and ritual. The word *as* refers to domesticated animals and to the shaman's familiar – a supernatural figure who imparts knowledge and skills. *Aluiis*, or "the act of looking up," speaks to the actions of dancers who looked up in the *Chanichñich* dance. *Chappiis* means "rain stopping." However, most of the verb forms are about the person who made the rain stop. Some words need interpretation. Though they translate, they lose their meaning. *Chocorris* is "to make like a mountain or wooded hill." Tac gave five related forms, including *chocorrimocui* – which, extrapolating from other entries, would mean "person who makes them act like a mountain or wooded hill." The concept makes no sense in Spanish and needs greater explication to be understood.

In California, as elsewhere in the Americas, Europeans confronted societies that allowed the body to produce knowledge through dance, and to render the spiritual world into corporal existence. Tac's descriptions of dance take into account the movement of the dancers, the direction from which they entered, the exact direction in which they moved, where they directed their gestures, and whether they looked up or down. These considerations have to do with the concerns of Luiseño astrologers who structured the ritual areas and movement to reflect their conceptions of the cosmos. Unlike Europeans, who considered dance "entertainment," indigenous people danced to rectify conditions and to speak through alternative vocabularies and historical concepts related to movement.

Dance is a site of alternative literacy in this society: it helps create, display, and convey knowledge and power.[6] Tac writes about dance in two different sections of his history. One deals with questions of group identity and speaks to conceptual change in that identity. Dance was among three subsections in the history. The other two concern "daily life" and the "ballgame." All three form part of a larger narrative that celebrates the ritual authority and knowledge of Luiseño elders, and the skills of new leaders who moved most easily between the two languages and cultures.

Within the tradition that Tac knew, dance produced knowledge and could regenerate power. Singers, dancers, and elders who trained villagers for different ceremonies participated in dance practice. The rehearsals also included those who prepared *toloache*, a deadly plant if not properly administered before certain dances and rituals, as well as those who created and stored the dance regalia, made the paints, and remembered and recreated the elements of ritual. Tac acknowledged that the dance of women was beyond his sphere of knowledge.

The overarching story of Tac's history is the encounter between the missionary, military, and an important Luiseño leader. Tac writes three different versions of the encounter, and in all three, the leader's friendship enables the Spanish to settle. In telling the story, Tac apparently worked in dialogue with Spanish histories of conquest. However, although Tac wrote during an enlightenment era, he inserted Luiseño narratives and stories of collective situations and imagination into his writing.

Asked to write a dialogue in Luiseño that he translated into Spanish, Tac told the story of Blood and Rabbit, both of whom have human qualities and go hunting together. Rabbit explains he is not a true rabbit. The process of metamorphosis, already important within the oral culture, then becomes part of the literature. The dialogue also goes over particular rules governing hunting. In all of this Tac explains non-western assumptions about nature and human beings. As he does so, elements of the oral tradition and underlying cultural norms become part of the literary history of Luiseños.

Mezzofanti must have asked Tac to write a Latin sketch of different Indian people in California. He includes people from missions San Fernando, San Diego, San Luis Rey, San Juan Capistrano, San Gabriel, and Santa Barbara, and comments on the Apaches and Yuma whom he met while traveling in California. He describes people by their dance, looks, and speech. Willing and confident to speak about people from the mission and their language, Tac seems reluctant to add his personal opinions. His hesitation might be attributed to the fact that indigenous people usually addressed their own history rather than representing other groups. Tac also stressed the importance of truth and accuracy in the manuscript.

For Pablo Tac, the colonial context emerged out of the political defeat of his ancestors. Yet he insisted on Luiseño land ownership, political leadership, ideas and practices, during a time of enormous change and population loss among indigenous groups. Tac reveals the striking differences in Luiseño/Spanish thought and culture. He speaks to the process of moving between, documenting the historical world under Spain. Although Tac wrote with humor, a shadow of sorrow and lament seemed to hover over the grammar. He frequently used the verb "to cry" in grammatical examples. When the term first appears toward the beginning of the manuscript, Tac sets it against the example of someone who laughs. However, although "to cry" reappears later, "to be happy" does not.

Tac's writing focused on Luiseño thought and social relationships during a time of political defeat for indigenous people, some of whose dances and languages he describes. He demonstrated how Luiseño elders accessed power through things such as dance and inherited status, and elaborated on the new forms of power that he used: writing, speaking, and dressing in certain ways. Tac recognized the hierarchies and distinctions in Luiseño, colonial, and Spanish society. He favored things that were distinctively Luiseño, referred to "we" or Luiseño practices, expressed allegiances with other Luiseños, and recorded the language and knowledge of his culture. His manuscript was more thorough and precise than other writings Mezzonfanti held in his collection.

The Painted Story

The Church meant to establish a new order within society and used images as much as words to convey it. Missionaries and soldiers brought paintings and statues to California. Spaniards used these images to heighten their own devotional practices and to convey Christian ideas and practices to indigenous people. Colonial Luiseños used the same word for "to write" as "to paint" and "to signal": *nauis*. Each word and practice had its own history in Spanish. However, the same word introduced painting and writing into Luiseño society. It identified two primary ways the Spaniards conveyed meaning during the process. The word *nauis* did not refer to Luiseño design, or body, rock, and sand painting.

European images first circulated in the environs of the missions as prints, further relating the visual world to print culture. They were ordered by the missionaries, often in enough numbers that they could have been given to every baptized person at the mission. Prints were framed and hung in mission chapels and passed out to the baptized indigenous converts. The missionaries also made large orders for pigments. Indigenous painters drew baroque configurations and framed the prints on church and chapel walls. Thus, the missionaries established a proliferation of Christian narratives concerning history and sacred events.

Images of the Virgin Mary, the cross, the Archangels, and the Stations of the Cross hung in all the mission chapels and churches. The paintings and statues conformed to the politics governing painting and the production of images established during the late sixteenth century due to the edicts passed by the Council of Trent. The Council produced legislation that determined new Church policies after the Reformation, as new Christians and potential painters entered the Church throughout Latin America. The edicts tried to impede popular religiosity and heretical representations. They preferred "stylistic realism": three-dimensional figures wearing conventional religious clothing, and icons of the virgin and various saints and Archangels. They encouraged the representation of biblical stories but not the recounting of popular legends. Local and national laws further governed colonial painting. They generally corresponded to guild restrictions that favored the Spanish and creole masters. The majority of native people either painted their stories under the supervision of shop masters or produced anonymous work. Even the well-known indigenous painters of the Cusco school in the Andes did not sign their paintings when patrons commissioned the pieces.

At Mission Santa Inés, a Chumash artisan painted a canvas picture that provided a particular interpretation of the story of the Archangel Raphael as both Catholic saint and Chumash leader. Indeed, the word for saint was translated in one California Indian language as Achachemem, referring to any great person of any lineage. In Santa Inés, artisans painted, carved, and produced cloths for the altar, and indigenous musicians and singers contributed to the mass. The missionaries allowed a Chumash painter to represent Raphael as a Chumash saint when the church was rebuilt after a war in the 1820s. The figure had the correct iconography to represent Saint Rafael: a healer with his healing pouch and a fish with which he had cured illness and blindness.

The overall image conformed to Chumash visual logic. The painter represented the Archangel by using a Chumash painting technique, outlining the image in red and black. He wore a traditional Chumash cape of hide. The fish resembled a whale effigy, a talisman in Chumash society. The Archangel cradled it in his arms.

Some members of a precolonial society of men and women leaders from different Chumash tribes belonged to the Antap organization. They also held prestigious positions within the missions as cantors, skilled artisans, painters, *alcaldes*, translators, and healers. Tac narrated indigenous lines of lineage and authority with words, whereas this painting of the Archangel Raphael represented narratives of indigenous lineage, authority, and power at the mission.

Mission San Fernando was founded in 1797 at a crossroads of tribal regions. Most of the land on its borders was held by autonomous tribes through the 1820s. The church décor included an indigenous tactile and visual narrative, featuring multiple colors, fabrics, and dimensions, and a certain vernacular style. The altar piece (*reredos*) behind the altar consisted of four large and four smaller mirrors, which reflected objects of radiance in the church. The mirrors also replaced the traditional painted altarpiece. Cloth was lavishly used to drape statues and dress saints. A statue of Saint Joseph in a colored garment stood in front of the altar railing, framed by a canopy of red cloth. The cloth had a vernacular meaning. It was a cornerstone of mission production and a crucial element in the dressing of indigenous converts. It was usually made in the mission textile rooms or imported. The mission church used an extensive number of wax figures that could have also been made in the mission's tallow factories. Artisans at Mission San Fernando painted the façade of the church red, and Indian painters reproduced European and indigenous motifs on church walls and corridors. The sculptures spoke to indigenous religious practices and aesthetics. One of the sculpted images presented Jesus Christ on the cross hanging in the skirt that male dancers in Southern California used for the Eagle dance. A sculpture of the Virgin Mary bore attributes of an indigenous woman with strong defined arms, bare breasts partly covered by long hair, and bare feet.

Indigenous artists produced fourteen paintings of the Stations of the Cross. Though copied from European paintings or printed images, the resulting visual narrative had an indigenous sensibility. The painters placed a single feather in a variety of shapes and sizes on the soldiers' helmets. Their paint strokes resembled the texture of feathers. The representation of the soldiers' cruel treatment of Jesus has few parallels in European art. The visceral rendition of the bloodied Christ in Stations Ten and Twelve was characteristic of the art work in heavily indigenous parishes. The women wear the same jewelry worn by settlers at the mission and *presidio*, and the men don clothing typical of the era's secular population. The story suggests a perspective drawn from indigenous experiences of colonial society.

The most interesting thing about the paintings are the horses present in eight of the fourteen paintings. They are the only figures that stare at the audience. Although their bodies are placed sideways, their eyes and heads look forward. In California, as in other areas of indigenous Mexico, the horse was a prominent cultural symbol – sometimes more important than the Catholic saints and angels. During most of the frontier colonial period, however, Indians were prohibited from riding horses. The animals, a symbol of colonial authority and military strength, became something else in indigenous thought and iconography. They supported the autonomy of Yokuts people who stole and traded in them.

For Luiseños, the word *as* referred to the shaman's familiar (a spiritual helper). The horse and the cow became "spirit helpers." The fact that they were painted on rocks at religious sites elsewhere in California suggests that they were incorporated into a wide range of indigenous beliefs. Chumash accounts of the 1824 war reported that many of the leaders jumped on horses, disappeared, and reappeared on mountain tops, evidence of the animals' service during wartime. In addition, the sound of the mare looking for her child became part of a Luiseño dance during the colonial era. The visual narrative of the horse shows one way that indigenous societies incorporated the horse into their systems of thought, political strategies, and imaginaries. They appropriated an instrument of colonial domination into one of their systems of power.

Narration and Power

Pablo Tac wrote down the many translations of Spanish concepts that his elders had made. Writing in Luiseño, Spanish, and Latin, he explained more than any other writer how Luiseños persisted under colonial conditions. Tac's writing is infused with the knowledge, ideas, and social relationships he grew up with in his youth. He conveyed a sense of Luiseño knowledge production, leadership, and imagination. Tac moved between cultures, and marked the verbal limits of that process.

Indian paintings, a form of indigenous writing, represented native peoples, their lineages, and elements of culture and knowledge. Painted images and written words contested the idea that these societies lacked knowledge and ancestry. Tac's manuscript, other writings by indigenous authors, and paintings offer ways of thinking about the difficult years of colonial and Mexican rule. They form part of an indigenous archive, together with other sources such as dance practice and oral narratives.

Narration in this society did not primarily take place in the realm of writing or painting, but through alternative practices of knowledge formation, dance, and stories (as other oral mediums). They embodied community memory and experience, and defined forms of leadership and power acquisition. In addition to writing, they expressed the sometimes incommensurate ways of seeing in indigenous and colonial thought.

Though dancing was popular during the mission era, it became more difficult to perform in later years. Fernando Librado, a Chumash man, described dancing in the Santa Barbara region in the mid-nineteenth century. All five Chumash dialects (from the missions) were used in some dances, as were certain Yokuts dialects. Few indigenous people knew the sacred languages except the singers. Librado tried to learn one song but the man who taught him finally stopped. He found Librados' voice too adopted to Spanish to intone the sound correctly.

For some dances, parts of the song had been lost and the song fragmented. Cycles of a particular dance may be interrupted by the death of one who specialized in the song. Skills were lost that were foundational to certain dances, such as the arrow dance. The cultural healing and ability to transform conditions, the knowledge gained from dance, and the many skills that made dance song and movement possible, shifted slowly but dramatically by mid-to-late nineteenth century.

Oral narratives, in contrast, were passed down from family to family, and foregrounded indigenous narrative structures. Three stories of the Chumash war were initially elaborated based on the experience of close relatives in the immediate communities.[7] They are dramatic stories that told sides of the four-month rebellion not available in other accounts of this event. They talk about forms of power and political visions that Chumash leaders held during the revolt, and foreground the power of Chumash leaders. They identify the causes and the major events of the revolt, as experienced by the indigenous people involved in the stories. All three blame the bloodshed on the betrayal of a native assistant too close to the priest. They express the people's vulnerability, their sense of impending death, and the determination to live or die together.

Indigenous writing in California focused on those with power in the community. The same emphasis can be seen in the Chumash painting of the Archangel Rafael, and in the stories of the Chumash war that became community narratives. The indigenous literary record is intertwined with other kinds of cultural and language productions in the colonial and

Mexican eras. Tac's writing responded to colonial representations of things indigenous, and presented a specific narrative voice and set of interests that defined an indigenous intervention into the production of knowledge about California.

Notes

1. I have used these sources and developed ideas presented here more fully in my recent book *Saints and Citizens: Indigenous Histories of Colonial and Mexican California* (Berkeley: University of California Press, 2014).
2. See Rose Marie Beebe and Robert Senkewictz, *Testimonios: Early California Through the Eyes of Women, 1815–1848* (Berkeley: Heyday Press and the Banroft Library, 2006).
3. To see Pablo Tac's entire manuscript published in its original and in translation, please see Lisbeth Haas, *Pablo Tac: Indigenous Scholar Writing on Luiseño Literature and Colonial History* (Berkeley: University of California Press, 2011). The book also gives a biography of Tac and analysis of his writing. See also the development of these ideas more fully in "'Raise Your Sword and I Will Eat You': Luiseño Scholar Pablo Tac" in Steven Hackel, *Alta California: Peoples in Motion, Identities in Formation, 1769–1850* (San Marino: Huntington Library Press, 2010).
4. Tac's manuscript in the original: under the title *Prose Lingua Californese*, "Studi grammaticali sulla lingua della California" n.d., Fondo Speciale Giuseppe Mezzofanti, cartone III, fascicolo I, Biblioteca comunale dell'Archiginnasio, Bologna.
5. See Sandra Chung, "Remarks on Pablo Tac's *La Lingua degli Indi Luiseño*," *International Journal of American Linguistics* 40.4(I) (October 1974). Eric Elliot, *Dictionary of Rincón Luiseño* (Ph.D. diss., University of California, San Diego, 1999).
6. Dance scholarship about non-western dance and indigenous records from California both offered ways to understand sound/dance in this tradition.
7. See an extended use of the narratives of Maria Solares, Lucrecia Garcia, and Luisa Ignacio and their placement among other narratives of the 1824 revolt in *Saints and Citizens*. See another use of a similar body of oral histories in Deborah Miranda's *Bad Indians* (Berkeley: Heyday Books, 2012).

CHAPTER 3

Spanish and Mexican Literature

Vincent Pérez

The name California has both Spanish and literary origins. The word was coined by the Spanish author of chivalric romances, Garci Rodríguez Ordóñez de Montalvo. Appearing in his early sixteenth-century novel *Las sergas de esplandián* (*The Exploits of Espandián*), it denoted an island, named after the fictional Queen Calafía, the leader of a tribe of "black Amazon women." Her kingdom was located "on the right hand of the Indies ... very near the Terrestrial Paradise." The weapons and other devices used by this tribe, according to the story, "are all made of gold," because "[i]n all the island there is no other metal." The names Calafia and California appear not to refer to any person or object in the physical world. However, they derive from the Arabic word *khalifa* (caliph). The term calls to mind the centuries-long wars, known as the *reconquista* (reconquest), completed in 1492. Though it is not clear when the name was first used to denote what is now Baja California, it probably "occurred sometime in the late 1530s or early 1540s as a sardonic acknowledgement that the legends of rich islands to the west ... had little basis in fact."[1]

While this etymology may be familiar to scholars and students of California history, the word's origin, which dates back some two decades before Hernán Cortés conquered the Aztec empire, suggests the problem of demarcating the dates of the Spanish era in California literary history. In a broad sense, the era begins with de Montalvo's novel, which was very popular in Spain in the early 1500s, and which fed the imagination of countless Spanish explorers who made their way to the "Indies" during that period. It officially ended approximately three centuries later, in 1821, with the conclusion of the Mexican War of Independence, when Mexico gained its sovereignty from Spain and in 1823 became a federal republic. Unofficially, because of its century-long duration and vast geographic scope, the Spanish era in California and Southwest (literary) history stretches into the modern period. However, the same chronological ambiguity characterizes the Mexican era. Though officially this

43

period lasted only twenty-five years (1823–48), in a broad sense the Mexican era continues to this day. The cultural legacy of Mexican California, sustained by the proximity of California to its home nation and multiple waves of Mexican immigrants to the state, indicate that the Mexican era did not end neatly when the United States annexed Alta (Upper) California in 1850. The combined cultural inheritance of the Spanish and Mexican periods forms a central current of California culture to the present, though this legacy is often narrowly identified with the nineteenth century.

The literary lives of three nineteenth-century writers – Mariano Guadalupe Vallejo (1807–90), María Amparo Ruiz de Burton (1832–95), and Helen Hunt Jackson (1830–85) – illustrate central themes and tensions that form the fabric of the literary history of Spanish and Mexican California. Their story, extended through Vallejo back to the Spanish colonial era and through Ruiz de Burton and Jackson to the U.S. era, serves as a template for the neglected literary history of this foundational period in California's past. This story, and related early narratives, also underscore the shameful vacancy that until recently marked the literary histories of California, the U.S. West, and the nation as a whole. Elaborated and historicized, the works of Vallejo, Ruiz de Burton, and Jackson frame three categories: 1) autobiographies (*testimonios*) and histories; 2) fiction and other literary genres, including print culture; and 3) literature of Spanish exploration, colonization, and settlement.

Vallejo's multi-volume historical autobiography, *Recuerdos históricos y personales tocante a la Alta California* [Historical and Personal Memoirs Relating to Alta California] (1875) was the first comprehensive history of Alta California. A primary source for countless later histories of the region, it nevertheless remained unpublished for more than a century. Not far from the original manuscript, housed at University of California, Berkeley, lies Hubert Howe Bancroft's thirty-nine volume collected works, including a seven-volume *History of California* (1884–90). Unlike this better-known history, Vallejo's work offers a Mexican Californian perspective on the pre-1850 era and ends with a scathing indictment of U.S. mistreatment of the conquered Mexican population.[2]

Vallejo and the seventy-seven other Californios (Mexican Californians), whose lives spanned the Spanish, Mexican, and U.S. eras, granted their dictated *testimonios* (testimonials) to Bancroft in good faith after he sought them out as primary sources for his *History of California*. Like Vallejo, they hoped that Bancroft would use their narratives to give voice to Californio history. As the first volume appeared, however, they discovered that their stories were silenced by the weight of Bancroft's massive history, "smothered [by the text] into footnotes below the main narrative, revised and in many cases discounted by Bancroft."[3] These two historians offer radically different interpretations of the Gold Rush years. Vallejo presents a narrative of collapse and betrayal, while Bancroft writes a history of progress and heroism. The story of Vallejo's text closely resembles that of fellow Californio Antonio María Osio's *The History of Alta California*, which, although written decades earlier in 1851, was not published in a complete English translation until 1996.

However, Bancroft's role in preserving the *testimonios* as well as thousands of other pre-1850 documents pertaining to Spanish and Mexican California cannot be overstated. The "Archive of California" is an enormous collection of documents that were copied or summarized by Bancroft's assistants in the 1870s. It comprises sixty-three volumes with nearly 300,00 pages of documents. Vallejo bequeathed his family's own large archive of historical documents to Bancroft at the same time that he submitted his *testimonio*. Following in Bancroft's footsteps, the historian Herbert Eugene Bolton (1879–1953) published a pioneering body of scholarship on the Spanish-American borderlands, inaugurating a new field in U.S. historiography. Equally important, Bolton's English-language editions of early Spanish Californian writers – such as the Catholic missionaries Francisco Palóu, Junípero Serra, Francisco Garcés, and others – brought recognition and interest to this period in California's past.

Just before Vallejo narrated his *testimonio* to Bancroft's assistants, his longtime friend, the Southern California rancher and writer María Amparo Ruiz de Burton, published her first novel, the historical romance *Who Would Have Thought It?* (1872). The work was a triumph for a western writer of that era, especially for a woman who learned English as a second language and who identified with her Californio and Mexican heritage. Ruiz de Burton published the novel with a major East coast press at a time when racial attitudes presented an almost insurmountable obstacle for both Mexican American and Black writers. A domestic novel set during the Reconstruction era, this remarkable book interrogates the racial and gender identities of the era, addressing the meaning of U.S. nationhood for Mexican Americans and other racial minorities as it depicts the disenfranchised status of women during the post-bellum period. Ruiz de Burton lost most of her ranch lands after the U.S. conquest. As White squatters and settlers took up residence on her land, corrupt officials helped these land grabbers exploit a legal apparatus that was inherently biased toward Mexicans. In a span of two decades Ruiz de Burton and Vallejo, like most other *Californio* landowners, were dispossessed from their land. As hundreds of thousands of American settlers arrived in the region following the Gold Rush, the Californios and their descendants became subject to the same social and legal barriers as African Americans and other racial minority groups.

A composite of the stories of these Californio ranchers, Ruiz de Burton's *The Squatter and the Don* (1885) narrates the story of Californio patriarch Don Mariano Alamar, a character closely modeled after Vallejo but also drawn from the author's own struggle to maintain possession of her land. Like several other better-known nineteenth-century novels, such as Harriet Beecher Stowe's *Uncle Tom's Cabin* (1852) and Helen Hunt Jackson's *Ramona* (1884), *The Squatter and the Don* draws from the tradition of sentimental or domestic fiction to address a great social injustice and call for immediate political change. With descriptive detail reminiscent of a nineteenth-century realist or naturalist novel, *The Squatter and the Don* depicts the appalling abuses of the newly established U.S. legal and political apparatus, which favored arriving U.S. settlers and squatters in California over Mexican American landowners who had acquired their properties as land grants during the Mexican era. Now formally included in the U.S. literary canon, since it was first republished in 1993 *The Squatter and the Don* has generated a large body of scholarship. Like Vallejo's "Historical and Personal Memoirs," it represses the submerged social and racial contradictions of Mexican Californian agrarian society, such as the oppressed status of Indian and Mexican *campesinos* (peasants) within the agrarian social economy. However, since the novel's republication its phenomenal influence across the disciplines makes it one of the most important literary works by an early Spanish or Mexican Californian.[4]

Unlike Ruiz de Burton's novels, which have only recently been re-printed, Jackson's *Ramona* was more popular in the nineteenth century than any other novel except *Uncle Tom's Cabin*. It was an immediate bestseller, and has since gone through hundreds of printings, making it the most famous California and Southwest novel of the nineteenth century. The novel inspired the mission revival movement, which the author Carey McWilliams in his 1948 book *North from Mexico* disparaged as a product of the region's imagined Spanish "fantasy heritage." The novel gave rise to John S. McGroarty's *The Mission Play* (1912), which for decades was performed at the San Gabriel Mission and elsewhere, becoming a regional institution and "part of the cultural fabric of the growing [Los Angeles] metropolis."[5] Though Jackson was not of Spanish or Mexican ancestry, her novel is set on a Mexican ranch, or hacienda, in the years following the U.S. possession. Jackson drew her setting and story in part from interviews with Antonio Coronel, a prominent Californio politician and rancher who contributed his own testimonial to Bancroft's research project. Through its narration of the story of Ramona, a bi-racial woman (*mestiza*) adopted by a landed Spanish/Creole family, the novel sought to address the plight of California's indigenous population after the U.S. takeover. This political purpose, however, was lost to most readers. Rather than embracing the novel's dramatic romance between Ramona and her Native American suitor Alessandro as an affirmation of these characters' racial difference, Jackson's mostly White audience identified with the Spanish cultural heritage symbolized by the hacienda setting. However, Ramona cannot be dismissed simply because it played a central role in generating the Spanish-focused mission revival movement. Comparing *The Squatter and the Don*'s and *Ramona*'s differing approaches to race, David Luis-Brown observes that "... while *Squatter* is concerned with carving out a space for *Californios* in whiteness, [*Ramona*] ... enacts a reformist project upsetting racial norms and establishing the personhood of Indians ..."[6] *Ramona* serves to highlight class and racial contradictions Ruiz de Burton overlooks. This may explain why the poet José Martí, founder of Cuba's movement to gain its independence from Spain, extolled *Ramona* and in 1888 translated it into Spanish.

Had they been available to her, Jackson would no doubt have been drawn to the testimonials by Mexican Californians compiled in the 1870s by Bancroft. Along with Vallejo's, these autobiographical works include Juan Bautista Alvarado's *Vignettes of Early California*, Josefa Carrillo's untitled *testimonio*, Antonio Franco Coronel's *Cosas de California* (Tales of Mexican California), Angustias De La Guerra's *Ocurrencias en California* (Occurrences in California), Apolinaria Lorenzana's *Memorias* (Memoirs), José Francisco Palomares' untitled *testimonio*, María Inocenta Pico's *Cosas de California* (Things about California), Eulalia Pérez's *Una vieja y sus recuerdos* (An Old Woman and Her Memories), Platón Vallejo's *Memoirs of the Vallejos*, and Salvador Vallejo's *Notas históricas sobre California* (*Historical Notes about California*).[7] Brigida Briones' autobiographical sketches, published in English in *Century Illustrated Monthly Magazine* in 1891, should also be included in this group even though they were not a product of Bancroft's research project. With the exception of Mariano Guadalupe Vallejo's much longer "Historical and Personal Memoirs," a number of Californio *testimonios* have now been published in English. However, until recently, these works usually appeared in anthologized fragments, sometimes with poor translations. Even today, only fifteen of a total of seventy-eight works have been published in their entirety.

Contemporary scholars approach the *testimonios* as both literary texts and historical documents, identifying the rich complexity of their double meaning. By telling their life stories, *Californio* narrators speak as foundational historians for the Mexican American and U.S. Latino communities. However, their double function opens up a further complication for readers. Because these works were elicited narratives, dictated to Bancroft's agents and structured around a set of questions that Bancroft wished to be asked, they are quite distinct from traditional autobiography. They more closely resemble the genre of testimonials, autobiographical narratives that must be understood as highly mediated works, the products of a collaborative process in which the interviewer plays a central role in shaping the narrative. Despite their differences from traditional autobiography, when set in the context of official history, like other testimonials from across Latin America these works are true counter-narratives that capture the oppositional viewpoint of a conquered and dispossessed population. Whether viewed as historical or autobiographical accounts, they provide a crucial critical perspective on Bancroft's and other standard histories.[8]

During the Spanish and Mexican periods, Alta California was a sparsely populated frontier region with an agrarian social economy comprised of hundreds of ranches that were owned by a group of elite families. As Jackson portrays in *Ramona*, Indians and *mestizos* comprised the *campesino* (peasant/peon) work force on these ranches. They were regarded by the landed classes as subordinate and racially inferior. Before the U.S. possession, the Vallejo family owned the largest group of ranch properties in the north. The Carrillo family accumulated the most land in the south. The Mexican population in 1848 was approximately 15,000. Following the discovery of gold the same year, the population increased more than tenfold to 200,000, transforming native Mexican Californians into a small racial minority amid a majority of European-Americans. This small Spanish-speaking population and its descendants were denied full rights of citizenship and were racially vilified by a dominant society fueled by the ideology of Manifest Destiny. Yet it produced a large body of writing, including landmark novels and an expansive print culture that continues to re-define early California and U.S. literary history.

From the mid-nineteenth through the early twentieth century, approximately 200 Spanish-language newspapers and periodicals were published by Mexican and Hispanic Californians. They were published in almost every region of the state, with many based in or near Los

Angeles and San Francisco. These and hundreds of other such newspapers from across the country comprise a substantial part of two new digital databases. Many writings from this archive have now been published in English in a variety of anthologies, academic journals, monographs, and scholarly studies. The archive includes the first Spanish-language newspaper in the United States, *El Misisipí*, published in 1808 in New Orleans, and the first two published in the region that became the U.S. Southwest, *La Gaceta de Texas* (The Texas Gazette) and *El Mexicano*, both of which were founded in Texas in 1813. California's Spanish-language newspapers included *El Clamor Público* (The Public Clamor, 1855–59) and *La Crónica* (The Chronicle, 1872–92), both based in in Los Angeles; *El Eco del Pacífico* (The Pacific Echo, 1856–?) and *El Nuevo Mundo* (The New World, 1864–68), which were located in San Francisco; and Santa Barbara's *La Gaceta* (The Gazette, 1879–81). The writer and publisher Francisco F. Ramírez (1837–?) is the most important figure in nineteenth-century Spanish-language journalism. For decades, he was a leading voice for the Mexican Californian community.

Along with presenting news, information, and entertainment, these newspapers also served "as forums for intellectuals, writers, and politicians, and often [spearheaded] political and social movements ... "[9] In California they championed the rights of Mexican and Hispanic Americans, working to promote ethnic unity, pride, and empowerment at a time when English-language conduits did little more than stigmatize this population. Ramirez's *El Clamor Público* published articles and editorials that directly challenged the practices of the new U.S. legal and political regime in the state. It called for Mexican Americans to resist the new order by reclaiming their constitutional rights as American citizens. Writings by Pablo de la Guerra and Ramírez illustrate this line of criticism in *El Clamor Público*. De la Guerra was a member of a landed family from Santa Barbara whose history spanned the Spanish, Mexican, and U.S. eras. In 1856, he published an indictment of the injustices against the native Mexican population. The piece was drawn from his speech, "The Californios," which he presented to the California constitutional convention in 1850. In his essay De la Guerra refers to Mexican Californians as "foreigners in their own land" – a phrase adopted by the Chicano Movement of the 1960s – and as a subjugated population now "prostrated before the [U.S.] conquerors."[10]

Many of Ramírez's editorials propose a similar argument, often with striking rhetorical flourishes, as, for example, when he refers to U.S.

democracy in California as a "lynchocracy." As the number of extra-legal executions of Mexicans and other Hispanics increased, the killings became a recurring subject in Ramírez's editorials in *El Clamor Público*. In contrast to the English-language press, Ramírez denounced these executions, placing them in the context of the land struggle between Mexican Californians and U.S. settlers as well as in relation to the expansionist policies of the United States. As the term "lynchocracy" dramatically asserts, Ramírez cited the killings not only to decry them as unjust, but also to condemn the hypocrisy of U.S. democracy he believed these executions symbolized.

El Clamor Público's commitment to creative literature exemplifies how Spanish-language newspapers in California and elsewhere in the United States became the primary publishers of a variety of literary genres, "including poetry, literary prose, serialized novels and even plays," works "often drawn from local writers as well as reprinted from the [books] of the greatest writers of the Hispanic world...."[11] As research by scholars such as Kirsten Silva Gruesz and Luis Torres has demonstrated, poetry was the most common literary genre to be published in Spanish-language newspapers in California. Along with translations of poems and other works by major European writers, and pieces by well-known writers from across Latin America, *El Clamor Público* published many Los Angeles poets. These local poets were often published anonymously, and have yet to be identified. This body of poetry comprises another formerly unknown aspect of Mexican Californian literary history.

Between 1890 and 1930, Mexican immigration transformed California society. A new generation of Spanish-language newspapers were founded by and directed toward immigrants and exiles, but also serving the larger Spanish-speaking California population. Among the notable periodicals from this group, representing primarily Los Angeles and San Francisco, were *Azucena* (The White Lily, 1907–16), *Regeneración* (Regeneration, 1910–18), *La Prensa* (The Press, 1912–24), *El Heraldo de México* (The Herald of Mexico, 1915–52), *Hispano América* (Hispanic America, 1917–34), *El Malcriado* (The Brat, 1923–30), and *La Opinión* (The Opinion, 1926–present). This list represents a cross section of what may be termed the second generation of California's Spanish-language newspapers. Like their forerunners, these newspapers embraced the fundamental assumption that news, politics, and culture were inseparably linked. However, some were primarily conduits of news and/or political ideas, while others, like *El Malcriado*, were literary and satirical newspapers. Collectively they comprise a newly recovered body of

Spanish-language print culture that extends the Mexican Californian literary tradition into the modern era.

Ricardo Flores Magón and Daniel Venegas – the founders of *Regeneración* and *El Malcriado*, respectively – embody two different political and literary approaches in second-generation newspapers. Recognized as one of the most important political theorists of the Mexican Revolution, and a lifelong activist for the working class, today Flores Magón is a revered figure in Mexico and throughout the Americas. Because of his criticism of the Mexican dictator, Porfirio Díaz, in 1903 Flores Magón was forced into exile in the United States. There, with his brothers Enrique and Jesús, he re-established *Regeneración*, a newspaper that they had founded in 1900 in Mexico City. Unlike most Spanish-language newspapers in California of that era, *Regeneración* voiced an openly radical and revolutionary perspective informed by Anarchist and Marxist theory. Political activists as well as writers and publishers, Ricardo and his brothers worked tirelessly to organize and empower working class people of all races both in Mexico and the United States. Their radical politics led to persecution by the FBI and eventually to Ricardo's imprisonment.

In 1923, Venegas founded *El Malcriado* in Los Angeles. Venegas' political, journalistic, and creative sensibility could not have been more different from that of the Flores Magón brothers. His 1928 novel *Las Aventuras de Don Chipote* (*The Adventures of Don Chipote*, English translation, 2000) reveals Venegas' identification with the Mexican working class and immigrant communities. This sentiment defines *Don Chipote* from beginning to end, and obviously parallels the Flores Magón brothers' political solidarity with these groups during the same period. Based on his extant writings, Venegas was not a political theorist, nor an activist. Rather, he was an author of satires, plays, and fiction who during the 1920s worked as a journalist for various Los Angeles newspapers. Before founding *El Malcriado*, "Venagas had worked for *El pueblo* newspaper in Los Angeles and, because *El heraldo de México* published his *Don Chipote*, he may have been a staff writer for that paper as well."[12] Venegas' advocacy for Mexican workers and immigrants took a variety of literary forms, including vaudeville entertainment, musical comedy, and literary burlesque. The hallmark of Venegas' writing, as illustrated in *Don Chipote*, is his use of satirical humor and vernacular language to portray sympathetically the lives of Mexican laborers and immigrants. However, his many works for the theater, which are known today only from newspaper reviews, points to the large body of Spanish-language theatrical works that were written and performed from the mid-nineteenth through the early twentieth centuries.

This is another branch of U.S. Hispanic literary history that has only recently been charted.

Though many Mexican Californian writers identified with the region's Spanish past, Mexico's own relationship to its Spanish colonial history has always been fraught with staggering contradictions. Today there are likely more statues of Spanish explorers in the United States than there are in Mexico. The statue of Juan de Oñate, the conqueror and first Spanish governor of New Mexico, dedicated in 1991 and located near the town of Española, New Mexico, serves as a reminder of this historical anomaly. In California, the 1940 statue of Juan Bautista de Anza in Riverside and the 1988 statue of Gaspar de Portola in Pacifica offer other examples. Mexican nationhood, especially after the Mexican Revolution, was forged through the creation of a cultural identity that embraced the nation's *mestizo* past. As a result, Hernán Cortés and other conquistadors, who symbolized the period of Spanish colonialism, were toppled from their historical thrones. In contrast, after the U.S. conquest and well into the twentieth century something close to the opposite occurred in the U.S. Southwest. Taken by the romance of the Spanish legacy, European-Americans erased the Mexican and *mestizo* past from California history as they developed an affection for everything "Spanish." *Ramona*'s public appropriation as a novel extolling the romance of California's pre-1850 Spanish/Creole ranch culture provides the most conspicuous example.

The literature of Spanish California comprises a variety of genres, including travel chronicles, autobiographical works, religious narratives, biographies, histories, diaries, and letters. Though their subjects may vary, collectively these works posit a set of Spanish/Creole identities constructed through an ideology of racial difference. This ideology marks indigenous peoples as "other" – i.e., savage, uncivilized, and heathen – while establishing the Spanish/Creole colonists and settlers as the standard bearers of civilization and (Christian) morality. The Spanish settlers referred to themselves as *gente de razón* (people of reason) to further assert this distinction. An analysis of Spanish California literature must begin with this assumption and should be carried out in comparative relation to Native American literature and the cultural memory from which it draws. One of the recurring subjects in this body of Alta California writing is native resistance, which took a variety of forms including violent rebellions against Spanish colonization. When the first Spanish expedition arrived in 1769, Alta California's native population numbered between two and three hundred thousand. In 1800 the Spanish/Creole population amounted to approximately 18,000, and as late as the mid-nineteenth century the Mexican and Spanish/Creole population was still relatively small.

California's Spanish myth of origins today continues to shape the region's culture and identity. Popularized by European-American writers and artists in the late nineteenth and early twentieth centuries, the Spanish period in California history is often identified with this picturesque "fantasy heritage." Famously debunked by McWilliams, this view of the Spanish era pervaded California historical and literary discourse for much of the nineteenth and twentieth centuries. The Spanish narrative of origins formed the basis for a cultural and arts movement perhaps best exemplified by the Mission Revival and Spanish Colonial Revival styles in architecture. Along with its architectural expression, the movement encompassed a multitude of products for popular consumption, including novels, plays, prints, paintings, postcards, travel narratives, and newspaper and magazine articles. However, from its inception, the cultural memory of an idealized Spanish past was underwritten by a longstanding racial animus toward the predominantly dark-skinned *mestizo* (Mexican) population. For much of the twentieth century, the popular narrative erased the Mexican, *mestizo*, and indigenous past from the region's historical ledger, transforming the early period into a tale designed to satisfy the European-American imagination.

The appeal of the romantic narrative suggests the problematic status of writings by Spanish and Mexican Californians in the English-language discursive framework that emerged after 1850. Today a new literary history of Spanish and Mexican California is being written. In its broadest sense, this project involves shifting the geographic center of U.S. literary history from the Northeast to the Southwest, where the first (Spanish) European settlement was established in 1598 in present-day New Mexico and where the first North American literary text, Álvar Núñez Cabeza de Vaca's 1542 *Relación* (*The Narrative of Cabeza de Vaca*) was set. Scholars across the Humanities, and especially those working in U.S. Hispanic literary recovery research and Hemispheric American Studies, have contributed greatly to this project.[13] Their scholarship rests on an assumption that Thomas Jefferson recognized as early as 1787: in a letter in which he encouraged a friend to study the Spanish language, Jefferson noted that "the ancient part of American (hemispheric) history is written chiefly in Spanish."[14] When Jefferson penned this letter, the Spanish had already established ten missions in Alta California, most with accompanying forts (*presidios*) and towns (*pueblos*) stretching from San Diego to San Francisco. The Spanish place names across California and the Southwest reflect this colonization, attesting Jefferson's observation, but the Spanish writings of this period have only recently begun to be recognized as foundational texts in U.S. and Southwest literary history.

Much of the first volume of Vallejo's *testimonio* narrates events set during and before the Spanish colonial period and includes descriptions of the indigenous cultures, the process of colonization, and the establishment of the missions. Many other Californio *testimonios*, such as Alvarado's, harken back to the Spanish era as they trace their narrators' family histories. Vallejo proudly asserts his family's roots in the colonial period; his father, Ignacio, was a soldier who was posted in Alta California in 1774 and remained there for the rest of his life. Vallejo also refers to the two earliest Spanish (European) expeditions to Alta California, the first in 1769–70 led by Gaspar de Portola de Rovira (1716–84) and the second in 1774–76 led by Juan Bautista de Anza (1736–88). The latter was the first colonizing expedition to travel by land to Alta California. Beginning with an expedition led by Juan Rodríguez Cabrillo (1500–43) in 1542, in the sixteenth and seventeenth centuries the coast of Alta California had been charted by sea by the Spanish. Cabrillo's expedition marked the first time that Europeans set foot in the region that became the western United States. In 1949, a fourteen foot statue of Cabrillo was dedicated at Point Loma, in San Diego, the bay where Cabrillo touched shore and which he had named San Miguel. Though a summary of the official report of the Cabrillo expedition survives, there is no extant diary or journal by Carrillo himself. Both Portola and De Anza kept travel diaries which, along with several other journals from these land expeditions, have survived, including accounts by the Franciscan missionaries Junípero Serra (1713–84), Juan Crespi (1721–82), and Francisco Garcés (1738–81). Though today Garcés is remembered for his participation in the De Anza expedition, his name stands out for the many expeditions that he led throughout the regions that became Arizona and California, journeys documented in the two-volume *Diary and Itinerary of Francisco Garcés*.

Early travel narratives set in the Americas have generated a large body of scholarship. In the past several decades especially, with the emergence of transnational, hemispheric, comparative, and borderlands approaches to American (U.S.) literature, renewed critical scrutiny has been brought to travel literature of the Spanish colonial period. Though this literature has always been regarded as canonical in countries that were colonized by the Spanish, increasingly many of these works are also being embraced as foundational to North American (U.S.) literary history.

In 1994, *The Norton Anthology of American Literature* created a new section, "Literature to 1620," in which an abridged version of Cabeza de Vaca's account was anthologized. Since then, the effort to expand traditional models of U.S. literary history has led to the addition of other Spanish/Creole colonial-era writers, such as *Sor* (Sister) Juana Inés de la Cruz, a poet, essayist, and early feminist who lived in New Spain in the second half of the seventeenth century. This critical endeavor rests on the assumption that these and other early Spanish writings are the products of complex historical, cultural, economic, and literary currents, and that their lineages therefore rarely conform to a single national or regional tradition. At the same time, informed by fields such as U.S. Ethnic, Hemispheric, Latin American, and Post-Colonial studies, the new model highlights the key role that early travel writing played in the Spanish imperial project in the Americas. This project involved not only the conquest and colonization of vast reaches of the hemisphere, but the conversion to Catholicism of tens of millions of indigenous inhabitants. Much like travel narratives discussed by Mary Louise Pratt, works by early Spanish travel writers employ "strategies of representation" whereby Spanish "subjects seek to secure their innocence in the same moment as they assert European [Spanish] hegemony."[15] Early travel writing, according to Pratt, fashioned a view of the non-European world which served Spanish and European colonialism, paving the way for economic exploitation as well as further imperial expansion.

Much like Cabeza de Vaca's narrative, early California travel writings may be placed in this hemispheric context even as they may also be defined regionally as the earliest Spanish (European) writings from California. And like other early Spanish writings, they may be claimed as landmark literary works in diverse fields including the Spanish-American, U.S., U.S. Latino/a, and Chicano/a cultural traditions. These disparate claims enhance rather than detract from their interpretive richness.[16] Their literary qualities as historical chronicles only add to this richness. Like many other Spanish writings of exploration and discovery, the complexity of early California narratives derives from their multiple functions as travel chronicles, autobiographical narratives, and military or ecclesiastical accounts. Most important, and bridging these multiple roles, these early works both document and interpret the writers' lived experiences as travelers in the unexplored northwest frontier. They are not only highly inflected personal accounts; like all autobiographical writing, they also exhibit creative and fictional qualities. At the time of the first expeditions to Alta California between 1769 and 1776, a long tradition of colonial travel writing, beginning with Cortes' *Cartas de relación* (*Letters from Mexico*, 1519–26) had been established. Cortés, Cabeza de Vaca, and other sixteenth- and seventeenth-century travel writers drew from literary models such as the medieval chivalric romance as they narrated adventures which often seemed to exceed the fantastic events described in this early genre. The accounts by Portola, De Anza, and the missionaries who accompanied them differ in many ways from those of other early Spanish explorers. What stands out, however, is the manner in which the journey of discovery rehearses scenes and motifs from the literary world.

Garcés' travels as described in his *Diary and Itinerary* captures the ways in which the journey motif, structured around the struggle to survive in a desert landscape inhabited by Indian tribes, embodies the interwoven Catholic missionizing and Spanish colonizing ideals. Unlike Serra and Palou, Garcés often traveled only with Indian guides. He led several expeditions from Mission San Xavier del Bac (near Tucson, Arizona) into the uncharted expanses of Alta California. His travels far exceeded those of any other missionary of that era who went unaccompanied by Spanish soldiers. He made a total of five *entradas* (exploratory trips) from 1768 through to 1776. In 1771, he "undertook an eight-hundred mile journey through the desert regions around the Colorado and Gila Rivers," an expedition that helped establish the route for De Anza's first expedition in 1774, which Garcés also joined.[17] His journey of 1775–76 was his fifth. In it he accompanied De Anza's (second) expedition, which was charged with finding an inland route to the San Francisco Bay. Following the orders of the Viceroy of New Spain, Garcés then left De Anza to lead a separate expedition that explored regions of southern and central (Alta) California including the Mojave Desert. Like other early Spanish missionaries, Garcés was driven by the power of Catholic faith and its uncompromising belief in its mission to save the souls of native peoples.

Of all of the Spanish and Mexican Californians examined, several associated with the founding of California's missions, particularly Junípero Serra and his colleague Francisco Palóu, remain today the most well-known figures of the pre-1850 era. Serra's fame extends well beyond California and the United States, where in 1931 a statue of him was unveiled in the Capitol's National Statuary Hall. As the founder of the first nine missions in Alta California, and the president of the mission system from 1769 to 1784, he was beatified in 1988 by Pope John Paul II, and will likely become the first Catholic saint from California. However, long before his beatification, Serra had already become a legendary figure within the Church, and, more generally, in early California and Southwest history. Along with his travel journal, Serra's writings include an extensive body of correspondence, which was published in English in four volumes between 1955 and 1965. His fame has its origins in Palóu's 1787 biography of Serra, *Relación histórica de la vida y apostólicas tareas del venerable Fray Junípero Serra* (Account of the Life and Apostolic Labors of the Venerable Father Junípero Serra). This hagiographic account not only inaugurated Serra's legend in New Spain; it also served to validate the Church's narrative of the Alta California missions at a time when it was not at all clear that the missions would be able to weather the various threats to their existence. A prolific writer, Palou's most important work is the four-volume *Noticias de la Nueva California*, first published in 1857 (*Historical Memoirs of New California*, 1926), a history of the California missions from 1767 to 1784. Palóu's narrative of mission history in this work stands in stark contrast to Vallejo's anticlerical argument in "Historical and Personal Memoirs," where Vallejo draws from Enlightenment philosophy to mount a sustained attack on the missions and their leaders. Juan Crespi, another colleague of Serra whose name also runs through early Alta California history, is best known for his first-hand account of the Portola expedition. The most comprehensive of the three diaries from this journey, the first English translation of Crespi's diary was included in Bolton's *Fray Juan Crespi* (1927).

Bolton's role in the historiography of Spanish California parallels that of Bancroft's influence in creating the long-dominant narrative of Mexican California history. Though both historians recovered and preserved historical and literary works by California's Mexican and Spanish writers, these primary works were usually subsumed by the historians' wider historical projects. Their value as historical sources eclipsed their importance as the literary and cultural inheritance of Mexican and Hispanic Californians. This exemplifies the intrinsic relation between power and knowledge (discourse) as lived by early Mexican and Spanish Californian writers and the urgency of recent U.S. Hispanic literary recovery research. Only in the past several decades has the literature and print culture of Spanish and Mexican California become the subject of scholarly inquiry that would fully rescue this writing from what the poet Derek Walcott has called the "amnesia of the races."

Notes

1. Rose Marie Beebe and Robert Senkewicz, *Lands of Promise and Despair: Chronicles of Early California 1535–1846* (Berkeley: Heyday Books, 2001), 30.
2. In Californio works such as Vallejo's the struggle over the ownership of land parallels the struggle over the ownership of history.
3. Genaro Padilla, *My History, Not Yours: The Formation of Mexican American Autobiography* (Madison: University of Wisconsin Press, 1993), 107.
4. See Amelia Montes and Anne Goldman, eds., *María Amparo Ruiz de Burton: Critical and Pedagogical Perspectives* (Lincoln: University of Nebraska Press, 1987) and The Modern Library (Random House) 2004 reprint.
5. William Deverell, *Whitewashed Adobe: The Rise of Los Angeles and the Remaking of Its Mexican Past* (Berkeley: University of California Press, 2004), 230.
6. David Luis-Brown, *Waves of Decolonization: Discourses of Race and Hemispheric Citizenship in Cuba, Mexico, and the United States* (Durham: Duke University Press, 2008), 62.
7. See Rose Marie Beebe and Robert Senkewicz, *Testmonios: Early California through the Eyes of Women, 1818–1848* (Berkeley: Heyday Press and the Bancroft Library, 2006); and Rosaura Sanchez et al., *Nineteenth Century Californio Testimonials* (La Jolla: Crítica Monograph Series, 1994).
8. See Rosaura Sanchez, *Telling Identities: The Californio Testimonios* (Minneapolis: University of Minnesota Press, 1995).
9. Nicolás Kanellos and Helvetia Martell, "A Brief History of Hispanic Periodicals in the United States," in *Hispanic Periodicals in the United States, Origins to 1960: A Brief History and Comprehensive Bibliography* (Houston: Arte Público Press, 2000), 7.
10. Quoted in Nicolás Kanellos, *Herencia. The Anthology of Hispanic Literature of the United States* (New York: Oxford University Press, 2002), 111.
11. Kanellos and Martell, "A Brief History of Hispanic Periodicals," 13.
12. Ibid., 13.
13. The Recovering the U.S. Hispanic Literary Heritage Project, founded and directed at the University of Houston by Professor Nicolás Kanellos, has begun the task of recuperating the early U.S. Hispanic literary tradition. This project involves locating, preserving, publishing, and disseminating U.S. Latino-Hispanic culture in its written form from the Spanish colonial era to 1960.
14. Cited in Rolena Adorno and Patrick Charles Pautz, *The Narrative of Cabeza de Vaca, by Álvar Núñez Cabeza de Vaca* (Lincoln: University of Nebraska Press, 1999), 1.
15. Mary Louise Pratt, *Imperial Eyes: Travel Writing and Transculturation* (New York: Routledge, 1992), 7.
16. Adorno and Pautz, 35.
17. Beebe and Senkewicz, *Chronicles of Early California*, 193.

PART II

The American Presence

CHAPTER 4

White Explorers and Travelers
David Wyatt

Despite being reputedly located near the Terrestrial Paradise, California inspired in the early arrivers from the United States a set of tensions and ambivalences it could arouse but not entirely resolve. This mixture of incompatible feelings was summed up by Hinton Rowland Helper in *The Land of Gold: Reality versus Fiction* (1885). "California can and does furnish the best bad things that are obtainable in America."[1] Helper had reason to complain. After three months of prospecting, he realized a profit of only 93 and ¾ cents. Helper was a latecomer compared to other writers featured in this chapter. He came not for furs or hides, but for the mines. However, like his fellow adventurers he was unable to reconcile his ambivalent feelings about this land of extremes.

The key opposition for Richard Henry Dana, Jr., was between "dreary" and "dear." Returning to California more than two decades after his arrival in the 1830s, Dana found himself in "a dream of San Diego ... not a vessel pursues the – I was about to say the dear – the dreary, once hated business of gathering hides upon the coast, and the beach of San Diego is abandoned and its hide-houses have disappeared."[2] Dana linked the "California ambivalence" to the gap between emotions felt upon arrival and return. First encounters produce resistance. California only becomes a paradise once it is lost.

California is fortunate to have *Two Years before the Mast* (1840) as its foundational American English text. A masterpiece of nineteenth-century autobiography, Dana's "Personal Narrative" is also the first and best book about dropping out of college and finding yourself in California. However, what Dana found remains a matter of dispute. Is his book one more "captivity" narrative, as Thomas Philbrick argues, or a sly if un-self-aware fantasy of crossing over, as I argued in *Five Fires*?[3] "And there I found myself more truly and more strange." The line from Wallace Stevens captures the uncanny doubleness of Dana's experience in the Far West.[4] To give oneself over to Dana's "magical chance" is to enter into a paradigmatic experience of self-fashioning and cross-cultural encounter, a dance whose contours continue to be reenacted in California lives and literature.[5]

Dana articulated a number of enduring California themes: place as a site of entrapment and nostalgic return; the correspondence between "the single body" and the "solitary character" of California landscape; the pleasure of physical as opposed to "head work"; the Far West as the junction point for "all manner of languages"; and a California sojourn having the power to undo one's identity and to alter the color of one's skin.[6]

Dana arrived in Santa Barbara in January 1835. Six months earlier he had shipped out from Boston as an ordinary sailor on the hide ship *Pilgrim*. Like Francis Parkman, the Harvard sophomore decided to head west in order to cure "a weakness of the eyes." He spent eighteen months in California, sailing hides off of Dana Point, floating into "the vast solitude of the Bay of San Francisco," and living with a motley crew of hide curers on the beach at San Diego.[7]

In San Diego, Dana surrendered to the "grand carnival" of California life. There he met Hope, his favorite of the Sandwich Islanders, the "most kind-hearted people I ever fell in with." He later secured the medicine that allowed Hope to recover from a serious illness and confessed to feeling "an affection" for Hope and his fellows "such as I never felt before but for a near relation." In San Diego, the "unvarying repetition" of shipboard routine gave way to long intervals of "much leisure," which Dana spent "reading, mending, sleeping" – and partying. His night at the *Rosa*'s hide house was the most memorable:

> We had songs of every nation and tongue. A German gave us "Och! mein lieber Augustin!" and three Frenchmen roared through the Marseilles Hymn; the English and Scotchmen gave us "Rule Britannia," and "Wha'll be King but Charlie?" the Italians and Spaniards screamed through some national affairs, for which I was none the wiser; and we three Yankees made an attempt at the "Star-spangled Banner." After these national tributes had been paid, the Austrian gave us a very pretty little love-song, and the Frenchmen sang a spirited thing called "Sentinelle! O prenez garde à vous!" and then followed the *melange* which might have been expected.[8]

Such an array of California characters and voices would not again be reassembled until Dame Shirley began recording her experience of miner-speak in her letters from Rich Bar. There "wanderers from the whole broad earth" formed "a living polyglot of the languages, a perambulating picture gallery, illustrative of national variety in form and feature."[9]

D. H. Lawrence calls Dana "a perfect tragic recorder."[10] In California, he is much more than that: he is an impassioned if conflicted participant. Dana no doubt lived through an intense period of sexual and social emancipation in the months spent at San Diego, although much of this experience can be inferred from what is not said. He makes only a passing mention of "squaws" coming down "to the beach." In "An Autobiographical Sketch," Dana admitted "that 'many things' were omitted from the book 'from necessity,' principally 'much of the wickedness which I was placed in the midst of.'"[11] After reading Dana's book, shipmate Ben Stimson was to chide him in a letter for having omitted mention of "*the beautiful Indian lasses*, who so often frequented your humble abode in the *hide house*."[12] That abode consisted of a small room "in which four berths were made" and where Dana not only consorted with Indian lasses but worked and ate quite happily with men of color.[13]

The pattern of Dana's California experience takes the repeated form of assent and regret. Impassioned straying is followed by self-laceration over "sins of the flesh."[14] His "hated" California works to call up its felt opposite, burdening Dana with an approach-avoidance response difficult to distinguish from a kind of love. His deepest feeling can perhaps be inferred from the objects compelling his gaze: the "bare" and "loose" bodies of California women and the dancing figures of its men. In his famous description of the airborne Don Juan Bandini, we glimpse Dana's attraction for a road not taken:

> His slight and graceful figure was well calculated for dancing, and he moved about with the grace and daintiness of a young fawn. An occasional touch of the toe to the ground, seemed all that was necessary to give him a long interval of motion in the air. At the same time he was not fantastic or flourishing, but appeared to be rather repressing a strong tendency to motion.

In such passages we see Dana drawn toward an activity he will later deem "offensive." His longing to enter the dance is offset by his identification with solitary objects–an iceberg, an albatross, Dead Man's Island. Dana first signs on as a common sailor, then reasserts his special status as "a gentleman's son" and alienates the crew of the *Pilgrim*. He appears to be repressing "a strong tendency to motion" when surveying the people and culture of Mexican California.[15]

Dana presents California as an inversion of the Yankee world. "Among the Spaniards there is no working class," he discovers. Every man considers himself "a gentleman." Indians do the heavy lifting at work; otherwise the Californios scarcely seem "to earn their sun-light." Living in rough simplicity in a two-room adobe house with only "the ground for a floor," they are distinguished by a "fondness for dress" and by "the fineness of their voices." Their politics consist of "revolutions ... of constant occurrence." Dana finds their "hydrophobia" – a refusal to wash – to be "a national malady." Their funerals are as celebratory as their weddings, involving bear-baitings, musket firings, and cockfights. As for virtue, "the men are thriftless, proud, and extravagant, and very much given to gaming; and the women have but little education, and a good deal of beauty, and their morality, of course, is none of the best."[16]

California is the home of the pleasure principle, a place where Dana is no longer hindered by the constrictions of class and his professional "duties."[17] Thomas Philbrick writes of Dana's choice to go before the mast as entailing "the risk of the annihilation of his social identity," as if this was not what he wanted. However, California spoke enticingly to Dana of "the hope of change." He wanted to escape from his sheltered upbringing and his New England life of conformity. Had he not traveled to California, he would have been one of those people who "never lived anywhere but in their own homes, and never walked but in one line from their cradle to their graves":

> We must come down from our heights, and leave our straight paths, for the byways and low places of life, if we would learn truths by strong contrasts; and in hovels, in forecastles, and among our own outcasts in foreign lands, see what has been wrought upon our fellow-creatures by accident, hardship, or vice.[18]

Truths by strong contrasts: the words can be taken as a motto for Dana's California experience.

Dana's frequent references to "complexion" may remind a reader that skin color was the contrast most strongly enforced in antebellum America. In his opening chapter, Dana appears to resist the "transformation" brought about by donning a sailor's clothes and comforts himself that "doubtless my complexion and hands were enough to distinguish me from the regular *salt*." On his return to Boston harbor two years later, however, he greets a member of the ship's firm with "a face burnt as black as an Indian's." He also finds himself becalmed in a "state of indifference" about homecoming as the long anticipated feeling of glad return is met with "a state of very nearly entire apathy." Biographer Charles Francis Adams captures a Dana whose sense of the "regular shades" of things may have been permanently altered.[19] "Accustomed to seeing rough, hardy, sunburnt faces, the men he reencountered in New England seemed like convalescents from some epidemic fever, while the women were "mere shades."[20] Like sailor George Marsh, a man "tattooed from head to foot," one's complexion ought to render one distinct and "distinguishable."[21] Having strayed beyond the reach of such hierarchies, Dana had come to embody the meaning of the color brown. As Richard Rodriguez argues, "Brown made Americans mindful of tunnels within their bodies, about which they did not speak; about their ties to nature, about which they did not speak; about their ties to one another, about which they did not speak." Dana spoke, if only in code, about these tunnels and ties. In doing so, he celebrated "the undermining brown motif" that was to prove, in Rodriguez's words, "the private history and making of America."[22]

Jonathan Arac argues that personal narratives like Dana's have "the circular shape of descent and return."[23] Dana quit sailing and went back to Boston to get his Harvard degree. But did he ever really return? Going back to California twenty-four years later, he wandered through the old spots around San Diego, "and it seemed to me that I remembered them better than any other place I had ever been in."[24] In the ensuing years, Dana had attended Ralph Waldo Emerson's "Divinity School Address," had befriended Herman Melville, and had dined with John Brown. As a lawyer, he defended escaped slaves in the 1850s. However, in a letter to his wife in 1854, Dana confessed, "my life on shore is a mistake."[25] "My great success," he came to believe, "my book – was a boy's work, done before I came to the Bar."[26] He may have come back to the East, but he left his heart in San Francisco.

Dana came to California by sailing around Cape Horn. The first Americans had reached the Pacific Slope nine years earlier by traveling overland. The mountain men who entered California in the 1820s and 1830s were often looked upon by the Mexican authorities as illegal immigrants. In 1826, after Jedediah Smith made his way across the Mojave Desert into southern California, he was "Detained by the Governor."[27] His journals present Smith as a man of "movement,"[28] motivated by the same impulse that drove the Joads toward California, an impulse that Steinbeck called "westering."[29] Smith's crossings and recrossings of the Rockies, the Sierra Nevada, and the Great Basin left him not tired but rather "weary of rest."[30] Smith might have agreed with mountain man Charles Olson, who claimed, "We must go over space, or we wither."[31] Three of the trappers who came after him – James

Ohio Pattie, James Clyman, and Zenas Leonard – demonstrated a similar restlessness.

James D. Hart described Pattie's *Personal Narrative* (1831) as "very likely quite fictional."[32] It certainly reads like a tall tale. He was jailed after entering California in 1827 and was allegedly released after agreeing to vaccinate Californios and Indians against smallpox, "twenty-two thousand persons" in all.[33] In exchange, Governor Echeandía offered Pattie land and cattle and pressured him to become a Catholic and a Mexican citizen.

Pattie told his story to a New England minister named Timothy Flint, who converted the narrative into "a Protestant psychomachy of wilderness travail."[34] Pattie is a stranger in a strange land; the Mexicans are Canaanites. His autobiography becomes "the withering remembrances of an unhappy wanderer."[35] Pattie and Flint can be credited with investing the California sojourn with one of its most enduring narrative frameworks, the myth of Exodus. And, like Dana, Pattie is more a Moses than a Joshua figure – he glimpses the promised land but is prevented by his adopted angle of vision from fully entering into it.

James Clyman was a more agreeable visitor to the Far West, and his account of his sojourn is the least conflicted and most lighthearted narrative written by a mountain man. Clyman entered California in 1845 and traveled from Napa to Sacramento to Monterey. First edited for publication in 1928, his inventively spelled journals are sardonic and witty examples of Southwestern humor:

> Toward sundown the moskitoes made a general and simultanious attact on ourselves and animals and although I had fought mosketois through the Wabash Illinois and Mississippi vallies yet I never met with such a Quantity of Blood thirsty animals in any such country as we found here your mouth nose Ears Eyse and every other assailable point had its thousand Enemies striving which should be formost in their thirst for Blood.

Clyman loved a tall tale, he was also a keen social observer. He described how Indians were fed at Sutter's Fort. "10 or 15 troughs" were brought out and placed in "the Broiling Sun. The laborers "ran to the troughs like somany pigs and [fed] themselves with their hands as long as the troughs contain[ed] even a moisture." Clyman was also charmed by the way Mexican marriage resolved the problem of having only one horse: "the husband takes his wife on before him and takes hold of the logerhead of his saddle with his arms around his bride and this method looks Quite loveing and kind and might be relished by the single."[36]

Clyman admired Mexican government, calling it "the most free and easy government Perhaps on the civilized globe no Taxes are imposed on any individual what ever I saw nor heard of no requirement for Roade labour no Military tax no civil department to support no Judiciary requiring pay and in every respect the people live free."[37] Clyman differed from other Anglo visitors who criticized Californio life and who supported the region's conquest by the United States.

Nevertheless, Clyman offered his services to the "conqueror" of California – John Charles Frémont – in the spring of 1846. Instead of traveling with Frémont back east after his victory, he accompanied the author of *The Emigrant's Guide to Oregon and California* (1845), Lansford Hastings. Hastings' expansionist fantasy described a new and "most direct route" to California. The book advised emigrants to bear southwest from the Oregon Trail about two hundred miles east from Fort Hall and continue "down to the bay of San Francisco."[38] Hastings recommended a route he had never fully explored. It later became known as Hastings' Cut-off.

Clyman met James Reed at Fort Laramie. He recommended that Reed and his party avoid the Cut-off and stick to the California Trail. Most of Reed's wagons headed north. However, Reed and approximately seventy emigrants turned south toward the Cut-off. By the time they hacked their way through the Wasatch Mountains, they had fallen behind the rest of the wagons. Renamed after the man who elected to lead them at the parting of the ways, they were now known as the Donner Party. Virginia Reed wrote after her ordeal by hunger, "never take no cutofs and hury along as fast as you can."[39]

Unlike the *Emigrant's Guide*, which promoted a route its author had never taken, the *Narrative of the Adventures of Zenas Leonard* (1839) was a product of "*personal observation.*" Leonard was twenty-one when he served as a clerk with the Walker Expedition on an overland trip that ended in Monterey. The first American explorers to cross the Sierra from east to west, Walker and his men encountered a remarkable obstruction along the way:

> Many small streams which would shoot out from under these high snowbanks, and after running a short distance in deep chasms which they have through ages cut in the rocks, precipitate themselves from one lofty precipice to another, until they are exhausted in rain below.[40]

In prose at once awestruck and off-hand, Leonard here offers up the first description in English of Yosemite.

Committed to a vocabulary of "profit" and loss, Leonard was seldom able to stop on his journey "to view an occasional specimen of the wonders of nature's handy-work." He made $1,100 during his four years on the trail. Travel provided other non-material benefits, as Leonard acknowledged upon first hearing waves on the California coast in 1834:

> The idea of being within hearing of the *end* of the *Far West* inspired the heart of every member of our company with a patriotic feeling for his country's honor, and all were eager to lose no time until they should behold what they had heard. We felt as if all our previous hardships and privations would be adequately compensated, if we would be spared to return in safety to the homes of our kindred and have it to say that we had stood upon the extreme end of the great west.

Here, Leonard experiences a sense of arrival. Having survived the Battle of Pierre's Hole, the death of his horses, a nine-days' diet of beaver skins, and thoughts of suicide, he turns up in California "like that of one risen from the dead," another providential survivor of the ordeal of westering who has converted his material losses and sufferings into spiritual capital. "Every man expressed himself fully compensated for his labour, by the many natural curiosities which we had discovered."

Leonard is awed by the nature of the "Far West" but dismayed by its culture. The adobe houses contain "no floor, partition, or work of any kind except bare walls." The "Spaniards ... are very ignorant and much more indolent ... and only seem to enjoy themselves when engaged in the chase." Herds of cattle run free; the place has no boundaries. "These people have no fences round their cleared or cultivated land ... During our whole stay in this country I have never seen any thing like a stable or a barn." California needs to be contained; "our government should be vigilant," Leonard wrote. "She should assert her claim by taking possession of the whole territory as soon as possible."[41]

Walter Colton renewed Leonard's call a few years later. A bureaucrat with a taste for apocalypse, he described the Bear Flag Revolt in *Three Years in California* (1850) as the "final conflagration." Along with Edwin Bryant's *What I Saw in California* (1848), Colton's book provides the best blow-by-blow account of the "quasi war" in which the United States took possession of California.[42]

Colton arrived in California in 1846 as the Chaplain of the *Congress*. He was appointed *alcade* of Monterey soon thereafter. Colton designed a Greek Revival town hall and founded the territory's first newspaper. He participated in the conquest of the region as the administrator of a major northern settlement and "fell passionately in love with California,"[43] according to Kevin Starr.

Colton dedicated his book to General Mariano Vallejo, who had been imprisoned by the Bear Flaggers, and announced his sympathy for a disappearing California. The emigrants from the United States "sweep in like a cloud" and "roll down like a current." In "Notes by Flood and Field" Bret Hart displayed a fellow feeling for the passing of the Californios and predicted the eventual engulfment of the invaders through the figure of the flood. Colton's allusions simultaneously heralded and condemned westward emigration. It was an event of Biblical proportions. "[T]he Israelites took the promised land of the East by arms, and the Americans must take the promised land of the West in the same way." Their actions sounded a blow "on the great anvil of time"; "They have pitched their tents by the water-courses, and those tents they will never strike."[44]

At the same time, Colton found the emigrants lacking in nerve. "They arrive here with very slender means; and the idea of paying twenty dollars a barrel for flour covers them with dismay." The war had created a food shortage. "Instead of having reached a land of plenty, [the emigrants] hastily conclude that they are to suffer the miseries of destitution, and yield to a despondency deeper than that which shook the faith of the Israelites before their wants were miraculously supplied." In a starving time, "give me the Californian," Colton wrote. "If he has a farm, and I have none, he will divide with me; but who ever heard of a Yankee splitting up his farm to accommodate emigrants?"[45]

Colton's uneasy admixture of metaphors of process and providential rhetoric anticipates the debate over "Naturalism" later to be carried out in the writings of Frank Norris, Jack London, Robinson Jeffers, and John Steinbeck. On the one hand, Colton celebrates the "traits of individual character."[46] On the other hand, he suggests that history is made by "forces," not "men,"[47] echoing one of Norris's characters. Colton articulates a tension between freedom and fate that would remain a touchstone of the California experience.

Colton describes American California as a land unrelieved "by the smiles and soothing cares of woman."[48] The first co-ed wagon train reached California in 1841 and was led by John Bidwell. *A Journey to California, 1841* (1843) was followed by Bidwell's posthumous *Echoes of the Past* (1928). Sarah Royce's *Across the Plains* (1932 and 2009), a narrative of her nineteenth-century travels, offers a more dramatic account than Bidwell's pedestrian narratives. It provided her son Josiah with "the underlying story line" for his brilliant and angry history of California.[49]

The first female citizen of the United States to write about California didn't receive credit for her work during her lifetime. The first bestseller about a journey to California was partly the creation of a woman giving voice to a less than articulate man.

When John C. Frémont's *Report of the Exploring Expedition to Oregon and North California* was printed in 1845, his wife Jessie wrote, "You are ranked with Defoe. They say that as Robinson Crusoe is the most natural and interesting fiction of travel, so Frémont's report is the most romantically truthful."[50] The most widely read official document to come out of the West, the *Report* sold 10,000 copies and was used by many emigrants, including the Royce family, as a guide to the Overland Trail.

Jessie paid herself a compliment in praising the romantic truth of the *Report*. Frémont experienced "writer's block" and "incessant nosebleeds" while working on the book, which conflated the accounts of his first two western expeditions. Jessie suggested that her husband dictate his thoughts. As David Roberts argues, Frémont was a pompous letter writer who relied on his wife's sprightly eloquence to transform the *Report* into a highly readable narrative.[51]

Ironically, Jessie created a husband whose work became an advertisement for the fashioning of the imperial self. Emerson believed the *Report* was obsessed with "this eternal vanity of *how we must look*."[52] Frémont focused on his own perceptions and self-development rather than on the landscape he was hired to survey – as did later writers, such as Clarence King, Gary Snyder, and Joan Didion.

Frémont wrote about planting the flag on Frémont Peak, careening after buffalo, and entering California. Although he wasn't ordered to do so, the Frémonts suggested he had no choice. Frémont was ostensibly in search of a mythical river – the Buenaventura – promising a waterway to the Pacific. He arrived in the Truckee Valley of Nevada in January 1844. Realizing it was impossible to cross the country because his horses lacked shoes, he decided to attack the highest mountain wall in North America in midwinter instead. "The course of the narrative will show . . . how we were forced" to turn toward the Pacific," the Frémonts maintained.[53]

Frémont was a great disobeyer. When ordered to leave California by Governor José Castro in 1846, Frémont established a defensive position in the nearby Galiban Mountains, then grudgingly marched his armed party of sixty men north across the Oregon border. Frémont was appointed military governor of California during the Bear Flag Revolt. He refused to obey General Stephen Kearney, was removed from his post, charged with mutiny, and subjected to a court-martial. Frémont was also headquartered in St. Louis during the Civil War while commanding the Department of the West. He angered President Lincoln by freeing the slaves in Missouri and was removed from his post.

One of Frémont's jobs was to make a map of California. He might have been satisfied simply to *see* the Far West. However, a sense of manifest destiny began to compete with the gratitude he felt toward his Mexican hosts, as it did for Dana and Leonard. Each author agitated for conquest. However, only Frémont had the means to capitalize on this imperial project.

The rhetoric of destiny obscures the fact that on both occasions when Frémont marched into California he either encountered tortuous terrain and inhospitable weather or was commanded to leave. It is Frémont's will, not his unavoidable fate, that reveals itself in his writing – even when he represents himself as a soldier merely responding to secret orders.

The orders were given by A. H. Gillespie, a lieutenant in the U.S. Marines. In October 1845 Gillespie spoke with President Polk "on the subject of a secret mission" to California.[54] Gillespie set out with messages for the commander of the Pacific Squadron, the U.S. consul in Monterrey, and Frémont. Agitated about impending war, he committed a number of the documents to memory while traveling through Mexico, then destroyed them. Among those documents were the orders for Frémont.

Gillespie reached Frémont at his camp in southern Oregon two weeks after fighting began. In his *Memoirs* (1887) Frémont claimed that the lieutenant ordered him to return to California and the territory for the United States. "How fate pursues a man!" he claimed as the "faint sound" of Gillespie's horses approached. The information "absolved me from my duty as an explorer, and I was left to my duty as an officer of the American Army with the further authoritative knowledge that the Government intended to take California."[55]

Frémont resolved to return to the Sacramento Valley, a decision that represented "the first step in the conquest of California." For Frémont, that conquest was a matter of personal honor. In a letter to his father-in-law, Senator Thomas Hart Benton, Frémont wrote that he was "humiliated and humbled" by Castro's order to leave the country. Blaming Castro for "his determination to proceed against me," Frémont had no choice but to take measures that might "justify my own character."[56] However, Frémont and his men never fought a major engagement during the Mexican-American War. It was Kearney who faced defeat at the Battle of San Pasqual. Refusing to recognize Kearney's authority, Frémont was found guilty of mutiny. He resigned his army commission in February 1848. The publicity machine maintained by his wife worked so well, however, that despite the compromised nature of his achievement in California, Frémont later became the first presidential nominee put forward by the Republican Party.

Of all the early American arrivers in California, Frémont was the most successful at identifying the fate of the emergent state with that of a single man. California was the geographical endpoint and the most valuable prize yielded by the destiny Frémont worked so hard to make manifest. However, everything about the Bear Flag Revolt, an unruly uprising of which Frémont eventually took control, spoke of bathos. The Bear Flaggers insisted on jailing Mariano Vallejo, a man who was in fact sympathetic with American intentions in California. After invading his house, they found his whisky and got drunk. Led by one William Ide, a man who harangued the crowd at Sonoma on "the common rights of man" in an English "not the twentieth part interpreted,"[57] the Bear Flaggers adopted as their standard a strip of cloth on which was "badly painted" an animal that "looked more like a pig than a bear." In consenting to exploit the energies of the revolt, Vallejo wrote, Frémont became "a leader of thieves."[58]

The revolt was quickly caught up in the war that broke out between Mexico and the United States. However, the damage to a possible California comity had been done. Josiah Royce would look back on Frémont's introduction of "civilized warfare" into California as the poisoned apple. In the impassioned argument made by Royce's *California* (1886), the conqueror's actions led to "the degradation" of the "Californian people by our own." Frémont "brought war into a peaceful department; his operations began an estrangement, ensured a memory of bloodshed, excited a furious bitterness of feeling between the two peoples that were henceforth to dwell in California, such as all his own subsequent personal generosity and kindness could never again make good."[59] The long fandango was ending, and generations were to pass before the Reconquista began.

Notes

1. Hinton Rowland Helper, *The Land of Gold: Reality versus Fiction* (Baltimore: Henry Taylor, 1855), 68.
2. Richard Henry Dana, Jr., *Two Years before the Mast* (New York: Penguin, 1981), 506.
3. Ibid., 25.

4. Wallace Stevens, *The Palm at the End of the Mind* (New York: Random House, 1972), 55.
5. Dana, *Two Years*, 7.
6. Ibid., 158, 109, 221.
7. Ibid., 40, 497.
8. Ibid., 199, 205, 323, 357, 240, 228, 222.
9. Louise Clappe, *The Shirley Letters 1854–55* (Santa Barbara: Peregrine Smith, 1973), 108, 109.
10. D. H. Lawrence, *The Works of D. H. Lawrence: Studies in Classic American Literature* (Cambridge University Press, 2003), 108.
11. Dana, *Two Years*, 225, 12–13.
12. Richard Henry Dana, Jr., *Two Years before the Mast and Other Voyages* (New York: Library of America, 2003), 877.
13. Dana, *Two Years*, 202.
14. Dana, *Two Years before the Mast and Other Voyages*, 879.
15. Dana, *Two Years*, 362, 126, 317, 350.
16. Ibid., 123, 261, 127, 234, 284, 236.
17. Dana, *Two Years before the Mast and Other Voyages*, 886, 880.
18. Dana, *Two Years*, 11, 143, 335.
19. Ibid., 40, 41, 458, 459, 127.
20. Charles Francis Adams, *Richard Henry Dana: A Biography* (Boston: Houghton Mifflin, 1890), 18.
21. Dana, *Two Years*, 275.
22. Richard Rodriguez, *Brown: The Last Discovery of America* (New York: Penguin, 2002), 133.
23. Jonathan Arac, *The Emergence of American Literary Narrative, 1820–1860* (Cambridge: Harvard University Press, 2005), 77.
24. Dana, *Two Years*, 515.
25. Adams, 332.
26. Dana, *Two Years*, 16.
27. Dale L. Morgan, *Jedediah Smith and the Opening of the West* (Indianapolis: Bobbs-Merrill, 1953), 331.
28. John Steinbeck, *The Grapes of Wrath and Other Writings* (New York: The Library of America, 1996), 224.
29. Ibid., 204.
30. Jedediah Smith, *The Travels of Jedediah Smith, A Documentary Outline Including the Journal of the Great American Pathfinder*, ed. Maurice S. Sullivan (Lincoln: University of Nebraska Press, 1992), 63.
31. Charles Olson, *Call Me Ishmael* (New York: Reynal & Hitchcock, 1947), 114.
32. James D. Hart, *A Companion to California* (New York: Oxford, 1978), 323.
33. James Ohio Pattie, *The Personal Narrative* (1831; Philadelphia: Lippincott, 1962), 198.
34. Kevin Starr, *Americans and the California Dream* (New York: Oxford, 1973), 18.
35. Pattie, 229.

36. James Clyman, *American Frontiersman, 1792–1881*, ed. Charles C. Camp (San Francisco: California Historical Society, 1928), 170, 173, 178.
37. Ibid., 187.
38. Lansford Hastings, *Emigrant's Guide to Oregon and California* (Cincinnati: George Conclin, 1845), 137.
39. George R. Stewart, *Ordeal by Hunger* (1936; New York: Simon & Schuster, 1960), 287.
40. Zenas Leonard, *Narrative of the Adventures of Zenas Leonard* (1839; Lincoln: University of Nebraska Press, 1978), 3, 129.
41. Ibid., 139, 129, 146, 58, 139, 155.
42. Walter Colton, *Three Years in California* (New York: A. S. Barnes, 1850), 335, 17.
43. Starr, 30.
44. Colton, 1, 118, 84.
45. Ibid., 157, 360.
46. Ibid., 1.
47. Frank Norris, *Norris: Novels and Essays* (New York: The Library of America, 1986), 1037.
48. Colton, 6.
49. Sarah Royce, *Across the Plains: Sarah Royce's Western Narrative*, ed. Jennifer Dawes Adkinson (Tucson: The University of Arizona Press, 2009), 11.
50. Allan Nevins, *Frémont: Pathmarker of the West* (New York: D. Appleton-Century, 1939), 303.
51. David Roberts, *A Newer World: Kit Carson, John C. Frémont, and the Claiming of the American West* (New York: Simon & Schuster, 2000), 125.
52. Bernard DeVoto, *The Year of Decision: 1846* (Boston: Little, Brown, 1943), 196.
53. John Charles Frémont, *The Expeditions of John Charles Frémont, Volume I, Travels from 1838 to 1844*, eds. Donald Jackson and Mary Lee Spence (Urbana: University of Illinois Press, 1970), 611, 575.
54. Tom Chaffin, *Pathfinder: John Charles Frémont and the Course of American Empire* (New York: Farar, Straus & Giroux), 298–299.
55. John Charles Frémont, *The Expeditions of John Charles Frémont, Volume II, The Bear Flag Revolt and the Court-Martial* (Urbana: University of Illinois Press, 1973), 107, 111.
56. Ibid., 111, 181, 182.
57. Josiah Royce, *California; from the Conquest in 1846 to the Second Vigilance Committee in San Francisco* (1886; New York: Knopf, 1948), 60.
58. Mariano Vallejo, "Recuerdos historicos y personales tocante a la alta California," in *The Heath Anthology of American Literature*, vol. 1, ed. Paul Lauter (Lexington, MA: D. C. Heath & Co, 1990), 1957, 1955.
59. Royce, 25, 88.

CHAPTER 5

The Gold Rush

Nicolas S. Witschi

The California Gold Rush was, as the saying goes, many things to many people. To the New England essayist, poet, and fiction writer Elizabeth Drew Stoddard, it offered women who were stuck in unhappy marriages an opportunity to change their situations for the better. In one of her regular contributions as a "Lady Correspondent" to San Francisco's *Daily Alta California*, Stoddard satirically advised such women to "Send your husbands to California!"[1] By encouraging their men to take off for the West, unhappy or abused wives might prompt them to seek divorce (which, Stoddard assures, the men wouldn't even have to pay for), since any man who makes his way to the goldfields would inevitably be caught up in a world of carousing bachelorhood and, hence, would no longer wish to be married. Such was the danger and the promise of what was happening in the far West. From her vantage point in New York City, Stoddard had seen ample evidence of the ill effects felt by families whose fathers, brothers, and sons had exchanged their community responsibilities for a highly questionable search for faraway treasure. She thus concluded that the wives they had left behind were actually better off without them.

By the time the *Daily Alta California* ran this column in June 1856, the social and cultural effects of the search for wealth in the streambeds and hillsides of the Sierra Nevada had become abundantly clear. As Stoddard's satire implies, and as historical analyses confirm, the Gold Rush exerted a great deal of pressure on models of community organized around traditional gender roles.[2] As an easterner writing for a western daily paper, Stoddard no doubt recognized that her audience was much more likely to consist of men who had come in search of fortune, not the families they had left behind (two of her brothers had immigrated to San Francisco, and critics have speculated that she was writing for them). Her essay prompts men who had gone away to contemplate their own recent acts of self-redefinition to reflect on the consequences of their actions and on the danger to community posed by the hunt for gold. On a broader scale, the new world being carved out of the hills in California also compelled reconsiderations of the social and political power held by laborers and the rapidly emerging merchant class, just as it posed distinctive challenges for the longstanding Native and more-recently established Hispanic communities that had largely defined the region prior to 1848.[3] Ultimately, the Gold Rush confronted just about everyone who was already in or who came to California with the need to define themselves anew. Some thrived under these conditions, while others struggled tremendously.

Stoddard's essay also serves as an example of what is perhaps the most salient genre in the literary history of the Gold Rush, namely nonfictional prose. A handful of drama, a smattering of mostly satirical or sentimental verse, and only one novel of any genuine consequence may be found amidst an extraordinary and vast archive of letters, diaries, newspaper articles, magazine features, pamphlets, letter sheets, and book-length personal narratives.[4] When one consults accounts of mid-nineteenth-century American literature, discussions of the novel and the poem clearly predominate. Nathaniel Hawthorne's *The Scarlet Letter* (1850) and Harriet Beecher Stowe's *Uncle Tom's Cabin* (1852) are examined for their challenges to long-held pieties and social policies, while Walt Whitman's *Leaves of Grass* (1855) is typically hailed for its poetically innovative celebrations of a diverse and expanding nation. With respect to nonfiction, Henry David Thoreau's *Walden* (1854) receives attention for its intellectual examination of living deliberately in nature. However, his contemporaries in the far West seldom concerned themselves with philosophical and metaphysical issues. The mostly nonfictional texts that emerged out of the California Gold Rush demonstrate an abiding concern with material well-being. Although some of their concerns were financial, many writers dwelled on physical threats to life and limb. In so doing, they also chronicled the extent to which traditional notions of communal and even national identity were strained and the ways in which different modes of self-definition evolved (along racial, gendered, and even class lines) to address those strains. Thus, for all the attention given to the first spoken whispers of James Marshall's discovery in January 1848 – "Boys, I believe I have found a gold mine," he reportedly told his workmates[5] – the California Gold Rush is a profoundly writerly event. Its literary history is marked by a variety of noteworthy prose efforts to report, mediate, and meliorate the experiences of those affected by it. A second generation of writers in the 1860s and 1870s used the fictional short story to define the event retrospectively as something other than a time of disruption and trauma.

In an era before the telegraph and the transcontinental railroad, when word of any newsworthy event in the West might take weeks or months to spread, newspapers were the primary form of mass communication. Of course, news outlets in such large cities as Boston, New York, Philadelphia, Washington, New Orleans, and St. Louis reported on the Gold Rush. As the examples collected in Peter Browning's *To the Golden Shore: America Goes to California – 1849* (1995) demonstrate, Gold Rush reporting comprised a mix of good and bad news that could range in tone from wild boosterism to cautious optimism to extreme warnings to stay away. Among the first professional journalists to offer eyewitness accounts were the prominent travel writers Bayard Taylor, sent by Horace Greeley to report for the New York *Herald Tribune*, and Frank Marryat, who had come from England to the goldfields more interested in sport hunting than in mining. Their respective books, *El Dorado* (1850) and *Mountains and Molehills* (1855), paint a picture of a people and a region in the midst of a dazzlingly great adventure. Both the optimistically cheerful Taylor and the delightedly amoral Marryat depict the virtually overnight rise of often chaotic human communities and urban spaces. Neither one suggests that such developments are anything but the inevitable and much-wished-for progress of civilization. A more realistically sober assessment may be found in the Scottish journalist J. D. Borthwick's *Harper's Weekly* stories, which were eventually gathered together under the title *Three Years in California* 1857). However, in terms of style, such professional accounts suggest that many of the more prominent periodicals embraced a mode of reportage that was designed to increase readership through largely positive, even exciting accounts of the Gold Rush.

Generally less enthusiastic evaluations were recorded by gold seekers themselves. A surprisingly high number of them, in fact, documented their experiences in print, often at the request of small-town newspaper editors. Indeed, the majority of articles, features, and notes in Browning's collection are from travelers to California who sent back letters and diary extracts to their hometown, local, or regional papers. These remarkably literate and compelling narratives describe what it was like to cross the arid plains and snowy mountains or to travel by ship to the Isthmus of Panama, struggle through the jungle to the Pacific, and then board another ship bound for San Francisco Bay. They portray mining as a difficult, bone-chilling, illness-inducing, labor-intensive task that frequently yielded little reward. The daily experiences of the average miner were, to say the least, far from comfortable.[6] Browning's collection includes the work of dozens of such authors, some identified by name but just as many anonymous.

A number of the more informative and well-written dispatches sent home were gathered for publication as books, often in an apparent effort to discourage further emigration to California. Taking stock of the region's climate extremes, the apparently limited supply of gold, the difficulty of manual labor, and the overall lack of social and material infrastructure, the somewhat dilettanteish Leonard Kip advises in *California Sketches, with Recollections of the Gold Mines* (1850) that the region was destined to fail in attracting and sustaining any sort of significant population and industry. Daniel B. Woods, perhaps more directly reliant on earning his keep from mining than Kip, also collected his journals and letters, publishing them as *Sixteen Months at the Gold Diggings* (1851). Recounting a series of miserable and often near-death experiences, the self-identified "Rev." Woods advises the family men among his readers to stay home for their health and sanity. For those who would still emigrate, however, he hoped his book would serve as a miner's manual that could inspire a well-informed and distinctly Christian composure in its readers. And in *Sights in the Gold Region and Scenes by the Way* (1853), Theodore Johnson also counsels against traveling West, as he too had found life in the goldfields to be more dispiriting, unprofitable, and dangerous than he had imagined.

One particularly significant instance of a traveler's keeping in touch with a local readership may be found in the Ottawa *Free Trader*, the Northern Illinois newspaper that published the adventures of Alonzo Delano. A native of upstate New York who had come to the Midwest in the hopes of finding success as a merchant, Delano left Ottawa with a party of fifty fellow gold-smitten townsfolk in April 1849. The letters he submitted to the *Free Trader* over the course of the next two years not only kept his wife and children apprised of his undertakings, they also informed the broader community about what was happening with some of the other men and boys from Ottawa who had made the journey. Delano does not seek to dissuade emigration, though he does caution his readers not to expect endless sunshine and riches. Through eloquent and descriptive prose, Delano reports on the arduous nature of the overland journey as well as on his subsequent failure to establish himself in business, first in the mines and then in San Francisco. His descriptions of the illnesses he suffers on the plains are by turns amusing and harrowing, while his tales of women emigrants who were widowed while en route and of the impoverished state of the many men and boys he meets in the mines paint a grimly realistic picture.

Upon arriving in California after a four-month journey, and perhaps feeling pressured by his inability to re-establish himself as a merchant,

Delano expanded his prospects for publication. In Sacramento, he entered into an agreement to send dispatches about his experiences to the New Orleans *True Delta*, and, soon after this, he also began submitting satirical sketches about mining culture under the penname "Old Block" to San Francisco's *California Daily Courier*. The former endeavor continues his self-presentation outside of California as an earnest and realistic chronicler of the Gold Rush, while the latter rapidly establishes a persona that became a favorite among miners. When writing for a local and regional audience, Delano is less of a reporter, becoming instead more Hogarthian in his approach to material, employing numerous self-reflexive literary techniques and subjecting himself as much as anyone else to satirical lampooning. As "Old Block," he blends humor with sentimental literary conventions in an effort to document and meliorate the difficulties faced by laborers in the mountains, whom he treats sympathetically. His oft-repeated depiction of the effigy of a broken-down miner he had found by an abandoned cabin strikes a figure that will become a standard trope of Gold Rush literature: the young man emaciated to the point of seeming old and decrepit. "Old Block" was among the first to record this image, just as he was the first to present the image of a hungry miner who resorts to eating his boots in a pamphlet called "The Miner's Progress" (1853), illustrated by his friend Charles C. Nahl.

Like his colleagues before him, Delano combined his various newspaper contributions with the more detailed diary he had kept during his overland trek for publication as a book, the indispensable *Life on the Plains and Among the Diggings* (1854). Meanwhile, his collected "Old Block" writings were published in a pair of widely read books called *Pen Knife Sketches, or, Chips off the Old Block* (1853) and *Old Block's Sketch Book* (1856). He even published, though never produced, a very readable play called *A Live Woman in the Mines* (1857). After becoming a banker in his new adopted hometown of Grass Valley, CA, Delano continued until his death in 1874 to contribute essays about California mining and political culture to periodicals ranging from his local newspapers to the *New York Times* and the *Saturday Evening Post*.

Delano was thus both a contributor to and a product of the prolific rise of periodical culture during the Gold Rush. San Francisco in the 1850s was a time and a place in which a remarkable number of printed serials were available to readers of all kinds who wished to make sense of their individual and collective experiences. During the city's rapid early expansion, prominent newspapers such as the *Daily Alta* and the San Francisco *Chronicle* began publication, as did the *Morning Call*, the *Evening Bulletin*, and the *Mirror of the Times*, the first newspaper west of St. Louis published by and for African Americans. The Sacramento *Union* established itself as a solid daily, while magazines such as *The Pioneer*, *The Hesperian*, *The Golden Era*, and *The California Farmer and Journal of Useful Sciences* competed for the attentions of a literate and growing population.[7] And their reach was significant, too. The *Daily Alta* contracted with New Yorker Elizabeth Stoddard to provide routine updates about the social scene on the East coast, while the *Mirror of the Times* had a regular correspondent in Japan.

One widely circulated publication, *Hutchings' Illustrated California Magazine*, was founded with profits earned from the sale of one of the more intriguing textual artifacts of the Gold Rush, a letter sheet by James M. Hutchings called "The Miner's Ten Commandments" (1853). Letter sheets were large pieces of printed and illustrated stationery that, when folded a certain way, provided space for writing and served as their own envelopes. They were useful not only for sending news about oneself but also as souvenirs from the diggings. The most popular of these was Hutchings's, which on the printed side offered readers advice about how to ward off threats to one's physical and emotional integrity, including the commandments "Thou shalt not kill thy body by working in the rain" and "Though shalt not grow discouraged."[8] The commandments about respecting one's marital vows and about not forgetting one's children at home no doubt appealed to buyers of the sheet as a sort of shorthand reassurance to their families that they had not been entirely left behind. The letter sheet's success allowed the entrepreneurial Hutchings to partake in the rapid emergence of a strong periodical culture.

In 1850s California, letters and periodicals clearly served complementary purposes, and the crowning achievement of this relationship was the publication of an epistolary account of life in the mines signed by an anonymous author named "Shirley." Louise Amelia Knapp Smith Clappe was a well-bred native of Massachusetts who in January 1850 arrived by boat in California with her health- and gold-seeking husband, Dr. Fayette Clapp [*sic*]. In September 1851, the couple settled into Rich Bar on the Feather River, which at the time was a booming camp of roughly 2,000 men and 5 women. By this time Clappe had already published several poems and essays in the Marysville *Daily Herald*, and she now began writing letters to her sister "Mary Jane" back in Amherst that were eventually published in *The Pioneer* (1854–55). Although she never collected them in book form, Clappe's twenty-three epistles have long been valued for their richly textured depiction of mining and their evocative, sympathetic representation of the social environment Clappe experienced over the course of a year. Dated September 13, 1851, to November 21, 1852, and issued serially more than twenty-four months, the so-called "Shirley Letters" demonstrate a quality of prose that clearly suggests that their author was an adept manipulator of genre conventions. In addition to the knowledge displayed through her many allusions to familiar literary texts and figures, Clappe exhibits a mastery of the epistolary form that allows for the reader to feel the immediacy of her descriptions. Indeed, on several occasions she laments that due to her inability to draw a picture, she must rely on words to convey her impressions. The most vivid passages – recounting a scenic mountain vista, the trauma of a woman's death from peritonitis, the amputation of a miner's crushed leg, and the brutal consequences of both crime and vigilante justice – are strikingly and emotionally rendered.

In Rich Bar and nearby Indian Bar, Clappe experienced a truly international, polyglot, and multiracial community. Aside from her sympathy for Mexicans, whose treatment by Anglo miners she vehemently decried, Clappe generally did not express very positive feelings about the Native Americans, Chinese, and African Americans whom she had but briefly encountered in the mines. However, her encounters with races and cultures about whom she acknowledges she has only the barest of reading-based knowledge actually reinforce the greater point toward which Clappe draws her letters. In addition to the immediacy of experience it conveys, the epistolary form also strongly suggests a narrative of unanticipated change, a sort of fish-out-of-the-water tale in which a woman of some refinement, a "Dame" as she calls herself in the letters, gives her readers access to her progressive transformation. The initial set up suggests that as a good wife, "Dame Shirley" will endure all manner of physical and psychological discomforts in support of her husband's futile search for wellness. Eventually it becomes clear that Clappe is the true survivor, the person best able to adapt and thrive in the camp environment. She observes in her final letter, "everybody ought to go to the mines, just to see how little it takes to make people comfortable in the world," and she signs off by calling herself "your *now* perfectly healthy sister" (emphasis in original).[9] With Fayette's return to Massachusetts in 1854 and the couple's divorce in 1856, Louise Clappe's self-reinvention was complete. She did not have to send her husband to California; instead, she effectively left *him* behind as she sought a revitalized identity for herself.

Among the noteworthy persons to visit at least once with Clappe at her sociable table in Indian Bar was a fur trapper and mountain guide named James Beckwourth. Having spent the better part of the 1830s and 1840s living among the Crow and scouting throughout the American West, Beckwourth moved to California in 1851 with the hope of securing a steadier income. Notably, he never seemed to consider mining as an option. In the as-told-to autobiography he published in 1856, he recounts how during his one gold-seeking expedition in the Feather River region, he was much more interested in establishing a lucrative new route through the mountains to Marysville. To this day, the gently sloped, wagon-accessible passage across the crest of the Sierra Nevada that he located is still called Beckwourth Pass. Unfortunately, his efforts in the nearby camps and towns to finance development of the route weren't successful.

Strictly speaking, *The Life and Adventures of James P. Beckwourth* is not a Gold Rush text but an account of the narrator's adventures prior to 1848. However, as a frontier memoir published during the height of interest in literary Gold Rush nonfiction, it was no doubt designed to capitalize on the popularity of such narratives as Clappe's and Delano's (Delano had briefly met Beckwourth, an event he recounts in *Life on the Plains*). Beckwourth allegedly dictated his story to a former journalist named Thomas D. Bonner, and the finished product is replete with exciting adventures and dramatic self-invention. Beckwourth was part African American, though he presents himself to readers as white and describes times when he passed as an Indian.[10] In this respect, the narrative epitomizes the Gold Rush dialectic of reinvention that deflects one mode of identity from another while in the service of crafting a third. Delano the family man employs "Old Block" to become Delano the gold-country bachelor, while Louise Clappe uses "Dame Shirley" to reinvent a third version of herself as well. This process, moreover, is clearly at work in the career of Cincinnatus H. "Joaquin" Miller, a self-styled frontiersman/poet who became a celebrity in England with his cloyingly romantic *Songs of the Sierras* (1873). It is also evident in both the life and work of John Rollin Ridge, whose 1854 literary creation, the social bandit Joaquín Murieta, provided the name source for Miller's fantasy of frontier identity.

Ridge's first and only novel, *The Life and Adventures of Joaquín Murieta, the Celebrated California Bandit*, is perhaps the most influential and enduring of all Gold Rush texts. It tells the story of a charismatic miner from Sonora who turns to vengeful outlawry when his wife is raped, his brother is lynched, and he himself is severely beaten by Anglo miners. It is a sensational tale, told with the expert swiftness of a series of newspaper dispatches and the breathlessness and gore of a dime novel. However, it is also a cogent, albeit deeply ambivalent examination of the fluidity of individual and national identities that were being negotiated by border communities in the wake of the Mexican-American War and the influx of tens of thousands of immigrants. Ridge culled much of his material from the newspapers of the day, condensing and consolidating many of the vague whispers and often paranoid assertions about banditry and bigotry running rampant in the mining country at the time. There may have been several actual outlaws in the hills known as Joaquín, including one with the surname Murrieta [*sic*]. Ridge crafts a fiction that captures the essential nature of the fear felt in the diggings by Mexican and Anglos. It is also a pulpy narrative that offers its own critical self-diagnosis of popular culture. While Ridge's name is rarely still attached to the popular legend he more or less initiated, schoolchildren throughout California are still taught the story, while in Sonora the Murrieta clan continues to pass along the oral history of their ancestor. The telling and re-telling of the legend have also continued through such forms as Mexican *corridos* in the 1930s, Chicano poetry since the 1960s, and seemingly endless iterations in film and television of the story of Zorro.

Ridge's own identity usually factors into critical evaluations of the text as well. He was the son of a prominent leader in the Cherokee Nation and a white woman, and he published the novel under his Native name, Yellow Bird. *The Life and Adventures of Joaquín Murieta* is thus considered the first novel ever published by a Native American, and consequently the question of Ridge's racial and political allegiances is often debated in assessments of the work. Some critics have suggested that the novel should be read as an allegory for Ridge's anger at the assassination of his father and the general dispossession of Native Americans in the southeastern United States. Others have cautioned against reading it as anything other than a sympathetic treatment of Mexicans in their fight against Anglo incursions. It has even been suggested that *The Life and Adventures of Joaquín Murieta* is a racist declaration of support for the largely imperial legal system being imposed on California by the United States (even to identify the title character as a "social bandit" is to wade into the debate). Each of these readings is certainly plausible, given the striking ambivalence of the novel's dramatic construction. The most compelling case for the meaning of *The Life and Adventures of Joaquín Murieta*, in addition to the significance of its expert manipulation of genre, centers on Ridge's insistence on the recognition of individual autonomy, regardless of skin color or national ideology, that is nevertheless framed within an appeal to the rule of law founded on racial stereotype. Ambivalence and contradiction seem to define the history of this text, characteristics that may well define the true legacy of the Gold Rush.[11]

The robust periodical culture from which Ridge gleaned much of his material (and which would provide him with a livelihood when he became the editor of the *California American*) also nurtured the early careers of many writers who emerged in the 1860s, the second generation of writers to chronicle the memory and legacy of the Gold Rush. One of these was Samuel Clemens, who sat out the Civil War in the silver-mining region of Nevada. Here he developed the persona of Mark Twain while serving an apprenticeship with some of the most talented newspapermen and humorists in the region, including William Wright ("Dan De Quille"), Rollin Daggett, James Townsend ("Lying Jim"), Alf Doten, and other members of the Sagebrush School. Twain's experiences in the silver mines of the Comstock are humorously dramatized and embellished in his quasi-memoir *Roughing It* (1872). However, his sojourn in California's gold country in 1864–65 truly established him as a Gold Rush writer. After a stint as a reporter with the San Francisco *Call*, Clemens spent several months in the southern mines near Angel's Camp, during which time he learned the curious story of a gambler's being duped in a jumping frog contest. Within a year, his rendition of "Jim Smiley and His Jumping Frog" (1865) had made Twain a bona fide literary star. By framing the story as a letter to Artemus Ward, the pseudonym of the humorist and lecturer Charles Farrar Browne, Twain was explicitly entering a tradition of humor writing that included his Virginia City, NV, colleagues and such Gold Rush humorists as Alonzo Delano and George Horatio Derby ("John Phoenix" and "Squibob"). As the story's narrative structure demonstrates, Twain had by this time become an expert in conveying the story of a self-deprecating narrator who has little awareness of the true significance of his own tale. This technique, which reached its pinnacle with *Adventures of Huckleberry Finn* (1885), was a mode of meta-storytelling that Twain first learned to deploy in the hills of Calaveras County.

Another member of the second generation to arise out of the periodical world to transform the Gold Rush through fiction was Bret Harte, frequently though not entirely accurately considered the event's foremost fabulist and romanticist. Arriving in the gold country in 1854, Harte worked briefly as a miner, a Wells Fargo agent, and a schoolteacher, before settling into a career in writing and publishing. When his readers became disenchanted with a series of editorials he wrote for the weekly *Northern Californian* (in Uniontown, CA; now Arcata) decrying the brutal mistreatment of Native Americans by Anglo miners, Harte was forced to move back to the city. Once in San Francisco, he became quite prolific, publishing reviews, satires, articles, short stories, and poems in such prestigious periodicals as the *Golden Era* and the *Californian*. Over the course of the ensuing decade, Harte became the leader of San Francisco's literary elite, extending his friendship and mentorship to such young and promising writers as Ina Coolbrith, Ambrose Bierce, Henry George, Charles Warren Stoddard, and Clemens. In the spring of 1868, Harte was offered the position of editor-in-chief of the newly formed *Overland Monthly*, a highbrow magazine modeled loosely on Boston's *Atlantic Monthly*. With this move, his rise to the heights of both literary celebrity and influence began in full.

In the second issue of the *Overland*, Harte published a tale about a mining camp full of coarse but honorable miners who are compelled to deal with the presence of a newborn child. The first in a series of comic tales set in the same mining region as Ridge's novel and Twain's frog story, "The Luck of Roaring Camp" (1868) is an ironic satire of the Nativity that challenges the formulaic conventions of sentimental literature. Its representation of backcountry earnestness has also prompted some readers to interpret the story as pleasingly sentimental itself, a conundrum that haunted much of Harte's career. Subsequent tales collected in his landmark first book *The Luck of Roaring Camp and Other Sketches* (1870) include "The Outcasts of Poker Flat," "Miggles," and "Tennessee's Partner." These stories crystalize such character types as the golden-hearted prostitute, the honorable gambler, and the grizzled '49er. However, the ironic distinction between Harte's genteel narrators and such dialect-speaking characters as Kentuck and Miggles is frequently missed. The reception of Harte's wildly popular 1870 poem, "Plain Language from Truthful James," has proven even more vexing in this regard, as Harte's viciously satirical condemnation of anti-Chinese racism in California has a long history of being used to justify deeply racist representations and formulations.[12] Eventually, Harte found himself more committed to confirming his facility with the cliché's of Gold Rush characterization than to continuing his initially parodic take on the whole literary enterprise. Nonetheless, as an innovator of vernacular dialect, Bret Harte is a significant predecessor to the realist and regionalist writers who followed him at the end of the nineteenth century. Like Twain, Harte transformed the raw literary material of the Gold Rush into metafiction. He was less interested in documenting history than reinventing it.

By 1875, the naturalist John Muir had begun to establish himself in San Francisco's publishing world, starting with pieces for the *Daily Evening Bulletin* and the *Overland Monthly*. Several of his essays about California's natural wonders take a few potshots at Harte, and he even briefly engages a familiar trope in his depiction of John Nelder, an old and decrepit but lovable former miner who had tucked himself away in a giant Sequoia grove in the hills near Fresno ("The Royal Sequoia," *Daily Evening Bulletin*, 1875). When he combined and revised these early publications during the composition of *The Mountains of California* (1894), though, Muir greatly diminished the sections about the mining country, and he completely eliminated all mention of Nelder. Thus, the literary history of a lingering yet still living remnant of the Gold Rush figuratively gave way to a vision of the California mountains that was largely devoid of human presence.

Nonetheless, Delano, Clappe, Ridge, and even Harte have ensured that the California Gold Rush remains known in all of its traumatic and fantastical dimensions. Born chiefly of a need to document a set of events that seemed astonishingly unusual to those who experienced them firsthand, the literary history of the Gold Rush rapidly evolved into a profoundly literate, engaging, often funny, yet always sobering record of people involved in making and remaking both themselves and their communities. The effect has been a lasting one. The material traces of mining in the 1850s mark the landscapes of California to this day. Similarly, when one speaks of things not "panning out," or roots for a particular professional football team from San Francisco, or talks of visiting the town of Oakhurst just outside of Yosemite National Park, one is invariably quoting the Gold Rush.

Notes

1. E. D. B., "From Our Lady Correspondent," *Daily Alta California*, June, 8 1856: 1. Stoddard, who married in 1852, signed her columns for this newspaper with the initials of her maiden name, Elizabeth Drew Barstow.
2. Susan Lee Johnson, *Roaring Camp: The Social World of the California Gold Rush* (New York: Norton, 2000); JoAnn Levy, *They Saw the Elephant: Women in the California Gold Rush* (Norman: University of Oklahoma Press, 1992).
3. Rudolph M. Lapp, *Blacks in Gold Rush California* (New Haven: Yale University Press, 1977); Brian Roberts, *American Alchemy: The California Gold Rush and Middle-Class Culture* (Chapel Hill: University of North Carolina Press, 2000); Malcolm J. Rohrbough, *Days of Gold: The California*

Gold Rush and the American Nation (Berkeley: University of California Press, 1997).

4. This essay concerns itself with texts actually published during the Gold Rush era. Of course, historians have over the years also told the story of the Gold Rush by using extensive archives of unpublished letters and diaries. Arguably, the most impressive of these studies remains J. S. Holliday's treatment of the journals of William Swain and the many letters of his contemporaries in *The World Rushed In* (1981), a study that further demonstrates the highly literate nature of Gold Rush writing.
5. Rohrbough, 7.
6. With the exception of a relative few like Frank Marryat, emigrant-writers typically wrote nothing for the printed press about the more profligate lifestyles adopted by many of the young men involved. See Johnson (156–183) for an analysis of unpublished diaries that record such behavior. As Stoddard's essay affirms, though, news of that kind did nevertheless filter back east.
7. On the proliferation of periodicals during the Gold Rush era, see Franklin Walker, *San Francisco's Literary Frontier* (New York: Knopf, 1939). Walker makes no mention, though, of *The Mirror*. Credit for most fully articulating its significance as a Gold Rush-era publication belongs to Eric Gardner's *Unexpected Places: Relocating Nineteenth-Century African American Literature* (Jackson: University Press of Mississippi, 2009).
8. James M. Hutchings, "The Miner's Ten Commandments," in *Gold Rush: A Literary Exploration*, ed. Michael Kowalewski (Berkeley: Heyday, 1997), 290–293.
9. Louise Amelia Knapp Smith Clappe, *The Shirley Letters from the California Mines, 1851–1852*, ed. Marlene Smith-Baranzini (Berkeley: Heyday Books, 1998), 177, 179.
10. Blake Allmendinger variously refers to Beckwourth's autobiography as a "literary charade" and a "fiction of passing." *Imagining the African American West* (Lincoln: University of Nebraska Press, 1998), 12.
11. Especially useful recent analyses of the entanglements of history, memory, literature, and popular culture in the story of Murieta (or Murrieta, as it is sometimes spelled) may be found in Johnson (25–53); and Shelley Streeby, *American Sensations: Class, Empire, and the Production of Popular Culture* (Berkeley: University of California Press, 2002), 251–287.
12. Gary Scharnhorst, "'Ways That Are Dark': Appropriations of Bret Harte's 'Plain Language from Truthful James.'" *Nineteenth-Century Literature* 51 (1996): 377–399.

CHAPTER 6

California Nature Writers

Steven Pavlos Holmes

Beginning in the middle of the nineteenth century, early California nature writers drew upon and transformed a wide range of cultural sources to address a variety of societal needs. Clarence King, John Muir, Mary Austin, and Robinson Jeffers combined scientific observation and theory, religious and philosophical concepts, imagery from artists and poets, local color and folk tales, and dramatic stories of adventurers and mountaineers in creating compelling descriptions of the state's varied natural features – mountains, deserts, and coast. They created a literary tradition that expressed the ethical and political goal of cultivating an appreciative, meaningful, and respectful relationship with the natural environment on its own terms, apart from the dictates of human use.

Beginnings: Tourism, Art, and Politics in Yosemite Valley

Although Spanish, French, Russian, and English explorers, surveyors, military leaders, and others had been writing about the geography, resources, and natural features of California for hundreds of years, literary nature writing about California emerged in association with a more specific time and place: Yosemite Valley and the High Sierra in the third quarter of the nineteenth century. Yosemite Valley first became known to white Americans in 1851, when it was "discovered" by a military battalion commissioned to make the Sierra Nevada safe for gold miners and other settlers by pacifying or eliminating the Native inhabitants. In the case of Yosemite, those inhabitants were the Ahwahneechee, who had lived in the valley (which they called "*Ahwahnee*") for some 4,000 years. They managed their environment in part through the use of periodic burning to keep down underbrush and facilitate hunting. Disease and military action soon decimated the Ahwahneechee, leaving a park-like valley open and accessible to the imaginations and lifestyles of newly arrived Americans – not miners but tourists.

In 1855, James Mason Hutchings of San Francisco began a multilayered effort to create a tourist mecca. Hutchings arranged transport from the city, started a hotel, led tours of the valley, and spread information and images of the valley through publications such as *Hutchings' California Magazine* (1856–61) and a series of popular guidebooks. The first article of the first issue made clear Hutchings' interest in promoting Yosemite (identified by an alternate spelling of the name): "There are but few lands that possess more of the beautiful and picturesque than California .... Among the most remarkable [of California scenes] may be classed the Yo – Ham – i – te Valley."[1]

Hutchings' use of the term "picturesque" is significant. On a basic level, the phrase signaled the importance of visual artists in creating a powerful and enduring image of the valley as a centerpiece of California identity and American culture. The article was accompanied by a sketch of the valley as first viewed from the trail by the artist Thomas Ayres. The iconic view became a model for subsequent artists, including photographers Charles Weed (also an associate of Hutchings) in 1859 and Carleton Watkins in 1861. Watkins' large-format photographs and stereoscopic views soon made their way east, to the parlor of Oliver Wendell Holmes (where they were viewed by Emerson and others) as well as Goupil's gallery in New York. They provided visual confirmation of the descriptions that Unitarian minister Thomas Starr King (a transplanted New Englander) had written as letters to the *Boston Evening Transcript* in December 1860 and January 1861. Starr King and Watkins brought Yosemite to the attention of the nation and attracted even more prominent artists and writers, including the German painter Albert Bierstadt (already famous for his views of the Rockies) and the writer Fitz Hugh Ludlow. Writing in the *Atlantic Monthly* in June 1864, Ludlow reported himself profoundly moved by the same scene that had captivated (and been captured by) Ayres, Watkins, and others.[2]

Along with the emphasis on visual scenes, Ludlow's prose reminds us of the deeper meanings of the term "picturesque" in nineteenth-century American culture – often associated with a companion term, the "sublime." The ideals of the picturesque and the sublime were originally developed by artists and writers who depicted European scenery. Later, American painter Thomas Cole and members of the Hudson River school emphasized aesthetic composition and balance as a means of unifying contrasting themes of beauty and awe, comfort and danger, intimacy and grandeur, approachability and remoteness, humanity and divinity. Thus, for a scene in Switzerland, the Catskills, or Yosemite to be termed "picturesque" or "sublime" meant that it was more than just a pretty picture – it was a scene that moved you emotionally and intellectually, that simultaneously humbled and exalted you, that made you feel alive in the present yet with some touch of eternity. At the same time, Ludlow's narrative also includes humorous passages on camping and food, tales of strenuous travel, local color-style sketches of stereotypic Westerners (akin to the Gold Rush tales of Bret Harte and Mark Twain), and practical recommendations for tourists – all *de rigueur* for Eastern audiences. With its combination of art and practicality, adventure and philosophy, high-brow description and low-brow tales, Ludlow's article illustrates the basic elements of countless other traveler's accounts and guidebook descriptions of Yosemite popularized throughout the 1860s and 1870s. Many of them reached national and international audiences in illustrated magazines such as the *Atlantic Monthly* and *Harper's* and in the two-volume *Picturesque America* (1872–74).

However, tourist popularity came at an environmental cost. As early as 1860, Starr King decried the adverse impact of thoughtless visitors and commercial exploitation on scenery. These concerns were echoed by Horace Greeley, editor of the *New York Tribune*, and landscape architect Frederick Law Olmsted. In 1864, California senator John Conness brought forth a bill setting aside more than sixty square miles of federal land to be cared for by the state of California for purposes of "public use, resort, and recreation." The bill, signed into law by President Abraham Lincoln later that year, was the first federal act protecting wilderness. Although Olmsted and Starr King were aware of the ecological destruction being wrought by gold mining on Sierra streams and forests, the concern over Yosemite focused on protecting a certain sort of human experience rather than the natural environment. Olmsted and others offered cultural and psychological arguments for governmental action to protect and manage natural scenery for the public good – an idea that over the next fifty years would form the core of the movement for national parks, and contribute to other forms of environmental protection as well.

Clarence King: Romantic Geologist

Interestingly, it took a mountain-climber and geologist, Clarence King, to produce the first real classic of California nature writing, *Mountaineering in the Sierra Nevada* (1872). The book grew out of King's work as part of the California Geological Survey, which emerged during the Gold Rush as a means of gathering scientific information to aid mining development. In

1860, the legislature named as State Geologist Josiah D. Whitney, a Massachusetts native and Yale graduate who had participated in a number of scientific surveys in the East and Midwest. Whitney enlisted the prominent botanist William Henry Brewer, another Yale graduate, whose letters about his travels were published in 1930 as *Up and Down in California, 1860–64*. Over the next few years Whitney added King (a Yale student at the time) and other scientists. The survey undertook fieldwork until 1870, and although state funding ended in 1874, various members published a variety of reports on geology, paleontology, botany, and ornithology through 1880. For a more popular audience, in 1868 Whitney published *The Yosemite Book*, a scientifically informed guidebook that included photographs by Carleton Watkins.

Coming from a prominent and wealthy New England family, King had cultural as well as scientific interests. The Alpine writings of John Tyndall and John Ruskin were as important as the geological insights of Louis Agassiz in sparking his interest in the mountains of California. Combining Eastern culture with Western adventurousness, King was known to lounge around the campfire in white linen dinner jackets, and this breadth of background, interest, talent, and connections is part of what made *Mountaineering in the Sierra Nevada* a breakthrough book at the time. The book was distinctive for its scientific perspective and for its compelling account of daring exploits of Alpine-style mountain climbing. The first chapters offer a broad geological overview of the Sierra, explicitly acknowledging the work of Whitney and the California Survey. Later chapters include specific descriptions of landscape and botany. Geological analysis flows into picturesque fancy, as when King describes Mt. Tyndall as "purely Gothic."[3]

The dramatic core of the book is a series of accounts of mountaineering adventures. Inspired by the English Alpinists, King dramatizes the human encounter with the mountains on physical as well as mental levels. He and his companions test their strength, skill, and fortitude against the highest peaks in the Sierra, and are rewarded at the summit with sublime scenery. At times, the intense relationship of trust and dependence between King and his companion takes center stage. On their descent from Mt. Tyndall, King and his friend Dick Cotter find themselves on a narrow ledge, facing a sheer rock wall on one side and a precipitous drop on the other.

The dramatic high point of the book comes in the penultimate chapter, with what King believed to be the first-ever ascent of Mt. Whitney, already understood to be the highest peak in the continental United States. After the book's publication, however, it was discovered that King had climbed not Mt. Whitney but the next peak over, Mt. Langley. Accordingly, in 1873 he corrected his mistake, though only after others had reached the peak first. The controversy occasioned a new edition of the book in which King recounted the successful ascent and reflected further on "the unperishing germ of primitive manhood that is buried within us all under so much culture and science."[4]

Anticipating the interest in human consciousness later explored by pioneering California-based ecopsychologists such as Paul Shepard and Theodore Roszak, King unified culture, science, and elemental encounters with nature. After leaving the California Survey, he participated in other Western explorations before being named the first director of the U.S. Geological Survey in 1879. In later years, he gradually withdrew from public sight to pursue more personal passions – including a double life in which he passed for an African American Pullman porter in order to marry a former slave named Ada Copeland, with whom he lived for thirteen years and had five children before his death in 1901.

John Muir: Wilderness Prophet

A very different – though more enduring – public persona associated with Yosemite and the Sierra was that of a young Scots immigrant, John Muir. Born in Scotland, raised on the Wisconsin frontier, with only a few years of schooling at the University of Wisconsin, Muir had none of the cultural background, formal scientific training, or social and professional connections of King. When he arrived in Yosemite in 1868, he worked as a mechanic at a sawmill. Over the next five years he taught himself geology, met Emerson in Yosemite, collected plant specimens for Harvard botanist Asa Gray, and collaborated with University of California scientist Joseph LeConte, whose *Ramblings in the High Sierra* (1875) describes some of their early encounters in Yosemite. Muir soon published original studies arguing for the glacial origins of Sierra valleys such as Yosemite, disagreeing with Josiah Whitney, who believed that the valley was created by an ancient catastrophe. The established scientist mocked the young upstart, but in the end Muir was proved correct, and the controversy ended up enhancing his reputation.

Muir also had a literary turn, reading Milton and Thoreau and writing nature and travel essays. Wintering in the Bay Area, he met fellow-contributors to the *Overland Monthly* such as editor Bret Harte and the poet Joaquin Miller, another "frontier original." Born Cincinnatus

Heine Miller in Indiana, he moved with his family to Oregon as a child, and played up his frontier origins in self-consciously creating a popular persona as a rough-and-ready outlaw poet. *Songs of the Sierra* (1871) and *Songs of the Sun-Lands* (1873), epic ballads of stereotypic Western characters and scenes, made him a minor celebrity in California and England. In 1887, he contributed four essays to a descriptive travelogue edited by Muir entitled *Picturesque California* (modeled explicitly upon the earlier *Picturesque America*). Even more important to Muir were his friendships with poets Charles Warren Stoddard and especially Ina Coolbrith, the first Poet Laureate of California, whose presence as librarian in Oakland and San Francisco for many years provided stability to the Bay Area literary scene. Her own poetry, lyrical ballads, and short pieces imported classical styles into local scenes and presented natural beauty as central to a more cultured and spiritual California than Miller's frontier. Her 1895 *Songs from the Golden Gate* included engravings of paintings by another of Muir's close friends, the landscape painter William Keith. As did the painters and photographers of the 1860s, the California poets and artists of the 1870s, 1880s, and 1890s helped shape the nature writing of the day – including that of Muir.

Most of his first book, *The Mountains of California*, was published as magazine articles in the 1870s and early 1880s. They appeared in book form in 1894. The book differs from King's in its focus on the mountains rather than on the human act of mountaineering. Muir's *Mountains* includes no local color stories and places much less emphasis on the narrator, offering instead a fuller geological and biological description of the Sierra as an ecological whole. After an introductory chapter, the book is structured not with respect to narrative incidents (as in King) but with regard to landscape features considered in the light of geological evolution. Beginning with the formative power of the glaciers, the book in effect proceeds downhill to passes, lakes, meadows, forests, and the lowlands beyond, including chapters on animal inhabitants as well. Within this naturalistically structured presentation, the authorial persona makes regular appearances as a human lens through which the reader may better experience the deeper meanings of the mountains. This happens most famously in the dramatic mountaineering adventure narrated in the third chapter, "A New View of the High Sierra," where Muir explicitly contrasts his artist-companions' quest for "picturesque views" with his own more intense spiritual and bodily contact with the dangers and glories of Mt. Ritter. More often, though, Muir portrays a right relationship with the mountains not through manly adventure but through a contemplative and receptive stance reminiscent of Emerson, Thoreau, and poets such as Coolbrith.[5]

Although *Mountains* is not an overtly political book, certain passages suggest the origins of Muir's conservationism, especially his observations on the range and health of the sequoia forests. The time at which the book was published was one of emerging activism. In 1890, a series of articles in *Century Magazine* had helped shape public and political opinion in support of the creation of Yosemite National Park. Two years later Muir and others founded the Sierra Club to consolidate and extend the conservation message. In this context, the appreciation of nature expressed in *Mountains* was immediately understood as having political implications, and the popular and financial success of the book contributed to increased activism by Muir and the Sierra Club as well.

Muir's second book, *Our National Parks* (1901), was his most explicitly political. The book begins in an Olmstedian mode, noting the public interest in the spiritual, health, and social benefits of nature that characterized the broader "back-to-nature" movement of recent years, and taking this as a mandate for political action to protect the forests from increasing destruction at the hands of loggers, tourists, and others. Muir used political sarcasm to address these threats:

> Any fool can destroy trees. They cannot run away; and if they could, they would still be destroyed – chased and hunted down as long as fun or a dollar could be got out of their bark hides, branching horns, or magnificent bole backbones. . . . Through all the wonderful, eventful centuries since Christ's time – and long before that – God has cared for these trees, saved them from drought, disease, avalanches, and a thousand straining, leveling tempests and floods; but he cannot save them from fools – only Uncle Sam can do that.[6]

Muir's pen and persona contributed much to the emergence of conservation as a political force both in California and nationwide, typified by the famous 1903 photograph of Muir and President Theodore Roosevelt standing atop Glacier Point, with Yosemite Valley stretching out behind them. In a few years Roosevelt would increase federal control of the valley, one of many federal acts extending protection to national parks and forests throughout the country.

Even as he continued to engage in political activism, Muir struggled to find time and focus to write. His later books were more autobiographical and less explicitly political, including *My First Summer in the Sierra* (1911), a revised version of his early Yosemite journals and one of his most-read works today. Combining elements of travelogue, scientific observation, and local color, the most memorable passages evoke a youthful transcendentalist encounter with the mountains: "We are now in the mountains and they are in us, kindling enthusiasm, making every nerve quiver, filling every pore and cell of us."[7] Reaching back further in his life, *The Story of My Boyhood and Youth* (1913) explores Muir's formative experiences in Scotland and Wisconsin. Other reminiscences were published posthumously, including the edited journals of his trip through the South, *A Thousand-Mile Walk to the Gulf* (1916). The book contains philosophical passages that have influenced environmental thinkers throughout the twentieth century. "Why should man value himself as more than a small part of the one great unit of creation? And what creature of all that the Lord has taken the pains to make is not essential to the completeness of that unit – the cosmos?"[8] Other reminiscences included *Stickeen* (1909) and a posthumous collection of edited journals, *Travels in Alaska* (1915).

Muir's career was not without defeats. He participated in the unsuccessful movement to stop the flooding of Hetch Hetchy Valley. The struggle brought out some of his most powerful language. "These temple destroyers, devotees of ravaging commercialism, seem to have a perfect contempt for Nature, and, instead of lifting their eyes to the God of the mountains, lift them to the Almighty Dollar. Dam Hetch Hetchy! As well dam for water-tanks the people's cathedrals and churches, for no holier temple has ever been consecrated by the heart of man."[9] Even in defeat, such rhetoric became part of the enduring myth of Muir as a wilderness prophet, combining science, ethics, and ecstasy in the service of political action.

Mary Austin: Voice of the Desert

Another early-century urban water project – this time involving the flooding of Owens Valley, on the east side of the Sierra, to feed an aqueduct carrying mountain water to Los Angles – was a pivotal event in the career of the next great California nature writer, Mary Hunter Austin. Born in Illinois in 1868, Mary Hunter moved with her family to the San Joaquin Valley in 1888, marrying Stafford Wallace Austin three years later. The couple moved frequently in search of work, and during a stint in San Francisco Mary met Ina Coolbrith, who helped the novice writer publish her first story in the *Overland Monthly* in 1892; other stories, poems, and essays appeared in various venues, including the *Atlantic Monthly*. That same year, the Austins moved again, this time to the town of Lone Pine in the Owens Valley. Over the next seven years – despite (or perhaps because of) the pressures of chronic poverty, marital difficulties, and a developmentally disabled daughter – Austin made close observations of the geography, animals, and Native inhabitants of the desert around her, which became the subject of her first and best known book, *The Land of Little Rain* (1903).

Before Austin, the desert was not a favored subject in American literature, as suggested by the complete absence of desert settings in *Picturesque America* or *Picturesque California*. The only significant literary writing about deserts before Austin, the art critic John C. Van Dyke's *The Desert* (1901), approaches the Arizona desert primarily from an aesthetic perspective (as suggested by the book's subtitle, *Further Studies in Natural Appearances*). By contrast, Austin's intimate experience of the desert led her to an ecocentric perspective, placing the land itself rather than human consciousness or concern at the center of the text. Combining the cadences of the King James Bible with Transcendentalist imagery, Native and Mexican-era folk tales, local color characters, and her own observations and experiences, Austin produced an allusive and evocative book, as hard to pin down as the desert itself.

In contrast to the relatively straightforward personas of nature writers such as King and Muir, Austin's narrative voice is guarded, even secretive – telling other people's stories more than her own, blurring fact and fiction, always emphasizing that second-hand reports (including her own) can't be completely trusted, yet still might contain some grains of truth. All such assertions must be brought to the test of the desert itself, where humans don't have the luxury of either mountaineering – style conquest or mere aesthetic contemplation; rather, knowledge and action must always be keyed to survival – on the desert's own terms, which can only be divined slowly, by long experience in specific surroundings: "The manner of the country makes the usage of life there, and the land will not be lived in except in its own fashion." At the same time, for all its uncertainties and dangers, the desert can be an object of beauty and even love: "None other than this long brown land lays such a hold on the affections. . . . For all the toll the desert takes of a man it gives compensations, deep breaths, deep sleep, and the communion of the stars."[10] Austin goes on to describe the land and its inhabitants – plants, animals, and humans – all of whose lives are shaped and constrained by the presence or absence of water. In "Jimville – A Bret Harte Town" she shows the baleful results of the typical American prospector's refusal to take the land on its own terms; by contrast, the final chapter presents a semi-mythical Old Mexican town, The Little Town of the Grape Vines, as having achieved a more convivial culture and a more workable, productive (if still tenuous) relation to the land.

It was around the time of the publication of *The Land of Little Rain* that the Owens Valley water project brought controversy to Austin's desert. With none of the cultural prominence or political associations of Muir's Hetch Hetchy campaign, opposition to the project took the form of local farmers and grazers banding together to keep control of their water by establishing their own cooperative, in which cause Wallace and Mary Austin both took an active role. They stood little chance against the economic and political power of Los Angeles, however, and by 1905 the debate was over. Pushed by the controversy and pulled by the fame of *Little Rain*, Austin left the valley with a clearer sense of its fragility at human hands. Separating from her husband and placing her daughter in a sanatorium, she moved to Carmel, where she completed her next nonfiction book, *The Flock* (1906). In line with her and Wallace's response to the Owens Valley water project, in *The Flock* Austin explores the possibilities for appropriate, sustainable use of arid landscapes by surveying the history of sheepherding in the region, portraying traditional shepherds (many of them, at least) as dignified, responsible stewards, attuned by experience to the subtle rhythms of the land. The book thus offers a sharp contrast to Muir's *My First Summer in the Sierra,* which portrays shepherds as slow and dim-witted and sheep as "hoofed locusts," inherently destructive to the land, as part of Muir's overall campaign to prohibit all such economic activity from national parks and other wild places. For Austin, the experience helped sharpen her social justice vision and her interest in traditional peoples and societies in their relation to the land, concerns that would guide her later writings about Native Americans and made her a forerunner of the environmental justice movement that emerged later in the century.

Austin found a congenial home among the artists and writers of Carmel, and would return there periodically for the rest of her life, but after a diagnosis of breast cancer she chose to travel in Europe for a few years, returning to the United States in 1910 to settle in New York. Despite her wanderings, the desert remained central to her writing. In *Lost Borders* (1909), Austin explores the lives of people trying – and usually failing – to impose some external order or purpose on their lives in the trackless desert. Austin, more than King or Muir, was aware of the potential negative forms of dissolving the boundaries between self and nature: "Out there, then where the law and the landmarks fail together, the souls of little men fade out at the edges, leak from them as water from wooden pails warped asunder."[11] For Austin, it was women who were most likely to have the strength to accept the unbounded existence the desert offered and demanded, as typified in the final story of the collection, "The Walking Woman." Clearly inspired in part by the stresses and dreams of Austin's own life, the Walking Woman "had begun by walking off an illness. There had been an invalid to be taken care of for years, leaving her at last broken in body, and with no recourse but her own feet to carry her out of that predicament. "An enigmatic figure, flawed yet powerful, the Walking Woman embodies the elemental human needs and desires – work, love, a child – that life in the desert unveils: "She had walked off all sense of society-made values, and, knowing the best when the best came to her, was able to take it. Work – as I believed; love – as the Walking Woman had proved it; a child – as you subscribe to it. But look you: it was the naked thing the Walking Woman grasped, not dressed and tricked out, for instance, by prejudices in favor of certain occupations."[12]

A prolific and varied writer, Austin also explored the California environment in fiction such as *Isidro* (1905) and *The Ford* (1917) and a nonfiction collaboration with the artist Sutton Palmer, *California, Land of the Sun* (published in England in 1914 and in the United States in 1927). She also wrote novels, plays, and essays on topics including women's capacities and rights, religion and spirituality, Native Americans, politics, and (after moving to New Mexico in the 1920s) the land and peoples of the desert Southwest. Her autobiography, *Earth Horizon* (1932), confirms the importance of the natural world in her life and work.

Robinson Jeffers: Mythopoetic Inhumanist

Mary Austin was not alone in her strong associations with Carmel, for in the few decades after the San Francisco earthquake of 1906 the town served as the unofficial artistic and literary capital of California. "Discovered" by the poet Charles Warren Stoddard, Carmel was brought to cultural and social prominence through the presence and energy of another minor poet, George Sterling, who was part of San Francisco's Bohemian Club and who introduced Jack London, Sinclair Lewis, Upton Sinclair, and others to the town's dramatic seaside setting. The Carmel Arts and Crafts Club promoted literature, theater, handicrafts, and painting. Later, Carmel attracted prominent photographers such as Edward Weston and his friend Ansel Adams, both of whom moved there (in 1929 and 1962, respectively). Of the poets associated with Carmel, by far the most enduring and influential was Robinson Jeffers, who lived there from 1914 until his death in 1962.

Jeffers was born in 1887 in Pittsburgh, where his father was a seminary professor of the Old Testament. He was educated in a series of European boarding schools in Europe, which grounded him in classical literature and languages. The family moved to Pasadena in 1903. Jeffers graduated from Occidental College at age 17, then studied comparative literature and medicine at the University of Southern California and forestry at the University of Washington. His engagement with modern science was deepened further by contact with his brother Hamilton, a prominent astronomer who spent much of his career at the Lick Observatory, where he collaborated with luminaries such as Edwin Hubble. In 1913, after a complex personal odyssey, Jeffers married Una Call Kuster, and the following year the two settled in Carmel, where Jeffers used local stone to build a home, Tor House, and an accompanying tower. Integrating his immersions in classical poetics, myth, and modern science, Jeffers wrote about the coast around Carmel, using concrete descriptions as well as a philosophical sense of humanity's embeddedness in the natural world.

Much of Jeffers' early literary works – and the basis of his initial fame – were long narrative poems based on ancient mythological themes. These pieces offered environmental perspectives, stressing the notion that past cultures were "closer to nature." For example, the novels of Sir Walter Scott depicted medieval Scotland in terms of timeless allegiance to the land, cultural images reflected in Muir's memories of the "inherited wildness" that characterized his own childhood in Scotland. Later in the nineteenth century, William Morris lauded the social, spiritual, and environmental virtues of traditional economic systems and local handicrafts over the modern machine-based economy, ideas that informed Austin's positive interpretation of the sheepherders of the Owens Valley. For Jeffers, as for others of his generation, such antimodernist ideas were amplified by the catastrophe of World War I, which seemed to signal a final judgment on the path taken by modern Europe and America.

Influenced by new theories of primitive mythology and mentalities such as Frazier's *The Golden Bough*, and powerful patterns of the unconscious offered by Freud and Jung, Jeffers's early long poems reworked Greek mythology in contemporary settings, often emphasizing darker aspects of primal human existence. Poems such as *Tamar* (1924), *Roan Stallion* (1925), and *Cawdor* (1928) explored the inchoate forces of death, sex, spirit, law, and violence in the lives of isolated, rural inhabitants of the Carmel coast. Jeffers's characters attain understanding or authority only when their humanness has been sheared away by struggle or violence, as the protagonist of *Tamar* rising to her feet on a beach between cliff and sea at night:

> She in the starlight
> And little noises of the rising tide
> Naked and not ashamed bore a third part
> With the ocean and keen stars in the consistence
> And dignity of the world. She was white stone ...

And underlying the human story is the foundational, timeless strength and beauty of the coast itself:

> Old cypresses
> The sailor wind works into deep-sea knots
> A thousand years; age-reddened granite
> That was the world's cradle ... [13]

Such ideas and imagery – but without the mythopoetic narrative – appear also in his shorter poems, which are more easily recognizable as nature poetry and which, after a slump in his critical reception in the middle of the century, have formed the basis of his more recent popularity. Many of the poems offer exquisite descriptions of the Carmel coast along with explicit statements of his belief in the inherent beauty and worth of nature, apart from human presence or interpretation. In "Hawk and Rock" (1935), he rejects all ideologies, from Christianity ("the cross") to collectivisms such as communism ("the hive"), taking instead as his "emblem" a falcon sitting on a gray rock:

> bright power, dark peace;
> Fierce consciousness joined with final
> Disinterestedness;
> Life with calm death; the falcon's
> Realist eyes and act
> Married to the massive
> Mysticism of stone.[14]

Jeffers rejected many currents of modern American life. He suited his actions to his words by taking a strong stand against the United States' entry into World War II and decrying the consumerism and suburban expansion that was defacing his beloved Carmel coastline. These positions contributed to the mid-century decline in his reputation but also set the stage for a resurgence of interest in his work beginning in the 1960s, when such stances became more popular. Later in his career he described this outlook as "inhumanism," which was "based in a recognition of the astonishing beauty of things and their living wholeness, and on a rational acceptance of the fact that mankind is neither central nor important in the universe."[15] Note that while this definition includes the core of the late-century concept of ecocentrism – the denial of human *centrality* in the universe – Jeffers goes further in refusing to accord any fundamental *importance* to human existence. As a purely philosophical doctrine, such assertions seem nihilistic and contradictory. But Jeffers's genius lay in his poetic expression of the power and beauty of nature on its own terms. He recognized and celebrated such beauty and power with a detached but ultimately religious sense of awe.

For much of his career, Jeffers was friends with the photographer Ansel Adams, whose work reflects the legacy and influence of all the major authors explored above. In 1927, Adams (an avid mountaineer) included in his first published portfolio an image of Mt. Clarence King. Three years later he collaborated with Mary Austin, whom he had met in Carmel, on his first book project, *Taos Pueblo*. In 1938, he contributed to the Sierra Club's effort to create Sequoia and Kings Canyon national parks through the photographic book *Sierra Nevada: The John Muir Trail*, whose cover featured the earlier image of Mt. Clarence King. In 1948, he published some of his most famous images in *Yosemite and the Sierra Nevada*, with words drawn from Muir's writings. In 1965, Adams participated in another landmark Sierra Club publishing project, *Not Man Apart*, which paired lines from Jeffers's poetry with stunning images of the Big Sur coastline contributed by a number of prominent photographers. The title came from Jeffers's poem "The Answer" (1937):

> Integrity is wholeness, the greatest beauty is Organic wholeness, the wholeness of life and things, the divine beauty of the universe. Love that, not man Apart from that, or else you will share man's pitiful confusions, or drown in despair when his days darken.[16]

King, Muir, and Austin surely would have agreed.

Notes

1. James M. Hutchings, "The Yo-Ham-i-te Valley, and Its Water-falls," *Hutchings' California Magazine* 1: 1 (July, 1856), 2.
2. Fitz Hugh Ludlow, "Seven Weeks in the Great Yo-Semite," *Atlantic Monthly* 13: 80 (June 1864), 746.

3. Clarence King, *Mountaineering in the Sierra Nevada* (rev. ed., 1874; New York: Norton, 1935), 67–68.
4. Ibid., 305.
5. John Muir, *The Mountains of California* (1894), in *Nature Writings*, ed. William Cronon (New York: Library of America, 1997), 395.
6. Muir, *Our National Parks* (1901), in *Nature Writings*, 720.
7. Muir, *My First Summer in the Sierra* (1911), in *Nature Writings*, 161.
8. Muir, *A Thousand-Mile Walk to the Gulf* (1916), in *Nature Writings*, 826.
9. Muir, *The Yosemite* (1912), in *Nature Writings*, 817.
10. Mary Austin, "The Land of Little Rain" (1903), in *Stories from the Country of Lost Borders*, ed. Marjorie Pryse (New Brunswick, NJ: Rutgers University Press, 1987), 57, 15, 17.
11. Austin, "Lost Borders" (1909), in *Stories from the Country of Lost Borders*, 156.
12. Ibid., 257, 261.
13. Robinson Jeffers, "Tamar" (1924), in *The Selected Poetry of Robinson Jeffers*, ed. Tim Hunt (Stanford University Press, 2001), 56–57, 80.
14. Jeffers, "Rock and Hawk" (1935), in *Selected Poetry*, 502.
15. Jeffers, preface to *The Double Ax and Other Poems* (1947), in *Selected Poetry*, 719.
16. Robinson Jeffers, "The Answer" (1937), in *Selected Poetry*, 522.

PART III

Contested Spaces

CHAPTER 7

The Black Frontier

Aparajita Nanda

As a nationalistic concept, *frontier* refers to America's westward expansion, which was propelled in the nineteenth century by Manifest Destiny. Culturally, *frontier* promises even more: the creation of communities, the development of markets and states, the merging of peoples and cultures, and the promise of survival and persistence based on values of equality and democracy. Thousands of people left their homes in the East to pursue these ideals, including large communities of African Americans. However, African Americans, like many other cultural groups who moved westward, encountered struggles when they reached the new frontier. In some cases, they faced the same problems they left the East to escape.

As new frontier territories and states were founded, new regional policies on slavery were also created. When the Treaty of Guadalupe Hidalgo (1848) ceded the territories of California and New Mexico to the United States, it outlawed slavery in the new territories. California entered the Union in 1850 as an officially free state. Before the Civil War, about one thousand slaves lived in California, which despite its status as a free state remained inconsistent in defining its anti-slavery laws. The state continued to label as "property" both fugitive slaves and those who entered the state with their masters before 1850. As a result, de facto slavery continued in California. The state had the largest number of bondservants west of Texas, working in fields and households.

Gold was discovered in northern California near the end of the Mexican-American War. By 1852, the region's population soared to 200,000. When slavery was abolished in 1865, African American migration to the West increased significantly. By 1870, African Americans comprised 12 percent of the West's inhabitants. Yet racial discrimination was rife in the state.

Despite their sizeable presence in the area, African Americans have been largely ignored in frontier history and lore.[1] Romanticized stories of the frontier have long revolved around "[t]he mythical American West ... filled with strong and often heroic men and women – the sons and daughters of stout European forebears."[2] The black man's alleged inferiority to the white man denied him the heroic qualities traditionally associated with the vaunted frontiersman in the popular imagination. Yet nineteenth-century black frontiersmen like James P. Beckwourth – a mountain man, Chief of the Crow Tribe, and fur trader – shattered the racial stereotype of the Anglo-Saxon frontiersman. Inspired by pioneering figures like Beckwourth, black authors such as Alvin Coffey, Mifflin Wistar Gibbs, Wallace Thurman, Langston Hughes, and Chester Himes sought to reclaim the black frontier.

James P. Beckwourth (1798–1866) was an African American born into slavery in Virginia. His father and owner, Jennings Beckwith, a descendant of Irish and English nobility, raised James as his own son and later manumitted him around 1824. Beckwourth joined Ashley's Fur Trading Company and became a prominent trapper and mountain man, buying furs from Pawnee Indian traders. His pioneering feats in the wilderness of the West culminated when he was captured by Crow Indians while trapping between the Crow, Cheyenne, and Blackfoot territories. For almost a decade, Beckwourth lived with a Crow band, eventually becoming a chief. He later moved to Fort Vasquez, Colorado, and, with a few partners, built a trading post there. Beginning in 1844, he traded along a portion of the Old Spanish Trail between Arkansas, California, and Nevada that now bears his name as the Beckwourth Trail. In fact, Beckwourth's ranch, trading post, and hotel in Sierra were the first settlements of Beckwourth, California, another frontier landmark that bears his name. In the winter of 1854–55, Thomas D. Bonner stayed in the hotel and recorded Beckwourth's exploits, as reported to him by the frontiersman himself, in *The Life and Adventures of James P. Beckwourth* (1856). The book blends fact with fiction in a way that anticipates Toni Morrison's famous postmodern challenge of autobiography's foundation in "fact." Citing the proverbial axiom "truth is stranger than fiction," Morrison argues that, in fact, fact (or truth) is really only distinguished from fiction (or lies) by a comparative – not an absolute – degree.[3] Autobiography, then, emerges not as a simple recounting of lived events but as a story that in itself pioneers a self-inventive narrative, which introduces the narrated self as "my first other."[4]

Beckwourth's rendering of himself defied the limiting stereotypes of minority culture and strove to portray a legendary hero, a true black pioneer (though he often wanted to pass himself off as white) whose daring exploits, careful strategic planning, and near-death encounters followed by instant resurrections, imbued him with an indestructible, mythic quality.[5,6] Being African American allowed Beckwourth to move freely among Native Americans even as he worked for the American Fur Company. First nicknamed the "Morning Star" – clearly promising a day full of glory – Beckwourth graduated to the appellation "the Bobtail Horse" when he scalped an Indian, and then to "Bloody Arm" when he was deemed "the only brave [man] who can keep the nation together."[7] These multiple titles not only seem to give his personality a superhuman power but also complement his lived reality, as he juggled the roles of fur trapper, trader, guide, hotelier, and trailblazing mountaineer. The variety of his professional ventures again added to his aura of being multifaceted – a man who could "adapt to any group or environment by reinventing himself ... to change names and identities, to enjoy physical freedom, social fluidity, and economic mobility."[8] Therefore, the concept of the frontier, with its sense of fluidity and possibility, was well represented by the mythic figure of James Beckwourth.

The Gold Rush in California was a turning point in the history of the African American frontier. It promised black migrants the possibility of buying back freedom and family with the gold they hoped to excavate for their masters. By 1849, thousands of people had reached California, either by sailing around South America (a journey that could take as long as six months) or by walking the California trail, an almost 2000-mile, 6-month long trek via wagon train from Missouri.

Alvin Coffey (1822–1902), born a slave in Mason County, had accompanied his master to the northern California goldfields in 1849. He writes about the hardships on the trail, of strenuous night guard duty, and of driving "night and day"[9] in panic to escape from a cholera epidemic. As they trudged through a desert to get to Black Rock, a great number of cattle perished. Despite the odds, Coffey's acts of courage and empathy are as remarkable as his resilience. Coffey recalls how he worked tirelessly for 13 months making "$5500 in gold dust"[10] for his master and $616 for himself. On their way back through New Orleans, his master, who carried Coffey's share with him, took it to "the mint [to get their] gold coined."[11] When they got to Missouri, however, he sold Coffey for "a thousand more [than $616]."[12] In 1854, with his new owner, Coffey crossed the plains into California once again. This time he made enough money, and when, in 1856, his owner emancipated him, he went back to Missouri and finally bought back his wife and children. They settled in Shasta County. In the latter years of his life, Coffey was involved in organizing the Home for the Aged and Infirm, to which he donated his total income. Alvin Coffey died in 1902 and was buried at Oak Hill Cemetery in Red Bluff, California. Coffey's story is most importantly one of chattel slavery, but it also exemplifies two key themes specific to the regional history of California. On the one hand, it delineates California as a land of opportunity, a place of possibility where one's freedom can be secured. On the other, ironically, it demolishes the concept of California as a state free from racism. The latter half of Coffey's narrative, though, proves him to be a true frontier man, who despite all odds, exploited every opportunity available to him until he finally achieved his goal of securing freedom for himself and his family.

Unlike Beckwourth and Coffey, Mifflin Wistar Gibbs (1823–1915) was born a free man. His father, Reverend Jonathan Gibbs, enrolled his son in one of the few all-black schools in Philadelphia, Pennsylvania. Soon thereafter, however, the Reverend died and Gibbs's mother withdrew her son from school. Gibbs was hired out to a white lawyer. In one of his expeditions with his employer, Gibbs first encountered slavery. It awakened in him the desire to rebel and by the time he was twenty, he was secretly working in the Underground Railroad to free slaves in the South. During this time he became acquainted with the African American abolitionist Frederick Douglass, and often shared the speaking platform with him. However, in his autobiography Gibbs admits he became depressed until at the age of twenty-five he received the encouraging injunction – "go do some great thing" – of Julia Griffiths, who Gibbs adds is "a renowned wom[a]n, who at home and abroad ... hasten[ed] the downfall of slavery and encourage[d] the weak and lowly to hope and effort."[13]

By 1850, Gibbs had arrived in San Francisco, drawn to California by the Gold Rush. He knew that the West was extremely hostile toward African Americans. Though California was admitted to the Union in 1850 as a free state, the state's ban on slavery was in reality an attempt to ensure an all-white population. Its first legislature failed, however, to ban completely the entry of African Americans into the state. Within this climate, Gibbs's West Coast hopes were born more out of desperation than genuine optimism. Penniless in San Francisco, he encountered severe racism in the segregated mining fields. He went on to work as a carpenter and then as a bootblack who "scraped mud and animal droppings from boots and then applied polish."[14] By 1851, Gibbs was able to quit boot blacking and open a shoe store with his acquaintance Peter Lester, a former slave from Maryland.

For African Americans, California proved to be a unique site of residence. No white person had forced the black migrants to relocate there; in fact a number of them, like Gibbs and Lester, were free men. And yet slavery was an overwhelming presence in this ostensibly free state, raising legal and moral issues in cases like Dred Scott and Archy Lee. Verdicts jostled between the notorious Dred Scott decision, which asserted that Negroes had no citizenship rights at all, to the dramatic course of the Archy Lee case, which, after Lee's exoneration and re-arrest, granted him his freedom on the grounds that, because the man who claimed to own him could be deemed a California resident, Lee himself was never a fugitive slave crossing state lines, but instead a man held in illegal servitude in a free Union state. The set of legal acrobatics that freed Archy, however, did nothing to settle the larger question of California's policy of allowing nonresident slaveholders to bring people as property into the state. Gibbs spearheaded protests against these verdicts in his *Mirror of the Times* (1855–57), the first black newspaper in California, which grew out of the work of the San Francisco Atheneum Institute, the primary seat of black intelligentsia in San Francisco. Along with other black leaders, Gibbs went on to publish a series of antidiscriminatory resolutions and to protest against the state legislature's 1858 limitation of black immigration into California.

Violence against African Americans in California escalated in the late 1850s, including an incident when two white men posing as customers deliberately created havoc in the shoe store owned by Gibbs and Lester. In his autobiography, Gibbs recalls how "[o]ne of two mutual friends (both customers) came in looking over and admiring a display of newly acquired stock."[15] One of them tried on a pair of boots but laid them aside on the pretense that he had not yet made up his mind. Shortly thereafter, his friend arrived, asked to "try on his friends selection," and bought them, despite the shop owners' insistence that his friend had put the shoes aside for himself.[16] The man who had bought the shoes promised that nothing would happen and "he would clear [Gibbs and Lester] of blame."[17] Both customers soon came back, however, and while the first asked for his boots his friend stood mute. As a result, the former went on to "assault [Gibbs's] partner, who was compelled tamely to submit, for had he raised his hand he would have been shot, and no redress." "I," Gibbs adds, "would not have been allowed to attest to 'the deep damnation of his taking off.'"[18] Even as he recognizes the heinousness of the crime, Gibbs's narration of the futility of the situation remains unnerving. He must "tamely" watch his friend Lester being viciously assaulted, and quietly acknowledge that the miscreants got away, because African Americans according to California Criminal Procedure's existing (1850) exclusion could not testify in court against white men.

Thus though the Gold Rush had brought freedom to some and jobs for others, the African Americans in California were still very much victims of unjust laws. Gibbs went on to petition for the testimony law to be changed. The petition, however, was initially rejected by the state legislature at Sacramento in 1852, and crimes against African Americans continued rampantly. Gibbs and Lester, however, did not give up on their mission. When the resolution was finally approved by the three-day convention held at Barney Fletcher's African Methodist Church at Sacramento, it had been revised in such a way that it glossed over the brutal reality of black life in California, but began to recognize the wealth and intelligence of the black man by granting him permission to testify in California courts. As a next step, Gibbs looked for white support to petition for basic human rights. His strategy was to emphasize the benefit whites would reap if black men were granted their rights. When the legislature convened in April of 1856, however, the petition was once again turned down. Finally, after eight years, six failed petitions, and three conventions, Gibbs sold his shoe company and left California for Victoria, British Columbia.

By 1858, about ten percent of the black Californian population had left San Francisco, bound for Victoria, British Columbia, after the Canadian province invited free Negroes to come and settle there. Mrs. Priscilla Stewart, a teacher of the Broadway School at San Francisco complains, in "A Voice from the Oppressed to the Friends of Humanity" (1858), about "our sad despair/Our hopes and prospects fled." She refers to the homeless state of her fellow black men, answering the call from Canada, which she characterizes as emanating from Queen Victoria herself, who "looked on us with sympathy/ And offered us a home." Mrs. Stewart, who played an active role in a number of movements in support of African American rights, was a true pioneer of the black frontier, trumpeting a message of courage and determination. "May God inspire your hearts, / A Marion raise your hands; / Never desert your principles/ Until you've redeemed your land."[19]

Quite different from the reality-driven autobiography of Gibbs or the clarion call of Priscilla Stewart are the early writings, primarily poems of Christian piety and morality, by Eloise Bibb Thompson (1878–1928). Born in New Orleans, Thompson published her first book of poems when she was only seventeen. After being educated at Oberlin College's

Preparatory Academy and Howard University Teacher's College, she became head resident of Howard's Colored Social Settlement House. In 1911, she left that job, married, and moved to Los Angeles, where her work was published in the *Los Angeles Tribune*, *Out West*, and the *Morning Sun*. Her marriage to journalist Noah Davis Thompson, a devout Catholic, likely strengthened her interest in religion. Whether this interest was directly linked with the uplifting of the black race in the United States is hard to tell. Thompson's primary contributions to the *Tidings* (1895), a Catholic publication, were an article entitled "The Church and the Negro" (1917) and a poem called "A Garland of Prayer" (1917). Her poetic style and subject matter resonate with the fervor and vintage tone characteristic of Victorian poetry of the nineteenth century. The lyric poem is sincere in its appeal to God, its note of supplication underscored by a voice that begs for "devotion," "chastity," "meekness," and "mercy." The total surrender to a Higher Power evinced in "A Garland of Prayer" recalls her earlier poem "An Offering" (1895): "Lord, all I am and hope to be, / I humbly offer, King, to thee!"[20] The lyric's simple statement is energized by a willed surrender. The even metrical rhythm of the sestets moves through an ordered time sequence manifest in floral analogies – "the Elder flower," "the Heliotrope," "the Orange flower," and "the Lilac wild," ending in "And thus each day shall be my care / To add another flower of prayer, / Until complete."[21] Thompson's work consciously follows in the footsteps of Phyllis Wheatley; she dedicates her religious poems to Mrs. S. F. Williams, President of the Phyllis Wheatley Club of New Orleans. This dedication traces an important genealogy that links Victorian poetry of the nineteenth century to the Harlem Renaissance literary arts movement of the twentieth and provides a space, cordoned off from lived reality, for the female voice to come into its own in African American poetic history.

In complete contrast to the work discussed above, though, stand Thompson's plays. In 1915, she wrote *A Reply to the Clansman* (1920) in response to Thomas Dixon's 1905 novel *The Clansman*, the infamous inspiration for D. W. Griffith's film *Birth of a Nation* (1915). Between 1920 and 1924 Thompson wrote three one-act plays – *Caught* (1920), *Africans* (1922), and *Cooped Up* (1924). In *Cooped Up* she unflinchingly portrays black people with all their virtues and their flaws. Thompson was also recognized for her short stories "Mademoiselle Tate" (1925) and "Masks" (1927) both of which were published in *Opportunity* magazine. Thompson stands out as a unique literary pioneer on the emerging black frontier of California. She was a woman writer who transformed herself from a religious poet to a socially vocal, politically aware, and racially conscious playwright.[22]

Another distinctive poetess of the times was Eva Carter-Buckner, a personal friend of Paul Lawrence Dunbar. Her poems were published in notable periodicals in Colorado and later in both black and white newspapers in Mexico. Her greatest honor, though, came when her musical composition, "City of Sunshine" (1905) was included in a 1912 book of poems called *Gems of Poesy*. Apart from inspiring club songs like "Colorado & California State Federation," Carter-Buckner also wrote a number of short stories and articles.[23] Her work is memorable for articulating her commitment to the uplifting of her race, with soul-inspiring lines that call for recognition of the black man, and ring out loud and clear against the irrationality of the "one drop rule." She recognizes the arduous task ahead of her and yet unflappably carries on her crusade as voiced in the last stanza of "What Constitutes a Negro?" (n.d.):

> But, there, friends,
>   Join us in life's great combat,
> Though your skin be dark, what matter?
>   You're a man, e'en for that;
> And we are using every effort
>   To make good where e'er we trod,
> One hand with the flag a-waving,
>   And the other stretched to God.[24]

Eva Carter-Buckner, hailed by Delilah Beasley as the most popular Negro poetess, was an ardent admirer of Abraham Lincoln and a strong advocate of the National Association for the Advancement of Colored People (NAACP). On Lincoln's birthday, February 12, 1909, the *Los Angeles Daily Times* published an excerpt from her poem "Whittier":

> We boast of the freedom thou so longed to see
> And each generation sings praise;
> And while the vast number thy name celebrate
> We, too, our voices shall raise.
> Oh long may our country do honor to men
> Whose stand for the right will not sway,
> And now with the nation we breathe a prayer,
> "God bless thy natal day."

Some of the finest protest poetry of the nineteenth century appeared before the Civil War. James Monroe Whitfield (1822–71) worked as a barber and in his spare time wrote poetry. Frederick Douglass, a former slave and also the nation's most powerful anti-slavery speaker, inspired him to become a spokesperson for abolitionism and pursue a writing career. In "America" (1853) and "How Long?" (1853) Whitfield's anti-slavery tirades come alive with a bitter cynicism. Despite the metrical smoothness of his poetry, "Self-Reliance" (1849), "Delusive Hope" (1853), "Yes, Strike Again That Sounding String" (1850), and "The Misanthropist" (1852) remain dark imprecations against a world that is corrupt and meaningless. The lofty ideals that the enthusiastic voice in the opening stanza of "Self-Reliance" hails are dogged by life's treacherous hypocrisy and resultant misery. The answer to overcoming adversity seems to lie in listening to God, "In bonds mysterious to unite / The finite with the infinite."[25] No such solace, however, brightens "The Misanthropist," where no "ray of hopeful light" penetrates the gloom of the lived experience of the black man. This poem rejects religion as "a false and empty name," while nature and books appear in their "sternest moods" and fiercest visages, reinforcing a sense of doom and desolation. Whitfield's poems testify to the African American experience of brutal discrimination that would foment the Civil Rights movement.

Along with Whitfield, one of the primary voices of the nineteenth century that spoke of racial oppression and the African American struggle for recognition and equality was James Madison Bell (1826–1902). Born in Gallipolis, Ohio, Bell later moved to Ontario, where he met and befriended John Brown and raised funds for the 1859 raid on the arsenal at Harper's Ferry. In 1860, after Brown's execution, Bell moved to San Francisco, where he remained committed to activist politics. As an active member and steward of the African Methodist Episcopal Church, Bell worked untiringly for abolition during the Civil War. Some of his most rousing poems, like "A Poem Entitled the Day and the War" (1864) and "A Poem Entitled the Triumph of Liberty" (1870), dramatize slavery, Civil War, emancipation, and reconstruction to create a radical voice of protest.

On April 18, 1865, Bell recited a piece simply titled "Poem," commemorating the death of Abraham Lincoln, to a public gathering of colored citizens in Sacramento, California. The sonorous opening stanza, burdened with repeated questioning – "wherefore" and "why" "those marks of grief and sorrows / So visible on every place?" – ends with a fatal declaration of Lincoln's assassination: "Our Nation's father has been murdered! / Our Nation's Chieftain has been slain! By traitorous hands most basely ordered."[26] With these lines, Bell recalls the intonation of Macduff as he reports the death of King Duncan, the Lord's anointed temple, in Shakespeare's *Macbeth*. The poem ends with a call to "avenge the death of Lincoln . . . . Till every base inhuman falcon / Is swept from freedom's broad domain."[27] For Lincoln's successor, Andrew Johnson, Bell has only scathing disdain couched in vitriolic humor. Johnson is "My liege of graceless dignity," a false prophet whose "hours of reign" have "brand[ed] him with the mark of Cain."

Another poet who tirelessly fought for equal opportunity in California for African Americans was Charles Alexander (1818–1923). Born in Mississippi, Alexander's work as a journalist brought him to Los Angeles, where he went on to become the editor of the *Los Angeles Times*. Actively involved in the NAACP, Alexander served on the committee that accompanied attorney Edward Ceruti when he made a second plea to the board of supervisors in Los Angeles County not to rescind their vote to admit African Americans to the nurses' training school there. "My Kind of Man" (n.d.), originally published in the *Los Angeles Times*, hails the man whose courage and patience, resolve to work hard and achieve success despite all odds, makes him "the man of the hour."[28]

At the turn of the century, concerns regarding the fate of African Americans in the urban West went through sharp ups and downs. In the 1920s, racial hostility and public apathy took on monstrous dimensions. This was also, though, the exciting era of Marcus Garvey's "Back to Africa" call and the rise of Black Nationalism. By the mid-1920s, a rising young generation of educated, optimistic, and confident "New Negroes" had virtually taken over Harlem in Manhattan, New York. Notable among them were Langston Hughes, Arna Bontemps, and Wallace Thurman, who resembled "the old pioneers" of the Western frontier, only this time "moving in the opposite direction, relocating in a modern eastern metropolis."[29]

One of these "old pioneers" was Wallace Thurman (1902–34), who was born in Salt Lake City and had moved to Los Angeles, where he contributed to the black newspaper *The Public Defender* and established *The Outlet*, a magazine that lasted for six months. Inspired by the Harlem Renaissance, Thurman tried to create a similar movement on the West Coast. Failing that, he migrated to Harlem in 1925, where he published the very short-lived magazine *Fire!!* (1926). In 1929, he published his first novel, *The Blacker the Berry*, which tells the story of Emma Lou Morgan, a dark-skinned black woman whose internalized intra-racial color prejudice causes a number of her personal calamities. *The Blacker the Berry* has been taken to be an autobiography of sorts, with critic Thadious M. Davis claiming that Thurman adopted the female voice of Emma Lou as a textual strategy to facilitate a radical interrogation of race.[30] Emma Lou, enthusiastically rushing around the campus of the University of Southern California trying to connect to her colored peers, becomes a pathetic figure seeking familiarity in a society defined by the hierarchy of complexion snobbery. Because of her dark skin, Emma Lou is labeled "hottentot," a "discomfort and embarrassment to others of her race, more civilized and circumspect than she."[31] After a year in college, Emma drops out, much like Thurman himself did, concluding that racism had infiltrated all regions of the United States, from Utah to California. "She was now determined to go East where life was more cosmopolitan and people ... more civilized."[32] History, however, repeats itself in Harlem and the end of the novel finds Emma Lou resigned to fight through her struggles in life.

Much like Emma Lou is Langston Hughes's Flora Belle in the short story that bears her name. Haunted by memories of the lynch mob and ostracized by blacks and whites alike, Flora Belle flees with her family from Montana to California. She contemplates suicide in Fresno, California, stoically accepting that there is no comfort of community or belonging for the black man or woman.[33]

Langston Hughes (1902–67), born in Joplin, Missouri, spent his childhood years in Kansas, Illinois, and Ohio before enrolling in Columbia University in 1922. He left school to travel through Africa and Europe. Between 1926 and 1929, Hughes, then in New York City, published his first book of poems, *The Weary Blues* (1926), followed by *Fine Clothes to the Jew* (1927), his famous essay, "The Negro Artist and the Racial Mountain" (1926), his novel, *Not Without Laughter* (1930), and two autobiographies, *The Big Sea* (1940), and, *I Wonder as I Wander* (1956).

In 1939, Langston Hughes spent time in California, where he collaborated on various projects with the black actor Clarence Muse. Despite the glitter of Tinseltown and the glamorous frontier it projected, racism and discrimination were rife in Hollywood. In 1940, Hattie McDaniel became the first black actor to win an Academy Award for her portrayal of Mammy in the film *Gone with the Wind*. In his unpublished one-act play, *Hollywood Mammy* (1940), Hughes responds to this event. African Americans were pleased that a black actor had finally won an Academy Award, but they were frustrated that it was for a stereotypical role. With seething irony, Hughes chronicles the rise of the Mammy, secure in her career path, as she compromises her aspirations: "I used to want to play Shakespeare but I put that on the shelf. I found it better business to pretend to be the kind of dear old 'Darkie' that the studios like to see."[34] She is quick to deny her roots ("I'm not from Alabama – except in publicity") and claim access to a luxurious life style ("hats from Hattie Carnegie," "got a chauffeur, cook, and maid to wait on me hands and feet") even as the chorus satirically describes her as a hypocrite paying lip service to Scarlett O'Hara for fifty grand a year and packaging herself as a "Hollywood Mammy in a great big way!"[35]

A close friend of Langston Hughes, born the same year, Arna Bontemps (1902–73) was a Louisiana Creole whose family moved to Los Angeles when he was four. He grew up in California and graduated from Pacific Union College at Angwin in 1923. When his father sent Arna to a virtually all-white boarding school in San Fernando Valley, he had advised him "[n]ow don't go up there acting colored."[36] The words stayed with Bontemps and ironically made him more interested in his black culture. Bontemps later left California and moved, at the peak of the Harlem Renaissance, to New York, where he accepted a teaching position at the Seventh-Day Adventist Harlem Academy and began to publish poetry and write novels.

Region played a complex and seminal role in Bontemps's writings.[37] The West was marked by his father's exhortation that young Bontemps strive to be "colorless," while the South was aligned with his great uncle Buddy's countervailing pride in regional heritage and the legacy of Afro folkways. Bontemps published three stories – "Why I Returned" (1965), "The Cure" (1973), and "Three Pennies for Luck" (1973) – about Los Angeles. In his novel *God Sends Sunday* (1931) he describes Mudtown, the black neighborhood of Los Angeles, as "a tiny section of the deep south" with scenes of black community life as easily plucked from rural Georgia as urban California.[38] In "Why I Returned," Bontemps has new hopes as he cheerily notes that "[s]egregation, the monster that had terrorized my parents and driven them out of the green Eden in which they had been born, was itself vulnerable and could be attacked, possibly destroyed."[39] Shortly after the publication of *God Sends Sunday*, Bontemps accepted a faculty position at Oakwood College in Alabama. The acute racism and discrimination that he faced in the "real" South led to the attitude he expresses in *Black Thunder* (1936), a novel he published in 1936 as he fled from Alabama back to Watts in California. *Black Thunder* paints the South with decidedly different strokes than Bontemps's previous work did. Though racial tensions ran high in the post-1930s Los Angeles, it seemed more peaceful than Alabama to the freshly relocated writer.

A defining moment for blacks in California was the 1928 NAACP convention held in Los Angeles. It established an important connection between the East and West Coasts, as the NAACP took on a truly national character. As unemployment soared, black workers were the last hired and first fired from jobs, and the political arena, in response, was a site of an important and lasting sea change. With the rise of the Democratic Party and the victory of Franklin Roosevelt in 1932 came the "New Deal" program that promised poor blacks blue-collar mainstream jobs in which their race would cease to matter.[40] A forceful backlash of Jim Crowism in the U.S. Senate forced New Deal leaders to recognize and grapple with the deep rootedness of U.S. racism and, with time, pushed the liberal elements within the Democratic Party to put Civil Rights on the agenda. It also made many African Americans leave the Republican Party of Lincoln and move into the Democratic Party. In California, Democrat Gus Hawkins unseated Republican Fred Roberts in the 1934 State Assembly election. Hawkins continued his winning streak through 1962, when he was elected to a seat in the U.S. Congress from which he voted for the Civil Rights legislation of the mid-1960s.

By the mid-1940s, World War II and its aftermath ushered in a radical transformation – demographically, economically, and politically – for African Americans. Countless black workers flocked to the shipbuilding and aircraft plants that proliferated across the West Coast. As defense jobs opened up, labor unions became stronger and housing strained to accommodate the population boom. California seemed to live up to its image of a frontier province, one that promised new opportunities in life; only this time it was no longer on the periphery of American life – it had moved to the center.

This Second Great Migration saw African Americans pouring into California, seeking out business opportunities and striving once more to win equal rights for themselves. History, in fact, was repeating itself. The elusive dream of the possibility of democracy at home, a dream that African Americans had when the United States entered World War I in 1917, had been shattered when soldiers returned from the war to rampant racial violence. However, the New Negro Renaissance of the 1920s and the New Deal Coalition in the 1930s, which had included the black man, revived hopes of a better tomorrow. It is possible, too, that Roosevelt's "Four Freedoms" (1941) articulation of his policy goals, with its repeated rhetorical promises of "Freedom from Fear and Want," kindled the imagination of Civil Rights activists. Roosevelt's Executive Order 8802, which prohibited racial discrimination in federally funded defense plants, also renewed hopes for a less racially segregated world.[41] The reality, however, was different. California was rife with tense race relations, white backlash, acute class conflict, and random greed.

Chester Himes (1909–84) was born in Jefferson City, Missouri, and moved to Los Angeles, California in 1940. Prior to this, he had been dismissed from Ohio State University, become involved in gambling and drugs, and been arrested for armed robbery in 1928 and sentenced to twenty years in prison. Granted parole after serving seven years, Himes moved to California in search of employment. His brutal encounters with blatant racism formed the basis of his protest novels, *If He Hollers Let Him Go* (1945) and *Lonely Crusade* (1947), where the protagonists Bob Jones and Lee Gordon battle racial intolerance in alienating urban environments. The semi-autobiographical *If He Hollers Let Him Go* revolves around a black shipyard worker, Bob Jones, who, like Himes himself, had migrated from Ohio to Los Angeles only to find his workplace embroiled in racism and gross discrimination. Prevented from joining the labor union, Jones is asked to supervise a blacks-only crew. Caught between his ambitious, light-skinned African American girlfriend who would like him to land a white-collar job, and a seductive white coworker who ultimately accuses him of rape, Jones singlehandedly maneuvers his way through the dangerous "postlapsarian paradise"[42] of California, an illusive "frontier" reality that had beckoned the black man with its booming defense industries only to crush his dreams of equal job opportunity and upward social mobility.

What Himes says in *The Quality of Hurt* (1973) – "I was thirty-one and whole when I went to Los Angeles and thirty-five and shattered when I left to go to New York"[43] – is portrayed in the five weekday span of the narrative in *If He Hollers Let Him Go*. Monday finds Jones demoted from a leader to a mechanic after he retorts "cracker bitch" to the white woman's "nigger," and given a neatly typed note that reads, "We served you this time but we do not want your patronage in the future," when he takes his fiancée, Alice, to dinner in an upscale restaurant.[44] Helpless and isolated in a hostile world, humiliated by sadistic bigots in the shipyard, and traumatized by nightmares of a black boy slashed to death with a razor blade, Bob Jones is virtually paralyzed, overwhelmed by his subconscious, which keeps repeating "Bob, there never was a nigger who could beat it."[45] At the end of the fourth day, Thursday, he is brutally beaten by his white coworkers on a fake charge of rape and arrested by the police as he tries to flee in his car. On the last day, Friday, Jones is hauled up to the judge's chamber, told that the "rape" charges have been dropped by the white woman in the interest of racial harmony and pushed off to "join the armed forces," bestowed as a cynical gift to help him "stay away from white women and keep out of trouble."[46]

In a society where blackness is a handicap in itself, Bob Jones is an iconic example of the victim hero protagonist of black protest novels. Himes continued his exploration of interracial dynamics in his other "protest" novel, *Lonely Crusade*. The novel spans fifty days in the life of Lee Gordon, who, after a period of unemployment becomes a union representative for black workers at Comstock Aircraft. Snubbed by the union's white organizer, Joe Ptak – "the union can't show any special interest in your people or we antagonize the Southern whites."[47] Gordon single-mindedly seeks to salvage the black man who "was more firmly convinced of his own inferiority than were those who had charged him thus."[48] Lee gets involved with a young white woman, communist Jackie Falks. He defends Jackie against threats of expulsion from the union. As a result, his wife forces him to leave home, and Jackie also renounces him, fearful of his wife's retaliation. Himes's second novel ends with Gordon being charged for a crime he did not commit and is killed by the police even as he leads a union demonstration.

The novels' historical backdrop – wartime Los Angeles, labor unions, black racial consciousness stratified along class lines – is further darkened by the era's widespread violence against young Mexican Americans sporting zoot suits and internment of Japanese American citizens after the Pearl Harbor bombings. Even as his fictional characters were exposed to the racist grime and slime that formed the underbelly of the Golden State, Himes moved to Manhattan, on the East Coast. He went on to publish *Cast the First Stone* (1952), *The Third Generation* (1954), and *The Primitive* (1956). Disillusioned by the racism and lack of opportunities in America, Himes ultimately decided to settle in Paris in 1953. There he went on to write best-selling crime novels, and was awarded the Grand Prix de la Litérature Policière in 1958. By 1969, he had settled in Spain, where he lived until his death in 1984.

In the aftermath of World War II, job opportunities again shrunk and African Americans still remained the victims of ongoing racism. Nevertheless, blacks' wartime victories against white domination of labor unions and fights against housing segregation contributed to the Civil Rights movement in the postwar era. By 1948, black Civil Rights became an official agenda item of the Democratic Party. With the 1954 *Brown v. Board of Education* ruling that struck down the "separate but equal" clause, followed by the Montgomery Bus Boycott, the Civil Rights movement that "climaxed in the mid-1960s was already running in 1945, and [was] . . . very apparent in the urban West."[49]

Even as the concept of the frontier recalls promises of expansion, opportunity and advancement, further investigation reveals that these promises were illusory for the black man. From the mid-nineteenth century to the mid-twentieth, the black frontier was defined by dreams that were pursued only to be shattered by the reality of racism and discrimination. Black California literature remains a testament to these stories. James Beckwourth's mythical autobiography of a frontier man who exists beyond the brutal reality of his time and place, the narratives of betrayal and survival during the Gold Rush and after, the protest poetry of Whitfield, Bell, Alexander, and their female counterparts, the writings of the West Coast Harlemites and the novels of Chester Himes – all provide literary strategies of survival as they relate fictional stories that acknowledge or deal with the brutal racist reality the best they can.

Notes

1. Kenneth Porter, *The Negro on the American Frontier* (New York: Arno Press, 1971).
2. John W. Ravage, *Black Pioneers: Images of the Black Experience on the North American Frontier* (Salt Lake City: University of Utah Press, 1997), xi.
3. Toni Morrison, "Site of Memory" in *Inventing the Truth: The Art and Craft of Memoir*, ed. William Zinsser (New York: Houghton Mifflin, 1995), 93.
4. Helene Cixous, *Rootprints: Memory and Life Writing* (New York: Routledge, 1997), 53.
5. Blake Allmendinger, *Imagining the African American West* (Lincoln: University of Nebraska Press, 2005), 1–12.
6. Laura Browder, "'One Hundred Percent American' : How a Slave, a Janitor, and a Former Klansman Escaped racial Categories by Becoming Indian" in *Beyond the Binary: Reconstructing Cultural Identity in a Multicultural Context*, ed. Timothy Powell (New Jersey: Rutger's University Press, 1999), 107–116.
7. James Beckwourth, *The Life and Adventures of James P. Beckwourth as told to Thomas D. Bonner* (Lincoln: University of Nebraska Press, 1981), 149, 201, 263.
8. Allmendinger, 8.
9. Alvin Coffey, *Autobiography and Reminiscence of Alvin Aaron Coffey* (Mills Seminary P.O., 1901), 46.
10. Ibid., 50.
11. Ibid., 50.
12. Ibid., 50.
13. Mifflin Wistar Gibbs. *Shadow and Light: An Autobiography* (New York: Arno Press, 1968), 36, 37.

14. Jerry Stanley, *Hurry Freedom* (New York: Crown Publishers, 2000), 24.
15. Gibbs, 46.
16. Ibid.
17. Ibid.
18. Ibid.
19. Delilah Beasley, *The Negro Trail-Blazers of California* (Los Angeles, CA: Times Mirror Printing and Binding House, 1919), 263.
20. Joan Rita Sherman, *Collected Black Women's Poetry*, vol. 1–4 (New York: Oxford University Press, 1988), 107.
21. Aparajita Nanda, *Black California: A Literary Anthology* (Berkeley: Heyday, 2001), 43.
22. Sharon Lynette Jones, "Thompson, Eloise Bibb" *African American National Biography*, ed. Henry Louis Gates, http://www.oxfordaasc.com/article/opr/t0001/e0966?hi=1&highlight=1&from=quick&pos=1.
23. "Negro Women's Club Convene: State Federation Delegates Open Annual," *Los Angeles Times*, July 24, 1918.
24. Beasley, 270.
25. Nanda, 5.
26. Ibid., 20.
27. Ibid., 21.
28. Ibid., 26.
29. Allmendinger, 46.
30. Daniel M. Scott III, "Harlem Shadows: Re-Evaluating Wallace Thurman's *Blacker the Berry*" *MELUS* 29:3/4 (Fall/Winter, 2004), 327.
31. Wallace Thurman, *The Blacker the Berry* (New York: Arno Press, 1969), 41.
32. Ibid., 71.
33. Allmendinger, 56–57.
34. Nanda, 58.
35. Ibid., 58, 60.
36. Arna Bontemps, *The Old South "A Summer Tragedy" and Other Stories of the Thirties* (New York: Dodd, Head and Company, 1973), 10.
37. Douglas Flamming, "A Westerner in Search of Negroness: Region and Race in the Writing of Arna Bontemps" in *Over the Edge: Remapping the American West*, eds. Valerie Matsumoto and Blake Allmendinger (Berkeley: University of California Press, 1999), 85.
38. Arna Bontemps, *God Sends Sunday* (New York: Washington Square Press, 2005), 118.
39. Bontemps, *The Old South*, 20.
40. Douglas Flamming, *African Americans in the West* (Santa Barbara, CA: ABC Clio, 2009), 150.
41. Ibid., 161.
42. Allmendinger, 87.
43. Chester Himes, *Quality of Hurt* (New York: Thunder Mouth Press, 1972), 75–76.

44. Chester Himes, *If He Hollers Let Him Go* (New York: Thunder Mouth Press, 1986), 59.
45. Ibid., 140.
46. Ibid., 190.
47. Chester Himes, *Lonely Crusade* (New York: Alfred Knopf, 1947), 25.
48. Ibid., 61.
49. Flamming, 193.

CHAPTER 8

California as Political Topography: Asian American Literature before 1980

Catherine Fung

California has played a central role in Asian American history, political formation, and cultural production. While laborers began migrating from Asia to the Americas in the sixteenth century, the first large-scale migration of Asians to the United States was prompted by California's Gold Rush during the mid-nineteenth century. The region became a hotbed for anti-Asian legislation, including the Chinese Exclusion Act of 1882 and California's Alien Land Act of 1913. During World War II, the forced incarceration of Japanese Americans marked another instance of Asian Americans being excluded and displaced from a place in which they had built their lives. This period of exclusion effectively ended with the Immigration Act of 1965 (also known as the Hart-Cellar Act), which dismantled the national origins quota system, allowing more immigrants to enter the country. California became the birthplace of the Asian American movement during the late 1960s and early 1970s. Gaining traction from the Civil Rights' movement, and employing strategies that involved collective efforts to claim the right to space, the Asian American movement both formed and was formed by a shifting political topography.

This essay charts the history of Asian American literature in California before 1980. Historical accounts often mark the late 1960s as a watershed moment, for the dramatic political changes of the time brought about the invention of the terms "Asian American" and "Asian American literature." As Keith Lawrence and Floyd Cheung assert, "[D]uring this period, concerted efforts were made by Asian American writers and scholars, especially in California, to define, codify, and stimulate appreciation for Asian American literary production."[1] The new trend prompted the "recollection" of early Asian American literature that had largely been forgotten or overlooked until the 1970s.[2] In terms of literary history, 1980 can mark a shift from developing "Asian American literature" as a category to its institutionalization and recognition in the contemporary era. This essay explores Asian American literature up to 1980, focusing specifically on what Hsuan Hsu terms "the racial specificity of chronotopic experience."[3] For different groups and in different historical moments, California's landscape can be experienced as vast and liberating, violent and chaotic, constricting and comforting. Examining how California is depicted in these early works tells much about Asian American experience during this period.

Migration, Exclusion, and Containment

One of the earliest known pieces of Asian American writing is *An English-Chinese Phrasebook*, by Wong Sam and Assistants, published and distributed by Wells, Fargo Company in 1875 as a bilingual dictionary of useful phrases.[4] While not a literary text per se, this document offers a glimpse into Chinese immigrant life in the American West. After the Gold Rush ended and the Transcontinental Railroad was completed, the Chinese attempted to build lives in spaces where they were often unwanted.[5] Many of the phrases provided in the book are for business purposes, such as "Will you sell on credit?"[6] and "Tell me when the lease of my store is expired."[7] However, the phrasebook also reveals the violence and danger that the Chinese routinely encountered in the United States: "He was choked to death with a lasso, by a robber," "He was smothered in his room," "He was strangled to death by a man," "He tried to assassinate me."[8] These phrases not only address an authority of the law, but offer strategies and tactics for dealing with law enforcement: "The confession was extorted from him by force."[9] "He has to hire a very good lawyer to defend himself."[10] These phrases can be read as responses to events such as the California Supreme Court case *People v. Hall* (1854), which determined that Chinese Americans and Chinese immigrants had no right to testify against white citizens, effectively making white crime against the Chinese unprosecutable. In July 1877, white citizens of San Francisco, gathering for a meeting organized by the Workingman's Party, launched a two-day pogrom against the Chinese, resulting in four deaths and at least $100,000 worth of property damage.[11] The San Francisco Riot of 1877 marked the beginning of anti-Chinese campaigns, which led to the passage of the Chinese Exclusion Act of 1882. Wong Sam and Assistants appear to have anticipated the legislation against Chinese immigration, including in their book the phrase, "The immigration will soon be stopped."[12]

With the Chinese Exclusion Act, which would not be repealed until 1943, Angel Island, a military garrison off the coast of the San Francisco

Bay, served as an immigration station and detention center. Approximately 175,000 Chinese immigrants were imprisoned there from 1910 to 1940.[13] The poems that detainees inscribed on the walls of their barracks (more than 135 have been recorded) express the bewilderment, despair, and anger of having one's body inspected, of being interrogated, and of waiting indefinitely to find out whether entry will be granted or denied. Many poems refer to the geography of the island, such as this one that contrasts the boundlessness of the ocean and the confinement of the prison: "The seascape resembles lichen twisting and turning for a thousand *li*./ There is no shore to land and it is difficult to walk./ With a gentle breeze I arrived at the city thinking all would be so./ At ease, how was one to know he was to live in a wooden building?"[14] The Angel Island poems testify to feeling at once suspended in time and trapped as time passes, to being acutely aware of being excluded from and contained within spaces.

The Chinese immigrants who managed to settle in the United States were forced to retreat into their own ethnic enclaves, which would become known as Chinatowns. As Marlon K. Hom notes, Chinatown did not emerge because of Chinese immigrants' unwillingness to assimilate, but "as a means of survival during a time of rampant racial intolerance, when the Chinese were forced to retreat from an integrated existence to an alienated one."[15] The opium dens, gambling houses, and brothels that operated in Chinatown became fodder for the perception of the Chinese as the "Yellow Peril." Contemporary Chinese American writers attempted to dispel the popular myths about Chinatown and the xenophobia that the myths engendered, but they also appealed to those stereotypes in order to establish themselves as "native informants" who could speak on behalf of the Chinese. Yan Phou Lee, who came to the United States not as a laborer but as a student via the Educational Mission in Hartford, Connecticut, briefly referred to San Francisco as "the paradise of the self-exiled Chinese" in his memoir, *When I Was a Boy in China* (1887)[16]; however, he also responded directly to the treatment of the Chinese in California and pleaded for their rights in an essay entitled "The Chinese Must Stay" (1889).[17] Edith Maude Eaton, a writer of English and Chinese descent known by her pen name Sui Sin Far, used conventions of sentimental fiction to depict the alliances forged between middle-class Chinatown merchants and American missionaries in her collection of short stories, *Mrs. Spring Fragrance* (1912). In the story, "Its Wavering Image," a half white, half Chinese girl leads a white American visitor through Chinatown: "[S]he led him about Chinatown, initiating him into the simple mystery and history of many things, for which she, being of her father's race, had a tender regard and pride."[18] While Eaton's portrayals of the Chinese were sympathetic and favorable, her Chinatown was nonetheless an Orientalized space: foreign, mysterious, the site of ancient practices. Jade Snow Wong's memoir *Fifth Chinese Daughter* (1950) described Chinatown in similar terms in its opening pages: "Chinatown in San Francisco teems with haunting memories, for it is wrapped in the atmosphere, customs, and manners of a land across the sea."[19] In his book about his family's life in Chinatown, *Father and Glorious Descendent* (1944), Pardee Lowe noted its location on the Barbary Coast, among brothels and gambling houses: "It was part and parcel, Father said, of the Chinamen's burden in San Francisco. Families living in buildings adjoining the bawdyhouses always hung up CHINESE FAMILY – RESPECTABLE – PLEASE DO NOT RING BELL signs."[20] For its residents, Chinatown certainly housed "vices," but it was also a vibrant place in which community organizations were formed, schools and churches operated, and families established their legacy. For Chinese American writers, Chinatown was both strange and familiar: a comfortable home that they felt compelled to defend to a larger audience.

Unlike the Chinese who came to the United States as contract laborers, Japanese immigrants came to the United States largely motivated by the Meiji Restoration, an industrialization campaign launched by the Japanese government that lasted from 1868 to 1912. Among the student-laborers who arrived in the United States during this period was Yone Noguchi, who immigrated to San Francisco in 1893. After meeting Joaquin Miller, who introduced Noguchi to San Francisco's bohemian scene, he became a fixture in the Bay Area literary scene and began a prolific writing career that took him to Chicago, New York, and London. While Noguchi's writing is not known for offering place-specific or historically situated portrayals of life in California, another Japanese student-laborer, Henry Yoshitaka Kiyama, who immigrated in 1904 and studied at the San Francisco Art Institute, represents the discrimination that the Japanese faced in the United States in *The Four Immigrants Manga* (1931). An underground text that was unknown until its discovery in 1980, *The Four Immigrants Manga* is a series of comic strips representing Japanese experience in California (mostly San Francisco, but also Sacramento) from 1904 to 1924. Loosely autobiographical, and written in both Japanese and English, the comics reference specific conditions of Japanese immigration and settlement: The Russo-Japanese War (1904–05), which was used to portray Japan as a threat and agitate against

Japanese immigrants in California; the 1906 decision on the part of the San Francisco Board of Education to order all Japanese and Korean school children to join the Chinese in segregated schools; the 1906 San Francisco earthquake, which ignited fires all over the city and killed more than 3,000 people; the 1907 Gentleman's Agreement, which was meant to cease Japanese immigration into the United States; the "picture bride" system by which Japanese women were able to enter the United States; the Turlock Incident in 1921, in which Japanese laborers in the town were awakened by an armed band of white men who loaded them into trucks and drove them out of town; California's Alien Land Act of 1913, which prohibited all "aliens ineligible for citizenship" (as all Asian immigrants were) from owning or leasing land; and the Immigration Act of 1924, which signed into law racial quotas that would effectively end immigration from Japan to the United States. This history serves as a backdrop for humorous and bittersweet vignettes about a group of four friends beginning their lives in America, working as "schoolboy" servants in San Francisco households. Due to a series of cultural misunderstandings and accidents, the characters are dismissed from these jobs with the repeated command, "GO HOME."[21] That "home" could be their native Japan, but also spaces of community they would form in the United States. By the 1920s, a number of Japanese American newspapers were established on the West Coast, in which *issei* (first generation) and *nisei* (second generation) Japanese American writers published poems and stories. These include San Francisco's *The New World-Sun*, as well as Los Angeles's *The Rafu Shimpo* and *Kashu Mainichi*.

Rather than treat their country of origin and the United States as mutually exclusive spaces of home, Asian immigrants often maintained a connection to the "homeland" as a means to establish their presence as Americans. The first significant waves of South Asian migration to the United States were Sikh farmers and laborers from the Punjab region in India. The immigration movement began in the late nineteenth century, during British rule, and lasted until 1947. The Ghadar Party was an organization founded by Punjabi Indians in the United States and Canada with the aim of gaining India's independence from British rule. Many of its founding members, including Har Dayal and Taraknath Das, were students at the University of California at Berkeley. The first issue of the Ghadar Party's weekly newspaper was published in San Francisco in 1913.[22] Dhan Gopal Mukerji, who immigrated to the United States in 1910, was not among this community of radical activists, though he was invested in Indian independence. His autobiography, *Caste and Outcast* (1923), is split into two parts: the first devoted to his Brahmin childhood in British colonial India, the second to his time as an impoverished student at University of California, Berkeley. Mukerji wrote of socializing with leftists and anarchists, and expressed an affinity with the underclass. However, he critiqued the "typical Indian revolutionist" he met in San Francisco for being unfeelingly violent.[23] Most of Mukerji's prolific body of work – including poetry, drama, fiction, philosophy, translations, and children's books – delved into spiritualism more than politics. However, *Caste and Outcast* offered a glimpse of the political unrest brewing in a race and class stratified in the San Francisco Bay Area. While Mukerji presented a vivid picture of a local scene, he also showed how that scene was part of larger transnational forces. South Asian immigrants were subject to some of the same discriminatory laws that applied to all Asian immigrants, including the 1917 Asiatic Barred Zone Act, which effectively ended Asian immigration to the United States, and the 1923 Supreme Court decision in *US v. Bhagat Singh Thind*, which determined that "Hindoos" were racially ineligible for citizenship. The court based its decision on a precedent established three months earlier, in *Takao Ozawa v. US*, which denied citizenship to Japanese residents. (Both Ozawa and Thind lived in California.) Many South Asian immigrants, like Mukerji, believed that the injustices they experienced in the United States were similar to the injustices of colonialism in British India.

Korean migration to the United States was also linked to colonialism. Prior to the 1860s, Korea was generally a secluded nation. It began sending its subjects abroad after the Sino-Japanese War (1894–95) and the Russo-Japanese War (1904–05), both of which were fought on Korean soil. These events were followed by Japan's annexation of Korea in 1910, and the arrival of American medical missionary Horace H. Allen, whose friendship with King Kojong opened doors for American Methodists and Presbyterians to proselytize in Korea. Few Koreans responded to the recruitment efforts of the Hawaiian Sugar Planter's Association until the missionaries persuaded members of their congregations to go to Hawaii. From there, some Koreans proceeded to the mainland. Younghill Kang, an anti-Japanese and pro-independence activist who was educated in both Confucian and Christian missionary schools, fled to the United States in 1921. He settled on the East Coast, where he attended Boston University and Harvard University. His autobiographical novels, *The Grass Roof* (1931) and *East Goes West* (1937), trace the journey of a young man from Japanese-occupied Korea to the United States.

Ronyoung Kim's novel, *Clay Walls* (1987), chronicles a Korean immigrant family living in Los Angeles from the 1910s to the 1940s. Anchoring the community depicted in the novel is both the church and the Korean independence movement. Mary Paik Lee's autobiography, *Quiet Odyssey: A Pioneer Korean Woman in America* (1990), testifies to Korean American life in Riverside, California, during the early twentieth century.

The American colonial occupation of the Philippines prompted a wave of migration to the United States, starting in 1898. Carlos Bulosan worked as a farmworker in central California and became active in the labor movement. In his semi-autobiographical novel, *America Is in the Heart* (1946), the protagonist travels up and down the Pacific Coast as a migrant farmworker during the Great Depression. Bulosan portrayed California as a dangerous landscape, full of exploitative employers, co-ethnics who cheat their own compatriots for survival, and hateful white nativists who attack a Filipino without provocation. In one scene, Bulosan referenced the anti-miscegenation laws affirmed by the 1933 California Supreme Court case, *Salvador Roldan v. Los Angeles County*, to explain why a white restaurant owner attacks a Filipino patron accompanied by his white wife. Bulosan also placed his character in the 1930 Watsonville riots, in which local white men raided the dance halls frequented by Filipino men. The fictional Carlos continues to shuttle from one place to the next, as a labor activist, organizing for a movement that Bulosan depicted as both bustling and contentious. Carlos's "place" in America is constantly moving; he stays in one place only to be hospitalized for tuberculosis. A social worker interrogates him in order to find reason to deny him a stay at a sanitarium for his recovery. The novel ends with Carlos anticipating certain death and watching his friends scatter as World War II begins. However, the California landscape inspires an insistent faith in the American Dream: "I glanced out of the window again to look at the broad land I had dreamed so much about, only to discover with astonishment that the American earth was like a huge heart unfolding warmly to receive me."[24] This passage can be read as particularly melancholic, given that by 1934 the United States had passed the Tydings-McDuffie Act, which established Philippine independence but also restricted immigration.

Internment

World War II had a profound impact on Asian immigrants and their U.S.-born descendants. China, Korea, the Philippines, and India were allied with the United States. Some positive changes occurred for people with ancestral ties to those countries. Immigration and naturalization exclusion for the Chinese was lifted with the Magnuson Act of 1943. The 1946 Luce-Celler Act allowed Filipinos and Indians to gain naturalization. The Japanese, however, were viewed as enemies of the state after the attack on Pearl Harbor. Executive Order 9066 authorized the Secretary of War, John L. DeWitt, to designate military areas "from which any and all persons may be excluded as deemed necessary or desirable." Military Areas 1 and 2 comprised the entire Pacific Coast: the western halves of Washington and Oregon, the southern half of Arizona, and the entire state of California. All persons of Japanese ancestry in these zones were uprooted from their homes, forced to sell their property, and relocated to assembly centers, where they awaited assignment to more permanent camps that were hurriedly being built. The internment camps were located on federal land in desolate places: Tule Lake and Manzanar, California; Minidoka, Idaho; Heart Mountain, Wyoming; Topaz, Utah; Poston and Gila River, Arizona; Amache, Colorado; and Rohwer and Jerome, Arkansas. Of the more than 120,000 men, women, and children who were interned, nearly two-thirds were U.S.-born and American citizens.

Internees produced literature, art, music, and drama and published their work in camp newspapers. After the war their work reached a wider audience. Miné Okubo, who was born in Riverside, California, and interned at Topaz, made more than 2,000 drawings of daily life in the camp. Many were included in her graphic memoir, *Citizen 13660* (1946). After the war, Okubo relocated to New York to continue her career as an artist. Hiroshi Kashiwagi, born in Sacramento and interned at Tule Lake, produced his first one-act play for the Nisei Experimental Group, a theater group formed in Los Angeles, in 1949. His 1953 play, *Laughter and False Teeth* (1953) is a comedy of manners set in a camp. Toshio Mori, born in Oakland and interned at Topaz, wrote the stories in *Yokohama, CA* (1949) in the late 1930s and early 1940s. The volume was accepted for publication in 1941, but did not appear until 1949. The inaugural story, "Tomorrow Is Coming, Children," was written while Mori was interned at Topaz, and was published in the camp newspaper.[25] The speaker is a grandmother who describes her journey from Japan to California. She proclaims, "Ah, San Francisco, my dream city. My San Francisco is everywhere. I like the dirty brown hills, the black soil and the sandy beaches. I like the tall buildings, the bridges, the parks and the roar of the city traffic. They are of me and I feel like humming."[26] The grandchildren do not understand her platitudes in a time when war is raging. The grandmother says that the war gives her "an opportunity to find where her heart lay." She appears to affirm her American loyalty, yet acknowledges what she has lost: "If there were no war we would not be in a relocation center. We would be back in our house on Market Street, hanging out our wash on the clothesline and watering our flower garden. You would be attending school with your neighborhood friends. Ah, war is terrifying. It upsets personal life and hopes."[27] Mori takes his place alongside his Seattle-born counterparts Monica Sone (*Nisei Daughter*, 1953) and John Okada (*No-No Boy*, 1957), all of whom can be considered internment and post-internment writers.

Hisaye Yamamoto represents Japanese American life before, during, and after the war. She was born in Redondo Beach, California, and interned at Poston, where she wrote for the camp newspaper. She was one of the first Japanese American writers to gain national recognition after the war, at a time when anti-Japanese sentiment was still prevalent. Her stories "The High-Heeled Shoes" (1948), "The Brown House" (1951), and "Epithalamium" (1960) appeared in Martha Foley's list of "Distinctive Short Stories," and "Yoneko's Earthquake" (1951) was included in *Best American Short Stories: 1952*.[28] The volume *Seventeen Syllables*, first published in 1988, compiles stories Yamamoto wrote over a span of forty years. Many of her stories are site-specific, featuring familial and interracial dynamics, gender roles, and labor conditions in rural and urban California. In "Wilshire Bus" (1950), the Los Angeles landscape bears markers of the past, present, and future. The protagonist, Esther Kuroiwa, is a former internee on her way to visit her husband, an injured Japanese American veteran. She witnesses a white bus passenger tell a Chinese couple, "Why don't you go back to China, where you can be coolies working in your bare feet out in the rice fields?"[29] After he departs, another white man consoles the couple. "We don't all feel the way he does. We believe in an America that is a melting pot of all sorts of people. I'm originally Scotch and French myself."[30] In this compactly narrated scene, Yamamoto offers a nuanced meditation on interracial conflict and internalized racism. Esther is self-conscious about being recognized as Japanese so soon after the war, and notices a man on the bus wearing an "I AM KOREAN" button. She feels "betrayed" by being disavowed by a fellow Asian, but she is also relieved that she is not being targeted by the harasser. Esther realizes how racism can affect anyone when the harasser yells, "So clear out, all of you, and remember to take every last one of your slant-eyed pickaninnies with you!,"[31] using a derogatory term referring to African Americans. Though the kinder man gestures to a more egalitarian and multiculturalist future, his words ring hollow and trite after this confrontation. As a public mode of transportation, the bus navigates through a landscape delineated by race and class. Yamamoto begins the story with a topographical description:

> Wilshire Boulevard begins somewhere near the heart of downtown Los Angeles and, except for a few digressions scarcely worth mentioning, goes straight out to the edge of the Pacific Ocean. It is a wide boulevard and traffic on it is fairly fast. For the most part, it is bordered on either side with examples of the recent stark architecture which favors a great deal of glass. As the boulevard approaches the sea, however, the landscape becomes a bit more pastoral, so that the university and the soldiers' home there give the appearance of being huge country estates.[32]

Given the diverse passengers on this route, one wonders what communities reside in the areas "scarcely worth mentioning." Los Angeles, its buildings coexisting with pastoral stretches of landscape, reflects a burgeoning industrialization and vestiges of an earlier frontier. The view of the Pacific is a reminder of the bodies, capital, and ideas that travel across the ocean. The UCLA campus and the veterans hospital represent knowledge production and empire. Yamamoto depicts Los Angeles as a dynamic space that constantly changes as its people navigate through and within it.

The Cold War and Civil Rights

The Cold War impacted Asian Americans in contradictory but equally dramatic ways. After the Chinese Revolution of 1949, the United States vowed to contain communism in Korea. After anti-colonial forces under Ho Chi Minh defeated the French in 1954, the United States took a larger role in Southeast Asia, determined to maintain the partition between North and South Vietnam and prevent unification under communist rule. Domestically, anticommunist paranoia merged with xenophobia, leading to the McCarran-Walter Act of 1950, which enabled the "Chinese Confession Program," initiated in 1955. INS (Immigration and Naturalization Service) officials asked Chinese Americans who had fraudulently established their U.S. citizenship or had otherwise entered the country illegally to come forward. While no formal provisions were made for the amnesty of confessors, people were urged to confess and disclose the names of relatives and friends who had entered the country illegally. Abuse of the program was widespread. INS agents frequently entered

Chinatowns, stopping people on the streets to see their documents. Most of the 13,000+ confessors were able to stay, but several were deported. C. Y. Lee's novel *The Flower Drum Song* (1957), which was turned into a popular stage musical and film by Rodgers and Hammerstein, mediated the anxieties produced within San Francisco's Chinatown during the Cold War period. The novel centers on Wang Chi Yang, a 63-year-old man who fled communist China. Living in Chinatown and stubbornly resisting assimilation into American culture, he argues with his sister-in-law, Madam Tang, who takes citizenship classes and urges Americanization. After a series of conflicts involving finding a suitable wife for his older son, Wang demonstrates his willingness to accept American culture by going to a Chinese-run western clinic when he develops a chronic cough. The novel depicts assimilation as a life-or-death matter, and anticipates that the space of Chinatown will become increasingly incorporated into mainstream American society. As it did for all Americans, the Cold War drew lines between "loyal" and "disloyal" Asian Americans. While Jade Snow Wong was sent by the U.S. State Department on a tour through Asia, where she spoke about life as a Chinese American, Bulosan was blacklisted for his communist sympathies.

The Cold War atmosphere of competition, anti-radicalism, and fear of nuclear war generated much domestic anxiety. It also prompted the United States to assume the role as leader of the "free" world. This position required changes to immigration policy, often with the purpose of "rescuing" women and children. The War Brides Act of 1945 allowed the alien spouses and the minor children of citizen members of the U.S. armed forces to enter the United States as non-quota immigrants. Thousands of Chinese wives, not necessarily married to servicemen, immigrated under the Chinese Alien Wives of American Citizens Act of 1946. The adoption of Asian children, particularly Korean war orphans, into American families began in the 1950s. These developments prompted dramatic demographic changes to Asian American communities, particularly in regard to gender distribution, given that earlier migrations consisted primarily of male laborers. The 1965 Immigration Act abolished the national origins quota system established in the 1920s and fulfilled the United States' Cold War imperatives of industrialization and "rescue" by creating a preference system that privileged immigrants' professional skills and kinship with U.S. citizens. With restrictions to Asian immigration dismantled, the number of immigrants increased dramatically. These new immigrants also comprised of greater proportions of educated and professional classes. The greater visibility of upwardly mobile Asians in America seemingly proved that Asians were the "model minority." As Robert G. Lee asserts, the model minority myth fulfilled the imperatives of the Cold War because it promoted ethnic assimilation while sending a message to all minorities that "accommodation would be rewarded while militancy would be contained or crushed."[33]

In spite of these pressures to assimilate, the term "Asian American" largely came from radical resistance. The Vietnam War struck many as a racist war because the "enemy" was racialized just as Asians had been for decades. Certain Asian American activists were inspired by the Black Power Movement. Richard Aoki was a member of the Black Panther Party and Yuri Kochiyama belonged to Malcolm X's Organization of Afro-American Unity. Both organized for minority liberation and self-determination. The Asian American movement largely took shape in California. The Asian American Political Alliance at San Francisco State College was formed in 1968, and was the first organization to use the pan-ethnic designator "Asian American" in its name. The Third World Liberation Front (TWLF) organized strikes at San Francisco State College and University of California, Berkeley in 1968 and 1969. The TWLF featured an unprecedented coalition of African American, Chicano, Native American and Asian American students, and resulted in the establishment of the first School of Ethnic Studies in the United States. The fight against the evictions at the International Hotel, which not only housed older working class Chinese and Filipino residents, but also served as the headquarters for many community organizations that served San Francisco's Asian American community, lasted from 1968 to 1977. In this manner, the Asian American movement was about space and history. Through the formation of a collective identity and an affinity with other groups that experience racial oppression, Asian American activists sought to change and determine their place in America.

The redress movement during the 1960s led to a reexamination of Japanese American internment and a renewed interest in internment literature. Works that had gone out of print were republished, and works that had remained underground were finally published. Related new works were published as well, including Jeanne Wakatsuki Houston's memoir, *Farewell to Manzanar* (1973), and Edward Miyakawa's novel, *Tule Lake* (1980). Miyakawa's book portrays Executive 9066 as an unjust violation of the Bill of Rights. Focusing on the most conflict-ridden camp, and the one that imprisoned the most "disloyals" based on a questionnaire administered by the War Relocation Authority, Miyakawa presents internees who refused to cooperate, who staged protests in camps, and who continued to resist in spite of being treated violently by the government and fellow internees. In 1980, the U.S. Congress established the Commission on Wartime Relocation and Internment of Civilians, which produced a report condemning the internment as unjust and motivated by racism and xenophobia rather than military necessity. The Commission's recommendation that $20,000 be paid to each interned individual was fulfilled in 1988, when President Ronald Reagan signed the Civil Liberties Act.

Political activism and cultural production went hand-in-hand in the formation of Asian America during the 1960s and 1970s. East West Players, one of the first Asian American theater organizations, was founded in Los Angeles in 1965 by a group of actors including Mako, Soon-Tek Oh, and James Hong. Kearny Street Workshop, a multi-disciplinary Asian American arts organization, was founded in San Francisco in 1972, its first home situated in the International Hotel. The Asian American Theater Company in San Francisco was founded in 1973 by Frank Chin, author of *The Chickencoop Chinaman* (1971) and *The Year of the Dragon* (1974), which were both produced on major New York stages. This kind of institutional support was key in launching the career of Wakako Yamauchi, whose play *And the Soul Shall Dance* was adapted from a short story of the same name and produced by East West Players in 1977. Her second play, *The Music Lessons*, was produced by Joseph Papp for the New York Public Theater in 1980. Jessica Hagedorn, who was active in San Francisco's progressive art scene, published poetry and music starting in the early 1970s. Her first play, *Mango Tango*, was produced by Joseph Papp in 1978. Philip Kan Gotanda got his start during this period with *The Avocado Kid* (1979) and *A Song for a Nisei Fisherman* (1980). David Henry Hwang's play *FOB* premiered at the Stanford Asian American Theater Project in 1979, and debuted off-Broadway in 1980, winning the Obie Award. The 1970s marked the beginning of a thriving Asian American theater scene. Most of these playwrights continued to produce work into the 1980s and 1990s.

Asian American literature arguably became established as a field due to the groundbreaking of *Aiiieeeee!: An Anthology of Asian-American Writers*, edited by Frank Chin, Jeffery Paul Chan, Lawson Fusao Inada, and Shawn Wong, published in 1974 by Howard University Press. All of these contributors were California writers. The pan-Asian anthology collected literature by Chinese, Japanese, and Filipino American writers from the past fifty years. Its goal was explicitly political. The editors' opening essay laid out Asian American writers' concerns about Orientalism and ghettoization. It argued for a distinctly Asian American sensibility, which some would criticize for being masculinist and heterosexist. The volume was updated and expanded in 1991. Its opening essay, Chin's "Come All Ye Asian American Writers of the Real and the Fake," lambasted some Asian American writers for being inauthentic, appealing to stereotypes, and pandering to white feminism. Among those that Chin condemned was Maxine Hong Kingston, whose phenomenally successful *The Woman Warrior* was published in 1975. Her second book, *China Men*, was published in 1977 and won the National Book Award. Though many critics and scholars have problematized Chin's arguments, the debates about representational politics continue among Asian American writers and scholars.

By the late 1970s, many Asian American poets from California published their first volumes, including Janice Mirikitani (*Awake in the River*, 1978), Geraldine Kudaka (*Numerous Avalanches at the Point of Intersection*, 1978), and Alan Chong Lao (*Songs for Jadina*, 1980). Garrett Kaoru Hongo, Alan Chong Lau, and Lawson Fusao Inada performed a collective concert of poetry and music in 1977 at California State University, Long Beach. Echoing the ethos of the Beat poets, in particular Gary Snyder's "Night Highway 99," *Buddha Bandits Down Highway 99* is a poetic meditation on the highway that runs up and down central California. Calling the highway "THE YELLOW STRIPE DOWN THE BACK OF AMERICA,"[34] Inada signals to the "yellow" of ethnic nationalism and inscribes an Asian presence into the American landscape. Dedicating the piece to their ancestors, "who led us to California/ and traveled 99,"[35] Hongo, Lau, and Inada recreate a road trip, filling the sites with their own experiences and the histories of those who came before them. This insistence on an Asian American presence is echoed in Shawn Wong's novel, *Homebase* (1979). The novel literalizes the Asian American's search for his place in America. The Chinese American protagonist, Rainsford Chan, is named after a town in the Sierras in which his great-grandfather supposedly settled. He reenacts a transcontinental journey made by his deceased parents, moving across the American landscape "picking up ghosts."[36] Rainsford contemplates his predecessors who built the railroad, mined for gold, were driven out and buried in settlement towns. The journey concludes with an emphatic declaration: "We are old enough to haunt this land like an Indian who laid down to rest and his body became the outline of the horizon. This is my father's canyon. See his head reclining! That peak his nose, that cliff his chin, and his folded arms are summits."[37] The Asian American body not only belongs in the California landscape, but becomes it.

The California landscape arguably created Asian American literature as a space in which so many Asian American writers came to be. At the same time, Asian American writers changed how that landscape would be imagined and understood by constantly rewriting their place in it. Asian American history and experience are defined by specific relationships to space. Moreover, the political topography shifts as individuals and communities redefine those relationships, whether by dodging the danger that chases them, insisting on their right to stay where they do not belong, finding resistance within contained spaces, or imagining lives that are boundless.

Notes

1. Keith Lawrence and Floyd Cheung, eds. *Recovered Legacies: Authority and Identity in Early Asian American Literature* (Philadelphia: Temple University Press, 2005), 2.
2. Josephine Lee et al., eds. *Re/collecting Early Asian America: Essays in Cultural History* (Philadelphia: Temple University Press, 2002).
3. Hsuan Hsu, "Chronotopes of the Asian American West," in *A Companion to the Literature and Culture of the American West, First Edition* (Oxford: Blackwell Publishing, 2011), 146.
4. Little is known of the identities of Sam Wong and his assistants, or why Wells, Fargo & Co. published this phrasebook. Included in the phrasebook is a complete list of Wells, Fargo & Co.'s offices in California and Nevada.
5. The driving out of Chinese Americans is thoroughly documented by Jean Pfaelzer in *Driven Out: The Forgotten War against Chinese Americans* (Berkeley: University of California Press, 2008).
6. Sam Wong and Assistants, "An English Chinese Phrasebook," in Jeffery Paul Chan et al., eds., *The Big Aiiieeeee!: An Anthology of Chinese American and Japanese American Literature* (New York: Meridian, 1991), 94.
7. Ibid., 110.
8. Ibid., 98.
9. Ibid., 97.
10. Ibid., 109.
11. Selig Perlman, "The Anti-Chinese Agitation in California," in John R. Commons et al., eds., *History of Labour in the United States* (New York: Macmillan, 1918), 253.
12. Wong Sam and Assistants, 105.
13. Angel Island Immigration Station Foundation. "Life on Angel Island." *Angel Island Immigration Station Foundation.* http://aiisf.org/education/station-history/life-on-angel-island.

14. Him Mark Lai et al., eds. *Island: Poetry and History of Chinese Immigrants on Angel Island, 1910–1940* (Seattle: University of Washington Press, 1980), 34.
15. Marlon K. Hom, *Songs of Gold Mountain: Cantonese Rhymes from San Francisco Chinatown* (Berkeley: University of California Press, 1992), 15.
16. Yan Phou Lee, *When I Was a Boy in China* (Boston: Lothrop, Lee, and Shepard Co., 1887), 106.
17. Yan Phou Lee, "The Chinese Must Stay." *North American Review* 148 (April 1889): 476–483.
18. Edith Maude Eaton (Sui Sin Far), *Mrs. Spring Frangrance* (Toronto: Broadview, 2011), 81.
19. Jade Snow Wong, *Fifth Chinese Daughter* (1950, Seattle: University of Washington Press, 1989), 1.
20. Pardee Lowe, *Father and Glorious Descendant* (Boston: Little, Brown and Company: 1944), 38.
21. Henry Kiyama (Yoshitaka), *The Four Immigrants Manga: A Japanese Experience in San Francisco, 1904–1924*, trans. Frederik L. Schodt (Berkeley: Stone Bridge Press, 1999).
22. See Gordon H. Chang's introduction, "The Life and Death of Dhan Gopal Mukerji," in Dhan Gopal Mukerji's *Caste and Outcast* (Stanford: Stanford University Press, 2002).
23. Dhan Gopal Mukerji, *Caste and Outcast*, 194.
24. Carlos Bulosan, *America Is in the Heart* (1946, Seattle: University of Washington Press, 1973), 326.
25. According to Lawson Fusao Inada's introduction to the 1985 edition.
26. Toshio Mori, *Yokohama, California. 1949* (Seattle: University of Washington Press, 1985), 20.
27. Ibid., 21.
28. According to King-Kok Cheung in her introduction to '*Seventeen Syllables*': *Hisaye Yamamoto* (New Brunswick: Rutgers University Press, 1994).
29. Hisaye Yamamoto, *Seventeen Syllables and Other Stories* (1988, New Brunswick: Rutgers University Press, 2001), 36.
30. Ibid., 37.
31. Ibid., 37.
32. Ibid., 34.
33. Robert. G. Lee, "The Cold War Origins of the Model Minority Myth," in *Orientals: Asian Americans in Popular Culture* (Philadelphia: Temple University Press, 1999), 146.
34. Garrett Kaoru Hongo et al., *The Buddha Bandits Down Highway 99* (Mountain View: Buddhahead Press 1978), n. p.
35. Ibid.
36. Shawn Wong, *Homebase* (1979; Seattle: University of Washington Press, 2008), 29.
37. Ibid., 96.

CHAPTER 9

Mexican American Literature
Manuel M. Martin-Rodriguez

The first half of the twentieth century represents a dynamic and diverse period for Mexican Americans in California. Changes in population and culture were largely determined by a remarkable sequence of major historical events whose significance cannot be understated. At the turn of the century, the original Mexican-origin population of the state was increased by an influx of workers recruited to construct the railways and to work in the mines. Because of the restrictions on Chinese labor brought about by the Chinese Exclusion Act of 1882, Mexican laborers were seen as the most reasonable replacement. Then in 1898, a mere fifty years after the signing of the Treaty of Guadalupe-Hidalgo, which settled the Mexican American War, the United States of America declared war on Spain, a country for which many Mexican Americans in California – and elsewhere in the United States – still felt a strong attachment. Twelve years later, in 1910, the Mexican Revolution began in Mexico, launching a decade of continuous fighting, and sending a large mass of Mexicans of all social classes to the United States. With the situation in Mexico still unresolved, the United States became a formal participant in World War I in 1917, resulting in increased military and labor needs that impacted Mexican Americans in California. The Great Depression led to massive deportations in the early 1930s, disrupting Mexican American communities and sending families and individuals (many of them American citizens) south to Mexico. In 1942, when the United States joined World War II, the war effort required large numbers of laborers, and Mexicans were recruited once again, both informally and through official government initiatives such as the Bracero Program (1942–65). The arrivals tried to acclimate themselves to their new environment. But scores of urban Mexican American youngsters were targeted by angry mobs of U.S. sailors and marines in Los Angeles and other cities during the so-called Zoot Suit Riots of 1943, reflecting deep social and ethnic tensions, some of whose consequences are visible still today.

Each of these historical developments contributed to making Mexican American California a rather complex society in the early twentieth century. This rapid succession of major historical events resulted in the coming together of groups that, united as they were by their common Mexican roots, were nonetheless quite different in their experiences and in their understanding of what it meant to be Mexican or Mexican American. Mexican Americans in California included the following groups or subgroups during the first half of the twentieth century: 1) the descendants of the original Hispanic population of California; 2) workers who migrated at the turn of the century; 3) refugees from the Mexican Revolution, in themselves a diverse group comprising working-class and middle class-individuals, progressives and conservatives, highly educated people and their illiterate counterparts; 4) large numbers of working-class men who migrated during the 1940s; and 5) second- and later-generation Mexican Americans whose own hybrid culture puzzled both U.S. dominant society and Mexican immigrants.

Because of these internal differences, political and cultural allegiances also differed. Some thought that their presence in the United States was only temporary, and they attempted to preserve Mexican customs and traditions as much as possible. Others had never been to Mexico, and their cultural allegiance was not to Mexico per se, but to *Mexicanness*, understood as the product of the interaction of inherited cultural practices with new ways of life in California. A prime arena for observing this tension was language: some Mexican Americans insisted on the need to maintain their Mexican Spanish free of interference from English, while others grew up mixing both languages on a daily basis.

In literature, the internal diversity of the Mexican American population resulted in a rich tapestry of writings whose artistic means and goals were as varied as was their social and cultural impact. While much of this literature is yet to be rescued from oblivion and endowed with the appropriate public visibility, the analysis of those works identified and located thus far allows us to conceptualize Mexican American California literature in the following phases and/or categories.

Turn-of-the-Century Literature

Adolfo Carrillo was one of the earliest refugee journalists in California. His criticism of dictator Porfirio Díaz's regime resulted in prosecution and jail time in the infamous San Juan de Ulúa prison. After serving his sentence, Carrillo went into exile in Cuba, and then moved to the United States, spending time in Texas and New York. In New York, Carrillo met Mexican ex-president Sebastián Lerdo de Tejada (ousted by Díaz in 1876), and from the notes taken during his meetings with the politician Carrillo wrote *Memorias inéditas del Lic. Don Sebastián Lerdo de Tejada* (Unpublished Memoirs of Mr. Sebastián Lerdo de Tejada, Attorney at Law). This book was published anonymously, but Carrillo's biographer Luis Leal has made a persuasive case for his authorship.[1] *Memorias inéditas* became an instant success, and it was reprinted several times in the United States and Mexico.

In 1897, after several years spent in Spain and France, Carrillo relocated to California, where he married and opened a printing shop in San Francisco. His *Memorias del Marqués de San Basilisco* (Memoirs of the Marquis of St. Basilisk) also appeared that year anonymously. This work adopts the structure of the picaresque novel – an extremely popular genre throughout the Hispanic world – to present a picture of Mexican and U.S. society. Its protagonist, Jorge Carmona (also known as Camomina) is the typical antihero of picaresque narratives. He eats as often as he can while working as little as possible. His constant job changes and travels allow the narrator to comment on multiple trades, social classes, and types of life. In San Francisco, for example, Camomina finds out that making a living entails too much work and he returns to Mexico as soon as he can. In Europe, on the other hand, he finds no trouble buying a title, which makes him a Marquis and a man of leisure overnight.

Carrillo's most relevant book is *Cuentos californianos*, published in Los Angeles around 1922. At some point after losing his only daughter and his business during the San Francisco earthquake of 1906, Carrillo moved to Los Angeles, where he died in 1926. *Cuentos californianos* is deeply informed by the author's experiences in California, as well as by his knowledge of literary trends elsewhere in the world. The collection opens with the autobiographical story "El Budha de Chun-Sin" (Chun-Sin's Buddha), which chronicles life in San Francisco before and after the earthquake and fire of 1906. The eyewitness perspective of the narrator complements a portrayal of multi-ethnic San Francisco that owes many of its features to the Orientalizing trend that had impregnated Latin American literatures with the advent of *modernismo* at the turn of the century. The combination of literary Orientalism, the eyewitness chronicle, and autobiographical details produces perhaps the best results in the entire collection, and the short story allows us to witness the transformation of Carrillo's artistry as he transitions from a Mexican-Latin American perspective to a U.S. Latino viewpoint.

The rest of the *Cuentos californianos* are mostly based on legends and nineteenth-century episodes of (Hispanic) California. Carrillo writes extensively about the missions, combining a heavy dose of anticlericalism with a flair for intrigue and impossible love stories. For Carrillo, the missions represented a social system that oppressed the local population, and he was critical of the effect of the priests in arresting progress. Carrillo eschews the mission romanticization then in vogue. As for the legends, which are almost always intertwined with historical occurrences, Carrillo's pen flies from notorious social bandit Joaquín Murrieta to the Gold Rush and its effects on Californian society, tapping into issues likely to attract a wide audience.

An important aspect of *Cuentos californianos* that should not be overlooked is the brief introduction signed by E[steban] V. Escalante, a fellow journalist and Los Angeles playwright, who discusses the genesis of the stories and the overall literary context in which they were written. Escalante presents the stories as pieces written by Carrillo for the Los Angeles newspaper *La Prensa*, and suggests that the author's intention was not to produce high culture but popular literature, which would appeal to the masses. Stories of love and violence are based on legends that would have been known by his audience, especially women who represented a large segment of the audience for newspapers and their cultural supplements.[2]

Mexican Revolution Refugee Literature

The Mexican Revolution was a decade-long succession of military and social movements that profoundly disrupted and transformed the country. As revolutionary armies battled one another across the Mexican territory, thousands of civilians and defeated soldiers sought safety in the United States, crossing a border that was easier to negotiate than today. Two features of this mass migration are worth highlighting. First, those who left Mexico were a diverse group that included large numbers of unskilled illiterate workers as well as intellectuals and professionals who were already part of the lettered society in Mexico. In addition, these new immigrants tended to relocate in existing Mexican American communities in cities throughout the U.S. southwest and California. This was particularly important for educated refugees, who benefitted from an existing cultural infrastructure that included scores of theatres, newspapers, and printing shops. Because of their experience and talents, many literate refugees found jobs in and around those existing cultural networks, which they in turn helped revitalize by creating new periodicals, plays, novels, and even audiences.

One of those who successfully relocated to California was Julio G. Arce, who wrote under the pen name "Jorge Ulica," a thinly disguised anagram of his real name. In California, Arce was a newspaper editor and a prolific author of sketches about life in the United States. Most of his writings are characterized by his quick wit and tongue-in-cheek satire of Mexican life in California. Arce's journalistic activity had been intense in Mexico. In Sinaloa, he had openly opposed presidential candidate Francisco I. Madero, the revolutionary leader who would become president shortly afterwards. In 1915, after being imprisoned by the forces of Venustiano Carranza, Arce left Mexico for San Francisco, where he started writing for journals such as *La Crónica*, *Mefistófeles*, and *Hispano-América*, the latter two founded by him. Like Carrillo, Arce died in 1926, leaving behind a rich legacy of *crónicas*, short journalistic pieces that combined observations of daily life with social commentary.

In his "Crónicas diabólicas" (Diabolical chronicles), Ulica's most successful pieces explore cultural transformation, contact, and conflict. Afraid of any change that would take his compatriots away from their Mexican roots, Ulica ridicules acculturation, using clever linguistic strategies. Like other recent arrivals, Ulica marveled and snickered at the mixture of English and Spanish that Mexican Americans used on a daily basis. In pieces like "Do You Speak Pocho," Ulica censors Mexican American Spanish as *pocho*, contaminated and spoiled by contact with English. Implicit (and often explicit) in that criticism is the idea that Mexican Americans are no longer true Mexicans, that they have lost their cultural purity, assimilating into the dominant U.S. culture. A fierce enemy of what that transformation entailed, Ulica was particularly harsh with his acculturated characters, many of whom don ridiculous names, the product of an all-too-quick translation to English.

Ulica was also anxious about the social transformation of Mexican women. Like many of his contemporaries, Arce subscribed to an idealized vision of Mexican femininity that defined women as the (submissive) center of traditional home life, at the same time portraying women as preservers of culture. Women were entrusted with passing on traditions to subsequent generations, and were expected to have little or no social life of their own. Much to his irritation, Arce observed that in the U.S. women (both married and single) freely came and went without permission from their parents or husbands, and that many of them worked outside their homes, as secretaries or in other skilled capacities. Arce's worries about the financial independence of women are masked under the motif of the flirting female worker, as in "La estenógrafa" ("The Stenographer"). However, they reveal his unease with the transformation of the idealized traditional Mexican home in the United States. Mexican women in California enjoyed greater freedom and exercised more decision-making power in private and public matters than their counterparts in Mexico, and Ulica's sketches present us with a refracting mirror of that situation by ridiculing those *pochas* and their husbands.

The reader is able to witness some of the transformations wrought by Mexican immigrants and refugees. A substantial market waiting to be tapped by businesses, Mexicans indirectly created the need for "Spanish departments," personnel in charge of conducting transactions with the new arrivals in their mother tongue. Having censored the linguistic shortcomings of the *pochos* elsewhere, Ulica focuses now on the atrocious Spanish spoken by these dedicated sellers. In the hilarious "Los 'Parladores de Spanish'" (The So-Called Spanish Speakers), he criticizes the schools that confer useless certificates of proficiency on students who are utterly unable to speak the language.

While Jorge Ulica and others like Benjamín Padilla (who wrote under the pen name "Kaskabel") cultivated mostly the humorous side of journalism, other refugee intellectuals took a more political approach to their situation and that of their host country and country of origin. Ricardo Flores Magón has come to epitomize revolutionary journalism through his writings on both sides of the border. Flores Magón and his brother Enrique were among the earliest intellectual leaders of the impending Mexican Revolution, a role that forced them into exile at the beginning of the twentieth century. By 1904, Ricardo was publishing the journal *Regeneración* (Regeneration) in San Antonio, TX. Eventually he was forced to move to St. Louis, and then to El Paso in 1906. His writings inspired the Cananea, Mexico miners' strike in 1906. By 1907, he was publishing *Revolución* (Revolution) in California, contributing to the journal from jail. In 1910, at the start of the Mexican Revolution, Flores Magón resumed the publication of *Regeneración* in Los Angeles, but his activities were marred by numerous problems, including the cancellation of postal privileges for his newspapers, and five stints in prison in quick succession. Flores Magón remained undeterred in his commitment to proletarian internationalism, as a sample of his articles indicates: "El deber del revolucionario" (The Revolutionary's Duty), "¡Fuera la propiedad individual!" (Down with Private Property), and "La revolución agraria" (The Agrarian Revolution). An antiwar manifesto published in 1918 earned him a twenty-year prison sentence. Flores Magón died at Leavenworth Penitentiary in 1922. Other political writers of the time included Blanca de Moncaleano, founder of *Pluma Roja* (Red Pen, published in Los Angeles from 1913 to 1915), a newspaper addressed to women that supported the idea of pan-Americanism and international solidarity.

As for lyrical poetry and other forms of creative literature, it is worth noting that many of the Spanish-language periodicals in California included literary pages or sections in which the works of famous international writers were interspersed with pieces by local authors. Newspapers with literary content included Los Angeles' *El Eco de México* (The Echo from Mexico), *La Prensa* (The Press), *El Heraldo de Mexico* (Mexico's Herald), as well as San Francisco's *Hispano-América* (Spanish-America), *Mefistófeles* (Mephistopheles), *El Imparcial* (The Impartial), and *Semanario Imparcial* (Impartial Weekly). Much of that literature is yet to be catalogued and studied. However, a cursory look at the surviving issues of the periodicals cited reveals a wealth of compositions by the likes of Nicaraguan Rubén Darío, Spain's Francisco Villaespesa and Concha Espina, Peruvian José Santos Chocano, Colombian Adolfo León Gómez, Cuban Mariano Ramiro, Mexican authors Amado Nervo, Efrén Rebolledo, Miguel D. Martínez Rendón, Alfonso Iberri, and Sixto Spada; and by non-Hispanic writers like Rabindranath Tagore and Johann W. von Goethe. There were also local writers like Domingo N. Nava, Zoila Rosa Cárdenas, political poems by Popotillo (unidentified pen name), and a popular humorous poetry section "Carta de Medina" (Medina's Letter), whose verses were reprinted in publications as far as New Mexico. Thematically, these compositions are as varied as their authors. Newspaper editors seemed to favor love poetry, patriotic verses, fantastic short stories, and convoluted stories of the feuilleton type. The richness and variety of these contributions extended to the sports pages. *El Eco de México*, for instance, printed "El Base Ball," a whimsical bilingual poem by Mariano Ramiro, who switches freely from Spanish to English to explain the baseball craze in mid-1920s Cuba.

Hispanophile Literature

In California, as well as in other states that were formerly part of Spain and Mexico, segments of the local population have stressed at different times their ties with Spain, rather than Mexico and the United States. Even though critics have dismissed these claims as part of a "fantasy heritage," the idea of a direct Spanish lineage has proven popular. In literature, this sentiment is often associated with an interest in old customs and history. In 1920s California, María del Sacramento López de Cummings (1850–1930) represented this trend. The López family owned a large tract of land in Paredón Blanco (now Boyle Heights, Los Angeles). In 1869, María del Sacramento married George Cummings, a real estate developer and landowner in Boyle Heights. Like many other Californios who had lost much of their land and social position, the Lópezes must have welcomed this marital alliance with new capital. However, long after starting her mixed marriage and family, López de Cummings wrote one of the most pristine examples of fantasy heritage or hispanophile literature, *Claudio and Anita: A Historical Romance of San Gabriel's Early Mission Days* (1921). It featured an introduction by John McGroarty, author of the very successful San Gabriel Mission play.

This short novel uses race and ethnicity to separate its noble characters from others of lower stock. Anita, the female title character, is blonde and blue-eyed, and Claudio (whom the author claimed for a grandfather) arrives directly from Spain to help Father Salvidea develop the San Gabriel Mission. María del Sacramento's great-granddaughter (and family historian), Catherine L. Kurland, has exposed this genealogy as false, revealing that Claudio was born in Baja California and that other relatives came from Jalisco and other Mexican states.[3] Regardless of the personal motivation for such a fabrication of the past, the author may have been responding to social pressures that had codified recent Mexicans arrivals as inferior and uneducated. The so-called civilizing efforts of Claudio during the Mission era could also be read as a thinly disguised paean to the Lópezes and Cummings' land development businesses. The romance not only responds to a desire to idealize the past, but also to an interest in depicting the present as the logical continuation of a history of developing California in which the author and her family occupy a central position in both the old and the new order.

In other ways, *Claudio and Anita* is typical of the fantasy heritage genre. The Spanish Californios are presented as hardworking entrepreneurs and as refined lovers of entertainment. The book also offers scenes with bandits, buried treasures, and magical elements. The author is critical of the transition from Spanish to Mexican rule after Mexico's independence in 1821, and the ensuing secularization of the missions. López de Cummings presents the Mexicans as politically motivated new arrivals, thus farther distancing her Spanish characters from any association with Mexico, and maintaining the claim that the true California population was of Spanish – not Mexican – origin.

Proletarian and Popular Culture in California during the 1920s and 1930s

While López de Cummings chose to focus on noble, well-to-do characters in *Claudio and Anita*, other writers turned their attention to the urban working class that populated California's big cities. The success of these playwrights rested upon a tradition of popular performances with which they could easily connect, as well as on the availability of numerous venues in which to present their pieces. Nicolás Kanellos' extensive research on this period has identified performances in such venues as Teatro Hidalgo, Teatro México, Teatro Zendejas, Teatro Capitol, Teatro California, and Teatro Principal, among others.[4] The same newspapers that carried poems and stories by local and international writers also chronicled successful Mexican American stage life. Audiences seem to have favored traditional genre pieces of the *zarzuela* (a type of musical operetta), *revista* and *variedades* (variety shows) nature, frequently presented by touring companies. These pieces allowed for the exploration of cultural differences, the critical examination of life in Mexico and the United States, and the venting of frustrations and grievances. Melodramas were also quite popular, and they easily tapped into the audiences' cultural sensibility.

The roster of playwrights during these two decades is ample. Most of their works have not survived, or are yet to be found, although newspaper chronicles have helped scholars piece together their literary biographies and output. One of the most successful authors was Adalberto Elías González, whose works include *La muerte de Francisco Villa* (The Death of Francisco Villa), *La asesina del martillo o la mujer tigresa* (The Assassin of the Hammer, or the Tiger Woman, 1923), *Los amores de Ramona* (Ramona's Loves, 1927, an adaptation of Helen Hunt Jackson's novel *Ramona* that broke all attendance records), *Los expatriados* (The Expatriates), *Los misioneros* (The Missionaries), and *Sangre Yaqui* (Yaqui Blood, 1924). González dramatized sensational episodes in Mexican and California history, and the life of the expatriate community who was eager to see itself on stage. A native of Sonora, Mexico, González was also a journalist for *El Heraldo de México*.

Eduardo A. Carrillo migrated from Veracruz, Mexico, to Los Angeles in 1922. He authored *Heraclio Bernal, o El rayo de Sinaloa* (Heraclio Bernal or Sinaloa's Lightning, 1923, a play inspired by the Mexican Revolution), *Los hombres desnudos* (Naked Men, 1922, a play about *machismo*), and *El proceso de Aurelio Pompa* (The Trial of Aurelio Pompa, 1925), a socio-political drama about the persecution of a Mexican worker that enjoyed multiple productions in the 1920s and 1930s. Other playwrights include Brígido Caro, Gabriel Navarro, Esteban V. Escalante, and Romualdo Tirado. Caro's interest in history is evident in plays like *Joaquín Murrieta* (1926) and *Mexico y Estados Unidos* (Mexico and the United States, 1927). Navarro, a journalist who arrived in Los Angeles in 1922, is credited with the plays *Los emigrados* (The Emigrants, 1928), *El precio de Hollywood* (Hollywood's Prize, 1933), *Alma Yaqui* (Yaqui Soul, 1932), and *Cuando entraron los dorados* (When the Golden Ones Arrived, 1932, reflecting his experiences in the Mexican Revolution). Escalante, a playwright-journalist wrote the prologue to Adolfo Carrillo's *Cuentos californianos*, as well as the plays *La pura verdad* (The Naked Truth, 1926) and *Las mariposas de Hollywood* (Hollywood's Butterflies, 1928). He returned to Mexico in 1933, after spending fifteen years in Los Angeles. His contemporary Romualdo Tirado was a successful impresario and coauthor (with Antonieta Díaz Mercado) of an adaptation of Mariano Azuela's novel *Los de abajo* (The Downtrodden, 1930).

Playwright Daniel Venegas was one of the most active and well-rounded intellectuals in Los Angeles during these decades. Venegas was a journalist, playwright, and novelist whose output has secured him an important place in Mexican American and Chicano/a literature. As a newspaperman, Venegas was responsible for *El Malcriado* (The Ill-Behaved), which included pieces on various hot social issues. His humor was often coarse and unsubtle.

Though none of his plays have been located, they always attracted a full house, according to contemporary newspaper articles, because the author's reputation as a satirist was well known throughout the Mexican American community. *El maldito jazz* (That Darned Jazz, 1930) and *El con-su-lado* (The Consulate, 1932) appear to have been comic pieces, while *Esclavos* (Slaves, 1930) probably combined humor with serious social commentary about labor issues, a problem he had already explored in his novel *Las aventuras de Don Chipote, o cuando los pericos mamen* (The Adventures of Don Chipote, or When Parrots Breastfeed, 1928).

Venegas's novel chronicles the trials and tribulations of Don Chipote, a poor Mexican farmworker who works hard without ever getting ahead. Enticed by the tall tales about the United States of his neighbor Pitacio, Don Chipote decides to try his luck in the country where allegedly money can be swept off the streets. With a heavy dose of coarse humor, the novel describes his border crossing and the travails that await him on U.S. soil. The narrator interrupts the story frequently to insert commentary about the treatment of Mexicans in the United States, lamenting their working conditions, discrimination, and abuse by employers and others who prey on them. After suffering an accident on the job, Don Chipote goes to Los Angeles for treatment. Here he discovers others like himself. He becomes infatuated with a waitress, frequents variety shows and similar forms of popular entertainment, and buys a songbook to try his luck at the talent shows so that he can impress his paramour. In the end, his wife shows up in Los Angeles with their many children and Pitacio just when Don Chipote is performing on stage. After a comic fight between the spouses, Don Chipote is sent back to Mexico, where he resumes his former life, thus suggesting a return to the status quo before immigration.

Las aventuras de Don Chipote is a complex text in which multiple discourses intersect. On the one hand, it can be read as part of the literary effort to discourage Mexican migration to the United States. The work seems to suggest that Mexicans will never succeed in the United States and therefore should not leave their country. However, the chapters that describe Don Chipote's life in Los Angeles offer a fascinating portrait of a vibrant community in which Mexican-owned or Mexican-serving businesses thrive by providing a host of goods and services. The authorial voice, moreover, while denouncing abuses and working conditions, speaks nonetheless from a Californian point of view. The ensuing contradiction articulates much of the novel's complexities.

Las aventuras de Don Chipote is deeply rooted in Hispanic folkloric and literary motifs such as *la tierra de Jauja* (the land of milk and honey) and Miguel de Cervantes' *Don Quijote*. However, it also reveals striking coincidences with the song "El corrido del lavaplatos" (The Dishwasher's Ballad), recorded in 1938 by Los Hermanos Bañuelos. Like Don Chipote, the nameless protagonist of the ballad migrates from Mexico to the United States, where he works in agriculture and railroads before moving to Los Angeles and finding employment as a dishwasher. After realizing that his dream of obtaining fame and riches was not meant to be, he returns to Mexico, advising others not to come to the United States. Researchers have not been able to determine whether the song was inspired by the novel or vice versa, or if both derive from a common source or set of sources.

Literature by the Descendants of the Nineteenth-Century Californios

Other authors explore family history as part of the general history of California. Poets Francisca Vallejo McGettigan and Inés de la Guerra

Dibblee work mostly with symbols and images that transcend their immediate textual value to connect with larger socio-historical forces in subtle, yet traceable ways. The most important of those referents is the hacienda that, as Vincent Pérez has suggested, functions as a mimetic image and icon of pre-1848 Californio community, and as a symbol of land ownership and social power, the famous Californio gentility.[5] Pérez also suggests that this mythologizing of the hacienda responds to the social displacement of Californios by capitalist modernity. One may be tempted to dismiss these authors' emphasis on their *hacendado* origin as an unproblematic celebration of the past, or as another iteration of the fantasy heritage discourse. However, as a potential response to social disenfranchisement, this "return to the past" also serves as a symbol of rootedness and belonging, which contrasts with dominant narratives that portray the Mexican as a recent arrival.

Francisca Vallejo McGettigan (1875–1962) was the granddaughter of General Mariano G. Vallejo, one of the leading figures of early California. She attended Dominican College, graduating with a degree in music in 1902. Her musical contributions include more than one thousand songs, operas, and mission plays. In addition, McGettigan wrote scripts for a weekly radio program on the history of California, from the Spanish period to the 1930s. She recorded more than one hundred programs of the show, entitled "Padres, Gringoes and Gold," for station KYA in San Francisco.

McGettigan published two poetry books, *Along the Highway of the King* (1943) and *San Francisco Souvenir* (1956). The former, whose title alludes to *el camino real* (also known as the California Mission Trail), is a collection of seventy-nine poems with a preface by notable California writer Gertrude Atherton. Her poems revere the Golden State, its history and its landscape. However, they also reveal the author's struggle with reconciling past and present. The title poem advises the reader to embrace change. The poetic voice observes how a traffic sign has replaced the mission bell, and feels a mixture of excitement and sadness: enthusiasm for the progress of the state, but nostalgia for the ways of the *padres*. The second part of the book, entitled "Suisun Indian Legends," centers on Native American lore. The author draws from the folklore of the Suisun, while presenting a romanticized portrait of the tribe. The final two sections, "Sonnets" and "Reveries," celebrate California and its peoples.

McGettigan's second book, a tribute to San Francisco, serves as a poetic guide for the visitor. The author writes about most of the city's attractions (the Golden Gate, the Twin Peaks, Fisherman's Wharf, the Ferry clock, Chinatown, Alcatraz), painting a vibrant picture of the Bay Area and its inhabitants. The poems explore the tension between history and change, embracing the latter but reminding readers of the importance of preserving an understanding and knowledge of the past. The author repeats stories that her father (Platón Vallejo) told her as a child. For Latino/a literatures in general, recovering lost voices or texts is an effective tool for cultural survival.[6] Thus, McGettigan ensures that early California voices are not forgotten.

A descendant of the influential De la Guerra family, from Santa Barbara, Inés de la G. Dibblee published only one book, *Hacienda Memories and Caravans of Thoughts* (1955). Most poems in the collection are presented as remembrances of a not-so-distant past in which the speaking subject lived as a youngster. "Hacienda Memories," the first section, revolves around the natural cycle of harvesting and animal husbandry at the hacienda. The pastoral setting reveals abrupt class divisions. Ethnic lines are also clearly drawn, and the poetic voice identifies (and characterizes by speech) a multicultural labor force that includes Basques and other Spaniards, Portuguese, and Chinese men. The author emphasizes autumn as the end of the season, symbolizing the disappearance of the Californio way of life. In the second section, "Caravan of Thoughts," the inevitable passage of time has religious significance. The final section, "Remembered," brings the social and the natural worlds together in a final effort to keep memories alive. The last poem, "In the Old Mission," describes the garments of an old lady (a regular visitor to the mission church) as shadows of her vanished world, perhaps an apt metaphor for her Inés' own writings.

The Autobiography of Migration

As editor Lauro Flores has suggested, *El Coyote, the Rebel* by Luis Pérez should be read as an autobiography with certain novelistic embellishments.[7] Narrated almost matter-of-factly, with a characteristic use of subdued humor, *El Coyote* tells the story of a young orphan who survives war and poverty by making the most of life's opportunities. In his preteen years, Pérez joins the Mexican Revolution in Sonora. He participates in several military campaigns, deserts twice, loses a finger, and keeps reenlisting until he receives an honorable discharge. El Coyote's adventures resemble a picaresque novel in which frequent changes in occupation and great geographical mobility are essential. Pérez sees multiple segments of Mexican society, from military commanders to prostitutes, and his narrative straddles the U.S.–Mexico border, which he crosses several times. Though he acquires a modest fortune in Mexico by panning gold, Luis often ends up in economically precarious situations. Having no family roots and no formal education, Luis soon finds himself among the ranks of Mexican laborers, subjected to the whims of the U.S. job market. On one of his trips to the United States, he picks cotton at an Arizona farm where he is cheated out of his earnings. During World War I, Luis works at an ore smelter, where he befriends a Mexican American who has been drafted but wants to go with Luis to Mexico. On his final return to the United States, Luis receives help from a missionary who arranges for him to receive an education in New Mexico, and then attend a seminary in Los Angeles. Pérez leaves the seminary once his love for another missionaries proves impossible. He continues his acculturation by getting a college degree. After getting his American citizenship, Luis goes to meet his love interest, Dolores, who is returning from a trip to Mexico, and who has promised to answer his marriage proposal. The book ends ambiguously with the protagonist thinking that an affirmative answer would be the perfect climax to a picture-perfect present and a hopeful future. Editor Lauro Flores observes that the real-life Luis Pérez did not marry a woman of Mexican descent,[8] which makes this ending even more ambiguous. Nevertheless, the author sees citizenship and marriage as liminal points that transform one's identity. The old Luis (a Mexican without a family) becomes the new Louis (the name he used to publish the novel *The Girls of the Pink Feather* in 1963), an American citizen about to start a family and a new life.

The Mexican (American) as Field Worker

Born in Madera, California, Emmanuel J. Camarena worked as a farmworker in California, Texas, and Mexico. As an author, Camarena is best known for the novel *Pancho* (1958), which he wrote for those readers unfamiliar with the situation of the undocumented workers. Camarena privileges many themes and settings that would later become popular in Chicano Movement narratives: the traumatic moment of the crossing of the river, a season picking cotton in Texas, relocating in California's San Joaquin Valley, deportation, and the attempt to return to the United States by any means possible. As a literary text, *Pancho* may not be the most artistically accomplished novel, but it serves an important historical purpose, signaling a transitional moment, from the urban proletarian texts of the 1920s and 1930s to the rural-based Chicano/a narratives that dominated much of the 1960s and early 1970s.

Conclusion

Most of the aforementioned writers deal with the question of identity. For Carrillo, Venegas, and Pérez, identity is connected with transculturation, or the process of identity transformation that occurs when subjects move from one country to another. Others, like Ulica, confront the same problematic of displacement but reject change and embrace the ideal of cultural continuity. U.S.-born authors, like López de Cummings, McGettigan, and Dibblee negotiate change from a historical (not a geographical) perspective, appeal to alternative genealogies (Spain and Hispanic California, rather than Mexico). Identity negotiation entails an interrogation of subjectivity, and many authors insert their own speaking selves in their works through autobiographical writing or by appealing to family history and tradition. Geographical change enables authors to explore the border and the notion of transnationalism that permeates the works of non-U.S. born writers. Pérez offers the most detailed examination of the transnational self.

Flores Magón and Moncaleano approach this question from a political view, stressing international solidarity among workers, rather than national allegiance. They are not the only authors to stress the significance of class in Mexican American literature. The 1920s witnessed an explosion of proletarian writers who understood that the Mexican American population was predominantly of working-class extraction. Camarena's *Pancho* signals a return to the working-class ethos and aesthetics by the end of the period under scrutiny. Even those writers who came from well-to-do backgrounds (López de Cummings, McGettigan, Dibblee) had to reconcile their elite status as part of the Californio upper class with the change and alliances demanded by the new social powers. Their literature entails a complex process of balancing past and present, rootedness and displacement in ways that are rather distinct from those of their working-class colleagues.

Language is a major theme for all of these writers as well, not just a vehicle for their creative endeavors. Language choice determined not only the target audience for their works but also the set of cultural referents that a writer expected her/his readers to recognize. When Jorge Ulica makes fun (in Spanish) of the *pochos* and the *parladores de Spanish,* he ridicules a linguistic deficiency that can also be interpreted as a cultural and social commentary on identity. Daniel Venegas writes in vernacular Spanish, using malapropisms, crude humor, and slang. He caters to a specific segment of his Mexican American audience, but at the same time addresses his readers as equals.

These authors were always aware of their readers. Those who wrote for newspapers could count on subscribers who had patronized the same periodicals for decades. Playwrights realized that their success depended on how well they presented their pieces, as well as on their ability to satisfy their audiences' need to see themselves on stage. English-language novelists and poets addressed a larger, less clearly defined audience than those writing for a Mexican American readership.

A diverse group, Mexican American writers in the first half of the twentieth century were nonetheless united in the common goals of asserting their own subjectivities, inscribing their personal and collective experiences in print, and struggling for cultural survival. The fact that we are studying them in the twenty-first century indicates that their voices are still relevant for our own time.

Notes

1. Luis Leal, "Adolfo Carrillo," in *Dictionary of Literary Biography: Chicano Writers Second Series* 122 (Detroit, MI, and London: Bruccoli Clark Layman, 1992), 53.
2. Miguel López Rojo, "Introducción," in *Cuentos californianos*, by Adolfo Carrillo (Guadalajara, Mexico: Secretaría de Cultura de Jalisco, 1993), 14.
3. Catherine L. Kurland, "Pobladores to Mariachis: A Personal Journey," in Miguel A. Gandert et al., eds., *Hotel Mariachi: Urban Space and Cultural Heritage in Los Angeles* (Albuquerque: University of New Mexico Press, 2013), 2.
4. Nicolás Kanellos, *A History of Hispanic Theatre in the United States: Origins to 1940* (Austin: University of Texas Press, 1990), and *Hispanic Immigrant Literature: El Sueño del Retorno* (Austin: University of Texas Press, 2011).
5. Vincent Pérez, *Remembering the Hacienda: History and Memory in the Mexican American Southwest* (College Station: Texas A&M University Press, 2006), 92.
6. Manuel M. Martín-Rodríguez, *Life in Search of Readers: Reading (in) Chicano/a Literature* (Albuquerque: University of New Mexico Press, 2003).
7. Lauro Flores, "Introduction," *El Coyote, the Rebel*, by Luis Pérez (Houston: Arte Público Press, 2000), viii.
8. Ibid., xxiii.

PART IV

Social Change and Literary Experimentation

CHAPTER 10

The Protest Fiction of Frank Norris, Upton Sinclair, Jack London, and John Steinbeck

Susan Shillinglaw

In the first few decades of the twentieth century, social protest writers called attention to the unprecedented industrial and agricultural growth that characterized a new era of prosperity, while seldom benefitting the workers themselves. Edmund Wilson, in "The Boys in the Back Room" (1940), insisted that California fiction more insistently dramatized class warfare and socialist ideals than did fiction from other regions of the country. Fiery socialist Jack London argued that the closing of the western frontier created surplus capital that "roams for investment and nips in the bud the patient efforts of the embryo capitalist to rise through slow increment from small beginnings." On California's intemperate shores, the socialist party established deep roots, solace to the turn-of-the-century working man. A quarter century later, John Steinbeck also believed that continent's end would be the stage for a dramatic showdown between workers and owners. For Oklahoma migrants "suddenly confronted with our capitalist industrialism" – California's corporate farms – "the ridiculous thinking of that system is doubly apparent."

Writers working in this political genre typically focused on a moment when the people's expectations were thrown into high relief; when dreams and failures violently collided; when the gap between powerful and powerless was raw, violent, and disturbing. The shared turf of Frank Norris, Jack London, Upton Sinclair, and John Steinbeck is the dark underbelly of California's golden dream – systemic failures, absence of social parity, of homes for all, of land for the little guy, of a living wage. Each yearned to pen a California epic. Steinbeck probably would have agreed with Norris, who asserted that westward movement was the "last great epic event in the history of civilization." And yet, Norris complained at the turn of the twentieth century, the only western genre was the dime novel. He meant to correct that with "real thing," with what he identified as the highest form of the novel, the "Novel of Purpose" with its "great force, that works together with the pulpit and the universities for the good of the people." These four writers had something of the same aim – a broad grasp, wide and lasting impact.

All have been labeled as naturalists, a literary movement that began in the late nineteenth century, and that aligned itself with the scientific theories of the late nineteenth century, particularly social Darwinism. Naturalists believed that humans, like other species, were impacted by the laws of evolution, heredity, and atavism. They argued that instead of controlling their destinies, people were impacted by natural forces and physical laws. Naturalist writers recognized that environment, heredity, instinct, and chance shaped human lives – as did poverty, industrial might, and fluctuations of the economy. "Change the system and you will change the people," barked Upton Sinclair. "Blame conditions not men" the representative of the railroad tells Presley, the observer and poet in Norris's *The Octopus*. Presley doesn't know quite how to respond to that. Have humans no control over corporate might? For all four, in varying degrees, the answer to that was yes, they do. These writers believed in resurgent regional communities and what London called "plasticity" and Steinbeck "survivability." Humans adapt.

Indeed, the mid-nineteenth-century scientific work of Charles Darwin on natural selection and Herbert Spencer on survival of the fittest impacted not only the ideologies but also the methodologies of these four novelists. In a 1899 essay, author Maurice Thompson argues that writers of fiction should study Darwin's "double method" of "microscopic analysis" as well as "stupendous synthesis" of facts. In *Sea of Cortez* (1941) Steinbeck expressed appreciation of Darwin's exacting methodology: "out of long long consideration of the parts [Darwin] emerged with a sense of the whole." That's a fairly good description of what these novelists intended. All had journalistic roots; all were impacted by turn-of-the-century muckraking zeal (and legacy) – bearing witness to human misery transformed their own sensibilities, and they reworked facts into fiction. Rooted in the particular, these novels move to broad, intersecting visions, what Norris calls "the larger view." Each is a hybrid text, delivering both factual punch and trenchant critiques of power, drawing from a variety of genres to limn social upheaval. Crises were, for them, personal as well as political, historical as well as environmental, economic as well as sociological.

Outrage as well as empathy are, perhaps, the two most essential qualities of a socially engaged writer. Sinclair put it another way in his introduction to a collection of global protest literature published the year he moved to California, 1915. In selecting writers for his anthology,

Cry for Justice, he writes, "Two questions have been asked of each writer: Have you had something vital to say? And have you said it with some special effectiveness?"

The Disturbers

In 1902, Steinbeck was born and Norris died. London researched the slums of London, England, publishing *The People of the Abyss* in 1903: "for years afterwards," said his friend Sinclair, "the memories of this stunted and depraved population haunted him beyond all peace." Sinclair first learned about socialism in 1902. It was an "amazing discovery," he wrote, to learn that "I did not have to carry the whole burden of humanity's future!" At the cusp of a new century, with Teddy Roosevelt in the White House, and Progressive reform gathering momentum, and a middle class attuned to abusive corporate power, these California writers intersected in a symbolic moment. Each contributed to a decades-long struggle for economic and social equity.

Their biographical roots also intertwined. To varying degrees, assertive mothers shaped sensitive sons; weak fathers left psychic wounds – and those sons wrote furiously to achieve what philandering, inebriated, absent, or disappointed fathers had not. As children, London, Sinclair, and Steinbeck were often lonely. Works of fantasy and romance offered solace, as well as clear moral dictates that may have determined their later ideological sympathies. Their first publications were romances, and subsequent writings were characterized by an extraordinary depth of feeling.

All were largely self-educated (only Sinclair graduated from college). At a time when Teddy Roosevelt was celebrating the virtues of "the strenuous life," many intellectuals considered physical and personal experience more important than higher education. All four writers would have agreed with Roosevelt's observation that to know working men and women, one had to live and work with them.

Frank Norris (1870–1902)

When reviewing *The Octopus* (1901), London heralded Norris as a troubadour of the "great, incoherent, amorphous West! . . . Who could grip the spirit and the essence of it, the luster and the wonder"? he asked. "Frank Norris has done it."

That was generous praise for a wealthy midwestern transplant, coming from a scrappy Californian native. When Norris moved from Chicago at age fifteen, he seemed the least likely candidate to "grip" an amorphous West. The son of an actress and a businessman, young Norris studied art in San Francisco and Paris and writing at Berkeley and Harvard. He went to South Africa to become a travel writer and then returned to San Francisco to work as a journalist for a weekly magazine, *The Wave*. Up to age twenty-seven, Norris might aptly be called a dilettante, as his biographers note. However, he was beginning to develop his life's ambition: to reshape the fiction of the West, to eschew the "commonplace people" and "restricted emotions, dramas of the reception-room" characteristic of realist William Dean Howells's work. By his late twenties, Norris envisioned hybrid narratives that blended the deep truth of the romance – "the black, unsearched penetralia of the soul of man" – with a broad understanding of the ways that natural laws determined human action. He aspired to write a kind of regional literature that was "relentlessly and remorselessly true."

Gradually, Norris became the novelist he had theoretically nursed into being. In 1899, with two novels published (*Moran of the Lady Letty* and *McTeague*), Norris envisioned a "great work with the West and California as a background, and which will at the same time be thoroughly American." Like other social protest writers, he wished to balance region and nation, to write a stinging California epic as well as achieving a "stupendous synthesis." His "Trilogy of the Epic of the Wheat" served this purpose. Volume one, *The Octopus*, was "a story of California," the region's greatest wheat producer; volume two, *The Pit*, focused on Chicago, the city that distributed wheat throughout the world; volume three, dealing with the international consumption of grain, was never written (McE 334). Norris, formerly an investigative reporter working for S. S. McClure, thoroughly researched the relationship between California agriculture and the Southern Pacific Railroad, intending to champion the people's perspective. However, his understanding broadened after he interviewed a railroad executive and spent several weeks at a ranch near Hollister, interviewing his hosts, observing the wheat harvest, and connecting with the land.

In *The Octopus*, Norris surveys the state's surging economic growth and layered cultural history: the vast fields of wheat and grain that were California's primary agricultural product from the 1870s into the early twentieth century; the great herds of sheep that were once driven east from Hollister; the bustling village of Bonneville, modeled on Hollister, laid out in the late 1860s; and the seventh of the California Spanish missions – San Juan Batista – which is Guadalajara in the novel. And at the center of *The Octopus* is a violent scene of class conflict, Norris's fictionalized version of a

1880 shootout between settlers and railroad representatives in the Mussel Slough section of the southern San Joaquin Valley. Ranchers had homesteaded land offered years earlier by the Southern Pacific Railroad on odd numbered tracks on either side of the proposed line. With faith in the brochures produced by the railroad, which pledged to sell "ordinary agricultural, vineyard, and grazing lands, at from $2.50 upwards per acre," once the railroad was completed, the ranchers created homesteads in good faith and chipped in to bring water from the Kings River to their dry acres. However, when the railroad charged higher prices per acre than originally quoted – twenty to thirty dollars – the ranchers resisted, forming a Settlers' Land League to fight the eviction of those who refused to pay inflated prices.

Seven men were killed on Henry Brewer's ranch when railroad officials came to his homestead to reclaim the land that farmers had leased from the railroad years before. In this bloody clash between ordinary folk and the railroad monopoly, Norris finds complex motives. While the ranchers are industrious, visionary "westering" settlers, they are also naive, often greedy, sometimes dismissive of those less fortunate. The railroad represents a vast corporate power in this novel. Its high tariffs to ship wheat are "legitimate profit," in the words of the unlikeable railroad representative Behrman. And although running a railroad, like homesteading, is the work of tough and determined men, theirs is less a communal than a commercial venture, a monopoly that engages in price fixing, control of public lands, suppression of labor. Those who hold a monopoly on land and river transportation wield great political clout – and engage in bribes and corruption. What is sacrificed in the brutal confrontation between the corporate power of the railroad – the octopus – and the fierce individualism of the ranchers is a frontier dream – a landed community, home and kinship ties, self-determination, freedom. Families are shattered in this novel. Nearly all the men are maimed or die in the end, with the women widowed, left starving, or forced into prostitution.

Stitching together the saga of ranchers, the railroad, and the unearthly romance of Vanamee allows him to create a "composite" central character modeled partly on Norris and partly on California poet Edwin Markham (1852–1941), author of the popular "The Man with a Hoe," a work of social protest published in newspapers around the country in 1899. Poet Presley yearns to write an epic of the West, but initially finds that realism has "disfigured" his chimerical West and is thus a detached witness to the ranchers' long fight with the railroad. Violence snaps him to attention, and he sees in a "true light" the conflict as a "war between Freedom and Tyranny." Presley composes "The Toilers" because his sympathies have been "stirred to his lowest depths." His poem plunges into the "primal heart of things," his friend tells him, touching both regional and universal truths.

Presley is a fictional exemplar, a figure vital to social protest fiction, argues Mark Bracher in *Literature and Social Justice*. The character's transformation results from his being malleable and "situated" with others, becoming empathetically "of the People," able to feel their pain and loss.

Jack London (1876–1916)

By 1903, with the publication of *The Call of the Wild*, Jack London himself was the iconic western writer he heralded in Norris – famous in California and around the country as hobo on the road, sailor on the Pacific, Alaskan miner, and San Francisco Bay oyster pirate, stealing from the private oyster beds that, since the 1870s, had been seeded with hearty Atlantic coast oysters. London rewrote versions of his remarkable life in book after book, shifting his scrappy poses, tapping down and ramping up his socialist zeal: "He was a Socialist," said a friend, "but he wanted to beat the Capitalist at his own game." Janus-faced London was a roughneck and a ragged childhood victim of poverty; a champion of the people as the "boy socialist" of Oakland and someone who scorned the effect that poverty had on individuals weaker than himself. He called them "People of the Abyss" in his 1903 account of the London poor. In "War of the Classes" (1905), London insisted that the "capitalist class offers nothing that is clean, noble, and alive." However, he also fancied himself a self-made writer with a socialist soul.

For London, the personal was political. His social protest writings were rooted in psychic pain. As critics have noted, London's interior landscape was vertiginous. The abyss of his early poverty always loomed before him. "I was down in the cellar of society, down in the subterranean depths of misery about which it is neither nice nor proper to speak," he noted in "What Life Means to Me" (1906), piling image upon image. "I was in the pit, the abyss, the human cesspool, the shambles and the charnel-house of our civilization." Equally compelling was his ability – his determination – to claw his way out of that chasm. London's heroes, dogs and men, generally do the same. His memories of childhood squalor and his subsequent valor in overcoming his lot was far more real to him than the external vistas of Oakland or the Alaskan ice sheets that he described in his tales of the Klondike. At age twenty, London joined the socialist party, whose ideology served as a hammer to attack the abuses of capitalist society. In scores of essays and speeches, collected in *War of the Classes* (1905) and *Revolution and Other Essays* (1910), as well as in his fiction, London traced the high costs of industrial progress and the equally appalling cost to human lives ground down by power.

London can hardly contain his anti-capitalist rage in *The Iron Heel* (1908), a novel that is part romance, part ideological tract, part *bildungsroman*, and part hagiography (socialist hero Ernest Everhard has brows "bright with the divine that was in him"). It is a dystopian novel in which the socialist revolt is a terrifying failure, as well as a jeremiad that conveys anxiety about both America's imperialist powers at the beginning of the twentieth century and the workers' suffering under a capitalist system. The novel notes the impact of British imperialism as well: "The natives [of India] died of starvation by the millions while their rules robbed them of the fruit of their toil." And the novel's *donnée* is equally arresting: in the Foreword readers learn that a 700-year-old manuscript has been found in a tree trunk by Anthony Meredith, scholar. This "flawed" and unfinished document, composed by Ernest's wife, covers the years between 1912 and 1932, Anthony writes, and is primarily interesting for the "psychology of the persons that lived in that turbulent period" before "many Revolts" in the centuries following that finally bring about the Brotherhood of Man, a socialist fulfillment never actually described in the narrative.

Like Norris, London yearned for the "stupendous synthesis" that would convey the Progressive era's urgent message – the widening gap between labor and capital, between corporate control and frontier freedoms.

Originally entitled *Oligarchy*, the novel contains London's socialist speeches and tracts, delivered by his startling hero, Ernest Everhard – a man whose resonant moniker suggests his oratorical and physical gifts. To convey his allure, London – like Norris, Sinclair, and Steinbeck – creates a pupil for Everhard, a political novice who assumes the stance of an untutored writer/observer. Ardent socialist convert Avis Everhard serves the same function as the poet Presley in *The Octopus*, young Bunny in *Oil!*, and paroled Tom Joad in *The Grapes of Wrath*. Each character respects, even reveres, the more experienced activist. Each gathers evidence in assessing that activist's stance. Each bears witness to a social crisis and reassesses his/her moral stance.

In *The Iron Heel*, Avis is the liberal daughter of a professor, a comfortably situated woman with "strong class instincts." She meets Ernest Everhard, who has the "neck of a prize-fighter" and is a "natural aristocrat ... a super-man ... aflame with democracy." Avis is lured to his bedrock ideals and his bed, as she moves through initiatory stages of recognition, sympathy, education, and participation in a turbulent Chicago workers' strike. As Jane Howard notes, writing about *The Jungle* (1906): "Portraying a political awakening is one way of suggesting the possibility of profound social change without violating the conventions of realism, and it is a strategy that emerges still more strongly in a later genre that has many affinities with naturalism, the proletarian novel" (Norton 496).

First-hand experience alters beliefs – that point is repeatedly made in these novels of social protest. Each one owes something to a documentary impulse and to the fact that these novelists were also journalists familiar with the "muckraking closeups" of the turn-of-the-century journalism. After Ernest Everhard tells Avis that "the gown you wear is stained with blood" – the blood of working men like Jackson, who lost his arm in the Sierra Mills – Avis talks to Jackson, listening to the "terrible details" of his story. She then seeks out "the lawyer who had handled Jackson's case, and the two foremen and the superintendent at the mills who had testified." Avis's research upends her life: "The more I thought of Jackson's arm, the more shaken I was. I was confronted by the concrete. For the first time I was seeing life." Avis's path to socialism is replicated by the Bishop's education (the church itself, like the press, is part of the oligarchy, the "Iron Heel" of power). Ernest takes the Bishop on a "journey through hell ... through the homes of a few of our factory workers. I showed him the human wrecks cast aside by the industrial machine, and he listened to their life stories." Her father, a chemistry professor, writes a sociological text after meeting Ernest and ends up on the streets of San Francisco, trying out various laboring jobs. He too is a fact finder, a man on the ground.

Their educations become that of the startled reader, both then and today. Anthony Meredith's footnotes – which reflect London's own wry historical commentary – add heft to the novel's critique: "Even as late as 1912 AD, the great mass of the people still persisted in the belief that they ruled the country by virtue of their ballots" (72). Another quotes the cool Mr. Wickson, voice of the oligarchy: "We are in power. Nobody will deny it. By virtue of power we shall remain in power."

As in *The Octopus*, the novel churns toward a violent confrontation between the powerful and the powerless, a nightmarish Chicago riot where disruption erases civilized restraint. Chaos results. In turbulent scenes, the revolution fails. To a greater extent than any other writer of his day,

London "broke the ice that was congealing American letters and brought life and literature into a meaningful relation to each other" (quoted in Raskin 6). The source of that ice-breaking power was his "passionate, awkward, hyperbolic, and frequently overwrought prose style and plotting." Fellow ice-breaker Frank Norris barked: "Who cares for fine style! Tell your yarn and let your style go to the devil. We don't want literature, we want life" (107 *Manhood in America*). Hybrid, unruly texts barely contain the full-throated masculine outrage of these two, young turn-of-the-century novelistic disturbers.

Upton Sinclair (1878–1968)

"Readers of my novels know that I have one favorite theme, the contrast between the social classes," Upton Sinclair wrote in his autobiography. "There are characters from both worlds, the rich and the poor, and the plots are contrived to carry you from one to the other" (Norton 347). Sinclair himself had been carried between poverty and wealth as a child, growing up in Baltimore, Maryland, where he was born on September 20, 1878. His alcoholic father spent his earnings on liquor, insuring that his wife and young son sometimes slept on a "vermin-ridden sofa in a lodging house" as he put it, and "the next night under silken coverlets" in the sumptuous rooms of his grandfather or his mother's sister. Back and forth the family swung, and it was a pattern that Sinclair would never forget. In the socialist movement, which he joined in 1904, Sinclair, much like London, "learned to identify [his] own struggle for life with the struggle for life of humanity" (349). In 1918, three years after he moved to California, Sinclair declared that his "trade-mark" of "Social Justice" would brand each issue of his self-published monthly magazine, *Upton Sinclair's*.

Although the journal was short lived, Sinclair and his campaign for Social Justice had a long and energetic life, both literary and political (in 1934 he ran for governor of California on the EPIC platform, "End Poverty in California"). During his ninety years he published ninety some works that wrestled with the profit system. Sinclair's best-known novel is, of course, the muckraking exposé of the meat packing industry, *The Jungle*, published in 1906 when he was twenty-five. Other works burn with similar indignation: the novel *King Coal* (1917) is based on a large miners' strike against the Colorado Fuel and Iron Company, where women, children, miners, and soldiers died when the militia was brought in. (In New York City, Sinclair delivered a lecture luridly entitled "Shall We Murder

Rockefeller," owner of the mine? No was his response to the audience. It's the "phantom" Rockefeller who had to die, that "specter of power, of predatory force, of murderous inspiration.") Sinclair's defense of striking Los Angeles longshoremen resulted in the play *Singing Jailbirds* (1924) about the imprisonment of World War I protestors. His "Dead Hand," social critiques of the early 1920s – a "dead hand" was strangling Americans – tackled contemporary religion, journalism, education (submissive students), and literature. *Money Writes* (1927) dismisses the notion of "art for art's sake" as well as nihilist modern art and America's "celebrity culture" that degraded taste. The proper aim of art was propaganda, he thought, presenting a strongly felt view of the world.

The broad social critiques of the "Dead Hand" series are enfolded into *Oil!* (1927). Although the plot steadily explores predatory and corrupt oil leases in California, Sinclair also takes pock shots at religious zealotry, tepid higher education and the repression of radical ideas, the blind zealotry of World War I, journalistic bias, the lurid film industry, and corrupt presidential politics. Sinclair's campaign for Social Justice recognized few boundaries. Indeed, critic Lawrence Clark Powell declared that *Oil!* was "the largest scale of all California novels." In Sinclair's eyes, the need for social reform was evident in every institution.

Sinclair started gathering material for *Oil!* in 1924, inspired by the Teapot Dome scandal of 1922, when the Secretary of the Interior leased oil-rich land to private oil companies without competitive bidding. Closer to home, oil wells in Long Beach had yielded huge quantities of oil – all of it in a fifteen-square mile urban area. When his wife bought lots on the west slope of Los Angeles' Signal Hill, where oil had been struck, Sinclair attended nasty meetings of property owners who were struggling to agree on sales – these gatherings recreated in early pages of *Oil!*. "I am devoting all my time and energy to writing a novel about the class struggle in California," he wrote a friend in 1926. "This must be accepted as my contribution to the welfare of the California working class" (Coodley 56).

Sinclair's young hero Bunny is another composite central character who explores the contradictions and conflicts of capital and labor. Bunny adores his powerful, self-made father, J. Arnold Ross. His socialist friend Paul is an equally compelling mentor to the "little idealist." While Dad's mind was ever "on his money – or on the things he wanted to do, and that his money enabled him to do," Paul's mind dwells on equity and, after fighting in World War I, on labor organizing. Physically and ideologically, Bunny shuttles back and forth between silken and socialist enclaves, making an "earnest and devoted" effort to "ride on two horses at once! And the horses kept getting farther and farther apart, until he was all but split in the middle!" While Bunny's mind and heart are aligned with the workers' strikes and arrests and injustices, his body is lured again and again into the boudoirs of wealthy women. Out of Bunny's discomfort and indecision Sinclair traces the woe of the worker as well as the allure of wealth and ease. If Bunny's amorous exploits sometimes threaten to swamp the novel's political exposé, his sympathies are unwavering. Again and again, he returns to the homes and jails of his revolutionary friends. Sinclair's great talent as a writer was in marshaling evidence and providing detailed accounts of systemic failures.

Dad himself also contains the tensions of the corporate/labor clash. Once a working man, J. Arnold Ross, oilman, is a loving and attentive father who listens to his son's appeals for worker housing and a library and for funds to free jailed strikers. However, as Bunny recognizes, Dad's code is not his own. Dad blithely robs a farmer of valuable oil land and cheerfully bribes the chair of the county board of supervisors in Paradise Valley. Dad is a liar, a hypocrite, manipulative and ruthless. Dad is a foil to empathetic Bunny. When Bunny learns of the compromises Dad makes to the powerful Federation, Bunny cries out: "Why, Dad, we don't own our own business! We don't even own our own souls." Like Presley, Bunny grapples with the limits of human freedom in a world shaped by capitalist greed.

In these protest novels, edenic California is blighted by the corporate power of oilwells, railroads, and agribusiness. If a distant oilfield seems a fairyland and if oil is also necessary to fight wars and run automobiles, an oil field is also a place where "an army of men were ... working hard in twelve hour shifts, and in peril of life and limb" with "blasted hopes." Dad's oil wells banish quail and bougainvillea from idyllic Paradise Valley and smoke curls over the hills in "a curtain of black mist." Irresistibly, the "little idealist" Bunny hopes for a renewed Paradise, where he and Dad could "tear down that barbed wire fence that separated capital from labor! In the new world there would be no more barbed wire and no more bad feelings – the roses would bloom on the hedges." However, that hope is faint at the novel's conclusion. Paul is dead and Dad disgraced.

Both the idealist's future and the ecological health of the California landscape are uncertain in these books. While raw facts convey the urgency of the moment and help to shift the central character's consciousness, breaking down the fence is a Herculean endeavor.

John Steinbeck (1902–68)

When eastern publishers asked the young Norris, London, and Steinbeck for biographical sketches, all three lied about their western bloodlines. Norris sent a resume to the *Louisville Times* declaring that "I was 'bawn 'n raise' in California" (McE 30), erasing his first fifteen years in Chicago. London informed Houghton Mifflin that his father was a "soldier, scout, backwoodsman, trapper, and wanderer" – his unassuming *stepfather* was none of these western types. And Steinbeck wrote to Robert Ballou, publisher of his first novel set in California, *To a God Unknown* (1933), that he – unlike nearby Carmel poet Robinson Jeffers – truly grasped the West: "I know the god better than he does," Steinbeck insisted, because "I was born to and my father was. Our bodies came from this soil ... and our blood is distilled from the juices of this earth." Steinbeck told a stretcher as well. Mr. Steinbeck had been born in Florida, not California. Each writer's concern with lineage was less about Anglo-Saxon purity (although in other instances, both London and Norris asserted white racial superiority) and more about western patrimony, the right to speak Californian. It was a tall order and they knew it. It meant translating a region that covered two-thirds of the Pacific coast, reached from sub sea-level Death Valley to Mt. Whitney, the highest peak in the nation, and included incredibly diverse ecological systems. The complex social structure of the state was equally challenging.

Verdant landscapes and cantankerous citizens imprinted a young John Steinbeck, born in Salinas, one of the richest agricultural regions of California. More thoroughly than London, Norris, or Sinclair – largely city boys – Steinbeck developed a deep attachment to the valley where "oaks wore hoods of golden green" and "hills were brown and baked in the summer." Equally strong was his disdain for Salinas's complex social hierarchy. Wealthy growers and shippers created a cultural dynamic of haves and have-nots – and the have-nots were Chinese and Filipino field workers and Mexican factory workers at the nearby Spreckels Sugar plant. Although John Steinbeck's family was, in the main, middle class, he empathized with those at the bottom, perhaps because he too felt a sense of dislocation in his hometown. In Salinas, power was entrenched in land production. And in many ways, land use and yearning for land ownership became the most compelling story he would tell in his California novels, from *To a God Unknown* to *East of Eden*.

The Great Depression of the 1930s did not, of itself, turn Steinbeck into a partisan writer. *The Grapes of Wrath* was written out of his own simmering disgust with what was the latest chapter of a grim, 75-year-old California story, one he knew since youth: the poverty of field workers, the inadequacy of migrant housing, the lack of sanitation or job security or health care or decent wages. Steinbeck became a partisan in the fall of 1936, when, on a journalistic assignment for the liberal *San Francisco News*, he recognized the urgency of that old story of abject field workers. As witness to a terrible human drama of homelessness and hunger, with wages nearly 40 percent below what workers were paid a decade earlier, he immediately launched into his "big" novel with a clear "thesis" in his mind: California agriculture depended on "serf labor" and "[t]hat is not a popular thesis in California," he wrote.

The fourteenth chapter of *The Grapes of Wrath* is the keystone of the novel, laying out, in effect, that thesis. It excoriates "the great owners" of California who fail to grasp the whole picture and instead strike out at "the immediate thing," labor unrest or "reds" in their midst – "not knowing these things are results, not causes." Owners are blind to the root causes of unrest: the fact that humans (serfs/migrants/field workers) need to work and to eat and to have shelter – all basic needs. (Later in the book Casy reiterates this message, telling Tom that when he, Casy, was in jail, other prisoners helped him realize that "It's need that makes all the trouble.") *The Grapes of Wrath* insists that migrants forced from their land will have their needs fulfilled, somehow, somewhere. Steinbeck writes in Chapter 14: "Having stepped forward, [a human] may slip back, but only half a step, never the full step back." That is Steinbeck's bedrock optimism, the capacity of humans to survive, to endure. Serfs will revolt rather than slip back a full step. Chapter 14 closes by noting the chasm separating the great owners – who abide by the gospel of self sufficiency and the power of "I" (the American way) – from the poor people who band together in order to survive. "Is a tractor bad? Is the power that turns the long furrows wrong?" Steinbeck's answer to both questions is no. "If this tractor were ours it would be good – not mine, but ours." And that awareness, that there is profound difference between "mine" and "ours," is the fulcrum upon which the book tips.

Tom Joad is, of course, the central consciousness, his vision altered by what he witnesses. A recently paroled Tom is introduced sauntering up to a truck that bears the sign, "No Riders" – corporations owning trucks give no free rides. Like the railroad whistle that Presley hears in the opening chapter of *The Octopus* and like Dad's 90 horsepower engine in the first chapter of *Oil!*, the "huge red transport truck" represents power, the "rich bastard [who] makes him carry a sticker." While machines are not inherently evil in any of these novels – the Joads' jalopy is their home, after all; the oil rigs in *Oil!* are powerful and necessary; the railroad is a lifeline for wheat farmers in *The Octopus* – the destructive power of the machine is, from the opening pages of each novel, a foreboding presence, a symbol of industrial might.

True in *The Grapes of Wrath*, true in each protest novel, characters are largely white. Sidestepping race, these writers build cases that are socio-economic, about the haves and have-nots, about power that is often insidious and unseen, without contours or borders. They examine another kind of enslavement, "wage slavery" and economic entrapment under the "iron heel" of legal, religious, journalistic, economic, and political power that was increasingly evident during the first decades of the twentieth century. The scourge of the present day, insisted Sinclair in 1903, was a "gigantic, all-consuming, all-debasing Materialism" (Herms 13). Clearly the cultural dialogue had shifted fifty and seventy-five years after Harriet Beecher Stowe published her trailblazing novel of social protest, *Uncle Tom's Cabin*, and these four novelists, consciously I believe, wrote in response to her model, shifting the dialectic. What they witnessed was the rise of industrial and corporate power and the widening gap between wealth and poverty. By implication and direct statement in the novel itself (Chapter 19), Steinbeck associated destitute, despised, and hungry field workers with slaves. "I've seen such terrific things in the squatters' camps that I can't think out of them right now," he wrote to his agent after his first investigative trip into the Central Valley of California in the fall of 1936. "There's Civil War making right under my nose. I've got to see it and feel it." After seeing, feeling, and writing for two years, he wrote a book that helped bring the Congressional LaFollette Committee, charged with investigating migrant conditions around the country, back to California for a full-scale inspections. Housing for field workers in California improved.

Direct political and social change are the barely hoped for consequence of novels of social protest. In his Foreword to *American Protest Literature*, John Stauffer notes that Kenneth Burke's term "symbolic action" is the aim of all protest literature – a phrase that "implies indeterminacy of meaning, rich ambiguity, and open-endedness in the text, which goes beyond the author's intent." Lightening passes from writer to reader, what Steinbeck called "participation." Of these four California protest novels, only *The Grapes of Wrath* is a novel of social reform in the tradition of Stowe's book, effecting real and immediate change. However, "symbolic action" and reformist zeal were polestars for each.

CHAPTER 11

Dreams, Denial, and Depression-Era Fictions

Jan Goggans

An estimated 350,000 people entered California during the Great Depression, seeking employment and economic relief. However, the literature published during this period suggests that the state wasn't an actual refuge for immigrants. According to John Kenneth Galbraith, the nation's financial collapse in 1929 was "the most devastating in the history of the New York stock market."[1] Investment and construction drastically declined. Soon there were bank closures and home foreclosures. The unemployment rate rose to 25 percent, and underemployment hovered at fifty percent. Blaming the current president, Americans turned to a new candidate, handing Franklin Delano Roosevelt an overwhelming victory over Herbert Hoover in 1932. That winter, before Roosevelt's inauguration, the economy hit a new low.[2]

Studies of the Great Depression often focus on the Dust Bowl population of the South and Midwest, or on the unemployed on the East Coast, where the stock market crashed. California was a long way from New York. The factory closures paralyzing the nation seemed irrelevant to the state's economy. Kevin Starr suggests that it took longer for the Depression "to make itself fully felt" in California's agricultural areas.[3] However, it was here that writers found the most moving examples of economic exhaustion and human despair.

People who came to California were driven by a combination of hope and futility. These competing motivations expressed themselves in two types of works. One looked at the plight of everyday people who came to California believing its promise of fertile farms and abundant employment. The second explored the lure of Hollywood, which promised a different kind of reality. Both promises were illusory, a fact that reveals itself in the literature published during this era. In *The Grapes of Wrath* (1939), the Joads leave Oklahoma for California, which they perceive as a modern-day Eden. However, their car also carries Grandma's corpse, a grim reminder that the state is "an ironic ending point for a misbegotten manifest destiny."[4]

There had been earlier versions of the same story, from the travelogues of the pre-Gold Rush era to the tragic tale of the Donner Party. When George R. Stewart published *Ordeal by Hunger* (1936), his account of the Donners' ill-fated journey, it resonated with Depression-era America. During this decade, the majority of fiction focused on the struggles of contemporary sojourners. James Gregory suggests that there were "two separate streams of migration within California's borders: one from former urban residents to the distressed metropolitan areas of California, the other from distressed rural areas to the fertile valleys of the state."[5]

> We might . . . suspect there were but two signposts on Highway 66, the road that brought most families west. Migrants either stayed on that highway all the way to Los Angeles or turned off at Barstow and followed the still practically unpaved road that led over the Tehachapi Mountain into the valley of the San Joaquin.[6]

There was a similar split in California fiction: accounts of hardworking farmers and their families, and pursuers of the Hollywood dream. The type of narrative appeared not only in *The Grapes of Wrath*, but also in Dorothea Lange and Paul Taylor's *An American Exodus: A Record of Human Erosion* (1939). These two works contributed to the genre of social realism, drawing attention to the everyday conditions of the working classes and the poor. At a time when proletarianism and Communism were both on the rise in America, the books took a political stance, suggesting that once injustice was eradicated society could be rebuilt for the better. Tom Joad insists he will be "Wherever they's a fight so hungry people can eat."[7] He muses that perhaps "a fella ain't got a soul of his own, but on'y a piece of a big one," believing that communal solidarity could improve the plight of the poor and oppressed.

Carey McWilliams' *Factories in the Fields* also appeared in 1939. McWilliams exposed the deplorable industrial conditions in California's fields and the lack of worker safeguards. Like his artistic counterparts, McWilliams was interested in mixing literary narrative with historical documentation. *You Have Seen Their Faces* (1937), a similar enterprise, paired text with photography. Playwright Erskine Caldwell provided quotations for pictures taken by *Life* magazine's Margaret Bourke-White. The book was inspired by the reports and essays of Paul Taylor and Dorothea Lange. Taylor was an influential figure in migrant studies who, in addition to teaching at the University of California–Berkeley, produced significant government work. Lange, a studio photographer in San Francisco, abandoned her practice when the government hired her to document the nation's response to the Depression. Together, they published three government reports in 1935, all of which included Lange's photographs.

Their culminating California project on migrant labor catapulted the photo-text into a new realm. *An American Exodus* builds on an earlier essay Taylor had published in *Survey Graphic*, "Again the Covered Wagon" (1936), using Lange's photographs. Taylor began the essay – "Vast clouds of dust rise and roll across the Great Plains" – by invoking the visual, and he compared the dispersion of soil to the waste of human life. "After the drifting dust clouds drift the people; over the concrete ribbons of highway which lead out in every direction come the refugees. We are witnessing the process of social erosion and a consequent shifting of human sands in a movement which is increasing and may become great."[8]

Taylor and Lange culled their book's title and theme from this earlier essay. They built their book on "a tripod of photographs, captions, and text," illustrating "themes [that] evolved out of long observation in the field."[9] Unlike Bourke-White and Caldwell, who were suspected of making up quotations and taking photographs with a concealed camera, Taylor and Lange stated: "We adhere to the standards of documentary photography as we have conceived them. Quotations which accompany photographs report what the persons photographed said, not what we think might be their unspoken thoughts." A productive scholar since the 1920s, Taylor had been working on labor and agriculture in a number of places for years. Lange was unused to photographing field workers and migrants, and the work she did in California was the first of its kind. Lange believed that the impact of the Depression could only be felt by allowing people to tell their own stories. "Our work has produced the book, but in the situations which we describe are living participants who can speak," Taylor and she wrote in their book. "So far as possible we have let them speak to you face to face." In doing so, Lange and Taylor took social realism to a new level, combining sociological analysis, textual montage, oral testimony, and photographs. Lange and Taylor drew on a number of modernist conventions. To paraphrase the forefather of modernism, Ezra Pound, they "made it new." Enjambing news articles with personal quotes, and juxtaposing contemporary and historical photographs, they created a pastiche that covers the initial western migration and concludes in California. *An American Exodus* makes one thing perfectly clear: for better or worse, all roads lead to "The Last West."

People were still streaming into California when *An American Exodus* was published in November 1939. As Steinbeck revealed in his novel, growers were distributing handbills to migrant workers, advertising jobs that didn't exist. The government programs created by the New Deal failed to account for what was happening in California. Steinbeck's main concern, like Taylor and Lange's, was the state's lack of housing and employment. Steinbeck wrote that "the new barbarians wanted only two things – land and food; and to them the two were one."[10] The Joads' quest to find employment, dignity, and safety in California is based in part on a belief in their own abilities. However, that belief was also supported by widely circulated handbills, which offered "plenty work, an ever'thing nice an' green, an' little white houses, an' oranges growin' aroun'."[11]

The Grapes of Wrath decries the conditions California seemed willing to tolerate. Steinbeck's sympathy for the "forgotten man" stemmed from an earlier political awakening, and the 1930s saw him socializing with supporters of the Cannery and Agricultural Workers' Industrial Union (CAWIU) and the John Reed Club in Carmel. He turned from the psychological tenor of his earliest novels, *Cup of Gold* (1929) and *To a God Unknown* (1933), to the social-realist fiction he produced in *In Dubious Battle* (1936), a fictionalized recreation of California's massive cotton strike of 1933. That book's publication led to a visit from George West, a government camp supporter and the *San Francisco News* editor whose article "Starving Pea Pickers" (1936) came out after he had seen Dorothea Lange's famous photograph, "Migrant Mother." West suggested a series on migrants and Steinbeck agreed to do it.

According to Steinbeck's journals[12] and letters,[13] "The Harvest Gypsies" was the beginning of *The Grapes of Wrath*. However, although the novel was inspired by the photo-realist tradition of the 1930s, it also broke new literary ground. Steinbeck created "inter chapters," which alternate with the story of the Joad family to tell the larger story of the Okie migration. The author believed that the individual was ideally part of a collective community that had embarked on the hazardous journey out West. As Steinbeck explained to Louis Owens, "it means very little to know that a million Chinese are starving unless you know one Chinese who is starving."[14]

Those who didn't go to California looking for work in the fields often had their sights set on Los Angeles. As Gregory notes, during the Depression "most Americans kept going to the movies. And quite often they found there confirming images of California's appeal."[15] Just as one type of literature detailed the harm done by false advertisement and unfair practices in the agricultural industry, so another type of narrative exposed the hollowness of the Hollywood dream.

Hollywood novels weren't necessarily critical of capitalism, as the studios were one of the largest employers and sources of revenue in southern California. The industry enticed such writers as Tennessee Williams and F. Scott Fitzgerald. Others who came here wrote about their own attempts to "make it" in Hollywood. Horace McCoy published two Hollywood satires, *They Shoot Horses, Don't They?* (1935) and *I Should Have Stayed Home* (1938). Robert Syverton, a would-be film director in the first novel, like McCoy originally, came to California hoping to work in the industry. Falling inadvertently into a dance marathon contest, Robert finds himself the willing but unwitting partner of Gloria, who is destined for death from the start.

The majority of the novel takes place on an amusement pier built over the Pacific Ocean. Robert constantly feels the tide rumble beneath his feet, an echo of the dance marathon with its constant, non-stop movement. Couples rotate without cessation, guided by an emcee, supervised by a doctor and nurse, and rewarded occasionally with breaks for rest and food. They endure this punishment because they are desperate to win the $1,000 grand prize.

Structurally, the novel alternates between scenes that show Robert being sentenced for Gloria's murder and those that flash back to the moments leading up to her death. When Robert asks Gloria why she doesn't leave the movie industry, her answer mocks the golden dream and those who believe in it: "Why should I? I may get to be a star overnight. Look at Hepburn and Margaret Sullivan and Josephine Hutchinson."[16] If Gloria can't succeed in Hollywood, her only other wish is to enlist and "get killed in a war." McCoy's character is yet another example of someone who vacillates between hope and despair. The novel exposes Hollywood's theatrical falseness and ultimate emptiness. When the police ask Robert, "Why did you kill her?" he answers, "They shoot horses don't they?"

McCoy returned to Hollywood in his third novel, *I Should Have Stayed Home*. The story follows a hapless young man who opens the novel bemoaning the loss of "Mona," without whom he feels "alone and friendless." Even before the reader knows who the characters are, it is clear that the speaker is not an object of genuine pathos or tragedy. Instead, he has swallowed the Hollywood myth, hook, line, and sinker. The novel's structure reveals Hollywood's faux theatricality. McCoy unveils the plot in three acts, and the characters mimic Hollywood stereotypes. The novel descends into a shrill madness that revolves around the protagonist's stubborn and increasingly hysterical insistence that he cannot go home because everyone there has read his fictional accounts of his success in Hollywood. Like the author, Ralph leaves home because he fantasizes about fame and fortune. Deceiving his family and friends, Ralph transforms from a victim of illusion into a creator and perpetuator of lies.

Ralph nearly embraces his self-deception. Early in the novel, he writes, "I did not want to take a chance on seeing anything that might have made me wish I had stayed home, and this is why I waited for the darkness. That is when Hollywood is really glamorous and mysterious and you are glad you are here, where miracles are happening all around you, where today you are broke and unknown and tomorrow you are rich and famous."[17] Significantly, the deception comes in the form of a woman. McCoy personifies Hollywood as the kind of *femme fatale* who dominates the hard-boiled fiction of California writers Dashiell Hammet, James M. Cain, and Raymond Chandler. McCoy worked with Hammet and Chandler on the pulp magazine *Black Mask*, and his "really glamorous" version of Hollywood is deceptive, deceitful, and deadly.

McCoy earned a medal in World War I and toiled as a sports writer and editor before arriving in Hollywood. Like Hammet, who also served in the war, and Chandler, who returned to California after it ended, McCoy helped forge a decidedly masculine genre of popular literature. These men wrote about women from a male perspective. None of them created realistic depictions of women during the Depression. Because of rising unemployment in the 1930s, women left the workforce and returned home, where they were forced to economize. The lives of migrant women were even more depressing and unstable. No chronically mobile woman could "keep" house. As a song from the Dust Bowl indicates, women who came West carried a different burden than men.

WHY WE COME TO CALIFORNY

Flora Robertson
Shafter, 1940

Here comes the dust-storm
Watch the sky turn blue.
You better git out quick
Or it will smother you.

Here comes the grasshopper,
He comes a-jumpin' high.
He jumps away across the state
An' never bats an eye.

Here comes the river
it sure knows its stuff.
It takes our home and cattle,
An' leaves us feelin' tough.

Californy, Californy,
Here I come too.
With a coffee pot and skillet,
I'm a-comin' to you!

Robertson hopes that she and other women will be able to recreate their former lives in California. Because of their unstable existence, they search out a unifying factor, one that could cross the boundaries of place. Codes of fashion and make-up provide a common reference point, enabling migrant women to transcode their lives into something shared. One California writer who understood this need to belong was poet Wilma McDaniel. Known in later life as the "Okie Poet Laureate," McDaniel accepted her position as a migrant worker, yet at the same time desired to be something more, "whatever a girl desired."

McDaniel noticed how Hollywood revered women: their form, their beauty, and their power. Her writing expresses a woman's need for beauty and glamour, and her emotional pain at being unable to achieve those desires. Working in fields, living an impoverished existence only a few miles away from the screen stars they longed to emulate, California's female field workers and those who wrote of them articulated their relationship with Hollywood very different way than their male counterparts did. Kathy Peiss argues that because of their cultural position, the movies influenced the way both sexes looked at women. Advertisements encouraged women to use cosmetics and fashion as the means by which they could transform themselves into something better. "You can select ten ordinary girls from a factory and by the skillful use of such preparations as Kiija and proper toilet articles . . . you can in a short time make them as attractive and good looking as most an ten wealthy society girls," claimed one advertisement of the era.[18] The Hollywood movie star seemed more within reach of those women who could afford to purchase certain clothes and cosmetics. Lawrence Levine quotes one radio listener in the 1930s: "I like Helen Trent. She is a women [sic] over 35. You never hear of her dying her hair! She uses charm and manners to entice and she does. If she can do it, why can't I?"[19]

Because McDaniel didn't publish her work until she was in her fifties, it is difficult to date much of her poetry. However, one poem is entitled

"Picking Grapes 1937." McDaniel's youthful persona, "new in California" and "magic seventeen," speaks of both the "sweet vineyards" in which she labors and the "one strap held by a safety pin" her position as a field laborer demands. McDaniel migrated with her family when she was a teenager. Her poetry reconciles her work in the fields with her yearning belief in something beyond the scope of her own existence. "Picking Grapes" focuses on her belief that "a girl could be whatever/she desired/the first breath of/Eve in Paradise/the last gasp of Jean Harlow/in Hollywood." That desire is expressed through a female persona that is very different from the *femme fatale*. In spite of her overt sexuality, Harlow is an innocent girl, tender, and unable to survive in the film industry. McDaniel laments Harlow's passing, as well as the death of a dream. In "No Girl Could Ever Be Young Again," the connection is clear. "Jean Harlow died today," the narrator learns. Her "legs turned to rubber/Moroni's peacocks screamed in agony/pieces of sky began to fall." She turns "old at seventeen" because "no girl could ever be young again/bold enough to use platinum for hair."

California has always been the land of dreams. However, during the Depression those dreams became fragile. In 1933, gubernatorial candidate Upton Sinclair wrote a futurist fantasy entitled "I Governor of California, and How I Ended Poverty – A True Story of the Future." Set five years in the future, after Sinclair has served one term as governor, the pamphlet/manifesto/campaign propaganda piece explains how Sinclair was able to end all poverty and change society by implementing EPIC (End Poverty in California). After Sinclair lost the actual election, he published "I Candidate for Governor of California and How I Got Licked" (1933). In 1935, he published *Depression Island*, hoping it would be turned into a film. Alas, Sinclair found his submission met the "usual fate" of his efforts for the screen: "it was 'different'," he writes, "and that is the worst that can be said about movie material."[20] The erstwhile Hollywood screenwriter and governor never saw *Depression Island* made into a movie. However, he did see it performed as a play. Later, he changed the script, devoting the second half of the play to women, as the first half was about men, "and that was unprecedented for the movies."[21] The resultant screenplay (also unfilmed) was influenced less by Marx and more by the Marx Brothers. It featured three brothers who turn the island into a capitalist economy based on coconut production, as well as three feminists who work unsuccessfully to produce an artificial egg. All the characters abandon their efforts in the pursuit of love.

Food-faddist, egotist, and dreamer of impossible dreams, Sinclair would have easily fit into Nathanael West's *The Day of the Locust*. The novel was published in 1939, which is considered the greatest year in the history of American cinema, and it featured such classics as *The Wizard of Oz* and *Gone with the Wind*. *The Day of the Locust* is the quintessential California novel and the ultimate Hollywood satire. It offers a darkly humorous indictment of the entertainment industry, and a despairing portrait of the people on the fringe of that culture who are searching during the Depression for their version of the American dream.

Tod Hacket serves as the novel's protagonist. A former Yale School of Fine Arts student, Tod has been lured to California by a talent scout who gets him a job doing set and costume design. In his spare time he works on his "masterpiece," a mural entitled "The Burning of Los Angeles." The canvas is filled with characters he has come to know, including a dwarf and a would-be Hollywood starlet. They are products of their environment, grotesque and pathetic, filled with rage, bitterness, and seething frustrated desires.

West blurs the line between cinematic performance and reality, exposing the falseness of the Hollywood dream. Abe is a misfit, an outcast – but more importantly, a survivor. Harry Greener, a former vaudevillian unable to make the transition to film, dies halfway through the novel. His daughter, Faye, lacks the qualities necessary to become a successful screen siren and uses her attractiveness to manipulate men. One of her victims is Homer Simpson, a Midwest transplant with "fever[ish] eyes and unruly hands,"[22] whose impotence eventually gives way to anger, precipitating the novel's incendiary climax.

Following a series of increasingly violent set pieces, *The Day of the Locust* concludes with a riot at the red carpet premiere. Homer attacks a young child and the crowd of autograph-seekers suddenly turns into a mob, determined to have their piece of flesh when they can't get Gary Cooper's signature. As he clings to an iron railing with a broken leg, Tod mentally begins to compose his picture. His subjects are the people who discovered when they came to California that the sunshine isn't enough. Their boredom grows, he imagines, as does their sense of betrayal. Tod realizes that these disaffected residents have no other choice but to riot. Cultists, religious zealots, disaster watchers: they are all "poor devils who can only be stirred by the promise of miracles and then only to violence."[23]

Like McCoy, West came to Hollywood to write screenplays. Like Hammet, Chandler, and Cain, he created female characters who embodied the dark side of the American dream. And like F. Scott Fitzgerald, he was fascinated by the movie studios and film impresarios. Jack Hicks writes that West "saw misfits everywhere, people who never quite felt they are getting what was promised to them when they left Des Moines, people who felt, in short, cosmically cheated."[24] Perhaps it was fitting that West and his wife died in a car accident on their way to attend Fitzgerald's funeral.

In 1940, Fitzgerald's Pat Hobby stories were published in *Esquire* magazine in monthly installments. The author began writing a novel originally entitled *The Love of the Last Tycoon* that same year. The unfinished work, published after Fitzgerald's death, would ultimately change the course of the Hollywood novel. The author drew on the eighteen weeks he spent under contract to MGM in 1937, during which time he faced personal and financial turmoil. Unlike West and McCoy, who wrote about industry dreamers and hangers-on with a certain detachment, Fitzgerald wrote from a more personal perspective. The novel reflected his own struggle with alcohol, and his inability to adapt to innovations within the industry and society as a whole. Steinbeck made a similar shift, moving from the kind of social protest novels that focused on politics and government to the more intimate exploration of human behavior in *East of Eden* (1952). California literature began to change as well, allowing for the inclusion of minority voices, as Toshio Mori, Jade Snow Wong, Carlos Bulosan, and Chester Himes arrived on the scene.

During the Great Depression, the state produced some of the most profound social-realist works ever written. Simultaneously, it explored the burgeoning of a Hollywood culture based on artifice, money, and manufactured dreams. Mark Arax has praised California's "vastness of idea, and projection, and execution."[25] If we are a state of "dreamers, believers, builders, and killers," as the title of his book suggests, then we must cohabit, coexist, and even cooperate with each other. The twin poles of despair and desire that mark California literature in the 1930s are still valid reference points in California, the land Theodore Roosevelt once called "west of the west."

Notes

1. John Kenneth Galbraith, *The Great Crash 1929* (Boston: Houghton Mifflin, 1955), 116.
2. Robert McElvaine, *The Great Depression: America, 1929–1941* (New York: Three Rivers Press, 1984), 134.

3. Kevin Starr, *Endangered Dreams: The Great Depression in California* (New York: Oxford University Press, 1994), 121.
4. Jack Hicks et al., eds. *Literature of California,* vol. I (Berkeley: University of California Press, 2000), 394.
5. James Gregory, *American Exodus: The Dust Bowl Migration and Okie Culture in California* (New York: Oxford university Press, 1989), 41.
6. Ibid.
7. John Steinbeck, *The Grapes of Wrath* (New York: Penguin Centennial Edition, 2002), 419.
8. Paul Taylor, "Again the Covered Wagon," *Survey Graphic* 24 (7): 348 (1936).
9. Paul Taylor and Dorothea Lange, *An American Exodus: A Record of Human Erosion* (New York: Reynal and Hitchcock, 1939), 6.
10. Steinbeck, *The Grapes of Wrath*, 233.
11. Ibid., 91.
12. John Steinbeck, *Working Days: The Journals of* The Grapes of Wrath, ed. Robert De Mott (New York: Penguin Books, rpt. 1990).
13. John Steinbeck, *Steinbeck: A Life in Letters*, eds. Elaine Steinbeck and Robert Wallsten (New York: Penguin Books, rpt. 1989).
14. Louis Owens, "The Culpable Joads: Desentimentalizing *The Grapes of Wrath*" *Critical Essays on Steinbeck's* The Grapes of Wrath, ed. John Ditsky (Boston: G. K. Hall, 1989), 108–116.
15. Gregory, 22.
16. Horace McCoy, *They Shoot Horses Don't They?* (London: Serpent's Tail Classic, rpt. 2011), 23.
17. Horace McCoy, *I Should Have Stayed Home* (New York: Signet reprint, 1951), 4.
18. Kathy Peiss, *Hope in a Jar: The Making of America's Beauty Culture* (New York: Metropolitan Press, 1998), 145.
19. Lawrence Levine, *The Unpredictable Past: Explorations in American Cultural History* (New York: Oxford University Press, 1993), 306.
20. Upton Sinclair, *Depression Island* (Pasadena, CA: Published by the author, 1935), 7.
21. Ibid., 8.
22. Nathanael West. *Miss Lonelyhearts & The Day of the Locust* (New York: New Directions Publishing, 1962), 70.
23. Ibid., 184.
24. Jack Hicks et al., 543.
25. Mark Arax, *West of the West: Dreamers, Believers, Builders, and Killers in the Golden State* (New York: Public Affairs, 2009), xii.

CHAPTER 12

Modernism in the Early Twentieth Century
Geneva M. Gano

The fundamental impetus of literary modernism – the creative attempt to capture and reflect the new realities of modern life – emerged across the arts around the turn of the twentieth century. According to intellectual historians, this cultural phenomenon is identified with the upheavals of technological modernity and the social, political, and economic dominance of the western metropolis. Indeed, merely conjuring up the names of cities such as London, Berlin, and Paris brings to mind the dynamic experimentalism of modernist activity in the early twentieth century; as scholars such as Perry Anderson and Raymond Williams have demonstrated, it is difficult to imagine modernism developing outside of an old-world metropolis. Within the United States, New York City came closest to replicating the conditions for modernist activity described by Anderson: it was the nation's historical seat of economic and imperial power and it was established as a center, insofar as the United States had one, for the arts and the intellect. If New York City barely met the necessary social and economic conditions for the emergence of modernist activity, California's major cities, San Francisco and Los Angeles, most certainly did not. They could hardly be described as developed cultural capitals in the European sense, and they were physically removed from the United States' centers of economic and political power. Nonetheless, *avant garde* thinking and creating was happening in the "deprived hinterlands" at continent's end (47).

The established metropolises on the East Coast – most notably New York City – remained crucial nodes for publishing, exhibition, and commercial exchange in the professional lives of California's modern artists during the early twentieth century, even as Los Angeles and San Francisco served as important regional hubs for cultural and social networking, and exchange. In California, however, modernist activity and production was able to develop along a different trajectory than it had developed elsewhere, most notably in its decentralized, suburban character. Crucial to the development of an emergent modernist culture in early twentieth-century California were recent technological innovations, swiftly implemented, in transportation and communications. Both railroad- and automobile-based transportation networks grew especially rapidly alongside urbanization in California, allowing modern artists and writers to circulate and commune physically as they shared new ideas and techniques. Also important were reliable, fast communications systems that enabled artists and writers to carry on active publishing and exhibition programs no matter where they were, arranging the business of their work (which still primarily took place in cities) from afar. A politicized life was also possible in the provinces. One could communicate news of protests and strikes, for instance, in a timely fashion, and even in the so-called hinterlands artists and workers were able to forge mutual supports. These infrastructures ensured that California's modernists were not isolated and provincial in character: they were linked into an international, cosmopolitan modernist network made up of dispersed, loosely cohesive sites of social, intellectual, and artistic exchange.

Newly able to break from the city yet also to grow and maintain careers and friendships, artists, writers, and thinkers could form distinctively modern brave new worlds and worldviews in relatively secluded places including Carmel-by-the-Sea and Edendale. Their connections to other California artists certainly touched those small coteries that had formed in the cities – they shared aspirations with Charles Lummis' Arroyo Set in Los Angeles and the Bohemian Club of San Francisco, both of which were established before the turn of the century. However, by the outbreak of World War I, the writers and artists considered here were not bound absolutely and solely to the metropolis. Indeed, in some sense, the spectacular expansion of California's major cities in the twentieth century actually impeded the direction and growth of modernism as it was developing in these small communities. As suburban sites of modernist activity, these communities looked and operated very differently than those located in the familiar cultural centers of the old world.

Modernism emerged in California as a cosmopolitan phenomenon while remaining grounded in place. The state's little arts communities were "translocal" in the sense that they drew simultaneously from local and transnational sources for aesthetic experimentation, political engagement, and community-building. This essay first defines and distinguishes what "modernism" and modernity looked like in California and why California's modernism looked a bit different than modernism elsewhere, even as it retained key aspects of modernism that developed in cities across the United States and Europe. The rest of this chapter focuses on the literary works produced in the most important of the non-metropolitan sites of California modernism, Carmel and Edendale.

1. California's Unique Modernism

At the dawn of the twentieth century, the United States' literary reputation was as dismal as it had ever been: the entire country was considered a cultural backwater even as the nation was beginning to flex its economic and technological might. In 1904, Gertrude Atherton, one of California's first transnational literary sensations, decried most of American literature – and particularly the dominant realist mode that then defined it – as "the most timid, the most anemic, the most lacking in individualities, the most bourgeois, that any country has ever known." Such denunciations, echoed within the decade by East Coast literary critics such as Van Wyck Brooks, Randolph Burke, and Waldo Frank, announced the defiant spirit of the age and ushered in the experimental, novelty-seeking ethos that would define literary modernism in the United States over the coming half-century. Disenchanted with the examples of their literary forebears as well as with the rapid industrialization and capitalist expansion of the United States, these Young Americans, as they were known, sought to develop along new lines and cast about for new and undiscovered impulses.

It was a point of pride for Atherton, a native Californian, that a marked change in both attitude and literary style came from western writers. At the turn of the century, two young writers from the San Francisco Bay Area, Frank Norris and Jack London, pointedly rejected the genteel realism that defined literature on the East Coast in favor of a gritty, vigorous naturalism. Norris and London frequently made California their fictional settings as they registered the rapid technological, social, and economic changes of modernity that were roiling the state as it surged from frontier region to modern state in a few short generations. These authors recorded tensions that resulted variously from the state's dynamic, multi-ethnic demographic mix of natives and immigrants, its still-emerging intellectual, artistic, and civic institutions, and its voracious, booming economy. Indeed, in California, the transformations wrought by modernity seemed magnified and accelerated: from its beginnings at the turn of the century through World War II, the particular version of literary modernism that emerged in California reflected these changes in distinctive ways.

First, California modernist literature was especially attentive to the political and economic shifts that marked modernity. Frank Norris' incomplete trilogy, "The Epic of the Wheat" [which included *The Octopus* (1901), *The Pit* (1903), and the projected but unwritten novel, *The Wolf*] dealt with struggles between farmers, railroad magnates, stock market speculators, and consumers within a global economic network: a set of concerns that has continued to feel relevant, even urgent, more than 100 years later. Jack London was also attuned to California's rapidly changing economy, and paid particular attention to the struggles of its working classes in his novels *The Iron Heel* (1908), *Martin Eden* (1909), and *The Valley of the Moon* (1913). London, who was internationally famous for his socialist views as well as for his prolific writing career, simultaneously contributed to the West Coast-based *Industrial Worker*, "the voice of revolutionary industrial unionism," and to decidedly middlebrow magazines such as the East Coast-based *Collier's*, *The Atlantic Monthly*, and *The Saturday Evening Post*. London didn't need to look far for his material, but rather drew his characters and scenarios from the hotbed of labor activity up and down the West Coast, from British Columbia to Baja California.

London incorporated regional, transnational labor activity and political upheaval in one of his many remarkable short stories, "The Mexican" (1911). The story, which is set in Los Angeles, traces the tribulations of a group of exiled Mexican revolutionaries who publish a radical newspaper and provide material support to revolutionaries just across the border in Mexico, where the intensive fighting of the Mexican Revolution (1910–20) had just begun. In this story, London alludes to the particularly radical ideals of the *Partido Liberal Mexicano* (PLM), a group that had been instrumental in fomenting the revolution, but which rejected the more moderate proposals of the California-educated Brahmin and newly elected President of Mexico, Francisco I. Madero. Instead, they favored a much more radical vision for Mexico that included the abolition of private property, empowerment of workers, and dissolution of government. London not only had personal knowledge of this radical group, but had thrown his support behind them publicly at a Socialist Party benefit in Los Angeles for Ricardo Flores Magón, its leader and figurehead, in early 1911. London's short story de-emphasizes the role played by Magón and the *junta* of professional revolutionaries who directed the PLM in favor of concentrating on the motivations and heroism of an unknown young worker. "The Mexican" of the title is a young man who had been personally affected by the brutal anti-labor and pro-business regime of former Mexican president Porfirio Díaz: his family and entire village were slaughtered by Mexican troops after a government-supported factory lockout. It is through his personal, physical labor and bodily sacrifice as a prizefighter that he is able to purchase arms for the revolution and prove his commitment to the cause.

Like many literary naturalists who were the immediate precursors to California's modernist movement, London was both a fiction writer and a journalist and much of his work (such as "The Mexican") blended the two by using current events as a springboard for an imaginative scenario or, alternatively, by examining them through a heightened, subjective perspective. Stylistically, the combination of literature with popular journalism typical of London's writing anticipated the much broader blending of "high" and "low" cultural forms that would surface in California literature over the next generation, particularly in subgenres such as California noir and the Hollywood novel. Though stylistically London's dual literary forms informed one another, their content was frequently at odds. A case in point was a series of articles that London agreed to write – for a fabulous price – for *Collier's Magazine* about the U.S. military occupation of the Mexican port of Veracruz during the Mexican Revolution. In these articles, London lionizes the U.S. military's efficiency, precision, and might, contrasting it with a mocking, blatantly racist portrayal of Mexican soldiers as disorganized, lazy peons. His conclusion in these articles – one totally at odds with the values celebrated in "The Mexican" – is that Mexico needs U.S. capitalism (especially its extractive industries) and military protection in order to become a civilized and modern participant in a new world order. Even though Jack London openly acknowledged that his commitment to the socialist cause had been waning over the years, the ideological discrepancy between the pieces – written just four years apart – is confounding. Nonetheless, London's work illustrates the fact that many California writers necessarily wrote for multiple and competing audiences, from Hollywood moviegoers to the U.S. government, or from exclusive, *avant garde* coteries to members of the Communist Party and the Industrial Workers of the World (IWW). This was part of the fabric of modern authorship in California and it informed the direction of California modernism over the decades to come.

Though London's journalism was aimed at a popular press, and perhaps therefore tended to reflect the broadest mainstream, "American values" of the time, much of the journalistic writing produced in California between World War I and World War II was politically progressive, or even radical in nature. These writings ranged from the aggressive "muckraking" work of Lincoln Steffens and Upton Sinclair (both former New Yorkers who had relocated to California) to the more sentimental, personalized portraits popular among those employed by the Federal Writers' Project during the New Deal. Important book-length examples of creative, imaginative writing blended with investigative journalism, aimed at exposing class inequalities, environmental injustice, and racial discrimination include Upton Sinclair's *Oil! A Novel* (1927), Carey McWilliams's *Factories in the Field* (1939), and Carlos Bulosan's *America Is in the Heart* (1943). This tradition of passionate, engaged, activist literary writing continues in contemporary works by California authors such as Mike Davis and Rebecca Solnit.

As the works by the authors mentioned in this essay indicate, the sudden appearance of modern business practices in the state of California reverberated significantly in the lives of its workers. They also had a huge impact on California's landscape and environment, which had been romanticized and celebrated nationally and regionally since before it became a state in 1850. At the turn of the century, the regional magazine *Sunset*, which was published in San Francisco but distributed nationally, promoted tourism in the state primarily by extolling the beauty and sublimity of its natural environment. Over the coming decades, the magazine published well-known writers including John Muir and Mary Austin, who recorded the feelings of ecstasy, renewal, and spiritual rebirth that they felt in the California wilderness. Modernist writing in California extended that tradition, though it also tended to emphasize the negative repercussions of modernity. For these writers, California's natural world was frequently portrayed as an endangered or lost Eden and they drew upon comparisons with the broader Mediterranean that had been made by artists and poets as well as architects, dancers, tourist agencies, and city boosters alike: if tourists wanted to catch a glimpse at California's pristine, unparalleled natural environment, they needed to hurry up and come out West. While the rhetoric of the vanishing wilderness may have been useful in bringing folks to California, in the age of steel and precision, the language of imperiled transcendental beauty opened up California's nature writers to charges of engaging in an escapist and "soft," nostalgic romanticism or what T. J. Jackson Lears has described as "antimodernism."

Most significant among the modern nature writers was Robinson Jeffers. Jeffers' immensely popular narrative poems and lyrics contrasted the awesome beauty of the inhuman natural world with the ugliness of the one humans had made. While his themes were sublime and drew upon his background in religious and philosophical inquiry, his poems are particularly distinctive for their sensitive responses to even the most minute and mundane aspects of the material world. One of Jeffers' better-known short poems, "Granite and Cypress," exemplifies the wild power that he attributed to the inanimate landscape of the Central California Coast, a power he understood as both overwhelming and eternal. In this poem, Jeffers praises the endurance of the granite rocks and cypress trees that are native to the region, noting that they have felt – and will feel in the future – the pounding of many furious tempests. Characteristically, Jeffers here extends his thoughts about the immediately apparent natural world to comment on the human tendency to be "shaken" by such transitory storms, comparing these natural ones to the man-made "tempests" that defined this period: World War I and the impending World War II.

Like his fellow modernists on the East Coast and abroad, Jeffers was transformed as a writer and thinker by the experience of living through war. Though he did not serve in World War I, Jeffers saw it as a horrific, nightmarish abomination for all of mankind. Many of his lyric poems record his attempt to come to terms with war on a philosophical level, and often propose that the equanimity of nature might serve as a model for man. Jeffers' longer narratives, in particular, tend to portray mankind as a tragically limited, self-important mote struggling to survive in an awesome, uncaring universe. As a number of his contemporary reviewers noted, Jeffers' pessimistic vision reverberated with the sense of disillusion that many American modernists, including T. S. Eliot and Ezra Pound, felt just after the Great War. In this sense, Jeffers was a man of his time within a cosmopolitan and interconnected world, and like the poetry of these other high modernists, Jeffers' poems resound with his revulsion at the thought that man's accomplishments on earth – in science, in philosophy, in religion – had come to this. Despite Jeffers' avowed wish to distance himself and his family from what he called the "thickening center" of corruption in the cities, he was typical of California modernists in that he was physically, emotionally, intellectually, and socially embroiled in the modern world.

Promiscuous and fertile interactions between the arts – a key element of modernist activity across the world – were made possible not only by fast and efficient transportation and communications systems, but also by the dissemination of the arts through widely accessible media. Art found its way out of the private collection or museum and into the typical home by way of cheaply produced books, on postcards, through newspapers and magazines, on movie screens, and over the radio, exposing people from a wide range of backgrounds to great works, experimental essays, and foreign styles and techniques. In California, as elsewhere, modern art drew from both "high" and "low" traditions to create something new: dance, theatre, sculpture, photography, comics and cartoons, and popular music all influenced the formal and thematic concerns of literary modernism. Perhaps because California did not have a publicly accessible, longstanding, native tradition of the fine arts – including the literary arts – for the new generation to learn from or react against, a notable portion of California's modernist literature responds particularly to the popular art forms that were emerging and flourishing on the West Coast, from modern journalism and newspaper cartoons to the movies.

In California, the influence of Hollywood on the thematic and formal directions that modernist literature took cannot be underestimated. Entire subgenres of literature specific to California, each with their own thematic and stylistic conventions, emerged from the relationship between the movies and literature during this period; one of the most important of these, California noir, is treated in Chapter 13 in this volume. Just as many California writers plied their trade in newspapers and mass-circulated magazines while simultaneously producing "serious" work for a learned or specialty literary market, a considerable number of established authors also moonlighted for the movies. Meanwhile, not a few considered themselves screenwriters first, and novelists and essayists second, reversing the conventional hierarchy that would place the "high art" of the novelist or poet at the apex of the writerly craft. These may have been nice distinctions: though writing for popular and coterie audiences has been thought of as two very different activities, many authors including William Faulkner, F. Scott Fitzgerald, Aldous Huxley, Nathanael West, Dorothy Parker, Anita Loos, and James Agee straddled the "Great Divide" between high and low art with varying degrees of success. Nevertheless, literary critics have vigorously disputed the ways in which these authors absorbed their experiences in Hollywood and the degree to which it informed their more properly literary endeavors.

The social, political, and cultural conditions of California in the early twentieth century clearly influenced the state's distinct version of modernism. Despite the fact that it developed out of very different conditions than its old-world iterations in Europe, literary modernism in California responded thematically and formally to the new ways of living in and understanding the modern world.

II. California's Suburban Modernism: Carmel-by-the-Sea and Edendale

It may come as something of a revelation that much of California's modernist activity – that is, the lively discussion of new social, political, and aesthetic ideas within a cosmopolitan framework as well as the production of challenging and experimental art across a wide range of forms and genres – occurred not in the urban centers of cities but in suburban locales. The most prominent of these was Carmel-by-the-Sea, which self-consciously considered itself a village. One of the key factors that made Carmel an important site for California's modernist artists and writers was its central physical location between Los Angeles and San Francisco along the California Coast. In its early years, it was accessible by way of the Southern Pacific railroad and, later, by automobile via the rapidly expanding state highway system. Carmel was situated just far enough away from the highways and major cities to be exclusive, but not impossibly removed – particularly for the wealthy and elite classes who had come to know the Monterey Bay, home of the exclusive coastal resort, the Hotel Del Monte, as a site for luxury and leisure. Even in the Depression Era, while much of the state was suffering economically, Carmel-by-the-Sea continued to thrive, attracting vacationing members of established families from all over the West as well as professors, movie stars, and oil tycoons.

At the turn of the century, Carmel-by-the-Sea was intentionally marketed toward artists and creative types; then, as now, arts and culture were good for tourism and the real estate market, and the Carmel Development Company intended to turn a nice profit in bringing the two together. Before the village had officially incorporated in 1916, the Carmel Arts and Crafts Club had been formed and the town's early bohemians, including writers George Sterling, Mary Austin, Jack London, Sinclair Lewis, and photographer Arnold Genthe, were well on their way to becoming well-known attractions for visitors. Described in 1910 in an article in the *Los Angeles Times* as the "most amazing colony in the world," the Carmel bohemians were known as fun-loving artists and thinkers who were vitally connected to the beautiful California Coast and to each other. London's 1913 novel, *Valley of the Moon*, depicts the intimate "rituals" of the "tribe" of bohemians through a mock-ethnographic lens, recording the group at work and at play, singing, dancing, sporting, drinking, and laughing in the edenic setting of the village of Carmel. London's visitors, a working-class couple from Oakland, enjoy the spectacle and camraderie that they find within the group, but they also act as ideal tourists: they buy a picnic lunch in town, go window-shopping for jewelry made of abalone, visit the Carmel Mission and rehearse its history, explore the tide-pools, and watch the sea lions. Though *Valley of the Moon* is fictional, the songs and frolics recorded in the novel became part of local legend, reappearing as fact in travel guides, the village's promotional materials, and local histories such as Franklin Walker's *Seacoast of Bohemia*.

Robinson Jeffers, the poet who made his life and career in Carmel and whose name remains most closely connected with the village, arrived there shortly after the outbreak of World War I in 1914. He had not yet become a national figure, though he had published a slim volume of poetry and was actively working on refining his craft. Besides his marriage to his wife Una, Jeffers credited the "wild rock coast" of the region for the inspiration and direction he took in his long and distinguished career. It was a place that "cried out for tragedy," Jeffers insisted, and the interaction of the poet with the place produced fourteen volumes of narrative, lyric, and dramatic poetry over a fifty-year career.

> From the early years of his career, Jeffers named himself a recluse from modern society and a poet of the timeless – a claim that clung to him in the thirties, as engagement became an important watchword in modern literature and the city became the dominant site of national attention. His residence in the village of Carmel – geographically removed from the corruption and decay that he saw in the cities – was taken for proof of his presumably reactionary attitudes and an elitist reserve that combined to damn his career as the nation marched towards World War II. Yet, as his poems reveal, Jeffers was anything but disengaged with the politics of his time, writing scathing denunciations of Fascists and Nazis as well as the American capitalists and politicians that, in his opinion, had pushed the United States into war. Neither Jeffers nor his favored subjects, the simple, rural folk of the California Coast, could achieve a "flight from history" by way of their geographical seclusion from the centers of western political and economic life; the nightmarish narrative poems Jeffers became best known for revolve around the spectre of war and its emotional and psychological aftermath even in Big Sur. Though they would rather go about their business fishing, farming, mining, and writing poetry, Jeffers's characters find that isolation is an impossible fantasy, and all are profoundly impacted by the reverberations of war. More wishful than actual, Jeffers's self-positioning as an exile from the modern world, then, is refuted in the very subject matter of his work, a fact he acknowledges in a number of his poems. Indeed, his work was so politically engaged with his times that his publisher, Random House, heavily edited and expunged some of the poems Jeffers had included in

the manuscript of *The Double Axe* (1941). It provided a notice at the beginning of the volume explaining that the poetry was the work of the author and in no way reflected the views or ideas of the publisher: a highly unusual disclaimer that indicates just how pointed Jeffers's criticisms of the makers-of-war, on all sides of the conflict, really were. The fallout from the publication, as his publisher feared, was immense, and within a few years Jeffers had plummeted from his place as one of the most popular and successful poets of the century. It is only with the rise of the Environmental Movement in the late twentieth century, and only as a sensitive poet of the natural world, that Jeffers' work has seen a widespread, renewed interest from a popular and scholarly audience alike.

Just as the myth of Jeffers-as-disengaged exile is ironic, so too is the idea of Carmel-as-rural-and-secluded-village. Though superficially rustic – some of the homes were fashioned with anachronistically thatched roofs and village residents repeatedly fought to ward off "improvements" such as paved roads – Carmel was hardly secluded from the modern world. Despite the "Olde English" village vibe, a diverse, distinctly modern and American crowd bustled through the area. To poet Langston Hughes, who first visited Carmel on a reading tour in 1932, Carmel was a little New York: as he wrote to a friend, "it might as well be 42nd Street and Fifth Avenue – so many white folks and Negroes passing through." An examination of the *Carmel Pine Cone*, the local weekly paper, does not quite bear this out, but does indicate a lively social, cultural, and intellectual milieu.

While Jeffers was the best-known author from Carmel during this period, the renown of Langston Hughes would eclipse that of Jeffers as the century progressed. When Hughes first came to Carmel to read his work in 1932, he was arguably the best-known African American poet in the world, and his name was virtually synonymous with urban Harlem, where he had participated in the postwar creative burst of art and culture before moving to the little village on the West Coast. Throughout the 1930s, Hughes traveled the world but Carmel was where he came home to; it was the most stable place he'd lived, anywhere, up to that point in his life. While in Carmel, Hughes wrote poetry at a less feverish pace than in the previous decade, devoting himself instead to developing his craft in the genres of drama, nonfiction prose, and fiction. His first collection of short stories, *The Ways of White Folks* (1934), which was dedicated to his friend and patron in Carmel, Noel Sullivan, was highly praised. He also actively immersed himself in the social, cultural, and political life of the village and greater region, speaking in nearby Pacific Grove on the anniversary of the Emancipation Proclamation, protesting the working conditions of fieldworkers in nearby Salinas, and composing songs for a friend's music recital in the village. With Sullivan, Hughes worked tirelessly to secure the freedom of the Scottsboro Boys, hosting Janie Patterson (mother of defendant Heywood Patterson) during her national speaking tour and putting together a highly successful benefit auction that included donations from Ezra Pound, G. B. Shaw, Bertrand Russell, Claude McKay, and many others.

Hughes, as a well-known poet of the Harlem Renaissance, was known for his dynamic lyric poems that typically expressed racial pride, celebrated a rich African heritage, and recognized the humanity and poetry in the lives of what his former friend and collaborator from Harlem, Zora Neale Hurston, called "the Negro furthest down." The prosaic, politicized work that he produced in Carmel was quite different from his Harlem poetry, and is still not well known to either his wide popular audience or scholars. Indeed, much of the writing he produced in this period of his life has not been fully recovered, examined, and appreciated and remains out of print or unpublished today. The politically radical nature of his Carmel writings has undoubtedly contributed to this fact. The years in which Hughes used Carmel as a home base were those that coincided with his closest connection to the Communist Party, including during his tenure as the president of the communist-affiliated League of Struggle for Negro Rights (formerly the American Negro Labor Congress) in 1934. While it may seem almost ironic that Hughes's most pointed political activism came to a head in rural Carmel and not urban Harlem, Carmel was recognized nationally as a particularly dense hotbed of radicalism during this period; many of Hughes's neighbors and friends from Carmel, including Jeffers and Sullivan, were investigated by the FBI and some of these were questioned, in the fifties, by the House Un-American Committee (HUAC). Locally, the Carmel John Reed Club (which had fewer than two dozen members), sponsored literary and artistic events and, on at least one occasion, sent a few carloads of supporters to help agitate for farmworkers' rights. This act drew forth explicit, violent threats from an unamused citizenry that had – in this same period – formed much larger American Legion Chapters throughout the Monterey Bay area. "Red" Ella Winter, who co-authored a play with Hughes about the 1933 San Joaquin Valley cotton pickers' strike ("Harvest" was never produced), frequently was singled out in the local paper as a communist and a public nuisance but it was Hughes who was run out of town in the midst of the town's peak anti-communist hysteria in the summer of 1934. At the end of the decade, between and after travels to the Soviet Union, Japan, China, Mexico,

France, Spain, and the United Kingdom, as well as to other parts of the United States, Hughes intermittently returned to "*mi casa*" at Sullivan's Hollow Hills Farm in Carmel – his home whenever he wanted it – until he bought a home in Harlem in 1947.

Between the wars, the artists and writers of Carmel maintained the irreverence and radicalism of their bohemian predecessors, even as the times changed. In addition to Jeffers, the colony counted among its core the muckraking journalist Lincoln Steffens and his wife Ella Winter; photographer Edward Weston; architect Charles Sumner Greene; art patrons and socialites Noel Sullivan, Mabel Dodge Luhan and Pauline Schindler; novelists Harry Leon Wilson and Alice MacGowan; and poets Charles Erskine Scott Wood, Sara Bard Field, and on-and-off again, Langston Hughes. This congenial though always shifting group gathered periodically for social, cultural, and political events in the surprisingly busy village as well as for informal gatherings where they drank wine and discussed the Spanish Civil War, Nietzchean philosophy, and the new Disney films. They raised money for the Scottsboro Trials, debated the local library policies, and hosted friends from all over the world, from singer Roland Hayes to movie stars Greta Garbo and Charlie Chaplin. They took their aesthetic cues not only from the cubists in Paris but also from the muralists in Mexico; they venerated home-grown primitives including the local Native Americans and the working-class Mexican and Filipino farmlaborers; and they followed Yeats and Jung (but not Aimee Semple Macpherson, their Carmel neighbor) into the world of the spirit. The diverse activities and interests of Carmel's arts community indicate the wide-ranging character of modernism as practiced in the village: in such a small community, poets, photographers, actors, and musicians not only supported and critiqued one another's aesthetic endeavors but they also attended birthday parties, went hiking and picnicking in Big Sur, contributed articles to the alternative weekly paper, *The Carmelite*, and relayed neighborly gossip. This is to point out that the social formations of modernism were crucial to its aesthetic and political development in "minor," non-metropolitan sites such as Carmel. In such locales, women were recognized for the important roles they played in the development of a communal arts culture as hostesses, editors, muses, and nurturers but they also had unique opportunities to develop and practice their talents as artists in their own rights. Though the women who formed the backbone of Carmel's arts community did not become nationally or internationally recognized for their achievements in the ways that their male counterparts did, they were well respected within their circles and understood to be crucial drivers of modernism at the local level.

One might think that the wealth that made the village of Carmel possible and enabled its sustenance and growth would have doomed it as an artists' colony. George Sterling, Carmel's original "king of Bohemia," reportedly maintained that the two most essential elements of bohemianism were a "devotion or addiction to one or more of the Seven Arts" and poverty. By these standards, Carmel never truly had a bohemian community, even in the early days. It tended to be the artists who already had a private income and who were well connected to and supported by the wealthy, who could make a living in Carmel. As Carmel-by-the-Sea developed over the first part of the century and the town's survival depended on its wealthiest residents and visitors, this was increasingly true. Even as they lived comparatively meagerly, the artists and writers of Carmel maintained their bohemian identity primarily through cultural rather than economic means, through their art and their sense of themselves as an unconventional community.

In Southern California, the artist's community at Edendale developed along somewhat similar lines as the one at Carmel-by-the Sea during the first half of the twentieth century. A hilly, farm-dotted community located northwest of downtown Los Angeles, Edendale had attracted a distinctive, bohemian community of communists, artists, and immigrants in the years preceding World War I. As the movie industry grew dramatically over the next decades, Edendale attracted writers, artists, and performers to the region from all corners of the earth who thrived, like the Carmelites, because of their geographical proximity to wealth and potential patrons. Even while Edendale retained its rural feel, its survival and development was tied directly to the city: it was nestled so closely to the rapidly expanding city of Los Angeles that the metropolis ultimately surrounded and absorbed it.

Before World War I, Edendale was something of an immigrant farming community with a sizable proportion of residents from Eastern Europe. It was particularly tolerant of the city's radicals, including the anarchists, union activists, and communists who were active in the city's red-hot class war that reached a peak in the 1910 bombing of the *Los Angeles Times*. This perhaps made the community an ideal site for the commune established in 1914 by brothers Enrique and Ricardo Flores Magón. Inspired by their readings of nineteenth-century anarcho-communist Peter Kropotkin, the daily lives of the Magonistas involved small-scale farming as well as a blend of cultural and political work: they continued to issue Magón's anarchist magazine, *Regeneración*, and, in 1916, involved the greater community in the performance of a revolutionary drama, "Land and Liberty." Though their attention was focused largely on the bloody Mexican Revolution raging across the border, they were in communication with and received support from U.S.-based anarchists including Alexander Berkman, who had moved to San Francisco where he was publishing *The Blast*, and Emma Goldman, who regularly spoke in Los Angeles during this period. They were also allied with the Los Angeles International Workers of the World and the Los Angeles Radical Club, whose shared political affinities with the Magonistas crossed national and linguistic lines.

Edendale was in transition during the 1910s, as the area was directly affected by the money and madness of a frontier-era boom town. The movies had come to Los Angeles and had planted themselves in Edendale before migrating further west to Hollywood in the 1920s. Edendale was also geographically located at the center of an explosive expansion in the region's fine arts. The Art Students' League of Los Angeles, founded in 1906, was thriving downtown as a home for new directions in art. The Los Angeles County Museum of History, Science, and Art opened its doors in Exposition Park near the University of Southern California in 1913. The Camera Pictorialists of Los Angeles, a group that included Edward Weston, Margarethe Mather, and Louis Fleckenstien, formed in 1914; the modern dance school, Denishawn, first opened its doors downtown in 1916 before moving to Westlake Park. By the end of the decade, oil heiress Aline Barnsdall had commissioned Frank Lloyd Wright to build an artists' compound on the property she had purchased for that purpose at the western edge of Edendale. Barnsdall's Hollyhock House was designed to showcase the dramatic arts in particular, but was also intended as a home for an intentional community dedicated to the integration of the arts more broadly. It would be the first Los Angeles home for modern art collectors Walter and Louise Arensberg in the early 1920s, and headquarters for the California Art Club from 1927 until 1942.

Situated between Hollywood and downtown, north of the University of Southern California and south of Occidental College – sites that offered employment for intellectuals and artists – Edendale was geographically positioned to become a significant residential center for Los Angeles's emerging, spatially diffuse arts community. Edendale resident and bookseller Jacob Zeitlin was a key member of this community, bringing together writers, artists, musicians, and others for discussions, exhibitions, late-night pasta feeds, and legendary bacchanals. Investigative reporter and essayist Carey McWilliams was one of

Zeitlin's neighbors and fast friends, as were scholar and librarian Lawrence Clark Powell, writer and book designer Merle Armitage, and printers and book artists Ward Ritchie and Paul Landacre. All were involved in producing a short-lived little magazine centered on literature and the arts, *Opinion* (1929–30). Zeitlin's circle also included the photographer Edward Weston, who had built up a brisk photography business in a studio just northeast of Griffith Park in the 1910s and 1920s, and architect Lloyd Wright, who designed the interior of Zeitlin's bookshop in downtown Los Angeles near Bunker Hill. Zeitlin's wider circle of friends and associates also included art dealer Galka Scheyer, architects Rudolph Schindler and Richard Neutra, woodcut artist Rockwell Kent, novelist Aldous Huxley, composer John Cage, and a number of artists and writers involved in the nearby Disney studios, the Young People's Socialist League, and regional WPA works.

Just as the nation was gearing up for World War II, McWilliams and other Edendale residents and activists became involved in the Sleepy Lagoon Defense Committee, a group that formed in the wake of the miscarriage of justice during the 1942 murder trials of twenty-four Mexican American youths, many of whom lived in the far eastern portion of Edendale in a predominantly working-class Mexican American neighborhood, known as Palo Verde. The ad-hoc defense group transformed into a broad and powerful coalition formed through neighborly and political alliances between members of the American Civil Liberties Union, leftist labor groups including the Congress of Industrial Organizations (CIO), the Communist Party, *El Congreso Nacional del Pueblo de Habla Española* (National Congress of Spanish-Speaking Peoples), and an interrelated network of community residents and family members. Josefina Fierro de Bright, an orator, activist, and leader of *El Congreso*, had direct political ties to the Mexican anarcho-communists who had settled in Edendale during the Mexican Revolution, as she had been raised as a Magonista. She also had direct ties to the Hollywood left through her husband, screenwriter John Bright. Both communities would be crucial to the success of the defense, which followed the eclectic and coalition-based model of activism used in the efforts to free the Scottsboro Boys in Alabama. They hosted fundraising dinners in their homes, publicized the injustices in many formats, reached out to writers and editors of local Spanish- and English-language newspapers, and capitalized on the leftward tilt of the nation in this period to encourage stars such as Anthony Quinn, Rita Hayworth, Orson Welles, and Ira Gershwin to speak out in support of the defense.

As head of the Sleepy Lagoon Defense Committee in 1943, McWilliams enlisted fellow writers to produce two pamphlets that helped to foment public sentiment in favor of the defendants, *The Sleepy Lagoon Case* and *The Sleepy Lagoon Mystery*. Published in both English and Spanish and distributed locally, regionally, nationally, and internationally, these pamphlets capitalized on the recent spate of publications by writer-activists from California including Monterey Bay resident John Steinbeck and LA-based Carlos Bulosan as well as McWilliams himself. Throughout the coming decades, McWilliams would continue to understand his literary career to be deeply entwined with his anti-racist political and social views; he was especially vocal in agitating against the internment of Japanese Americans during World War II.

By this time, Edendale had begun to disintegrate as a community. The growth of the Los Angeles real estate market and the increasing importance of Hollywood's movie industry squeezed out the semi-rural homes and small farms that had given the neighborhood its character. The Pacific Electric's "red car" service to Edendale, which had linked it to downtown Los Angeles, closed in 1940, though rail service through the area would continue for another fifteen years. In this period, many of the working-class residents that had formed the core of Edendale had been squeezed out or forcibly removed to make way for urban renewal projects, commercial development, and the modern urban freeway infrastructure for which Los Angeles would become infamous.

The little arts communities at Carmel and Edendale were distinctly suburban, rather than metropolitan. What's more, the radical worldviews and experimental art that their members cultivated were actively nurtured by the experience of living in close contact with other likeminded people: that is, in proximate, "beloved communities" such as the ones described by American philosopher Josiah Royce, where groups of people are unified in feeling, thought, and will. On the ground, within the communities themselves, this utopian ideal was aspirational rather than actual, but the face-to-face experience of community was understood by the members of these communities to be a crucial element in the achievement of a modern perspective and the creation of modernist art. In California, these suburban enclaves were important hotbeds of modernist activity across the arts, engaging both long-term residents and short-term visitors in the political, social, and aesthetic concerns of the day.

CHAPTER 13

The Hard-Boiled California Novel

William Marling

The rise of the California detective novel between 1920 and 1955 often seems dramatic, as though the state's progressive history and pastel landscapes had suddenly been discovered to conceal "mean streets" awash in violent crime. But there was no more crime in California than elsewhere. More sober analysis might point out the rise of Hollywood film and its need for material. But that industry was just one part of California's economic and cultural surge. The nation was beginning to suspect that California portended the future, so it became the setting for many popular narratives.

Though Dashiell Hammett, James M. Cain, and Raymond Chandler are the most famous hard-boiled writers in this place and period, around them was a talented cohort: Horace McCoy, W. T. Ballard, Erle Stanley Gardner and Ross Macdonald, among others. Their writings were distinct from works by their East Coast counterparts, who focused on an older style of crime committed by gangsters such as Al Capone, Bonnie and Clyde Barker, and Pretty Boy Floyd. The Pinkerton detectives on whom Hammett modeled his hero were "scabs" in labor disputes and "rats" in domestic predicaments. *Black Mask* promoted the Pinkerton prototype, influencing numerous subsequent pulp fiction writers. The new "California hardboiled" style might not have lasted without the innovative plots of Cain and the high literary style provided by Chandler.

Hammett moved to San Francisco in 1921, fifteen years after a catastrophic earthquake rocked the city's foundations. By now San Francisco was a major western metropolis, where immigration, mining, agriculture, exports, industry, and culture converged. The city was the terminus of the transcontinental railroad. It had an opera house, an art museum, several newspapers and radio stations, and cable cars. San Francisco was much more cosmopolitan than its southern rival, Los Angeles.

Hammett was not raised on Edgar Allen Poe or Arthur Conan Doyle. He worked as a Pinkerton detective agent in the mining battles of the mountain states until he was stricken with tuberculosis. After he recovered, he moved to San Francisco with his new wife and family. Here, the frail twenty-six-year-old found part-time employment with the Pinkerton agency. Even that, said his wife, took a toll. Soon he quit his job and began writing advertising copy and reviewing books to earn a living.

Later, Hammett claimed to have worked on four celebrated cases as a Pinkerton agent. Whether true or not, each case captured his imagination as a writer. When silent movie star Fatty Arbuckle was tried in San Francisco for the rape and homicide of actress Virginia Rappe, Hammett was among the Pinkertons assigned to protect him. He wrote that the whole imbroglio was a frame-up, arranged by the Hearst newspapers to embarrass Los Angeles. But Hammett disliked Arbuckle, who was proved innocent. He used the portly Arbuckle as a template for his villains, including Gutman in *The Maltese Falcon* (1929). Hammett also claimed a role in the arrest of Nicky Arnstein, whose theft of $1.5 million in bonds from a New York brokerage company was a modern financial crime of the sort dramatized by F. Scott Fitzgerald in *The Great Gatsby* (1925). In addition, Hammett contended that he had fallen through a decaying porch roof in Vallejo while eavesdropping on bank robber Gloomy Gus Schaefer, an archetypal eastern criminal – highlighting Hammett's theories about chance and causality, which often played roles in his characters' lives. Finally, Hammett said that he once found a fortune in English gold sovereigns hidden in a smokestack of a freighter. He transformed the money into the Maltese falcon and the freighter into a ship renamed *La Paloma*.

When his tuberculosis returned, Hammett moved to a rented room to avoid infecting his family. During his convalescence, he attended Munson's Business College, where he took courses in stenography, newspaper writing, and advertising. Subsequently he was hired by jeweler Albert Samuels and began writing advertising copy such as this:

> It's nothing unusual to find a man of position and excellent standing who is temporarily short of cash. The average man figures a long time ahead on the spending of his income. Besides his fixed expenses of rent, meals, clothing and recreation, he usually carries some kind of an investment, a savings account or life insurance, that pretty well takes care of all he earns. So when he finds himself engaged he may not have the cash necessary for the ring. We try to take care of men like that.[1]

It is tempting to think of this "man" as Hammett's ideal reader, an urban office-worker a bit baffled by life's financial challenges. The publisher of the *Oakland Post Enquirer* wrote that Hammett's copy was the best advertising his paper had ever carried.

Hammett also read *Black Mask* magazine, published in New York by H. L. Mencken and George Jean Nathan. They used it to fund their literary magazine *Smart Set*, to which Hammett sent his first short story, "The Parthian Shot" (October 1922). Hammett also began writing for *Black Mask* on a regular basis, devoting more time to his fiction than to his copywriting. In 1923, he published "Crooked Souls," "It," "The Second-Story Angel," and "Bodies Piled Up" – all set in California.

Hammett wrote seven stories for *Black Mask* in 1925. Two of those, "Dead Yellow Women" and "The Gutting of Couffignal," show him reworking his California short stories into longer narratives. The next year the Hammetts had a second daughter, and the author's health seemed to recover. But in July Hammett was found unconscious at Samuels Jewelry, suffering from hemorrhaged lungs. There was a publication gap of almost a year before "The Big Knockover" appeared in February 1927. A novella ("$106,000 Blood Money") followed in May, as well as four stories that would become the novel *Red Harvest* (1929). By spring 1927, Hammett felt well enough to return to advertising work, though by now he was living apart from his wife and daughters. In 1928, he sent an unsolicited manuscript of *Red Harvest* to Alfred Knopf in New York. The publisher's wife discovered the novel in a "slush pile," liked it, and suggested revisions, which Hammett completed in eight days.[2]

Red Harvest is a California novel at one remove. The Continental Op (modeled on an ideal Pinkerton agent) investigates scandal in the copper mines and newspapers of Montana, which were sources of the Hearst family fortune. The fictional Montana town is controlled by ethnic mafias like those in San Francisco. In its cross-cutting, car chases, and shootouts, the novel is paced like a Keystone Comedy, though some scholars think it is also a cautionary tale about capitalism. Its up-tempo action and humorously terse dialogue made *Red Harvest* very different from any crime writing set in the East.

The Dain Curse (1929) was Hammett's first novel set in San Francisco, and also the first to explore California's religious cults. The Op is called into the Leggett household to investigate missing diamonds, but he ends up solving a series of murders caused by a dynastic family curse. Gabrielle Dain, a drug addict, belongs to the "Temple of the Holy Grail," and the Op has to track her from San Francisco to Reno to Quesada (modeled on Monterey) before he can solve all the murders. No California writer had put a religious cult at the center of a detective novel before, or ranged over so much ground in solving his case. However, the cult was disappointingly anglophile, drawing on material about druids and Grail tales.

The Maltese Falcon (1930), set in San Francisco, was Hammett's *tour de force*. Though resembling the Continental Op, hero Sam Spade was more modern, predatory, and self-reliant. His efficiency apartment, his lack of a car – he walks and takes taxis – and his network of contacts presage the modern office-worker in an appealingly dangerous way. The plot develops through telephone calls and newspaper items, rather than the older stock devices of tips and coincidences. Drama happens at specific locations, including Stockton Street and the Bellevue Hotel at Geary and Taylor ("Hotel Belvedere" in the novel). Spade gets off the Geary St. streetcar and walks up the hill toward Hammett's Nob Hill apartment at 891 Post. He goes to docks in North Beach and on a wild goose chase to Burlingame. This was the first detective novel to hew so closely to the real San Francisco.

The plot was also more realistic, as Spade exposes the romantic myths of Casper Gutman (an avatar of Arbuckle) and Brigid O'Shaughnessy, revealing them to be as money-hungry as the Crusaders whose mythic falcon they seek. Spade plays them against each other, just as San Francisco politicians manipulated the city's ethnic populations for their own purposes. In the final scenes, much to the disgust of his secretary Effie Perrine, Spade turns in his paramour Brigid. This is also new. The message is that the modern worker has to be ruthlessly self-interested, and Spade sets the bar extremely high. He understands the momentum of modernity, from the legal-police apparatus that confronts him to the warren-like streets he walks. Not only did this novel establish key features of the genre: the secretary as sidekick, good guy/bad guy cops, and homophobic portrayals of men who seemed effeminate compared to the "tough guy" protagonist. *The Maltese Falcon* created San Francisco as a detective novel imaginary. That setting can be embellished by fog, nighttime or romance. However, the detective must be a vector of modernity who cuts through them.

Only nine years after he arrived in San Francisco, Hammett returned to the East Coast. He left his family in LA and went to New York with his new love, Nell Martin. *The Maltese Falcon* achieved a renown that made Hammett the toast of Manhattan. Dorothy Parker, who "discovered" him in *The New Yorker*, wrote that "I went mooning about in a daze of love [for Spade] such as I had not known for any character in literature since I encountered Sir Launcelot."[3] The tall, sartorial Hammett, his prematurely silvered hair combed back in a pompadour, became a literary celebrity just as the stock market crashed. Warner Brothers bought the rights to *Red Harvest* in 1929 and Hammett signed a contract to write for Paramount. First, however, he finished his most celebrated hard-boiled work ever, *The Glass Key* (1931), which was set on the East Coast. Ned Beaumont, the hero, is a political fixer who works for Paul Madwig, boss of a construction company. He suffers beatings and denigrations, ponders his bad luck, and serves as a harbinger of the Great Depression.

Hammett then moved to Los Angeles to become a script writer. He also began an affair with Lillian Hellman, later a famous playwright. They lived well, shuttling between Los Angeles and New York, where Hammett finished a new book, *The Thin Man*, in 1934. The story of Nick and Nora Charles was set in New York, but was partly autobiographical. Nick is a *bon vivant*, his wife a charmer like Hellman. The dialogue consists of high-speed repartee with sexual overtones. The novel had all the makings of a first-rate Hollywood detective story, screwball romance, and high-society comedy. It was adapted into a successful film starring William Powell and Myrna Loy in 1934, the first in a series based on Hammett's original novel. The author received copious royalties, which he spent in a typically liberal fashion.

Over the next decade Hammett wrote little and drank much. Royalties from his early stories and from Sam Spade – who starred in comic books, radio shows, and three films – enabled him to live flamboyantly. Hammett came to Los Angeles to sign contracts, and after 1938 to play a role in the Screenwriters Guild, which led to a fight against MGM, one of his former employers. In 1941, John Huston filmed *The Maltese Falcon*, starring Humphrey Bogart. At the time, Hammett was trying to join the army because he wanted to fight Fascism. He was unable to do so because of his health. After the war, still a committed leftist, he lived outside New York on Hellman's estate. In 1951, he was sent to prison for refusing to testify in Federal court about the Civil Rights Congress, of which he was a trustee. He had a heart attack in 1955, and he died on January 10, 1961.

Before coming to California in 1931, James M. Cain was a teacher, insurance salesman, reporter, and editorial writer in the East. After writing for the Baltimore newspapers and serving in World War I, he found a job at the *New York World*, where he wrote "color" pieces for Walter Lippmann's editorial page. One of the sensational news stories at the time was the 1927–28 New York trial and execution of Ruth Snyder and her lover Judd Gray, who were convicted for murdering Snyder's husband. Ruth was a striking blond who supposedly convinced corset-salesman Gray to bludgeon her husband with a sash weight and then to strangle him with picture wire. A circulation war among East Coast newspapers kept the story on the front page for eight months, and a sensational photo of Ruth Snyder's electrocution in the *New York Daily News* in 1928 shocked the nation.

Cain didn't use this material until 1931, when he left New York after the stock market crash to become a Hollywood screenwriter. Cain, like Hammett, was never a great scriptwriter. Released after his first studio contract, he drove around southern California looking for magazine articles to write. In his early pieces, Cain praised the friendly Californians he encountered, the state's excellent schools, and its extensive roadway system. However, he couldn't get over the lack of heavy industry that he knew back East. How did everyone manage to live?

On one of his drives he discovered Gay's Lion Farm in El Monte. The business supplied animals to the Hollywood studios. Three lions had killed a manager there in 1928. Nearby was an ambitious young couple running a gas station. Cain imagined them engaged in a steamy affair, and combined these settings in "The Baby in the Icebox" (1933). In the story, the husband lets a five-hundred-pound cat into the house to kill his wife, who puts the baby in an unplugged freezer for safety. The parents both die, but the baby survives. It was arguably the most sensational, and suspenseful, California crime fiction ever published to that point.

Encouraged by Knopf, Cain then began a novel called *Bar-B-Que*. Seemingly innocent and pristine, California was the perfect ironic setting in which to retell the Snyder-Gray murder. The author believed that the public fascination with this story reflected the nation's disgust with the pre-Depression hedonism of the 1920s. Cain made Gray a hobo, acknowledging California's anxieties about the Okies who were pouring into the state. It took him six months to write the story of Frank Chambers, a drifter who finds work at the roadside gas station and sandwich joint of Greek immigrant Nick Papadakis and his sexy wife Cora in *The Postman Always Rings Twice* (1934). There were direct parallels between the Snyder-Gray case and the account of Frank and Cora's torrid relationship, their initial botched effort to murder Nick, their success in faking an auto accident, and Cora's confession under pressure.

Cain used the Santa Monica and San Gabriel Mountains as inspirations for his setting. However, his story stalled once Cora got to jail. Then Cain remembered either his job as a teen selling insurance or the "double indemnity" details of the Snyder-Gray trial. The economy emerging from the Depression was led by white-collar industries like insurance and by public works like Hoover Dam. Cain invented a defense lawyer named

Katz, whose rivalry with the district attorney leads him to trick the prosecution into a squeeze play between three insurance companies. Ideologically, this shows that "justice" is pure economic efficiency; since it is cheaper for the companies, they reverse their testimony.

Once the lovers are freed, Cora urges Frank to help her to "make something" of the restaurant, adding refrigerated draft beer and Tivoli lights and "radio music" under the trees. Indeed, business picks up. Technology and better merchandising lead to a temporary reversal of the characters' fortunes. However, Cora can still put Frank in jail for murder, a threat that she saves until she tells him she is pregnant. Frank kills Cora by staging a car accident. *Postman* was "the first novel to hit for what might be called the grand slam of the book trade," wrote biographer Roy Hoopes. It was a success in hardcover, paperback, and syndication; as a play and as a movie. It was so tough that the *New York Times*' reviewer called it a six-minute egg.[4]

In 1936, Cain wrote an eight-part serial for *Liberty* magazine. The insurance industry also played a role in *Double Indemnity*, which had a southern California setting. Sexual desire leads insurance agent Walter Huff to accept Phyllis Nirdlinger's proposition that they murder her husband. They stage a statistically improbable accident, allegedly having the husband fall off a slow-moving train. Huff's desires constantly change. The agent wants Phyllis, but he also wants to outwit the system, to have her daughter Lola, to save himself, and to kill Phyllis in the end. Huff was an appealing film noir hero because he was an existential rebel in a modern consumer society, the first confessional white-collar criminal in an American crime novel. The emerging post-Depression economy needed to limit his kind of aggressive rationality. His confession, followed by his death, made an example of Huff. He was the darkest character California had yet produced.

Cain's last major novel was *Mildred Pierce* (1941). Like *Double Indemnity*, this tale of economic ambition and manipulation was set in Glendale in the 1930s. The novel opens with Mildred's unemployed husband meticulously watering his lawn and tending his fruit trees. Mildred soon leaves him, setting out to support herself and her children during the Depression, first as a waitress, then as a restaurateur and pie manufacturer. However, her pretentious daughter Veda is embarrassed by her mother's ambition. When she meets the unscrupulous Monty, the pair consume Mildred's hard-won gains. Like so many small businesses in Depression California, Mildred's enterprise crashes. Cain keyed its demise to the New Year's Day flood of 1934 in La Crescenta, where fourteen inches of rain fell in two days. In reality, the flood was devastating. However, it became a major set-piece in the novel, illustrating Mildred's valiant attempts to overcome adversity.

Historic settings and plots dominated Cain's work for the next two decades. Although he published another nine books, none of them can be termed "hard-boiled." Cain moved to Hyattsville, Maryland, with his third wife, where they spent the rest of their lives. He died on October 27, 1977.

Arriving in California in 1912, Raymond Chandler also acquired a reputation as one of the leading writers in the genre. After going to school in England, Chandler came to the United States to meet some distant relatives. He ended up settling in the progressive "Arroyo Culture" near Pasadena, living among Anglo Americans who were influenced by Indian and Spanish traditions. Chandler set aside the literary ambitions he had cultivated in London, and began working as an accountant at a dairy. He fell in love with Cissy Pascal, a married woman who was eighteen years his senior, and joined the Canadian Expeditionary Force during World War I. At the battle of Vimy Ridge everyone in his unit was killed except Chandler. The author was so badly concussed that he had to be evacuated from the front.

On his return Chandler tried writing for the *Los Angeles Daily Express*. When his mother came from England to live with him, he found a job at the Dabney Oil Syndicate. He was still in love with Cissy Pascal. When they divorced, he rented an apartment for her in Hermosa Beach, and lived in nearby Redondo Beach with his mother. They married after his mother died in 1924.

The oil business was gamble and grab in the 1920s. Chandler knew con men like promoter C. C. Julian, sudden millionaires like Edward Doheny, pickpockets, Zoot-suiters, hookers, and cops on the take. Though Chandler ran the office for Dabney, where he was known for dictating flawless letters and rooting out inefficiency, he was often in the fields. Soon he developed a problem with alcohol. "At the annual oil and gas banquets of 1,000 rollicking oil men at the Biltmore," said one Dabney executive, "Chandler was a shadowy figure, stinko drunk and hovering in the wings with a bevy of showgirls, a nuisance." He disappeared from work, took up secretaries, and threatened suicide. He was eventually fired in 1932, during the cellar of the Depression.

Fleeing to Seattle, he lived with army buddies and wandered up and down the Pacific Coast, reading pulp magazines. "This was in the great days of *Black Mask* and it struck me that some of the writing was pretty forceful and honest, even though it had its crude aspect. I decided that this might be a good way to try to learn to write fiction and get paid a small amount of money at the same time."[5] He returned to Cissy, who stood by him and became his inspiration. Never a fast writer, Chandler spent five months producing his first story, "Blackmailers Don't Shoot." The author suggested that blackmail was a crime against a person's reputation, something that Hollywood considered important.

Los Angeles was undergoing significant changes at the time. Between 1912 and 1932, the population increased by almost two million people. The stately streets of Hancock Park, where the founding aristocracy lived, were growing frayed. The first immigrants had been white Midwesterners, often retired farmers (like the Iowans whom Chandler often caricatured), but later immigrants were Dust Bowl fugitives, or Chinese and Mexicans and blacks. In 1909, Los Angeles had more churches per capita than any other major U.S. city. However, by 1930, celebrity had become the new religion. The movie industry attracted starlets, cowboy crooners, and eastern mafiosi. The orchards disappeared under tract housing and highways replaced village lanes. These changes were wrenching for Chandler, who in his stories contrasted the Malibu coast and the inland orchards with the seamy side of Bunker Hill, the central district, and Venice Beach.

Knowing he needed to write a book, Chandler combined the plots of "Killer in the Rain" and "The Curtain," his fourth and tenth stories for *Black Mask*, and produced *The Big Sleep*. He sent the novel to Knopf, the same publisher used by Hammett and Cain. The novel sold well, and Hollywood purchased the film rights. The novel introduced Philip Marlowe, the genre's most influential series detective. The term "hard-boiled" developed a new meaning based on Marlowe's wise-cracking style and his capacity to endure physical punishment. Chandler's ironic tone and extraordinary metaphors focused readers on individual scenes, which the author excelled at writing. Many of these evoke southern California in the late 1930s so vividly that the setting seems to become part of the plot.

The Big Sleep begins as a "wandering daughter job" and ends as a prodigal son story. Marlowe meets General Sternwood in the orchid-filled greenhouse of his mansion and is hired to track down the gambling IOU's and nude photos of his daughter Carmen. On his way out, he meets Carmen and her older sister Vivian, who is married to the missing IRA veteran Rusty Regan. Marlowe tracks the photos through Arthur Geiger's pornographic bookstore, another new Los Angeles industry. He breaks into Geiger's house, where he finds Carmen naked and the homeowner dead. Geiger's body and Carmen's negatives disappear before Marlowe gets back from returning Carmen to her father.

A second plot begins as Marlowe tries to find Rusty Regan. The pursuit leads to a garage in Realito (Rialto), in the high desert east of Los Angeles, where Marlowe is sapped by gangster Lash Canino, the only man the detective ever kills in the series. He can't find Regan until he meets Carmen, who asks him to give her shooting lessons at an abandoned oil well on the Sternwood's property – a location that combines the former Hancock and Doheny estates. When she fires at him, Marlowe knows who killed Regan and where he is hidden: in the oil sump, sleeping "the big sleep."

The character of Philip Marlowe first takes shape in an interview with Gen. Sternwood, and is fleshed out during the novel. The private eye is thirty-three, college-educated, and an investigator for the DA who was fired for insubordination. Marlowe is unmarried, and drives a convertible (make unknown) in which he keeps a gun and a bottle of rye. He lives in an efficiency apartment at the Hobart Arms. "In it was everything that was mine, that had any association for me, any past, anything that took the place of a family. Not much; a few books, pictures, radio, chessmen, old letters, stuff like that."[6] Chandler's irony about chess suggests that the chivalric code is hopelessly out of date in modern Los Angeles. Marlowe lives by his own set of rules. Like Spade, he is redeemed by his commitment to his profession and his pragmatic view of the world.

Chandler's memorable metaphors reflect Marlowe's jaundiced view of California. General Sternwood's "dry white hair clung to his scalp, like wild flowers fighting for life on a bare rock." The old man saves his strength "as carefully as an out-of-work showgirl uses her last good pair of stockings." The Pacific coastline has "a loud sea-smell which one night's rain hadn't even dented," and Carol Lundgren has "moist dark eyes shaped like almonds." Marlowe's office has five green metal filing cabinets, "three of them full of California climate." As he drives to Realito, "the flawless lines of the orange trees [wheel] away like endless spokes into the night."[7] The prevailing tendency of these metaphors is to compare people to things, positing a mechanistic, post-Einsteinian world of time, space, mass, motion, and inertia. They build an alternate view of the world, deflating the pretensions of the tough-talking thugs and making the detective's ideals seem wistful but beautiful, because the comparative terms come from local California color.

The plot takes the ironic form of an unnecessary journey. Marlowe searches for a man whom everyone says he resembles. The search leads him through Rusty Regan's life. In the final scene, Marlowe learns that he caught the culprit in the first scene, when Carmen fainted in his arms. As for romance, all four of the female characters survive, but of the five men involved with them, only Marlowe remains.

Chandler's second big novel, *Farewell, My Lovely* (1940), took shape at a confusing time, during which he and Cissy were living in fifteen different apartments. When the novel appeared in August 1940, sales were disappointing. However, *Farewell* soon became famous as one of the richest troves of grotesque characters in American literature. Foremost is Moose Malloy, a giant lovelorn gangster who recalls Hammett's Gloomy Gus Schaefer. Marlowe meets him outside Florian's, a Negro bar in central Los Angeles. Malloy kills a bouncer while looking for his old flame, Velma. Lt. Nulty persuades Marlowe to help him solve the case.

A subplot concerns Lindsay Marriott, who asks Marlowe to ransom her jade necklace. The two drive a Rolls Royce to Malibu Canyon, where Marlowe remarks that the car "sticks out like spats at an Iowa picnic." Marlowe is sapped and Marriott killed. The detective is awakened by spunky Anne Riordan – "the kind of girl Marlowe would have married if he had been the marrying kind," Chandler later said.[8] The next day she tells him that a Mrs. Grayle owned the necklace. The plots of the two stories merge when it is revealed that Mr. Grayle owns KFDK radio station (modeled on KGEF), where Velma was once a singer. Marlowe arranges to meet Mrs. Grayle at Laird Brunette's gambling club. However, he is abducted by Second Planting, a "Hollywood Indian," who takes him to visit the psychic Jules Amthor. (Both characters reveal Chandler's disdain for religious cults and Hollywood.) Marlowe wakes in a private sanatorium in fictional Bay City (Santa Monica), suffering withdrawal from an unknown drug. He overpowers an attendant and escapes from the institution.

On the third day Marlowe learns that he can find Malloy at Brunette's "Montecito" gambling ship off the coast. Marlowe checks into a Speedway (Venice Beach) hotel and hires gentle giant Red Norgaard to sneak him aboard the ship. When Marlowe reveals that Mrs. Grayle turned Malloy in, Moose erupts from the closet. Velma shoots him five times and flees, later taking her own life back East.

Perhaps the most literate hard-boiled novel ever written, *Farewell* is cleverly written. When Chandler claims that Moose Malloy "looked about as inconspicuous as a tarantula on a slice of angel food," he alludes to the fact that Moose was black (and thus a rarity in hard-boiled fiction), and also to Charles Dickens' *Great Expectations*, in which a spider emerges from Miss Havisham's wedding cake. When Marlowe later tells Lt. Randall that "I like smooth shiny girls, hard-boiled and loaded with sin," he lovingly refers to the genre that invented the *femme fatale*. The novel has so many allusions, some of them self-referential, that it develops its own metaphoric systems.[9]

It's hard to find the novel's theme beneath the frantic action. Marlowe may say that all criminal rackets are linked, but all the crimes result from Velma's desire to become Mrs. Grayle. She believes in the great American myth of upward mobility, but must give up her profession, her boyfriend, and her name to succeed. Even then, she must live in fear of discovery. As an immigrant living in a city of immigrants, Chandler reveals the cost of success, and its antithetical relation to old-fashioned love, represented by Moose.

Although the novel had disappointing hardcover sales, Chandler was hired by Hollywood. He adapted *Double Indemnity* for Paramount in a mere three days, with marginal assistance from cowriter and director Billy Wilder. The two received an Academy Award nomination for best adapted screenplay in 1945.

Chandler and his wife moved to the desert near Palm Springs as the money began to roll in. However, when he returned to the studio, he wasn't able to repeat his initial success. Chandler completed *The Little Sister* in 1948, though by now he was becoming bored with Marlowe. Chandler's last major novel, *The Long Goodbye* (1953), was longer and more socially conscious. An immediate critical and commercial success, the novel launched a new era in hard-boiled fiction – that of the socially, politically, racially, sexually, and environmentally conscious detective, typified by Ross Macdonald's Lew Archer a few years later.

The plot stretches from The Dancers Club in Hollywood to Las Vegas, Tijuana, and the fictional Otatoclan, Mexico. As in *The Big Sleep*, Marlowe searches for an earlier version of himself, this one named Terry Lennox. He has been hired by the drunken novelist Roger Wade, a dark version of Chandler, who lives in the subdivision of "Idle Valley." The novel includes a depiction of Latino life, featuring yard and service workers, as well as tough guy Mendy Menendez. Hancock Park aristocrats like Sewell Endicott are still in control, but their police chiefs are racists.

Chandler didn't have time to revel in the novel's success. After he made a trip to England with Cissy, her health declined and she died in December 1954. There was a void in Chandler's life, which he filled with drink. He attempted suicide and eventually returned to La Jolla, where he died of pneumonia in 1959.

Hammett, Cain, and Chandler couldn't have envisioned that the hard-boiled genre they invented would achieve lasting acclaim. The California that many people know – or think they know – was created by these men during the early and mid-twentieth century. Later authors, such as Ross Macdonald, Joseph Wambaugh, James Ellroy, Michael Connelly, and Sue Grafton, have continued to develop the genre, expanding its national and international readership. It is a long way from Hammett's waterfront to Kem Nunn's Imperial Beach, where his surfer-detective smells something foul in the waters of the Tijuana Slough. However, the stink remains the same.

Notes

1. Diane Johnson, *Hammett: A Life* (New York: Random House 1983), 39.
2. Ibid., 71–73.
3. Dorothy Parker, "Oh Look – Two Good Books!" *The New Yorker*, April 25, 1931, 91.
4. Roy Hoopes, *Cain: The Biography of James M. Cain* (New York: Henry Holt, 1982), 244, 248.
5. John Abrams in Frank MacShane, *The Life of Raymond Chandler* (New York: Dutton, 1976), 36. Raymond Chandler, *Selected Letters of Raymond Chandler*, ed. Frank McShane (New York: Columbia University Press, 1981), 236.
6. Raymond Chandler, *The Big Sleep* (New York: Random House, 1988), 96.
7. Ibid., 6, 41, 90, 51, 170.
8. Raymond Chandler, in Phillip Durham, *Down These Mean Street a Man Must Go: Raymond Chandler's Knight* (Durham: University of North Carolina Press, 1963), 39.
9. Raymond Chandler, *Farewell, My Lovely* (New York: Random House, 1976), 3, 166–167, 50.

PART V
Alternative Voices

CHAPTER 14

Writing the Hidden California
Phillip H. Round

Between 1940 and 1963, California literature underwent a major transformation. Where earlier writers aspired to sell the state as "the land of sunshine," authors during this mid-century period were more interested in producing literary works that drew power from the increasingly visible disjunction between rich and poor, arid and irrigated, Anglo-Saxon and ethnic other. In nonfiction works like *Factories in the Fields* (1939) and *Southern California: An Island on the Land* (1946), Carey McWilliams rose to prominence as the region's preeminent cultural critic by employing a blunt, journalistic nonfiction approach to the places and states of being he would come to call the "hidden California." The story of this hidden land corresponded to the legends of sunshine, beaches and movie stars only as a dark inverted other. Its narrative arc was shadowed by violence and racial exploitation.

Working at the nexus of an economic depression and world war, California writers of this generation honed their craft during an era in which the state's "hidden" regions would develop into springboards for new styles of literary expression. Social realist novels, film noir screenplays, and nature writing all ripened in the confluence and collision of wildly divergent social interests, environmental depredation, and blistering economic growth. By 1963, when Edmund G. Brown defeated Richard Nixon in the race for governor, the state had become the epicenter of social, cultural, and economic contradictions that would become the hallmark of something American and European intellectuals alike labeled the "postmodern."

Topographically, this hidden California stretched across a broad swath of the state's coastal and rural regions. Limned by the White Mountains to the east, the lower Colorado Desert to the South, bordered by conifer groves and rugged seashores to the north and west – it was fig and sword fern, madrone and alfalfa, magpie and sandpiper. Intertwined here and there with the more glamorous beach communities and cityscapes of the coast, the hidden California of the 1940s and 1950s became entangled in a kind of pastoral/industrial economic complex that traced a continuum of mechanized natural resource extraction and low-skilled itinerant labor, from Pacific canneries to inland wheat fields.

The tension between this California and the golden one of sound stages, sandy beaches, and cable cars sparked a literary revolution when 1930s readers hungry for "modern" stories of the West increasingly embraced books that unflinchingly exposed the terrible hardships faced by Dust Bowl refugees. Nonfiction works like Dorothea Lange and Paul Taylor's *American Exodus* (1940) and McWilliams' *Factories* educated readers with case studies and documentary photographs detailing the injustices of the farm-labor system. However, it was the human element of the stories that mattered most to these readers, and John Steinbeck's (1902–68) novel *The Grapes of Wrath* (1939) elevated the plight of the common laborer to the level of the epic. Its wrenching portraits of "Hoovervilles" and vigilante justice stirred public passions about these lives and landscapes to a fever pitch. McWilliams called the book a modern *Uncle Tom's Cabin* and reviewers across the country traced its wild popularity to the way it viewed the West through "revolutionary eyes."[1]

However, Steinbeck's novel also did something more unexpected and unusual. It reacquainted urban Americans with the literature of rural life. Soon California's peach orchards, cotton and melon fields became interesting landscapes in and of themselves, as Americans sought representations of nature and country both nostalgic and in stark contrast to the sterile concrete and steel environments most came to inhabit. They were in the market for a different West from the one their parents and grandparents had read about. That rough-and-ready world was long gone. By the time *The Grapes of Wrath* hit bookstores, Mark Twain (1835–1910) and Bret Harte (1836–1902), the previous century's most famous expositors of rural California, had been dead for decades. Even early twentieth-century disciples of realism and naturalism like Jack London (1876–1916), who found the forgotten California to be a perfect backdrop for fierce battles of natural selection in a Godless cosmos, had receded. Mary Austin, one of the few authors to embrace California's neglected desert margin as a source of aesthetic beauty ("the land of little rain," she called it), died suddenly of a heart attack in 1934, leaving the region's aspiring nature writers bereft of a mentor.

As this great generation of literary Californians passed from the scene, California's rural environmental and social landscapes also underwent a radical transformation. From the seaside prairies north of Moro Bay, to the grasslands and oak savannas of the Central Valley, the redwood forests of the northern coastal range, and long stretches of Great Basin desert, the hidden California's landscapes came under enormous pressures from developers and engineers who tried to reshape them into something efficient and modern. These progressives liked to think they were improving a wasteland, making the "desert blossom as a rose." Yet in fact, because the hidden California had been home to Native societies for thousands of years, its topography and ecosystems had already been rationally husbanded in a yearly cycle of "land management" for untold generations.

Plants like mesquite and acorn oak made up about sixty percent of tribal peoples' diets. As a result, indigenous Californians' lives were deeply invested in enhancing hazelnut flats, shaping valley oak savannas, coppicing, broadcasting seeds, and burning undergrowth to kill parasites and reduce species competition. Place names in this hidden California derive from such activities: the Pit River in the northeastern part of the state refers to the deep pits the Achumawi fashioned as fish weirs; Hetch Hetchy Valley in the famous canyon on the Tuolumne River is from a Central Miwok word denoting a kind of grass with edible seeds flourishing in the valley; Jamacho, in San Diego County, originated in the Kumayaay word *Hamacha*, the dwelling place of a small wild squash plant.

Between 1850 and 1910, however, all this had changed. Whereas historical demographers estimate that California was at one time one of the most densely populated and culturally diverse places in the western hemisphere, with an indigenous population that probably reached about 310,000 by the fifteenth century, the Gold Rush and Mexican War had encouraged the wholesale slaughter of Native peoples.

The carnage extended to the region's fauna. The majestic grizzlies were routed from the state. Bighorn sheep and Tule elk became virtually invisible, while egrets, harvested for haberdashery feathers, were driven nearly to extinction. By 1910, only about fifty Pacific otters were known to remain. During this period of what anthropologist Kat Anderson has called the Europeanization of California, the state's agricultural regions were violently carved out from carefully tended indigenous landscapes, as irrigation, monoculture, and machines supplanted diverse ecosystems.

After 1940, these cataclysmic environmental changes were matched by upheavals in the social sphere. During the 1930s, an ascendant New Deal political class had overseen California's cornucopia of natural resources.

It included writers like Upton Sinclair (1878–1968), who ran for governor in 1934 campaigning on a platform called End Poverty in California (EPIC). Even Carey McWilliams found himself in the unlikely role of Sacramento bureaucrat. Governor Culbert Olson appointed him to head up the state's Division of Labor and Housing, a government body responsible for reporting on the conditions of the fields and work camps. For members of the political left, those were heady days. The hidden California seemed poised to become the place from which a utopian social order might spring. The dream collapsed in 1942, when Olson's New Deal populism was soundly trounced at the polls by Earl Warren's centrist boosterism. California's borderland communities – the Central Valley, the Modoc Plateau, and the coastal forests – had begun to appear backward, in need of an update.

World War II deepened federal involvement and investment in California's coastal cities, spurring lightening fast modernization. Its impact on the state's rural areas was, however, quite different. In 1942, the establishment of the Bracero Program, for example, not only guaranteed California growers a labor force of Mexican nationals but also instituted an inferior social caste of migrant workers whose race became a determining factor in their marginality. The war also further frayed Japanese Americans' already uncomfortable relationship with the state's farming communities, especially after President Roosevelt signed Executive Order 9066 authorizing the internment of all people of Japanese descent in hastily erected camps. These prisons were deliberately relegated to remote desert regions of the forgotten California to discourage escape. Completion of the state's major water projects (begun in the 1920s and 1930s) led to the increased consolidation of land holdings in fewer and fewer hands, and the mechanization of agriculture on a massive scale. For the rural laborers, small farmers, and loggers who made up the vast majority of the population of the forgotten California, the levers of power were receding ever further into the distance.

All these social, environmental, and political factors fed into a new style of literature that emerged from the hidden California in the 1940s. The catastrophe of the world wars and the collapse of the Left's hopes for field worker organization, exposed a fundamental and unbridgeable gap between what was in reality two Californias – of the haves and have-nots, of the powerful and disenfranchised, of the Hearsts and Joads. Intellectuals in both camps struggled to reconcile the state's long-standing regionalist fantasy of go-it-alone, Bear Flag Republic provincialism with the growing realization that the state was deeply implicated in a global economic and social sphere, and that it needed to come to grips with this fact and conduct itself accordingly.

Carey McWilliams' rise to literary fame is emblematic of the role writing played in this transformation. Working first at the *Los Angeles Times*, and then as a freelance cultural critic for the *Overland Monthly* and *Los Angeles Saturday Night*, McWilliams spent the 1930s honing a literary nonfiction style deeply indebted to H. L. Mencken. McWilliams' early work highlighted the unsentimental and ironic side of the West, assuming a superior attitude toward everyday people. As he matured, however, his approach changed dramatically, and in his effort to demythologize the West, he increasingly embraced California's immigrants and migrant laborers as an effective narrative point of view from which to dismantle the romantic West of Brete Harte and the progressive West of Harold Bell Wright. In 1937, while addressing a thousand walnut workers in East Los Angeles, McWilliams was instantly struck by how ethnically diverse the hidden California had become. As he spoke, his words were simultaneously translated into Russian, Armenian, and Spanish.

In *Factories in the Fields,* his most famous work, McWilliams made a case for socialism and collective agriculture by weaving statistics and historical detail into a readable "story." Calling the book a "chapter" in the state's "hidden history" of racial and labor exploitation, McWilliams tried to write a narrative of development centered on California's farm-labor practices. He felt that only the stories of the farm workers in this hidden California could bring the rest of the state's development into "proper perspective."

Throughout the war years, McWilliams turned his considerable writing talents to considerations of race relations in the Golden State. After an abortive attempt at a farm-labor sequel to *Factories* (1942's *Ill Fares the Land*), McWilliams penned *Brothers Under the Skin* (1942) and *Prejudice: Japanese Americans: Symbol of Racial Intolerance* (1944). By the end of the war, McWilliams had been named West Coast contributing editor to the *Nation*. Within five years, he would move east to take over the reins of the magazine.

When the *Nation* made McWilliams its editor, the hidden California's literary voice really came of age. The West had finally secured a place at the table in the eastern liberal elite's bastion of cultural commentary. However, McWilliams' race-based cultural critiques were just the start of a whole new movement in California literature. Other writers – some the sons and daughters of the immigrant laborers McWilliams lionized – seized the chance to speak for themselves. Their writing was accented with the ethnicities, labor, and prejudices that animated California's Central Valley, its deserts, and its timberlands.

This branch of the forgotten California's literary canon had its roots as much in the work of William Saroyan (1908–81) as in that of John Steinbeck. Saroyan was Armenian and his ethnicity was a central subject of many of his best stories. His career took off in 1939 when he won a Pulitzer Prize for his play, *The Time of Your Life*. Perhaps more than any other California writer, Saroyan explored the comic irony demanded of immigrants who toiled away as perpetual outsiders in the land of plenty. In works like *My Name Is Aram* (1940) and *The Human Comedy* (1943), he worked to create an ethnic regionalism of sorts, blending family memories of Armenia and his mother's experiences as a cannery worker into a series of portraits of a California that evoked the bittersweet joys of labor mixed with camaraderie and dreams only partly realized.

"The Pomegranate Trees," from *My Name Is Aram*, epitomizes Saroyan's comic approach to alienation. When the narrator describes his uncle's foolhardy purchase of 680 acres of marginal farmland, he observes that his immigrant relation thought he could recreate the Armenian homeland in California's Central Valley. As he shows his nephew the land he's purchased, he shouts in "poetic" Armenian: "Here in this awful desolation a garden shall flower, fountains of cold water shall bubble out of the earth, and all things of beauty shall come into being" (36). The poetry and the pomegranates ("practically unknown in this country," according to the narrator's uncle) highlight the uncle's elision of the California landscape into an imaginary Persia. In this story, as with so many dreams in the hidden California, the link is tenuous and transitory. The trees do not flourish, and buyers do not flock to purchase the few fruits that survive. The narrator and his uncle end up eating all the pomegranates themselves.

Saroyan was not alone in this effort to reinvest the hidden California with ethnicity, humor, and folklore – a process whereby land and story intertwined to provide a window into the broader human condition. Displaced by war or lured by stories of plentiful jobs, during World War II immigrants from across the world flooded into the hidden California. One among them who would achieve prominence was Carlos Bulosan (1913–56), a Philippine-born laborer who emerged as a powerful voice for the hidden California. With only a third-grade education, Bulosan struggled to learn English as he worked in fields and canneries. By chance, a labor contractor asked him to write up flyers to entice fellow Filipinos to come and work on California's ranches. Bulosan fell in love with writing. He soon shifted his efforts to literature, and his poetry was collected in the 1942 volume *Letter from America*. By 1944, he had completed a collection of short stories called *Laughter of My Father*. In the mode of Saroyan, it was singled out by critics for its bemused take on a life of labor. At the war's end, Bulosan produced his masterpiece, an autobiography entitled *American Is in the Heart: A Personal History* (1946). Looking back on his writing career years later, Bulosan explained that he had often written in anger. The essay "I am Not a Laughing Man," for example, attacks reviews praising the "pure comic spirit" of his early work. Bulosan wrote, he explained, not because of his comic spirit, but because he was "sore at a guy named Saroyan." He sought to tell stories of ethnic life in the forgotten California that were neither Saroyan comedy nor Steinbeckian tragedy. "What I am trying to do," he wrote, "is to utilize our common folklore, tradition and history in line with my socialist thinking" (181).

He was soon joined by other "outsiders" writing out of a furious desire to express themselves in a land where, as Bulosan put it in *America*, being an ethnic person was practically in and of itself "a crime." Mexican American writer José Antonio Villarreal, whose novel *Pocho* (1959) is considered by many to be the beginning of Chicano/a literature, sank his protagonist's roots deep into the soil of the forgotten California. His protagonist Richard Rubio's coming-of-age story begins with his birth in the Imperial Valley, where "the land had been reclaimed and the valley made artificially green and fertile, but the oppressive heat remained" to claim the lives of immigrants from the central plateaus of Mexico.

Meanwhile, for the second-generation Japanese American community of survivors of wartime internment, their emerging identities as *nisei* (the Japanese term for the first American-born generation) were intimately entangled with California farming and desert imprisonment. Writers such as Wakako Yamauchi used short stories and plays to come to literary terms with the alienation they had experienced as children of tenant farmers in desert internment camps. In a series of short stories and one particularly fine play, *And the Soul Shall Dance*, Yamauchi channeled her experience of the hidden California in the 1930s and 1940s into a literary clarion call for a new generation of Asian American writers.

Set in the Imperial Valley's reclaimed desert farmlands, *And the Soul Shall Dance* contrasts the Japanese love of water and bathing with the region's forbidding aridity. It opens with the main character's family bathhouse burning down due to her youthful negligence. For the duration of the play, Yamauchi thematizes aridity as un-Japanese. Besides the burnt bathhouse, her stories feature several drownings – in ditches and small tubs of water – to establish an ironic contrast between the immigrants and an environment that is culturally at odds with her Japanese characters' memories of Japan.

Although she never mentions it in her literary works, Yamauchi was herself interned at Poston in the Arizona desert, not far from her family farm. The desert thus takes on an added layer of symbolism, especially when in *And the Soul Shall Dance* she stages a Noh-like pantomime in which an *issei* woman dances in a kimono – very impractical for a desert farm wife – to melancholy Japanese songs played on her Victorola. The stage directions indicate that the color and texture of the silk kimono clash with the desert bleakness and the sound of Japanese songs drifting across the farmland establish audio cues that cast the landscape in a "cultural" light that is alienated from the Anglo-Protestant ethic of the progressives who irrigated the desert in the first place.

The hidden California of the 1940s and 1950s also produced new types of literary depictions of Native peoples. Anthropologist Jaime de Angulo's *Indians in Overalls* (1950) represents a departure from the practice of earlier California writers like Helen Hunt Jackson, whose *Ramona* (1886) dramatized Indian genocide within the contours of a romantic, tragic tale. As its title suggests, *Indians in Overalls* is concerned with Native Californians who are also modern peoples. In it we encounter American Indians who own cars and wear jeans while struggling to maintain their languages, ceremonial and storytelling traditions, despite the encroachment of mechanized agriculture, mining, hydroelectric projects, and tourism.

Indians in Overalls is a rollercoaster of a tale, alternately ethnocentric and condescending. De Angulo is drawn to study the Achumawi because they are, to his mind, California's most primitive people. And yet they drive automobiles and trucks. The old-timers still seek spiritual power from the land, and Achumawi, Paiute, and Modoc people of all ages still play the gambling hand games that mix chance with medicine power. Over the course of the book, de Angulo beds down with several families in the old style, out under the stars or in a small lodge under rabbit skin blankets, and then rhapsodizes about the strange beauty that is the juxtaposition of the modern and ancient in Achumawi life: "A broken coffee pot – but a beautiful panoramic view" (24).

Indians in Overalls was joined by Charles L. McNichols' *Crazy Weather* (1944), a coming-of-age tale whose hero, South Boy, is a non-Indian who was raised by a Mojave Indian mother and strikes out on his own, using Mojave storytelling and cultural practices to navigate the very modern complexities of a world emerging from total war. The genre reached its apex in 1960 with Scott O'Dell's (1898–1989) *Island of the Blue Dolphins*, a Newberry Award-winning work of juvenile literature that fictionalizes the historical figure Juana Maria, a young Nicoleño marooned on San Nicolas Island off the Santa Barbara coast for eighteen years in the nineteenth century.

By the time these works were printed, California had undergone a postwar boom that radically redirected the storytelling energies of writers who sought to confront the hidden California in its most contemporary forms. Between 1945 and 1964, the state's population grew from 9 to 19 million, with a disproportionate 72 percent of that growth swelling urban areas. Returning veterans needed homes, and aspiring young politicians like Orange County's Richard Nixon appealed to voters tired of slow, labyrinthine New Deal bureaucracies. Throughout the congressional campaign of 1948, Nixon returned again and again to a workhorse of a stump speech, "A Service Man Looks at the Future," urging his listeners to elect men like himself who believed in "practical liberalism" and in giving young people just starting out the chance to "get ahead in the world."

Lumber for the stick frame units of the new housing tracts that began to sprawl across the coastal valleys came from the hidden California's vast forests – places like Scotia, a company town in the northwestern redwoods operated by the Pacific Lumber Company. Gravel for concrete, oil for autos, and essential ores for industrial plants poured forth from the hidden California. The housing projects themselves, and the freeways connecting them, were carved out of agricultural and grazing land. Orange County, once carpeted with citrus groves and truck farms, had become a bedroom community. In 1955, it made the final break with its agrarian roots by hosting Disneyland, a utopian theme park "dedicated to the ideals, the dreams, and the hard facts that have created America."

The sudden growth and widening economic disparity, the reorientation of social life from agriculture and ranching to manufacturing and service industries, exposed a dark side of postwar California. Many left-leaning writers and filmmakers turned to a style of filmmaking called *noir* – a blend of German expressionism, low-key lighting, black and white cinematography, urban landscapes, and storylines bent on revealing that all was not right with the American Dream.

Perhaps the most surprising (and overlooked) 1940 noir settings for the novels, these films were based on lay nestled in the hidden California.

Although much has been made of Raymond Chandler's uncanny depictions of Los Angeles cityscapes, a substantial number of hard-boiled thrillers were inspired by California's forbidding deserts, underbelly border towns, and remote mountain hideaways. The quintessential practitioner of this subgenre was Daniel Mainwaring (1902–77). Originally from Oakland, Mainwaring began his writing career with the *San Francisco Chronicle*. During the 1930s, he embarked on a series of mysteries in which the protagonist, newspaperman Robin Bishop, covered a backcountry beat that gave him a front row seat for the murders of powerful mining magnates and rusticating poets. Writing under the pseudonym Geoffrey Homes, Mainwaring penned a succession of conventional detective novels – including *The Man Who Didn't Exist* (1937) and *The Man Who Killed Goliath* (1938) – each set in a California coastal town just on the cusp of development, clinging to an ambiguous social and environmental position between unspoiled seafront and scrub oak hills.

It wasn't until Mainwaring departed from convention to showcase California's wilderness landscapes as a potent backdrop for his readers' postwar anxieties that he became a sought-after screenwriter in Hollywood. In his breakthrough novel, *Build My Gallows High* (1946), Mainwaring's main character is a private eye who has retired to yet another remote town in the foothills of the eastern Sierra Nevada, leaving behind the dangerous urban jungle of New York City and some dark secrets. Between running a modest gas station and spending long afternoons trout fishing and courting a plain and wholesome local girl, Red Bailey is a contented man. That is, until Joe Stephanos, a thug from the past, arrives at the gas station to drag Red back into some unfinished underworld business. The eastern Sierra foothills, its streams and grassy slopes, interrupt the flashbacks of Red's criminal past, serving as images of what his life could have been had it not been tainted by East Coast city life. When Red must return to New York to settle the score, he thinks of the hidden California landscape – the Kings River, the West Walker, the Stanislaus, and the Tuolumne. They are "[g]ood names to roll around your mouth" (82). As the novel comes to a violent close, Red looks down from Reno-based gangster Guy Parker's Lake Tahoe lodge and is cheered by its view of a kind of noir sublime: "As always, when he looked down on the big lake, he felt his spirits lift. You didn't amount to anything and what happened to you didn't matter" (152).

In a similar way, Ramona Stewart's *Desert Town* (1947) mines noir conventions to recast hidden California desert peripheries as places of moral purity capable of sheltering Americans displaced by the Depression and World War, even though the isolation and sanctuary proffered were also attractive to fugitives and subterranean vices. Stewart (1921–79) explores these themes in a generational struggle between an East Coast mother and her western daughter in the town of Chuckawalla, a desolate settlement replete with a "Mexican district" made up of a hodge-podge of "shacks and mongrel dogs" (18). The mother, Fritzi Haller, is a New Jersey drifter who sets up a bar and a series of bordellos when she hits town. Her daughter, Paula, is fatherless, essentially raised by the desert itself. Fritzi's tavern is called The Purple Sage, suggesting that this urban easterner is playing out a Zane Grey fantasy in her new life. The local sheriff, Pat Johnson, embodies a tough-but-fair approach to frontier justice that comes from his having been raised in California's hot and desolate Imperial Valley. In the course of the novel, he is corrupted by Fritzi and becomes her lover, leaving his wife alone at home most nights.

Desert Town employs a plot device that would become quite common for noir stories set in the hidden California. Like *High Sierra* (1941), *Out of the Past* (1947), and *DOA* (1948), a remote desert or mountain landscape provides the perfect hiding place for mobsters on the lam. In *Desert Town*, it is LA gangster Eddie Benedict, who decides to lay low in Chuckawalla until the heat dies down from a drug deal.

The desert landscape around these characters serves as a foil for their moral weaknesses. The alcoholic wife of the town's mortician announces of the desert: "Nothing to do but drink and go to the movies" (56). For the sheriff, it represents a libertarian freedom. While on his late night rounds, he and his deputy revel in "the thought that the little town was falling asleep in the darkness, while they were awake, equipped with guns and blackjacks and ready for any excitement the night might bring" (48–49). Fritzi's freedom is economic and social. Her ill-gotten wealth allows her to build an incongruous plantation-style mansion on the edge of town.

Despite a bloody shoot out near the end, *Desert Town* ends with a fizzle. With the mobsters' deaths, Paula and Fritzi are somewhat implausibly reconciled. Only the desert has been constant and chaste, and the last lines of the novel enshrine its moral centrality to the postwar noir anxieties the story has tried to navigate: "Paula turned her gaze out over the desert which lay clear and brightly outlined below them" (141). There is no low-key light in the desert. Summer and winter, it reflects a bright moral clarity, an ethical line often obscured in LA's urban alleys and on Hollywood's klieg-lit street corners.

Against the strange sublimity of these noir landscapes, a countervailing current of earnest nature writing began to reassert itself. Before the war, Robinson Jeffers (1887–1962) had been the state's foremost nature poet. His famed cliffside residence at Carmel on the Pacific Coast was the salon-like center of an arts community. With the publication of *Tamar and Other Poems* in 1924, Jeffers gained notoriety as a proponent of something he called "inhumanism," the belief that humankind lived in a universe of incredible natural beauty presided over by a deity indifferent to human suffering. By 1946, Jeffers was a celebrity author. However, the postwar reading public soon soured on Jeffers' inhumanism, and by the time his collection, *The Double Axe*, appeared in 1948, his publishers felt the need to warn its readers of its sometimes "unpatriotic" verse.

Picking up the tradition cut short by Mary Austin's untimely death, an alternate strain of nature writing emerged to replace the distasteful elements of Jeffers' approach. This new work was often based in pastoral landscapes – sleepy ranches bordered by grassy hills and stands of live oak. It also centered on the experiences of women. Judy Van der Veer's *November Grass* (1940) is perhaps the best example of the genre. It is a paean to ranch women and the hidden California's unconventional seasons (autumns in which brown hills and dry creeks are matched by freezing mornings and hot afternoons) to which they turned for meaning in a troubled world. The interior thoughts of the novel's protagonist, known only as "the girl," shape the plot as it emerges during the long hours of ranch work that allow time for self-reflection. What she finds is a sobering solace. The landscape's primordial stillness delivers respite from the frenzied war effort on the coast. Its boulder-strewn hillsides bespeak the presence of time so deep and vast that even cataclysmic events such as war shrink in significance merely on strength of scale.

However, if the grassland ranches of the coastal range outside San Diego seem tranquil, *November Grass* reminds the reader that beneath the superficial beauty lie "terror and pain." The girl knows too well that something random (fate? natural selection?) has brought her here and given her a literary disposition by which to appreciate nature. After all, it was pure happenstance that her mother, a girl from the East Coast, married a California rancher and imparted to her daughter a hybrid personality able to enjoy books and ranching, music and animal life.

Van der Veer never allows her character's acceptance of chance to overshadow the essentially organic nature of life in this part of the hidden California. The girl's childhood was troubled by few of the racial ills that plagued the cities. She went to school with local Native children and was enchanted by the discovery of smooth indentations in hillside boulders where Indians had pounded acorns. Here was certain permanence. Here also were cultures that could find fulfillment in living a simple life to its fullest. The girl especially likes the Mexican people because their "unhurried way of living ... was like the slow way of summer turning to autumn" (51). Life in the hidden California teaches her that living and dying in the place where one is born completes the natural cycle and links humans together in one "long unbroken line."

Van der Veer's quiet epiphany about the relative unimportance of humans in the larger scheme of things harked back to Robinson Jeffers' inhumanism but was gentler in tone. However, 1950s California was still searching for a new breed of nature poet. Gary Snyder (1930–) took up the challenge. In 1952, the Washington-born student of classical Chinese at Berkeley was spending the summer looking out for forest fires in the Cascades. In his notebook he asked, "if one wished to write a poetry of nature, where [to] find an audience?" He soon realized that the postwar nature writer in the West would have to make the very impossibility of writing about nature his subject. He resolved to explore the "tension of/human events ... against a non-human background." In a 1954 review of Jaime de Angulo's *Indian Tales* (1953), Snyder began to refine this view of the poetic process and the poet's relationship to nature that would serve as the foundation for just such a new school of nature writing. De Angulo became Snyder's nature writing prototype. In the guise of Coyote Old Man, a culture hero of the Achumawi, Snyder had discovered a position from which to chant his innovative nature verse. By 1955, Snyder had become an integral part of what has since been called the San Francisco Renaissance in California literature.

His first book of poetry, *Riprap and Cold Mountain Poems* (1959), is set for the most part in the hidden California. It fashions lyric meditations from his observations of nature as a lookout and trailbreaker. In "Hay for the Horses," there are glimmers of the golden pastoral one finds in *November Grass*, but the poem's conclusion leaves the reader with a wry challenge to that vision. Another, "Above Pate Valley," finds its speaker meditating on his relationship to arrowheads he's found while breaking a trail. Like the Native peoples who came before him, Snyder claims the forgotten California as his own: "I followed my own/Trail here."

By 1963, the literary dynamic forged in the hidden California's immense contradictions shifted even more decisively. Although Steinbeck, Saroyan, and McWilliams would continue to write sporadically into the 1960s, the generation of writers who came of age after the war saw things in a very different light. Neither nature nor society nor race held the same meanings for them. The alarms McWilliams had raised about the social consequences of mechanized agribusiness had been joined by new evidence that the postwar boom in pesticide and herbicide use had begun to wreak environmental havoc. In 1962, all of America had its consciousness raised by biologist Rachel Carson's *Silent Spring*. The societal cost of the Bracero Program had exacerbated the deplorable working conditions on California farms, a situation thrown into sharp relief by Ernesto Galarza's *Merchants of Labor* (1964). From a global perspective, the constant threat of atomic attack and grinding rhetoric of the Cold War paved the way for the agnostic, disillusioned literary style that ushered in the irreverent experimentalism known as "postmodernism."

Among the poets who contributed to this new amalgam of social conscience and stylistic experimentation, perhaps the most important was Philip Levine. Named Poet Laureate of the United States in 2013, Levine began his writing career as a factory worker from Detroit who arrived at Stanford in 1957 to study with Yvor Winters. In 1958, he answered the call for applications for a professorship in literature at Fresno State, a land-grant college in the heart of the Great Central Valley. There the working-class urbanite encountered a natural world that amazed him, so much so that he called it "a holy land" in one of his early poems. However, he also saw it as a complex place, in need of a well-honed poetic voice to do it justice. Its Spanish place names were themselves musical, and he soon realized he would have to learn Spanish to recover the valley's linguistic rhythms. As a "city of cotton pickers," Fresno would reveal itself to this urban poet of industrial labor to be a kind of Detroit in disguise, and he soon found good ground for composing poetry. Levine's first glimpses of this land of magpie and Joshua tree, of majestic mountain passes and muddy low-land sloughs, were tempered by the sight of labor camps and migrant workers thumbing rides to follow the crops. *On the Edge*, published in 1963, described the place where Rust Belt activism met the rural beauties of the San Joaquin.

Around the same time, another writer who would help define the direction of American literature in the 1970s and 1980s, Raymond Carver (1938–88), published his first short story. It too was deeply invested in re-imagining the hidden California. After high school, Carver had followed his father to California and worked alongside him in a sawmill. Later, he attended Humboldt State University in northern California. His inaugural publication, "Furious Seasons (1961)," is set in a rainy, forested valley. Its protagonist, Lew Farrell, reacts to his wife's sudden announcement that she's pregnant by killing her. The endless rain and foggy hillsides darken Farrell's mood and anchor an airless depiction of marriage that would become a hallmark of Carver's mature work. It is the landscape as much as Farrell's stunted emotions that mark this tale of madness in the hidden California as a precursor to "dirty realism," the literary school most associated with Carver in his later life.

Exposing the hidden California's gritty ambiguities also became the stock-in-trade of Sacramento-born Joan Didion, descendent of a long line of Central Valley farmers. Berkeley educated and drawn to cosmopolitan life in New York, Didion yet found her literary voice in the Sacramento River delta and its people. Her first novel, *Run River* (1963), is a masterwork of California literature, marking the end of one literary era and the beginning of another.

Like the writers of the war years, Didion exhibits a great fondness for the rural landscape and its storied pioneer past, but she finds neither nature nor noir a viable aesthetic in the 1960s. Like Raymond Carver, she detected a crippling stasis in the previous generation's approach to society and land. *Run River* dissects the sterile marriage of Lily and Everett McClellan, whose wedding has united two of largest tracts of farmland in the area, spurring great hopes that the old way of life will be preserved. However, signs that the old world of rural California are gone for good are everywhere. Lily and her father ignore the fact that Douglas Aircraft has become the main employer in Sacramento, corrupting the agrarian visions of the pioneers. Lily's son has no plans to take over the ranch when he finishes at Princeton, looking instead to sell the farmland to developers for a housing subdivision. Most of the book (in a very long section labeled 1938–59) takes place in flashbacks that expose the false nostalgia that has guided Lily and Everett's lives. In doing so, Didion creates a space for wistful reminiscences about allowing the hidden California to thrive, only to snuff them out in the book's closing pages, where all that *could have been* is extinguished in a single gunshot.

Looking back on her rural California upbringing in a memoir entitled *Where I Was From* (2011), Didion confesses that her whole writing career has been founded on the cultural disconnect she experienced between her ancestors' Anglo-Protestant progressive vision of the Sacramento Valley and her own skepticism about it. She views herself in an ironic past tense, emphasizing that she *was* a Californian because being a Californian really entails seeing oneself "as affected only by 'nature.'" However, "nature" in the forgotten California primarily signified only irreconcilable contradictions: "inspiration and renewal … and as the ultimate brute reckoning, the force that by guaranteeing destruction gave the place its perilous beauty" (993).

The great writers from rural California who flourished in the 1990s owe much to this realization of Didion's and other writers of the 1940s and 1950s. Gary Soto's *Elements of San Joaquin* (1988) reflects his apprenticeship with Philip Levine, but moves beyond it to give voice to the farmer workers with whom he labored as a child. In much the same way, Helena Maria Viramontes's classic farm worker novel, *Under the Feet of Jesus* (1999), frames a young Chicana woman's coming-of-age within the racism and environmental degradation that continues to mark life in the hidden California. It wasn't until 1998 that an Auchumawi writer appeared to speak for his people in their own language and voice, when Daryl Babe Wilson produced *The Morning the Sun Went Down*, a memoir dispelling the notion that California Native people's had disappeared, their languages and stories lost to time. Esselen writer Deborah Miranda has followed suit, creating a wonderful mixed-genre pastiche of a memoir, *Bad Indians* (2011). Hidden California noir has even experienced a revival, with the film *Salton Sea* (2001), and the crime novellas of Mexicali writer Gabriel Trujillo Muñoz and Imperial Valley author Jimmy Shaw once again set their stories in pristine deserts and miraculous irrigated farmland that still cradle corruption and vice – now in the forms of border maquiladoras and transnational drug cartels.

The hidden California is no longer unknown the way it was when writers in the forties and fifties turned to its natural beauty, its social ironies and contradictions, for inspiration in shaping a new literary culture. However, it still beckons. Debates about immigration, environmentalism, and government overreach most often find their foundation in one of many wayward forgotten California places or situations – Taft and its oil fields, the mirror arrays of Mojave solar farms, the depleted salmon fisheries of the once fecund Trinity River. And writers are there, too. Their poems and stories, as yet unread chapters in the fertile life of letters born alongside sugar beets and sudan grass in irrigated desert valleys no one but laborers, truckers, growers, and poets dare inhabit or embrace.

Note

1. Peter Monroe Jack, "John Steinbeck's New Novel Brims with Anger and Pity," *New York Times*, April 16, 1939.

CHAPTER 15

The Beats

Kurt Hemmer

Name Games

Once, Herbert Huncke "beat" some hippies by selling them phony acid in the Haight-Ashbury district of San Francisco. They didn't know that the seedy-looking man in a trench coat filled with fake LSD was introducing a term that poets would later appropriate. When Huncke used the expression in front of William S. Burroughs, Jack Kerouac, and Allen Ginsberg, he meant to suggest someone who was "exhausted, trampled by life." This feeling was the antithesis of the enthusiasm and with-it-ness of the hippies Huncke encountered when he traveled with the poet Janine Pommy Vega from New York to California in 1967 to dig a new scene. Earlier that year, Ginsberg, Gary Snyder, Michael McClure, Lenore Kandel, and Lawrence Ferlinghetti had appeared on stage at the Human Be-In in Golden Gate Park. This event heralded in a period known as the Summer of Love. The event, also called "A Gathering of the Tribes," consisted of more than 20,000 people. They assembled for a peaceful party/protest over the illegalization of LSD, which had occurred in October 1966. Hippies danced to bands like Jefferson Airplane and the Grateful Dead. Several years earlier, *San Francisco Chronicle* columnist Herb Caen had referred to these people as "Beatniks," combining "Beat" and "Sputnik" to describe the "out-of-this-world" young freaks he saw on the streets. Caen associated them with the satellite sent into orbit by the Russians in October 1957 – the same month Ferlinghetti was found not guilty of publishing obscenity in the trial over Ginsberg's *Howl and Other Poems* (1956).

In the month previous to that landmark decision, Kerouac published *On the Road*, a bible for the burgeoning Beat Generation. Kerouac combined the word Huncke used, "beat," with "beatitude." For the Catholic writer, it suggested a state of blessedness in which suffering was an essential part of attaining enlightenment. In a conversation with Beat novelist John Clellon Holmes in 1948, Kerouac called his peers a Beat Generation, alluding to the earlier Lost Generation. Ginsberg hated the term "beatnik," which he saw as different from "Beat." "Beatniks" were poseurs. The Beats were poets expressing a new spiritualism through a concentrated examination of their extreme personal experience: dealing with and experiencing states of madness, experimenting with drugs, defying sexual mores, and exploring the underbelly of American life in search of spiritual authenticity. The East Coast Beats shared a number of interests with their West Coast counterparts. They were both opposed to war, materialism, and big business, and interested in the environment and Eastern religions, particularly Buddhism. All of the major Beat themes could be found in Ginsberg's groundbreaking poem "Howl," which was read in October 1955 for the first time in a former garage made into an art gallery in San Francisco.

Carpetbaggers Reading Poetry in a Garage

The most famous poetry reading to take place in the United States is commemorated with a plaque outside 3119 Fillmore Street, disregarded by most passers-by, in front of what in the past has been an automobile repair garage, a rug store, and many things in between. Who knows what it is now. You cannot step twice into the same San Francisco street. But the plaque tries to preserve the memory of an event the likes of which we may never see again – when people attending a reading truly believed poetry could change the world.

Beneath the first four lines of Ginsberg's "Howl" and a replica of the poet how he looked in the mid-1950s, in stark contrast to the bearded image of Ginsberg in the 1960s, the plaque reads:

> Presented to San Francisco on the 50th Anniversary of the first full-length public reading of HOWL at the Six Gallery.
> October 7, 2005
> San Francisco salutes the Beat Generation poets Jack Kerouac, Philip Lamantia,
> Michael McClure, Kenneth Rexroth, Gary Snyder, and Philip Whalen.
> By Supervisor Michela Alioto-Pier and Lawrence Ferlinghetti of City Lights Books.

Those who attended and performed at that reading – exactly one week after the tragic automobile death of actor James Dean (who would become a Beat icon) in Cholame, California – could not have expected officials of San Francisco to honor their relatively minor event fifty years later. Initially the presence of the Beats in San Francisco had led to their vitriolic condemnation by the city's custodians and an infamous censorship trial. The reading honored by the plaque has been called both "The Birth of the Beat Generation" and "The Birth of the San Francisco Renaissance," but these sobriquets, though understandable, are inaccurate. If Voltaire was still alive he would point out, like he did for the Holy Roman Empire, that what we have come to know as the San Francisco Renaissance was not strictly a San Franciscan phenomenon, nor exactly a "renaissance."

The start of the San Francisco Renaissance can be traced to the journal *Circle* published by George Leite in 1944. Henry Miller (1891–1980), Anaïs Nin (1903–77), Kenneth Patchen (1911–72), Robert Duncan (1919–88), and Rexroth were published in this avant-garde magazine. The two major poets of the San Francisco Renaissance were Rexroth and Duncan, who met in San Francisco in 1942, two years before Kerouac and Ginsberg met in New York City.

The Beat Generation began in the mid-1940s when Ginsberg (from Patterson, New Jersey), Kerouac (from Lowell, Massachusetts), and Burroughs (from St. Louis, Missouri) were introduced to one another through Lucien Carr, a Columbia University student ardently pursued by Burroughs's best friend, David Kammerer, who like Carr was from St. Louis. The bond between Ginsberg, Kerouac, and Burroughs was morbidly sealed by Carr's murder of Kammerer on August 14, 1944, depicted in the film *Kill Your Darlings* (2013). Before Ginsberg came to San Francisco in 1954, the adventures Kerouac had with Neal Cassady from Denver, that would be the basis for the novel *On the Road*, were a distant memory.

Ginsberg had been suspended from Columbia in 1945 for writing obscenity on his dorm window and being caught, though innocently, in bed with Kerouac. Ginsberg confessed his homosexual longings first to a sympathetic Kerouac and then had his first sexual encounter with a stranger shortly after being readmitted to Columbia. When Cassady was introduced to the Beats in 1946, Ginsberg fell in love and they had a brief affair. In 1948, Ginsberg had his "Blake visions," claiming the spirit of the nineteenth-century English poet had actually recited to him. After being busted in connection with a group of burglars, Ginsberg found himself at the New York State Psychiatric Institute, where he would meet Carl Solomon in 1949. Gregory Corso, freshly out of jail, entered the Beat scene when he met Ginsberg in 1951 in Greenwich Village. In 1952, Ginsberg met Philip Lamantia, originally from San Francisco, who gave

Ginsberg the address to the father of the San Francisco poetry scene, Rexroth, whose poetics and politics actually had been honed in Chicago.

When Ginsberg made it to California, he immediately began socializing with San Francisco poets. He got in touch with Ruth Witt-Diamant, the remarkable director of the Poetry Center at San Francisco State College. Ginsberg attended one of Duncan's workshops, but was not impressed. The feeling was mutual. Though Ginsberg later claimed that Duncan was fascinated with Kerouac's "Essentials of Spontaneous Prose," Duncan refuted such an absurdity. To Duncan, the New York Beats did not warrant much attention, but he soon resented their position in the San Francisco poetry scene.

In October, Ginsberg had a peyote vision of "Moloch," the avatar of the military-industrial-corporate complex mechanically sucking the soul out of America that Ginsberg later said "destroyed the best minds of my generation," while staring at the Sir Francis Drake Hotel and the Medical Arts buildings in San Francisco. Ginsberg had also fallen in love with a beautiful young man named Peter Orlovsky. An important breakthrough for Ginsberg came when his psychotherapist, Dr. Philip Hicks, encouraged him to embrace homosexuality and poetry. In August 1955, Ginsberg began the first section of "Howl." He wrote with the sound of Kerouac's prose in his mind. Originally calling the work "Strophes," Ginsberg later claimed that Kerouac suggested the title "Howl," though perhaps Ginsberg forgot that he had named the poem "Howl" himself. That same month the artist Wally Hedrick asked Ginsberg to help put together a poetry reading. The event was held at the Six Gallery, a space named after the six people who ran the gallery. According to Jack Spicer's biographers Lewis Ellingham and Kevin Killian:

> The "6" Gallery opened on Halloween 1954 in the Fillmore Street premises vacated months before by King Ubu, an artists-run space established by Jess, Harry Jacobus, and Robert Duncan that lasted from 1952 to 1953. The "6" were the visual artists Wally Hedrick, David Simpson, Deborah Remington, Hayward King, John Allen Ryan, plus [Jack] Spicer, who hung his own poems next to the paintings of his confreres for the opening show.[1]

Ginsberg spoke to Rexroth for advice about organizing the event. McClure, originally from Kansas and who was now studying poetry with Duncan, was recruited to help Ginsberg. Both Ginsberg and McClure knew Lamantia, who agreed to read the work of the recently deceased John Hoffman, eventually published in *Tau & Journey to the End*

(2008). Rexroth suggested Snyder, who was born in San Francisco but raised in Washington and Oregon. Snyder suggested his Reed College roommate Philip Whalen from Oregon. Ginsberg, who had moved to Berkeley, wanted Kerouac to read, but the latter was too shy to recite the poems that were later published in *Mexico City Blues* (1959).

Postcards advertised the event:

> 6 POETS AT 6 GALLERY
>
> Philip Lamantia reading mss. of late John
> Hoffman – Mike McClure, Allen Ginsberg,
> Gary Snyder & Phil Whalen – all sharp now
> straightforward writing – remarkable coll-
> ection of angels on one stage reading
> their poetry. No charge, small collection
> for wine and postcards. Charming event.
> Kenneth Rexroth, M.C.
> 8 PM Friday Night October 7, 1955
> 6 Gallery 3119 Fillmore St. San Fran

Around a hundred of these postcards were sent out. Somewhere between 75 and 150 people attended. Lamantia began with Hoffman's poetry. McClure, giving his first poetry reading, read "Point Lobos: Animism," "Night Words: The Ravishing," "Poem," "For the Death of 100 Whales," and a letter from Spicer asking for help so that he could leave Boston and return to San Francisco. Whalen read "*Plus Ça Change...*" and "If You're So Smart, Why Ain't You Rich?". Ginsberg read all of "Howl" that he had finished at that time. It was not his first reading, which had taken place weeks earlier when he had read "Supermarket in California" at the San Francisco Arts Festival. The first complete reading of "Howl" would occur in Berkeley at the Town Hall Theater on March 18. Snyder, who finished the program, read "A Berry Feast." Of all the poets on the stage, only Lamantia could really be called strictly a California poet, and he had not even read his own poetry. Ferlinghetti, who had been born just outside New York City, would refer to the Beats as "carpetbaggers."[2]

Kerouac fictionalized the famous reading in his novel *The Dharma Bums* (1958):

> Anyway I followed the whole gang of howling poets to the reading at Gallery Six that night, which was, among other important things, the night of the birth of the San Francisco Poetry Renaissance. Everyone was there. It was a mad night. And I was the one who got things jumping by going around collecting dimes and quarters from the rather stiff audience

> standing around in the gallery and coming back with three huge jugs of California Burgundy and getting them all piffed so that by eleven o'clock when Alvah Goldbrook was reading his, wailing poem "Wail" drunk with arms outspread everybody was yelling "Go! Go! Go!" (like a jam session) and old Rheinhold Cacoethes the father of the Frisco poetry scene was wiping tears in gladness.[3]

McClure would recall, "In all of our memories no one had been so outspoken in poetry before – we had gone beyond a point of no return – and we were ready for it, for a point of no return."[4]

Surprisingly, Kerouac praised Snyder's reading the most. However, after the reading Kerouac predicted that Ginsberg would become known throughout San Francisco. Rexroth countered that Ginsberg would become known throughout the *country*. Ferlinghetti, the City Lights publisher, sent a telegram to Ginsberg the next day echoing Ralph Waldo Emerson's words to Walt Whitman: "I greet you at the beginning of a great career – When do I get manuscript of *Howl*?" Ferlinghetti had established what was considered the first all-paperback bookstore in America with his partner Peter Martin in 1953. Having already published his own *Pictures of the Gone World* (1955) and two other works, Ferlinghetti was ready to publish a book by Ginsberg as the fourth in his Pocket Poets Series. Before "Howl" was published by City Lights, the article "Richard Eberhart Discusses Group of Young Poets on West Coast" in the *New York Times Book Review* on September 2, 1956.

So started the San Francisco Renaissance in the public imagination. But not everyone was pleased. When *Mademoiselle* came to town and took a picture of Ginsberg and Kerouac used in their February 1957 issue, there were murmurs among the poets about who really was part of the scene. Kerouac's insistence on poetry that revealed the unspeakable visions from within the individual was countered by Spicer's belief that the poet allows for a magical entrance of the poem from without. Duncan, who was part of the triumvirate that made up the Berkeley Renaissance with Spicer and Robin Blaser (1925–2009), said:

> The term that later got applied – the "San Francisco Renaissance" – in the first place shows that someone didn't know what a renaissance was at all. What did it mean? That we revived the Yukon poets or something? When Spicer and Robin and I were [Ernst] Kantorowicz's students [at Berkeley], in poems assuming medieval and Renaissance learning – Miss [Josephine] Miles dubbed us "the museum poets" – we called ourselves the Berkeley Renaissance. And although we wanted other poets to belong to it, we meant that our poetry was really a Renaissance poetry: that [Italian Renaissance

philosopher Marsilio] Ficino would come into it; that questions of Dante and Petrarch would underlie it.

The Berkeley Renaissance is where the *term* "Renaissance" came from. San Francisco liked the term – but they've never been closer to the Renaissance than looking at pictures.[5]

Naked Poet in Hollywood

The San Francisco Renaissance poet George Stanley (b. 1934) argues:

> If you could consider the group centering around Ferlinghetti, Ginsberg, Corso, and later on, McClure – and still later, the Oregon poets, Whalen, Snyder and Welch – if you consider that one group "Beatniks," then the group around Spicer and Duncan were anti-Beatniks. But we *were* all Beatniks; we didn't think we were Beatniks, but we were.[6]

Not many poets agreed. If they even cared, most of the poets around San Francisco in the 1950s did not know where exactly to classify themselves: Berkeley Renaissance, San Francisco Renaissance, Beat, Black Mountain? Most did not fit comfortably into any category, and many fit into multiple groups. One group thought of themselves as more Beat than the New York Beats. Their goal was not the transformation of society, but the creation of a society all their own. In the late 1950s Venice, California, a beachfront neighborhood of Los Angeles, became a Beat sanctuary before transforming into a menacing asylum of hip, a trajectory much like Haight-Ashbury in the late 1960s. The scene was promoted by Lawrence Lipton (1898–75), author of *The Holy Barbarians* (1959), who presented the first philosophical and sociological portrait of a Beat scene in America. Lipton's book ostensibly came from the perspectives of the Beats themselves. Lipton himself had published *Rainbow at Midnight* in 1956. The most important poet to emerge from Venice was Stuart Perkoff (1930–74), who came from St. Louis, though there were several talented artists that made up the loose collective over the years: Charles Foster (1922–67), Philomene Long (1940–2007), Frank Rios (b. 1936), Tony Scibella (1932–2003), and John Thomas (1930–2002). Jonathan Williams (1929–2008) published Perkoff's book *The Suicide Room* (1956) with illustrations by Fielding Dawson (1930–2002), who like Williams had attended Black Mountain College. For a time the Scottish novelist Alexander Trocchi (1925–84), author of *Cain's Book* (1960), some of which was written in Venice, was part of the scene and converted several of its members to the use of heroin.

Venice West, as Lipton called it, was not as glamorous as Greenwich Village or North Beach, but, at least at first, it prided itself on its authenticity. The point was not to become famous, or even publish for that matter, but to live as an artist. To be obscure was a point of pride. The desire to change American society was not the point; to disaffiliate from it was the point. The poets of Venice West were the outsiders of the outsiders. Poverty was part of the code of honor. Marijuana was ubiquitous. For some, heroin use was heroic. Jazz provided their background music.

Lipton was born in Poland and raised in Chicago. He wrote successful detective fiction in collaboration with his wife and published under her name, Craig Rice. He was an old-time bohemian and radical who was a friend of Rexroth. Believing that poetry should be shamanistic and communal, Lipton found himself in allegiance with the New York Beats and they shared a common hero – the Welsh poet Dylan Thomas (1914–53).

On October 31, 1956, Ginsberg and Corso made a stop in Los Angeles on his way to visit Kerouac in Mexico City. Ginsberg wrote a letter to Anaïs Nin, whom he admired for once being Henry Miller's muse, asking if he and Corso could give a reading for her and any literary and Hollywood types she could round up. Believing that the future of poetry was in the hands of the jazz writers, Nin decided to see the Beats for herself. Later she would praise Kerouac's *On the Road* for its primitive jazz lyricism and referred to Ferlinghetti as one of her favorite poets. Nin brought some of her friends to the reading, but not any of the Hollywood stars Ginsberg hoped to rub shoulders with. The event was sponsored by editors of the Los Angeles quarterly *Coastlines*. Lipton got the job of emceeing the event and brought Perkoff, who would later write a poem about the event. Nin admired Ginsberg's reading of "Howl," but another guest had been heckling Ginsberg during his performance and continued to do so throughout Ginsberg's reading of "America." When Corso followed Ginsberg with a reading of his own poems the heckler, who could not comprehend Corso's poems at all, challenged Corso to fight. Ginsberg stepped up to the drunk and took his own clothes off. A profound statement had been made. Nin was impressed with what Ginsberg had said: "The poet always stands naked before the world."[7] What could be more courageous? Duncan had stripped naked years earlier after his play *Faust Foutu* at the King Ubu Gallery, an old auto repair garage that was later called the Six Gallery. Ginsberg managed to eclipse Duncan's act with his own infamous defense of poetry in Los Angeles.

When Lipton's *The Holy Barbarians* was published in June 1959, describing in detail Ginsberg's naked stance, it helped make being a "Beat" a fad. It was only a matter of time before Venice was packed with Beatniks. On September 21, 1959, *Life* magazine ran an article called "Squareville USA vs. Beatville USA." Three high school girls from Hutchinson, Kansas, had written to Lipton asking him to speak to their class about being a Beat. The story was even promoted on a cover featuring the wives of astronauts. Millions of Americans now knew who Lipton was.

Unlike Lipton, Perkoff did not enjoy the spotlight. He was able to build on the attention given to Venice West by being included in Donald Allen's groundbreaking anthology *The New American Poetry, 1945–1961* (1960). He also appeared on *You Bet Your Life* hosted by Groucho Marx and won a significant amount of money, which led him to being asked on local newscaster Paul Coates's *Confidential File*. In 1959, Jack Kerouac, who was much more uncomfortable than Perkoff on television, made an appearance at Venice Beach when he was in town to do *The Steve Allen Show*, but he was unimpressed and morose. Kerouac had disdain for the cool posturing of what he saw as Beatniks.

The Gas House, the Venice West beatnik hangout, was demolished in September 1962. Several people from the scene committed suicide or at least tried. Others, like Perkoff, were arrested on drug charges. The streets of Venice became the prowling grounds of violent criminals. Eventually the beatnik poets were replaced by folk singers. Some of the old group survived. John Thomas, a poet championed by Charles Bukowski (1920–94), had hitchhiked to Venice after reading Lipton's book in 1959, and many years later married Philomene Long, who was named Poet Laureate of Venice in 2005. Lipton, who had been severely beaten by police while covering the 1968 Democratic National Convention in Chicago, died in 1975, a little more than a year after Perkoff's death. In 1960, Lipton had a small role as "King of the Beatniks" in the film *The Hypnotic Eye*. If his son, James Lipton, had him appear on *Inside the Actors Studio* he would have asked him, "If Heaven exists, what would you like to hear God say when you arrive at the Pearly Gates?" Perhaps Lawrence would have responded, "I'm sorry I didn't make you a more famous poet." Even so, John Arthur Maynard, author of *Venice West: The Beat Generation in Southern California* (1991) believes, "No one had done more than Lipton to turn an obscure and sincere doctrine of poetry and art into a recognized alternative to conventional life."[8]

Lipton's vision would go on to inspire people in ways he could not have imagined. In 1965, two former film students who were enamored with and inspired by the Beats bumped into each other on Venice Beach. They decided to start a rock band called The Doors, influenced by Aldous Huxley's book *The Doors of Perception* (1954), which had taken its title from a line by William Blake from *The Marriage of Heaven and Hell*: "If the doors of perception were cleansed every thing would appear to man as it is, Infinite." The two young men were Ray Manzarek and Jim Morrison.

The Marthe/Creeley Affair

Competition was in the air, and the Venice West poets, the Beats, the Berkeley Renaissance poets, the San Francisco Renaissance poets, the Black Mountain poets, and the older San Francisco poets did not always get along. What should have been relegated to a minor footnote of literary gossip became a major rift between the Beats, first major champion on the West Coast and the man who would be called "The King of the Beats."

When Black Mountain College in North Carolina closed in 1956, several of its members headed for the Bay Area, most significantly Robert Creeley and Ed Dorn, and naturally they looked up Rexroth. Duncan had even briefly attended and taught at Black Mountain where Charles Olson had been the father figure for the younger poets. In the West it was Rexroth. Creeley asked Rexroth to become an advisory editor for the *Black Mountain Review*, but Rexroth resigned after reading an attack on the poet Theodore Roethke in the first issue.

The Beats were initially taken under Rexroth's wings rather than the Black Mountain poets. Rexroth had heard of Ginsberg through Lamantia, and knew that Ginsberg was a protégé of William Carlos Williams. Ginsberg had been attending Rexroth's Friday gatherings by the end of 1954. Rexroth's poem "Thou Shalt Not Kill," written in memoriam for Dylan Thomas, can be seen as a primogenitor for Ginsberg's "Howl." Ginsberg introduced Rexroth to Kerouac, and Rexroth showed some admiration for Kerouac's piece "Jazz of the Beat Generation," which was published in *New World Writing* in 1955. Kerouac even attended one of Rexroth's Friday gatherings with Ginsberg. After the Six Gallery reading, Rexroth was generally seen as the doyen of the Beats.

Rexroth had trouble at home that disrupted his relationship with these young writers. Though he was still legally married to his wife Marie, Rexroth lived with Marthe Larsen. Rexroth's habit of openly discussing his affairs with other women, coupled with his physical and verbal abuse of Marthe, troubled Spicer and Blaser, and caused Marthe and their two daughters to leave Rexroth temporarily. After they returned, Rexroth invited Ginsberg, Kerouac, Snyder, and Whalen to dinner. The Beats showed up late and drunk. Kerouac insulted Rexroth, and Ginsberg declared himself a better poet than his former mentor. Rexroth believed they had disturbed Marthe and he would never forget the incident.

In May 1956, Creeley visited San Francisco while working on what would turn out to be the last issue of *Black Mountain Review* and to visit Dorn. Two things happened very quickly: Creeley became a drinking partner with fellow Massachusetts native Kerouac and, after a dinner at the Rexroths', Creeley and Marthe fell in love and began an affair. Marthe and the children went to New Mexico to be with Creeley. Rexroth's rage initially fell on McClure and Ginsberg, whom he also felt jealous of because of their growing reputations. He was having a nervous breakdown. Duncan tried to intervene on Rexroth's behalf. Eventually Marthe and the children returned to him. He would forgive McClure and Ginsberg for being Creeley's friend, and even publicly praise Creeley's poetry, but he would spend the rest of his life insanely criticizing Kerouac, whom he irrationally blamed for the dissolution of his family. Snyder, who was now studying in Japan, tried to ease Rexroth's feelings about Kerouac in his letters. Even Kerouac wrote to Rexroth claiming that he had not encouraged the affair and admired Rexroth's poetry. However, in several reviews of Kerouac's work, Rexroth criticized Kerouac's understanding of Buddhism; insulted his writing style as amateurish and indecipherable; claimed that Kerouac (who saw himself as a jazz aficionado) knew very little about jazz; and that Kerouac, for all his discussion of them, had little understanding of African Americans and was ultimately racist. Though Rexroth would champion the work of the Jewish, African American Beat Bob Kaufman (1925–86), he would never return to his former admiration for Kerouac's work.

The Trial That Created the Beat Generation

Spicer, who never warmed to the Beats, was incensed when one of his lovers became infatuated with Kaufman. The Berkeley Renaissance poets were not the only people wary eye of the upstart invaders of the Bay Area known as the Beats.

A thousand copies of *Howl and Other Poems,* printed in Great Britain by Villiers, were officially published by City Lights on November 1, 1956. Ginsberg himself found it unlikely that so many copies would be sold. The first printing was dedicated to Kerouac, Burroughs, Cassady, and Carr.

Upon finding out that his name would be on the dedication page of such a scandalous work, Carr demanded that Ginsberg take his name off of all subsequent editions.

A boost in sales occurred on March 25, 1957, when Chester MacPhee, the San Francisco Collector of Customs, had 520 copies of the second printing seized for being obscene. A thousand additional copies of the book inexplicably made it past Customs, and shortly thereafter Ferlinghetti had a third printing of 2,500 made in the United States to avoid Customs altogether. The prescient Ferlinghetti had contacted the American Civil Liberties Union (ACLU) before publishing the book and had their guarantee of support should charges be brought against *Howl and Other Poems*. The seized copies were returned when Lloyd H. Burke, the U.S. attorney in San Francisco, refused to go to trial against the ACLU.

However the San Francisco Police Department's Juvenile Bureau, in an effort to keep the community safe, refused to let the issue be dropped. Ginsberg was never arrested for writing an obscene work, but on June 3, 1957, store manager Shigeyoshi Murao, who had spent time in an internment camp as a child during World War II, was arrested by undercover police Russell Woods and Thomas Pagee for selling Ginsberg's book and William Margolis's magazine called *The Miscellaneous Man* at City Lights Bookstore. An arrest warrant was issued by Captain William A. Hanrahan for Ferlinghetti, who turned himself in a few days later when he returned from vacationing in Big Sur. He was released after the ACLU posted his bail. At the time, Ginsberg was in Tangier, Morocco, helping Burroughs with the manuscript that would become *Naked Lunch* (1959).

Without this trial it is arguable that the so-called "Beat Generation" might never have taken off as a cultural phenomenon that is now imbedded in the literary history of the United States, and would have suffered the fate of near obscurity allotted to the Berkeley Renaissance.

The focus of the trial fell almost strictly on a single poem: "Howl." Charges against Murao were dismissed after it was determined by the prosecution that they could not prove that he knew what he had sold was "obscene." Charges against the selling of *The Miscellaneous Man* were also dropped. Defense Attorney J. W. Ehrlich defended Ferlinghetti against Deputy District Attorney Ralph McIntosh. The trial took place in September 1957, the same month Kerouac's *On the Road* was published. *Life* magazine ran an article entitled "Big Day for Bards at Bay: Trial over *Howl and Other Poems*" on September 9, 1957, bringing national recognition to the Beats. Ruling that *Howl and Other Poems* did have some redeeming social value, on October 3, Judge Clayton W. Horn found Ferlinghetti not guilty of publishing and selling obscene material. Later that month 5,000 more copies of the book were printed.

Ferlinghetti believed the trial was the best possible publicity he could have received. The trial had made Ginsberg and his poetry infamous. After being in the limelight of notoriety, Ginsberg's talent made him famous. It also helped bring attention to Ferlinghetti, whose *A Coney Island of the Mind* (1958) would even outsell *Howl and Other Poems*.

Ferlinghetti believed that "Howl" was the most significant poem published after World War II, and his sentiment was echoed by Kenneth Rexroth when he appeared as a witness for the defense during the trial. The book was sold at City Lights throughout the trial and helped make the bookstore an official San Francisco landmark in 2001. Jeffrey Friedman and Rob Epstein's film *Howl* (2010), starring James Franco as Ginsberg, is based on the trial and uses actually testimony. Today there are more than 1,000,000 copies of *Howl and Other Poems* in circulation.

Corso would sum up the contemporaneousness of Ginsberg's poem: "'Howl' is the howl of the generation, the howl of black jackets, of James Dean, of hip beat angels, of mad saints, of cool Zen, the howl of the Withdrawn, of the crazy Sax-man, of the endless Vision whose visionary is Allen Ginsberg, young sensitive timid mad beautiful poet howler of Kerouac's Beat Generation."[9]

The Gathering of the Tribes

Manzarek and Morrison were among the crowd of more than 20,000 people wandering around Golden Gate Park on January 14, 1967, for the Human Be-In, known as the Gathering of the Tribes. Quicksilver Messenger Service, Big Brother and the Holding Company, Jefferson Airplane, and the Grateful Dead provided the music. It was a precursor to the Monterey Pop Festival later that Summer of Love, which would lead to Woodstock and Altamont in 1969, and later the plethora of music festivals around the country for years to come. The Hell's Angels acted as unofficial security, but without the horrific results that would occur at Altamont. On stage were Timothy Leary, Ferlinghetti, McClure, Snyder, Ginsberg, and Kandel. The Beats were passing the torch to the hippies.

A year and a half earlier, poets had gathered for the Berkeley Poetry Conference in July 1965 for the last major gathering of the San Francisco Renaissance. The program included readings by Ginsberg, Duncan, Snyder, Dorn, Creeley, Olson, and Spicer, who would die shortly after (and maintained his disdain for Ginsberg right up to his final poem). Younger poets at the conference included Anne Waldman (b. 1945), Ted Berrigan (1934–83), Ed Sanders (b. 1939), and Kandel.

Kandel's poem "First They Slaughtered the Angels" has been called "a kind of feminist *Howl*."[10] During the San Francisco Renaissance several women played prominent roles in the movement, including Helen Adam, ruth weiss, Barbara Moraff, Joanne Kyger, Joanna McClure, Madeline Gleason, Josephine Miles, and Diane di Prima. However, Kandel caused the most controversy. Clerks selling copies of her *The Love Book* (1966) were arrested for selling obscenity, a decade after the same thing had happened to *Howl and Other Poems*, at a bookstore in Haight-Ashbury and also at City Lights. On a similar note, the actors of McClure's play *The Beard* were arrested fourteen straight nights in 1968 after performances in Los Angeles. But these two events were the last sparks of controversy for the movement.

There were several characteristics that defined the poetics of the Beats who were part of the San Francisco Renaissance: radical politics and political activism; spiritualism, especially Buddhism and Eastern philosophy; attempts to capture drug-induced and visionary states; a connection to geography; a celebration and rediscovery of the body; antiwar sentiments; ecological and environmental awareness; rejection of middle-class mores and materialism; performative poetics; and the idea of poetry as communal experience. These aesthetic ideals were passed on to the rock musicians of the hippie movement. The Beat movement can be seen as the last literary movement that believed that poetry could change the world; the hippies believed it would be rock music that would crumble the walls. As Ed Sanders says, after the Human Be-In, the Beatniks became hippies.[11] The times were still changing, but no longer would literature point the way. Rather than poets, rocks stars became the shamans, and many of them, like Morrison, Dylan, Joplin, and Garcia, saw themselves as the progeny of the Beats.

Notes

1. Lewis Ellingham and Kevin Killian, *Poet Be Like God: Jack Spicer and the San Francisco Renaissance* (Hanover, NH: Wesleyan University Press, 1998), 58.
2. Chuck Workman, dir. *The Source* (Calliope, 2000).
3. Jack Kerouac, *The Dharma Bums* (New York: Penguin, 2006), 9.
4. Michael McClure, *Scratching the Beat Surface: Essays on New Vision from Blake to Kerouac* (New York: Penguin, 1982), 13.

5. Ellingham and Killian, 78–79.
6. Ellingham and Killian, 101.
7. Anaïs Nin, *The Diary of Anaïs Nin: Volume Six, 1955–1966*, ed. Gunther Stulmann (New York: Harcourt Brace Jovanovich, 1976), 65.
8. John Arthur Maynard, *Venice West: The Beat Generation in Southern California* (New Brunswick, NJ: Rutgers University Press, 1991), 197.
9. Bill Morgan and Nancy J. Peters, eds. Howl *on Trial: The Battle for Free Expression* (San Francisco: City Lights Books, 2006), 47.
10. Warren Fench, *The San Francisco Poetry Renaissance, 1955–1960* (Boston: Twayne, 1991), 65.
11. Chuck Workman, dir. *The Source* (Calliope, 2000).

CHAPTER 16

Bay Area Poetics, 1944–1981

Kaplan Page Harris

Kathy Acker stages *The Adult Life of Toulouse Lautrec by Henri Toulouse Lautrec* (1978) in a fin-de-siècle Paris, surrounded by icons of post-impressionism and the Moulin Rouge. The protagonist Giannina explains her desire to move to 1970s San Francisco, which she associates with the Language poet Ron Silliman, perverts, and criminals. She recalls her first visit, in which she seduced Silliman and talked about writing with other members of his circle. Her Parisian cohort doubts whether this story is true, and Acker may also want the reader to question her narrative. Is Giannina supposed to be a stand-in for the punk postmodernist Acker? What is the relationship between Giannina's Ron Silliman and the actual poet?

If Acker's characters were truly creatures of the 1890s, then Paris should have satisfied them with its roster of major world poets. By the middle of the twentieth century, however, the geography of literary value had dramatically shifted, making San Francisco the top destination, at least for poets of the counterculture. How did this change come about? According to Pascale Casanova, literary capitals exist in the world, as do political capitals. Over time the rankings of these capitals change, redistributing the mechanisms of prestige in a way that is not entirely tied to the political economy. Paris was central for the eighteenth and nineteenth centuries, and New York rose to prominence in the early twentieth century. San Francisco's crowning moment came after World War II, when the Berkeley Renaissance and the Beats established their residence there. It remained a hotbed of cultural production during the student activism and social justice movements, beginning in the 1960s and 1970s.

Literary capitals, moreover, are at once imaginative and real. In his foundational study, *The San Francisco Renaissance*, Michael Davidson describes the "enabling fictions" of the city's literary history, for which the definitive moment was the Six Gallery reading on October 7, 1955 (Davidson 1998). The event featured host Kenneth Rexroth and younger poets Allen Ginsberg, Philip Lamantia, Michael McClure, Gary Snyder, and Philip Whalen. Ginsberg's virgin performance of *Howl* was a publicity coup that launched the fame of the Beat Generation and ensured that artistically ambitious members of the postwar generation would soon gravitate to the Bay Area. With the advent of the Beats, San Francisco transitioned from a provincial port on the western frontier, populated mainly by regionalist writers, to a cosmopolitan city that figured in many imaginations as the world's leading avant-garde center.

Literary capitals are also real, however. They exercise control over their cultural institutions: publishers, book distributors, literary-focused media, and reading series. In these cities, the true power brokers are the figures who sit on boards of directors, who write reviews for well-distributed journals, who teach in academia, who master the art of grant-writing, and who edit prestigious small-press magazines. In the second half of the twentieth century, San Francisco was also home to labor organizers, conscientious objectors, and anarchists, who flourished at the outset of World War II and who set the stage for the sexual revolution and the coming decades of grassroots activism.

The career of Kenneth Rexroth reflects the history of the city's modernization. Upon arriving in 1927, he recalled finding it "very much a backwater town ... a long way from the literary marketplace" (Meltzer 1971, 10). Rexroth said the city sneered at resident poet Robinson Jeffers because he was seen as "terribly modernistic." Asked to name California's leading writer, Rexroth answered Gertrude Stein, but added that people only knew of her because of her brother. Rexroth recounted showing his paintings to the one major artist in San Francisco at the time: "Hmmmmm, I see you have been experimentin' with abstract form, like Matissey and Picassio!" Rexroth, in turn, was tireless in his effort to eradicate this small-town myopia. He built an international reputation based not only on a prolific outpouring of essays, reviews, and correspondence with modernist luminaries abroad, but also on an astonishing number of translations from Chinese, Japanese, French, Spanish, Italian, Latin, and Greek. His writings on jazz foreshadowed the embrace of Charlie "Bird" Parker by the New American Poets who followed. Behind the scenes, he hosted an anarchist study group that included members of the Berkeley Renaissance. Rexroth also launched the career of the Beat poet Philip Lamantia by sending the aspiring teenager to New York to meet up with Surrealist refugees from Nazi Europe.

The 1940s saw local writers and artists becoming widely known for their bohemian reputation. In a revealing article, "The New Cult of Sex and

Anarchy," Mildred Edie Brady claimed that San Francisco was a "new Paris" that had usurped the glamor held by the Left Bank and Greenwich Village (Brady 1947, 312–322). Writers who once sought to make a name elsewhere now flocked to this western cradle of anarchism and nascent free love values. Brady credited poetry with leading the attack on "old standards of communication," experimenting with verse that was emotional, antilogical, orgiastic, magical, fluid, natural, and sentimentally mystical. She characterized the reigning political ideology as a mixture of anarchism and psychoanalysis: "holding on the one hand that you must abandon the church, the state, and the family ... and on the other offering sex as the source of individual salvation to a collective world that's going to hell." Brady was avant-garde about sex, referring to the "gonadal revolution" that would not occur until several decades later.

Poets increasingly capitalized on themes of transgressive sexuality. In 1965, Michael McClure published a broadside, *Poetry as a Muscular Principle,* photographed in full frontal nudity, with werewolf facial makeup. Police repeatedly shut down performances of McClure's play *The Beard* (1965) due to its reportedly pornographic content. Police too seized copies of Lenore Kandel's *The Love Book* (1966), alleging it was obscene. And Diane di Prima's *Memoirs of a Beatnik* (1969) supplied the hippie-curious literary market with salacious details about the private lives of the celebrity Beats (Knight 1998).

The local small-press journals combined postwar geopolitical issues with the legacy of high modernism. *Berkeley: A Journal of Modern Culture,* founded by Bern Porter in 1947, featured a regular series on news and politics in China, as well as stories on Frank Lloyd Wright, James Joyce, Sherwood Anderson, Jean-Paul Sartre, Paul Éluard, Man Ray, and Gertrude Stein. The journal juxtaposed Cold War politics with the founding of the Composer's Forum and the Modern Ballet Centre Galleries in 1947, and highlighted "composers of international repute [who] identified with the Bay Area," including Ernest Bloch, Arnold Schönberg, and Roger Sessions. In another journal, *Berkeley Miscellany* (1948–49), Mary Fabilli and Robert Duncan asserted their cosmopolitan credentials by publishing Duncan's "A Description of Venice," which reimagined the city based on Shakespeare's *Othello*.

The decade that followed saw one acolyte after the next enthusing over the worldliness of the city's writers. In *Archetype West,* an overview of Bay Area poetry, William Everson (né Brother Antoninus) considered the starry-eyed Hellenistic pantheon of Rexroth, Lamantia, and Duncan, arguing that these writers achieved a poetic transformation from "traditional regionalism to revolutionary internationalism" (Everson 110–119). They paved the way for the "cosmic obscenity" that flourished with the Beats, notably in Ginsberg's synthesis of eastern and western influences, Surrealism, and Judaism. Lawrence Ferlinghetti's poetry was vastly "more cosmopolitanism" than anything published prior. In "Note on Poetry in San Francisco" (1958), Ferlinghetti described the emergent activity of "street poetry" in contrast to the navel-gazing of the academic poet, and an oral impulse that was different from the silent, deadening effect of print on a page. The new poetry "all adds up to the beginnings of a very inevitable thing – the resocialization of poetry." David Meltzer portrayed the internationalism of the new poetry as a "Babel" of teeming linguistic resources from regional dialects and ubiquitous media discourse to "shop-talk, cop-talk, bop-talk": "these sounds, the languages, these codes & messages, all meet in the ears & eyes of poets who have been Jacob-wrestling Europe since landing on Plymouth Rock" (Meltzer 1971, 2–3). Meltzer could be describing Ginsburg's *Howl* when he identified the "USA Babylon" of poetry in their time: "The poet's work is to activate the mind to its full measure of perception & receptivity. The poem is an event created from a fusion, a wedding of learned skills & unknown sources. After trying to get it all down – the faces, voices, dreams, & fears – the poet begin to realize that all the voices are one & it is his work to make it heard." Would-be writers soon felt the pull of "Café Society," as one portrait collection dubbed the scene on North Beach (Nowinski 1978). Cafés, more worldly than Western saloons, invited viewers to experience a Left Bank *savoir faire*.

The Beats capitalized on the local buzz. The 1957 obscenity trial for Ginberg's *Howl* is often taken as a watershed moment for the counterculture. But San Francisco had already achieved international fame long before the publicity storm that occurred during the trial. In 1957, the *Evergreen Review* editors Donald Allen and Barney Rosset featured an essay on "The San Francisco Scene," granting locals widespread exposure in New York publishing circles. Rexroth introduced the issue, which featured Brother Antoninus, Duncan, Lawrence Ferlinghetti, McClure, Josephine Miles, Spicer, James Broughton, Michael Rumaker, Gary Snyder, Philip Whalen, Kerouac, and Ginsberg. The longest contribution was made by Rumaker, a new arrival from Black Mountain College, who had come West because of the city's growing reputation. In the months leading up to the Gallery Six reading, two magazines that scouted for new talent in the international literary marketplace published Jack Kerouac. *Paris Review* published "The Mexican Girl," and *New*

World Writing published "Jazz of the Beat Generation," both excerpts from *On the Road* (Theado 2001, 5). Notoriety had thus arrived even before *The New York Times* blessed *On the Road* with a positive review the following year.

§

The local literati would likely not have achieved the reputation it did, however, without the political activism of its most prominent members. The grassroot causes ranged from anarchism, pacifism, labor organizing, and homophile societies at mid-century to New Left coalitions of Second Wave Feminism, gay liberation, Black Nationalism, El Movimiento, and Third-Worldism. The movements did not always find poets in leadership positions, much less on subcommittees where avant-gardists tended to avoid the stamp-licking jobs. But a steady production of political agitation took place behind the scenes in the small-press magazines of the Mimeo Revolution. A crucial early example was *Circle* magazine, published at the Civilian Public Service Camp at Waldport, Oregon, by William Everson and fellow conscientious objectors who in 1944 proclaimed themselves "a small circle of creation as opposed to a bursting Nova of destruction." Muriel Rukeyser in *Berkeley Miscellany* declared: "To be against the war is not enough, it is hardly a beginning... The truth here goes farther, there is another way of being against the war and the sources of war. They are everyday, these sources, as the sources of peace are everyday, infinite and commonplace as a look, as each new sun." Later area magazines that carried this activist torch included *The San Francisco Oracle* and *The Journal for the Protection of All Beings*.

San Francisco differed from other urban concentrations of activism because it was ground zero for gay liberation in the United States. The literature of the city is definitively bound up with that struggle. The Mattachine Society, a leading homophile organization, based its editorial offices for *The Mattachine Review* in San Francisco (Sears 2006). The editors of this enormously influential publication conceived of social justice on a global field. They republished in translation articles that originally appeared in non-English forums and showcased the legal and political headlines of gay communities around the world. After the British Parliament issued a 1957 report urging the repeal of anti-gay legislation, the cover article announced, "The Wolfenden Report: Is It a 'Magna Carta for Homosexuals?" (Trout 1957). The editors were especially keen to highlight scientific research that normalized homosexuality. Alfred C. Kinsey's work on the spectrum of human sexuality was front-page news in several issues. The editors, moreover, were among the earliest public critics of the conversion therapy doctrines supported by the American Psychological Association. One article wryly reported, "The San Francisco psychiatrist declared he was encouraged to find one old-fashioned treatment – arranging an alliance between a prostitute and a homosexual, to 'teach him the facts of life' – is now beginning to fall by the wayside."

The Mattachine Review published these journalistic features alongside a plethora of fiction and poetry. The poems in translation reinforced the cosmopolitan ideals of the journal, while the attention to U.S. writers bolstered the impression of a thriving, indigenous gay tradition that stretched from Walt Whitman's "Whoever You Are Holding Me Now in Hand" to Allen Ginsberg's "The Green Automobile." A brief profile of Ginsberg compared him to two earlier "homophile" poets, Walt Whitman and Hart Crane. It applauded his sensitivity for the feelings of "some millions of [gay] Americans," addressed in the final lines of *Howl*: "American I'm putting my queer shoulder to the wheel." In case readers didn't catch the queer subtext, Ginsberg explained that "The Green Automobile" was "addressed to a boyfriend ... It is an important poem for me" (Ginsberg 1959, 12–15). Although heavily international in its coverage, the *Mattachine Review* regularly painted San Francisco as a paradise for gay life. A two-page illustration advertised, "San Francisco's North Beach area is famous among tourists and natives alike as one of the most colorful yet cosmopolitan places in America. Gourmets know it as a place where, within a distance of a few blocks ... some of the finest chefs in the hemisphere prepare native foods that would qualify them to serve the United Nations. Filipino, Chinese, Italian, Basque, Mexican, Hawaiian, French, Tahitian, Spanish, Armenian and many other national menus are regular bills of fare in this area. Yes, and Swedish smorgasbord, Creole cookin', Sukiyaki and Kansas City steaks too" (Balfour 1956). *Mattachine* called to gay readers in the hinterland who bucked against the pressure to take out a mortgage in a cookie-cutter suburb of the Baby Boomer diaper brigade. Rather than be defined by a horizon of McDonalds franchises or pockets stuffed with A&P coupons, the Bay Area arrivals could explore exponentially richer flavors of the palate (never mind the imperialism of the dinner menu). In San Francisco, "an electric kind of worldliness grips this area," announced the guide for neo-foodies: pizza joints and chop suey were "all but a few yards (and a world) apart."

By 1970, Berkeley's Gay Liberation Front announced a more militant banner with the founding of the magazine *Gay Sunshine*. The editorial philosophy in the debut issue set forth a bold political platform: "Since all gays are oppressed by the society ... a gay newspaper would be a powerful tool in the homosexual fight for equal rights, as it would be a catalyst that could call forth the political potential of a subculture." In its early years *Gay Sunshine* produced a stream of impassioned columns, activist manifestos, notes on hate crimes and police oppression, pornography, prisoner advocacy, job classifieds, practical advice, health tips, and much more. On the local front, *Gay Sunshine* covered the nightlife of bars like The Stud and White Horse. It also reported internationally on gay politics in New York, London, Austin, and what one column called "Down South." Like its predecessor, the *Mattachine Review*, *Gay Sunshine* mixed political coverage with cultural features that came to dominate the magazine. The most significant contribution by far was a series of interviews delving into the personal lives of gay artists and writers, among them Allen Ginsberg, Harold Norse, William Burroughs, Christopher Isherwood, Jean Genet, Gerard Malanga, Taylor Mead, and Mutsuo Takahashi. Another ongoing, much-lauded series cast an unprecedented light on gay cultures in world history, with topics such as "Arab Civilization and Gay Love," "Living in Truth: Akheneten and Egypt (Reigned 1379–1362 BC)," "Russia's Gay Literature and History from the Eleventh to the Twentieth Centuries," "Gay London in the 1720s," "An Historical Study in Indian Homosexuality," "Homosexuality in 1920s Harlem," "Homosexuals in the Anti-Nazi Underground," and "Mexican Gaylife in Historical Perspective" (Leyland 1991). The focus was worldly, even as local coverage promoted life in and around the booming gay neighborhoods in San Francisco.

§

This local grassroots activity formed the backdrop of the Berkeley Renaissance, which was led by Robert Duncan and Jack Spicer and joined by Robin Blaser, Helen Adam, Madeline Gleason, Stan Persky, and George Stanley. Spicer, Duncan, and Blaser met as students at the University of California, Berkeley under the historian Ernst Kantorowicz, whose classic *The King's Two Bodies* inspired themes of medievalism in their writing. A native of Los Angeles, Spicer was on track for a promising academic career in linguistics, but his appointment in the University of California system was derailed after he refused to sign a mandatory anti-communist loyalty oath in 1950. Spicer was known for his aggressive convictions in both poetry and politics. In addition to his service in the Mattachine Society, Spicer composed open poems about sexuality that proved influential for generations to come. His characteristic tone was less rhetorical agitprop than camping on poetic conventions, as for instance in his mock treatise, "The Unvert Manifesto and Other Papers Found in the Rare Book Room of the Boston Public Library in the Handwriting of Oliver Charming. By S." (Spicer 2008).

Spicer famously theorized the emerging poetics in lectures in Berkeley and Vancouver. He spoke of poetry as deriving from "outside" the ego or self in a way that was diametrically opposed to then-reigning confessional poets like Robert Lowell. Spicer's idea of poetry as "dictated" from "martians" eventually became canonical for poets who rejected the transparency of the lyric self (in particular the Language poets). His notion of seriality conceived of writing through interconnected units that do not develop toward a pre-ordained architecture or narrative. The serial poem thus sustained the viability of the long poem without the totalitarian baggage associated with its modernist forerunners. Some of Spicer's manifestos were not exactly manifestos. In his "Magic Workshop" he distributed a questionnaire that asked for such responses as "If you had a chance to eliminate three political figures in the world, which would you choose?" and "Invent a dream in which you appear as a poet." In *After Lorca*, his most celebrated work, Spicer corresponds with Lorca about translations of his poems, even though Lorca had been killed by Fascist forces twenty years earlier. The resurrected Lorca chides the younger poet for the mixture of translations, half-translations that include Spicer's own insertions, and outright fake translations, which give the series "the effect of an unwilling centaur" (Spicer 2008, 107). On the publishing front Spicer had a reputation for angrily denouncing anyone who let his writing circulate outside of the Bay Area. The San Francisco writer Dodie Bellamy dubbed him the "father of narrowcasting." His poetry celebrated not the universal, but the local, also known as the regulars at his local bar. He kept at his favorite watering hole a dropbox for submissions for his mimeo magazine *J*. In terms of book design, the cover of his *Book of Magazine Verse* caricatured the logo of the establishment *Poetry* magazine. The book's acknowledgments show that no one says thanks quite like Spicer: "None of the poems in this book have been published in magazines. The author wishes to acknowledge the rejection of poems herein by editors Denise Levertov of *The Nation* and Henry Rago of *Poetry* (Chicago)."

Duncan was more itinerant than Spicer, at least in his early life, and he thrived on ever-widening audiences. Following medieval and renaissance studies at Berkeley, he embarked for stints in New York, Florida, Mallorca, and Black Mountain College (the experimental arts school), before settling with the painter Jess Collins in San Francisco in the 1950s. When Donald Allen edited *The New American Poetry* (1960), he placed Duncan with the Black Mountain group because he taught at the school for a semester, he was friends with Charles Olson, Robert Creeley, Denise Levertov, and Larry Eigner, and his writing reflected the open field poetics of Olson's manifesto "Projective Verse" (1950). The main difference was that whereas Olson draws on the historical archive, Duncan draws on the theosophical tradition. In this way Olson is more like Ezra Pound, and Duncan more like H. D. and Yeats. His serialized *ars poetica* known as *The H. D. Book* is part homage to H. D. and part encyclopedic rumination on modernist poetry and the occult. His nearly four decades of poetry developed through several distinct stages. *Writing Writing* (1953) grew out of two years of Stein imitations that taught him to estrange the lyric voice (Reed 2011). With *The Opening of the Field* (1960), Duncan allowed himself to combine varying forms such as stanzaic verse, prose poems, and epistolary letters. Two serial poems "The Structure of Rime" and "Passages" that run their course through the later collections evoke a metaphysical totality that readers perceive only in fragments.

Like Spicer, Duncan threw his energy behind the cause of gay liberation. In 1944, he published an essay "The Homosexuality in Society" that scandalized the literary establishment by comparing the persecution of gays to other oppressed groups. When John Crowe Ransom caught wind of the essay, he canceled plans to publish poems by Duncan that he had already accepted for *The Kenyon Review*. Later in the 1970s, Duncan publicly read from their correspondence over the incident at rallies for gay rights. In politics more generally, Duncan tended to lean toward anarchism. His 1945 essay in *Direct Action* magazine calls for the adoption of "Robin Hoodism," the redistribution of food on the black market, and the erection of clandestine safe houses for traveling anarchists. In the "Passages: Uprising" he attacks the outrages of Cold War imperialism: "the very glint of Satan's eyes from the pit of hell of America's / unacknowledged, unrepented crimes." That said, despite his stance against U.S. actions in Vietnam, Duncan was suspicious about subsuming poetry to the political speech. His long-time friendship with the poet Denise Levertov fell apart over the antiwar poetry that she wrote in protest of civilian deaths at the hands of the U.S. military. The letters of their debate have since become required readings about the relationship of poetry and politics. Regardless of his activist misgivings, Duncan became an icon for gay militancy in the 1970s. His poem "The Torso: Passages 18" was renowned for reversing the gendered binaries of the lyric through the open representation of two male lovers. Duncan's presence also loomed over *Manroot* magazine, which was founded by his student Paul Mariah and, in the late 1960s, featured the first appearance of Judy Grahn's classic "The Psychoanalysis of Edward the Dyke," and devoted an entire issue to Spicer a decade after his death when most of the work was out of print. The coveted issue decisively crowned the late poet as patron saint for the literary front of gay liberation.

The poets around Duncan and Spicer were more diverse both geographically and generationally than the designation "Berkeley Renaissance" might imply. A case in point is Robin Blaser, whose serial poem "Image-Nation" stretches from the 1960s to the 2000s, developing from the campy medievalism favored by Duncan and Spicer toward the phenomenological meditations of his collected poems in *The Holy Forest* (2008). Behind the scenes he performed a crucial service to the community by editing *The Collected Books of Jack Spicer* and writing an afterword, "The Practice of the Outside," that has long served as a guide to Spicer's critique of expressionist tenets (Spicer 1975). Blaser, moreover, provided a vibrant conduit to poets in Vancouver after he began teaching at Simon Fraser University in 1966. A second case in point is the Scottish balladeer Helen Adam, who provided a living, breathing connection to the folkloric tradition that Duncan and his fellow poets prized. Among her best-known writings were the ballads collected in *The Queen of Crow Castle* (1958) and *Ballads* (1964), which were both illustrated by the painter Jess, and *San Francisco's Burning* (1963), which is one of the few operas in the genre generally known as poets' theater.

The Berkeley Renaissance was of course not the only show in town. A tangential constellation that Ron Silliman usefully refers to as New Western or Zen Cowboy includes the poets Philip Whalen, Gary Snyder, Joanne Kyger, and later Leslie Scalapino (Silliman 2007). The writing is largely defined by its concern with the West as a site of ecological investigation and as a contact zone between the European, Native American, and Pacific Rim cultures. Snyder is best known for such works as his Pulitzer winning *Turtle Island* (1973) that merge both these senses of the landscape (Gray 2006). A headliner at the original Six Gallery reading, Snyder has since effectively become poet laureate of the environmentalist movement. Whalen, who also took the stage at the Six Gallery, went on to produce numerous poems that humorously play with New Age spirituality and the aging male body. Paul Carroll once dubbed him the "Old Faithful of contemporary American poetry" for his steady output; his collected poems cover more than 800 pages. When Allen's anthology *New American Poetry* only featured four women contributors, the most glaring omission was Joanne Kyger, who has proven a major voice the local community since the 1950s. In the books *The Tapestry and the Web* and *Joanne* she subverts the patriarchy not only of the Hellenistic canon but also the western Buddhism of her one-time partner Gary Snyder.

§

The debate between Levertov and Duncan foreshadowed the high stakes of poetry and politics in the 1970s. A brief survey of reading schedules and announcements in *Poetry Flash* (a monthly local newsletter) reveals that political rallies were the main occasion for poetry readings during the decade. The list does not show the countless benefits for magazines, books, and literary establishments, nor does it show festivals and group readings that celebrated the myriad alternative lifestyles of San Francisco, like poetry events for Equinox, the Solstice, the "Imagination," the Feast of Saint Eulalia (patron saint of the gypsies), His Holiness The XVI Gyalwa Karmapa, and the Eros-god – among others that are advertised in *Poetry Flash*. And a whole separate list could be made that centered on the poetry of the vibrant subcultures, like "The San Francisco Punk Poetry Festival" on August 28, 1977.

But out of this decade the most acclaimed movement to emerge was the Language poets, comprised on the West Coast of Rae Armantrout, Steve Benson, Carla Harryman, Lyn Hejinian, Bob Perelman, Kit Robinson, Ron Silliman, and Barrett Watten. The Language poets generally distrusted Levertov's use of the public voice, but they generally distrusted Duncan's preference for metaphysical abstractions too. Language poets instead shifted critique to the role of language in the uneven distribution of power. Robert Grenier's proclamation "I HATE SPEECH" defined the moment that poets began to treat the poem as a material object. The poems themselves tend to demolish syntax, estrange referentiality, and resist narrative beyond the level of the sentence. Put another way, while they were unlikely to be headliners at the kind of rallies and events listed above, they strongly argued for political critique at the level of form. Or as Watten writes, "the turn to language that took place in experimental poetry in the 1970s continues the politics of the 1960s by other means." Silliman theorizes the prose poetry of "the new sentence" as an anticapitalist critique, and he identifies its presence almost exclusively in poets of the Bay Area. "Sentence structure," says Silliman, "is altered for torque, or increased polysemy / ambiguity" (Silliman 1980). Language poets attacked the poetry establishment too, ranging from the lucrative MFA reading circuit to literary journals that exploit the labor of internships or university course credit. The venues for their work, by contrast, were largely self-operated: the magazines *THIS* and *Poetics Journal*, Hejinian's Tuumba press, and the Grand Piano reading series. At a talk-based series, first held in Perelman's apartment and later at the 80 Langton Street Arts Center, the poets drew on criticism and theory to reflect on their practice. This turn to poetics, for lack of a better term, caused no shortage of controversy because it departed radically from the poet as celebrity model that prevailed during the previous generation.

Language poems come in all sizes. Hejinian and Silliman specialize in techniques for composing long poems, and in some cases very long poems. Hejinian's *My Life* is an autobiography composed using a non-linear, sentenced-counting constraint. In 1980, at age 37, she published the first edition containing thirty-seven sections with thirty-seven sentences in each section. The next edition published in 1987 not only adds seven sections at the end, but it also goes back and adds seven additional sentences to each original section. In this way *My Life* suggests that conventional autobiography performs a degree of violence in the narrative representation of a person's life. Silliman solves the problem of writing long poems by using a Fibonacci sequence to extend paragraph size in the prose poem *Tjanting* (1981). Silliman generated an even longer poem *The Alphabet* by writing individual sections like *Paradise* for P or *Demo* for D. Each section employs a distinct compositional device and bears a dedication to a friend or fellow poet. The poem "R" he describes as about the "tension between the sentence and the line. For "Skies," he explains, "Every day for one year I looked at the sky & noted what I saw." But not all the poems require heavy lifting. Like other Language poets, Rae Armantrout is an anthropologist of late capitalist outrages, but her poems are closer to the lyric than any of her peers. Many of her poems visually resemble the small poems of Emily Dickinson or Lorine Niedecker. Armantrout's most memorable lines are as much about poetic practice as they are about late capitalist deprivations: "Ventriloquy is the mother tongue," "A career in vestige management," "One's a connoisseur of vacancies, / loud silences / surrounding human artifacts."

The poets associated with feminism, cultural nationalism, and gay liberation also sought to continue the politics of the 1960s, but unlike the Language poets, their writing often utilized narrative as a political tool for expressing identity. The governing idea was that patriarchy had denied full personhood to women and people of color in the past, and telling stories of their experience therefore constitutes a stage of political resistance. Bob Kaufman's *Solitudes Crowded With Loneliness*, for example, fuses bebop rhythms and intense psychological testimony about racial violence, especially police persecution, in a way that proves a lasting influence for the Black Arts Movement (Smethurst 2005). To take another example, coming-out narrative gay and lesbian movements produced the Judy Grahn's "The Psychoanalysis of Edward the Dyke," which, in one part, dramatizes the incommensurability of a heterosexist medical establishment and lesbian experience, and in another part, portrays a series of very different women who are alike or "common" in sharing the brutality inflected upon them by patriarchy: "the common woman is as common as the best of bread / and will rise / and will become strong – I swear it to you." The theoretical grounds for such narratives often hearkened back to a model of class struggle described by György Lukács, who was read by an important but contentious Marxism study group of the 1970s that counted among its participants the Language poets Ron Silliman and Steve Benson, the New Narrative writers Bruce Boone, Steve Abbott, and Robert Glück, and the avant-feminist poet Kathleen Fraser, who co-founded the experimental journal *HOW(ever)* with Beverley Dahlen and Frances Jaffer (Harris 2011). Among this group the feminists and gay activists generally sought ways to reinvent narrative, such as the prose meditations on the materiality of language in Fraser's *Each Next* and the autobiographical novel about writing, sex, friendship, and philosophy in Glück's *Jack the Modernist*.

The writers associated with New Narrative arguably reflect the culmination of San Francisco's history of experimental poetry and social activism across the timeline traced in this essay. In terms of form, New Narrative can often be thought of as a "fellow traveller" of the Language poets, as exemplified by the non-linear verbal gymnastics of Dodie Bellamy's *Letters of Mina Harker* and the reduction and redaction techniques in her later *Cunt Norton*, which uses as its source text the patriarchal canon of the 1975 *Norton Anthology of Poetry* (Glück 2004; Harris 2009). Unlike Language poetry, at any rate, New Narrative draws on a queer tradition that foregrounds the affect and sexuality, as exemplified again by these two works by Bellamy. Robert Glück and Bruce Boone also extend the non-standard translations of Spicer's *After Lorca* in their collaboration *La Fontaine*, in which their quotidian life experiences regularly interrupt the expected transparency of the translation process. The most significant activist work by New Narrative occurred after two of its leading members, Bruce Boone and Steve Abbott, organized the Left Write Unity Conference of 1981 and invited writers from across the progressive spectrum: ecological, labor union, feminist, gay/lesbian, and anticolonial. Bringing the diverse coalitions together was a risky move because the Left was beset by in-fighting in the wake of Reagan's election. Fireworks flew around the claims of feminist and queer activists, whose leadership positions were frequently dismissed by peers in more established factions of the Left. More importantly, the New Narrative writers anticipated a return to street-level activism among local literary communities in the coming decades, from ACT UP organizing in the face of the AIDS pandemic to the Occupy actions against the outrages of neoliberalism.

New Narrative was only one tendency in the widely diverse field of Bay Area writing, but it was finally distinctive in that the work grew and developed as only would have been imaginable in the literary capital of the Bay Area. Like Acker's Giannina at the start of this essay, many of the leading New Narrative writers testify to the freedom they felt after moving to the city: Robert Glück from Cleveland, Kevin Killian from Long Island, Camille Roy from Chicago, Steve Abbott from Nebraska, Dodie Bellamy from Indiana. Perhaps no other writer captures the gravitational pull of the city than Abbott, who first came up with the name New Narrative. As an undergrad at the University of Nebraska in the 1960s he helped orchestrate Ginsberg's infamous campus reading from the antiwar poem *Wichita Vortex Sutra*. As a graduate student at Emory University in Atlanta c. 1970 he got elected as student body president before coming out of the closet in the campus newspaper and organizing on behalf of the local gay community. As a single gay father, he next moved to San Francisco, became a writer for *Gay Sunshine*, produced a vast body of experimental fiction, poetry, and criticism, and edited the monthly newsletter *Poetry Flash* during the rocky emergence of the Language poets. This all came before his early death from AIDS in 1992. One sure sign of the literary prestige conferred by the city is that his daughter Alysia Abbott's recent bestselling memoir about their growing up together in San Francisco is soon to be filmed by Sofia Coppola.

CHAPTER 17

Los Angeles Poetry from the McCarthy to the Punk Eras

Brian Stefans

Poetry in Los Angeles starts with the oral songs and narratives of the native American Tongva tribe who came to be called "Gabrielinos" during the period of the Spanish conquest. However, its print origins – where one can see the themes and controversies that form the ideological roots of urban Angelino poetry for the next hundred years – lie in the Spanish-language poems published in newspapers such as *El Clamor Público* and the bilingual *Los Angeles Star/La Estrella*.[1] In these papers, Mexicans newly disenfranchised after California became the thirty-first U.S. state in 1850 argued their cases before the courts of literature in lieu of consistent civic justice. With its refrain of "seis azotes" ("six lashes"), the anonymous narrator of "Azotes" (1856) ably illustrates the absurdities of the judicial vacuum in this territory on the far margins of two countries:

> To the husband who, neither
> Poor nor ugly, is yet abandoned,
> And still consents to help his
> Former wife with her expenses;
> Though he does not preserve his honor
> Thinks he can preserve that of others;
> Who knowing that their children
> Are not his, still embraces them;
> Though fearful to join the military,
> Yet wears his beard in varied sizes;
> Like a prudent doctor
> I prescribe to him – *six lashes*.[2]

Though Bertolt Brecht wouldn't start his five-year sojourn in Los Angeles until 1942, the German's unique blending of parable-like tales with acute, satirical character sketches is anticipated in this poem in which a rich typology – a "dull, beardless youth," a "lunatic son of Mars," a shifty politician, a wealthy "venerable hypocrite," the "impudent author" himself, and not least the cuckolded husband of the verse above – are all prescribed an automatic "six lashes" by our "prudent doctor." These poets vividly illustrated the trials of being former citizens of the recently independent Mexico who have had, quite literally, a new form of government inserted under their feet.

This Spanish period came to an end abruptly around 1900. If there is a distinctive flavor to English-language Los Angeles poetry at the turn of the century, it is imbued with the spirit of boosterism that came in the wake of Charles Lummis's transcontinental walk in 1884 to the city. The title of Charles Farwell Edson's undated volume, *Los Angeles: From the Sierras to the Sea*, with seductive etchings by Marion Holden Pope, captures the spirit of the luck these wealthy settlers felt in the "land of sunshine," not to mention hints at the rampant real estate speculation that would transform the city from a mere 12,000 when Lummis arrived to 102,000 fifteen years later. A few exceptional poets did emerge at this time – the young suicide Nora May French (1881–1907), the gardener and amateur Sinologist Olive Percival (1865–1945), and the New York transplant Julia Boynton Green (1861–1957)[3] – but they remained ignored by their peers in the Northeast, though French, in the year before her death, was an intimate of George Sterling's "bohemian" circle in Carmel.[4] The break between the Spanish- and English-language traditions in Los Angeles presages what, until the 1980s at least, has been a central characteristic of the city's poetic culture. Periods of intense activity – the poetry of the McCarthy Era, the brief experiment in Beat poetics in Venice West, the Watts Writers Workshop, and the emergence of "punk" poetry around Beyond Baroque in the late 1970s – did not establish a local tradition so much as sink into the mist.

To the sense of civic disenfranchisement that the Mexicans first discovered can be added a distinctive geographical disenfranchisement. What little "nature" there is in the city is largely imported or supported by water from outlying regions, and everything else is covered with sand and asphalt, becoming the "plains of Id" in Reyner Banham's memorable phrase.[5] There was also an interpersonal disenfranchisement: the common alienations of living in a huge, loud city are aggravated by the demographic divide between the rich and poor and between any number of ethnic communities. This lack, until the latter decades of the twentieth century, of a public space or agora where people of different classes and ethnicities can mingle is one of the few things all Angelinos have come to share. The positive aspirations of certain forms of ideological aspiration, even the environmentalism that has characterized Bay Area poetics for decades or the European-inflected socialisms that animated New York culture in the

1920s and 1930s, seem to be defeated by the very *inauthenticity* of communication in a city of actors and popular dramatists:

> Every visit to the cinema leaves me, against all my vigilance, stupider and worse. Sociability itself connives at injustice by pretending that in this chill world we can still talk to each other, and the casual, amiable remark contributes to perpetuating silence, in that the concession made to the interlocutor debase him once more in the person of speaker. The evil principle that was always latent in affability unfurls its full bestiality in the egalitarian spirit. Condescension, and thinking oneself no better, are the same.[6]

Adorno's melancholic reflections in *Minima Moralia*, written during his own exile in Los Angeles during the latter parts of World War II, aptly describe the dilemmas facing the poet in Los Angeles, energized by the liberated discourse of *vers libre* but cut off – in the face of the overheated real estate market well documented by Mike Davis in *City of Quartz* and the equally booming film industry – from anything like social agency. What results is a poetics of social critique expressed as a *negative* power: as a refusal of bourgeois norms of decorum, of morality, of sociability, even of language. Tracing the rises and falls of these forms of negative poetics in Los Angeles poetry sketches the lineaments of a story that is distinct to the city even as it might, yet again, just dissolve without a trace.

1. Thomas McGrath and the McCarthy Era

The major German writers including Brecht, Adorno, Max Horkheimer, Thomas Mann, and Alfred Döblin who lived in exile in Los Angeles during the war years didn't engage with the local writers in the same way that countless European writers and painters became part of the New York scene in the same time period. However, North Dakota poet Thomas McGrath became a central figure among writers associated with the political left, a group he affectionately dubbed the "Marsh Street Irregulars." A collection he mostly wrote during his decade in LA, *Figures from a Double World* (1955), shows McGrath as a master of the short, satirical lyric, a late descendent of Edwin Arlington Robinson and T. S. Eliot, with a taste for elaborate off-rhymes reminiscent of Wilfred Owens. However, unlike Robinson, who at his best had the patience to tell a story in a plain style and reserve his ironies for a final line or couplet, McGrath can't help setting out his thesis early, as he does in "Fantastic Gentry Wakes Up Dead":

> Walking without a personal sense of disorder
> But aware he was dead, he saw the sun on high,
> Light of the world, a natural. Time made hay
> Of the clipt hours. A perfect day for the murder
>
> Of Mr. Gentry, who, poised, holding his shoes,
> Remembers he cannot put both on together,
> That the process of setting one foot ahead of the other
> Is life.[7]

Though McGrath was critical of the burgeoning movement of Beat poetry, noting early in his review of *Howl,* "When I first read it, this poem seemed to me very bad," he does eventually confess: "Since reading it, I've heard it recited by the author – a moving experience, one with a wallop. The poems turn out to have music, considerable metrical control, a painful sincerity beneath its stridor [sic]."[8] Perhaps inspired, like Robert Lowell during the writing of *Life Studies,* by Ginsberg's fusion of the poetics of Whitman and Pound, McGrath soon started his own long autobiographical poem *Letter to an Imaginary Friend,* in which the note of Los Angeles is struck in this encomium to sunlit blondes:

> The immortal girls, the summer manifestoes
> Startle the buzzard in the corpse-bearing tree.
> [. . .]
> Coiffeur of dream, oh bright improbable gold!
> The blonde-haired women, crowned as with surplus light,
> Curls crisp as lettuce on their bellies porch
> And slick and secret when the armpit yawns,
> Hair! dimension of heat!
>   Lit by subliminal suns
> That shrink their dresses half way up their thighs
> It ripens outward.
>   Furry as a peach
> It licks the hand that hungers at the knee;
> And where the back and buttocks sweetly mate
> Like queenly empires joined in natural peace
> (Equation of the palm! O sweet division!)
> Glints like shot silk. And where the pubis thrusts
> Into my world to light me into dark
> Is stiff and secret as a buried fence
> Or bristles friendly as a welcome mat.[9]

This section of *Letter,* which first appeared in the small anthology *Poetry Los Angeles* in 1958, culminates in a section that begins with the memorable apostrophe: "O great Kingdom of Fuck! And myself: plenipotentiary!" as if rising to the challenge of *Howl* to break the bonds of censorship and let bacchanalian Eros thrive.

Few of McGrath's "Marsh Street Irregulars" attained his technical facility or attempted a lyrical epic on the scale of *Letter*. Bert Meyers, for example, expressed his deep humanistic empathy with the working class by becoming a master of the miniature:

> **Picture Framing**
>
> My fingers feed in the fields of wood.
>
> I sand pine, walnut, bass,
> and sweat to raise their grain.
>
> Paints, powder and brush
> are the seasons of my trade.
>
> At the end of the day
> I drive home
> the proud cattle of my hands.[10]

McGrath's other peers included former student Mel Weisburd, soldier and activist Edwin Rolfe who moved to LA after fighting Franco in Spain with the Abraham Lincoln Brigade, Ukrainian-born William Pillin, Gene Frumkin (co-founder of *Coastlines* with Weisburd), Josephine Ain (then married to important post-Bauhaus architect Gregory Ain), experimental photographer Edmund Teske, music critic Peter Yates, Naomi Replansky, Lawrence Spingarn and James Boyer May, editor of the literary journal *Trace* (1952–70), which indexed small-press poetry journals in the United States and Europe.

Poets in McGrath's circle would go on to create substantial bodies of work, notably Spingarn, Pillin, Replansky, and the teacher Ann Stanford, but it's the Malibu poet Curtis Zahn who picks up on the strand of negative ideology coupled with an earthy, concrete storytelling mode that becomes notable as the Los Angeles street tradition. Zahn's scathing, if undisciplined, screed titled "Tijuana" ends on a note that conjures both spectacle and the impoverishment of folk cultures, and echoes the Frankfurt School's critiques of postwar consumer society:

> Tijuana? One can get into but not out of it
> and into it from the whole world
> have come seekers, drifters, escapes [sic];
> wanted men and unwanted women, come here
> for the final stalemate. Their shoes –
> their city shoes frozen by dust, and

> stomachs bleached by begged Tacos shot with horsemeat.
> Here to dry up while drinking and stealing
> and waiting. Converting their German, French,
> English, Chinese into the oiled, grey
> pidgin Spanish of bordertown; to wait
> beside the flagrant streets for new faces
> come to be horrified by sin, and to
> grovel in the spectacle
> of abortion and absorption. And to hear
> lame, warped, U.S. made guitars, chord-wreaked
> by Indians too poor to fatten
> their dogs for the eating.[11]

Zahn was also a satirical, absurdist playwright and fiction writer, with the collection *American Contemporary* published by New Directions in 1963. Nonetheless, his reputation, along with many poets inMcGrath's circle, would remain largely local.

11. The Venice West Beats

McGrath appeared before House Un-American Committee (HUAC) as an unfriendly witness in 1953, a summons that lost him his job at Los Angeles State College. He made a declaration of the total unity of art in life that wouldn't have been unamenable to the "outlaw" Beat-influenced poets then beginning to congregate in Venice Beach:

> [A]s a poet I must refuse to cooperate with the committee on what I can only call esthetic grounds. The view of life which we receive through the great works of art is a privileged one – it is a view of life according to probability or necessity, not subject to the chance and accident of our real world and therefore in a sense truer than the life we see lived all around us. I believe that one of the things required of us is to try to give life an esthetic ground, to give it some of the pattern and beauty of art. I have tried as best I can to do this with my own life, and while I do not claim any very great success, it would be anti-climactic, destructive of the pattern of my life, if I were to cooperate with the committee.[12]

McGrath is not arguing, like a latter-day Surrealist, for the complete merging of the dream and waking worlds. The key term here is "pattern." He had a love for baroque wordplay in his poems, and he argues that poems are "not subject to the chance and accident of our real world." However, one can hear the faint echoes of the much simpler anthem of the Venice West Beats – "Art is Love is God" – coined by the artist Wallace Berman and scrawled in ink on the wall of the Venice West Cafe by its founder, poet Stuart Perkoff, just minutes before the first customers sidled in. And if McGrath's vision of life with an "esthetic ground" eventually took him far away from Los Angeles and back to his home state of North Dakota, the lives of the Venice West Beats ended, as often as not, in tragedy.

The New American Poetry, edited by Donald Allen and published by New York's Grove Press in 1960, brought to national attention the careers of several "underground" poets – now considered canonical – such as Ginsberg, Philip Whalen, Frank O'Hara, James Schuyler, Robert Creeley, Charles Olson, Robert Duncan, Jack Spicer, and Denise Levertov. Tucked away in the non-geographical miscellany of section five – alongside Gary Snyder (San Francisco), John Wieners (Boston), and Leroi Jones (New York) – are three poems by Perkoff, the sole LA poet[13] in the collection. It's not surprising that Perkoff did not become an overnight star and acquire younger acolytes like his peers; his three contributions seem, at times, pastiches of Ginsberg and Olson, and can feel thin on visual and intellectual detail when compared to the large elaborate structures of the urbane O'Hara, the elegant Creeley or the erudite Duncan. However, in his poems, Perkoff *theorized* the life of voluntary poverty in the shadow of the Venice oil derricks, then the seediest part of Los Angeles:

The Recluses

They paper the walls of their world
with their strange rhythms,
visions of this, their sighted dreams.
They have with their deepest eardooms
fragments of freshest wildness.
        That of a woman
never feeling breastingly through their eyes,
they have no sin. But on their walls
of rhythmed visioned scenes
they often have lines about a mountain.

That black which is the greedy of the mind,
that reaches up and grasps from
the perceiving eye
all of the memoric stanzas brought on by the world
is their fine house.

They live there.
They have their own dark lines.
They are always

inside[14]

The seeds of Perkoff's own eventual ruin can be found in this poem as the very ambiguity of the word "sighted" suggests. Perkoff was neither confident that his "dreams" could "see" and therefore offer guidance as they had for the Surrealists (emboldened by the writings of Freud and Marx) nor that they were literally "sighted," like a ship on the horizon, in waking life. His "dreams" replace the vestiges of the *real,* whether of politics, art or other people, mainstays of highly referential poets like O'Hara and Ginsberg but rejected as corrupt by this writer intent on pure, monastic "vision." Perkoff's revisiting of the concept of the *domus,* however, has telling resonances with comments by Adorno just a decade earlier: "Private existence, in striving to resemble one worthy of man, betrays the latter, since any resemblance is withdrawn from general realization, which yet more than ever before has need of independent thought. There is no way out of entanglement."[15] Perkoff's language, whose only real adornment are the syncopations of jazz rhythms (hence the repeated synaesthetic equation of sight and sound), points no real way beyond the impasse of spectacular society.

Lawrence Lipton's misguided, now largely unreadable *Holy Barbarians* (1959) portrayed Venice's bohemian culture as equal to that of the more acclaimed San Francisco scene where Lipton's main rival, Kenneth Rexroth, flourished as an unwitting "father" to the Beats. Other poets decided to take advantage of the lively obscurity of the deleterious enclave. Notable among them was Charles Foster – "the Arrow Collar man, the man in the grey flannel suit, the congenital Man Most Likely to Succeed,"[16] according to John Arthur Maynard. Foster's choice to leave the dog-eat-dog world of business appeared to justify Lipton's vision of Venice as a magnet for creative dropouts. A "square" by the standards of the time – tall, blonde, good-looking, from New England money – Foster was a terrible alcoholic, which made him an easy fit in the community. He churned out long, glossolaliac improvisations but occasionally hit on the vignette that captured the anxious and indeterminate nature of this Cold War retreat. "One Man's Society Island" is nearly Mallarméan in its apotheosis of chance in both story and syntax:

> at solitaire
> impeccably he
> closed his eyes to what –
> if anybody – to see,
> that is,
> if anybody wasn't
> looking (& anybody

wasn't so –
he riffed a shuffle
& dealt a glancing
temporary deuce in
(spades, smile of it's
all over, spilled death, right off
the bottom of
the cold deck / cool hands
to
himself.[17]

A fascinating, though short-term, visitor to Venice was the Scottish poet, novelist, publisher, and agitator Alexander Trocchi, most known for his association with the Situationists and his autobiographical novel *Cain's Book*, a Burroughsian effort that charted his willing addiction to heroin and that included true vignettes of prostituting his own girlfriend to help him acquire cash for smack.[18] William Margolis, Tony Scibella, and Frank Rios were significant poets on the scene and published a few small volumes, but it wasn't until the arrival in 1960 of John Thomas – a computer programmer who had left behind a wife and kids to hitchhike across the country from Baltimore to the West Coast, only stopping in LA because his ride wouldn't take him to San Francisco – that Venice acquired its first significant poet. Though he mainly had ambitions for fiction, Thomas was an autodidact with a rich, transformative imagination. His work bridged the ancestral wisdom one associates with Ezra Pound (whom he visited at St. Elizabeth's) in his Chinese translations, the cosmological and anthropological musings (not to mention breath-based meters) of Charles Olson, a substantial knowledge of the English poetry tradition and the decadent stylings of Europeans, especially George Bataille in writings such as the pornographic novella *Story of the Eye*. Thomas had a bawdy, Rabelaisian sense of humor as evinced in this reworking of a theme by Christopher Marlowe:

The Passionate Shepherd to His Love

O if I had bunions & grey hairs sprouting from my ears
& your breasts were down limp near your waist
if you had liver spots & carried odds & ends in a knitting bag
all over town, muttering to yourself with bare gums

O if we lived on Social Security in a furnished room
cooking Cream-of-Wheat on a gas burner
if there were a Sacred Heart calendar on the nasty yellow wall
& the buffet full of rusty tools & rent receipts
[. . .]

O my light o' love, then I would have secrets from you
I would receive sex magazines in plain envelopes
& hide them in the back of the radio
I would take the bus downtown, secretly
to the Gayety Burlesk where I would
play with my limp old self under my hat

yes, I may as well be honest now
that's just what I would do
I'll write you a pretty poem tomorrow, love
tonight I feel the need to write an honest one
about what will surely never happen to us[19]

Called "the most un-Hollywood writer in Los Angeles" by Neeli Cherkovski,[20] Thomas produced a small but various body of work during this period, including evocative, moody prose poems, visionary Surrealist trances, collage work reminiscent of *Paterson*, blistering satires and intimate love poems in praise of the small pleasures of domesticity. However, Thomas, like Pound before him (and Baraka concurrently), was a victim of his own hubris: he died, aged seventy-one, in jail for having had oral sex with his daughter in a drug-fueled craze some time in the early 1970s.[21] Thomas pleaded no contest to the charges in 2002, but his conscience had been wracked by the crime, as his lifestyle and writing changed dramatically after the incident.[22] Once again, the "escape" of Venice West proved itself to be a rich ground for excesses – heroin addiction in the case of Stuart Perkoff, alcoholism for Charles Foster, and sexual deviance for John Thomas – thwarting any chance of a true Los Angeles "renaissance" in poetry.

III. Two Outliers: Charles Bukowski and Wanda Coleman

One question frequently asked of the scholar of Los Angeles poetry, as testified by Laurence Goldstein in his recent volume *Poetry Los Angeles*, is "How Good, or Bad, Is Charles Bukowski's Poetry?"[23] Born in Germany in 1920, Bukowski was brought to Los Angeles at the age of three; though he had great ambitions as a writer from an early age, he didn't publish his first small collection of poems, "Flower, Fist, and Bestial Wail" until 1960. His first novel, *Post Office* (1971) began to give him fame as a dissolute, working-class storyteller. His first major collection, *The Days Run Away Like Wild Horses over the Fields* (1969), shows a poet with more techniques in his toolbox than his later poetry might suggest. Bukowski can be as concrete and word-centered as Williams, as broadly satirical and absurdist and as obsessed by the fate of humanity as Vladimir Mayakovsky, and as willing to rest in repose, reserving judgment or elaboration, as a haiku poet. Reputed to be misogynistic, Bukowski's perspective in this early volume isn't far apart from Adorno's in lamenting the fate of high culture in the face of the trivialities of the culture industry:

Plea to a Passing Maid

girl in shorts, biting your nails, revolving your ass,
the boys are looking at you –
                you hold more, it seems,
than Gauguin or Brahms or Balzac,
more, at least, than the skulls that swim at our feet,
your swagger breaks the Eiffel tower,
turns the heads of old newsboys long ago gone
sexually to pot;
your caged malarkey, your idiot's dance,
mugging it, delightful – don't ever wash stained under-
wear or chase your acts of love
through neighborhood alleys –
don't spoil it for us,
putting on weight and weariness,
settling for TV and a namby-pamby husband;
don't give up that absurd dispossessed wiggle
to water a Saturday's front lawn –
don't send us back to Balzac or introspection
or Paris
or wine, don't send us back
to the incubation of doubts or the memory
of death-wiggle, bitch, madden us with love
and hunger, keep the sharks, the bloody sharks,
from the heart.[24]

Bukowski's address to a "maid," meaning maiden more than actual working "maids" who no doubt weren't identified by their shorts, clues us to the fact that he is addressing a lost gentility in sexual relations. In fact, the poem is conventional in its suggestion that unleashed libido permits the (male) poet to forget about culture, politics, and the imminence of death in favor of pure pleasure – John Donne's "To His Mistress Going to Bed" might be the exemplar of this poem. Bukowski, like everyone who has ever fallen in lust with a Hollywood starlet, is the voyeur in an abject, helpless position – "don't send us back" – and he retaliates, in a way, with the modest tools he has at his disposal, words. The poem is as ambivalent about the virtue of his own desires as it is a request for clarity. Another poem from *The Days Run Away* shows a side of Bukowski that his fans, his detractors, and perhaps even himself lost sight of as his career as a fiction writer took on tremendous heights, which is his stand-up Zen mode.

> **The Cat**
>
> the hunter goes by my window
> 4 feet locked in the bright stillness of a
> yellow and blue
> night.
>
> cruel strangeness takes hold in wars, in
> gardens –
> the yellow and blue night explodes before
> me, atomic, surgical,
> full of starlit
> devils . . .
>
> then the cat leaps up on the
> fence, a tubby dismay,
> stupid, lonely,
> whiskers like an old lady in the
> supermarket
> and naked as the
> moon.
>
> I am temporarily
> delighted.[25]

While this poem might not have the technical wizardry of Ted Hughes' or Elizabeth Bishop's poems about animals, it follows a Williams mode, most typified in "To Elsie," of starting from a small observation and opening the focus in an associative, non-syllogistic manner to include pointillist meditations on war (which cats apparently engage in), aging ("whiskers like an old lady"), and even art (the exploding "yellow and blue night" can't be anything but an allusion to Van Gogh's "Starry Night"). Bukowski aspired to a noble artlessness – perhaps due to a working-class suspicion of refined, even if underground, poets like one of his *bête noires*, Robert Creeley. However, in these early poems one sees an engagement with the line and phrase ("atomic, surgical" and "tubby dismay" are surprising, complexifying inclusions) that puts him squarely in world of the *New American* poets much as he abhorred their recourse to "poetics" and "theory" to explain their work.

Bukowski's example of unbridled satire, observational honesty, and determined rejection of spectacular society can be found in the poetry of Los Angeles' other great street poet, Wanda Coleman. Born in 1946 and raised in the Watts area of Los Angeles, Coleman had some association with the Watts Writers Workshop started by Bud Schulberg in the wake of the Watts Riots of 1965, an organization that fostered such poets as Eric Priestley, Jayne Cortez, and Quincy Troupe, among others. It was brought down, rather dramatically, by FBI informant Darthard Perry in 1973. The 1968 volume *Watts Poets: A Book of New Poetry and Essays* begins with a strident note: "There can never be a successful adjustment of black people to the American economic system. And what system there is, in reality, has everything to do with its anathema for the black population."[26] However, Coleman's intelligence and imagination provided her a much richer imagistic field, a fearless vocabulary, and an ambivalent but precise tone suggesting an angry, complex yet absurdist, underlying philosophy, not unlike that of the poet of "Azotes" who heads the present essay. Her mature voice is apparent in the second poem of her first full volume, *Mad Dog Black Lady* from 1979:

Where I Live

at the lip of a big black vagina
birthing nappy headed pickaninnies every hour on the hour
and soul radio blasting into mindwindow
bullets and blood
see that helicopter up there? like
god's eye looking down on his children
barsandbarsandbarsandbarsandbars
where i live
in the gap filled mouth of polly, the old black woman
up the street whose daughter's from New Orleans and who abandons
her every holiday leaving her to wander up and down
the avenue and not even a holiday meal. she collects
always in the same browns, purples and blues of her
loneliness – a dress that never fades or wears thin

[...]

where i live
at the lip of a big black vagina
birthing nappy headed pickaninnies every hour on the hour
the county is her pimp and she can turn a trick

swifter than any bitch ever graced this earth
she's the baddest piece of ass on the west coast
named black los angeles[27]

"At the lip of a big black vagina" might be the scariest invocation of a cityscape since Eliot's "Unreal city / under the brown fog of a winter dawn" in the *Waste Land*. A decidedly surreal way to begin a poem, the line signals that, for all of Coleman's devotion to reportage – the common goal of poets who wish to provide witness to social injustice – this is an imaginative realm that is Dantescan in flavor: a vision of hell, this poem charts a vast and eternal damnation. Coleman is also writing about a location identifiable as Los Angeles; the helicopters and bars tip us off, but the last line, "named black los angeles," signals that this is an open letter to all those who can't grasp the magnitude of this huge segment of humanity, people who don't live within close proximity to Hollywood or Beverly Hills and who never appear in their true light in exploitative *noir* fiction. Coleman famously wrote of one of Maya Angelou's volumes that it was "small and inauthentic, without ideas wisdom or vision." She was also known as the "unofficial poet laureate of Los Angeles" and went on to publish several books of poetry, fiction, and essays with Black Sparrow (not incidentally, Bukowski's publisher). Despite her relative lack of national acclaim (like her peer in the Watts Writers Workshop, Jayne Cortez, who died the same year as Coleman), she was confident in her freedoms as a poet and enemy of bourgeois norms. She wrote in her response to the criticism of her negative review of Angelou's work:

> In our post-9/11 America, where unwarranted suspicions and the fear of terrorism threaten to overwhelm long-coveted individual freedoms, a book review seems rather insignificant – until the twin specters of censorship and oppression are raised. What has made our nation great, despite its tortuous history steeped in slavery, are those who have persisted in honoring those freedoms, starting with the Constitution and its amendments. It is this striving toward making those freedoms available to every citizen, regardless of race, creed, color, gender or origin, that makes the rest of the insanity tolerable. It is what allows me to voice my opinion, be it praise song or dissent, no matter who disagrees.

This statement seems to allude to McGrath's appearance before HUAC nearly fifty years earlier. Like her predecessor, Coleman aligns poetry – configured here as a *civic* duty – with a challenge to the States and even literary culture's monopoly on what is acceptable social and political thought.

IV. The Punk Era and Little Caesar

By the late 1970s, Los Angeles had become one of the major centers of the punk movement in the United States, second only to New York. Bands such as Germs, The Weirdos, Geza X and the Mommymen, The Dickies, The Screamers, Black Randy and the Metrosquad, X, the Go-Go's, and numerous others tore up the stages in Hollywood and, when the rare opportunity arose, on the Sunset Strip. Inspired by the DIY ethos of fanzine culture and punk's lo-fi recording aesthetic, poet Dennis Cooper started *Little Caesar* magazine in 1976. Contrary to most of the poetry that sought to reject the influence of the entertainment industry, Cooper and coeditor Jim Glaeser exploited the fusion of pop music and the irreverent, nihilistic social critique that punk represented. Cooper wrote in the brief introduction to the first issue:

> I think there are already too many little magazines around, mostly uninteresting and virtually unread. So why are Jim and I adding this to the heap? Maybe we're crazy but we think there can be a literary journal that's loved and powerful. We want a magazine that's read by the Poetry fans, the Rock culture, the Hari Krishnas, the Dodgers. We think this can be done and that's what we're aiming at.
>
> I have this dream where writers are mobbed everywhere they go, like rocks stars and actors. A predilection? You never know. People like Patti Smith (poet/rock star) are subtly forcing their growing audiences to become literate, introducing them to Rimbaud, Breton, Burroughs and others. Poetry sales are higher than they've been in fifteen years. In Paris ten year old boys clutching well worn copies of Apollinaire's ALCOOLS put their hands over their mouths in amazement before paintings by Renoir and Monet. Bruce Lee films close in three days. This could happen here.[28]

"*Little Caesar* was strikingly of its time, perfectly Californian, new wave, and queer without providing a manifesto for anything, being in your face about most things and up front about a few,"[29] write Steve Clay and Rodney Philips in their nearly exhaustive survey of poetry zines from the years 1960–80, *A Secret Location on the Lower East Side*. The two young poet editors, along with their sympathetic friends – Bob Flanagan, Jack Skelley, David Trinidad, and Amy Gerstler, among others – used Venice's Beyond Baroque as the center of their activities. However, *Little Caesar* had no patience for the antisocial, genteel bohemian poverty of the latter-day Beats. They chose, instead, to synthesize elements of the New York School, transgressive French literature, the visual arts (often through the photography of poet Gerard Malanga), and popular culture. All of these elements feature prominently in Cooper's early poetry:

Being Aware

Men are drawn to my ass by
my death-trance blue eyes
and black hair, tiny outfit,
while my father is home with
a girl, moved by the things
I could never think clearly.

Men smudge me onto a bed,
drug me stupid, gossip and
photograph me till I'm famous
in alleys, like one of those
jerk offs who stare from
the porno I sort of admire.

I'm fifteen. Screwing means
more to the men than to me.
I daydream right through it
while money puts chills on
my arms, from this to that
grip. I was meant to be naked.

Hey, Dad, it's been like this
for decades. I was always
approached by your type, given
dollars for hours. I took a
deep breath, stripped, and they
never forgot how I trembled.

It means tons to me. Aside
from the obvious heaven
when cumming, there's times
I'm with them that I'm happy
or know what the other guy
feels, which is progress.

Or, nights when I'm angry,
if in a man's arms moving
slowly to the quietest music –
his hands on my arms, in my
hands, in the small of my back
take me back before everything.[30]

Cooper later became famous for his violent and sexually transgressive novels, including 1993's *Frisk*, an "unnervingly lucid account of a man whose fascination with snuff photos and murder leads to a killing spree in Holland."[31] His poetry anticipated those later themes in these visually tidy, but metrically variable, stanzas. They achieve their effects through the paradoxical depiction of a sexually precocious, damaged, vulnerable but unrepentant young boy, a reimagining of Rimbaud's own homage to abjection in "Mon triste coeur bave à la poupe."

Not all of the *Little Caesar* poets would aim for such unnerving pseudo-confessions, or even for narrative. Jack Skelley's devotion to the urbane Surrealism of the New York School, primarily expressed through collage, is on display in "Text":

> Mister Barney is in transit for the time being
> your check is in the mail
> my penis is in a yellow bag
> crumbs and threads on a torn hi-low carpet
> quick-drying ink on tennis shoes
> the Golden Princess will not answer the phone
> complaining of headings for each section but no text
> babies with bugs crawling on them
> occasional twitches of your muscles for no obvious reason[32]

Calling Cooper and Skelley "punk" poets – as if they were trying to incite the "decline of Western Civilization," Penelope Spheeris's title of her 1981 documentary on LA punk – is, of course, a little inaccurate. Unlike Germs and later hardcore bands, the *Little Caesar* poets, for all of their shock tactics, wanted to be seen as an extension of a sophisticated, recognized scene that was already happening in New York. This intent became clear as successive issues of the journal featured more poets and artists from outside of Los Angeles. Like most of the poetry movements in LA to this point, *Little Caesa*'s time was brief. The journal published twelve issues between 1977 and 1982, along with twenty-four books of poetry and fiction. Many of the writers, including Cooper, Trinidad, and the teen-aged Kim Rosenfield, chose to leave for New York. Bob Flanagan died, after a prolific career as a "super-masochist" performing artist, at age forty-three of cystic fibrosis. Signaling a change in poets' attitudes to Los Angeles that extends to the present day, Amy Gerstler, who first appeared in issue 11 of *Little Caesar*, chose to remain. She has published seven books since her debut volume, *The True Bride* in 1986, most with the Penguin Poets series published in New York.

This narrative of Los Angeles poetry from the McCarthy to the "punk" eras is, by necessity, a sketch. It doesn't include prize-winning formalist poet Henri Coulette, prolific outliers like the Holly Prado and the actor Harry Northup, experimental text artists like Guy de Cointet, or writers of even more indefinable vintage like Hugh Fox or Robert Crosson. It also doesn't extend to other important presses that emerged in the 1970s and 1980s, such as Paul Vangelisti's *Invisible City*, Bill Mohr's *Momentum*, or the several journals edited by Lee Hickman, most notably *Temblor*.[33]

Poet Clayton Eshleman started his important journal *Sulfur* while poet-in-residence at Caltech in 1981 but was famously hostile to Los Angeles writers: "There is no Los Angeles poetry. Los Angeles is a suitcase city. I just happen to live here."[34] The more gregarious poet and publisher Douglas Messerli moved his Sun & Moon Press to Los Angeles in the 1980s, where it proceeded to become one of the main publishers of Language School poetry for the next two decades. In the wake of the prominence of cultural studies – through which one could read pop culture *subversively* – poets who identify with the lingering remnants of the "counterculture" have embraced the ubiquity of the industry in Southern California. The trivialities of the "spectacle" have become the fodder for new avant-garde materialisms, notable in Kate Durbin's recent publication of "conceptual writing" titled *E! Entertainment*,[35] comprised of the author's transcriptions of reality TV events such as Kanye West and Kim Kardashian's wedding. While this *rapprochement* would no doubt make Adorno turn in his grave, it nonetheless offers hints as to what "Los Angeles Poetry" was or is: a search for commonalities – an aspiration for a civic but non-official language, a *vulgate* – as can be ephemerally gleaned in a city that is still ethnically, economically, and geographically divided, saturated by the entertainment industry and – dangling off the "left coast" – unhindered by the European bourgeois tradition not to mention a recognizable tradition of its own.

Notes

1. Rosaura Sanchez and Beatrice Pita, "The Literature of the Californios" in *The Literature of Los Angeles*, ed. Kevin R. McNamara (Cambridge University Press, 2010), 13–22.
2. *The World of Early Chicano Poetry*, comp., ed. and trans. Luis A. Torres (Encino: Floricanto Press, 1994), pp. 186–187.
3. Robinson Jeffers arrived in Los Angeles in 1903 to study at Occidental College and the University of Southern California and published his first book of

formal poems, *Flagon and Apples*, in 1912. He disliked the city intensely and moved to Carmel in 1913 with his wife Una, eventually to build Tor Castle and Hawk Tower.
4. French's poems have since been collected in *The Outer Gate: The Collected Poems of Nora May French* (New York: Hippocampus Press, 2009).
5. Reyner Banham, *Los Angeles: The Architecture of Four Ecologies* (London: Allen Lane, 1971).
6. Theodor Adorno, *Minima Moralia*, trans. E. F. N. Jephcott (London: Verso, 2005), 25–26.
7. Thomas McGrath, *Figures from a Double World* (Denver: Alan Swallow, 1955), 17.
8. "The Pocket Poet Series" Estelle Gershgoren Novak. *Poets of the Non-Existent City: Los Angeles in the McCarthy Era* (Albuquerque: University of New Mexico Press, 2002), 239.
9. *Poetry Los Angeles* (London: Villiers Publications, 1958), n. p.
10. *Poets of the Non-Existent City*, 141.
11. Ibid., 124.
12. *Modern American Poetry* (website), "McGrath's Statement to the House Committee on Un-American Activities (HUAC)." http://www.english.illinois.edu/maps/poets/m_r/mcgrath/huac.htm.
13. Bruce Boyd, an "original" member of the Venice West scene, would move back and forth from the Bay Area to Los Angeles during this period. He seems to have disappeared without a trace; little biographical information is available for him after the early 1970s.
14. Donald Allen, *The New American Poetry* (New York: Grove Press, 1960), 299. A slightly revised version appears in *Voices of the Lady: Collected Poems* (Ann Arbor: National Poetry Foundation, 1998).
15. Adorno, *Minima Moralia*, 27.
16. John Arthur Maynard, *Venice West: The Beat Generation in Southern California* (New Brunswick: Rutger's University Press, 1991), 83.
17. Charles Foster, *Victoria Mundi* (New York: The Smith, 1973), 48.
18. Trocchi was an excellent poet whose collection *Man at Leisure* first appeared in 1972. As it's unclear that he wrote any of these poems while in Venice, I've chosen not to include them. *Man at Leisure* was reprinted (Chicago: Oneworld Classics, 2009) with an introduction by William S. Burroughs.
19. John Thomas, *Epopoeia and the Decay of Satire* (Los Angeles: The Red Hill Press, 1976), 36
20. Quoted in Elaine Woo, "John Thomas, 71; Member of Venice Beats" (obituary) *Los Angeles Times*, April 7, 2002, http://articles.latimes.com/2002/apr/07/local/me-thomas7.
21. This is a huge issue to address in a footnote, but documentation about this incident is not readily available. Contrasting viewpoints on the case have been provided by Thomas's other daughter Gabrielle Idlet in "Hitting the Beats" (*LA Weekly*, July 17, 2002) and her many respondents, including Thomas's attorney, in an extensive correspondence section titled "Poetic

22. *The Selected Poetry and Prose of John Thomas* (Venice: Raven Productions Press, 2011) largely focuses on these later poems.
23. Laurence Goldstein, *Poetry Los Angeles* (Ann Arbor: University of Michigan Press, 2014).
24. Charles Bukowski, *The Days Run Away Like Wild Horses over the Hills* (Santa Barbara: Black Sparrow Press, 1969), 31.
25. Bukowski, 56.
26. Quincy Troupe, ed. *Watts Poets: A Book of New Poetry and Essays* (Los Angeles: House or Respect, 1968), 1.
27. Wanda Coleman. *Mad Dog Black Lady* (Santa Barbara: Black Sparrow Press: 1979), 13–14.
28. *Little Caesar 1* (Los Angeles, 1977).
29. Steven Clay and Rodney Philips, *A Secret Location on the Lower East Side* (New York Public Library/Granary Books, 1998), 217.
30. Dennis Cooper, *The Missing Men* (Los Angeles: Am Here Books/Immediate Editions, 1981), 6.
31. Accessed on Amazon, July 4, 2014, http://www.amazon.com/Frisk-Novel-Cooper-Dennis/dp/0802132898.
32. *Coming Attractions: An Anthology of American Poets in Their Twenties*, ed. Dennis Cooper (Los Angeles: Little Caesar Press, 1980), 123.
33. Further reading on these poets and presses can be found in Bill Mohr's *Hold Outs: The Los Angeles Poetry Renaissance 1948–1992* (Iowa City: University of Iowa Press, 2011) as well as in Mohr's contribution to *The Cambridge Companion to the Literature of Los Angeles* titled "Scenes and Movements in Southern California Poetry" (New York: Cambridge University Press, 2010).
34. *Hold-Outs*, 123
35. New York: Wonder Books, 2014.

Licentiousness" (*LA Weekly*, July 31, 2002). None of the poets who were friends or acolytes of Thomas in the thirty years between his crime and death were aware of this incident.

PART VI
Creating Communities

CHAPTER 18

African American Uprising

Charles Toombs

African American writers in California, whether born in the state or having migrated to it, create diverse subject matter and themes reflecting individual and communal thrusts of black experience. These writers represent various oppressions in people's lives and examine how best to resist these oppressions. Their works are part of the larger body of African American literature and its complicated historical and cultural experience. The literature documents cultural authenticity and identity, black history and cultural heritage, the importance of black communities in mediating black kinship and communal self, human dignity, social justice, and an awareness of the oppression of other ethnic peoples in California. These writers are also preoccupied with longing for some other place and time, connecting their texts to memory, history, heritage, and the values of black experience. This longing and connecting provides spaces for people to wrestle with identity concerns related to gender, race, and class in their struggle to empower themselves and their communities to deal with racism, discrimination, and the lunacy of California and America.

Black writers in California have been inspired by many events that have occurred in the 1960s and afterward. With the Modern Civil Rights movement reaching a peak in the 1960s, writers, acting as witnesses to their communities, have used the changing landscape in America and in California to chart a new path for literary production defined by black values. The breaking down of the barrier of Jim Crowism, represented with the 1964 Civil Rights Act and the 1965 Voting Rights, signaled a change in direction of racial matters. Connected to the Civil Rights Movement, though with an agenda not predicated on integration, were the Black Power, Black Revolutionary, and Black Arts Movements. The Black Arts Movement articulated ideas for the creation of black art in its theories of a Black Aesthetic. Hoyt W. Fuller, Maulana Karenga, Addison Gayle Jr., and Larry Neal, among others, identified key elements that must be a part of black artistic production. Hoyt W. Fuller wrote, "The young writers of the black ghetto have set out in search of a Black Aesthetic, a system of isolating and evaluating the artistic works of black people which reflect the special character and imperatives of black experience."[1] Maulana Karenga, an important scholar in Africana Studies, stated that "black art must expose the enemy, praise the people and support the revolution... it must be collective."[2] The poet-critic Larry Neal said, "The Black Arts Movement is radically opposed to any concept of the artist that alienates him from his community."[3] These ideas are a call to which California black writers respond. They become part of the thinking that Molefi Asante uses in creating his theory of Afrocentricity, as announced in *The Afrocentric Idea*, especially its chapter, "Rhetoric of Resistance."[4]

African American writers in California not only have a cultural mandate; they also have energy "(up)rising" from black communities which indicate a new day. In 1965, black riots occurred in Watts and Chicago and two years later riots broke out in Cincinnati, Atlanta, Newark, Tampa, and Detroit. After the assassination of Dr. Martin Luther King, Jr. in 1968, rioting in black communities became a common tactic used by residents to vent frustration and rage at an America that gave them little equal opportunity and social justice, that failed to respect minority culture and history, and that did not think "black is beautiful." During this period, blacks took control of their communities, creating black-centered schools, food programs, and sites for cultural expression. They protected their communities from outside white forces that could potentially harm them. The Black Panthers of Oakland are a case in point, but other community organizing occurred throughout California and the nation.

Al Young was an active community organizer. He was named Poet Laureate of the State of California by Governor Arnold Schwarzenegger in 2005 and served until 2008. Born in 1939 in Ocean Springs, Mississippi, he moved to the San Francisco Bay area in 1961. He published his first book of poetry, *Dancing*, in 1969, and has been a prolific writer of poetry, fiction, screenplays, and essays ever since. Although some of his major texts appeared during the 1960s and 1970s, Young's response to the call of the Black Aesthetic theorists has been muted. Race matters in his works, but radical and militant protest is largely absent in his first poetry collections and novels. Instead, Young centers his works on universal human concerns of family, religion, love, and individual journeys through life. His works do respond to Black Aesthetic values in using vernacular black culture, such as rituals of religious experience, music, and black idiom.

His first novel, *Snakes* (1970), reveals his concerns with these ideas. *Snakes* is a *bildungsroman*. MC, the narrator and protagonist, is a young man trying to discover his purpose in life. Music helps MC on his journey. The novel, set in Detroit and New York, is about MC's response to a single hit song, "Snakes," and his understanding that bands, promoters, record companies, and groupies are not important; only the music is. The novel offers authentic representations of urban landscapes, captures the character's soulful street slang, and posits that artistic expression is a way for some blacks to counter the lack of opportunity in the ghetto. While *Snakes'* overall themes highlight black cultural values, the novel does not directly blame white people for the problems blacks face. Young, however, does participate in the literature of the streets movement that documents white racism and oppression. In 1972, he joined Ishmael Reed and Steve Cannon in founding the multicultural *Yardbird Reader*, which published works by new ethnic writers who directly indicted whites. He also began writing scripts for major black movies (that were also emerging as a way to counter the white racist Hollywood-controlled images of blacks), but he did not receive screen credit at the time.

In 1975, Young published *Who Is Angelina?* Set in California in the 1970s, the novel tells the story of a black woman struggling with drugs and alcohol, and various romantic involvements. Her sick father in Detroit, as well as other family members, advise her to attend church. Doing so helps Angelina realize that she must return to California and deal with her personal problems, rather than run from them. Like MC in *Snakes*, Angelina has to grow up.

In 1980, Young's novel *Ask Me Now* became a *New York Times* Outstanding Book of the Year. In addition to several volumes of poetry published since them, Young has written novels, memoirs, musical memoirs, and essays.

His friend and co-founder of *Yardbird Reader*, Ishmael Reed, comments on various aspects of the black experience. Born in Chattanooga, Tennessee in 1938, Reed grew up in Buffalo and New York City. In 1967, he moved to Berkeley, California, and began teaching at the University of California. In the same year, he contributed poems to *Where Is Viet Nam?: American Poets Respond*. He has also taught at several universities and colleges. Although equally talented and prolific as a poet, Reed's novels usually receive the most popular and critical attention. His first novel, *The Free-Lance Pallbearers*, is a science fiction fantasy. His second novel, *Yellow Back Radio Broke-Down* (1969) is a western. *Mumbo Jumbo* (1972) and *The Last Days of Louisiana Red* (1974) are detective novels. *Flight to Canada* (1976) is Reed's take on re-writing and re-envisioning the classic slave narrative. Two novels – *The Terrible Twos* (1982) and *The Terrible Threes* (1989) – are political parodies, while *Reckless Eyeballing* (1986) is a trickster tale. *Japanese by Spring* (1993) is Reed's vision of life in academia. Some critics describe Reed's works as satire. Others focus on how his writings disassemble black literary, historical, and cultural structures to comment on America in the 1960s and 1970s.

Jazz and Spoken Soul/black dialect inspire the poet Quincy Troupe, born in 1939 in New York City. Troupe was raised in St. Louis and moved to Los Angeles in the 1960s. In 1968, as a member of the Watts Writers' Workshop, he edited *Watts Poets: A Book of New Poetry and Essays*. In addition to a prolific writing career, Troupe has taught creative writing and literature at several universities, including the University of California, San Diego. He was briefly Poet Laureate of the State of California, until it was discovered that he misrepresented his academic degree information. He won the American Book Award for poetry in 1979 for *Snake-Back Solos: Selected Poems 1969–1977*. His other major poetry collections include: *Embryo* (1972), *Skulls Among the River* (1984), *Weather Reports* (1991), *Avalanche* (1996), *Choruses* (1999), *Trancircularities: New and Revised Poems* (2002), and *Errancities* (2012). He has edited literary anthologies and has written two books on jazz legend Miles Davis. One of those volumes, *The Autobiography of Miles Davis* (1990), won the American Book Award.

For readers not familiar with Troupe's poetry, *Trancircularities* is a good place to begin, since it includes poems from throughout his career. "Ode to John Coltrane" incorporates ideas from the Black Aesthetic Movement. "Eye would remember new poetry/read in back rooms;/ eloquent statements on the pig's inevitable doom."[5] Troupe acknowledges the significance of the life and death of Malcolm X in "For Malcolm, Who Walks in the Eyes of Children." Alluding to the black experience, the speaker states, "he had been coming a very long time/had been here many times before/Malcolm... in the words of Nelson Mandela/in the rap of public enemy number one, ourselves."[6] In "Come Sing a Song," Troupe responds to the Black Aesthetic Movement's call to create art with meaning for black people: "Come sing a song, Black Man,/... sing a black-blues song/... sing a work song,/ sing a prison chain gang/... sing jazz, rock, or, R & B,/sing a song Black man,/sing a 'bad' freedom song."[7] Troupe's later poems also use idioms of black music (especially jazz) and black speech to foreground black self-definition in the black experience.

Paying attention to the unique cultural space of the black experience in Los Angeles is the grounding for the Easy Rawlins mysteries of Walter Mosley, born in Los Angeles in 1952. Best known as a mystery writer, Mosley has also authored nonfiction, short stories, science fiction, plays, young adult fiction, and screenplays. In 1990, Mosley published his first novel in the Easy Rawlins series, *Devil in a Blue Dress*, introducing readers to Ezekiel "Easy" Rawlins, a World War II veteran who has been laid off from work at a defense plant. To make ends meet, Easy begins doing private detective work for a sleazy white gangster, Dewitt Albright. His assignment: to locate Daphne Monet, a young white woman who likes to hang out at black night clubs. In order to do so, Easy moves in and out of black and white establishments, from barber shops, blues joints, and the night clubs of Watts to the homes of corrupt white racist political figures. Mosley notes that many characters have migrated to Watts in search of better opportunities, yet find themselves in segregated communities with only slightly better living conditions than in the South. The author explores themes of survival, oppression and resistance, black manhood, and communal kinship. Other novels in the Easy Rawlins series move forward in time as Rawlins deals with similar issues. Albert U. Turner, in his analysis of the entire Rawlins series, observes that the novels' merits should be evaluated by considering how they tie Easy Rawlins (and his co-protagonists) to the black community. Turner writes: "On one hand, Easy is employed by whites or white public authorities to provide the 'favor' of searching Los Angeles's African American spaces for clues.... On the other hand, Easy is also in the habit of openly providing favors for members of his African American community. Engagement in discourse to which whites have little, if any, access makes these labors on the behalf of members of his African American community possible."[8]

Access to the black community is a feature of the novels of Jervey Tervalon, born in New Orleans in 1958, and raised in the Jefferson Park-Crenshaw area of Los Angeles. In his first novel, *Understand This* (1994), Tervalon gives voice to mostly young adult members of the black community, as they struggle with romantic love, dreams of moving beyond the hood, crime, gang culture, lack of social justice, and other concerns in South Central Los Angeles. The novel was published two years after the Los Angeles Riots of 1992, in which the media portrayed black and brown people as animals and savages. The novel focuses on the humanity of its characters, like Smith's play.[9] Her characters speak of police brutality and racial profiling, the loss of young people to gang violence, and lack of opportunity that makes everyday living difficult. Like the people in *Twilight: Los Angeles*, the characters in *Understand This* tell their own stories. Tervalon debunks the stereotypes of the hood by describing the reality of living in urban Los Angeles.

The novel's central protagonists are Francois and Margot, high school seniors who are in love, yet aware that their pending graduation from high school might end their relationship. As this possibility looms, Francois and Margot contend with gang activity, drugs, death, overly concerned parents, and making the transition from the childhood to adulthood. Richard Yarborough writes that "*Understand This* ... forces us to engage with open minds the diverse lives of black characters whose voices yield to the attentive listener a rich complex awareness of human experience and thus our own struggles to make sense of the world."[10] *Understand This* won the QPB's 1994 New Voices Award.

Although he has written several novels and other works, Tervalon's *Dead Above Ground* (2000) has received the most critical and commercial success. In *Dead Above Ground*, Tervalon uses 1946 New Orleans Creole society to tell the story of seventeen year old Lita Du Champ and to engage the peculiar race relations that are a part of Creole society. Lita, her sister Adele, and their strong-willed mother, Helen, are the main female characters. Helen wants the best for her daughters in their relationships with men and is willing to do anything to make sure their happiness, even if she has to commit murder. The novel provides an array of historically accurate characters and situations – including pimps, prostitutes, murder, love, romance, and the underworld – as family secrets are unveiled.

Al Young, Ishmael Reed, Quincy Troupe, Walter Mosley, and Jervey Tervalon write about black history and cultural traditions, emphasize "things black," and foreground race and class oppression and social and cultural justice in their works. Interestingly, these writers emerged as major figures in African American literature and California literature at the same time as Black Studies. The first Black Studies program in the country began at San Francisco State University in 1969. Black Studies not only developed its own theory and methodological practices; it created a space where the literature of these writers could be studied.

Black women writers in California from the 1960s to the present also tell the stories of African Americans. Like their male counterparts, they are influenced by the Civil, Black Power, and Afrocentric Movements. However, they focus on black women who are oppressed by race, gender, and class, and on female characters who discover – often in their cultural history – the tools for healthy survival. Joyce Carol Thomas, Shirley Anne

Williams, Wanda Coleman, and Octavia Butler write about an "invisible" California, one that black men, and white people, often ignore.

Like so many black writers in California, Joyce Carol Thomas migrated to the state from Ponca City, Oklahoma, in 1948. Her memory of her childhood in Ponca City figures in her novels and poetry. She has remained a resident of California, and has received many awards, including the Danforth Graduate Fellowship from the University of California at Berkeley, the Djerassi Fellowship for Creative Writing at the Stanford University, and the Columbus American Book Award for *Marked by Fire* (1982). She currently lives in Berkeley, where she writes children's literature.

Although primarily known as a writer of children's literature, Thomas began her career as a poet and playwright. Her poetry volumes, *Bittersweet* (1973), *Crystal Breezes* (1974), and *Blessing* (1975), were published by small, community-based presses. In these poems, Thomas intermingles memories of growing up as a child in Oklahoma with her experiences working in the fields of California with other people of color who have also been marginalized by race and class. Her poetry captures the nuances of the human condition. Her lyrical songs deal with nature, death and birth, hope and recovery, black women and black spirituality, racism, suffering, and black traditions and rituals. In "Little Girl Born Black," Thomas chronicles the historical and contemporary lives of black women. The speaker says, "They plan/your murder/while you are yet/in your/mother's womb." Yet there is hope for black girls, despite their lack of opportunities. "Now remembering/that she/always knew/what it was/to be queen/lover mother... Little girl born Black/please take your station."[11]

Inside the Rainbow: A Collection of Poems (1982) highlights many issues important to black readers. The speaker in "Where Is the Black Community?" seeks to dismantle stereotypes about African Americans. Thomas presents street people ("Holding down the corner/Where Third Street meets B"), black academics, professionals, and members of the middle class ("the Delta sisters," "Transplanting kidneys/In a university hospital," and "Teaching English/At Duke and Purdue"). At the same time, she depicts the marginalized work and living opportunities of African Americans ("Scrubbing chitlin grease/Off a kitchen stove eye," "And plowing cotton/In a Mississippi" to "arranging four kids/In a twin-sized bed").[12] Thomas also acknowledges the suffering of other people of color in California, especially in the poem, "To a Chicano," where the speaker records the plight of a Chicana welfare mother whose child dies in a fire. The speaker insists: "We must do more than/Cry."[13]

In the early 1980s, Thomas began to receive national critical attention and praise, as her works benefitted from the nation's growing interest in black women's writings. Her first two novels, *Marked by Fire* (1982) and *Bright Shadows* (1983), were initially considered young adult fiction. But both works addressed the subject of invisible black girls growing up in America, like Toni Morrison's *The Bluest Eye*, Alice Walker's *The Third Life of Grange Copeland* and *The Color Purple*, and Paule Marshall's *Brown Girl, Brownstones*.

Marked by Fire, an award-winning and critically celebrated novel, tells the story of Abyssinia Jackson, who grows up in the cotton fields near Ponca City, Oklahoma. Abyssinia is horribly raped at the age of ten by an elder in her church and spends her childhood coping with the memory of this terrible incident. With guidance from her mother and other adult women in the community, she works through her trauma and emerges at the end of the novel as a young woman willing to give back to the very community that saved her, becoming a community folk healer.

In *Bright Shadows*, the first of several sequels to *Marked by Fire*, Abyssinia, now a woman of twenty, takes her first forays into romantic love. She sets her heart on Carl Lee Jefferson, but her father does not approve. Soon the conflicts with her father over Carl Lee pale, as her Aunt Serena is brutally murdered. Abyssinia must come to terms with this tragedy while at the same time struggling with romantic love. Carl Lee helps her through her grief, as Abyssinia comes to understand that life has as much brightness as it does darkness.

While Joyce Carol Thomas draws on her memories of Oklahoma, Wanda Coleman (1946–2013), foregrounds the urban world of Los Angeles in her works. Although Coleman wrote poetry as a child, the Watts Riots convinced her that her writing could make a difference in people's lives. Coleman showed a concern for blacks who live in poverty; who are bombarded by racism, sexism, and classism; and who lack equal opportunity. She believed that corrective measures could help those living in Watts and other urban locales. After the Watts Riots, Coleman became involved in several community-based organizations that benefitted disadvantaged black individuals. She also became an active member of organizations devoted to developing the talent of black writers.

Known as the "LA Blueswoman" and considered by many to be the "unofficial" poet laureate of Los Angeles, Coleman published numerous volumes of poetry, short stories, and essays. In the 1983 volume of poetry, *Imagoes*, she indicted the white system, as well as black people who fail to support the African American community. In "Burglars," the speaker says, "yes, there are sneak thieves, pick pockets & purse snatchers/a veritable crime wave in the heat/heart/hearth of city/they creep & crawl thru streets & alleys/our perceptions/they are never caught."[14] People vent their problems and issues, instead of resolving them, in "The Saturday Afternoon Blues." The speaker states: "Saturday afternoons are killers... suicide line I can't get you ... the man i love is a killer/the man i love is a thief/the man i love is a junky/the man I love is grief."[15] Coleman's poetry covers a range of subjects, from failed romantic relationships to poems about death, aging, beauty, and nature. Her speakers are usually black women struggling to survive. In Coleman's world, people cannot get a break. The difficulty of living in Los Angeles is illustrated in "South Central Los Angeles Deathtrip 1982." She details a number of assaults against residents: racial profiling, young blacks being arrested and sometimes killed. One man "became combative in the rear seat of/that sleek zebra maria. they say/it took a chokehold to restrain him/and then they say he died of asphyxiation/on the spot."[16]

In her essays, Coleman writes: "I am dismayed by how frequently I have been invited to write about the Watts and South Central riots, yet how seldom I've been asked to discuss, in any real depth, other facets of the African American experience in Southern California.... It is a terrain with which I'm fascinated, the birthplace I've yet to abandon."[17]

In her work, Coleman never leaves Los Angeles, whereas Octavia Butler takes readers to other worlds and other times. Butler (1947–2006) was born in Pasadena, California, and lived there most of her life. She was an only child whose father died when she was an infant. Butler was raised by her mother, grandmother, and other relatives. Communities of black women appear in several of her novels. Although Butler was known for writing science fiction, she incorporated elements of the slave narrative in *Kindred*.[18]

Race and gender play central roles in her fiction. The Patternist series includes *Patternmaster* (1976), *Mind of My Mind* (1977), and *Survivor* (1978). These novels tell the story of Doro and Anyanwu, who are members of a genetically engineered society. Over the course of the series, spanning more than four thousand years, Doro survives by taking over other bodies, male and female. He is, as Margaret Anne O'Connor describes, "a powerful masculine hunter, progenitor of a race of superbeings gifted with physical and psychical powers that promise to take mankind to the next level of evolutionary development."[19]

In *Kindred*, which is part slave narrative and part science fiction, Edana (Dana) Franklin is transported from 1976 Los Angeles to a Maryland plantation, where she "must (re)live certain aspects of the lives of her ancestors in order to insure her present existence."[20] Dana experiences miscegenation, and comes to appreciate the importance of freedom, the viciousness of the master class, and the cruelty of a slavocracy. "The whipping served its purpose as far as I was concerned. It scared me, made me wonder how long it would be before I made a mistake that would give someone reason to whip me. Or had I already made that mistake?"[21] Dana loses her left arm, symbolizing how slavery still has an impact on African Americans.

Shirley Anne Williams (1944–99) also revisits the slave past in her novel *Dessa Rose* (1986). Williams was born in Bakersfield, California, where her family worked in the fields. She wrote a children's book, *Working Cotton* (1992), which was loosely autobiographical. After graduating from high school, she enrolled at Fresno State University, where she completed the BA in 1966. She earned her MA at Brown University in 1972, and in 1973 became a professor of literature at the University of California, San Diego, where she remained until her death.

In *Dessa Rose*, Williams uses Spoken Soul to capture the cultural specificity of her slave characters. In the novel, the impact of slavery is conveyed by the titular character's memory of events, her telling of these events to a white man, and his understanding of these events. The novel differs from slave narratives that were told to whites or that presented a white person's perspective on slavery. *Dessa Rose* is based on a 1929 Kentucky slave uprising, led by a pregnant slave woman and a white woman who used her own home to safeguard runaway slaves.

In her poetry, Williams writes about more recent past, including her hometown of Bakersfield, a highly segregated city inhabited by black field workers. Her most important and critically acclaimed volume of poetry, *The Peacock Poems* (1975), was nominated for the National Book Award. Like Coleman's poems, the works in this collection focus on the pain and suffering of black women. In "Any Woman's Blues," the speaker laments her lover's absence, while accepting the way he manipulated her: "My bed one-sided/from me sleepin alone so mucha the time./ My bed one-sided, now,/cause I'm alone so mucha time./But the fact that's empty/show how this man is messin with my mind."[22] "This Is a Sad-Ass Poem for a Black Woman to Be Writing" is also preoccupied with black male–female relationships. Here, the speaker reveals her ambiguous feelings about a potential sexual partner. The sex has not yet happened, and all she has so far is "good jive, a light rap/and fly speech over /a public table."[23]

The Peacock Poems also navigate the social, cultural, and economic terrain of the central valley of California, where black and brown bodies toil and work for almost nothing. Interspersed between several of the poems are statements concerning the valley, which read like dictionary or encyclopedia entries. Williams writes: "The economy of the region is based on agriculture and related business and industry, food-processing, the manufacture of farm equipment, and the like... The Valley is not the most fertile farming area in the world. It is the richest."[24] In one poem, a female field laborer says, "I wish I could still stay/down by the fire at the end of the row/and jes watch the baby but Daddy/say I'm a big girl now/ not big enough to have my own sack/jes only to help pile the cotton/in the middle of the row for momma to put/in her'n."[25]

African American writers in California have done what all African American writers do in their works: capture authentic black humanity from past and contemporary times in such a way as to authenticate the African American experience and to dispel stereotypes and distortions about it. These works pay tribute to black people in their communities who use their cultural traditions and resources to resist oppression, to document their struggles with white authority and with each other, and to express personal and communal identity.

Notes

1. Hoyt W. Fuller, "Towards a Black Aesthetic," in Addison Gayle, Jr. *The Black Aesthetic* (Anchor Books, 1972), 8–9.
2. Ron (Maulana) Karenga, "Black Cultural Nationalism," in Gayle, Jr., *The Black Aesthetic*, 32–33.
3. Larry Neal, "The Black Arts Movement," in Gayle, Jr., *The Black Aesthetic*, 257.
4. Molefi Asanate, *The Afrocentric Idea* (Temple University Press, 1987).
5. Quincy Troupe, *Transcircularities: New and Selected Poems* (Coffee House Press, 2002), p. 5.
6. Ibid., 14.
7. Ibid., 19.
8. Albert U. Turner, "At Home on 'These Mean Streets': Collaboration and Community in Walter Mosley's Easy Rawlins Mystery Series," in Owen E. Brady and Derek C. Maus, eds., *Finding a Way Home: A Critical Assessment of Walter Mosley's Fiction* (University of Mississippi Press, 2008), 113.
9. Anna Deavere Smith, *Twilight, Los Angeles, 1992* (Anchor Books, 1992).
10. Richard Yarborough, "Forward," *Understand This*, by Jervey Tervalon (University of California Press, 2000), p. 5.
11. Joyce Carol Thomas, *Bittersweet* (Firesign Press, 1973), 42, 44.

12. Joyce Carol Thomas, *Inside the Rainbow: A Collection of Poems* (Penny Press/Zikawuna, 1982), 57.
13. Ibid., 32.
14. Wanda Coleman, *Imagoes* (Black Sparrow Press, 1983), 28.
15. Ibid., 160.
16. Wanda Coleman, "South Central Los Angeles Deathtrip 1982," *Mercurochrome* (Black Sparrow Press, 2001), in *African American Literature*, eds. Keith Gilyard and Anissa Wardi (Penguin Academics/Pearson Education: 2004), 752.
17. Wanda Coleman, *The Riot Inside Me: More Trials & Tremors* (A Black Sparrow Book, 2005), xv.
18. Robert Crossley, "Critical Essay," in Octavia Butler, *Kindred* (Beacon Press, 1979), 265.
19. Margaret Anne O'Connor, "Octavia E. Butler," in *Afro-American Fiction Writers After 1955, Dictionary of Literary Biography, Volume Thirty-three* (Gale Research, 1984), 36–37.
20. Gregory Jerome Hampton, *Changing Bodies in the Fiction of Octavia Butler: Salves, Aliens, and Vampires* (Lexington Books, 2010), 1.
21. Octavia Butler, *Kindred* (Beacon Press, 1979), 92.
22. Shirley Anne Williams, *The Peacock Poems* (Wesleyan University Press, 1975), 11.
23. Ibid., 18.
24. Ibid., 12.
25. Ibid., 43.

CHAPTER 19

Of Carnales and Coyotes: Chicana/o Literature of California

Anne Goldman

I Aquí and Allá

He thought of all the beautiful people he had known. Of his father and mother in another time; of Joe Pete Manôel and of Marla Jamison; of Thomas and of Zelda and of Mayrie – the Rooster and Ricky . . . . He thought of this and he remembered, and suddenly he knew that for him there would never be a coming back.

– José Antonio Villarreal, *Pocho* (1959)

"You told me a crazy story, I remember. You were going to smuggle wets back into Mex. Isn't that right?"

– Luis Alberto Urrea, *Into the Beautiful North* (2009)

Thematically as well as chronologically, *Pocho* and *Into the Beautiful North* bookend California Chicana/o literature. Their characters' travels plot the complicated relationship between identity and origin. At the close of Villarreal's novel, Richard faces west toward the breakers that dash themselves against the cliffs of San Francisco. The young man initiates a break with his immigrant parents (themselves on the cusp of divorce) when he enlists in the Navy. At the same time, his decision to cross the ocean to aid the struggle against Fascism permits Villarreal to retell the Manifest Destiny mythos: Go West, young man, and make your fortune. Villarreal ends his story with Richard caught between possibility and peril, his fate unknown.

Half a century later, at the close of *Into the Beautiful North*, Urrea recalls his seventeen-year-old village girl Nayeli to Sinaloa. The teenager's trip to the United States midway through the book repeats the northbound trajectory that has become iconic for California Chicano literature since *Pocho*. But her quest is anything but conventional. Nayeli travels to Kansas to beg her father to come back home – not to join him in the town whose image is barely visible on the beat-up postcard she carries with her. Together with the three friends who travel alongside her on this quixotic adventure (in which Urrea gestures simultaneously toward *The*

295

Magnificent Seven and Cervantes), Nayeli aims to repopulate the village in Sinaloa that has been plagued by drug traffickers in the absence of the men who have gone north to find work. Tres Camarones is a fictional ghost town, but its deserted aspect gestures toward the actual villages emptied of people since NAFTA left Mexicans unable to compete with U.S.-produced grain and other commodities. However, Urrea refuses to represent Nayeli's home as the bleak no-man's-land envisioned by film noir and television border drama. Impoverished and imperiled, Tres Camarones remains fragrant with trumpet flowers and cheerfully loud with the cries of the parrots roosting by the brightly painted houses that line its narrow streets. The novel's comic tone, as well as its character's joyful return to Mexico, recall Daniel Venegas' 1929 border-burlesque *The Adventures of Don Chipote*.

Villarreal and Urrea dignify their characters as warriors, but the half century that elapses between their novels encourages the writers to articulate different arguments. In Richard, Villarreal honors Americans of Mexican origin, the people who will call themselves Chicanos a decade later when longstanding demands for civil rights culminate in the Movimiento. During this collective *grito* (shout), thousands protested the U.S. involvement in the Vietnam War, while an equal number of high school students from Colorado to California walked out demanding equal access to education. The literary flowering of drama, prose and poetry that developed alongside the Movement was correspondingly activist. In foregrounding Richard's struggles to define himself over and against his Mexican-born parents, Villarreal's 1959 novel anticipates this Chicano Renaissance, whose works include the code-switching poetry of California-based poet Alurista, Denver-born writer Corky Gonzales' 1967 poem *I am Joaquin*, the agitprop theater Luis Valdez wrote for Teatro Campesino (the Delano, California farm workers' dramatic troupe, he founded in 1965), Texas author Tomás Rivera's postmodern novel honoring migrant workers *Y no se lo tragó la tierra* (1971), and New Mexico native Rodolfo Anaya's lyrical *bildungsroman Bless Me, Ultima* (1972). Richard flails against the impossible demands of his immigrant parents and lashes out against the blatant prejudice of *Anglos*, but his struggles to articulate his own way are hindered by the political realities of mid-century America and his decision to join the U.S. military – itself a virtual laboratory of racial strife.

Villarreal, who was raised in Santa Clarita, California, spent four years in the Navy before attending the University of California at Berkeley. Rather than accord Richard a trajectory as exceptional as his, however, Villarreal wrote his central character into a position consonant with the straitened circumstances of the Mexican American majority.[1] A half century later, the reassessment of American identity Villarreal inaugurates in *Pocho* remains at the heart of Chicano literature. Roughly speaking, the literary works produced in the decades since this novel adopt two distinct strategies to revisit and revise the wrenching difficulty Richard experiences as a Mexican American "ni de aquí, ni de allá." One group focuses upon the relationship between "here" (aquí – that is, the United States) and "there" (allá – or Mexico) to further Villarreal's focus on the bond to Mexico that California Chicanos simultaneously long for and chafe against.

Arturo Islas' explorations of family life in *The Rain God* (1984) and *Migrant Souls* (1990) take place in California and Texas. But the desert bordering the United States and Mexico inserts itself into both works as a primary character, just as it will in Luis Urrea's recounting of the nightmare journey migrants make toward the United States in *The Devil's Highway* (2004). Islas invokes the desert's blowing sand and scant water as figures for the wants and needs of those whose houses overlook it. Luis Rodriguez's story collection *Republic of East LA* (2002) encompasses "here" and "there" less by straddling the border than by shuttling characters back and forth across this divide – sometimes physically, and in other instances figuratively, as they return in imagination to the landscapes of their birth. The Los-Angeles-based characters who people many of Dagoberto Gilb's gorgeously written collection of stories *The Magic of Blood* (1993) remember Mexico while they drive by billboards for tanning oil on California freeways. Urrea's Nayeli and company sojourn near the border, but in *By the Lake of Sleeping Children* (1996) and *Across the Wire: Life and Hard Times on the Mexican Border* (1993), the books of reportage that precede this novel, the author focuses upon Tijuana, a sister city inextricably bound to San Diego and Los Angeles.

Another set of writings insist upon "here," foregrounding a deep-seated relation to the Golden State. Floyd Salas situates readers of his first novel, *Tattoo the Wicked Cross* (1967), in a California prison. In *Emplumada* (1981) and *From the Cables of Genocide: Poems on Love and Hunger* (1991), poet Lorna Dee Cervantes evokes the smells of tomatoes and peaches ("Cannery Town in August") and the "shore where grebe / and egret print the beach in black and white" ("Point Lobos"). Alejandro Morales's historical fiction *The Brick People* (1988) honors the nineteenth-century Californios who owned land grants originally proffered by New Spain and whose patronyms still reside in street signs and the names of towns and cities from Portola to Coronado. Gary Soto's wryly affectionate reflections in the memoir *Living up the Street* (1985) and *A Summer Life* (1990) root characters in Fresno by offering readers a vivid map of his Braly Street neighborhood, complete with junkyard and the Sun-Maid Raisin and Challenge Milk factories fronted by "scraggly sycamores" (*Living up the Street*). Helena María Viramontes' lyrical evocation of landscape in *Under the Feet of Jesus* (1995) places a migrant family in the Central Valley. Like Soto's memoir (as well as Floyd Salas's 1992 memoir *Buffalo Nickel* and Mary Helen Ponce's 1993 *Hoyt Street: An Autobiography*), Viramontes' first novel insists on place to maintain the rights of the Chicano protagonists who inhabit such ground.

Even works that hold steadfastly to California locales cannot always avoid allusions to the line that divides and stitches together people who live on different sides of the border. When Gary Soto explores a boarded-up store with his friend Jackie in *Living up the Street*, for instance, the two encounter a broken mirror, cracked "like the border between Mexico and the United States." The final chapter of this Fresno-based autobiography finds the narrator in Mexico City, where he encounters a blind harp player, a modern-day Tiresias who advises the grown-up Soto to "Be a Mexican and go on." In the years that follow the Movimiento, writers like Soto address the difficulty of maintaining a metaphorical foot in two nations obliquely, describing the journey from Mexico as a one-time event. However, increasingly since the 1990s, both immigrant- and U.S.-born writers represent the return to Mexico as a cyclical movement, one as natural as the wheeling seasons. Ultimately, however, California Chicana/o literature across the decades remains of one mind in its refusal to make its people strangers to U.S. shores.

II From Acculturation to Rootedness: "So here I am well settled in the US.?"

Ernesto Galarza published *Barrio Boy: The Story of a Boy's Acculturation* in 1971, but his memoir owes as much to the early twentieth-century immigrant narratives written by Russian Jewish refugees as to the literary work of the Movement – a fact less surprising given that the author and his family fled Mexico only thirty years after the peak influx of Eastern Europeans to Ellis Island. Galarza announces himself as an immigrant in his opening sentence. Unlike those who greet the world in a hospital, ambulance, or taxicab, he is born "in an adobe cottage with a thatched roof" on "the only street of Jalcocotán." The book's last sentences show him settled – more or less – "on the edge of the barrio" in Sacramento.

The book's five chapters chart the child's northward movement as inexorably as arrows in cinematic newsreels diagrammed the advance of the U.S. military through Europe during World War II. As in *The Promised Land*, Mary Antin's 1912 recollection of acculturation, the tone of Galarza's book is resolutely upbeat. *Barrio Boy* describes a world riven by conflict, disease and poverty, but in the rainy dark the child smiles while being carried off a train by an American soldier, the "moral enem[y] of our country," who deposits the boy carefully next to his mother. The author's development across chapters mirrors the processes of uprooting, transportation, and replanting Antin describes in her autobiography. While she insists in one breath on her successful "acclimatization" and confesses in the next that it "is painful to be consciously of two worlds," Galarza strenuously disavows the host of "psychologists" and "social anthropologists" who "have spread the rumor that these Mexican immigrants and their offspring have lost their 'self-image.'" Instead, he declares in his preface, "I can't remember a time I didn't know who I was." The author's stout refusal to be redefined flies in the face of critical readings that fault him for failing to indict U.S. racism overtly. Granted, the book is not framed in the rebellious voice of the corrido. But the boy who grows up to work as a labor organizer does not forget his native land: fully half of this book takes place in Mexico.

Despite its appearance during a time of political ferment, *Barrio Boy* discloses none of the anger that lacerates Villarreal's *Pocho* and stabs through the lines of Gonzales' "I Am Joaquin." If outrage propels the Chicano Renaissance, however, its writers do not speak of unjust treatment in a single voice. Mexican-born, San Diego-based poet Alurista galvanized Chicano literature with the multilingual poetics of his ground-breaking collection *Floricanto en Aztlán* (1971), exploiting a sinuous weave of Spanish, English, and Nahautl in poems such as "Tarde Sobria." Then as now, however, his narrators often temper as they collocate the noises of the city – the "barking multitude of dogs," a "roar of wheels" and the "hammering of stone," for instance, which produces a chord that leaves the "heart at peace" in the poem "go ya go" (*Et Tú ... Raza?* 1996).

José Montoya code-switches between Spanish, English, and the Chicano vernacular of Caló with equal deftness in "El Louie," a poem that eulogizes a Korean War veteran and "vato de atolle" with the ebullience and energy of the zoot-suiter. The poet speaks in an entirely different key in "La Jefita," training the reader's ear on the "small cough" and "Clik-clok" of a mother's rolling pin to honor a hardworking woman with wry tenderness. Like Alurista and Montoya, legal-aid lawyer Oscar

Zeta Acosta worked both as author and activist. In his two memoirs, *Autobiography of a Brown Buffalo* (1972) and *The Revolt of the Cockroach People* (1973), Acosta faces readers head-on, exploiting humor to upset stereotypes of the bean-eating Mexican. The soliloquy that opens his first book styles him as Falstaffian in energy and appetite even as it lampoons the self-absorption that is the autobiographer's stock in trade. "I tighten, suck at the air, and recall that Charles Atlas was a ninety-nine-pound weakling when the beach bully kicked sand in his girl friend's pretty face," Acosta admits as he stands in front of the mirror. "Perhaps my old mother was right. I should lay off those Snicker bars" and "those liverwurst sandwiches with gobs of mayonnaise."

Though he comes of age during the Movement, Gary Soto does not linger on politics in his narrative recollections *Living up the Street* (1985) and *A Summer Life* (1990). Instead, he fixes attention on children who grow up "Mexican poor" and for whom backbreaking fieldwork is a synonym for what it is to "stoop like a Mexican." In the first memoir, Soto uses wry humor throughout his memoirs to confirm and critique the blessings and difficulties of Chicano family life in Fresno – as will Victor Martinez a decade later in the 1996 National Book Award-winning *bildungsroman Parrot in the Oven: Mi Vida*. In *Living up the Street*, Soto describes himself as a "page turner" in school who becomes a poet with a Guggenheim to his credit. Sitting cross-legged in his living room, "eager to reinvent" his childhood, Soto scratches out lines "to show others the chinaberry tree, ants, shadow, dirty spoons – those nouns" that compose his poetry. Even as his work "uses the mind," friends and neighbors remain yoked to "muscle" work. Elsewhere, Soto recapitulates in a single sentence the trip north from Mexico that Galarza unspools in *Barrio Boy*. Exiting from a movie theater after seeing *Gandhi*, Soto recalls the Indian masses on screen and connects them with the bone-wearying work his family undertakes, "beginning with Grandmother who came to the United States after the Mexican revolution to settle in Fresno where she met her husband and bore children." When his grandmother is not "dragging a large white sack like a sled" to the fields, she stands over a conveyor belt at the Sun-Maid Raisin factory plucking leaves and pebbles from the fruit.

Meanwhile, children jump from trees laughing, "unkillable kids of the very poor." There is rue in the writer's retrospective glance, but Soto consistently stares back at pity and foregrounds the imagination that flourishes even in industrial Fresno. When Gary and his siblings are not pushing each other out of an open window, pretending sharks are "ready to snack" on their skinny legs, the narrator and his friend

Jackie move forward through the dark of an abandoned store, curious as astronauts. There is anger here as well. After his father dies two days after suffering a neck injury at work, Soto describes a game of marbles he plays with his siblings in a house newly stripped of its furniture. "We separated," Soto writes, "each to a corner, where we swept them viciously with our arms – the clatter of the marbles hitting the walls so loud that I could not hear the things in my heart." In the poem "Braly Street," the adult narrator in a meditative vein upon death, finding loss in the "browning sage" and the "wine bottles / Whose history / Is a liver." In *Elements of San Joaquin* (1977), Soto's foundational second collection of poems, as well as in his prose, the author invokes the small nouns that compose the child's view of the world as objective correlatives that refract feeling.

In her 1995 novel *Under the Feet of Jesus*, scholar-writer Helena María Viramontes revisits fields like those which bedevil Soto's family. At the same time, her novel recalls *The Grapes of Wrath*. The old station wagon that ferries Estella and her family from worksite to worksite gestures toward the Joad family truck, reminding readers that the working poor who pick grapes and cotton and beets are not a historical anachronism in the late twentieth-century, but remain the mainstay of U.S. agribusiness. The bucolic landscape Viramontes conjures at the outset of her *bildungsroman* is more lyrical than Steinbeck's apocalyptic representation of the Dust Bowl. The rural beauty of the scene Estella observes from the inside of the station wagon echoes her youthful promise: "Sunlight weaved in and out of the clouds. Wisps of wind ruffled the orange and avocado and peach trees which rolled and tumbled as far back as the etched horizon of the mountain range." The sentence that follows this description – "A cluster of amputated trees marked the entrance to the side road" – cuts short its pastoral quality, signaling as it anticipates Estella's constricted circumstances. Before the novel's end, the protagonist suffers the loss of the boy who labors in the fields alongside her and to whom she develops a romantic attachment when this child wastes away in the hospital, sickened by spray from a crop duster. The unsympathetic nurse who attends the teenager (and who recalls the uncaring receptionist in Martinez's *Parrot in the Oven*) is a synecdoche for the shoddy care the United States' hardest and least-paid workers receive. And yet, Viramontes insists in her book, such families carry on – in Fresno and Modesto as in East Los Angeles and Chicago. Here they remain: as if to underscore their continuing presence in a U.S.-centered political geography, Viramontes invokes "Aquí" as the novel's first vocalized word.

The poems collected in Lorna Dee Cervantes' astonishing first volume of poetry, *Emplumada*, which earned her a 1982 American Book Award, offer readers portraits of girls and women who reflect on their lives as they escape poor work conditions and sometimes repressive families. The personas in this collection use words to build themselves up against what the 1994 poem "Astro-no-mia" calls "the fathers of fate, heavy like mercury" who "would trash / our stomachs into our wombs." Cervantes denies contemporary masculine retellings of stories that insist women deserve their sexual punishment by punning on their blamelessness when she yokes chastened factory workers to the "chased women set in the sky" of Greek myth. The resisting female speaker of this poem earns its final words, claiming the weapon of language against men who define themselves as warriors only by reducing women to prey.

As its title implies, flight is a prevailing motif in *Emplumada*.[3] Images of feathers and wings ineluctably lead in this collection to the writing quills fashioned from such plumage. The narrator of "Crow" watches this bird and recognizes herself, "flushed" out of her childhood house. However, women's words teach her how to build her own house. "*Learn hammer and Phillips*," they urge. "*Learn socket and rivet.*" In "Communication," a daughter speaks to her mother "long distance," imagining that "the humming telephone wires" telegraph the rapport, as well as the hostilities, that connect them. The persona whose voice speaks this fraught communication into being becomes a "foot" at the close of the poem who pedals her bicycle away. Nonetheless, the words hang over her head, as alive with electricity as are the wires. In "Beneath the Shadow of the Freeway," the poet explores another vexed mother–daughter relationship; again, from the younger woman's point of view. Her mother, the speaker tells us, prefers to style herself using the childish rhetoric of the "Princess," though she is both brave and strong. "Even now she dreams of taffeta," the daughter muses, "and foot-high tiaras." In a nod to the "antique Volume / Written by faded men" in Emily Dickinson's poem #1545, Cervantes' speaker announces herself as a "Scribe" who turns "to books, those staunch, upright men" to speak herself into a less restrictive role.

Indeed, the writer's project in *Emplumada* is in part to reject damaging fables – whether the grown-up canonical variety underwritten by Greek precursor narratives honoring male warriors or the Grimm Brothers' narratives Disney repackages to feed young readers. Unlike the Chicago-born writer Sandra Cisneros, whose revisionary fairy tales in *The House on Mango Street* (1984) foreground women trapped by husbands in Rapunzel-like fortresses and girls lured to surreal, blighted gardens, Cervantes honors the gritty and sometimes beautiful actual: the durable materials of "rocks and gravel" ("Crow"), the feathers, eel bones, and small mussels in "Starfish," the "spinach-specked shoes" of women working the graveyard shift in the poem "Cannery Town in August." Like Soto, Cervantes frames California places through the mixed feelings of the Chicanas/os who view their pasts through the lens of landscape. The trees the narrator of "Freeway 280" lovingly catalogues and the wild mustard growing nearby recall homes built near the cannery, residences unwillingly sacrificed to the San Francisco Bay Area's newest freeway. Cervantes invokes the freeway throughout her poetry, usually to indict it as a metaphor for social and political ravaging. In "Poema para Los Californios Muertos," the freeway scars the land, cutting a "clean cesarean" through Los Altos. Images such as this one indicate actual destruction, however, even before they stand in as figures of speech for social damage. Through he weals, welts, and mutilations left in the land the poet continuously draws our attention to anticipate Gloria Anzaldúa's now iconic representation in *Borderlands*/La Frontera (1987) of the "open wound" the border traces hundreds of miles south.

III   "Vamos a salir del pais y es algo natural, cosa de todos los días.[4]"

The line in the dirt that divides people residing in the United States from those who live in Mexico has been mythologized well in advance of Anzaldúa's study. In journalistic accounts and political rhetoric, the division between nations is less ground than ground for argument; not so much a place to be crossed as a conflict over language, the swirl and disputation of "illegals" and "undocumented people," of "mojados/wetbacks" and "aliens," of "Mexican workers" and "mexicanos." Scholars often follows Anzaldúa's lead by framing the border as the pivot around which the world of Mexican immigrants turns. However, in much of this criticism and theory, "the border" is an abstract space rather than a place that can be located on a map. Featureless no man's land, it functions as an acronym for discussions of federal and state immigration policy. At the same time, it becomes in the mass media a container for various "leyendas negras" – black legends – literalized in forms of violence such as drug trafficking, prostitution, and murder that are glamorized in television series and feature films. Contemporary "narco-corridos" or drug ballads often savage the desert in the same way, representing the land as a faceless void through which celebrated violent figures travel. Lost in the rush to deliver political critique and the desire to pander to the black legends are the people living in the California, Arizona, Texas and New Mexico towns that border Mexico, as well as their families and neighbors who inhabit the sister cities to the south.[5]

Theorists of "border identities" tend to leave people idling at checkpoints. But Chicana/o authors of memoir and story are not so quick to abandon them. Frequently, writers explore what happens after a mother or brother or father crosses the line. The *frontera* (border) is becoming increasingly militarized, but writers insist that life goes on alongside military encampment and fence. In much of the literature published within the last two decades, the self-divided figure Villarreal introduces in *Pocho* gives way to more cosmopolitan and forgiving characters. Notwithstanding corrosive political conflict, the characters who travel north and south and back again in the works of California-based writers like Dagoberto Gilb, Luis Urrea, and Luis Rodriguez do not see themselves as afflicted by Chicanismo.[6] Rather than framing racial identity as a cross to bear, an "either/or" they cannot negotiate, the men and women represented in fiction and nonfiction see the "both/and" experience of maintaining ties with two countries and several peoples as an enriching one. The unnamed narrator of Dagoberto Gilb's beautifully rendered titular story "The Magic of Blood," for instance, has moved to Hollywood, but he recalls the relatives converging upon Los Angeles to celebrate his great-grandmother's party who come "from everywhere, from every state in the Southwest, from Mexico." The very casualness of this phrase reinforces links across national lines.

While Luis Rodriguez's *Always Running: La Vida Loca: Gang Days in L.A.* (1992), currently in its eighteenth edition, continues to be featured at universities across the country, the writer's move to fiction in *The Republic of East LA* (2002) affords him greater flexibility to consider a range of relationships between self and nation. Several of the characters in this story collection take reflective attitudes toward the Mexican villages of their birth. In "Pigeons," for instance, the matriarch Socorro drowns out her two sons' argument over Chicanismo by looking "straight ahead, into the trees, into someplace else, among the heart-shaped faces of another land." With Rosalba, the strong-minded protagonist of "Sometimes You Dance with a Watermelon," Rodriguez concludes his story collection on a guardedly affirmative note. Like Luis Urrea, Rodriguez refuses to romanticize Mexico. Rosalba acknowledges that life was difficult in her village of Nayarit, but knows that Los Angeles is "far more threatening." Although she has made peace with her place in this country, she wishes to be buried "deep in Nayarit soil." With her "bright face and brash approach" to life, Rosalba defies the gray specters critical and theoretical studies that "do not exist" but paradoxically continue to float "unregistered, undocumented, unrecorded" through the pages of cultural studies articles.[7] Rosalba lacks legal status, but this uncertainty does not prevent her from claiming space in an LA Rodriguez represents as loud with shrill factory whistles and hammering machines, a city that is at the same time vibrant with children who speak a mixture of Spanish and English and a Grand Central Market whose stands of papaya, mango, watermelon, and oranges enable the writer to splash artful color before the reader's eye. In this story as in "Chicas Chuecas," Rodriguez offers portraits of Chicanas who negotiate difficult circumstances with poise. (Such women, "bent, but not broken," as he writes in "Chicas Chuecas," also provide Helena María Viramontes with her central focus in *Their Dogs Came with Them* (2007), a novel that returns readers to the gang conflicts LA-based writer-attorney Yxta Maya Murray explores in her 1998 novel *Locas*).

In "La Operación," Rodriguez does not commute imaginatively between the United States and Mexico, but instead follows two families who move from their home in Michoacán to a makeshift house in Los Angeles. The doubled narrative structure lets readers follow Carlos and his family between the United States and Mexico without forgetting its "special language," this "refugee tongue, written on scabbed and broken feet." Rodriguez's description of the border as "a festering sore that had never healed, had never closed up or scarred over" (207) recalls Gloria Anzaldúa's "herida abierta," but his story does not linger here. Instead, "La Operación" tacks between the United States and Mexico in alternative paragraphs that permit Rodriguez to insist upon the links between the two countries rather than the line that divides them. In this piece as elsewhere in the book, Mexico is not a dark continent, but simply one of two mirror images in which the difficulties and occasional small triumphs of life for working people play out.

The connection between nations rather than the partition between them characterizes Luis Urrea's work as well, notwithstanding the metaphor of division that opens his often humorous retelling of conflicted boyhood in *Nobody's Son* (2002). The Tijuana-born, San Diego-educated, Illinois-residing writer-professor announces himself to a journalist as a "son of the border" whose heart is neatly bisected by a barbed-wire fence. But in this memoir as elsewhere Urrea refuses self-pity, exchanging drama for comedy. The journalist responds to Urrea's announcement with an "Aha!" and begins scribbling "with real vigor." After the article is published, however, Urrea's metaphor is scrambled. "It said 'If you were to cut Urrea's heart open, you would find a border patrol truck idling between his ribs' .... I'm still not sure what it means." Like the protagonist of Tijuana-born writer Luis Humberto Crosthwaite's story "La fila," who understands border crossing as "natural, an everyday occurrence," Urrea does not recreate the dark glamour that has characterized pictorial and scholarly treatments of the border since Orson Welles' 1958 film *A Touch of Evil*.

Instead, in *By the Lake of Sleeping Children* (1996) he hedges surrealistic descriptions of garbage snowing the Tijuana dumps with down-to-earth oral histories of the people who labor in them in order to produce a collective portrait laced with a demonic humor that Salvador Dalí might have admired. In *The Devil's Highway*, Urrea dignifies the testimony of one man who survives the trek through the desert by recasting his words as verse. He also leavens grisly clinical accounts of heat stroke with ironic commentary: one chapter about a hapless coyote who leads other boys and men to their deaths, for instance, is titled "A Pepsi for the Apocalypse." Indeed, Urrea has afforded the United States and Mexico equal representation throughout his career, from his 1993 book of reportage *Across the Wire: Life and Hard Times on the Mexican Border* to the 2009 picaresque fiction *Into the Beautiful North*. In many of his books, Los Angeles jostles for center stage alongside sister city Tijuana, whose 1889 plan was modeled not after Mexican cities, but rather Indianapolis, and whose bars, cabarets, and houses of prostitution burgeoned in the 1920s for the benefit of those U.S. citizens making their way south to buy alcohol during Prohibition. In both nonfiction and fiction, Urrea insists on foregrounding Tijuana and the enduring if vexed relationship it maintains with those U.S. metropolises that develop symbiotically alongside it.[8]

Ultimately, constant people-traffic between border cities must complicate notions of what it is to be a "migrant," just as the multiple locations many people inhabit across long lifespans demand we take a more nuanced approach to "home." In Europe, a French high school teacher who lectures on the golden age of French literature marries a Catalan and sojourns in Madrid to study Spanish, while a teenager with a German father and Spanish mother divides his time between these two countries. However, neither teacher nor student appears unduly vexed when describing themselves. The Californian who buys a seaside villa on the Mexican coast in which to retire is an immigrant no less than the Michoacán native who builds a suburban home in Tracy or Stockton, but few Americans would expect the retiree to be hobbled by the fact of his migration. At what point, then, will we cease to understand the immigrant history of Chicanos as a "problem"? The variegated trajectories Chicana/o writers delineate in their prose and poetry encourage readers to explore, if not to resolve this question. From a focus on narrating the journey north, Mexican American writers of California have begun offering readers round trips and multiple stops in place of restrictive one-way tickets. Perhaps, reading their work, we may begin to take a wider view as well.

Notes

1. In choosing to focus upon the blighted fate of the majority rather than offering a model of the exceptional individual who, by a combination of gift and luck, distinguishes himself from the common fate, Villarreal defined his novelistic project in a manner similar to that of Richard Wright. In *Native Son*, published nineteen years before *Pocho*, Wright backs Bigger Thomas into a more malign corner than the one Villarreal reserves for Richard but in their outcries of anger and frustration, both characters demand the United States account for the savage treatment of its Native sons.
2. "La Jaula de Oro/The Gilded Cage," Los Tigres del Norte, 1986.
3. In this sense, Cervantes' work anticipates the announcement Sandra Cisneros' narrator makes in the final sentence of *House on Mango Street*, who insists she speaks for "The ones who cannot out." But the clear-voiced inflections that sustain *Emplumada* refuse the 1984 novel's revisionary fabulizing.
4. "We're going to leave the country and its normal/OK, an everyday thing." Luis Humberto Crosthwaite, "La fila," cited in Santiago Vaquera-Vásquez, "Notes from an Unrepentant Border Crosser," *South Atlantic Quarterly* 105: 4 (Fall 2006): 699.
5. More often than not, work in cultural studies takes its cue from Gloria Anzaldúa's feminist revision of Aztlán in *Borderlands*/La Frontera (1987). Anzaldúa transformed the geographical mapping that divides Texas and Mexico into a metaphorical, multi-state "*herida abierta*/open wound." Interestingly, her defiant "*atravesados*" – Chicanas/os marginalized and othered as the ill-intentioned "squint-eyed, the perverse, the queer, the troublesome" (3) and who share more than a little of the anger of the rebellious feminine characters in Sylvia Plath's *Ariel*, who "eat men like air" – have been divested of volition in much contemporary theory. Representative of "a condition of statelessness or nonexistence" (102), as Auerbach suggests in "Noir Citizenship," his excellent study of national identity in film noir, such people have become for too many theorists featureless shades, ghosts who drift in and out of accounts of "transnationalist migrations" and studies of "border identities." As one example, note what happens to immigrants in the pages of

the following essay. "As the migrants cross the border," Ana Maria Manzanas Calvo writes in "Contested Passages: Migrants Crossing the Rio Grande and the Mediterranean Sea," "they go through what Mary Pat Brady calls an 'abjection machine' that metamorphoses them into something else' ... and renders them 'unintelligible (and unintelligent), ontologically impossible, outside the real and the human'" [*South Atlantic Quarterly* 105: 4 (Fall 2006): 765]. Such criticism is intended as a correction and indictment of unjust state and federal policies towards immigrants. But, enchanted with its own rhetoric, a great deal of this work runs the risk of estranging readers from the people who live in this existential void. It is not, after all, always dusk in the twilight zone where such individuals rise for work, raise their children, cook their dinners, and go to sleep each night. See Santiago Vaquera-Vasquez's innovative hybrid of memoir and criticism in "Notes from an Unrepentant Border Crosser" for a particularly interesting assessment of the relationship between "old-style border studies, grounded in history and the empiricism of the social sciences" (702) and contemporary cultural studies.
6. I have not categorized Ana Castillo or Alicia Gaspar de Alba as California writers, but the former's work demystifying the glamor of desert violence in *The Guardians* (2007) and the latter's in *Desert Blood: The Juarez Murders* (2005) demand and deserve special mention here.
7. Auerbach, 113. This language is Auerbach's, but it could have been drawn from any number of critical studies.
8. "Imperceptibly and almost without comment," as Michael Dear and Gustavo Leclerc write in "Tijuana Desenmascarada," Tijuana has "emerged as the second largest city on the western seaboard of North and Central and Central America." [*Wide Angle* 20.3 (1998): 219 (211–221)]. I have drawn on their account of Tijuana, which enables them to argue that Mexican and U.S. border cities develop and evolve in tandem, throughout this paragraph.

CHAPTER 20

Interracial Encounters: Face and Place in Post-1980 Asian American Literature

King-Kok Cheung

Asian American writers who try to capture the interactions among peoples of diverse ethnicities arguably have offered some of the most prismatic views of California. This essay concentrates on selected post-1980 fiction and memoirs set against various historical currents of the twentieth century: emigration of Koreans after Japanese annexation of their country, postcolonial migration of Filipino Americans in search of the American dream, the Japanese American internment during World War II, the Korean War, the Vietnam War, the Civil Rights and the attendant Asian American movements, the 1965 Watts Riots, and the 1992 Los Angeles uprising. I use 1980 (the year in which an ancestry question appeared for the first time in the U.S. census) as a marker because the rise of multicultural curricular reform during the 1980s had ushered in an unprecedented number of publications by people from hitherto marginalized groups, including Asian American writers.[1] The texts selected, representing a much wider array of nationalities than those published previously, are quite dense in historical, social, and cultural contexts; they also have a distinctly regional flavor that against another backdrop would be lost. Instead of discussing the works according to their dates of publication, I have grouped them around common concerns and geographical settings, holding up a literary mirror to the polyglot state in all its faces.

Suspended Between Shores

This section covers fiction that straddles Asia and the United States. In *Clay Walls* Ronyoung Kim tells the story of a Korean couple who arrive in Los Angeles in the 1920s, after the Japanese annexation of Korea in 1910 and the Declaration of Korean Independence on March 1, 1919 – a campaign of resistance against the Japanese that led to a violent suppression in which more than 7,000 Koreans were killed.[2] Although the novel is divided into three parts, told from the perspectives of Haesu (a Korean woman from a *Yangban* or aristocratic family), Chun (her peasant-stock husband), and Faye (the sole daughter among their three American children) respectively, it centers on the transpacific vicissitudes of Haesu, who flees Korea involuntarily with Chun, after he is mistaken for a student protester during the March 1 movement. She sorely misses her homeland and her *Yangban* status.

Haesu nevertheless survives her double estrangement in Korea under Japanese occupancy and in the United States as a déclassé exile. At first, she clings to her dream of returning to an independent Korea, supporting the Independence movement from Los Angeles and buying land in Korea. At one point, she takes her children back to Korea with the intent of settling, but is appalled by the Japanese subjugation of her people, feeling homesick in the very presence of her homeland. All the same, she uses the money won by Chun through gambling to buy land there, expecting Korea to be independent some day. Ironically, the situation hardly improves after Japanese defeat and the partition of Korea into two countries at the end of World War II; Haesu loses her homecoming dream along with the land she has purchased in North Korea. Meanwhile, her family must confront numerous racial barriers in Los Angeles. The book opens with her cleaning a toilet under the patronizing gaze of a white housewife who calls her "insolent yellow," whereupon Haesu quits her cleaning job. Because of Alien Land laws and housing segregation, the couple must use the names of their white associates to rent a place and, later, to buy a house. After their son John is called a "chink" at public school, Haesu tries to enroll her two sons in Edwards Military Academy, only to be told that the school does not admit Orientals. Also on account of race her son Harold is turned down for officer-training in the marines during World War II. However, Haesu's rancor toward the Japanese far exceeds her vexation with whites. Not so with Faye: though forbidden by her mother to befriend Japanese, her closest buddy is Japanese American.

Raquel "Rocky" Rivera and Gabe Sullivan, the first-person Filipino narrators of mixed descent in Jessica Hagedorn's *Gangster of Love* and Brian Ascalon Roley's *American Son* respectively, grapple with their ethnic identities while interacting with people of heterogeneous backgrounds.[3] In *Gangster of Love* Rocky, her brother Voltaire, and their mother Milagros arrive in San Francisco in 1970 – the year Jimi Hendrix (Voltaire's idol) died. Growing up as a young adult in the Bay Area in the 1970s, Rocky falls in love with Elvis Chang, a Chinese American guitarist and rock musician, and meets Keiko Van Heller, a bisexual photographer who becomes her lifelong friend. Together they launch the eponymous rock band and head for New York, where Rocky remains in constant contact with her mother on the West Coast via phone calls. After a miscarriage and Elvis's love affair with Keiko, Rocky has a daughter with Jake Montano, a Cuban American sound engineer. When Milagros's health declines, Rocky shuttles between New York and San Francisco until her mother's death. Rocky then returns to the Philippines and reunites with her dying father.

This picaresque mosaic evokes what Ketu Katrak calls "simultaneity of geography" – the state of living in one place physically and in another place psychically.[4] Rocky longs simultaneously to reinvent herself and belong to a community. Her life in San Francisco is shot through with memories of the Philippines, and her time in New York is filled with reminiscences about San Francisco. The liaisons among Rocky, Elvis, and Keiko attest to the fluid connection among Asians of assorted nationalities on the West Coast. At the same time, despite the novel's motley ensemble that reflects the sweeping pop cultures of San Francisco and New York, Rocky often finds herself an outsider. Like the people closest to her – Voltaire (who wishes he were Jimi Hendrix), Elvis (the Presley wannabe), and her gay Uncle Marlon (an actor manqué) – she is enthralled by a Hollywood that eludes Asian American aspirants. Her decision to return to the Philippines might be seen as her attempt to reassert her indigenous identity and as her disillusionment with cultural Americana, which is at once enchanting and tantalizing. If Manila represents the pull of the homeland and New York demands complete assimilation, San Francisco seems to offer Rocky the possibility of intersecting ethnic tradition (embodied by Milagros) and American culture. Ultimately, she is like the yo-yo – the novel's recurrent trope for Filipino ethnicity – fluctuating between coasts.

Unlike Rocky, Gabe (the fifteen-year-old biracial narrator in Roley's *American Son*) and his older brother Tomas are totally alienated from their Filipino heritage, as promulgated by their Uncle Betino in the Philippines. This novel follows the two brothers' wanderings in contemporary California, from upscale mansions in the Hollywood Hills to dilapidated Los Angeles barrios. Tomas breeds pricey attack dogs, trains them in German using Nazi techniques, and foists them on Hollywood celebrities. Gabe tries to steer clear of Tomas's delinquent ways, but is hopelessly enmeshed in his brother's shady schemes. Their Filipina mother has moved from Manila to America with her abusive white husband, who marries her because he wants someone "meek and obedient." Now divorced, she tries in vain to instill Filipino values and Catholic faith in her sons while holding down two dead-end jobs.

Two instances of racial passing illustrate the Sullivan brothers' disavowal of their Filipino origin and the entanglement of masculinity, race, and class. Tomas models himself on a Mexican gangster, sporting a shaved head and copious tattoos. Trying to pass for Mexican, he is caught out by a potential buyer's Mexican wife, whom he ironically has mistaken for a maid. His appropriation of machismo extends to vicious behavior toward his own brother, at whom he lashes out frequently. Gabe tries to run away after Tomas brutally cuts his chest with a broken beer bottle. He is offered a ride by a white tow truck driver, who spouts demeaning slurs about Mexicans, Cambodians, Vietnamese, and Laotians without realizing that Gabe is of partial Asian ancestry. When his mother and his white aunt finally catch up with Gabe, he tells the driver that the aunt is his mom and the Filipina is their maid. Although the two brothers respond to racism differently – one passes for Mexican and the other for white – their common need to eclipse their Asian identity illustrates the prevalence of social bigotry and the extent of self-hate. Tomas dissembles as Mexican to slough off the stereotype of the feminized Oriental; Gabe pretends to be white to set himself apart from the minorities that the white driver denounces. The two brothers have moved away from the religion and obligations of the old world only to be stranded in the new.

In Lê Thi Diem Thúy's "The Gangster We Are All Looking For," published separately in *Massachusetts Review*, *Harper's Magazine*, and *The Best American Essays* (1999) before it became a chapter in a novel with the same title, a number of metaphors connect a Vietnamese family's displacement in Vietnam and in San Diego.[5] A barbed wire gate in a reeducation camp separating the father from his wife and daughter in South Vietnam resurfaces as a chain-link fence that cordons off their apartment complex in Linda Vista, San Diego, about to be razed to make way for condominiums priced above the means of the evicted residents. Tropical fish from a broken tank that the father throws outside their American apartment's door are reminiscent of the narrator's brother's body pulled from the South China Sea and the bodies of boat people washed to various shores. A photo of the mother's parents, taken in the courtyard of their home in Vietnam, sits forgotten in the Linda Vista attic; the mother, once a Catholic schoolgirl disowned by her parents for marrying a Buddhist gangster and further cut off from them in leaving Vietnam, undergoes yet another wrenching valediction when the photo is annihilated along with their apartment. Adjustment to San Diego is made the more difficult for the young narrator by ogling neighbors and white classmates, who call all their Southeast Asian peers "Yang" – refugees who reflexively deem themselves to be wanting in beauty, popularity, and intelligence. The sobriquet, like the eponymous "gangster," speaks to identities vacated on crossing the ocean.

Angie Chau's chapter "Quiet as They Come" (from a novel with the same title) and Andrew Lam's short story "Show and Tell" also feature newcomers suspended between Vietnam and the United States.[6] Their experiences are likewise shaped by the "simultaneity of geography," beset by racial discrimination, and aggravated by their designation as refugees. Chau's novel follows extended family members who have fled to San Francisco in the mid-1970s; this particular chapter revolves around Viet Tran, a father of two daughters who once envisioned himself a chancellor at a Vietnamese university but who now holds a monotonous job sorting mail by zip code at a post office. His coworkers consider Vietnamese immigrants to be as quiet as they come and Viet to be the mutest. The truth is that Viet's heavy accent makes him self-conscious. After his attractive daughter visits him at the post office, a black coworker named Melvin, a playboy, makes lewd remarks about her, unaware that Viet is hanging on his every obscene word. Tension mounts as the seething father, who obviously suffers from post-traumatic syndrome, recalls how he once killed a pirate about to rape his wife during their harrowing voyage as boat people, as though he were poised to pounce on Mel in like fashion. However, the chapter ends with Mel apologizing to Viet and enfolding him in a warm embrace.

Andrew Lam's "Show and Tell" traces the painful initiation in an American classroom of seventh-grader Cao Long Dinh (Kal), a Vietnamese refugee who speaks broken English, and his evolving friendship with Robert, the story's white narrator tasked by the teacher to show Cao around during the first day of school. Both Kal and Robert are teased by Billy, a bully who calls Kal a Viet Cong and Robert his new boyfriend. During Show and Tell, Billy brings in his father's old army uniform and talks pointedly about the wounds his father has received from fighting in Vietnam. Kal, in turn, communicates by drawing on the chalkboard and prompting Robert to supply the verbal narrative. After scribbling two boys (he and his friend) on buffaloes, a couple (his parents) holding hands, a man (his Dad) behind a barbed wire fence with chains on his ankles, a small boat, an island, and an airplane, and sketching a map of America along with its famous landmarks, Kal draws a heart around the Vietnamese scenes and another around the American ones. Robert effectively transforms Kal's illustrations into words and, in the process, overcomes his own inhibition and fear of Billy. Two boys differently marginalized – one by race and the other by sexual orientation – have found each other and connected across language barriers.

Creating Communities in San Francisco

Gus Lee's *China Boy* and William Poy Lee's *The Eighth Promise* chronicle the struggles of two Chinese Americans, China-born and U.S.-born respectively, in San Francisco.[7] *China Boy* (a novel that according to the author is a thinly veiled autobiography) describes the tribulations and eventual triumph of Kai, a seven-year-old immigrant growing up in the Panhandle (a predominantly black ghetto) and trying to become an accepted black male youth in the 1950s. The novel abounds in interracial contact: Kai's abuse by an Irish stepmother, friendship with an African American boy and a Jewish boy, verbal and corporal assault by black bullies, and tutelage by multi-ethnic YMCA coaches. Enmity and amity are dealt by those of varied hues in equal measure in Kai's path to manhood.

Edna, Kai's stepmother, resembles the wicked stepmother in fairytales, but her vicious power is bolstered by whiteness. Compared by Kai to German Nazis, she tries to crush any vestiges of Chineseness in her stepson, whose very facial expressions and indeed face can trigger slapping. By compelling Kai to stay outdoors except during meal times and bedtime, she also exposes him to bloody street fights. If Kai is subdued at home by oppressive whiteness in the person of Edna, he is literally hobbled on the street by a black bully named Big Willie. But numerous affectionate relationships between Kai and other people of color make up for the torments these two antagonists inflict. Most significant are the trainers Kai encounters at the Golden Gate YMCA, where he receives boxing lessons for self-defense under surrogate father figures of African American, Italian, Puerto Rican, and Filipino descent, who take the place of Kai's negligent biological father in shepherding their Chinese protégé, much as his black buddy's mother cares for him maternally.

William Poy Lee's *The Eighth Promise: An American Son's Tribute to His Toisanese Mother* spans three generations, linking the mother's upbringing in a Chinese village with the author's coming of age in San Francisco's Chinatown, where he becomes engaged with the Civil Rights Movement and a prolonged battle with the American legal system. Structurally, the memoir alternates between the voice of the American-born son and that of his emigrant mother, whom the author has interviewed in her Toisanese dialect. The mother has made eight promises to her own mother before leaving war-torn China to join her husband in San Francisco as a young bride in 1949. The eighth promise is to live with compassion toward all – an ethos that sustains her sons through a family tragedy when William's brother is convicted of murder.

Born in 1951 and living in San Francisco for more than four decades, William witnesses vociferous confrontation as well as mutual respect and caring among people of different races. When he is suspended from school for joining a Civil Rights protest, his father belligerently confronts the white principal. Ruthless inmates of color assault William's brother, sentenced to life in a California prison. However, remarkable racial harmony exists in the neighborhood of their boyhood home in the International Section across the street from Portsmouth Square, a multi-hued urban village that shares the communal ethos of their mother's Chinese hamlet. William and other kids are watched over by many beloved figures: Benny Beltran, a trustworthy Filipino American shop owner; a local beat patrolman nicknamed Danny the Wop; and Molly, an Irish prostitute who is also a lover of Sam, proprietor of Sam's Cleaners & Alterations. As in *China Boy*, a strong friendship develops between young William and a black boy when both of them are confined to the TB ward of San Francisco General Hospital, where the patients are offspring of a cross section of San Francisco's working class – Mexican, Irish, Italian, Chinese, and black.

Both Maxine Hong Kingston's *Tripmaster Monkey* and Karen Tei Yamashita's *I Hotel* capture the vibrant counterculture and political activism of the Civil Rights and Vietnam eras, especially the bids to usher in distinctive Asian Pacific American artistic expressions and to build coalitions and communities among the disfranchised.[8] However, neither author idealizes their main characters. Wittman Ah Sing, Berkeley graduate and *Tripmaster Monkey*'s bohemian protagonist (who reminds readers of Frank Chin, writer, playwright, and Kingston's most severe critic), must overcome his own ambivalence toward his Chinese ancestry and his sexist attitude toward women. A fifth generation Chinese American residing in San Francisco, Wittman looks askance at Chinese immigrants and yet he chastises Asian American women for their ignorance of Chinese classics. He bristles at any tendentious comments directed at people of color but cannot refrain from off color remarks and shenanigans. Pitching himself as the modern reincarnation of the intelligent but intractable Monkey King in the famous Chinese epic *Journey to the West*, he is fired from a toy store after positioning a wind-up brown monkey atop a white Barbie Bride.

The unemployed Wittman decides to start a theater company named Pear Garden Players of America (in Chinese "Pear Garden" refers to operatic circles in general) in which he is the playwright, producer, and director and in which the actors can be of any shade. Connecting his effort directly with the Civil Rights Movement, Wittman seeks to bring together not only Asian Pacific Americans but also anyone who has been sidelined. The play integrates the old and the young, foreign-born and American-born, poets and hobos. In the course of production, Wittman is tamed by women such as Nanci Lee, his Chinese American date; Tana De Weese, a white woman who marries him so he can dodge the draft; and the omniscient narrator, who assumes the voice of the Goddess of Mercy. His exceptionally long play, performed at a community center, epitomizes communal art. On the closing night, Wittman delivers a monologue that signals his transformation. Though still incorrigibly egotistical, he has learned to accept his Chinese ancestry, treat women more or less as equals, and foster camaraderie and even kinship among strangers to combat the loneliness of the American West.

I Hotel, a fusion of prose, drama, and graphic art set primarily in San Francisco's Chinatown, can be read as a companion novel or a sequel to *Tripmaster Monkey*, for Yamashita not only includes Kingston and Frank Chin (the duo appears in a series of cartoons in the middle of the text) but also populates her tome with simian mavericks and rebels. The panoramic novel opens in the Lunar New Year of 1968, when ethnic studies was birthed in San Francisco, and ends in 1977, panning a racially diverse political movement to save the International Hotel from being demolished by developers. Located on the corner of Kearny and Jackson Streets in the Manilatown-Chinatown section of San Francisco, I Hotel was home to hundreds of Filipino and Chinese bachelors, mostly retired migrant workers who had worked along the Pacific Coast. Chockfull of historical and biographical details, the historical saga brings together the activists of the Asian Community Center, the Black Panthers, the Native Americans taking over Alcatraz, the United Farm Workers, the protesters against nuclear proliferation, the veterans of the International Hotel Tenants Association, the artists of the Kearny Street Workshop, and the Maoists of the Chinese Progressive Association. The kaleidoscopic cast of historical and fictional figures encompasses a gay Chinese poet, a Japanese American Black Panther acolyte, a Filipino migrant worker and union activist, a Native American Vietnam War veteran, and a Samoan who escapes being arrested by the police for illegal fishing.

Interracial Relations in Post-1980 Asian American Literature 317

Most chapters contain a local, national, and international coordinate, linking California and elsewhere stateside and in the Third World, and connecting people of miscellaneous stripes. For example, in the first chapter, set in 1968, a Chinese boy's father drops dead on Grant Avenue during the Chinese New Year; Martin Luther King, Jr. is assassinated in Memphis, Tennessee; and the Tet Offensive makes headlines. Just as the demise of King – the symbol of nonviolence and integration – leads to the hardening of the Black Power movement, the debacle in Vietnam reminds Asian Pacific Americans of the discrimination against them in the United States and crystallizes the Yellow Power Movement. Paul, the orphaned Chinese boy, is symbolic of the many Americans bereft after the assassinations of King and Bobby Kennedy, their spiritual and political leaders. Affinities are also forged among New World Asian activists and other ethnic contingents, particularly the Black Panthers. Yamashita tracks the emerging Afro-Asian alliance and fissure, along with other attempts at political coalitions, during the turbulent decade. Although the many groups that rally to save the I Hotel fail to prevent the tenants from being evicted in 1977, the movement succeeds in bringing divergent constituencies together. Toward the end the narrator explains how the hotel has become a symbol of Asian Pacific and multiracial activism, of unity amid palpable disparities.

Unlike the other works in this section, which incorporate many details from lived realities, an imaginary frame surrounds Chitra Banerjee Divakaruni's *One Amazing Thing*.[9] Its nine characters – an Indian graduate student, an African American ex-soldier, a Chinese grandmother and her teenage granddaughter, an Indian officer and his secretary, a Muslim American man, and a Caucasian couple – are trapped in a passport and visa office at an Indian consulate after a massive earthquake. Although the city remains unnamed, one can infer from the thinly veiled allusions to a famous university and the Bay Bridge that the setting is the San Francisco Bay Area. At first the visa office workers and applicants eye one another with prejudice and suspicion. When conflicts erupt and rescue seems remote, the graduate student, who has been reading Chaucer's *Canterbury Tales*, proposes that each person recounts "one amazing thing" in their life to diffuse tension and distract the group from their anxiety.

Their individual narratives, in contrast to the fictional frame, are very much grounded in sociopolitical reality. For instance, the Chinese grandma reminisces about falling in love with an Indian in the Chinese quarter of Calcutta and being forced to leave India on account of the 1962

Sino-Indian War; FBI agents arrest the Muslim American's father after the 9/11 attacks on the World Trade Center, inducing a fatal stroke later. Together the vignettes illuminate how personal experiences are caught up in the riptides of history and how storytelling can bridge differences by revealing the stinging secrets buried in the human heart.

Tripping across Racial Borders in Southern California

Hisaye Yamamoto's memoir "A Fire in Fontana" and Ty Pak's historical fiction "The Court Interpreter" end respectively with the 1965 Watts Riots and the 1992 Los Angeles uprising; what precedes both urban upheavals is the reckless killing of African Americans.[10] After a hate crime in Fontana the Nisei writer feels deepening empathy with the black victims. Pak's Korean narrator, on the other hand, sides with the Korean grocer who shot a black teenager in the back and whose acquittal, along with that of the officers who beat Rodney King, unleashes the 1992 Los Angeles uprising. Guilt plagues both the Japanese American author and the Korean American narrator, the former for her inability to foil the crime and the latter for his role in extenuating the grocer's lethal act.

In "A Fire in Fontana," the author tells how she unwittingly has been burnt "black." Yamamoto, a Nisei born in 1921 in Redondo Beach, California, was interned in a detention camp in Poston, Arizona during World War II. After the war she worked from 1945 to 1948 as a staff writer for the *Los Angeles Tribune*, a black weekly. This memoir revisits an incident she has to "report" for the *Tribune* in 1945, shortly after the war. It concerns a young black man named Short, who appears at the editorial office one day to inform the staff that he has been getting threatening notes from his white neighbors ever since buying a house in Fontana. He hopes to enlist the *Tribune*, along with other black newspapers, to muster support for his right to live in the white neighborhood. Later that week his house goes up in flames, killing Short, his wife, and their two children. The police close the case by assuming that Short set the fire himself. Yamamoto, convinced of the contrary, blames herself as a journalist for her failure in preventing the hate crime. Twenty years later, the unspooling of the 1965 Watts rebellion on television revives her memory of the 1945 tragedy. To her, who has been gnawed by remorse in the intervening years, the urban violence in Watts seems to be a repercussion of the earlier wrong. Her visceral account evinces the importance of overcoming debilitating silence in the face of social iniquities. By memorializing the fire in Fontana, albeit decades later, she has ensured that this heinous crime will never be forgotten.

"The Court Interpreter," a thinly veiled fictional rendering of Soon Ja Du's shooting of Latasha Harlins in 1991, is told from the perspective of the court interpreter for the Korean grocer, renamed here Moonja Joo. The narrator deplores the shooting of the black girl, but takes umbrage at the way the national media and the African American press lump together all Korean Americans as repugnant. He decides to help the defendant during the trial by making her *sound* educated and eloquent. Later, he believes his superb performance as court interpreter accounts for the defendant's lenient sentence. The fictional trial is followed by a concatenation of events including the controversial police-brutality trial over the beating of motorist Rodney King, the acquittal of the four white police officers involved, and the ensuing conflagration that engulfs Los Angeles, in which the narrator's brother-in-law is killed. The story magnifies the various obstacles to sound judgment, most notably racial stereotypes, reciprocal prejudice, the burden of representation that racial minorities shoulder, and print and visual media's inflammatory role. The interpreter, who has intentionally mitigated the grocer's culpability during the trial, experiences a blackout during the insurrection, overwhelmed by his own complicity.

Russell C. Leong and Marilyn Chin also use first-person points of view to register the crosscultural encounters of their narrators, a gay middle-aged Chinese American man and an elderly Chinese female immigrant respectively.[11] Leong's narrator in "No Bruce Lee," a 44-year-old Chinese American aging alcoholic, has taken a Wilshire bus to the Greyhound station downtown, where he meets an African American man in a seedy bar on Sunset Boulevard. Mutual stereotyping accounts for both the incipient romance that results in a one-night stand and the distrust and recrimination the morning after. The black customer calls himself Brother Goode and the narrator "Bruce" after Bruce Lee, and other exotic images about Orientals roll off his tongue. The narrator soon becomes so inebriated that he has to be taken to a hotel by his black companion, who spends the night with him. Upon getting up, the narrator looks for his wallet and counts the bills, ticking off Goode, who tells the narrator disdainfully that after all he is "No Bruce Lee." Through the use of color imagery Leong intimates that skin pigmentation is misleading, that no one should be judged according to complexion alone.

A much more upbeat portrayal of interracial bonding is found in Marilyn Chin's "Monologue: Grandmother Wong's New Year Blessings," which tracks the phenomenal friendship between a Chinese grandma and three other elderly women of disparate ancestry. All four of them are intrepid grannies. In addition to raising twin granddaughters by herself, Grandma Wong runs a Chinese restaurant that employs workers and serves customers of sundry nationalities. During the Chinese New Year she asks the reluctant twins to drive her to visit her three dear friends. Mrs. Faith, a refugee from Sudan, raises two grandchildren whose parents have been slaughtered by the Janjaweed. Mrs. Wong gives her a big cleaver in the hope of dispelling her recurrent nightmares about the massacre. Mrs. Maria Gonzalez cares for four grandchildren so her daughter can work two jobs during the day and attend college at night; she lives in an apartment complex filled with drug addicts and wakes up at 3 a.m. to make a thousand Mexican dumplings to sell at market. Mrs. Wong gives her a bottle of tiger-bone wine to boost her energy. Mrs. Goldstein, an affluent Holocaust survivor, is dying of cancer; she worries about her grandson Benny, whose father has divorced a good Jewish wife and fallen in love with a shiksa. Mrs. Wong brings Mrs. Goldstein her favorite dish from the restaurant and promises to keep an eye on Benny after Mrs. Goldstein's death. The story, at once hilarious and poignant, highlights the extraordinary mingling of immigrants in Southern California and commemorates the resilience of the elderly whose checkered life histories allow them to identify across race and class.

Among the works discussed in this chapter, Nina Revoyr's *Southland* unfolds against the longest duration, shifting back and forth through five decades, from 1942 to 1994.[12] The novel focuses on the mystery surrounding the murder of four black boys in a grocery store owned by Frank Sakai in the multi-ethnic Crenshaw district during the Watts Riots of 1965. When Frank dies some thirty years later, his granddaughter Jackie, a lesbian law student, discovers that Frank intended to bequeath his store to someone she doesn't know. In the process of finding out who that beneficiary is, she stumbles upon the fact that four boys were found frozen to death in Frank's meat locker. Jackie tries to solve the puzzle with James Lanier, an African American worker in a social service center in Crenshaw. They learn about the interracial liaison between Jackie's grandfather and the mother of one of the murdered boys. Part mystery, part urban fiction, *Southland* probes into the historical significance of the variegated Crenshaw neighborhood in shaping race relations, Frank's ambivalence in serving as a Japanese American soldier during World War II, the self-hatred of a black policeman, and the dilution of Jackie's ethnic identity as her folks move up the economic ladder.

The personal quest of Jackie, who has grown up in suburban Los Angeles and who has drifted away from her grandfather, involves venturing into a new neighborhood and being enlightened by successive crosscultural encounters. After Frank's death, Jackie ends her lukewarm love affair with a Jewish woman who is indifferent to social inequalities. By contrast, her friendship with James deepens and she also becomes drawn to a progressive Japanese American social worker. By reopening the murder case, Jackie unearths not only the secrets of her family past but also a forgotten chapter of Los Angeles – a time when the Crenshaw district was a multiracial hub, a far cry from the highly segregated metropolis today. By the end of the novel, it is this racially integrated LA that Jackie wishes to reclaim as home.

The tapestry of faces in this chapter furnishes a rainbow cross section of California through Asian American lenses. Unsettling memories and invidious racial preconceptions stalk all the characters and render tenuous their footholds on the West Coast. The Korean, Filipino, and Vietnamese newcomers are haunted by a sense of simultaneous geography – by a superimposition of the Asian cultural landscape on their American experience. *Clay Walls* documents Haesu's double exile. *The Gangster of Love* and *American Son* reflect the colonial and neocolonial legacies of the Philippines. Awash in American pop culture and Hollywood ideals, Rocky and the Sullivan brothers hanker in vain after the image, glory or fortune celebrated in the U.S. media. Rocky's rock band falls through the cracks in the black and white counterculture. Tomas and Gabe try to live like the Joneses in Westside suburbs by acquiring wealth and consumer goods illegally. The transplanted family in "The Gangster We are All Looking For" suffers repeated evictions in San Diego. Viet in "Quiet As They Come" is perceived as an inarticulate Vietnamese refugee despite his multiple advanced degrees from another shore. Kal in "Show and Tell" is denounced by a classmate as a Viet Cong when his own father has died in a Viet Cong reeducation camp. The last two stories nevertheless end with a gesture of friendship, offered by a black worker and a white classmate respectively.

Gus Lee, William Poy Lee, Kingston, Yamashita, and Divakaruni all envision the possibility of building an inclusive community in the San Francisco Bay Area. Kai in *China Boy* survives a violent boyhood in the Panhandle through taking boxing lessons from instructors of diverse descent, who take him under their wing. William in *The Eighth Promise* finds sustenance and a sense of belonging in successive "villages" with mixed populations: SF Chinatown, the San Francisco General Hospital, City Lights Books, Galileo School, and Il Piccolo Cafe. Wittman in

Tripmaster Monkey assembles a humungous theater troupe that accommodates amateurs of all colors, ages, and political persuasions. Similarly, a movement that cuts across ethnicity, class, sexual orientation, and nationality mobilizes the activists in *I Hotel*. The nine pilgrims in *One Amazing Thing* learn to pool their resources in their effort to survive a devastating earthquake; their separate stories uncover hidden links among people who hail from dispersed geographical locales.

Compared with the works set in the Bay Area, the Southern California counterparts, with the exception of Marilyn Chin's "Monologue: Grandmother Wong's New Year's Blessings," paint a dimmer picture of race relations, exposing mutual prejudices and structural inequalities that erupt in hostile behavior and urban strife. Leong's "No Bruce Lee" and Pak's "The Court Interpreter" manifest reciprocal stereotypes' splintering effects. Just as the Chinese American's distrust of his black escort brings their relationship to a bitter halt, the Korean grocer's suspicion of a black teenager leads to a senseless killing and xenophobic retaliation. Depicting atrocious hate crimes in which the perpetrators go unpunished, Yamamoto's memoir and Revoyr's novel show how the wounds of the past continue to bleed into the present. Through Yamamoto's strong identification with blacks, Jackie's friendship with Lanier, as well as Grandma Wong's solicitude for her three elderly friends, we also see the special opportunities for reaching out to the Other in Southland.

Whether set in Northern or Southern California, individual quests are embedded in the broader canvass of historical drama, social movement, or urban unrest. While focusing on specific characters and their encounters with people of dissimilar ethnicities, the authors address issues that potentially affect everyone. Along with the characters we are taken for many a ride – from shore to shore, from coast to coast, and especially up and down the West Coast – and given close-up glimpses into interracial encounters that lead to empathy or misunderstanding, communal art or protracted silence, that galvanize a broad-based coalition or explode in a firestorm. It is up to the passengers, the authors seem to imply, to forestall a Californian apocalypse.

Notes

1. The curricular reform took place in response to both the post-Civil Rights efforts to desegregate education and the demographic shift caused by the arrival of Third World immigrants and refugees. Because of the proliferation of works by writers of Asian descent subsequently, there are many more texts set in

California than I am able to cover, such as Frank Chin, *Gunga Din Highway* (Minneapolis: Coffee House Press, 1995); Sesshu Foster, *Angry Days* (Los Angeles: West End Press, 1987); Wakako Yamauchi, *Songs My Mother Taught Me: Stories, Plays, and Memoir* (New York: Feminist Press, 1994). I have also omitted Cynthia Kakohata's *In the Heart of the Valley of Love* and Karen Tei Yamashita's *Tropic of Orange*, which are covered in Lynn Itagaki's chapter. I warmly thank Russell Leong and my research assistants Hannah Nahm and Robert Kiriakos Smith for their valuable suggestions.
2. Ronyoung Kim, *Clay Walls* (Sag Harbor, NY: Permanent Press, 1986).
3. Jessica Hagedorn, *The Gangster of Love* (New York: Houghton Mifflin, 1996); Brian Ascalon Roley, *American Son* (New York: Norton, 2001).
4. Ketu H. Katrak, "South Asian American Literature," *An Interethnic Companion to Asian American Literature*, ed. King-Kok Cheung (New York: Cambridge University Press, 1997), 201.
5. Lê Thi Diem Thúy's "The Gangster We Are All Looking For," *The Best American Essays* (Boston: Houghton, 1999); *The Gangster We Are All Looking For* (New York: Anchor-Random House, 2003), 78–107.
6. Angie Chau, "Quiet as They Come," *Quiet as They Come* (New York: Ig Publishing, 2010), 68–81; Andrew Lam, "Show and Tell," *Birds of Paradise Lost* (Pasadena, CA: Red Hen Press, 2013), 21–32.
7. Gus Lee, *China Boy* (New York: Penguin/Plume, 1991); William Poy Lee, *The Eighth Promise: An American Son's Tribute to His Toisanese China-Born Mother* (New York: Rodale, 2007).
8. Maxine Hong Kingston, *Tripmaster Monkey: His Fake Book* (1987, New York: Vintage, 1990); Karen Tei Yamashita, *I Hotel* (Minneapolis: Coffee House Press, 2010).
9. Chitra Banerjee Divakaruni, *One Amazing Thing* (New York: Hyperion, 2010).
10. Hisaye Yamamoto, "A Fire in Fontana," 1985; *Seventeen Syllables and Other Stories*, revised and expanded edition (New Brunswick, NJ: Rutgers University Press, 2001), 150–157; Ty Pak, "The Court Interpreter," *Moonbay* (New York: Woodhouse, 1999), 89–117.
11. Russell C. Leong, "No Bruce Lee," *Phoenix Eyes and Other Stories* (Seattle: University of Washington Press, 2000), 145–153; Marilyn Chin, "Monologue: Grandmother Wong's New Year Blessings," *Revenge of the Mooncake Vixen: A Manifesto in 41 Tales* (New York: Norton, 2009), 39–47.
12. Nina Revoyr, *Southland* (New York: Akashic Books, 2003).

PART VII

The Search for Utopia

CHAPTER 21

California and the Queer Utopian Imagination: 1981–2014

Cael Keegan

Nothing's lost forever. In this world, there is a kind of painful progress. Longing for what we've left behind, and dreaming ahead. At least I think that's so.

– Tony Kushner, *Angels in America*

... there is no there there.

– Gertrude Stein, *Everybody's Autobiography*

Gertrude Stein's often-repeated phrase "there is no there there" is arguably the most infamous queer utterance regarding California. Returning to Oakland during the Great Depression after decades abroad in Paris, Stein found that her pastoral childhood home had disappeared, swallowed up by the rapid urbanization of the early twentieth century. Where her house had stood there were now hundreds of homes, bisected by paved roads and telephone wires. Stein records this alienating encounter with industrialized California in *Everybody's Autobiography* (1937), during her continental tour of the United States:

> ... anyway what was the use of my having come from Oakland it was not natural to have come from there yes write about it if I felt like it or anything if I like it but not there, there is no there there. (...) ... the big house and the big garden and the eucalyptus trees and the rose hedge naturally were not any longer existing ... (...) what is the use of having been if you are to be going on being and if not why it is different and if it is different why not. I did not like anything that was happening.[1]

While specific to her own *nineteenth century* expatriate experience, Stein's memorialization of California as a place simultaneously found and lost has been echoed by generations of other queer writers. In the queer literary archive, California often appears as a utopian space that is alternately desired, anticipated, and grieved by authors struggling with the romantic call of the open West and the bloody legacy of Manifest Destiny.

This essay connects Stein's infamous line marking her newly discovered loss of Oakland to more recent queer struggles over the meaning of California in the late twentieth and early twenty-first centuries. Linking the literary image of California to the queer political and aesthetic movements of the post-AIDS era, it considers the symbolic role California has played in queer longing for spaces of possibility: for homelands lost, found, or yet to arrive. As the original site of both gay liberation and the AIDS crisis, California is a crucial landscape in the queer utopian literary imagination of the late twentieth century. In the white queer archive, California often appears as a "wide-open"[2] space of political dreamwork that predicts queer Americans' future citizenship in the national body. In queer of color[3] literature, a reparative utopian urge often reaches backward to a "then" before California's theft and decimation by white settler colonialism. Whether as a heaven on earth or a conquered territory, the queer utopian imaginary of the late twentieth and early twenty-first centuries represents California as a place that is paradoxically here and yet not quite – always approaching on the horizon, always receding under our feet.

Queer literature and art contains, according to the late José Muñoz, an inherently utopian desire for the horizon of possibility. In *Cruising Utopia* (2009), Muñoz writes, "Queerness is that thing that lets us know that this world is not enough, that indeed something is missing."[4] While Muñoz is generally concerned with queer desires for the future, he acknowledges that there is a concurrent, backward-facing quality of utopian thought that works to distinguish now and here from then and there. This bi-directional shuttling between negation and possibility is inherent to the concept of utopia itself. Conceived by Sir Thomas More as a name for his fictional island in *Utopia* (1516), the word can be translated as either "no place land" (*Utopie*) or "good place land" (*Eutopie*). In an appendix to subsequent editions of *Utopia*, More himself sought to clarify the English translation of his Latin word in a line that reads, "Wherfore not Utopie, but rather rightely my name is Eutopie, a place of felicitie."[5] While More clearly preferred the positive interpretation of the word, in English "utopia" has come to name the paradoxical state of the perfectly impossible or impossibly perfect. The contradictory nature of the term points to the essential irony of utopian desire: the perfect place can only be perfect because it does not exist, cannot ever exist. In this way, utopian formations require both romantic and critical aesthetic practices, since it is only through the creative disavowal of what "is" that we might imagine otherwise.

Muñoz's point that a utopian vision is fundamental to queer thought and aesthetics helps ground us in a discussion of how various queer writers, both popular and artistic, have looked to California as a symbol of simultaneous loss and possibility. California has historically served as "both model and antimodel" for the United States as well as the globe.[6] Centering the state as a site of queer literary production therefore helps us understand its generative role in the arc of queer political history over the late twentieth and early twenty-first centuries. California has been the origination point of U.S. history's most purely utopian and dystopian queer moments: the initial sparks of gay liberation that led to the post-Stonewall 1970s,[7] followed by the AIDS crisis and its attendant Reagan-era neoconservatism.[8] In the early twenty-first century, this dystopian/utopian motif was repeated by the passage and eventual striking down of Proposition 8. Over the course of the past four decades, queer literary representations of California as an ideal "golden" land and a paradise lost point to the inherent volatility in the concept of utopia itself.

1980–89: Falling from Grace

No conversation of how California is represented in queer literature would be complete without an extended consideration of Armistead Maupin's *Tales of the City* novels (1978–2014). Due to their serialized nature,[9] the novels provide a contemporaneous window into the life and politics of post-Stonewall San Francisco more than nearly forty years. Maupin's initial two books, *Tales of the City* (1978) and *More Tales of the City* (1980) radically altered the representation of queer life in California, revising the exotic and satirical depictions of queerness in John Rechy's *City of Night* (1963) and Gore Vidal's *Myra Breckinridge* (1968) into an optimistic vision of San Francisco as a site of the queer quotidian. Maupin's early novels make use of broad genre elements, such as melodrama and mystery plotting,[10] to draw readers into the lives of his quirky and fallible characters. The best-selling series would continue until 2014, carrying with it four decades of readers and functioning as a fictional anthropology of San Francisco queer life, in which he explored the queer subcultures and skewered the high societies of San Francisco as well as Marin and Napa counties.

Maupin's first novel, *Tales of the City* (1978), articulates the quintessential utopian vision of 1970s queer San Francisco, mediated through a motley cast of characters living at 28 Barbary Lane under the watchful eye of pot-smoking transgender landlady Anna Madrigal. Madrigal operates as the moral center of Maupin's universe: as mysterious as she is sensual and wise, she frames the city as a paradise for wayward souls. Early in the first novel, city newcomer Mary Ann Singleton encounters Anna while attempting to rent an apartment. Madrigal opens the conversation by quoting from Alfred Lord Tennyson's "The Lotus-Eaters":

The landlady nodded. "The look's a dead giveaway. You just can't wait to bite into that lotus."

"What? I'm sorry . . . "
"Tennyson, you know: 'Eating the lotus day by day, To watch the crisping ripples on the beach, And tender curving lines of creamy spray; To lend our hearts and spirits wholly To the influence of . . . something, something . . . You get the point."
"Does the . . . furniture go with it?"
"Don't change the subject while I'm quoting Tennyson."[11]

Maupin's utopian vision of gay San Francisco was an intervention into previous depictions of queer life as criminal, dangerous, and corrupt that dominated the popular literature and news media of the 1950s and 1960s. While Mary Ann carries some of these assumptions with her from Cleveland, she is quickly reformed by friendships with Madrigal and the gay Michael Tolliver that will last nearly forty years. A midwestern transplant to California, Mary Ann is a prosthetic character through which the (presumably heterosexual) *Tales* reading audience is permitted to witness the queer wonders of San Francisco social life. However, there is also trouble in paradise, a sense that California is wandering from its progressive, postwar ideals. Later in the first *Tales* novel, Anna Madrigal is confronted by one of the series' more overtly political lesbian characters, Mona Ramsey:

"It was fucking beautiful, because it was . . . was, like, history. We were history. We were on the cover of Time magazine, man!"

Mrs. Madrigal was polite. "What do you think happened, dear?"
"They killed it. Not the Pigs. The Media."
"Killed what?"
"Nineteen sixty-seven."
"I see."

"Nixon, Watergate, Patty Fucking Hearst, the Bicentennial. The Media got bored with 1967, so they zapped it. It could have survived for a while. Some of it escaped to Mendocino . . . but the media found out about it and killed it all over again. Jesus ... I mean, what's left? There's not a single fucking place where it's still 1967!"[12]

This sense of drifting from an ideal, golden period in California's queer history accelerates throughout the *Tales* series, as the political tenor of the Golden State shifts rightward, gay rights come under attack, and the AIDS crisis begins to loom over Maupin's characters. By the early 1980s, the utopian vision of liberation politics was giving way to a living nightmare in which an entire generation of young gay men, many of them writers, artists, and performers,[13] vanished into death seemingly overnight. Those who did not succumb to the disease were left to try to make sense of the catastrophe,[14] a newly ascendant conservative movement, and the Reagan administration's stupefying inaction in response to the epidemic. The fourth *Tales* novel, *Babycakes* (1984),[15] which ran serially in 1983, became the first piece of fiction to deal with the AIDS crisis. In his introduction to the anthologized version, Maupin discusses his difficult decision to confront AIDS in the series, writing "I had two options as the author of a fictional series purporting to record the times: I could end my 'Tales of the City' then and there, bidding an era farewell, or I could somehow incorporate the epidemic into what was basically a comedic work."[16] Maupin, who had begun to lose friends to the disease, decided to drop his more light-hearted plot outline for Babycakes and craft a new story in which several of his much-beloved characters become infected and/or die of the plague. By introducing a popular reading public to the issue of AIDS, as well as the plague's effects on queer subculture and its sexual practices, Maupin was able to bridge the enforced silence surrounding the disease in both media and political discourse. After *Sure of You* (1989),[17] Maupin would remain silent for eighteen years, but by then other California AIDS literature had emerged: perhaps most importantly Los Angeles-based poet Paul Monette's searing memoir, *Borrowed Time* (1988).[18]

Maupin's popular approach to representing queer California was true of three other long-running California-based crime novel series – written by Joseph Hansen, Michael Nava, and Katherine V. Forrest – that would counteract the association of queer life with criminality that dominated the 1950s McCarthy period: Joseph Hansen's *Dave Brandsetter* novels (1970–91) featured Brandsetter as an openly gay Los Angeles insurance investigator; Michael Nava's *Henry Rios* series (1982–2001), followed a gay Latino criminal defense attorney across the Golden State; and Katherine V. Forrest's *Kate Delafield* mysteries (1984–2013) introduced LAPD detective Delafield as the first fictional lesbian police operative.

These series place queer protagonists in the position of defending justice precisely because the corrupt political, police, and legal systems are incapable of doing so. In them, queer characters with utopian impulses are empowered to confront and aid in resolving the corrupt legal and moral climates of 1980s California. The Henry Rios series, especially, connects the venality of California's political class to the state's depraved colonial history, emphasizing the dark realities of California's looted past.[19] In these novels, justice, when it is reached, is often accomplished through semi-legal means, and is never permanently achieved. All three series present interesting analogs to AIDS activism in the 1980s, when groups such as ACT UP sought to seize control of the medications and funding that the federal and state governments were failing to make available.

In an important contrast to Maupin's *Tales*, texts from this period featuring queer of color characters and by queer of color authors remind readers that California is contested ground, not just in terms of sexuality, but also in terms of race and class. Hansen's and Nava's novels center the experiences of queer of color characters, who assert distinctly dystopian insights into the realities of California: insights that their white characters struggle to perceive.[20] Queer of color California-born authors writing in the 1980s provide another set of counterpoints to Maupin's sanguine representations of California as a "paradise found" for white liberals seeking to escape from the suburban suffocation of middle America. While Maupin's Mary Ann Singleton infamously visits San Francisco from Cleveland and decides – just like that – to stay, emerging writers Cherríe Moraga, Chrystos, and Richard Rodriguez thematize the ongoing violence inflicted by the romanticized American impulse to "go West". These queer of color writers highlight the continuing effects of capitalism, white supremacy, and Manifest Destiny that brought California under the influence of white settler colonialism in the mid-nineteenth century.

Published in the same year that the AIDS crisis emerged, the now-famous anthology *This Bridge Called My Back* (1981) initiated a new complexity in discussions of race, class, and sexuality in American feminism. The book represents California as a primary site of contestation between white feminists and feminists of color – a conversation historically framed by the state's shrinking white majority and its increasingly popular anti-tax and anti-immigrant sentiments.[21] In their editorial introduction,[22] Chicana lesbian authors Cherríe Moraga and Gloria Anzaldúa describe being inspired to create the work after learning that several Third World women were denied access to a 1979 women's retreat just north of San Francisco. The resulting anthology posed a trenchant critique to the whiteness and middle-class liberalism of Second Wave Feminism while simultaneously highlighting the male-dominated white supremacy of existing gay and lesbian thought. Challenging prevalent assumptions that the women's movement and its separatist communities were utopias of sameness, the volume called for a new feminism capable of addressing the fragmented political reality of the 1980s.

Other queer of color writers also extended similar critiques of California as a white queer or feminist utopia. Chrystos, a San Francisco-born Menominee lesbian and Two-spirit poet, emphasized the themes of white supremacy and the theft of California from its indigenous peoples in her contributions to *This Bridge* and in her first book of poems, *Not Vanishing* (1988). Chrystos' poem "I Have Not Signed a Treaty With the U.S. Government", is an expression of "psychic reterritorialization"[23] in which the ideology of illegal immigration is reversed: "We signed no treaty/WHAT are you still doing here/Go somewhere else and/Build a McDonald's/We revoke your immigration papers".[24] Although he did not come out as gay until 1992, Richard Rodriguez explored the contradictions of being a bilingual, middle-class Chicano raised in Sacramento, "a comic victim of two cultures",[25] in his autobiography *Hunger of Memory* (1982). As queer writers of color, each of these authors extends a challenge to the golden ideal of California as a "good place" for white migrants, drawing attention to the still-unfolding consequences of settler colonialism.

1990–99: Aftermath and Dreaming Forward

In the decade following the height of the AIDS crisis, writers who had devoted themselves to dystopian representations of the plague years turned to a consideration of the aftermath and an analysis of California's surviving queer subcultures. Tony Kushner's *Angels in America* (1993) weighs heaviest in this period as the quintessential articulation of late *twentieth century* queer utopian thought about California. Other writers, such as Maupin, Hansen, Nava, and Forrest, continued series begun in the 1970s and 1980s, thematizing queer survival of the AIDS era through the lives of their familiar, aging, and (in the case of Maupin) infected protagonists. The AIDS years, which oversaw the deaths of thousands of gay male cultural producers, ironically allowed queer female writers to step into the creative gap left behind by the epidemic. Emerging lesbian and bisexual female writers, including Jewelle Gomez and Michelle Tea, represented a generation of younger authors scanning the California landscape and considering what possibilities for queer life and meaning might remain. Works by queer women, particularly from queer of color writers such as Gomez and Chrystos, present sharp rebukes to Kushner's dominant image of California as a queer utopia.

The period arguably begins with Paul Monette's *Afterlife* (1990), a transitional novel in which Monette's characters struggle to make meaningful lives after surviving the plague years. The book's first line –"If everyone hadn't died all at once, none of this would have happened."[26] – can be read as an opening statement for the entire post-AIDS era. Temporal dislocation over living past the AIDS crisis also appears in Richard Rodriguez's second memoir, *Days of Obligation* (1992), in which Rodriguez explores his experience as a second-generation gay American immigrant who was anachronistically "born at the destination."[27] Recounting his experiences living in the Castro era at the height of the epidemic, Rodriguez muses over the philosophical and moral implications of his being spared from death. A Chicano equally isolated from his Mexican heritage as from the implicit whiteness of queer culture, Rodriguez is skeptical of ever fully belonging to America; his years of living through the plague have instructed him against any sort of utopian impulse: "Lonely teenagers still arrive in San Francisco aboard Greyhound buses. The city can still seem, by comparison with where they came from, paradise." But, he writes, "I have never looked for utopia on a map."[28]

However, searching for utopia is precisely Tony Kushner's project in *Angels in America* (1993), which dominates late *twentieth century* representations of California in queer literature. The Pulitzer Prize-winning two-part play is Kushner's attempt to reassert a redemptive, utopian narrative for American democracy and religion after the political toxicity and cultural devastation of the AIDS epidemic. The play is heavily influenced by Walter Benjamin's concept of the angel of history in his *Theses on the Philosophy of History* (1940), as well as Ernst Bloch's *The Principle of Hope* (1986), in which Bloch argues for the moral force of utopian thought and desire.[29] In Kushner's play, an angel appears to the twentieth century prophet, Prior Walter – a gay man dying of AIDS in the 1980s – pleading with him to stop humanity's progress forward in time. Throughout the play, various characters describe heaven as "a city much like San Francisco".[30] During the play's second half, "Perestroika",

Prior visits a heaven that looks like a ruined San Francisco City Hall to confront the stymied angels, reject the prophecy, and demand a blessing of "more life."[31] In Kushner's play, California is both a site of ruination and redemption, of apocalyptic ending and renewal – a "disaster" that becomes simultaneously a sign for and an incitement to contemplate paradise.[32]

Kushner's sharpest articulation of the dystopian/utopian dialectic contained in the queer aesthetics of California appears in a discussion about the nature of heaven between Belize, a black nurse, and Roy Cohn, Kushner's fictionalized version of the closeted McCarthyite lawyer who died of AIDS in 1986. Kushner's version of Cohn has been admitted to the hospital where Belize works, suffering with terminal AIDS. In the agony of his final few hours of life, Roy asks Belize "What's it like? After?" Belize responds to this question with another:

> Belize: Hell or heaven?
> [Roy indicates "Heaven" through a glance]
> Belize: Like San Francisco.
> Roy Cohn: A city. Good. I was worried ... it'd be a garden. I hate that shit.
> Belize: Mmmm. Big city. Overgrown with weeds, but flowering weeds. On every corner a wrecking crew and something new and crooked going up catty corner to that. Windows missing in every edifice like broken teeth, fierce gusts of gritty wind, and a gray high sky full of ravens. (...) And everyone in Balenciaga gowns with red corsages, and big dance palaces full of music and lights and racial impurity and gender confusion. And all the deities are creole, mulatto, brown as the mouths of rivers. Race, taste and history finally overcome. And you ain't there.
> Roy Cohn: And Heaven?
> Belize: That was Heaven, Roy.[33]

Belize's speech to Roy depicts a utopian heaven full of democratic racial mixing and apocalyptic queer beauty, a place that appears as a dystopian hell when viewed from Roy's neoconservative, homophobic, white supremacist perspective. This heaven, which is "like San Francisco," is a place "after" – race, taste, and (apparently) capitalism. It is a queer of color vision of history's end that precisely articulates Munoz's concept of "cruising utopia,"[34] an aesthetic gesture that renders a queer future out of the very pinnacle of unimaginable crisis and desolation. Belize's heaven is a "no place land" that rejects the facticity of death, disease, and destruction by reworking those realities into an impossible future, a "good place land" that nonetheless appears to Roy as a nightmare. "I'll be coming for you soon," Belize tells Roy, "Everything I want is in the end of you."[35] The line is a flawless example of the queer utopian impulse as articulated through the force of negation, through the refusal of the now and all it contains.

Despite Kushner's powerful articulation of queer utopianism, lesbian and bisexual women writing about California during the same period present challenges to Kushner's political idealism. Jewelle Gomez's *The Gilda Stories* (1991), a speculative novel about a black lesbian vampire, contains a section set in "Yerba Buena" in 1890 – the booming San Francisco of exactly a century earlier, when the U.S. census instituted the "one drop rule" to enforce legal distinctions segregating black bodies from white ones. Gomez therefore points to California's always-already colonized and racialized history. While Gomez's vampires practice a form of communitarian lesbian feminism, it is in Yerba Buena that Gilda meets a murderous white vampire, Eleanor, who rejects vampire law and tortures her victims for entertainment. Eleanor internalizes the "wide open" ideology of Gold Rush capitalism as an excuse to destroy human life and flout vampire morality[36] – an apt metaphor for the racialized violence lurking beneath the surface of California's romantic, utopian appeal.

The heightened visibility of lesbian writing in the 1990s also brought renewed attention to California authors at mid-career. Chrystos' poetry, particularly her erotic collection *In Her I Am* (1993), enjoyed a new level of popularity within the materializing dyke-chic culture of the early 1990s. Claiming her right to the Native female body through what Qwo-li Driskill has called a "sovereign erotic,"[37] Chrystos draws parallels between the occupied bodies of Native women and the colonized landscape of California. In "Against" she writes,

> your skin red under my hand against every
> political principle we both hold you want
> me to spank you & I do
> We're survivors of childhood violence with black eyes
> in common from mothers who hated our difference
> Neither loves our love
> they'd beat it out of us if they could
> Your people as well as mine slaughtered in millions
> Queer we're still open season[38]

Here, the "still" in "still open season" works in contradistinction to utopian visions of California that would easily dismiss the violence of colonization as "then" and assert the "political principles" of liberalism, feminism, or queer community as solutions to the wounds of history. For Chrystos, these wounds are self-constituting, the proposed principles are insufficient solutions, and the war of colonization is not and will never be "then". Later in *Fire Power* (1995), Chrystos writes, "This continent is morally and legally our land, since no treaty has been observed.... Logically, then, we remain at war in a unique way – not for a piece of the 'white pie,' but because we do not agree then there is a pie at all."[39] Here and elsewhere in her work, Chrystos presents Native and Two-spirit challenges to an idealistic queer futurity, locating the true utopian potential of California as always in the past, always lost.

2000–2009: Not (Quite) Dying

Queer California literature dating from 2000–09 is dominated by disillusionment, as writers express further disaffection from the state's flagging progressive ideals. By the first decade of the twentieth century, the political successes and grassroots activism of the ACT UP generation had subsided under neoliberal pressure into a privatized system of non-profits and corporate lobbying. The dot com crash and ensuing national recession, as well as the recall of California Democratic Governor Gray Davis and his replacement by Republican Hollywood actor Arnold Schwarzenegger, all mark this era as a time of emerging dysfunction and increasing fiscal conservatism. The period comes to a dismal close in 2008–09 with the Great Recession and the passage of Proposition 8, a state-wide ballot initiative that amended the California constitution to ban same-sex marriage. By the end of Schwarzenegger's second term in 2011, California was staggering under a 25.4 billion dollar deficit, and what remained of its progressive-era public institutions were under threat of total defunding.[40] California's Golden Era was truly over, replaced by existential questions about its ability to cohere.

Michelle Tea is perhaps the principle voice of the queer generation coming of age in California after AIDS. A co-founder of the San Francisco-based lesbian-feminist spoken word troupe Sister Spit, Tea's memoir *Valencia* (2000) and her later graphic novel *Rent Girl* (2004) chronicle the post-punk dyke culture of the Mission District in San Francisco. The anarchically structured works follow Tea through an underworld of radical lesbian sex, drug experimentation, willful unemployment, and survival sex work. Tea's San Francisco is a used-up shell of its former glory, a city brought low by recession and crowded with derelicts, punks, prostitutes, drug addicts, and the mentally ill. The memoirs revel in the dystopian landscape of the low-rent Mission district, populated by misfits drawn together by a shared sense of alienation from mainstream corporate culture. In *Valencia*, Tea describes walking in the Castro and being suddenly overcome by the "millions of gay people shopping. I just started sobbing. ... It was miserable, life was suddenly terrible and I felt like a chump, like I had been viewing reality through some inauthentic window that made everything look happy when it really wasn't. ... I cried openly through the throngs of cheerful lesbians and boys with neat haircuts and why does everyone in the Castro look so fucking healthy?"[41] In Tea's work, California is a queerly antisocial space, a place cut off from any sort of historical consciousness, unmoored in time by the deep crevasses created by AIDS, identity politics, and corporate capitalism. Emptied of any substantial queer political movement, Tea's California offers escape from the past, but withholds transformation.

A combination of nostalgia and longing for redemption features in other queer literature from the period. In transgender author Mattilda Bernstein Sycamore's *So Many Ways to Sleep Badly* (2008), former ACT UP member Sycamore meditates on the hypocrisy of San Francisco's "Gay People"[42] and the city's vapid culture of consumerism, objectification, and casual sex. Sycamore dedicates the novel, "For San Francisco, or what's left of it."[43] Similarly, Carla Trujillo's *What Night Brings* (2003) tells the tale of Marci Cruz, a young queer Chicana growing up next to a Chevy plant in the slums of San Lorenzo, who dreams of transforming into "Supergirl" and flying away.[44] In his third memoir, *Brown* (2002), Richard Rodriguez writes, "Californians have been trying to tell Eastern America that our nation is, after all, finite. Only within the last few years – a full century after the closing of the frontier – have we gotten a bite on the cliche ... Is the Golden State tarnished?"[45] Maupin's first *Tales* book in nearly two decades, *Michael Tolliver Lives* (2007), features an aging Tolliver who is living with AIDS. Now middle-aged, Tolliver recalls the AIDS crisis with an ironic nostalgia: "We were knee-deep in catastrophe ourselves – the last Big One of the century – and bracing for the worst. But then I didn't die."[46] While not all queer people died in the AIDS epidemic, the question of whether gay liberation and its utopian visions of sexual freedom and democratic community had perished, remained unanswered.

2010–2014: The End of California

After AIDS, after propositions 22 and 8, after the crash years, what remains of California and its utopian queer imaginary? Queer of color literature has always been skeptical of the utopian image of California: as Cherríe Moraga reminds readers in *A Xicana Codex of Changing Consciousness* (2011), "We are not headed for an apocalypse; the apocalypse has already occurred."[47] In contrast to the queer of color archive, white queer literature after 2010 appears to have arrived back at Stein's conundrum of nearly a century earlier: the "there" that California was, is no longer, or perhaps never quite was at all. Mattilda Bernstein Sycamore's aptly titled *The End of San Francisco* (2013) delivers a scathing indictment of the "new San Francisco,"[48] its gentrification by consumer-driven corporate capitalism, and the assimilationist effects on queer life. Sycamore's memoir is an elegy to the radical queer sensibility that drew her to San Francisco in her youth, but that has been supplanted by skyrocketing rents, gutted social services, and a city politics increasingly catering to elite, white gay men. "I mean," she asks wryly, "what could be worse than gay culture?"[49] Once again, it would seem, California is wide open to the highest bidder.

Does this current historical moment mark the end of California as site of queer utopian thought? In 2012, Armistead Maupin, the writer most associated with the everyday life of queer California, announced that he would leave San Francisco for Santa Fe, New Mexico. When interviewed about his decision to leave the state after forty-one years, Maupin reported that the relocation was giving him "new dreams. There's nothing wrong with that."[50] The move coincided with the release of Maupin's final *Tales* novel, *The Days of Anna Madrigal* (2014), which takes ninety-one year-old Anna Madrigal far from San Francisco into the high desert mountains of Nevada and finally to the Burning Man festival. There, surrounded by friends and family, Anna is honored with a ride in a butterfly shaped art car bearing her name. During the ride, she dies, transported back to the moment she left Nevada on a train to San Francisco, decades earlier. The novel ends with a simple line; "There was a city waiting for her."[51]

While California may now be waning in the queer utopian imaginary, we must remember Jose Muñoz's point that the utopian force of queer possibility cannot ever be exhausted. In turning elsewhere, by refusing the California of today as "not enough," queer writers and artists cruise for utopia by insisting on something better than now and here. The very act of refusal is itself an insistence on the possibility of something else, some time yet to come, some place as yet unseen. As Muñoz reminded us before his untimely death in 2013, "Queerness is essentially about a rejection of a here and now and an insistence on potentiality or concrete possibility for another world."[52] Impossibly perfect and therefore perfectly impossible, utopia is always in the horizon, always approaching or receding, never quite arrived. Like Anna, in letting go of one landscape, we may find another.

A city waits for us.

Notes

1. Gertrude Stein, *Everybody's Autobiography* (London: Cambridge University Press, 1993), 298–300.
2. Nan Alamilla Boyd, *Wide Open Town: A History of Queer San Francisco to 1965* (Berkeley: University of California Press, 2005), 2.
3. In *Aberrations in Black: Toward a Queer of Color Critique* (Minneapolis: University of Minnesota Press, 2003), Roderick A. Ferguson defines queer of color analysis as "an interrogat[ion] of social formations as the intersections of race, gender, sexuality, and class, with particular interest in how those formations correspond with and diverge from nationalist ideals and practices" (149).
4. Jose Esteban Muñoz, *Cruising Utopia: The Then and There of Queer Futurity* (New York University Press, 2009), 1.
5. Sir Thomas More, *The Utopia of Sir Thomas More* (New York: Macmillan, 1912), 230.
6. Peter Schrag, *California: America's High-Stakes Experiment* (Berkeley: University of California Press, 2006), 1.
7. See Susan Stryker, *Transgender History* (Berkeley: Seal Press, 2008). On pages 59–60, Stryker describes a 2005 interview with John Rechy in which he recounts a riot by a group of drag queens, transsexuals, and hustlers at Cooper's Donuts in Los Angeles in 1959. A similar incident, Compton's Cafeteria riot, took place in San Francisco in 1966 – well before the Stonewall riots in Greenwich Village in 1969.
8. See Susan Stryker and Jim Van Buskirk, eds. *Gay by the Bay: A History of Queer Culture in the San Francisco Bay Area* (San Francisco: Chronicle Books, 1996), 85–86. On November 25, 1980, San Francisco resident Ken Horne became the first person with AIDS to be reported to the U.S. Centers for Disease Control.
9. Maupin's first four *Tales* novels were serialized in the *Pacific Sun* and the *San Francisco Chronicle*; the fifth ran in the *San Francisco Examiner*.
10. Robyn R. Warhol, "Making 'Gay' and 'Lesbian' into Household Words: How Serial Form Works in Armistead Maupin's *Tales of the City*" *Contemporary Literature* 40.3 (Autumn 1999): 378–402.
11. Armistead Maupin, *Tales of the City* (New York: Harper, 2007), 13.
12. Ibid., 48.
13. Patrick Moore, *Beyond Shame: Reclaiming the Abandoned History of Radical Gay Sexuality* (Boston: Beacon Press, 2004), 191–221.

14. See Elizabeth A. Armstrong, *Forging Gay Identities: Organizing Sexuality in San Francisco, 1950–1994* (University of Chicago Press, 2002), 154. In *White Nights and Ascending Shadows*, activist Cleve Jones comments on the period, "It was not at all clear how gay people would respond [to AIDS]. We had political power because we all came to live [in San Francisco]. Why was it that we lived here? Was it only for sex? If we couldn't have sex, would we still want to live together? Would we have a community?"
15. Armistead Maupin, *Babycakes* (New York: Harper, 2007).
16. Maupin, *Tales*, i.
17. Armistead Maupin, *Sure of You* (New York: Harper, 2007).
18. Paul Monette, *Borrowed Time: An AIDS Memoir* (New York: Mariner Books, 1998).
19. Michael Nava, *The Little Death* (New York: Alyson Books, 1982), 46, 117.
20. Joseph Hansen, *Gravedigger* (New York: Holt, Rinehart, and Winston, 1982), 53–54.
21. Schrag, *California*, 1–22.
22. Gloria Anzaldúa and Cherríe Moraga, eds. *This Bridge Called My Back: Writings by Radical Women of Color* (Watertown, MA: Persephone Press, 1981), xxiii–xxvi.
23. Donelle N. Dreese, "Psychic Reterritorializations of Self and Place in the Poetry of Chrystos" *Interdisciplinary Literary Studies* 3.2 (Spring 2002): 40.
24. Chrystos, *Not Vanishing* (Vancouver, BC: Press Gang Publishers, 1989), 71.
25. Richard Rodriguez, *Hunger of Memory: The Education of Richard Rodriguez* (New York: Bantam, 1983), 4.
26. Paul Monette, *Afterlife* (New York: Crown Publishers, 1990), 1.
27. Richard Rodriguez, *Days of Obligation: An Argument with my Mexican Father* (New York: Viking, 1992), 208.
28. Ibid., 27–9.
29. Joshua Takano Chambers-Letson, "The Principle of Hope: Reflections on a Revival of Angels in America" *The Drama Review*, 56.1 (Spring 2012): 144.
30. Tony Kushner, *Angels in America: A Gay Fantasia on National Themes* (New York: Theatre Communications Group, 1995), 194, 272.
31. Ibid., 266.
32. David Savran, "Ambivalence, Utopia, and a Queer Sort of Materialism: How *Angels in America* Reconstructs the Nation" *Theatre Journal* 47.2 (May 1995): 212.
33. Kushner, *Angels in America*, 209–210.
34. Muñoz, *Cruising Utopia*, 18.
35. Kushner, *Angels in America*, 209.
36. Jewelle Gomez, *The Gilda Stories* (Ithaca: Firebrand Books, 1991), 53–101.
37. Qwo-li Driskill, "Stolen From Our Bodies: First Nations Two-Spirits/Queers and the Journey to a Sovereign Erotic" *Studies in American Indian Literatures* 2.16.2 (Summer 2004): 51.
38. Chrystos, *In Her I Am* (Vancouver, BC: Press Gang Publishers, 1993), 24.
39. Chrystos, *Fire Power* (Vancouver, BC: Press Gang Publishers, 1995), 127.

40. "Bark if you don't like deficits" *The Economist* 01/25/2014.
41. Michelle Tea, *Valencia* (Berkeley: Seal Press, 2008), 72.
42. Mattilda Bernstein Sycamore, *So Many Ways to Sleep Badly* (San Francisco: City Lights, 2008), 65.
43. Ibid., i.
44. Carla Trujillo, *What Night Brings* (Willimantic, CT: Curbstone Books, 2003), 5.
45. Richard Rodriguez, *Brown: The Last Discovery of America* (New York: Penguin, 2003), 174.
46. Armistead Maupin, *Michael Tolliver Lives* (New York: Harper Perennial, 2008), 5.
47. Cherríe L. Moraga, *A Xicana Codex of Changing Consciousness* (Durham: Duke University Press, 2011), xviii.
48. Mattilda Bernstein Sycamore, *The End of San Francisco* (San Francisco: City Lights Press, 2013), 128.
49. Ibid., 130.
50. Leah Garchick, "Armistead Maupin Leaving SF, Setting for His 'Tales'" *San Francisco Chronicle* 06/20/2012.
51. Armistead Maupin, *The Days of Anna Madrigal* (New York: Harper, 2014), 270.
52. Muñoz, *Cruising Utopia*, 1.

CHAPTER 22

Modern California Nature Writing

Michael Kowalewski

"Nature writing" is a broad umbrella term that covers a wide range of literary works. At the heart of the genre are nonfictional personal narratives that combine close observation of the physical world and personal experience. As John Elder notes, nature writing represents a "vivid edge – between literature and science, between the imagination and the physical processes of observation, and between humanity and the many other forms of life with which we share this earth."[1] Memorable writing about nature does not only take the form of the personal reflective essay. It also appears in poetry, fiction and journalism, and many nature writers work in several genres simultaneously. Some nature writers have academic credentials in the sciences while others are self-taught. Some writers are happy to be thought of as "nature writers" while others feel that designation is too narrow and implies that nature writing deals only with nature, not people and culture. The multiplicity of literary responses to the natural world encompassed by nature writing calls for a wide-angle inclusiveness of approach and this is especially true of modern California nature writing.

California has a rich heritage of nature writing that includes such now-iconic figures as John Muir, Mary Austin, and Robinson Jeffers. Some of these writers focused on a form of the wilderness sublime – a celebration of the glaciers, waterfalls, and wildlife of Yosemite National Park (Muir) or the vertical cliffs and kelp-beds of the Big Sur coastline (Jeffers). Others, like Austin, focused on less outwardly scenic areas such as the rain-shadow deserts on the eastern slope of the Sierra Nevada. These earlier writers often decried human intrusion and alterations of the landscape. However, despite concerns about hydraulic mining, logging, dam-building, species extinction, and large-scale engineering projects in California, most earlier nature writers still felt confident in celebrating the power, beauty and resiliency of the California landscape. California nature writing since World War II has retained some of that confidence, with a persistent lyrical celebration of the state's stunning topographical and ecological diversity. The California nature writing of the last seventy years, however, is also frequently shadowed by an urgent concern about the consequences of profligate overdevelopment and runaway growth in the nation's most populous state.

California has grown from a population of 8.5 million people at the end of World War II to more than 38 million in 2014, with estimates of 60 million people by the middle of the twenty-first century. That exponential growth has led to a host of environmental challenges from traffic congestion and deformed wildlife to industrial agriculture and Superfund sites. Nature writers have been acutely aware of these changing conditions and have responded in a wide variety of ways. A heightened awareness of the state's ecological history has sparked a new emphasis on the fragility and vulnerability of the state's natural resources and on the possibilities for renewing, restoring, and re-inhabiting previously damaged ecosystems. Modern California nature writing has also expanded its focus beyond wilderness areas to address topics as diverse as viticulture, organic agriculture, and outdoor sports like fishing, surfing, and mountaineering. Modern environmental writing in California – in multiple genres – remains a potent, sometimes contradictory mix of lyrical observation, grassroot activism, melancholy elegy, and stubborn expressions of hope.

During World War II, the federal government spent more than $35 billion in California for shipbuilding, aircraft factories, and troop training. The overnight transformation of the state into a shining high-tech embodiment of the "military-industrial complex" brought prosperity to many in the state and sparked a population boom and a matching construction boom, with ten thousands of new homes being built each year after the end of the war. (California became the most populous state in the nation in 1962.) Postwar growth in California also featured massive new freeway and infrastructure construction projects, a rise in automobile air pollution, an increased dependence upon pesticides (many dispersed aerially and allowed to drift), and a sharp rise in consumerism that would generate millions of tons of new landfill garbage. Not all nature writing at the time registered the presence of the war or the postwar boom. For example, Sally Carrigher's book *One Day on Beetle Rock*, which was published during the war in 1944, presented interlocking portraits of nine different animals on one specific day in Sequoia National Park. However, many writers did express their concern for the way postwar prosperity was altering the landscape and taking a toll on

California's ecosystems. Hildegarde Flanner, for instance, wrote evocatively about living for thirty-six years in the foothills of Altadena in a booklet (written in the 1950s and published in 1980) that was tellingly entitled *A Vanishing Land*.

At the end of World War II, a lively avant-garde literary scene took shape in the San Francisco Bay Area and focused in part on the fragile beauty of California's land and seascapes. Important writers in San Francisco included the poets Kenneth Rexroth, William Everson, Robert Duncan, Josephine Miles, Philip Lamantia, and Robert Duncan. The novelist Henry Miller added to the mix when he moved to a remote coastal outpost in the Big Sur area in 1944. His *Big Sur and the Oranges of Hieronymus Bosch* (1957) detailed the isolated landscape – the creeks, canyons, and rattlesnakes – of California's central coast. All these writers laid the groundwork for what Everson, who had spent World War II in a camp for conscientious objectors on the Oregon coast would later describe in *Archetype West* (1976), as a distinct Pacific Coast aesthetic, one that colorfully combined a relaxed bohemianism, a love of small-press printing and close contact with nature. As Linda Hamalian notes, the dramatic natural setting of the West Coast infiltrated the sensibility of these writers: "they slipped into the spell of the California spaces, of its mountains, its forests, its wild terrain, and of the Pacific ocean itself," creating "a sense of sacramental presence in all things."[2] Rexroth, in particular, had worked in his youth in fire lookouts and on Forest Service trail crews, and he brought a detailed knowledge of western landscapes to bear in poetry collections such as *The Dragon and the Unicorn* (1952).

Beat Generation writers such as Jack Kerouac, Allen Ginsberg, Philip Whalen, Gary Snyder, and Lew Welch arrived in the Bay Area in the mid-1950s. Beat writers felt alienated from a society shadowed by the nightmare of nuclear annihilation and awash in consumerism, suburban conformity, and the bullying tactics of anti-communist crusaders like Senator Joseph McCarthy. Their social alienation relied less on social activism than on a poetics of immediacy and a ragged yearning for enlightenment that valued intensely lived experience and an immersion in the natural world. In Kerouac's novel *The Dharma Bums* (1958), narrator Ray Smith (based on Kerouac himself) is a scruffy spiritual vagabond or "Dharma bum," a rucksack pilgrim cooking pork and beans on the beach, exploring San Francisco, and searching for the Buddhist principle of Dharma or the Path of Truth. He befriends Japhy Ryder (based on the poet Gary Snyder), a former logger who grew up in the wet woods of the Pacific Northwest. Studying Chinese and Japanese literature and wearing Salvation Army hand-me-downs, Japhy is a poet woodsman who instructs Ray about Zen Buddhism as they hike together in the high Sierras or on Mt. Tamalpais. Japhy teaches Ray that the close, patient observation of nature can bring about a fresh new vision of the world. As Japhy puts it: "the closer you get to real matter, rock air fire and wood, boy, the more spiritual the world is."[3] The solitary, introspective adventures of Kerouac's characters on mountain trails and in fire lookouts helped engender what would become the literary and spiritual values of the emerging environmental movement of the 1960s.

Entering the 1960s, California and the country as a whole witnessed a drastic increase in environmental challenges such as the need to save wild areas before they were destroyed by urban sprawl. The novelist, historian, and conservationist Wallace Stegner became actively involved in such issues. Stegner founded the Stanford Creative Writing Program in 1946. He had written *Beyond the Hundredth Meridian* in 1954, an environmental history of the American West that focused on the life of John Wesley Powell, and he had worked with the executive director of the Sierra Club, David Brower, to help defeat plans to build dams in Dinosaur National Monument in Utah. In 1960, two years before Rachel Carson would write her landmark book *Silent Spring*, Stegner wrote a private letter to a commission charged with gathering information pertaining to wilderness legislation being debated in congress. In the letter, now widely known as "The Wilderness Letter," Stegner argued for the value of wilderness as an intangible and spiritual resource. "Something will have gone out of us as a people," he claimed, "if we ever let the remaining wilderness be destroyed; if we permit the last virgin forests to be turned into comic books and plastic cigarette cases." We need wilderness areas, he said, because they refresh the psyche and reassure us of our sanity: they are "a part of the geography of hope."[4] The letter is widely credited with aiding the passage of the 1964 Wilderness Act, which established a national system of wilderness areas on federal land that now includes dozens of areas in California (the federal California Wilderness Act of 1984 later extended the Wilderness Act and authorized an additional 3 million acres of designated wilderness within California). Stegner was a brilliant essayist and conversationalist and he would continue for many years to be a powerful voice on environmental issues in California and the American West in collections such as *The Sound of Mountain Water* (1969), *One Way to Spell Man* (1982), *Conversations with Wallace Stegner on Western History and Literature* (1983), and *Where the Bluebird Sings to the*

Lemonade Springs (1992). His Pulitzer Prize-winning novel, *Angle of Repose* (1971), which is partly set in California, also dramatized the environmental history of the arid West.

By the late 1960s and early 1970s, environmentalists and conservationists had much to be heartened by in terms of new environmental legislation and grassroots efforts to preserve open spaces near where people lived. Environmental successes in California during this era included the passage of the National Wild and Scenic Rivers Act in 1968 (which would eventually include more than 20 rivers in California), the designation of the 2,663-mile Pacific Crest Trail as a national scenic trail in 1968, President Lyndon B. Johnson's 1968 signing of a bill creating Redwood National Park (later designated a UNESCO World Heritage site) in Humboldt and Del Norte counties, the passage of the National Environmental Policy Act in 1969, the establishment of the California Coastal Commission and the creation of the stunning Pt. Reyes National Seashore, north of San Francisco in 1972, and the creation of the Marine Animal Protection Act (which called for an ecosystem approach to natural resource management) in 1972. In addition to these gains, many environmental organizations either headquartered or actively engaged with green issues in the Golden State were founded during this time: the World Wildlife Fund in 1961, the Environmental Defense Fund in 1967, Friends of the Sea Otter in 1968, Friends of the Earth and the New Alchemy Institute in 1969, the National Resources Defense Council in 1970, Greenpeace in 1971, and the Planet Drum Foundation (founded by noted ecologist and environmental activist Peter Berg) in 1974. All these groups joined the continuing efforts of longstanding environmental organizations in California like the Save the Redwoods League and the Sierra Club (whose membership had rapidly grown from 7,000 members in 1952 to more than 70,000 by 1969) to help address new environmental threats in California.

Still, many of these new organizations and new legislation had originated in response to a deepening sense of the environmental crisis in California and the nation. In 1965, the conservationist and wildlife biologist Raymond Dasmann sounded an alarm with his *cri de coeur* entitled *The Destruction of California*, which detailed how the state had squandered its resources, degraded its ecosystems and continued its patterns of conspicuous consumption and overdevelopment. Environmental Journalist Harold Gilliam reported on the struggle to save the San Francisco Bay in *Between the Devil and the Deep Blue Bay* (1969). Increasing media coverage of air pollution in Southern California in the 1960s and 1970s (most cars at the time used leaded gas to power oversized V-8 engines) made "smog" and "LA" synonymous in the minds of many Americans. Then in late January of 1969, the blowout of a Union Oil drilling platform off the Santa Barbara coast spewed out 235,000 gallons of crude oil into the ocean, fouling 30 miles of high-quality beach on the mainland as well as on the Channel Islands with thick layers of tar and oil. The spill killed thousands of seabirds and marine animals such as dolphins and elephant seals. At the time, it was the largest oil spill in American history and it still ranks as the largest oil spill in California waters. The blowout sparked a public outcry that brought about stricter environmental regulations on offshore drilling.

The Santa Barbara oil spill was an environmental disaster with national significance. Along with the burning of the Cuyahoga River in Ohio a few months later, the oil spill galvanized a bipartisan coalition of congressmen to take action. Gaylord Nelson, a Democratic senator from Wisconsin and Representative Paul ("Pete") McCloskey from California, a conservation-minded Republican, worked to organize a national "teach-in" on the environment to help raise public awareness of air and water pollution across the nation. The result was what many see as the birth of the modern environmental movement: the first Earth Day, held on April 22, 1970. An estimated twenty million Americans (still the largest public turnout for any social movement in American history) listened to speakers in university plazas or turned out for large-scale rallies and demonstrations or smaller, local events where people could plant trees or clean up litter. Californians participated up and down the state. A group of fifty walkers on a six-week "survival walk" from Sacramento to Los Angeles organized by the Berkeley Ecology Action group spent Earth Day in the small town of Newhall. As it had in other towns, the group organized a small "eco-fair," distributed information about recycling, water pollution, and overpopulation and flew a green and white American flag over their exhibits. One walker played a guitar and sang "Welcome, Carbon Monoxide" from the musical *Hair* while a group of third-graders responded on cue with a chorus of coughing. The extraordinary grassroots success of Earth Day led to the creation of the Clean Air Act (1970), the Clean Water Act (1972), and the Endangered Species Act (1973). The phrase "teach-in" (taken from the anti-Vietnam war movement) to describe Earth Day events pointed to a demographic shift in the environmental movement, one the media dubbed a "Youthquake." Whereas earlier conservation organizations had tended to be comprised primarily of middle-aged white professional men, most of the participants on Earth Day were school children or college-age adults. The majority of them were still white but they included men and women and there was notable participation by people of color. As historian Adam Rome puts it, Earth Day helped create a new "green generation" of environmental activists who "were convinced that young people could change the direction of society."[5]

The youthfulness of the participants at the first Earth Day events was also tied to the rise of the hippie counterculture during the late 1960s, which was largely centered in northern California. The counterculture was a complex congery of multiple groups of younger adults who questioned traditional social, sexual, and spiritual mores and who, like the Beats before them, were alienated from the culture of consumerism that had characterized the 1950s and early 1960s. An important element of the 1960s counterculture was the rise of intentional communities and "back-to-the-land" communes that featured "off the grid" lifestyles incorporating gardening, baking, carpentry, homemade auto repair, shared child-raising, and the construction of geodesic domes for homes. Stewart Brand, a Stanford-educated writer and maverick environmental thinker, tapped into a new burgeoning interest in ecological design and alternative technology. Brand was inspired by the first NASA photographs, taken in 1967 and 1968, of the earth as seen from outer space. The image of a blue and green planet bedecked with clouds and juxtaposed against the blackness of space or the dead craters of the moon highlighted the fragile, anomalous beauty and color of a living earth. Brand used the image as the cover for a new, carefully crafted large-format publication called *The Whole Earth Catalog*, which he published from 1968 to 1972 from his home in Menlo Park. Brand advocated positive environmental pragmatism, a DIY sharing of helpful advice, and direct grassroots problem-solving. As Andrew Kirk notes, *Whole Earth* offered "a simple proposition to readers: empower yourself in an increasingly homogenized modern culture through access to creative information about alternate paths and good tools to get the job done." *Whole Earth*, as Kirk puts it, was "a breath of fresh air for a generation suffocating on relentless bad news."[6] The catalog sold millions of copies and won the National Book Award in 1972.

The writer who best embodied the holistic ecological sensibility Brand championed was Gary Snyder, who quietly but surely became a seminal figure in modern California nature writing. Snyder's collections of poetry – *Riprap* (1959), *Myths and Texts* (1960), *Riprap and Cold Mountain Poems* (1965), *The Back Country* (1968), and *Turtle Island* (1974), which won the Pulitzer Prize – employed deceptively simple verse forms to evoke a rich, precisely delineated sense of nature and place. His poetry combined his interest in Buddhism, Native American cultures, and the landscapes of the West Coast. After studying Zen Buddhism for twelve years in Japan, Snyder returned to California and settled with his family in 1970 on a 100-acre parcel of land at 3,000 feet on the south fork of the Yuba river. With friends he constructed a *zendo* (a Buddhist temple) and a house constructed from the wood of local hardwood trees, and named the place *Kitkitdizze*, a Wintun word for an aromatic ground shrub. He has been living, working and writing there for more than forty years. Snyder's lifestyle – a combination of manual labor, spiritual practice and literary culture – was a powerful example of the "back-to-the-land" movement. His poetry combined the elegance of Italic calligraphy with the goofy irreverence of the counterculture. His poem "Smokey the Bear Sutra," for example, which Snyder distributed as a free broadside at a San Francisco Sierra Club Wilderness Conference in 1969, raised environmental consciousness by re-imagining the famous mascot of the U.S. Forest Service as a manifestation of the Great Sun Buddha, with a shovel and a broad-brimmed hat, eating blackberries and saving planet Earth from freeways, suburbs, and oil slicks. "Sutra" shared whimsical affinities with the work of other counterculture writers such as Richard Brautigan, whose comic antiestablishment novella *Trout Fishing in America* (1967), achieved tremendous – and paradoxical – mainstream success, eventually selling more than four million copies worldwide. In the decades to come, Snyder would remain a powerful voice for environmental concepts like "bioregionalism" (the conception of regions in both ecological and human terms) and "watershed consciousness" (using watersheds as a conceptual model in thinking about nature and culture) in essay collections like *The Practice of the Wild* (1990), *A Place in Space* (1995), and *Back on the Fire* (2007). He continued to write poetry and in 1996 he published his book-length poem *Mountains and Rivers Without End*, a work he had first begun forty years earlier in 1956. The poem – whose title refers to an ancient Chinese scroll painting – interweaves East Asian, Native American and western American history, spirituality, and landscape. The poem shifts between various geographical locations and explores the possibility of simultaneously having a local, bioregional vision of nature on a planetary scale.

The 1970s saw the rise of the environmental justice movement and the fashioning of a more aggressively confrontational and media-oriented style of environmental activism in groups like Earth First! and Sea Shepherds, both founded in 1979. It also witnessed less publicized but no less significant literary activity in California that emerged from the counterculture but began to move beyond it. In 1974, Malcolm Margolin, who was born in Boston and had been educated at Harvard, arrived in the Bay Area and founded Heyday Press in Berkeley by writing, typesetting, and distributing a personal guide to the natural history of the Berkeley/Oakland foothills entitled *The East Bay Out*. The book was a quirky example of the dozens of hiking and field guides to the various regions of California, which, along with botanical guidebooks and manuals on ecological restoration, became increasingly popular with outdoor-oriented Californians. These field guides were and remain an important part of California nature writing. Heyday would go on to establish itself as a premier press for works on California nature and culture, with a particular focus on Native American culture and artistry in California. Margolin wrote and edited several important books about native cultures in California, including *The Ohlone Way* (1978) and *The Way We Lived* (1981). In 1987, he also founded the quarterly magazine *News from Native California*, devoted to the Indian people of California. The magazine has helped connect native and non-native communities within the state and it has highlighted works by native authors – such as Darryl Babe Wilson's memoir, *The Morning the Sun Went Down* (1998) and Greg Sarris' biography of a Pomo basket-weaver, *Mabel McKay* (1994) – which have explored the deep history and spirit dimensions of native responses to the California landscape. In 2001, Margolin, along with David Loeb, also founded the magazine *Bay Nature*, which explores the landscapes and wildlife of the Bay Area and consistently features some of the best natural history writing in California.

The 1970s saw the appearance of other significant works. In 1973, T. H. Watkins, a protégé of Wallace Stegner, published his California memoir, *On the Shore of the Sundown Sea*. Watkins spent fifteen years as the editor of *Wilderness* magazine and published more than two dozen books and hundreds of articles. While much of his writing focused on wilderness issues and the American West more broadly, several of his books focused on California, including *Time's Island* (1989) on the California desert. In 1975, Ernest Callenbach published his futuristic utopian novel *Ecotopia*, which used emerging notions of ecological sustainability to imagine a small country, Ecotopia, consisting of northern California, Oregon and Washington, that had broken away from the United States in order to live out its values of environmental and social stability (Callenbach followed up on the popularity of this novel with a sequel entitled *Ecotopia Emerging* in 1981). *Ecotopia* was an important precursor of later "eco-fiction" that conjured futuristic visions of environmental flourishing and collapse: works such as Ursula K. LeGuin's intricately imagined novel, *Always Coming Home* (1985), set in northern California, and Octavia Butler's "Earthseed" novels, *The Parable of the Sower* (1993) and *The Parable of the Talents* (1998), set in the ecologically ravaged California of the 2020s. In 1976, Barry Lopez, who grew up in the semi-rural San Fernando Valley of the 1950s launched an acclaimed career as a nature writer with a collection of short stories entitled *Desert Notes*, set in the austere landscapes of the Great Basin and Mojave deserts. In that same year, writer and painter Russell Chatham published *The Angler's Coast*, which recorded fourteen fishing adventures on the West Coast, including accounts of shad fishing on the Feather river and angling for striped bass in the San Francisco Bay.

In 1978, David Rains Wallace's *Dark Range* was published. Subtitled "A Naturalist's Night Notebook," the book was a study of nocturnal ecology in the Yolla Bolly-Middle Eel wilderness of northern California and it marked the beginning of Wallace's distinguished and prolific career as a California nature writer. Wallace, who was raised in Connecticut and first came to the Bay Area in 1969, has published more than a dozen books of natural history. He gained national attention with *The Klamath Knot* (1983), a book focused on the Klamath Mountains in northwest California and southwest Oregon. The Klamaths prompt Wallace's philosophical and psycho-cultural reflections on evolution and he explores everything from geology to legends of Sasquatch or Bigfoot, a giant hominoid said to live in these remote mountains. Wallace fashioned a distinctive style of reportage that is, by turns, observant and playful, fussy and genial, scientific and literate. He is as likely to quote Dante or Tolstoy as he is to refer to Mr. Mole in *The Wind in the Willows*. His other California works include *Neptune's Ark* (2007), about maritime evolution and *Chuckwalla Land* (2011), about the California desert. Wallace also wrote two "eco-thriller" novels: *The Turquoise Dragon* (1985), set in the Trinity Alps, and a sequel, *The Vermilion Parrot* (1991), set in Big Sur.

The 1980s and 1990s witnessed a continuing explosion of California nature writing. David Darlington's *In Condor Country* (1987), traced the efforts in San Joaquin county to save the California condor, the largest bird in North America, with a nine-foot wingspan and the capability of soaring for more than an hour without flapping its wings. Several important works of California environmental history also appeared, many of them with a narrative sweep like that of good fiction. Notable examples include Marc Reisner's *Cadillac Desert* (1986) about water management in the American West, Ted Simon's *The River Stops Here* (1996), an account of a rancher's landmark environmental battle in the mid-1960s to stop the Army Corps of Engineers from building a dam on the Eel River, and Philip Fradkin's *A River No More* (1996), about the Colorado River, and *The Seven States of California* (1997). The acclaimed *New Yorker* writer John McPhee profiled geologist Eldridge Moores of U.C. Davis in *Assembling California* (1993). Several compelling works about outdoor sports in California also appeared. Bill Barich and Russell Chatham published collections of essays about fishing in California: Barich in *Traveling Light* (1985) and Chatham in *Dark Waters* (1988). Daniel Duane's *Lighting Out* (1994) dealt with big-wall climbing in Yosemite and *Caught Inside* (1996) chronicled a surfer's year on the northern California coast. Interest in all forms of nature writing was also buoyed at this time by the rise of "eco-criticism," an environmental form of literary criticism. (An important scholarly organization – the Association for the Study of Literature and Environment (ASLE) – was formed in 1992 and its membership grew rapidly.)

An important but sometimes neglected sub-genre of California nature writing consists of literature about food, wine, and cooking. Although this genre particularly flourished in the 1980s and 1990s, it had an impressive pedigree that extended back to Mary Frances Kennedy (M. F. K.) Fisher, a prominent food writer raised in Whittier who spent many years living in the South of France as well as in vineyards and ranches in the hamlets of St. Helena and Glen Ellen in northern California. Her writing career spanned more than sixty years and included fifteen books of essays and reminiscences on culinary subjects. Works such as *An Alphabet for Gourmets* (1949), *The Art of Eating* (1954), *The Story of Wine in California* (1962), and *With Bold Knife and Fork* (1969) featured Fisher's cosmopolitan sophistication and her celebration of the sensual pleasures of artfully prepared food. She influenced many writers exploring California's food and wine cultures, including Alice Waters, who founded Chez Panisse restaurant in Berkeley in 1971. Waters' memoir, *40 Years of Chez Panisse* (2011), recounts her pioneering creation of a new California cuisine that emphasized cooking with the freshest locally sourced seasonal ingredients. Other works in this vein include David Darlington's *Angels' Visits* (1991), an exploration of the Zinfandel grape, and his study of iconoclastic winegrowers, *An Ideal Wine* (2011). David Mas Masumoto, a third-generation farmer who grows organic peaches and grapes on an 80-acre farm south of Fresno, also emerged as an important writer about California agriculture in the 1990s. In books such as *Epitaph for a Peach* (1995), *Harvest Son* (1998), *Four Seasons in Five Senses* (2003), and *Wisdom of the Last Farmer* (2009), Masumoto writes about farm labor, the Japanese American internment experience, and contemporary rural life in California and Japan. His writing is a blend of multigenerational memoir, environmental commentary, and an evocative celebration of the sensory pleasures of working the land and growing fresh fruit. Most recently, Michael Pollan, of Berkeley, has risen to prominence as a food writer in books such as *The Botany of Desire* (2001), *The Omnivore's Dilemma* (2006), *In Defense of Food* (2008), and *Cooked* (2013), all of which critiqued modern agribusiness and suggested alternatives to the mass production and consumption of food. Pollan argued that our daily choices of how and what we eat represent our most intimate engagement with the natural world. His work helped initiate the "slow food" and local foods movements in California and beyond.

By the early 2000s California was the fastest growing state in the nation, growing at twice the national rate. Since 1964, seven million acres of farmland had been lost to development, much of it to seemingly indistinguishable housing tracts, industrial parks and shopping malls. In 2001, the U.S. Environmental Protection Agency noted that Sequoia National Park had higher ozone levels than those of Los Angeles and New York City combined. Persistent worries about water shortages prompted engineers to dream about 1,400-mile long ocean pipelines designed to bring fresh water from Alaska to Los Angeles. Hurricane Katrina in 2005 prompted worries about Sacramento's aging levee systems. Contaminated groundwater was blamed for causing birth defects in the Salinas Valley and the spraying of pesticides on nearby strawberry fields sickened schoolchildren in Ventura County. Perhaps no other work of nature writing captured the downbeat tone of the times better than the collaboration between historian Gray Brechin and eco-photographer Robert Dawson entitled *Farewell, Promised Dream*. Published in 1999, this large-format book, with its valedictory, Chandleresque title and ominous subtitle ("Waking from the California Dream") focused on ominous signs of collapse and ruination: abandoned mining sites, high-tension wires, "bathtub ring" reservoirs, and industrial landscapes. Brechin provided a grim assessment of California's environmental prospects. "If California were to be allegorically portrayed on its 150th birthday," he wrote, it would look not like "a virgin flourishing in immortal youth" but like "a badly used whore – chemically dependent and disfigured by abuse – who has seen and tried everything."[7] The book ends with heartening stories of California community activists who have won local environmental victories, but its dark message remains solidly in the tradition of the environmental jeremiad, a mournful and bitter lament about a society's present condition that prophesizes dire consequences.

The interdisciplinary format of Brechin and Dawson's book is part of a long-standing tradition of collaborative volumes that pair nature writing with photographs, paintings or field sketches. From 1960 to 1969, David Brower created the Sierra Club Exhibit Format series: large, heavy coffee-table books that combined text and high-quality reproductions of large-format photographs that required a viewer's eye to move about within the picture rather than being able to encompass it in a single glance. While the compelling nature of visual imagery in these books sometimes overshadowed the text, the popularity of such volumes has never completely disappeared. In 1984, the Sierra Club revived the Exhibit Format with a volume entitled *The Wilder Shore* (1984), a collaboration between David Rains Wallace and photographer Morley Baer that explores the influence of the California landscape on writers. Focusing upon different regions of the state, Baer's photographs are interspersed with a blend of Wallace's literary criticism and impressionistic journal entries from various locations. *The Wilder Shore* is a remarkable work of literary geography (Wallace's text from the book was reprinted in his collection, *Articulate Earth*, in 2014). Other notable examples of large-format books that combine artwork and nature writing include Stephen Johnson, Gerald Haslam, and Robert Dawson's *The Great Central Valley* (1993); William DeBuy's study of the Imperial Valley, *Salt Dreams* (1999) with photographs by Joan Myers; William Kittredge's collaboration with photographers Tupper Ansel Blake and Madeleine Graham Blake in *Balancing Water* (2007), about restoring the Klamath Basin; and Gary Snyder's collaboration with the painter Tom Killion in *Tamalpais Walking* (2009). Two inventive, smaller-format variations on these combinations of images and text are David Robertson's *Real Matter* (1997), a personal tribute to California nature writers illustrated with his own blurred-motion polaroid prints and Rebecca Solnit's multi-layered "atlas" of San Francisco, *Infinite City* (2010), which features work by multiple artists, writers, and cartographers that conveys the seeming inexhaustibility of nature and culture in San Francisco.

A writer, historian and environmental activist, Solnit has emerged in the last decade as a trenchant cultural commentator who sees nature not as separate from human culture but as always implicated in multiple coexisting contexts of history, politics, technology, and globalization. She has written about aspects of past and present California landscapes in books like *Savage Dreams* (1999), *River of Shadows* (2003), and *Yosemite in Time* (2005), a re-photographic project coauthored with Mark Klett and Byron Wolfe. Solnit's advocacy of multiple perspectives in conceptualizing environmental issues seems appropriate for the first decade and a half of the twenty-first century, when the scale of environmental problems in California expanded far beyond the boundaries of the state. Concerns about global climate change, warming oceans and sea-level rise, new possibilities of tsunamis, earthquakes and volcanic activity, invasive species, foodborne diseases, bioterrorism, and new extractive industries like fracking are all putting unprecedented demands on California nature writers seeking to evoke and understand the full scale of these issues. The range of their writing has remained refreshingly eclectic.

Jennifer Price explored the intersections of nature and popular culture in *Flight Maps* (1999) and wrote an important essay entitled "Thirteen Ways of Seeing Nature in LA" (2005). Botanists John O. Sawyer in *Northwest California* (2006) or Michael Kauffmann in *Conifer Country* (2012) continued to write traditional natural history guides, though now often with an eye to how climate change has altered the timing of annual events in species' life cycles. Some works – such as Freeman House's account of salmon restoration in the Mattole River, *Totem Salmon* (1999) or Kenneth Brower's *The Winemaker's Marsh* (2001), about the restoration of a wildfowl marsh in Sonoma county – focused on efforts to restore habitat or repair damaged landscapes. Eco-activist Julia Butterfly Hill wrote a popular arboreal memoir, *The Legacy of Luna* (2000), about living for more than two years on a makeshift platform in a Humboldt County redwood as a protest against old-growth logging. David Ulin, in *The Myth of Solid Ground* (2004) and Philip Fradkin, in *Magnitude 8* (2014), both explored life along California's seismic fault-lines. Bob Madgic wrote a riveting account of a climbing disaster in Yosemite in *Shattered Air* (2005). Judith Larner Lowry celebrated wildland ecology and native plant horticulture in *Gardening with a Wild Heart* (2007) and Richard Preston wrote about redwood canopy botanists in *The Wild Trees* (2007). In 2009, Yosemite Park Ranger Shelton Johnson published his novel *Gloryland*, whose narrator, Elijah Yancy, is an African American "Buffalo Soldier" whose journey takes him from the Reconstruction South to Nebraska, the Phillipines and eventually to a post in Yosemite in 1903. Cheryl Strayed's bestselling account of hiking the Pacific Crest Trail in *Wild* (2013), proved that many readers still value stories of personal redemption in wilderness. Still others such as artist-naturalist Laura Cunningham, in her lavishly illustrated *A State of Change* (2010), used their historical imaginations to evoke the deep ecology of California's past landscapes in the hopes that Californians might yet "re-localize" themselves and live in harmony with healthy local ecosystems while still acknowledging the omnipresence of change in nature. The California nature writing of the past seventy years has been strikingly rich and varied. Whatever new directions California nature writers take in the coming decades, they will undoubtedly continue, as have so many of their remarkable predecessors, to represent the stunning but also vulnerable landscapes of the Golden State with precision, apprehension, and an inspiring obstinacy of hope.

Notes

1. John Elder, "Introduction," *American Nature Writers*, vol. 1 (New York: Charles Scribner's Sons, 1996), xii.
2. Linda Hamalian, "Regionalism Makes Good: The San Francisco Renaissance," in *Reading the West: New Essays on the Literature of the American West*, ed. Michael Kowalewski (New York: Cambridge University Press, 1996), 219.
3. Jack Kerouac, *The Dharma Bums* (1957, New York: Penguin Books, 2006), 157.
4. Wallace Stegner, *The Sound of Mountain Water* (Garden City, New York: Doubleday & Company, 1969), 146, 153.
5. Adam Rome, *The Genius of Earth Day: How a 1970 Teach-In Unexpectedly Made the First Green Generation* (New York: Hill and Wang, 2013), 77.
6. Andrew G. Kirk, *Counterculture Green: The "Whole Earth Catalog" and American Environmentalism* (Lawrence: University Press of Kansas, 2007), 3.
7. Robert Dawson and Gray Brechin, *Farewell, Promised Land: Waking from the California Dream* (Berkeley: University of California Press, 1999), 175.

CHAPTER 23

Making California's Towns and Small Cities Visible in the Twenty-First Century

Nancy S. Cook

By the early 1990s, academic studies of the American West moved from a scholarly emphasis on unpeopled regions toward considerations of urban and suburban areas. Scholars in Western American Studies developed a critical regionalist strategy by clarifying connections, flows, disruptions, and displacements within and beyond locations in the western United States. However, little of that work has taken up the town, the exurb, or the smaller city as its subject.

Popular depictions of California tend to focus on two urban areas – Los Angeles and San Francisco – or the wide-open spaces of the state's so-called unpeopled places. Towns and small cities, which are neither urban hives of activity nor examples of pristine nature, refuse to fit these mythologies of California. In literature and media, a town or small city is not depicted as a reality in and of itself, but instead serves as a means of comparison to an urban area, often playing its binary opposite: provincial vs. cosmopolitan, rustic vs. urbane, periphery vs. center, static vs. mobile, past vs. future, and redneck red vs. metropolitan blue. Although contemporary writers have attempted to reclaim these areas – viewing them as relational and essential spaces – in the larger public imaginary, as well as in a good deal of political discourse, California's inland towns and smaller cities have often been seen as bastions of conservatism, anti-intellectual zones, or simply irrelevant.

My essay examines social entanglements and engagements in two kinds of places: agriculturally based smaller cities that operate as a center around which the action unfolds; and towns, primarily coastal, which have become havens for those escaping from metropolitan life, an edge where life proceeds in relation to a largely absent, but powerful metropolitan center.

California writers have been looking at these places critically for a long time. Building on a long tradition, many contemporary California writers have worked to represent the vitality of towns and smaller cities in a matrix of flows and nodes, pathways, networks, and edges that intersect with class, gender, the environment, race, sexual orientation, and broadly conceived cultural differences, while tracing these connections back to regional, urban, national, and global economies and social structures. As Rob Shields asserts, "marginalized places expose the relativity of the entrenched, universalizing values of the centre, and expose the relativism of cultural identities. The small city's very mediality and peripherality predisposes it to flexible representation – and to unique ways of seeing" (217). By decentering the metropolis and rethinking California literature from the perspective of towns and smaller cities, we are offered a new window into these areas. While some writers use old mythologies to restore towns and small cities to sites of nostalgic simplicity and others warn us that no safe haven exists, still other writers drill deeper, disrupting old binaries and hierarchies that demarcate periphery and center to depict complex webs of family and community relationship experience in economic hardship

Once upon a time, readers knew that California literature was from and about California, because it was steeped in place – real or imagined. The California mystique helped sell stories, magazines and novels ranging from Mark Twain's "The Celebrated Jumping Frog of Calaveras County" (1865) to Bret Harte's "The Outcasts of Poker Flat" (1869); from Mary Austin's *The Land of Little Rain* (1903) to John Muir's *My First Summer in the Sierra* (1911); from the celebration and promotion of California writers by *The Overland Monthly* to books such as *The Life and Adventures of Joaquín Murieta* (1854) or *Ramona* (1884). Much of the literature that circulated outside California was about the less-populated places – Dame Shirley's mining camps, the *rancherias*, and the nearly unpeopled expanses beyond the developing metropolises. This tendency continued well into the twentieth century with the international recognition of work by writers such as Jack London, John Steinbeck, Aram Saroyan, and the Beats.

Nineteenth-century representations frequently offered up the small town as a foil to the city. Elements of the pastoral, the picturesque, and local color occur in the work of Twain and Harte, Dame Shirley, Elizabeth Stoddard, Gertrude Atherton, and Mary Hallock Foote, among others. Norris, London, Austin, and later Steinbeck and Kerouac revised these earlier visions of California. However, they did so for a largely white and middle-class audience.

By the 1970s, this had changed – and California's two great cities, San Francisco and Los Angeles, captured the nation's and the world's attention. Currently the region outside the metropolitan areas receives less critical scrutiny or has become severed from this more metropolitan notion of place. These late twentieth- and early twenty-first-century writers self-consciously play off existing representations of California. In earlier traditions, a sophisticated outsider often encountered a local rustic culture and described it for an audience that imagined itself to be sophisticated. Twain exploited this paradigm, even reversed it for comic effect. The joke was sometimes on the outsider, but the humor often required a cosmopolitan knowledge, as in Twain's "Whittier's Birthday Speech" given on 17 December 1877 in honor of the poet John Greenleaf Whittier. The story features rough characters called Longfellow, Emerson, and Oliver Wendell Holmes, who abuse the hospitality of a rugged miner in the Sierra foothills. Now, it takes a roomful of Twain scholars to unpack the literary and cultural politics that made the speech both humorous and scandalous.

Tourists continue to flock to Twain's Calaveras county, Jackson's Ramona, London's Valley of the Moon, and Steinbeck's Monterey as literary landmarks, but the serious literature of the 1990s and 2000s does not attract local color or tourists. Instead, this is the contested California, where the stakes include the places themselves and the people who try to live there.

While earlier generations of writers such as Steinbeck and Saroyan wrote about the places where they lived, writers from the 1990s forward privileged their identities over their connections to place. How many people know that Maxine Hong Kingston writes about Stockton, California? Certain authors were also concerned more with the connections between places, rather than the places themselves. In *Play It as It Lays* (1970), Joan Didion connects the tony beach towns of southern California with bedraggled desert outposts without settling down anywhere. Just as the two great urban areas, Los Angeles and San Francisco, seemed disconnected from the towns and cities surrounding them, these surrounding towns – places such as Big Sur, Marin, and Mendocino, as well as agricultural communities, such as those in Sonoma County, the Salinas and Great Central Valley – are also places of contestation. How can such communities sustain themselves in a time of crisis, and how can diverse subcommunities survive and coexist? This essay takes a core sampling of writers who link, explicitly or implicitly, what happens in California's towns and smaller cities to the issues and challenges that determine the state's future.

Popular literary genres such as romance and crime present small-town California as a haven from the ills of modernity. Robert Pinsky found that in the late twentieth century, in a culture "notionally built on speed, change, mobility, and expansion, the thought of a quiet, human-scale community has been comforting – a half-real, half-invented shelter"(13). In genre fiction, places are idealized or mythologized. Romance novels, for example, often use coastal California towns, Sierra Nevada foothill towns, or the wine country as their setting. Historians and sociologists have shown how the towns in the Sierra foothills ravaged by placer mining, the wine country's mono culture and industrial practices, and the landscape dotted with warehouses and dense commercial development can't possibly match their literary counterparts.

In romance novels, the city is depicted as soul-destroying. Romance heroines often come to a small town in retreat from cosmopolitan modernity. Characters hunger for simplicity, honesty, and community in the sleepy places they have chosen. In books by writers such as Casey Dawes, Robyn Carr, and Shirlee Busbee, charming small towns feature cafés and bookstores or ranches, vineyards, and gardens where women try their hands at agriculture. During the course of these novels, the heroines must let down their urban guard, relinquish their hard-nosed individualism, and embrace the "natural" rhythms of these California Edens. In turn, they become attuned to the natural world, marry, and join the community in earnest. Rural towns and agricultural settings become part of a larger fantasy that preserves heteronormativity and promises a retreat from modernity. Ryan Poll observes: "The small town that is ostensibly 'our heritage' is a retroactive, reactive, and romanticized narrative. The dominant small town is not killed by modernity; rather modernity proves the condition of possibility for the dominant small town" (13).

In crime fiction, the protagonist often hones his or her detective skills in the metropolis, only to find that those skills are needed in the hinterlands. In Marcia Muller's *Burn Out* (2008), detective Sharon McCone retreats to her ranch for physical and psychic healing, only to discover trouble. However, in a small town, solving a crime restores the torn fabric of a community in a way that it rarely can in urban crime fiction. By the novel's end, the perpetrator, guilty of rape and multiple murders, has killed his long-suffering brother, severing his last connection to family, sanity, and place. He is institutionalized, saving the community the expense of a trial. With the murderer put away, one family, traumatized by the events is "pulling together, doing better" (312), while the investigating officer has resolved her drinking problem and put her life back on track.

Through contrast, the city defines the town. Romance and crime novels present small towns as safe, "authentic" places where community is valued. Outside of genre fiction, these retreats retain their appeal. California literature includes many examples of the writer in voluntary exile, from the nineteenth- and early twentieth-century arts colonies to the woodsy Marin county locales of the Beats to Henry Miller's extended stay in Big Sur.

California's nonfiction writers share a fascination with the contemporary rural retreat. In the 1990s, Daniel Duane rejected the most rudimentary demands of post-college adulthood when he gave up a dull job in Berkeley and headed for Santa Cruz to spend a year surfing. In his memoir, *Caught Inside: A Surfer's Year on the California Coast* (1996), he offers a day-to-day account of the sensual pleasures and dangers of surfing, along with a history of the sport, as well as a depiction of an international surfing community and a natural history of the coastal regions around Santa Cruz – while downplaying his other Santa Cruz identity, that of a doctoral student in literature. As a surfer and outsider, he copes with locals who loathe newcomers, earns his way into the surfing community, and finds a more authentic version of himself through a community that shares his obsession. People fight over the best surfing spots and debate who owns the culture of surfing. While the tensions he depicts are real, they are about choices, pleasure, and pastimes, not race, citizenship, or economic survival. By the end of the book, Duane has become more insider than outsider. Santa Cruz, then, has fulfilled its promise and allowed him to fulfill his fantasy. Duane can, stay or leave, know that he has earned a place in a community of men he respects and admires.

For several literary fiction writers, the small community as safe haven fails, and characters learn, sometimes at the price of their own lives, that the complications and violence of urban life follows them into the hinterlands. Thomas Pynchon's Zoyd Wheeler seeks to escape from the wars and failed revolutions of the 1960s by fleeing to a freewheeling northern California town until the U.S. government unfurls its tentacles. In *Vineland* (1990), Pynchon refuses to idealize the 1960s or northern California as a post-hippie retreat. He reminds readers that the decade abounded in trauma and betrayal and that Vineland affords no safety. The characters return "home" at the novel's end, but they have been transformed by their engagement with a sordid past and a collision with the government in the present. Even if readers tune out a global culture of violence, repression, and capitalism, forgetting is not an option.

Denis Johnson wreaks havoc with the dream of small towns as safe retreats in *Already Dead* (1997). Johnson's Mendocino county towns and countryside offer no respite from intrigue, bad behavior, and hit men. Although they are living in a nightmare version of small-town California, his characters still cling to the fantasy. The small towns along Highway 101 in northern California "felt like little naps you might never wake up from – you might throw a tire and hike to a gas station and stumble unexpectedly onto the rest of your life, the people who would finally mean something to you, a woman, an immortal friend, a saving fellowship in the religion of some obscure church" (3). In *Nobody Move* (2009), set in the Central Valley and Sierra foothills, where towns are invaded by criminals and littered with dead bodies, Johnson's characters still yearn for the a simpler life even as their actions foreclose the possibility.

Roy Parvin and Katherine Haake portray individuals who must cope with isolation. In *The Loneliest Road in America* (1996) and *In the Snow Forest* (2000), Roy Parvin's characters struggle between solitude and loneliness. In the small towns of the Trinity Mountains simple conviviality feels impossible. Haake imagines our connections to nature and the body: through rivers, through thirst. In her book, *That Water, Those Rocks* (2002) – a mixed-genre look at the far north dammed rivers – she insists that wherever we imagine isolation, instead we find connection. The water from those reservoirs "goes south" to Los Angeles and not west to the sea, connecting the sacrificed rivers of northern and central California to the hunger and thirst of the south. Haake also writes about the uprooted, including the workers who follow the work of dam construction. The losses, both human and environmental, not only are the result of greed, but also because of the engineers' faith in their ability to improve on nature. T. C. Boyle aligns with Pynchon and Johnson. In *A Friend of the Earth*, Boyle illustrates that rural safe havens are unsustainable. As long as California's biota are threatened, he points out throughout the novel, even the most charming cabin in the woods can't provide safety.

California towns and cities have experienced enormous population shifts over time, as have so many states in the intermountain West. While the people and places of origin change, the migration continues and is reflected in a variety of ways in California literature. From wealthy individuals seeking retreats, to artists searching for a more "authentic" California, to people fleeing the city because they can no longer afford a metropolitan lifestyle, to laborers looking for work, these "strangers" feel like outsiders once they leave the comfortable anonymity of urban life.

When outsiders disrupt congenial, homogenous communities, "old timers" become elegiac and a bit testy, as in Annie Lamott's *All New People* (1989). Sometimes characters use a community's instability strategically. In *Mañana Means Heaven* by Tim Z. Hernandez (2013), the fluctuating population of a labor camp helps an informer for "La Migra" blend in as just another migrant laborer. William T. Vollman examines both the strivers who cross the United States/Mexico border looking for work in his sprawling nonfiction book *Imperial* (2009), and considers the consequences of these crossings for Imperial Valley communities. In *Grand Avenue* (1994), Greg Sarris follows his Pomo Indian characters as they endure a number of micro-migrations after they are displaced from their *rancheria* and move from place to place within a run-down Santa Rosa neighborhood.

Industrial agriculture – with its labor practices, ecologically unsound land practices, inequitable resource allocations, and hierarchical corporate structures – has created worlds of conflict. Many of these contestations worry ideas of cultural and environmental sustainability. Rigoberto Gonzalez and Manuel Muñoz write about the contests and tensions between social and political conservatism and those who are punished by such ideologies. In the literature about Central Valley farm labor, or for the "invisible" Indians of Greg Sarris's Sonoma County, class tensions also play out as racial tensions. Characters in many of these works provoke questions of stasis and mobility – physical mobility, (should they stay or should they go?), class mobility, and the mobility of identity.

If California's northland coasts and mountains seem to offer the promise of retreat, California's interior valleys might be the places one retreats *from*. However, it is in California's heartland, where an abundance of stories and poems are placed, we find work that focuses everyday life, reveals it unflinchingly as it occurs there, nowhere else. In everyday life, as Ben Highmore contends: "our feelings, emotions and passions that seem so 'private' and 'internal' are, in actuality, social-material forces that circulate externally. ... It is the world that has got under our skin and has stirred us to the core" (33). As Gerald Haslam and James D. Houston pointed out in their pioneering collection, *California's Heartland: Writing from the Great Central Valley* (1978), a lot of valley writers have insisted that everyday life merits close attention. Philip Levine's tenure at Fresno State, beginning in 1959, influenced a number of new poets to go on to write powerfully about the Central Valley: Larry Levis, Greg Pape, David

St. John, Gary Soto, Roberta Spear, and Shirley Anne Williams, among them. It is the writers of the Great Central Valley who have given us portraits of working-class Californians, those who spend their daily lives on farms and ranches to serve the cities on the coast.

Since the nineteenth century, immigrants from around the world have moved to the Central Valley, making it a multivocal, contested place. With each new generation of immigrants, some moved up the economic and social food chain, some slipped down, some were deported, some escaped, some hobbled away, looking for work elsewhere. California's Central Valley industrial agriculture produced a culture deeply diverse, as well as socially hierarchical, while providing commodities for world export. Agribusiness, Haslam observes, "uses people as it uses water and sunlight" (The *Sacramento Bee* 15A).

Since the first incursions of non-Natives, the literature of California's heartland registers the push-back from the laboring classes. Among the books from valley writers in the last two decades, we find those of Wilma McDaniel, whose death in 2007 ended a long poetic engagement with Okie culture and working classes of the San Joaquin Valley. Gerald Haslam demonstrates his sensitivity to the land, its history, and the laboring classes that keep the valley growing in the 1994 enlarged edition of *The Other California: the Great Central Valley in Life and Letters*. He continues to produce work about the Central Valley and to promote both established and up-and-coming California heartland writers in his newspaper editorials, anthologies, and book reviews.

On the occasion of President Barack Obama's visit to Fresno, Haslam wrote a February 14, 2014 editorial in the *Sacramento Bee*, recalling a sign that hung in a "beer bar" in his hometown of Oildale: "We don't care how they do it in LA." Obama was travelling to California's Great Central Valley, where much of the nation's food has been produced for more than a century, to see the consequences of extended drought, but Haslam reminded urban readers that "President Barack Obama will be entering a part of California today that plays by its own rules and expectations – Los Angeles and San Francisco (and maybe Sacramento) be damned." Haslam, always attentive to the class and racial politics of California's interior, pointed out that "three of the five worst metropolitan areas in terms of population below the poverty line are also found in the Valley – Fresno, Modesto and Delano-Bakersfield – along with much wealth concentrated in few hands. Gated communities sprout and economic segregation increases." While acknowledging that water, and the agribusiness it supports, would be the focus of presidential attention, he hoped to shift the question to the region's economic woes, urging the president to ask himself "how more water will help abate the endemic culture of poverty and lack of opportunity that is the San Joaquin Valley's least-discussed crop. The region is both a best and a worst component of California, and certainly is not an unimportant one." Haslam points out that the Great Central Valley of California has several cities that continue to grow at a terrific rate: Fresno has a population of more than 500,000 and Bakersfield has more than 350,000 residents. Although agribusiness and petroleum industries are booming in the region where the cities are located, the area also houses many of the poorest people in the nation.

Despite the fact that this area has been portrayed in literature for years, these large and growing California cities are not visible to the media, politicians, and policymakers – they are not yet as important to the California imaginary. Haslam's editorial underscores the relationships between metropolitan areas and the places that serve their interests. San Francisco, Los Angeles, and the rest of the nation depend on water or food from California's interior, but the urban centers only fitfully consider the lives of those who nourish them. Indeed, in the face of drought, economic hardship and a lack of water, we must turn to people most at risk – which is complicated by the increasingly volatile subject of immigration and the militarized southern border of the United States. And those most at risk are undocumented workers and the children and grandchildren of undocumented workers. While public discourse routinely overlooks the relationships between labor, place, and the circulation of commodities, many contemporary writers examine these circuits of economic stasis and physical mobility, the relationships between the metropolitan center and the places that feed it, and the cultural consequences of stagnation and movement.

Towns and small cities can function as "canaries in the coalmine" because they are often on the front line of metropolitan and global relationships, flows, and exchanges. Connected to global matrices of commodity prices, labor, and environmental degradation, such places assert their singularity and small-town status as they struggle with issues shared by towns worldwide. Several California books look at routes and circuits of environmental change, economics, and power as practiced in the cities and towns of the Central Valley, including James Gregory's *American Exodus: the Dust Bowl Migration and Okie Culture in California* (1989) and Mark Arax and Rick Wartzman's *The King of California:*

J. G. Boswell and the Making of a Secret American Empire (2003). Along with memoirs by working-class residents of these valley towns, the literary fiction from this region has powerfully shown, again in Highmore's terms, how "the world has got under our skins and has stirred us to the core."

Frank Bergon, raised in the valley near Madera, takes up his homeland in *Jesse's Ghost* (2011), and considers difference – historical, hierarchical, perspectival, embodied – with its lethal *and* redemptive consequences. The novel insists that the legacies of difference are place-specific – played out in one small section of the Great Central Valley. By the late 1950s, when Bergon's narrator, Wade "Sonny" Childers, was in junior high school, two generations of Okies; Issei, Nisei, and Sansei; and innumerable generations of "Mexicans" took turns as reviled, repatriated, and interned underclasses in the Central Valley. Those legacies persisted through the 1960s, the historical terrain of the novel. In terms of class dynamics, it is the Okies, and Sonny in particular, who merit Bergon's evaluation. As it analyzes cultures of violence amid the agricultural community, Bergon's novel explores the complex and shifting alliances among agricultural workers in the valley.

Writers such as McDaniel, Soto, Haslam, and Bergon complicate ideas about white privilege and the social and political conservatism often attributed to the California's white population. By focusing on class in the Central Valley, they offer nuanced portraits of the shifts in cultural and economic capital in California's heartland. Again, as Haslam has pointed out, with the exception of the valley's indigenous people, everyone there is an immigrant and a striver.

As California's Latino population edges toward majority in the state, three Chicano writers from the valley, all born in the 1970s, have embraced their home as a setting for their work, pushing representations of the valley into the twenty-first century. In the books of Rigoberto Gonzalez, Manuel Muñoz, and Tim Z. Hernandez, we find communities where there are ongoing negotiations in the neighborhoods, factories, and fields between grandparents, parents, and children; between straight and gay people; young and old; the desperately poor and the working poor; the fearful and the bold.

In his two short story collections, *Zigzagger* (2003) and *The Faith Healer of Olive Avenue* (2007), as well as in his novel *What You See in the Dark* (2011), Manuel Muñoz interweaves striving and reticence in his characters. He observes and carefully calibrates the action, while he articulates and subverts a range of stereotypes, including what Judith

Halberstam calls metronormativity – "the conflation of urban and visible in many normalizing narratives of gay/lesbian subjectivities" (36). Muñoz deftly analyzes this conservative culture:

> The Valley is a place in which all the tension of social clash is underneath the fabric of the community. With the exception of the UFW marches in the 60s and 70s, major pushes for political change remain the domain of the big cities. I've always seen the Valley as a place of observers: if you're not watching the neighbors, you're watching the news, waiting to see how what happens next door or in the big cities will change your life. It's a place of reaction, rather than action. It makes change slow to arrive.

All of his work examines the politics of looking: neighbors watching neighbors, employers watching employees, family members watching each other. Concepción, or "Connie," as she is named in her fake birth certificate and by her white employer, is the mother of a teenaged son killed in an accident. She knows her neighbors are watching her for signs of grief or recovery while she watches her employers, looking at their "closet shelves and the kitchen drawers and the laundry hamper," and she knows "the husband's habit of leaving socks around" (*Faith Healer* 3–4). However, observation does not lead to intimacy. In fact, it leads to its reverse: estrangement. Connie, as a single mother living in close quarters with her son might have enjoyed a close relationship with him, but she discovers only after his death that he was in love, and with a young man.

Muñoz's characters routinely move back and forth between the small towns and cities of the Central Valley and the metropolis, San Francisco, with its promise of a vibrant gay culture. However, life "Over There" can't erase the pull homeward, nor can it transform characters' relationships with family at home. In most of his short stories and in the novel, characters hold their secrets closely and remain profoundly alone.

Rigoberto Gonzalez, who writes poetry, fiction, nonfiction, and criticism, has produced two young adult novels, *Mariposa Club* (2009) and *Mariposa Gown* (2012) that capture the milieu of gay teens in California's interior cities. Characters yearn for the metropolis as a means of fulfilling their dreams, including the fantasy of sexual expression. They struggle with the social strictures of high school, with their conservative families, with racial and social difference or economic precariousness while dreaming of sexual fulfillment and urban sophistication. In *Mariposa Club*, one member of their group seems to achieve all this when he runs away to Los Angeles and is sheltered by an older man. When he returns home for a short time, the others see through the fantasy to much harsher realities. Gonzalez captures the desire for mobility and the compensation of stasis for characters who are at an age when getting out of town is a major preoccupation and apparent solution to all of life's problems.

In *Breathing, in Dust* (2010), Tim Z. Hernandez tracks the seasonal movements of workers and families throughout west and into Mexico, but his twenty linked stories focus on characters who live in a Central Valley farming town he calls "Catela." In capturing the rhythms of life for the valley's underclasses, Hernandez keeps his characters in motion. His character are restless: whether they imagine a way to counter the relentless labor and scarcity in the valley, or whether they travel to another state for a harvest, or go to Mexico for dental work. Zones of contestation abound: Hernandez's characters struggle to stay in the United States; they scramble for food and shelter; they hide from the police even when guilty of no crime, they strive to keep their families together in spite of deportations, migrations, and incarcerations; and they conquer astounding odds to find a community in which to flourish. In the penultimate story, "The Eleventh Step," Tlaloc, the protagonist of many of the stories, takes a bus to LA in order to read his poems to a writer's group. The walk from the bus station to his destination is harrowing, recounted nearly step by step. The group is friendly, but the gulf between Tlaloc and the group is enormous. After the reading, while the others drive to another reading elsewhere in the vast city, he waits overnight in the station for his bus home in the morning. The story plays with concepts of distance, and the social and experiential differences between Tlaloc and the Chicano writer who hosts him as well as the spatial distances that the story enhances.

These three writers offer portraits of young adults who must negotiate the economic realities of the underclasses and their desire for access to a larger world while simultaneously feeling bound to the place, with its web of family and community relationships. Each writer insists on the importance of the everyday, on the small details of people getting by. They render the complexity of their characters' feelings about a place, one frequently imagined as somewhere one wants to be *from*, not living *in*. Their characters' attachments and sense of home come without title or deed and they are always suspect, always labeled as "foreign." As California changes demographically, and the Central Valley with it, these writers insist that readers see California's heartland as it is in the twenty-first century: a place in ecological, economic, social, and cultural crisis.

If there is a renaissance in the Great Central Valley, as Gerald Haslam claims, it is largely due to publishing houses well outside the mainstream. While the University of California Press publishes California history and has reprinted some California classics, its catalogs no longer classify literary texts as Californian. Steinbeck and Saroyan were published by major New York publishers, but the next generation of valley writers' books came out with Santa Barbara's eclectic Capra Press. University presses, particularly the University of Nevada Press, or the nonprofit Heyday publish many contemporary heartland writers. Of the many prose books mentioned here that are set in the Valley and written by Valley natives, only Muñoz is published by a trade press (Algonquin). Of the publishers, only Heyday is a California press. While there is an abundance of powerful books that provide critical views of California's past and present as they nudge readers toward a more socially, economically, and environmentally equitable future, those books must find readers without benefit of advertising campaigns or author tours. They do lead readers beyond the metropolis and toward meaningful conversations about what's at the heart of California dreaming, but they need champions.

This chapter has necessarily included only a core sample of those who have been or will be important to any history of California literature. In earlier chapters, contributors have discussed the ways identities form outside the metropolises, how power is negotiated within California's towns and smaller cities, and how people, ideas, and goods move between California's imagined centers and peripheries. Many of the writers considered earlier in this book have become identified with California's major urban centers, but often they migrated from inland California. How has their experience of those homelands, even temporary ones, affected their ideas about California? Let us recall Rob Shields' claim: "marginalized places expose the relativity of the entrenched, universalizing values of the centre, and expose the relativism of cultural identities. The small city's very mediality and peripherality predisposed it to flexible representation – and to unique ways of seeing" (217). I say we turn the conversation on its head: How would Gerald Haslam respond to Joan Didion's fleeting representations of Okies or her nostalgia for the white pioneer grandees? What kind of conversation might Greg Sarris and Anthony Barcello have about dairies and the Portuguese families who owned them? The workers they hired? What if we put African American, Asian American, Latino, Armenian American, Native American and European American writers into conversations with each other about place? By decentering the metropolis and rethinking California literature from the perspective of small towns and cities, not only do we see California more clearly, but also, we see Californians more clearly, and in conversation with each other.

CHAPTER 24

Science Fiction and Mysterious Worlds

Lynn Mie Itagaki

At the continental end of U.S. westward expansion, California has long held the imagination of a nation building a global empire, at the forefront of technological innovations, and increasing economic dominance. As the eighth largest economy in the world, California, with its myriad peoples, industries, and ecologies, has inspired the speculative fantasies of many writers, filmmakers, and, more recently, videogame designers. Their futuristic visions have influenced the architecture, city planning, and politics that shape the built environments and landscapes of California and make these settings iconic for audiences the world over. California has been the backdrop for hundreds of apocalyptic world-ending or world-beginning scenarios in science fiction, whether precipitated by nuclear fallout, alien invasion, natural disaster, viral epidemics, biochemical contamination, or civil disorder. These catastrophic futures and new world orders galvanize the deepest fears of audiences terrified of foreign invasion, religious end times, environmental collapse, urban unrest, immigration from Asia and Latin America, as well as white and black migration from the Dust Bowl and U.S. South.

The utopias and dystopias imagined for California are shaped by its particular amalgam of diverse climes, terrains, peoples, and histories. Since statehood, California has been a popular destination for Anglo-American migrants trying to practice their religious and philosophical beliefs in utopian communities. This legacy of possible futures is rooted in the very founding of California. The region was once a spiritual homeland of the Aztec people, a mythical kingdom of female Amazonian warriors, an outpost of the Spanish empire, and later a U.S. territory and the thirty-first state. In the mid-nineteenth-century, the Gold Rush brought prospectors to the state from across the United States and around the world. Turn-of-the-nineteenth-century real estate developers depicted California as a Garden of Eden. It was a place of refuge for whites after Reconstruction and for African Americans during World War II.

While some of these Californian dreams and nightmares have been captured by the naturalist Frank Norris and the Beat poet Allen Ginsberg, the possibility of utopian existence allows speculative fiction writers to explore the depths of human weakness and the unintended consequences of well-meaning practices. Often claimed to take place in California, Ray Bradbury's most famous novel *Fahrenheit 451* (1953) describes a future society in which firefighters set fires to homes rather than extinguish them. Books are made illegal as society's attempt to eradicate social and political conflicts, media entertainment is purposely mind-numbing and plotless, and public spaces such as roads are death traps filled with thrill-seeking drivers who run down pedestrians. The protagonist, Guy Montag, is a fireman whose increasing fascination with books is heightened by the insistent build-up to war. Ironically, a society without books is one without imagination or the ability to negotiate conflict effectively and avoid its own annihilation. In Octavia Butler's "The Evening and the Morning and the Night" (1987), the discovery and use of a cure-all drug for cancer and other diseases causes the descendants of those cured to become carriers of a violent illness who are ostracized and shut away in mental institutions if they don't first kill themselves and their loved ones in brutal, disfiguring ways. These cruelly hierarchized and repressive societies are cautionary tales of the utopian life for some at the expense of the many, often people of color, impoverished, enslaved, queered, weakened by environmental pollutants or medical experimentation. Writers explore the paradoxes of technological innovation and scientific advances that facilitate or enhance lifestyles yet cause environmental degradation or irrevocable biological disasters. The fantastic cures for cancer or other epidemics come with horrifying psychological side effects or create new incurable illnesses. Tremendous scientific advances also bring catastrophic unforeseen consequences – freedom and life for some entails the enslavement and suffering for everyone else. California's wide range of social, economic, and political histories and possibilities encompass these paradoxes.

Mythic States

Speculative fiction revises and often parodies the powerful, pervasive mythologies of California by providing alternative pasts and futures. The state's built environment is famous as a backdrop to its uniquely American lifestyles: car culture, Hollywood celebrity culture, and counterculture. Its world-famous amusement parks, such as Disneyland

and Universal Studios, have globally disseminated their visions of Tomorrowland and Tinseltown. Aspects of urban and suburban Californian environments look as though Hollywood set designers have staged the daily lives of residents. In his famous postmodern treatise *Simulacrum and Simulation* (1981), which inspired a generation of speculative writers, Jean Baudrillard uses Disneyland and other amusement parks in California to explain how the mimicking of real-life processes or lived environments can no longer be considered "false" or "fictional" since this mimicry is increasingly believed to be "the real" without original or referent: "Disneyland is presented as imaginary in order to make us believe that the rest is real, whereas all of Los Angeles and the America that surrounds it are no longer real, but belong to the hyperreal order and to the order of simulation."[1]

Limning the real and hyperreal, William K. Gibson founded the cyberpunk genre of science fiction with his masterpiece *Neuromancer* (1984), followed by his award-winning collection of short stories *Burning Chrome* (1986). "The Gernsback Continuum" (1986) surveys contemporary Californian and other Sun Belt landscapes psychically littered with past futuristic dreams and desires. The short story functions as an allegory for dystopic speculative fictions at the end of the twentieth century. It parodies and rejects these technological e/utopias after the genocidal horrors of Nazi totalitarianism. The main character, a photographer, is commissioned for a book-length photo-essay to detail what he calls the "ray gun gothic" architecture "of Coca-Cola plants like beached submarines and fifth-run movie houses like the temples of some lost sect that had worshiped blue mirrors and geometry."[2] He describes a West Coast landscape of Hollywood film sets merging with Art Deco, Streamline Moderne, or Googie-style buildings: "[T]hey put Ming the Merciless in charge of designing California gas stations. Favoring the architecture of his native Mongo, he cruised up and down the coast erecting ray gun emplacements in white stucco. Lots of them featured superfluous central towers ringed with those strange radiator flanges.[3] In referring back to one of the founders of modern science fiction,[4] "The Gernsback Continuum" focuses on the protagonist's increasing interactions with the "America-that-wasn't" in his encounters with long-forgotten imagined futures, what Gibson calls "semiotic ghosts": "bits of deep cultural imagery that have split off and taken on a life of their own, like the Jules Verne airships that those old Kansas farmers were always seeing."[5] The photographer finds himself simultaneously fascinated by, nostalgic for, and contemptuous of these gleaming cities of "white marble and slipstream chrome, immortal crystal and burnished bronze" that were so naively or sinisterly a part of 1930s utopic fantasies.[6]

While Gibson thinks of the futures that never came to pass, experimental poet and writer Sesshu Foster thinks of alternative pasts that result in new possibilities for the present. In *Atomik Aztex* (2005), Foster upends one of the most famous origin stories of the Americas: the Spanish army's subjugation of the Aztec empire in the sixteenth century. Instead, it is Aztec culture and civilization that has dominated the world for the past four centuries. Foster combines the gritty urban realism of low-wage, dangerous work at a meat-processing plant in east Los Angeles with an alternative 1940s past as a prominent "Aztek" official. The main character encounters an immigrant worker in the familiar present and the Aztek Zenozatli, who is assigned to the Russian front to help defeat the Nazis. Descriptions of this Aztek-ruling civilization in the present-day allows Foster to subvert the notion that the Spanish were civilized and the Aztecs barbaric. Zenozatli excoriates the inhuman apathy and entertainment spectacle with which "Europians" silently witnessed atrocities, genocides, disappearances, civil wars, and the desecration of human life: "while this happened, entire populations of Spanish-style nations went about their daily business like sleepwalkers like zombies ... conscripting leftover children .... This was the civilization those Europians [sic] sought to bring us .... this was the reality they sought to invoke upon our land ... and while it all was happening as they delivered it across the world they would have watched it replayed in movies to musical accompaniment! *Auschwitz, the Musical! Mauthausen Off-Broadway!*"[7] In an interview, Foster discussed his desire to critique the legacies of European and U.S. imperialism and its assumed advances:

> "Part of the intent of the book is to talk about the sorry state of America that almost everybody – left, right, and center – hates," Foster says. He waves one hand above the steering wheel, his gesture encompassing the miles of minimalls, the passing cars, the stench-soaked air. "Is that it?" he laughs. "That's it? That's all we get?"[8]

The unsatisfactory present is hardly a reward for the centuries of violence and human misery.

Psychological States

In his 1998 study of Los Angeles, Mike Davis identifies the "ecology of fear" that the Golden State has long evoked in its residents and the rest of the nation. As the most populous state, it is renowned or reviled for its diversity, the xenophobia of immigrant hordes, Communists, foreign corporations, and terrorists. The fears linked to the futures of California often stem from the assortment of natural disasters that periodically threaten it: landslides, earthquakes, droughts, floods, torrential rains, wildfires, and insect infestations. At the height of US–USSR tensions, nuclear catastrophe seemed imminently possible for a region with military bases, ports, and concentrations of weapons research laboratories and government contractors. In her increasingly speculative novel *Golden Days* (1986), which portrays life after a nuclear holocaust, Carolyn See adapts to the aftermath with bewilderment, rising anxiety, and resignation. When the main character's fears of nuclear war are belittled, she insists, "It's *my* view that the other fears, all those of which we have spoken, are a metaphor for my fear of nuclear war!"[9] Ray Bradbury's landmark collection, *The Martian Chronicles* (1950), also includes a brief consideration of life on earth after a nuclear holocaust. Written after Hiroshima and Nagasaki, "There Will Come Soft Rains" (1950) provides a haunting vignette of a fully automated home in Allendale, California, that continues to facilitate the routines of its former occupants until its own extinction by fire. The only testaments to the existence of this young family are their individual silhouettes vaporized against the charred side of the house, victims of one of the "ten thousand explosions ... and a rain of ashes and radioactivity."[10]

Other famous writers have taken a more tongue-in-cheek approach to the end of the world – as seen from California. Set ten years in the future, Robert Heinlein's "The Year of the Jackpot" (1952) compresses myriad scenarios for apocalypse into the economical space of one short story. Potiphar Breen and his girlfriend Meade escape a deluge of biblical proportions, the atomic bombing of Los Angeles, a cataclysmic earthquake, and Russian paratroopers. Their survivalist narrative ends at their isolated cabin in the mountains of northern California, where they watch the sun explode, calmly witnessing the end of the world. At time, Heinlein writes with irreverent humor. "This year the human race is letting down its hair, flipping its lip with a finger, and saying '*Wubba, wubba, wubba.*'"[11] For everyone except Potty, the story's ill omens are submerged in the larger cacophony of strange events that are part of the everyday life of the region. Meade experiences "Gypsy Rose syndrome," as a group of women inexplicably strip in public. The passersby, "with the self-conscious indifference to the unusual of the true Southern Californian, ... went on their various ways."[12]

L. Ron Hubbard's runaway bestseller, *Dianetics: The Modern Science of Mental Health* (1950), posited the mind as a perfect computational and memory-recall device thwarted by "engrams" or psychic scars that created "aberrant" perceptions. To become a "Clear" or unaberrated person, the "pre-clear" must work with an auditor who asks a series of questions intended to spark increasing awareness and free the mind. Foundational to the Scientology religion, Dianetics has earned sensational headlines and celebrity converts. It has also received scathing criticism from the medical establishment since its inception in 1950. The formation and institutionalization of Dianetics and Scientology is a case study for how science fiction functions akin to religious origin stories and how religious discourse has shaped science fiction. Hubbard had a long and successful career as a commercial science fiction writer. He understood that the creation of worlds and societies can often mirror the creation stories of existing religions. For Scientologists, the founding cosmogony begins 75 million years ago with a ruler named Xenu who tyrannized the 76 planets that formed the Galactic Confederation:

> To control overpopulation and solidify his power, Xenu instructed his loyal officers to capture beings of all shapes and sizes from the various planets, freeze them in a compound of alcohol and glycol and fly them by the billions to Earth ...
> The beings were deposited or chained near 10 volcanoes scattered around the planet. After hydrogen bombs were dropped on them, their thetans were captured by Xenu's forces and implanted with sexual perversion, religion and other notions to obscure their memory of what Xenu had done .... During the last 75 million years, these implanted thetans have affixed themselves by the thousands to people on Earth. Called "body thetans," they overwhelm the main thetan who resides within a person, causing confusion and internal conflict.[13]

These initially secret origin stories reserved for higher levels of Scientologists parallel the plots of other religions. They also share certain features with post-World War II science fiction, focusing on the atomic age (hydrogen bombs), extinction (aliens exiled and murdered on earth), interplanetary travel (spaceships), and quasi-alien abduction or body snatching ("body thetans" who interfere with the individual's own "mind thetan").

Other works are concerned with distinguishing between truth and falsity, reality and simulation, in the same way that Hubbard's novel explores the paranoid possibility that engrams warp the mind. In Thomas Pynchon's *The Crying of Lot 49* (1966), Oedipa Maas becomes embroiled in the mystery of her former lover's estate. With increasing paranoia, she discovers a constellation of symbols that may or may not have significance. Southern California provides the ideal backdrop to Oedipa's panicked self-questioning, as the protagonist wonders whether she suffers from paranoia or is the unwitting target of an actual conspiracy. The fictional San Narciso appears "less an identifiable city than a grouping of concepts – census tracts, special purpose bond-issue districts, shopping nuclei, all overlaid with access roads to its own freeway."[14] These indistinguishable cities roll out endlessly throughout the region. Despite their "intent to communicate,"[15] they defy Oedipa's attempt to grasp their meaning.

Ecological Disasters and Ecotopic States

California is famous for its excessive waste and superficiality – expensive and inefficient cars, overwatered lawns, McMansions, and far-flung bedroom communities. However, it has also emerged as a leader in clean energy ("cleantech") with its environmental regulations, alternative energy use, and low per-capita emissions. With its politically innovative state constitution that includes electoral recall and voter initiatives and its well-known history of utopian communities, California seems the obvious setting of so many speculative futures involving ecological utopias and dystopias.

Ernest Callenbach's *Ecotopia* (1974) details the secession of northern California, Oregon and Washington from the rest of the United States. Since its independence nineteen years earlier, the new nation is completely closed off to the rest of the world. Although the founding principle is environmental sustainability, Ecotopia is an isolated nation filled with barbarians, gun-toting women, cannibals, and totalitarians. A U.S. journalist, William Weston, is allowed to visit the capital city of San Francisco and its environs. Governmental decisions are based on factoring in the "total social cost per person." The twenty-hour work week allows for almost full employment. "Mini-cities" are connected by magnetic propulsion trains. The famous streets of San Francisco have been turned into large park-like public spaces: "Market Street, once a mighty boulevard striking through the city down to the waterfront, has become a mall planted with thousands of trees. The 'street' itself, on which electric taxis, minibuses, and delivery carts purr along, has shrunk to a two-lane affair. The remaining space, which is huge, is occupied by bicycle lanes, fountains, sculptures, kiosks, and absurd little gardens surrounded by benches."[16] Personal cars are outlawed in most urban areas, and abandoned corporate offices in downtown San Francisco have been turned into affordable living spaces.

Kim Stanley Robinson's "Three Californias" triptych examines divergent Californian futures stemming from differently organized societies and political systems. Unlike most depictions of "ecotopian" worlds, Robinson focuses on southern California, and more specifically, Orange County, a region of suburban towns wedged between Los Angeles and San Diego. *The Gold Coast* (1988) describes an exaggerated landscape of minimalls, drug use, and suburban angst. *Pacific Edge* (1990) portrays a local municipality struggling to maintain its ecological values despite foreign investment and business pressures. *The Wild Shore* (1984) is set almost two generations after a nuclear apocalypse and details a future society. The post-apocalyptic southern Californian settlement is part of a communitarian bartering society, largely isolated from other communities. There are "scavenger" threats to the north. Japanese boats patrol off the coast of California, and bullet-riddled bodies occasionally wash up onshore as a reminder of the people's circumscribed existence. Tales circulate about how bridges are blown up to keep communities apart from each other. Only a handful of survivors remember the time before the United States was decimated by nuclear war. Continuing sanctions keep the United States from regaining its military might, and destroying itself and other countries again.

Also using the first-person point-of-view of a teenaged narrator, Cynthia Kadohata depicts a 2040s United States in her novel *In the Heart of the Valley of Love* (1992). Here, the government has gone bankrupt, people are dying of cancer or people inexplicably disappear, leaving generations of orphaned children. Everyone suffers from a skin condition in which they perspire hard black pearls, a forbidding sign of their own likely premature mortality. Kadohata's future southern California is dotted with half-finished freeway overpasses, memorials to the early twenty-first century anticipation of an endlessly prospering economy and a metaphor for the curtailed American dream. Writing in the late 1980s, Kadohata plays on the immediate fears of a region hard hit by the recession and the end of the Cold War. The novel imagines the building of the I-105 Century Freeway from the Los Angeles International Airport on the coast to the inland Orange County border and the controversial Malathion sprayings in the late 1980s, which controlled the devastating fruit fly infestation that ravaged the California agricultural industry. It is difficult for the main character

Francie to maintain familial relationships, and to sustain love and hope amid such uncertainty.

Xenophobic States

The presence of sentient beings and the arrival of aliens – whether human or extraterrestrial, friend or foe – bring concerns about national security, political stability, and even racial purity to the fore as Californians confront Communism, terrorism, or other world-views deemed un-American. California has a unique history of interracial alliances and conflicts. Its location as the gateway to the Pacific and to the United States has made the state a historic crossroads for migrations from all directions and all continents. More than two hundred languages are spoken in the state, and the number of Spanish-speaking households almost equals that of English-speaking ones. The struggles over immigration and language have dominated the state's politics, often resulting in restrictions on public services for immigrants and bilingual education.

Immortalized by Ridley Scott's 1982 cinematic classic, *Blade Runner*, Philip K. Dick's novel *Do Androids Dream of Electric Sheep?* (1968) analyzed the fundamental question of what separates humanity from other life forms. Unlike the film, which is set in a polyglot, multiracial, overcrowded, dystopic Los Angeles, the novel takes place in a sparsely populated San Francisco where the sun has ceased to shine through dense clouds of radioactive fallout. In the aftermath of a nuclear war, biological life is precious. For Detective Rick Deckard, an android bounty hunter with the San Francisco Police Department, empathy separates humans from androids – near-perfect human robots who are increasingly indistinguishable from their biologically human "masters." Earth is reserved for humans and their real or electric pets. Androids returning to the planet face the death penalty. They are "retired" if they escape from colony planets. Society classes humans based on their exposure to radiation. "Regulars" are able to reproduce, "specials" are contaminated by radioactive dust and sterilized, and "chickenheads" have severe mental disabilities. Empathy is reserved for the regulars, while everyone else is shunned, hunted, or killed.

In the Los Angeles of the near future, an orange in the northern tropic pulls the southern half of the continent across the U.S.-Mexico border and into Los Angeles. An allegory for current politics over border-crossings and immigration, Karen Tei Yamashita's *The Tropic of Orange* (1997) reorients readers along a north–south axis redefining "American" to include all of the Americas beyond the United States. The interactions among Yamashita's multiracial cast of characters lead to new kinds of social relations and community-formation based on different constructions of personhood and citizenship. The novel's seven protagonists include a Japanese American homeless man who conducts city noises from downtown LA freeway overpasses, a five-hundred-year-old undocumented Latino immigrant performance artist who witnessed Columbus' first voyage to the Americas, and an ethnic Chinese immigrant from Singapore who grew up in Koreatown and speaks Chicano slang and English with a Spanish accent. *The Tropic of Orange* ends with readers wondering if the future will be chaos or a utopic world without borders. This blending of continents distorts the time and space on which nation-states depend for their global circuits of capital and narrowly imagined communities of belonging. Using a characteristic technique of magic realism, Yamashita literalizes this exploitative exchange as the performance artist Arcangel contrasts the difficulty of crossing the United States/Mexico border to the easy transference of money in and out of nations: "but his voice was swallowed up by the waves of floating paper money: pesos and dollars and reals, all floating across effortlessly – a graceful movement of free capital, at least 45 billion dollars of it, carried across by hidden and cheap labor."[17] The orange's northward journey is a powerful allegory for the global reach of U.S. economic imperialism, manifested in organs such as NAFTA and the World Bank, which have pulled immigrants and resources into the United States and devastated the economies of their debtor nations.

Carceral States

California is home to a concentration of corporations that comprise world-leading industries: agribusiness, biotech, information technologies, and clean energy. The state is also a leader in the prison industry, infamous for its high rates of incarceration for African Americans and Latinos. Despite a nationally decreasing crime rate, California's "golden gulag" of prisons marks what some researchers identify as the biggest prison-building project "in the history of the world."[18] Writers explore the effect of subsuming government objectives under corporate profit motives and supplanting social welfare aims with capitalist exploitation models. Such public–private partnerships and governmental outsourcing inspire the corporate takeover of governmental functions and public services that, for many writers, lead to fewer individual freedoms or even totalitarian regimes.

In *Lunar Braceros, 2125–2148* (2009), the twenty-first century's most powerful corporations create a new nation from the most profitable regions and divide the population between the employed and unemployed. Rosaura Sánchez and Beatrice Pita describe a world several decades after this *coup d'état* backed by multinational corporations in 2068. The United States dissolves into "Cali-Texas," which includes much of northern Mexico, the U.S. Southwest, the West Coast, Alaska, and Hawai'i. Most of the new nation's populations who were rounded up from "the streets or living mega-slums"[19] are imprisoned on twenty-first century reservations, a repressive mixture of carceral practices from the nineteenth and twentieth centuries. The novel features labor camps, apartheid, residential segregation, concentration camps, Native American reservation systems, contract labor agreements, chain gangs, chattel slavery, and unregulated medical experimentation. The corporate oligarchy opens up waste disposal sites on the moon and finds human laborers more reliable and cheaper than machines. Given these repressive conditions and the mass murder of previous crews of lunar workers, one crew agitates against the system that perpetually oppresses and even murders them in the name of profit. The epistolary novel is comprised of "nano-texts" from this group of lunar workers-turned-revolutionaries to the next generation, recording their subversive knowledge and actions in these digital recordings.

Pasadena resident Octavia Butler frequently uses the city just north of downtown Los Angeles and its environs as settings for her dystopian short stories and novels. Her multiracial protagonists and interspecies reproduce in order to survive after the earth – or the United States – has been laid waste by environmental disaster, corporate greed, epidemics, or war. Her future worlds are filled with African American or multiracial protagonists and human slaves. However, Butler's fictive communities are grounded in her belief that humanity's hierarchical nature transcends racial categories: "I don't think we will get over racial problems, because they're just one more version of dominance games."[20] In her award-winning story "Speech Sounds" (1984), a stroke-like illness decimates the world's population and divides the severely impaired from each other. Society has disintegrated because most humans have lost the ability to read, write, or speak. Those who haven't are beaten and often killed. Body language and rudimentary gestures are all that most people can use to communicate. The resulting frustration more often than not ends in violence. Society descends into chaos, as it does in the Earthseed series, the *Parable of the Sower* (1993) and *Parable of the Talents* (1998). In the first novel, a multinational conglomerate creates new forms of bondage in a contract labor force held captive within walled cities of factories and living quarters. These corporate compounds promise to protect people from surrounding violence and threats to their safety. Families are forced to band together in compounds and develop rigorous security rituals and fortifications. In the sequel *The Parable of the Talents*, the residents of small communities are forced into Christian fundamentalist camps. Even the police gets involved in human trafficking and indenturing indigents: "The Thirteenth and Fourteenth Amendments – abolishing slavery and guaranteeing citizenship rights – still exist, but they've been so weakened by custom, by Congress and the various state legislatures, and by recent Supreme Court decisions that they don't matter."[21]

Walter Mosely's *Futureland: Nine Stories of an Imminent World* (2002) is an example of the cyberpunk genre. It describes a future world in which a corporate head, Dr. Ivan Kismet, owner of MacroCode International, conducts a series of business acquisitions and mergers. Black protagonists of the future battle the half-man, half-machine CEO. His company's computerized proxy programs have replaced criminal justice systems in the name of efficiency. Individual and collective freedom can only be won through human ingenuity that uncovers the flaws and weaknesses in these totalized networks of corporate capitalism and state power. The consequences of this centralized oligarchy, or technocracy, are evident in a rigid class system that permanently separates the unemployed – and their offspring – from those aboveground in a vast underground area called Common Ground. The prison-industrial complex uses the most sophisticated technologies to terrorize and murder unwanted populations.

In Mosely's short story, "Little Brother," an allusion to George Orwell's *1984*, Frendon Blythe is recruited by Kismet's top lieutenant to test the new computerized justice program on those who cannot afford a human lawyer in Sacramento. Trials are ten to twenty minutes long, there is no backlog of cases, and "politicians [claim] that justice had become objective reality for the first time in the history of the courts."[22] As Frend attempts to outmaneuver the system, he finds that when the program is perplexed by its unanticipated emotional response, it deems the defendant guilty as the default.

The Future Happens First in California

California is the land of extremes, home to the grandest American dreams and the harbinger of national or global collapse. Theodor Adorno has argued that Los Angeles marks the end of Western civilization, though promoters of the region might disagree. The state's unique interracial history and multiracial communities have sparked fear and loathing, as well as awe and admiration, because of repressive and innovative public policies. As California goes, so goes the rest of the nation. Some mourn the waning of American global dominance, while others see it as payback for centuries of material excess and oppression. As science fiction writers posit the destruction or utopias of California within these contexts, so go the world and its imagined futures.

Notes

1. Jean Baudrillard, *Simulacra and Simulation*, trans. Sheila Faria Glaser (Ann Arbor: University of Michigan Press, 1994), 12.
2. William K. Gibson, "The Gernsback Continuum," in *Burning Chrome* (New York: Omni, 1986), 27.
3. Ibid.
4. The story's title refers back to one of the founders of modern science fiction, Hugo Gernsback, whose contributions as promoter and publisher of science fiction have been recognized with the annual Hugo award from the World Science Fiction organization.
5. Gibson, 29–30.
6. Ibid., 27.
7. Sesshu Foster, *Atomik Aztex* (San Francisco: City Lights, 2005), 16.
8. Ben Ehrenreich, "Naked Lunch: Talking Beats, Alternate History, Talking 'Isaak' Babel with Sesshu Foster," in *The Village Voice* (November 15, 2005).
9. Carolyn See, *Golden Days* (Berkeley: University of California Press, 1996), 124–125, original emphasis.
10. Ray Bradbury, "There Will Come Soft Rains," *Collier's Weekly* (May 6, 1950), 34. In *The Martian Chronicles*, Bradbury republishes this story as "August 2026: There Will Come Soft Rains" and a 1997 edition changes the date of the story to August 2057, to project the stories further into the future. The first two paragraphs identifying the specific setting – the Californian city and the nuclear bombings – are also excised in all editions of the short story collection.
11. Robert A. Heinlein, "The Year of the Jackpot," in *The End of the World*, ed. Donald A. Wollheim (New York: Ace Books, 1956), 19, original emphasis.
12. Ibid., 10.
13. Joel Sappell and Robert W. Welkos, "Defining the Theology," in *The Los Angeles Times* (June 24, 1990).
14. Thomas Pynchon, *The Crying of Lot 49* (New York: Perennial Classics, 1999), 13.
15. Ibid., 14.
16. Ernest Callenbach, *Ecotopia: The Notebooks and Reports of William Weston* (New York: Bantam Books, 1990), 12.

17. Karen Tei Yamashita, *Tropic of Orange* (Minneapolis: Coffee House Press, 1997), 200.
18. Rudman and Berthelsen quoted in Ruth Wilson Gilmore, *Golden Gulag: Prisons, Surplus, Crisis, and Opposition in Globalizing California* (Berkeley and Los Angeles: University of California Press, 2007), 5.
19. Rosaura Sánchez and Beatrice Pita, *Lunar Braceros, 2125–2148* (Califia: Calaca Press, 2009), 19.
20. Charles Brown, "Octavia E. Butler: Persistence," in *Conversations with Octavia Butler*, ed. Consuela Francis (Jackson: University Press of Mississippi, 2010), 184.
21. Octavia Butler, *Parable of the Talents* (New York: Seven Stories, 1998), 42.
22. Walter Mosely, *Futureland: Nine Stories of an Imminent Future* (New York: Warner Books, 2001), 213.

Conclusion

Blake Allmendinger

Sometimes anthologies get a bad rep.

In *The History of Normandy and of England* (1851), Sir Francis Palgrave claimed that in order to appreciate the works of medieval historians, one must first "acquire a thorough liking for them." One cannot "enjoy a landscape reflected in the fragments of a broken mirror. Excerpts, selections, pieces picked for quaintness or curiosity, pall the intellectual appetite. Elegant extracts, Anthologies, are sickly things: cut flowers have no vitality – the single growing violet lives sweetly, and lasts: the splendid bouquet decays into unsavoury trash."

The word "anthology" derives from the Greek root "*anthológ(os)*," meaning a "flower-gathering." In English, the term refers to "a collection of the flowers of verse," or a selection of excellent literary works. No editor likes to think of an anthology as a mere assortment of extracts, or – even worse – as a pile of "unsavoury trash." At the same time, no anthology can be all-inclusive. An editor chooses the most important works in a field and allows scholars a brief amount of space to discuss them.

There are many writers worth reading, in addition to those who appear in this critical survey. They include the Depression-era novelist John Fante; English satirists Aldous Huxley and Evelyn Waugh; and contemporary authors such as Janet Fitch and Mona Simpson. Other groups may not be represented because they comprise a relatively small subfield. For example, the best-known contemporary Native American writers don't reside in California. Louise Erdrich, N. Scott Momaday, Leslie Marmon Silko, and Sherman Alexie chronicle other parts of the American West.

Certain kinds of writing also receive minimal coverage. Newspapers and magazines have played important roles in the history of California. Between 1868 and 1875, San Francisco's *Overland Monthly* published many of the region's top writers, including Mark Twain, Bret Harte, Ina Coolbirth, Joaquin Miller, and Clarence King. Charles Fletcher Lummis founded *Land of Sunshine* in 1894. "Boosters" used the magazine to promote California. They lured businesses from out of state by advertising California's ideal climate and robust economy. William Randolph Hearst used his newspaper to expose the state's flaws. He transformed journalism in the late nineteenth and early twentieth centuries by denouncing political graft and social injustices in *The San Francisco Examiner*.

In the late 1890s, *Sunset* magazine served as a promotional vehicle for the Southern Pacific Railroad and its luxury passenger train, the Sunset Limited. It evolved into one of the West's most prestigious literary forums, featuring pieces by Jack London, Mary Austin, and Aimee Semple McPherson. Newspapers have also fostered the careers of California writers, introducing them to millions of readers, often before their books appeared in print. For example, *The San Francisco Chronicle* published the first four novels in Armistead Maupin's *Tales of the City* series. Some California newspapers also devote space in their book review sections to regional writers who aren't heavily promoted by the East Coast publishing industry.

Although California has inspired artists working in different media, it has seldom attracted the interest of playwrights. Certain works celebrate the California frontier, superficially analyze the state's contemporary social problems and interracial dynamics, or gleefully satirize popular culture. Examples include David Belasco's *The Girl of the Golden West* (1905), Richard Rodgers and Oscar Hammerstein II's *Flower Drum Song* (1958), Neil Simon's *California Suite* (1976), and Charles Busch's *Psycho Beach Party* (2000). However, several plays have seriously considered the state's historical legacy, and received critical acclaim, among them Sam Shepard's *True West* (1980) and Jon Robin Baitz's *Other Desert Cities* (2011).

Musicals pose an interesting question for students of California literature. Should lyrics carry the same weight as the published or spoken word? The same question applies to popular music. California is associated with numerous musical genres, including Hollywood films such as *Singin' in the Rain* (1952), which examines the transition to talkies; surf music, which romanticizes a 1960s version of beach culture; and West Coast rap, which celebrates "bling," an inner-city, material manifestation of the American dream.

Films might also be evaluated on their textual merits. Writers seldom receive credit in Hollywood, where film is perceived as a visual medium, dominated by directors and movie stars. However, classic works, such as Robert Towne's screenplay for *Chinatown* (1974), remind us that every film is built on the invisible foundation of the written word. Literary adaptations can be as useful to study as original screenplays. Adapting another writer's work requires tremendous skill, as witnessed by the disappointment we sometimes experience when one of our favorite novels is transferred to film. John Huston acknowledged the indestructible power of a well-crafted novel by adhering to the original plot and retaining most of the dialogue in his 1941 adaptation of Dashiell Hammett's *The Maltese Falcon.*

Certain theorists argue that all objects are "texts," capable of being read and interpreted. Cartographers produced maps of California, beginning in the pre-discovery period and continuing through subsequent centuries of conquest and settlement. Some of these documents can be read as mythical narratives, revealing the map-makers' superstitions regarding the New World, or illustrating European cultural bias. Others chart the history of empire, the fluctuations of war, the changing borders of a region in flux, and the process of urbanization. In recent decades, writers have represented California as a social and industrial maze that can only be navigated by someone with a proper sense of direction. Consider Oedipa's quest through the suburbs of northern California in Thomas Pynchon's *The Crying of Lot 49* (1966), the protagonist's aimless wanderings on the Los Angeles freeways in Joan Didion's *Play It as It Lays* (1970), and the disorienting magical realism in Karen Tei Yamashita's *Tropic of Orange* (1997).

Works of art offer other ways to read California. Diego Rivera's murals have a narrative as well as a visual power. The communist revolutionary painted his allegorical ode to the working-class and people of color on the wall of the San Francisco Stock Exchange. Other minority artists have created murals on concrete freeway corridors and abandoned public properties, calling attention to their peripheral place in society. Like graffiti, these displays have alternately been interpreted as works of art, as acts of vandalism, and as politically subversive forms of expression.

Advertising presents an unambiguous, upbeat assessment of California. In the early twentieth century, citrus crate labels depicted local orchards as pastoral landscapes. They seduced consumers into buying regional produce by exporting a vision of California as Eden. Later, roadside billboards became popular as more people began purchasing automobiles. During the Depression, Dorothea Lange observed the billboards lining Route 66, which ironically greeted the unemployed immigrants who came to California looking for work. It sometimes seems that everything in the state is for sale. Movie posters on the Sunset Strip drape entire buildings.

Skywriters work the coastline, advertising tequila during the summer and sending loved ones messages on Valentine's Day. Tourists visit Hollywood Boulevard, reading the sidewalks, which are imprinted with the names of their favorite entertainers.

A literary work isn't written in stone. It can morph over time, taking different narrative forms. John Rollin Ridge's *The Life and Adventures of Joaquín Murieta* (1854) is either a sympathtetic portrayal of Mexicans during the Gold Rush, or an account of Mexican gangs robbing innocent miners, depending on how one interprets it. Other versions of the story offer more specific, and sometimes conflicting, messages. MGM's *The Robin Hood of El Dorado* (1936) transforms Murieta into a Mexican version of Zorro. In 1967, Rodolfo "Corky" Gonzales recast Murieta as a spokesperson for the Chicano movement. Two years later, his epic poem was adapted into a short film by Luis Valdez.

Sometimes the spirit of a work remains intact, despite its numerous reincarnations. Raymond Chandler published *The Big Sleep* in 1939. The 1946 film adaptation, co-written by William Faulkner, adds a romantic subplot involving Humphrey Bogart and Lauren Bacall. However, it retains a noir sensibility. Chandler's masterpiece has also inspired Aaron Silverman and Molly Maguire's *The Raymond Chandler Mystery Map of Los Angeles* (1985), featuring actual locations that appear in the book; the videogame *LA Noire* (2011); and Jules Feiffer's graphic novel, *Kill My Mother* (2014). Chandler's literature has influenced generations of writers, cartographers, gamesters, and filmmakers. They have transformed his fiction into a cultural myth that is more powerful than any historical truth.

It is almost as difficult to discover the real California as it is to define what constitutes literature. *Do Androids Dream of Electric Sheep?* (1968), by Philip K. Dick, is a generic hybrid – part science fiction, part noir. Like *The Big Sleep*, it has been adapted into a film (1982), as well as a videogame (1997), both entitled *Blade Runner*. In each version of the story, a bounty hunter tracks down "replicants," or androids, who have infiltrated human society. It seems fitting that the story takes place in California. Like botoxed movie stars, the replicants are capable of simulating genuine emotions. Only the bounty hunter can tell the difference between human beings and members of the bio-engineered species. The film and videogame also replicate Dick's novel. The game acknowledges its narrative artifice by allowing players to choose one of thirteen possible endings. In one scenario, the bounty hunter is revealed to be an android, like his prey. The game shares the same setting as the film, has a parallel plot, and features character voice-overs by some of the film's performers.

Do Androids Dream of Electric Sheep? is set in a specific geographic locale – in this case, the San Francisco Bay area. (Both versions of *Blade Runner* take place in Los Angeles.) Other dystopian novels often feature a futuristic community where conformity is the norm – see Lois Lowry's *The Giver* (1993) – or a post-apocalyptic America that has been ravaged by war – witness Suzanne Collins' *The Hunger Games* trilogy (2008–10). In a utopia, regional differences are eliminated, along with racial tensions, class distinctions, and unorthodox thinking. In a dystopia, there is no nation left to divide into regions. The surviving population lives within a constricted space, sometimes monitored by a ruling power.

Regional literature isn't as popular as it used to be. Maybe it's because the concept of region isn't as relevant in the twenty-first century. We live in a global society comprised of immigrants. Due to the affordability of air travel, there are few geographically isolated areas left in the world. We all live in a virtual worldwide community linked by the Internet.

California literature creates a sense of place. The writers who inhabit that space share a regional identity. However, they also have their differences. An anthology puts those writers and their critics in conversation with one another. Over time, certain themes emerge, disappear, and resurface. Cultural attitudes shift. Stereotypes persist, even though the literature reflects an increasingly wider range of individual experience.

Early works represent California from a single perspective. A specific world is created in Native American stories, one that looks different from the frontier Richard Henry Dana encounters. Some writers fail to appreciate other cultures they observe. Others, like Helen Hunt Jackson, err on the side of compassion, depicting the Mission era less critically than Luiseño Indian Pablo Tac. More recently, writers have attempted to achieve a balance, refusing to privilege one perspective over another; focusing on the tensions among California's inhabitants. This theme appears in the protest fiction of early twentieth-century white male writers such as John Steinbeck, as well as in literature that chronicles the modern urban underclass; in stories that contrast the experiences of first- and second-generation immigrants; and in fiction that documents the intersecting lives of the state's multiracial, straight, gay, and bisexual residents.

In a state known for its diversity, this seems like a positive trend.

Bibliography

PRIMARY SOURCES

Abbott, Alysia. *Fairyland: A Memoir of My Father*. New York: Norton, 2013.
Acker, Kathy. *The Adult Life of Toulouse Lautrec*. New York: TVRT Press, 1978.
Adam, Helen. *The Queen of Crow Castle*. San Francisco: The White Rabbit Press, 1958.
  Ballads. New York: Acadia Press, 1964.
Adorno, Rolena, and Patrick Charles Pautz, eds. *The Narrative of Cabeza de Vaca, by Álvar Núñez Cabeza de Vaca*. Lincoln: University of Nebraska Press, 1999.
Allen, Donald, ed. *The New American Poetry, 1945–1960*. 1960. Berkeley: University of California Press, 1999 rpt.
Alurista, Alberto Baltazar Urista Heredia. *Floricanto en Aztlán*. 1971. Los Angeles: UCLA Chicano Studies Research Center Press, 2012 rpt.
Alvarado, Juan Bautista. *Vignettes of Early California: Childhood Reminiscences of Juan Bautista Alavarado*. San Francisco: Book Club of California, 1982.
Austin, Mary. *Stories from the Country of Lost Borders*. 1903. Edited by Marjorie Pryse. New Brunswick: Rutgers University Press, 1987 rpt.
Beckwourth, James P. *The Life and Adventures of James P. Beckwourth, Mountaineer, Scout, and Pioneer, and Chief of the Crow Nation of Indians, Written from His Own Dictation by T. D. Bonner*. 1856. Lincoln: University of Nebraska Press, 1972 rpt.
Beebe, Rose Marie, and Robert Senkewictz. *Testimonios: Early California through the Eyes of Women, 1815–1848*. Berkeley: Heyday Press and the Bancroft Library, 2006.
  eds. *Lands of Promise and Despair: Chronicles of Early California, 1535–1846*. Berkeley: Heyday Books, 2001.
  Testimonios: Early California through the Eyes of Women, 1815–1848. Berkeley: Heyday Books, 2006.
Bellamy, Dodie. *The Letters of Mina Harker*. 1998. Madison: University of Wisconsin Press, 2004 rpt.
  Cunt Norton. Los Angeles: Les Figues, 2013.
Bergon, Frank. *Jesse's Ghost*. Berkeley: Heyday, 2011.
Bertholf, Robert J., and Albert Gelpi, eds. *The Letters of Robert Duncan and Denise Levertov*. Palo Alto, CA: Stanford University Press, 2003.

Bontemps, Arna. *The Old South: "A Summer Tragedy" and Other Stories of the Thirties*. New York: Dodd, Head and Company, 1973.
  1931. God Sends Sunday. New York: Washington Square Press, 2005 rpt.
Boyle, T. C. *A Friend of the Earth*. New York: Viking, 2000.
Bradbury, Ray. *The Martian Chronicles*. Garden City, NY: Doubleday, 1950.
  Fahrenheit 451. 1953. New York: Simon & Schuster, 2013 rpt.
Bukowski, Charles. *The Days Run Away Like Wild Horses over the Hills*. Santa Barbara: Black Sparrow Press, 1969.
Bulosan, Carlos. *America Is in the Heart*. 1946. Seattle: University of Washington Press, 1973 rpt.
  On Becoming Filipino: Selected Writings of Carlos Bulosan. Philadelphia: Temple University Press, 1995.
Butler, Octavia. *Kindred*. 1979. Boston: Beacon Press, 2003 rpt.
  Parable of the Sower. 1993. New York: Warner, 2000 rpt.
  Parable of the Talents. 1998. New York: Warner, 2000 rpt.
Cabeza de Vaca, Álvar Núñez. *The Narrative of Cabeza de Vaca, by Álvar Núñez Cabeza de Vaca*. 1542. Edited and translated by Rolena Adorno and Patrick Charles Pautz.
Cain, James M. *Double Indemnity*. New York: Knopf, 1943.
  Mildred Pierce. New York: Knopf, 1941.
  The Postman Always Rings Twice. New York: Knopf, 1934.
Callenbach, Ernest. *Ecotopia: The Notebooks and Reports of William Weston*. 1975. New York: Bantam, 1990 rpt.
Carson, Rachel. *Silent Spring*. New York: Houghton Mifflin, 1963.
Carter, Jennie. *Jennie Carter: A Black Journalist of the Early West*. Edited by Eric Gardner. Jackson: University Press of Mississippi, 2007.
Carver, Raymond. *Where I'm Calling From: Selected Stories*. 1961. New York: Vintage, 1989 rpt.
Cervantes, Lorna Dee. *Emplumada*. Pittsburgh: University of Pittsburgh Press, 1981.
  From the Cables of Genocide: Poems on Love and Hunger. Houston: Arte Público Press, 1991.
Chandler, Raymond. *The Big Sleep*. New York: Knopf, 1939.
  Farewell, My Lovely. New York: Knopf, 1940.
  The Long Goodbye. London: Hamish Hamilton, 1953.
  Selected Letters of Raymond Chandler. Edited by Frank MacShane. New York: Columbia University Press, 1981.
  The Simple Art of Murder. 1950. New York: Ballantine, 1972 rpt.
Chin, Frank. *The Chickencoop Chinaman/ Year of the Dragon: Two Plays by Frank Chin*. Seattle: University of Washington Press, 1981.
  Jeffery Paul Chan and Lawson Fusao Inada, eds. *Aiiieeeee!: An Anthology of Asian-American Writers*. Washington, DC: Howard University Press, 1974.
Chrystos. *In Her I Am*. Vancouver: Press Gang Publishers, 1993.
Clappe, Louise Amelia Knapp Smith. *The Shirley Letters from the California Mines, 1851–1852*. Edited by Marlene Smith-Baranzini. Berkeley: Heyday Books, 1998.

Clyman, James. *American Frontiersman, 1792–1881*. Edited by Charles C. Camp. San Francisco: California Historical Society, 1928.

Coffey, Alvin. *Autobiography and Reminiscence of Alvin Aaron Coffey*, Mills Seminary P.O., 1901.

Coleman, Wanda. *Imagoes*. Santa Barbara: Black Sparrow Press, 1983.

Mad Dog Black Lady. Santa Barbara: Black Sparrow, 1979.

Colton, Walter. *Three Years in California*. New York: A. S. Barnes, 1850.

Dana, Richard Henry, Jr. *Two Years before the Mast*. 1840. Edited by Thomas Philbrick. New York: Penguin, 1981 rpt.

Cooper, Dennis. *Coming Attractions: An Anthology of American Poets in Their Twenties*. Los Angeles: Little Caesar Press, 1980.

de Angulo, Jaime. *Indians in Overalls*. 1950. San Francisco: City Lights Books, 1990 rpt.

The Unique Collection of Indian Tales. 1953. New York: Ballantine Books, 1974 rpt.

Delano, Alonzo. *Life on the Plains and Among the Diggings: Being Scenes and Adventures of an Overland Journey to California; with Particular Incidents of the Route, Mistakes and Sufferings of the Emigrants, the Indian Tribes, the Present and the Future of the Great West*. 1854. Rpt. as *On the Trail to the California Gold Rush*. Lincoln: University of Nebraska Press, 2005.

Dick, Philip K. *Do Androids Dream of Electric Sheep?* 1968. New York: Del Rey, 1996 rpt.

Didion, Joan. *Run River*. 1963. New York: Vintage, 1994 rpt.

Where I Was From. New York: Vintage, 2004.

Duncan, Robert. *The Collected Early Poems and Plays*. Edited by Peter Quartermain. Berkeley: University of California Press, 2012.

The Collected Later Poems and Plays. Edited by Peter Quartermain. Berkeley: University of California Press, 2014.

The Collected Essays and Other Prose. Edited by James Maynard. University of California Press, 2014.

Eaton, Edith Maude (Sui Sin Far). 1912. *Mrs. Spring Fragrance*. Edited by Hsuan Hsu. Toronto: Broadview, 2011 rpt.

Ferlinghetti, Lawrence. *A Coney Island of the Mind*. Norfolk, CT: New Directions, 1958.

Flores Magón, Ricardo. *Dreams of Freedom: A Ricardo Flores Magón Reader*. Edited by Charles Bufe and Mitchell Cowen Verter. Oakland: AK Press, 2005.

Forrest, Katherine V. *High Desert*. Tallahassee: Spinsters Ink, 2013.

Foster, Charles. *Victoria Mundi*. New York: The Smith, 1973.

Foster, Sesshu. *Atomik Aztex*. San Francisco: City Lights, 2005.

Frémont, John Charles. *The Expeditions of John Charles Frémont, Volume I, Travels from 1838 to 1844*. Edited by Donald Jackson and Mary Lee Spence. Urbana: University of Illinois Press, 1970.

The Expeditions of John Charles Frémont, Volume II, The Bear Flag Revolt and the Court-Martial. Urbana: University of Illinois Press, 1973.

French, Nora May. *The Outer Gate: The Collected Poems of Nora May French*. New York: Hippocampus Press, 2009.

Galarza, Ernesto. *Barrio Boy: The Story of a Boy's Acculturation*. Notre Dame: University of Notre Dame Press, 1971.

Garcés, Francisco Tomas Hermenegildo. *On the Trail of a Spanish Pioneer: The Diary and Itinerary of Francisco Garcés (Missionary Priest) in His Travels Through Sonora, Arizona, and California, 1775–1776*. 1900. New York: Bibliobazaar, 2009 rpt.

Gerstler, Amy. *The True Bride*. Culver City, CA: Lapis Press, 1986.

Gibbs, Mifflin Wistar. 1902. *Shadow and Light: An Autobiography*. New York: Arno Press, 1968 rpt.

Gibson, William K. "The Gernsback Continuum." In *Burning Chrome*. 1986. New York: HarperCollins, 2003 rpt.

Gilb, Dagoberto. *The Magic of Blood*. Albuquerque: University of New Mexico Press, 1993.

Gilbar, Steven, ed. *Natural State: A Literary Anthology of California Nature Writing*. Berkeley: University of California Press, 1998.

Ginsberg, Allen. "The Green Automobile." *Mattachine Review* 5.6 (June 1959): 12–15.

— *Howl*. 1956. Edited by Barry Miles. New York: Harper & Row, 1986 rpt.

Gomez, Jewelle. *The Gilda Stories*. Ithaca: Firebrand Books, 1991.

Gonzalez, Rigoberto. *Butterfly Boy: Memories of a Chicano Mariposa*. Madison: University of Wisconsin Press, 2006.

Gotanda, Philip Kan. *Fish Head Soup and Other Plays*. Seattle: University of Washington Press, 1991.

Grahn, Judy. *Edward the Dyke and Other Poems*. Oakland, CA: Women's Press Collective, 1971.

Hammett, Dashiell. *The Dain Curse*. New York: Knopf, 1929.

— *The Glass Key*. New York: Knopf, 1931.

— *The Maltese Falcon*. New York: Knopf, 1930.

— *Red Harvest*. New York: Knopf, 1929.

— *The Thin Man*. New York: Knopf, 1934.

Harte, Bret. *The Luck of Roaring Camp and Other Writings*. Edited by Gary Scharnhorst. New York: Penguin Books, 2001.

Haslam, Gerald. *The Other California: The Great Central Valley in Life and Letters*. 1990. Reno: University of Nevada Press, 1994 rpt.

Hastings, Lansford. *Emigrant's Guide to Oregon and California*. Cincinnati: George Conclin, 1845.

Heinlein, Robert A. "The Year of the Jackpot." 1959. In *The Menace from Earth*. Riversdale: Baen, 1999 rpt.

Hejinian, Lyn. *My Life*. Los Angeles: Sun & Moon, 1987.

Helper, Hinton Rowland. *The Land of Gold: Reality versus Fiction*. Baltimore: Henry Taylor, 1855.

Himes, Chester. 1945. *If He Hollers Let Him Go*. New York: Thunder Mouth Press, 1986 rpt.

The Lonely Crusade. New York: Alfred Knopf, 1947.
The Quality of Hurt. New York: Thunder Mouth Press, 1972.
Hom, Marlon K. *Songs of Gold Mountain: Cantonese Rhymes from San Francisco Chinatown.* Berkeley: University of California Press, 1992.
Hongo, Garrett Kaoru, Alan Chong Lau, and Lawson Fusao Inada. *The Buddha Bandits Down Highway 99.* Mountain View: Buddhahead Press, 1978.
Houston, Jeanne Wakatsuki. *Farewell to Manzanar.* 1973. Chicago: Ember, 2012 rpt.
Hubbard, L. Ron. *Dianetics: Evolution of a Science.* 1950. Los Angeles: Bridge, 2007 rpt.
Hughes, Langston. *The Ways of White Folks.* New York: Knopf, 1934.
Hwang, David Henry. *FOB and Other Plays.* New York: Plume, 1989.
Islas, Arturo. *Migrant Souls.* New York: William Morrow, 1989.
The Rain God. 1984. New York: Harper Perennial, 1991 rpt.
Jackson, Helen Hunt. *Ramona.* 1884. New York: Penguin, 2002 rpt.
Jeffers, Robinson. *Flagon and Apples.* Los Angeles: Grafton Publishing Company, 1912.
Selected Poetry of Robinson Jeffers. Edited by Tim Hunt. Stanford: Stanford University Press, 2001.
Tamar and Other Poems. New York: P.G. Boyle, 1942.
The Double Axe. New York: Random House, 1948.
Thomas, John. *Epopoeia and the Decay of Satire.* Los Angeles: The Red Hill Press, 1976.
The Selected Poetry and Prose of John Thomas. Venice: Raven Productions Press, 2011.
Johnson, Denis. *Already Dead: A California Gothic.* New York: HarperCollins, 1997.
Kadohata, Cynthia. *In the Heart of the Valley of Love.* 1992. Berkeley: University of California Press, 1997 rpt.
Kandel, Lenore. *The Love Book.* 1966. San Francisco: Superstition Street, 2003 rpt.
Kanellos, Nicolás, ed. *Herencia. The Anthology of Hispanic Literature of the United States.* New York: Oxford University Press, 2002.
Kang, Younghill. *The Grass Roof.* New York: Scribner's, 1931.
East Goes West: The Making of an Oriental Yankee. New York: Charles Scribner's Sons, 1937.
Kashiwagi, Hirsoshi. "Laugher and False Teeth." In *The Big Aiiieeeee!: An Anthology of Chinese American and Japanese American Literature.* Edited by Jeffery Paul Chan, Frank Chin, Lawson Fusao Inada, and Shawn Wong. New York: Meridian, 1991.
Kaufman, Bob. *Solitudes Crowded with Loneliness.* New York: New Directions, 1965.
Kerouac, Jack. *Big Sur.* New York: Farrar, Strauss and Cudahy, 1962.
The Dharma Bums. New York: Viking, 1958.
King, Clarence. 1874. *Mountaineering in the Sierra Nevada.* New York: Norton, 1935 rpt.
Kingston, Maxine Hong. *The Woman Warrior: Memoirs of a Girlhood Among Ghosts.* New York: Vintage International, 1975.

China Men. New York: Vintage International, 1977.
Kiyama, Henry (Yoshitaka). *The Four Immigrants Manga: A Japanese Experience in San Francisco, 1904–1924*. Translated by Frederik L. Schodt. Berkeley: Stone Bridge Press, 1999.
Kudaka, Geraldine. *Numerous Avalanches at the Point of Intersection*. Greenfield: Greenfield Review Press, 1978.
Kushner, Tony. *Angels in America: A Gay Fantasia on National Themes*. New York: Theatre Communications Group, 1995.
Lau, Alan Chong. *Songs for Jadina*. Greenfield: Greenfield Review Press, 1980.
Lange, Dorothea and Paul Taylor. *American Exodus*. 1940. Paris: Jean-Michel Place, 1999 rpt.
Lee, C. Y. *The Flower Drum Song*. 1957. New York: Penguin, 2002.
Lee, Mary Paik. *Quiet Odyssey: A Pioneer Korean Woman in America*. Edited by Sucheng Chang. Seattle: University of Washington Press, 1990.
Lee, Yan Phou. *When I Was a Boy in China*. Boston: Lothrop, Lee, and Shepard, 1887.
"The Chinese Must Stay." *North American Review* 148 (April 1889): 476–483.
Levine, Philip. *The Bread of Time*. New York: Knopf, 1994.
On the Edge. Iowa City: The Stone Wall Press, 1963.
London, Jack. *Jack London: Novels and Social Writings*. New York: Library of America, 1982.
Jack London: Novels and Stories. New York: Library of America, 1982.
The Valley of the Moon. Cosmopolitan. April–December, 1913.
Lord, Albert B. 1960. *The Singer of Tales*. Cambridge, MA: Harvard University Press, 2000 rpt.
Lowe, Pardee. *Father and Glorious Descendant*. Boston: Little, Brown and Company, 1944.
Leonard, Zenas. *Narrative of the Adventures of Zenas Leonard*. 1839. Lincoln: University of Nebraska Press, 1978 rpt.
Mainwaring, Daniel [writing as Geoffrey Homes]. *The Man Who Didn't Exist*. New York: Dell, 1944.
Build My Gallows High. New York: William Morrow, 1946.
Marryat, Frank. *Mountains and Molehills, or, Recollections of a Burnt Journal*. 1855. Edited by Scott R. Grau. Santa Clara, CA: Santa Clara University; Heyday Books, 2009 rpt.
Martinez, Victor. *Parrot in the Oven: Mi Vida*. New York: Rayo, HarperCollins, 1996.
Masson, Marcelle. *A Bag of Bones*. Happy Camp, CA: Naturegraph Company, 1966.
Maupin, Armistead. *The Days of Anna Madrigal*. New York: Harper, 2014.
Tales of the City. 1978. New York: Harper, 2007 rpt.
McCoy, Horace. 1935. *They Shoot Horses Don't They?* London: Serpent's Tail Classic, 2011 rpt.
1938. *I Should Have Stayed Home*. New York: Signet, 1951 rpt.
McGrath, Thomas. *Figures from a Double World*. Denver: Alan Swallow, 1955.
Letter to an Imaginary Friend. Seattle: Copper Canyon Press, 1997.

and James Boyer May. *Poetry Los Angeles* London: Villiers Publications, 1958.
McNichols, Charles L. *Crazy Weather*. New York: MacMillan, 1944.
McWilliams, Carey. *Ill Fares the Land*. Boston: Little, Brown, 1942.
Brothers Under the Skin. Boston: Little, Brown, 1943.
Prejudice: Japanese Americans: Symbol of Racial Intolerance. Boston. Little, Brown, 1944.
Southern California: An Island on the Land. New York: Duell, Sloan and Pearce, 1946.
Merriam, C. *The Dawn of the World: Myths and Tales of the Miwok Indians of California*. 1910. Lincoln: University of Nebraska Press, 1993 rpt.
Meyers, Bert. *In a Dybbuk's Raincoat: Collected Poems*. Albuquerque: University of New Mexico Press, 2007.
Miyakawa, Edward. *Tule Lake*. 1980. Victoria: Trafford, 2002 rpt.
Monette, Paul. *Borrowed Time: An AIDS Memoir*. New York: Mariner Books, 1998.
Montoya, José. "El Louie," *Aztlán: An Anthology of Mexican-American Literature*. Edited by Luis Valdez and Stan Steiner. New York: Knopf, 1972.
"La Jefita," *El Espejo (The Mirror): Selected Mexican-American Literature*. Edited by Octavio Romano. Berkeley: Quinto Sol Publications, 1969.
Moraga, Cherríe. 1983. *Loving in the War Years: Lo Que Nunca Paso por Sus Labios*. Brooklyn: South End P, 2000 rpt.
Morales, Alejandro. *The Brick People*. Houston: Arte Público Press, 1987.
Mori, Toshio. *Yokohama, California*. 1949. Seattle: University of Washington Press, 1985.
Mosley, Walter. *Devil in a Blue Dress*. New York: Norton, 1990.
Futureland: Nine Stories of Imminent Future. New York: Warner Books, 2001
Muir, John. *Nature Writings*. New York: Library of America, 1997.
Mukerji, Dhan Gopal. *Caste and Outcast*. Stanford: Stanford University Press, 2002.
Muñoz, Manuel. *The Faith Healer of Olive Avenue*. Chapel Hill: Algonquin, 2007.
What You See in the Dark. Chapel Hill: Algonquin, 2011.
Zigzagger. Chicago: Northwestern University Press, 2003.
Nanda, Aparajita. *Black California: A Literary Anthology*. Berkeley: Heyday, 2011.
Norris, Frank. 1901. *The Octopus: A Story of California*. New York: Penguin, 1986 rpt.
Okubo, Miné. *Citizen 13660*. Seattle: University of Washington Press, 1946.
Olmsted, Roger R., ed. *Scenes of Wonder & Curiosity from Hutchings' California Magazine, 1856–1861*. Berkeley: Howell-North, 1962.
Otsuka, Julie. *The Buddha in the Attic*. New York: Knopf, 2011.
Palóu, Francisco. *Historical Memoirs of New California*. Edited by Herbert Eugene Bolton. 4 vols. Berkeley: University of California Press, 1926.
Palóu's Life of Fray Junípero Serra. Translated by Maynard Geiger. Washington, DC: Academy of American Franciscan History, 1955.
Parker, Dorothy. *The New Yorker*, April 25, 1931, 91.
Parvin, Ron. *The Loneliest Road in America*. San Francisco: Chronicle Books, 1996.

Pattie, James Ohio. *The Personal Narrative*. 1831. Philadelphia: Lippincott, 1962 rpt.
Pérez, Luis. *El Coyote, the Rebel*. Houston: Arte Público Press, 2000.
Perkoff, Stuart. *Voices of the Lady: Collected Poems*. Ann Arbor: National Poetry Foundation, 1998.
Ponce, Mary Helen. *Hoyt Street: An Autobiography*. Albuquerque: University of New Mexico Press, 1993.
Pynchon, Thomas. *The Crying of Lot 49*. 1965. New York: HarperCollins, 2006 rpt.
Rechy, John. 1963. *City of Night*. New York: Grove P, 2013 rpt.
Reed, Ishmael. *Mumbo Jumbo*. 1972. New York: Scribner, 1996 rpt.
   New and Collected Poems: 1964–2006. New York: Carroll & Graf, 2006.
Rexroth, Kenneth. *Selected Poems*. Edited by Bradford Morrow. New York: New Directions, 1984.
Ridge, John Rollin. *The Life and Adventures of Joaquín Murieta, The Celebrated California Bandit*. 1854. Norman: University of Oklahoma Press, 1955 rpt.
Robinson, Kim Stanley. *The Wild Shore: Three Californias*. 1984. New York: Orb, 1995 rpt.
   The Gold Coast: Three Californias. 1988. New York: Orb, 1995 rpt.
   Pacific Edge: Three Californias. 1990. New York: Orb, 1995 rpt.
Rodriguez, Luis. *Always Running: La Vida Loca: Gang Days in L.A.* 1992. New York: Touchstone/Simon & Schuster, 2005 rpt.
   The Republic of East L.A. New York: HarperCollins, 2002.
Rodriguez, Richard. *Days of Obligation: An Argument with My Mexican Father*. New York: Viking, 1992.
Royce, Josiah. *California; from the Conquest in 1846 to the Second Vigilance Committee in San Francisco*. 1886. New York: Knopf, 1948 rpt.
Royce, Sarah. *Across the Plains: Sarah Royce's Western Narrative*. Edited by Jennifer Dawes Adkinson. Tucson: University of Arizona Press, 2009.
Ruiz de Burton, María Amparo. *The Squatter and the Don*. 1885. New York: Modern Library, 2004 rpt.
   Who Would Have Thought It? 1872. Edited by Rosaura Sánchez and Beatrice Pita. Houston: Arte Público Press, 1995 rpt.
Salas, Floyd. *Tattoo the Wicked Cross*. New York: Grove Press, 1967.
The Salton Sea. Directed by D. J. Caruso. 2002.
Sánchez, Rosaura and Beatrice Pita. *Lunar Braceros, 2125–2148*. National City, CA: Calaca Press, 2009.
Sarris, Greg. *Grand Avenue*. New York: Hyperion, 1994.
Scott, Fitzgerald, F. 1941. *The Last Tycoon: An Unfinished Novel*. New York: Collier, 1988 rpt.
See, Carolyn. 1986. *Golden Days*. Berkeley: University of California Press, 2006 rpt.
Serra, Junípero. *Writings of Junípero Serra*. Edited by Antonine Tibesar. 4 vols. Washington, DC: Academy of American Franciscan History, 1955–1965.
Sherman, Joan Rita. *Collected Black Women's Poetry. 4 vols*. New York: Oxford University Press,1988.

Sinclair, Upton. *Depression Island*. 1935. Pasadena, CA: Privately published.
  Oil! 1927. New York: Penguin, 2007 rpt.
  The Jungle. 1906. New York: Norton, 2003 rpt.
Smith, Anna Deavere. *Twilight: Los Angeles, 1992*. New York: Anchor, 1994.
Soto, Gary. *A Summer Life*. 1990. New York: Laurel-Leaf, 1991 rpt.
  The Effects of Knut Hamsun on a Fresno Boy. New York: Persea Books, 2001.
  The Elements of San Joaquin. University of Pittsburgh Press, 1977.
  Living up the Street. New York: Bantam Doubleday, 1985.
Spicer, Jack. *The Collected Books of Jack Spicer*. Edited by Robin Blaser. Santa Barbara: Black Sparrow, 1975.
  My Vocabulary Did This to Me: The Collected Poetry of Jack Spicer. Edited by Peter Gizzi and Kevin Killian. Middletown, CT: Wesleyan University Press, 2008.
Stein, Gertrude. *Everybody's Autobiography*. 1937. London: Cambridge University Press, 1993 rpt.
Steinbeck, John. *Steinbeck: A Life in Letters*. Edited by Elaine Steinbeck and Robert Wallsten. New York: Penguin Books, 2001.
  In Dubious Battle. 1936. New York: Penguin, 2006 rpt.
  The Grapes of Wrath. 1939. New York: Penguin, 1986 rpt.
Strong, William Duncan. *Aboriginal Society in Southern California*. Berkeley: University of California Press, 1929.
Sycamore, Mattilda Bernstein. *The End of San Francisco*. San Francisco: City Lights Press, 2013.
Taylor, Bayard. *Eldorado, or, Adventures in the Path of Empire: Comprising a Voyage to California, Via Panama, Life in San Francisco and Monterey, Pictures of the Gold Region, and Experiences of Mexican Travel*. 1850. Lincoln: University of Nebraska Press, 1988 rpt.
Tea, Michelle. *Valencia*. Berkeley: Seal Press, 2008.
Tervalon Jervey. *Understand This*. New York: William Morrow, 1994.
Thomas, Joyce Carol. *Bittersweet*. San Jose: Firesign Press, 1973.
Thurman, Wallace. 1929. *The Blacker the Berry*. New York: Arno Press, 1969 rpt.
Trocchi, Alexander. *Man at Leisure*. Chicago: Oneworld Classics, 2009.
Troupe, Quincy. *Watts Poets: A Book of New Poetry and Essays*. Los Angeles: House of Respect, 1968.
  Transcircularities: New and Selected Poems. Minneapolis: Coffee House Press, 2002.
Twain, Mark. *Roughing It*. 1872. Edited by Harriet Elinor Smith, et al. Berkeley: University of California Press, 1993 rpt.
Urrea, Luis. *By the Lake of Sleeping Children*. New York: Anchor, 1996.
  Into the Beautiful North. New York: Back Bay Books, 2009.
  Nobody's Son: Notes from an American Life. Tucson: University of Arizona Press, 1998.
  The Devil's Highway: A True Story. New York: Little, Brown, 2004.
Valdez, Luis. *Zoot Suit and Other Plays*. Houston: Arte Público Press, 1992.
Vallejo, Mariano Guadalupe. "Historical and Personal Memoirs Relating to Alta California." 1874. Translated by Earl R. Hewitt, 1875. 5 vols. Unpublished

testimonial, BANC MSS C-D 17, 18, 19, 20, 21. Bancroft Library, University of California at Berkeley.

Venegas, Daniel. *The Adventures of Don Chipote or, When Parrots Breast-Feed*. Translated by Ethriam Cash Brammer. Houston: Arte Público Press, 2000.

Vidal, Gore. *Myra Breckinridge*. New York: Little, Brown, 1968.

Villarreal, José Antonio. *Pocho*. New York: Doubleday, 1959.

Viramontes, Helena Maria. *The Moths*. Houston: Arte Público Press, 1985.

Under the Feet of Jesus. New York: Penguin, 1996.

West, Nathanael. *The Day of the Locust*. 1939. New York: Time, 1965 rpt.

Whalen, Philip. *The Collected Poems of Philip Whalen*. Edited by Michael Rothenberg. Lebanon, NH: Wesleyan University Press, 2007.

Williams, Shirley Anne. *Dessa Rose*. New York: William Morrow, 1986.

The Peacock Poems. Middletown: Wesleyan University Press, 1975.

Wong, Sam, et al. "An English Chinese Phrasebook," In *The Big Aiiieeeee!: An Anthology of Chinese American and Japanese American Literature*, Edited by Jeffery Paul Chan, Frank Chin, Lawson Fusao Inada, and Shawn Wong. New York: Meridian, 1991.

Wong, Jade Snow. *Fifth Chinese Daughter*. 1950. Seattle: University of Washington Press, 1989 rpt.

Wong, Shawn. *Homebase*. 1979. Seattle: University of Washington Press, 2008 rpt.

Yamamoto, Hisaye. *Seventeen Syllables and Other Stories*. 1988. New Brunswick: Rutgers University Press, 2001 rpt.

Yamashita, Karen Tei. *Tropic of Orange*. Minneapolis: Coffee House Press, 1997.

Yamauchi, Wakako. *Songs My Mother Taught Me: Stories, Plays, and Memoir*. Edited by Garrett Hongo. New York: The Feminist Press, 1994.

Young, Al. *Heaven: Collected Poems 1956–1990*. Berkeley: Creative Arts Book, 1992.

Zahn, Curtis. *American Contemporary*. New York: New Directions, 1963.

SECONDARY SOURCES

Acuña, Rodolfo. *Occupied America: A History of Chicanos*. 7th edition. New York: Pearson, 2010.

Adams, James. *The American: The Making of a New Man*. New York: Scribner's, 1943.

Aldama, Frederick Luis. *Brown on Brown: Chicano/a Representation of Gender, Sexuality and Ethnicity*. Austin: University of Texas Press, 2005.

Spilling the Beans in Chicanolandia: Conversations with Artists and Writers. Austin: University of Texas Press, 2006.

Allen, Donald. *The New American Poetry*. New York: Grove, 1960.

Allmendinger, Blake. *Imagining the African American West*. Lincoln: University of Nebraska Press, 2005.

Anderson, Kat. *Tending the Wild: Native American Knowledge and the Management of California's Natural Resources*. Berkeley: University of California Press, 2013.

Angel Island Immigration Station Foundation. "Life on Angel Island." *Angel Island Immigration Station Foundation*. http://aiisf.org/education/station-history/life-on-angel-island.

Arax, Mark. *West of the West: Dreamers, Believers, Builders, and Killers in the Golden State*. New York: Public Affairs, 2009.

— and Rick Wartzman. *The King of California: J. G. Boswell and the Making of a Secret Empire*. New York: Public Affairs, 2003.

Armstrong, Elizabeth A. *Forging Gay Identities: Organizing Sexuality in San Francisco, 1950–1994*. Chicago: University of Chicago Press, 2002.

Arthur, Anthony. *Radical Innocent: Upton Sinclair*. New York: Random House, 2006.

Atherton, Gertrude. "Why Is American Literature Bourgeois?" *North American Review* 178.570 (May 1904): 771–781.

Auerbach, Jonathan. *"Introduction" to Jack London's* The Iron Heel. New York: Penguin, 2006.

— *Male Call: Becoming Jack London*. Durham: Duke University Press, 1996.

Avila, Eric. *Popular Culture in the Age of White Flight: Fear and Fantasy in Suburban Los Angeles*. Berkeley: University of California Press, 2004.

Balfour, Bruce. "Bohemian Saturday Night." *Mattachine Review* 2.3 (April 1956): 26–27.

Banham, Reyner. *Los Angeles: The Architecture of Four Ecologies*. London: Allen Lane, 1971.

Baudrillard, Jean. *Simulacra and Simulation*. Translated by Sheila Faria Glaser. Ann Arbor: University of Michigan Press, 1994.

Beasley, Delilah. *The Negro Trail-Blazers of California*. Los Angeles: Times Mirror Printing and Binding House, 1919.

Beers, Terry. *Gunfight at Mussel Slough: Evolution of a Myth*. Berkeley: Heyday Books, 2004.

Birrell, Anne. *Chinese Mythology: An Introduction*. Baltimore: The John Hopkins University Press, 1993.

Blodgett, Peter J. *Land of Golden Dreams: California in the Gold Rush Decade, 1848–1858*. San Marino: Huntington Library, 1999.

Bolton, Herbert Eugene. *Fray Juan Crespi: Missionary Explorer on the Pacific Coast 1769–1774*. 1937. New York: AMS Press, 1978 rpt.

Booker, Matthew. "Oyster Growers and Oyster Pirates in San Francisco Bay." *Pacific Historical Review* 75.1 (February 2006): 63–88.

Boscana, Geronimo. *Chinigchinich: A Revised and Annotated Version of Alfred Robinson's Translation of Father Gerónimo Boscana's Historical Account of the Belief, Usages, Customs, and Extravagancies of the Indians of This Mission of San Juan Capistrano Called the Acagchemem Tribe*. Morongo Indian Reservation: Malki Museum Press, 1978.

Boyd, Nan Alamilla. *Wide Open Town: A History of Queer San Francisco to 1965*. Berkeley: University of California Press, 2005.

Bracher, Mark. *Literature and Social Justice: Protest Novels, Cognitive Politics, and Schema Criticism*. Austin: University of Texas Press, 2013.

Brady, Mildred Edie. "The New Cult of Sex and Anarchy." *Harper's Magazine* 194 (April 1947): 312–322.
Brady, Owen E., and Derek C. Maus, eds. *Finding a Way Home: A Critical Assessment of Walter Mosley's Fiction*. Jackson: University Press of Mississippi, 2008.
Browder, Laura. "'One Hundred Percent American': How a Slave, a Janitor, and a Former Klansman Escaped racial Categories by Becoming Indian." In *Beyond the Binary: Reconstructing Cultural Identity in a Multicultural Context*. Edited by Timothy Powell. New Jersey: Rutger's University Press, 1999.
Browning, Peter, ed. *To the Golden Shore: America Goes to California—1849*. Lafayette, CA: Great West Books, 1995.
Buell, Lawrence. *The Environmental Imagination: Thoreau, Nature Writing, and the Formation of American Culture*. Cambridge: Belknap Press of Harvard University Press, 1995.
Casanova, Pascale. *The World Republic of Letters*. Translated by M. B. DeBevoise. Cambridge: Harvard University Press, 2004.
Cassuto, Leonard, and Jeanne Campbell Reesman. *Rereading Jack London*. Stanford University Press, 1996.
Castillo, Ana. *Massacre of the Dreamers*. 2nd ed. New York: Plume, 1995.
Chan, Sucheng. *Asian Americans: An Interpretive History*. Boston: Twayne, 1991.
Cheung, King-Kok, ed. *'Seventeen Syllables': Hisaye Yamamoto*. New Brunswick: Rutgers University Press, 1994.
    ed. *An Interethnic Companion to Asian American Literature*. Cambridge University Press, 1997.
Cixous, Helene. *Rootprints: Memory and Life Writing*. New York: Routledge, 1997.
Coodley, Lauren, ed. *Land of Orange Groves and Jails: Upton Sinclair's California*. Berkeley: Heyday Press, 2004.
    Upton Sinclair: California Socialist, Celebrity Intellectual. Lincoln: University of Nebraska Press, 2013.
Coehn, Michael P. *The Pathless Way: John Muir and American Wilderness*. Madison: University of Wisconsin Press, 1984.
Curry, Jane Louise. *Back in the Beforetime*. New York: McElderry Books, 1987.
Davidson, Michael. *The San Francisco Renaissance: Poetics and Community at Mid-century*. Cambridge University Press, 1989.
Davis, Mike. *City of Quartz: Excavating the Future in Los Angeles*. New York and London: Vintage Books, 1992.
    Ecology of Fear: Los Angeles and the Imagination of Disaster. New York: Metropolitan Books; Henry Holt, 1998.
Dégh, Linda. *Folktales & Society*. Bloomington and Indianapolis: University of Indiana Press, 1969.
De la Guerra Ord, Angustias. *Occurrences in Hispanic California*. Translated and edited by Francis Price and William H. Ellison. Washington, DC: Academy of American Franciscan History, 1956.
Deverell, William. *Whitewashed Adobe: The Rise of Los Angeles and the Remaking of Its Mexican Past*. Berkeley: University of California Press, 2004.

Dick, Bruce Allen, ed. *The Critical Response to Ishmael Reed*. Westport: Greenwood, 1999.
Dickstein, Morris. *Dancing in the Dark: A Cultural History of the Great Depression* New York: Norton, 2009.
Durham, Phillip. *Down These Mean Street a Man Must Go: Raymond Chandler's Knight*. Durham: University of North Carolina Press, 1963.
Ellingham, Lewis, and Kevin Killian. *Poet Be Like God: Jack Spicer and the San Francisco Renaissance*. Hanover: Wesleyan University Press, 1998.
Everson, William. *Archetype West: The Pacific Coast as a Literary Region*. Berkeley: Oyez, 1976.
Fender, Stephen. *Plotting the Golden West: American Literature and the Rhetoric of the California Trail*. Cambridge University Press, 1981.
Fisher, Anne B. *Stories California Indians Told*. Berkeley: Parnassus, 1957.
Flamming, Douglas. *African Americans in the West*. California: ABC Clio, 2009.
"A Westerner in Search of Negroness: Region and Race in the Writing of Arna Bontemps." In *Over the Edge: Remapping the American West*. Edited by Valerie Matsumoto and Blake Allmendinger. Berkeley: University of California Press, 1999.
Francis, Consuela, ed. *Conversations with Octavia Butler*. Jackson: University Press of Mississippi, 2009.
Fregoso, Rosa Linda. *The Bronze Screen: Chicana and Chicano Film Culture*. Minneapolis: University of Minnesota Press, 1993.
French, Warren. *The San Francisco Poetry Renaissance, 1955–1960*. Boston: Twayne, 1991.
Galbraith, John Kenneth. *The Great Crash 1929*. Boston: Houghton Mifflin, 1955.
Gardner, Eric. *Unexpected Places: Relocating Nineteenth-Century African American Literature*. Jackson: University Press of Mississippi, 2009.
Garraty, John. *The Great Depression: An Inquiry into the Causes, Course, and Consequences of the Worldwide Depression of the Nineteen-Thirties as Seen by Contemporaries and in the Light of History*. New York: Harcourt Brace Jovanovich, 1986.
Geis, Deborah R., and Steven F. Kruger. *Approaching the Millennium: Essays on Angels in America*. Ann Arbor: University of Michigan Press, 1998.
Gifford, Edward W., and Gwendoline Harris Block, eds. 1930. *California Indian Nights*. Lincoln: University of Nebraska Press, 1990 rpt.
Gilmore, Ruth Wilson. *Golden Gulag: Prisons, Surplus, Crisis, and Opposition in Globalizing California*. Berkeley: University of California Press, 2007.
Glück, Robert. "Long Note on New Narrative." In *Biting the Error: Writers Explore Narrative*. Edited by Mary Burger, Robert Glück, Camille Roy, and Gail Scott. Toronto: Coach House, 2004.
Goggans, Jan. *California on the Breadlines: Dorothea Lange, Paul Taylor, and the Making of a New Deal Narrative*. Berkeley: University of California Press, 2010.
Goldstein, Laurence. *Poetry Los Angeles*. Ann Arbor: University of Michigan Press, 2014.

Goodman, Susan, and Carl Dawson. *Mary Austin and the American West*. Berkeley: University of California Press, 2008.
Gray, Timothy. *Gary Snyder and the Pacific Rim: Creating Counter Cultural Community*. Iowa City: University of Iowa Press, 2006.
Gregory, James. *American Exodus: The Dust Bowl Migration and Okie Culture in California*. New York: Oxford University Press, 1989.
Gruesz, Kirsten Silva. *Ambassadors of Culture: The Transamerican Origins of Latino Writing*. Princeton: Princeton University Press, 2002.
Haas, Lisbeth. *Conquests and Historical Identities in California, 1769–1936*. Berkeley: University of California Press, 1995.
Pablo Tac, Indigenous Scholar Writing on Luiseño Language and Colonial History. Berkeley: University of California Press, 2011.
Saints and Citizens: Indigenous Histories of Colonial Missions and Mexican California. Berkeley: University of California Press, 2014.
Hackel, Steven, ed., *Alta California: Peoples in Motion, Identities in Formation, 1769–1850*. San Marino: Huntington Library Press, 2010.
Junípero Serra: California's Founding Father. New York: Farrar Straus, and Giroux, 2013.
Hagedorn, Jessica. "Jessica Hagedorn." In *Between Worlds: Contemporary Asian American Plays*. Edited by Misha Berson. New York: Theater Communications Group, 1990.
Hamalian, Linda. *A Life of Kenneth Rexroth*. New York: Norton, 1991.
Hampton, Jerome. *Changing Bodies in the Fiction of Octavia Butler: Slaves, Aliens, and Vampires*. New York: Lexington, 2010.
Hanhardt, Christina B. *Safe Space: Gay Neighborhood History and the Politics of Violence*. Durham: Duke University Press, 2013.
Hapke, Laura. *Daughters of the Great Depression: Women, Work, and Fiction in the American 1930s*. Athens: University of Georgia Press, 1995.
Harris, Kaplan. "New Narrative and the Making of Language Poetry." *American Literature* 81.4 (December 2009): 805–832.
"The Small Press Traffic School of Dissumulation," *Jacket2* (April 2011). http://jacket2.org/article/small-press-traffic-school-dissimulation.
Haslam, Gerald. *The Other California: The Great Central Valley in Life and Letters*. Santa Barbara: Capra Press, 1990.
Heizer, Robert F. 1978. "Mythology: Regional Patterns and History of Research." In *Handbook of North American Indians* 8: 654–657. Edited by William C. Sturtevant. Washington: Smithsonian Institution, 1978.
Herms, Dieter, ed. *Upton Sinclair: Literature and Social Reform*. Frankfurt: Peter Lang, 1990.
Hernandez, Tim Z. *Breathing, In Dust*. Lubbock: Texas Tech University Press, 2010.
Hicks, Jack, ed. *The Literature of California Volume I*. Berkeley: University of California Press, 2000.
Hine, Robert, and John Faragher. *The American West: A New Interpretive History*. New Haven: Yale University Press, 2000.

Holliday, J. S. *Rush for Riches: Gold Fever and the Making of California.* Oakland and Berkeley: Oakland Museum of California and University of California Press, 1999.

The World Rushed In: The California Gold Rush Experience. New York: Simon & Schuster, 1981.

Hoopes, Roy. *Cain: The Biography of James M. Cain.* New York: Holt, 1982.

Hsu, Hsuan. "Chronotopes of the Asian American West." In *A Companion to the Literature and Culture of the American West.* Edited by Nicholas S. Witschi. Oxford: Blackwell Publishing, 2011.

Hurtado, Albert L. *Intimate Frontiers: Sex, Gender, and Culture in Old California.* Albuquerque: University of New Mexico Press, 1999.

Irwin, Lee, ed. *Native American Spirituality.* Lincoln: University of Nebraska Press, 2000.

Itagaki, Lynn M. "Transgressing Race and Community in Chester Himes's *If He Hollars Let Him Go.*" *African American Review* 37:1 (Spring, 2003): 65–80.

Jarnot, Lisa. *Robert Duncan: The Ambassador from Venus, A Biography.* Berkeley: University of California Press, 2012.

Johnson, Carolyn. *Jack London: An American Radical?* Connecticut: Greenwood Press, 1984.

Johnson, Diane. *Dashiell Hammett: A Life.* New York: Random House, 1983.

Johnson, Susan Lee. *Roaring Camp: The Social World of the California Gold Rush.* New York: Norton, 2000.

Kanellos, Nicolás, and Helvetia Martell. "A Brief History of Hispanic Periodicals in the United States." In *Hispanic Periodicals in the United States, Origins to 1960: A Brief History and Comprehensive Bibliography.* Houston: Arte Público Press, 2000.

Hispanic Immigrant Literature: El Sueño del Retorno. Austin: University of Texas Press, 2011.

A History of Hispanic Theatre in the United States: Origins to 1940. Austin: University of Texas Press, 1990.

Keeling, Richard. *Cry for Luck : Sacred Song and Speech among the Yurok, Hupa, and Karok Indians of Northwestern California.* Berkeley: University of California Press, 1992.

Knight, Brenda. *Women of the Beat Generation: The Writers, Artists and Muses at the Heart of a Revolution.* Berkeley: Conari Press, 1998.

Kowalewski, Michael, ed. *Gold Rush: A Literary Exploration.* Berkeley: Heyday Books, in conjunction with the California Council for the Humanities, 1997.

Kurutz, Gary F. *The California Gold Rush: A Descriptive Bibliography of Books and Pamphlets Covering the Years 1848–1853.* San Francisco: Book Club of California, 1997.

Labor, Earle. *Jack London: An American Life.* New York: Farrar, Straus and Giroux, 2013.

Lai, Him Mark, Genny Lim, and Judy Yung, eds. *Island: Poetry and History of Chinese Immigrants on Angel Island, 1910–1940.* Seattle: University of Washington Press, 1980.

Laird, Carobeth. *Mirror and Pattern: George Laird's World of Chemehuevi Mythology*. Banning: Malki Museum Press, 1984.

Lapp, Rudolph M. *Blacks in Gold Rush California*. New Haven: Yale University Press, 1977.

Lattimore, Richmond, ed. *The Iliad of Homer*. Chicago: University of Chicago Press, 1951.

Lawrence, Keith, and Floyd Cheung, eds. *Recovered Legacies: Authority and Identity in Early Asian American Literature*. Philadelphia: Temple University Press, 2005.

Layman, Richard. *Shadow Man: The Life of Dashiell Hammett*. New York: Harcourt, 1981.

Lee, Don. L. "About Al Young." *Ploughshares* 19.1 (1993): 219–224.

Lee, Josephine, Imogene L. Lim, and Yuko Matsukawa, eds. *Re/collecting Early Asian America: Essays in Cultural History*. Philadelphia: Temple University Press, 2002.

Lee, Robert. G. "The Cold War Origins of the Model Minority Myth." In *Orientals: Asian Americans in Popular Culture*. Philadelphia: Temple University Press, 1999.

Lee, Shelley Sang-Hee. *A New History of Asian America*. New York: Routledge, 2014.

Levine, Lawrence. *The Unforgettable Past: Exploration in American Cultural History*. New York: Oxford University Press, 1993.

Levy, JoAnn. *They Saw the Elephant: Women in the California Gold Rush*. Norman: University of Oklahoma Press, 1992.

Leyland, Winston. *Gay Roots: Twenty Years of Gay Sunshine: An Anthology of Gay History, Sex, Politics, and Culture*. San Francisco: Gay Sunshine Press, 1991.

Link, Eric Carl. *The Vast and Terrible Drama: American Literary Naturalism in the Late Nineteenth Century*. Tuscaloosa: University of Alabama Press, 2004.

Lipton, Lawrence. *The Holy Barbarians*. New York: Messner, 1959.

Oeb, Edward M. "The Creator Concept among the Indians of North Central California." *American Anthropologist* 28 (1926): 467–493.

Loftis, Anne. *Witnesses to the Struggle: Imaging the 1930s California Labor Movement*. Reno: University of Nevada Press, 1998.

Loney, Glenn, ed. *California Gold-Rush Plays*. New York: Performing Arts Journal Publications, 1983.

Luis-Brown, David. *Waves of Decolonization: Discourses of Race and Hemispheric Citizenship in Cuba, Mexico, and the United States*. Durham: Duke University Press, 2008.

Lukács, György. *History and Class Consciousness*. Translated by Rodney Livingstone. Cambridge: MIT Press, 1972.

Maciel, David R., Isidro D. Ortiz, and María Herrera-Sobek, eds. *Chicano Renaissance: Contemporary Cultural Trends*. Tucson: University of Arizona Press, 2000.

MacShane, Frank. *The Life of Raymond Chandler*. New York: Dutton, 1976.

Madden, David. *Tough Guy Writers of the Thirties*. Carbondale: Southern Illinois University Press, 1979.
Maeda, Daryl Joji. *Rethinking the Asian American Movement*. New York: Routledge, 2012.
Dashiell Hammett. Boston: Twayne, 1983.
Raymond Chandler. Boston: Twayne, 1986.
The American Roman Noir. Athens: University of Georgia Press, 1998.
Martín-Rodríguez, Manuel M. *Life in Search of Readers: Reading (in) Chicano/a Literature*. Albuquerque: University of New Mexico Press, 2003.
Maynard, John Arthur. *Venice West: The Beat Generation in Southern California*. New Brunswick: Rutgers University Press, 1991.
McClure, Michael. *Scratching the Beat Surface: Essays on New Vision from Blake to Kerouac*. New York: Penguin, 1994.
McElrath, Joseph R., Jr. *Frank Norris Revisited*. New York: Twayne, 1992.
McElrath, Joseph R., Jr., and Jesse S. Crisler. *Frank Norris: A Life*. Urbana: University of Illinois Press, 2006.
McElvaine, Robert. *The Great Depression America, 1929–1941*. New York: Three Rivers Press, 1984.
McInnis, Jarvis C. "Writing around the Edges: A Praise Song for Wanda Coleman." *Callaloo* 37.2 (2014): 189–193.
Meléndez, A. Gabriel. *Spanish-Language Newspapers in New Mexico, 1834–1958*. Tucson: University of Arizona Press, 2005.
Meltzer, David, ed. *San Francisco Beat; Talking with the Poets*. San Francisco: City Lights, 2001.
ed. *The San Francisco Poets*. New York: Ballantine, 1971.
Mimura, Glen. *Ghostlife of Third Cinema: Asian American Film and Video*. Minneapolis: University of Minnesota Press, 2009.
Mohr, Bill. *Hold Outs: The Los Angeles Poetry Renaissance 1948–1992*. Iowa City: University of Iowa Press, 2011.
Montes, Amelia María de la Luz, and Anne Elizabeth Goldman, eds. *María Amparo Ruiz de Burton: Critical and Pedagogical Perspectives*. Lincoln: University of Nebraska Press, 1987.
Morgan, Bill. *The Beat Generation in San Francisco: A Literary Tour*. San Francisco: City Lights, 2003.
I Celebrate Myself: The Somewhat Private Life of Allen Ginsberg. New York: Viking, 2006.
Morgan, Bill, and Nancy J. Peters. *Howl on Trial: The Battle for Free Expression*. San Francisco: City Lights, 2006.
Mrozowski, Daniel J. "How to Kill a Corporation: Frank Norris's *The Octopus* and the Embodiment of American Business." *Studies in American Naturalism* 6.3 (Winter 2011): 161–184.
Muñoz, Jose Esteban. *Cruising Utopia: The Then and There of Queer Futurity*. New York University Press, 2009.

Murphet, Julian. *Literature and Race in Los Angeles*. Cambridge University Press, 2001.
Murray, David. *Forked Tongues*. Bloomington: Indiana University Press, 1991.
Nash, Roderick. 1965. *Wilderness and the American Mind*. New Haven: Yale University Press, 2001 rpt.
Nicosia, Gerald. *Memory Babe: A Critical Biography of Jack Kerouac*. Berkeley: University of California Press, 1994.
Nolan, William. *Dashiell Hammett: A Casebook*, Santa Barbara: McNally & Loftin, 1969.
Novak, Estelle Gershgoren. *Poets of the Non-Existent City: Los Angeles in the McCarthy Era*. Albuquerque: University of New Mexico Press, 2002.
Nowinski, Ira. *Café Society: Poetry from San Francisco's North Beach*. San Francisco: Seefood Studios, 1978.
Nunn, Kem. *Tijuana Straits*. New York: Scribner, 2004.
O'Grady, John P. *Pilgrims to the Wild: Everett Ruess, Henry David Thoreau, John Muir, Clarence King, Mary Austin*. Salt Lake City: University of Utah Press, 1993.
Osio, Antonio María. *The History of Alta California*. Edited by Rose Marie Beebe and Robert M. Senkewicz. Madison: University of Wisconsin Press, 1996.
Padilla, Genaro M. *My History, Not Yours: The Formation of Mexican American Autobiography*. Madison: University of Wisconsin Press, 1993.
Park, Josephine. *Apparitions of Asia: Modernist Form and Asian American Poetics*. Oxford University Press, 2008.
Pearl, Monica B. *AIDS Literature and Gay Identity: The Literature of Loss*. London: Routledge, 2012.
Peeler, David. *Hope among Us Yet: Social Criticism and Social Solace in Depression America*. Athens: University of Georgia Press, 1987.
Pérez, Vincent. *Remembering the Hacienda: History and Memory in the Mexican American Southwest*. College Station: Texas A&M University Press, 2006.
Perlman, Selig. "The Anti-Chinese Agitation in California." In *History of Labour in the United States*. Edited by John R. Commons et al. New York: Macmillan, 1918.
Pfaelzer, Jean. *Driven Out: The Forgotten War against Chinese Americans*. Berkeley: University of California Press, 2008.
Porter, Kenneth. *The Negro on the American Frontier*. New York: Arno Press, 1971.
Pratt, Mary Louise. *Imperial Eyes: Travel Writing and Transculturation*. New York: Routledge, 1992.
Raskin, Jonah. *American Scream: Allen Ginsberg's* Howl *and the Making of the Beat Generation*. Berkeley: University of California Press, 2004.
  ed. *The Radical Jack London: Writings on War and Revolution*. Berkeley: University of California Press, 2008.
Ravage, John W. *Black Pioneers: Images of the Black Experience on the North American Frontier*. Salt Lake City: University of Utah Press, 1997.
Rebolledo, Diana. *Women Singing in the Snow: A Cultural Analysis of Chicana Literature*. Tucson: University of Arizona Press, 1995.

Roberts, Brian. *American Alchemy: The California Gold Rush and Middle-Class Culture*. Chapel Hill: University of North Carolina Press, 2000.
Rohrbough, Malcolm J. *Days of Gold: The California Gold Rush and the American Nation*. Berkeley: University of California Press, 1997.
Rohrich, Lutz. 1979. *Folktales & Reality*. Bloomington: University of Indiana Press, 1991 rpt.
Rooth, Anna B. "The Creation Myths of the North American Indians." *Anthropos* 52 (1957): 497–508.
Rosenus, Alan. *General M. G. Vallejo and the Advent of the Americans: A Biography*. Albuquerque: University of New Mexico Press, 1995.
Saldívar, Ramón. *Chicano Narrative: The Dialectics of Difference*. Madison: University of Wisconsin Press, 1990.
Sánchez, Rosaura. *Telling Identities: The Californio Testimonios*. Minneapolis: University of Minnesota Press, 1995.
    Beatrice Pita, and Bárbara Reyes, eds. *Nineteenth Century Californio Testimonials*. La Jolla: *Crítica* Monograph Series, 1994.
Saroyan, Aram, *Genesis Angels: The Saga of Lew Welch & The Beat Generation*. New York: Morrow, 1979.
Schrag, Peter. *California: America's High-Stakes Experiment*. Berkeley: University of California Press, 2006.
Scott, Daniel M. "Harlem Shadows: Re-Evaluating Wallace Thurman's *Blacker the Berry*." *MELUS* 29.3/4 (Fall–Winter 2004): 323–338.
Sears, James. *Behind the Mask of the Mattachine: The Hal Call Chronicles and the Early Movement for Homosexual Emancipation*. New York: Routledge, 2006.
Shillinglaw, Susan. *On Reading The Grapes of Wrath*. New York: Penguin, 2014.
Shipley, William, ed. *The Maidu Indian Myths and Stories of Hanc'Ibyjim*. Berkeley: Heyday Books, 1991.
Silliman, Ron. "The New Sentence." *Hills* 6/7 (Spring 1980): 190–217.
    The Alphabet. Tuscaloosa: University of Alabama Press, 2008.
Smethurst, James Edward. *The Black Arts Movement: Literary Nationalism in the 1960s and 1970s*. Chapel Hill: University of North Carolina Press, 2005.
Smith, Larry. *Lawrence Ferlinghetti: Poet-at-Large*. Carbondale: Southern Illinois University Press, 1983.
Smith, Michael L. *Pacific Visions: California Scientists and the Environment, 1850–1915*. New Haven: Yale University Press, 1987.
Stanley, Jerry. *Hurry Freedom*. New York: Crown, 2000.
Starr, Kevin. *Americans and the California Dream, 1850–1915*. New York: Oxford University Press, 1973.
    Endangered Dreams: The Great Depression in California. New York: Oxford University Press, 1994.
    "Introduction" to *The Octopus: A Story of California*. By Frank Norris. New York: Penguin, 1986.
Starr, Kevin, and Richard J. Orsi, eds. *Rooted in Barbarous Soil: People, Culture, and Community in Gold Rush California*. Berkeley: University of California Press, 2000.

Steiner, Michael C. *Regionalist on the Left: Radical Voices from the American West.* Norman: University of Oklahoma Press, 2013.
Strong, William Duncan. *Aboriginal Society in Southern California.* Berkeley: University of California Press, 1929.
Stryker, Susan. *Transgender History.* Berkeley: Seal Press, 2008.
Stryker, Susan, and Jim Van Buskirk, eds. *Gay by the Bay: A History of Queer Culture in the San Francisco Bay Area.* San Francisco: Chronicle Books, 1996.
Sueyoshi, Amy. *Queer Compulsions: Race, Nation, and Sexuality in the Affairs of Yone Noguchi.* Honolulu: University of Hawaii Press, 2012.
Theado, Matt, ed. *The Beats: A Literary Reference.* New York: Carroll and Graf, 2001.
Thompson, Stith. *Folk Tales Of The North American Indians.* North Dighton, MA: JG Press, 1995.
Tichi, Cecelia. "Canonizing Economic Crisis: Jack London's *The Road.*" *American Literary History* 23.1 (January 2011): 19–31.
  Civic Passions: Seven Who Launched Progressive America (and What They Teach Us). Chapel Hill: University of North Carolina Press, 2009.
  Expose and Excell: Muckraking in America, 1900/2000. Philadelphia: University of Pennsylvania Press, 2004.
Tongson, Karen. *Relocations: Queer Suburban Imaginaries.* New York University Press, 2011.
Torres, Luis A. *The World of Early Chicano Poetry: California Poetry, 1855–1881.* Encino, CA: Floricanto Press, 1994.
Vickery, Ann. *Leaving Lines of Gender: A Feminist Genealogy of Language Writing.* Hanover, NH: University Press of New England, 2000.
Walker, Franklin Dickerson. *San Francisco's Literary Frontier.* 1939. Seattle: University of Washington Press, 1969 rpt.
Walker, Melissa. *Down from the Mountaintop: Black Women's Novels in the Wake of the Civil Rights Movement, 1966–1989.* New Haven: Yale University Press, 1991.
Wallace, William J. 1978. "Comparative Literature." In *Handbook of North American Indians.* Vol. 8. Edited by William C. Sturtevant. Washington: Smithsonian Institution, 658–661.
Wartzman, Rick. *Obscene in the Extreme: The Burning and Banning of John Steinbeck's The Grapes of Wrath.* New York: Public Affairs, 2009.
Watkins, T. H. *The Great Depression: America in the 1930s.* Boston: Little Brown, 1993.
  The Hungry Years: A Narrative History of the Great Depression in America. New York: Henry Holt, 2000.
Watten, Barrett. *The Constructivist Moment: From Material Text to Cultural Practice.* Middletown, CT: Wesleyan University Press, 2003.
Wilson, Charles E. Jr., ed. *Walter Mosley: A Critical Companion.* Westport, CT: Greenwood, 2003.
Wilson, Robert. *The Explorer King: Adventure, Science, and the Great Diamond Hoax: Clarence King in the Old West.* New York: Scribners, 2006.

Witschi, Nicolas S. *Traces of Gold: California's Natural Resources and the Claim to Realism in Western American Literature*. Tuscaloosa: University of Alabama Press, 2002.
Alonzo "Old Block" Delano. Boise State University Western Writers Series. Boise, Idaho: Boise State University, 2006.
Worster, Donald. *A Passion for Nature: The Life of John Muir*. Oxford University Press, 2008.
Wyatt, David. *The Fall into Eden: Landscape and Imagination in California*. Cambridge University Press, 1986.
Five Fires: Race, Catastrophe, and the Shaping of California. Reading, MA: Addison-Wesley, 1997.

Index

1964 Wilderness Act, 346
9/11 Attacks, 318

AIDS, 11, 259, 328–329, 331–35, 337–38; (see also, HIV)
Abbott, Alysia, 259
Abbott, Steve, 259
Achumawi, 217, 222, 227, 230
Acker, Kathy, 246, 259
   The Adult Life of Toulouse Lautrec by Henri Toulouse Lautrec, 246
ACT UP, 259, 332, 337–38
Acosta, Oscar Zeta, 299–300
   Autobiography of a Brown Buffalo, 300
   Revolt of the Cockroach People, The, 300
Adams, Ansel, 98, 101
   Not Man Apart, 101
   Sierra Nevada: The John Muir Trail, 101
   Taos Pueblo, 101
   Yosemite and the Sierra Nevada, 101
Adam, Helen, 244, 252, 255
   Ballads, 255
   Queen of Crow Castle, The, 255
   San Francisco's Burning, 255
Adorno, Theodor, 262, 267, 270, 277, 382
   Minima Moralia, 262
Agee, James, 189
Ain, Gregory, 264
Ain, Josephine, 264
Alcatraz, 150, 316
Alexander, Charles, 114, 120
Alexie, Sherman, 385
Alien Land Law (California), 7, 310
Alioto-Pier, Michela, 232
Allen, Donald (editor), 249, 254, 256
   The New American Poetry, 1945–1961, 254, 256
Altamont, 243
Alurista, 296, 299
   Floricanto en Aztlán, 299
   "Et Tú…Raza?", 299
   "Tarde Sobria", 299

Alvarado, Juan Bautista, 47, 54
   Vignettes of Early California, 47
Amamix, Agapito, 32–33, 34
American Civil Liberties Union, 197, 242
American Psychological Association, 251
Anaya, Rodolfo, 296
   Bless Me, Ultima, 296
Angel Island, 7, 124
   Angel Island Poems, 125
Angelou, Maya, 273
Antin, Mary, 299
   Promised Land, The, 299
Anzaldúa, Gloria, 303, 305, 332
   Borderlands/La Frontera, 303
   This Bridge Called My Back, 332 (see also, Moraga)
Apache, 34–36
Arbuckle, Fatty, 200, 202
Arensberg, Louise and Walter, 196
Armantrout, Rae, 256, 257
Armitage, Merle, 197
Art Students' League of Los Angeles, The, 196
Asian American Theater Company, 135
Asiatic Barred Zone Act (1917), 128
Association for the Study of Literature and Environment, 353
Atherton, Gertrude, 150, 184, 359
Atlantic Monthly, 85, 89, 90, 95, 185
Austin, Mary, 7, 88, 95–98, 99, 101, 187, 190, 216, 226, 343, 359, 386
   California, Land of the Sun (With Sutton Palmer), 98
   Earth Horizon, 98
   Isidro, 98
   Lost Borders, 97
   The Flock, 97
   The Ford, 97
   The Land of Little Rain, 7, 96–97, 216, 359
Autobiography, 6, 13, 44, 48, 61, 66, 82, 98, 106, 108–10, 114, 120, 128, 129, 151, 165, 221, 257, 286, 298, 299, 300, 314, 333

Ahwahneechee/Ahwahnee, 88
Ayres, Thomas, 89
"Azotes", 260, 272
Azuela, Mariano, 148
   Los de abajo (novel), 148

Bacall, Lauren, 388
Baer, Morley, 355
   The Wilder Shore, 355 (see also, David Rains Wallace)
Baitz, Jon Robin, 386
   Other Desert Cities, 386
Balancing Water (Sierra Club Exhibit Format; Madeline Graham Blake, Tupper Ansel Blake, and William Kittredge), 355
Ballard, W.T., 199
Bancroft, Hubert Howe, 44–5, 47, 48, 57
   History of California, 44
Baraka, Amiri, 269
Barcello, Anthony, 370
Barich, Bill, 353
   Traveling Light, 353
Barker, Bonnie and Clyde, 199
Barnsdall, Alice, 196
   Hollyhock House, 196
Baudrillard, Jean, 373
   Simulacrum and Simulation, 373
Bautista de Anza, Juan, 6, 47, 52, 54
Bear Flag Revolt, 68, 70, 72
Beatniks, 231–32, 237, 239, 244
Beats, 4, 10, 231–44, 246–49, 265–69, 349, 359, 362
Beckwourth, James, 13, 82, 106–7, 108, 120
   The Life and Adventures of James P. Beckwourth, 13, 82, 106–7, 120
Belasco, David, 386
   The Girl of the Golden West, 386
Bell, James Madison, 113
   "A Poem entitled the Day and the War", 113
Bellamy, Dodie, 253, 258, 259
   Cunt Norton, 258
   Letters of Mina Harker, 258
Benjamin, Walter, 334
   Theses on the Philosophy of History, 334
Benson, Steve, 256, 258
Berg, Peter, 347
Bergon, Frank, 367
   Jesse's Ghost, 367
Berkeley Renaissance poets, 10, 236, 237, 240, 241, 242, 246, 247, 252, 255 (see also San Francisco Renaissance)
Berkman, Alexander, 196
Berman, Wallace, 265
Berrigan, Ted, 244
Bidwell, John, 69
   A Journey to California, 69

Echoes of the Past, 69
Bierce, Ambrose, 85
Bierstadt, Albert, 89
Big Brother and the Holding Company, 243
bildungsroman, 163, 285, 296, 300, 301
Bishop, Elizabeth, 271
Black Arts Movement, 258, 283–84
Black Mask (pulp magazine), 176, 199, 201, 206
Black Mountain College, 237, 240, 249, 254
Black Mountain Poets, 10, 237, 240
Black Mountain Review, 240, 241
Black Nationalism, 114, 250
Black Panther Party, 134, 316
Black Power Movement, 134, 283, 288, 317
Black Revolutionary, 283
Black Sparrow, 273
Blackfoot, 106
Blade Runner (film), 379, 388–89
Blake, William, 240
   The Marriage of Heaven and Hell, 240
Blaser, Robin, 236, 240, 252, 255
   "Image-Nation", 255
   The Holy Forest, 255
   "The Practice of the Outside," 255
Bloch, Ernst, 248, 334
   The Principle of Hope, 344
Bogart, Humphrey, 203, 388
Bolton, Herbert Eugene, 45, 57
   Fray Juan Crespi, 57
Bontemps, Arna, 114, 116
   Black Thunder, 116
   God Sends Sunday, 116
   "The Cure," 116
   "Three Pennies for Luck," 116
   "Why I Returned," 116
Boone, Bruce, 258–59
   La Fontaine, 258
Boston University, 128
Bourke-White, Margaret, 172, 173
Boyle, T.C., 2, 363
   A Friend of the Earth, 363
   The Tortilla Curtain, 2
Bracero Program, 9, 139, 218, 228
Bradbury, Ray, 372, 375
   Fahrenheit 451, 372
   The Martian Chronicles, 375
   "There Will Come Soft Rains," 375
Brand, Stewart, 349
   The Whole Earth Catalog, 349
Brautigan, Richard, 10, 350
   Trout Fishing in America, 350
Brechin, Gray and Robert Dawson, 354–55
   Farewell, Promised Dream, 354–55
Brecht, Bertolt, 10, 260, 262

Brewer, William Henry, 91
  Up and Down in California, 1860–64, 91
Bright, John, 197
Briones, Brigida, 47
Brooks, Van Wyck, 184
Broughton, James, 249
Brower, David, 346, 355
Brower, Kenneth, 356
  The Winemaker's Marsh, 356
Brown, Edmund G., 215
Brown University, 292
Bryant, Edwin, 68
  What I Saw in California, 68
Buddha Bandits Down Highway 99 (Garrett Kaoru Hongo, Alan Chong Lau, Lawson Fusao Inada), 136
Buddhism, 10, 232, 241, 244, 256, 346, 250
Bukowski, Charles, 10, 239, 269–73
  Days Run Away Like Wild Horses Over the Fields, The, 269
  "the cat," 271
  "plea to a passing maid," 270
  "Flower, First, and Bestial Wail," 269
  Post Office, 269
Bulosan, Carlos, 129, 133, 180, 187, 198, 220, 221
  America is in the Heart: A Personal History, 129, 187, 221
  "I am Not a Laughing Man," 221
  Laughter of My Father, 221
  Letter from America, 221
Burke, Kenneth, 170
Burke, Lloyd H., 242
Burke, Randolph, 184
Burroughs, William S., 231, 233, 241, 242, 252, 268
  Naked Lunch, 242
Busbee, Shirlee, 361
Busch, Charles, 386
  Psycho Beach Party, 386
Butler, Octavia, 4, 11, 289, 291, 352, 372, 381
  Kindred, 291
  Mind of My Mind, 291
  Patternmaster, 291
  "Speech Sounds," 381
  Survivor, 291
  "The Evening and the Morning and the Night," 372
  Parable of the Sower, The, 352, 381–2
  Parable of the Talents, The, 352, 381–2

Cabeza de Vaca, Alvar Núñez, 53, 55–6
  Relación, 53
Cabrillo, Juan Rodríguez, 54
Caen, Herb, 231
Cage, John, 197
Cahuilla, 17–20

Cain, James M., 9, 176, 199, 203–6
  "The Baby in the Icebox," 204
  Bar-B-Que, 204
  Double Indemnity, 205
  Mildred Pierce, 205
  Postman Always Rings Twice, The, 204–5
Caldwell, Erskine, 172–73
California Art Club, 196
California Geologic Survey, 90
California Institute of Technology (Caltech), 277
California State University
  Fresno, 228, 292, 298, 364
  Long Beach, 136
California Wilderness Act of 1984, 346
Callenbach, Ernest, 351, 377
  Ecotopia, 351, 377–78
  Ecotopia Emerging, 351–52
Camarena, Emanuel J., 8, 152, 153
  Pancho, 8, 152, 153
Camera Pictorialists of Los Angeles, The, 196
Cannery and Agricultural Works' Industrial Union (CAWIU), 174
Cannon, Steve, 285
Capone, Al, 199
Capra Press, 370
Cárdenas, Zoila Rosa, 145
Carmel-by-the-Sea, CA (Carmel, CA), 9, 97–101, 168, 174, 184, 184, 190–95, 198, 226, 261
Carmel Arts and Crafts Club, 98, 190
Caro, Brígido, 148
  Joaquín Murrieta, 148
  Mexico y Estados Unidos, 148
Carr, Lucien, 233
Carr, Robyn, 361
Carranza, Venustiano, 143
Carrigher, Sally, 344
  One Day on Beetle Rock, 344
Carrillo, Adolfo R., 7, 140–42, 143, 148, 153
  Cuentos californianos, 141, 142
  Memorias del Marqués de San Basilico, 141
  Memorias inéditas del. Lic. Don Sebastián Lerdo de Tejada, 141
Carillo, Josefa, 47
Carrillo, Eduardo A. 147
  El proceso de Aurelio Pompa, 147
  Heraclio Bernal, o El rayo de Sinaloa, 147
  Los hombres desnudos, 147
Carson, Rachel, 228, 346
  Silent Spring, 228, 346
Carter-Buckner, Eva, 112
  Gems of Poesy, 112
Carver, Raymond, 228–29
  "Furious Seasons," 228
Cassady, Neal, 233, 231
Castro, (Fidel) Era, 334

Index

Catholic Church/Catholicism, 3, 5, 31, 33, 35, 38, 40, 45, 55, 56, 57, 66, 111, 231, 312
Century Illustrated Monthly Magazine, 47
Cervantes, Lorna Dee, 297, 302–3
  Emplumada
    "Astro-no-mia," 302
    "Beneath the Shadow of the Freeway," 302
    "Cannery Town in August," 302
    "Communication," 302
    "Crow," 303
    "Freeway 280," 303
    "Poema para Los Californios Muertos," 303
    "Starfish," 303
  From the Cables of Genocide: Poems on Love and Hunger
Cervantes, Miguel de, 149
  Don Quijote, 149
Chandler, Raymond, 9, 176, 179, 199, 206–10, 224, 388
  Big Sleep, The, 207–8, 210, 388
  "Blackmailers Don't Shoot," 207
  Farewell, My Lovely, 209–10
  "Killer in the Rain," 207
  Little Sister, The, 210
  Long Goodbye, The, 210
  "The Curtain," 207
Chaplin, Charlie, 194
Chatham, Russell, 352, 353
  The Angler's Coast, 352
Chau, Angie, 313
  "Quiet as They Come," 313
Chaucer, Geoffrey, 317
  Canterbury Tales, 317
Cherokee Nation, 83
Cheyenne, 106
Chez Panisse, 353
Chicana/o movement, 8, 10, 49, 152, 296–300, 388
Chicano Renaissance, 296, 299
Chin, Frank, 135–6, 315, 316
  Aiiieeeee!: An Anthology of Asian-American Writers, 135
  Chickencoop Chinaman, The, 135
  "Come All Ye Asian American Writers of the Real and the Fake," 136
  Year of the Dragon, The, 135
Chin, Marilyn, 319
  "Monologue: Grandmother Wong's New Year Blessings," 319–20
Chinatown (film), 386
Chinese Alien Wives of American Citizens Act of 1946, 133
Chinese Exclusion Act (California), 7, 123, 124, 139
Chinese Revolution, 1949, 132
Chocano, José Santos, 145

Chrystos, 332, 333, 334, 336–7
  Fire Power
    "I Have Not Signed a Treaty With the U.S. Government," 333
  In Her I Am, 336
    "Against," 336
  Not Vanishing, 333
Chumash tribe, 5, 31, 38–41
Cisneros, Sandra, 302
  The House on Mango Street, 302
City Lights Books/Publishing, 232, 236, 241, 242, 243, 244, 321
  Pocket Poets Series, 236
Civil Rights era, 7, 10, 11, 117, 119, 123, 283, 309, 315, 316
Clean Air Act, 348
Clean Water Act, 348
Clyman, James, 6, 66–7
Coates, Paul, 239
  Confidential File, 239
Coffey, Alvin 106, 107–8
Cold War, 132–4, 228, 248, 254, 267, 378
Cole, Thomas, 89
Coleman, Wanda, 269, 272–3, 289, 290
  Imagoes, 290
    "Burglars," 291
    "South Central Los Angeles Deathtrip 1982," 291
    "The Saturday Afternoon Blues," 291
  Mad Dog Black Lady, 272
    "Where I Live," 272–3
Collier's Magazine, 185
Collins, Suzanne, 389
  The Hunger Games, 389
Colton, Walter, 6, 68
  Three Years in California, 68
Columbia University, 115, 233
Commission on Wartime Relocation and Internment of Civilians, 135
Communist Party, 186, 193, 197
Congress of Industrial Organizations (CIO), 197
Connelly, Michael, 211
conservationism, 94
Coolbrith, Ina, 85, 93–5
  Songs from the Golden Gate, 93
Cooper, Dennis, 274
  "Being Aware," 274
  Frisk, 274
Coppola, Sofia, 259
Coronel, Antonio Franco, 47
  Cosas de California, 47
Corso, Gregory, 233, 238, 243
Cortés, Hernán, 43, 52, 56
  Cartas de relación, 56
Cortez, Jayne, 272, 273

Coulette, Henri, 277
Council of Trent, 38
Creeley, Robert, 240–1, 243, 254, 266, 271
Crespi, Juan, 54, 57
Crosson Robert, 277
Crosthwaite, Luis Humberto, 306
   "La fila," 306
Crow tribe, 82, 106
Cunningham, Laura, 257
   A State of Change, 257
Cupeño, 17

Daily Alta California, 75, 80
Dagget, Rollin, 84
Dahlen, Beverley, 258
Dalí, Salvador, 306
Dame Shirley (Louise Amelia Knapp Smith Clappe), 6, 13, 62, 80, 81, 82, 86, 359
Dana, Richard Henry, 3, 6, 61–66, 71, 389
   Two Years Before the Mast, 6, 61–66
Darío, Rubén, 145
Darlington, David, 352, 353
   An Ideal Wine, 353
   Angels' Visits, 353
   In Condor Country, 352
Darwin, Charles, 158
Darwinism, 158
Dasmann, Raymond, 347
   The Destruction of California, 347
Davis, Gray, 337
Davis, Mike, 187, 262, 374
   City of Quartz, 262, 374
Davis, Miles, 286
Dawes, Casey, 361
Dawson, Fielding, 237
de Angulo, Jaime, 222, 227
   Indians in Overalls, 222
   Indian Tales, 227
de Cointet, Guy, 277
de la Cruz, Sor Juana Inés, 55
De La Guerra, Angustias, 47
   Ocurrencias en California, 47
De Quille, Dan (William Wright), 84
de Rovira, Gaspar de Portola, 54
Dean, James, 232, 243
Declaration of Korean Independence, 309
Delano, Alonzo, 78–79, 82, 84, 86
   A Live Woman in the Mines, 79
   Life on the Plains and Among the Diggings, 79, 82
   Old Block's Sketch Book, 79
   Pen Knife Sketches, or, Chips off the Old Block, 79
DeLillo, Don, 1
   White Noise, 1

Democratic National Convention, 1968 (Chicago), 239
Denishawn, 196
Detective fiction (genre), 199, 238
di Prima, Diane, 244
   Memoirs of a Beatnik, 248
Díaz, Porfirio, 51, 140, 185
Dibblee, Inés de la Guerra, 149–50, 151, 153
   Hacienda Memories and Caravans of Thoughts, 151
Dick, Philip K., 379, 388
   Do Androids Dream of Electric Sheep?, 379, 388
Dickens, Charles, 209
   Great Expectations, 209
Dickinson, Emily, 257, 302
   #1545, 302
Didion, Joan, 70, 229, 230, 360, 370, 387
   Play It as It Lays, 360, 387
   Run River, 229
   Where I Was From, 229
Dime Novel, 157
Disney Studios, 197
Disneyland, 223, 272, 373
Divakaruni, Chitra Banerjee, 317
   One Amazing Thing, 317
Dixon, Thomas, 111
   The Clansman, 111
DIY magazines, 10
Döblin, Alfred, 262
Doheny, Edward, 206, 208
Donner Party, 67, 172
Doors, The (band), 240
Dorn, Ed, 240
Donne, John, 270
   "To His Mistress Going to Bed," 270
Doyle, Arthur Conan, 199
Douglass, Frederick, 108, 113
Du, Soon Ja, 319
Duane, Daniel, 353, 362
   Caught Inside: A Surfer's Year on the California Coast, 353, 362
   Lighting Out, 353
Dunbar, Paul Lawrence, 112
Duncan, Robert, 233, 238, 248, 252, 254–55, 266, 345
   "A Description of Venice," 248
   Direct Action, 254
   Faust Foutu, 238
   H.D. Book, The, 254
   Opening of the Field, The, 254
   "Passages: Uprising," 254
   "The Homosexual in Society," 254
   "The Structure of Rime," 254
   "The Torso: Passages 18," 255
   Writing Writing, 254

Durbin, Kate, 277
  E! Entertainment, 277
Dust Bowl, 8, 171, 176, 207, 216, 301, 371
Dylan (Bob), 244

Earth Day, 348–9
Earth First!, 350
East West Players, 135
Easy Rawlins Mysteries, 287 (see Mosley, Walter)
eco-fiction, 352
Edendale, 9, 183, 184, 190, 195–8
Edson, Charles Farwell, 261
  Los Angeles: From the Sierras to the Sea, 261
Ehrlich, J.W., 242
Eigner, Larry, 254
El Clamor Público, 49–50, 260
El Congreso Nacional del Pueblo de Habla Española, 197
El Movimiento, 250, 296, 298
Eliot, T.S., 188, 262, 273
  Waste Land, 273
Ellingham, Lewis, 234
Ellis Island, 298
Ellroy, James, 211
Éluard, Paul, 248
Emerson, Ralph Waldo, 65, 70, 89, 92, 94, 236, 360
  Divinity School Address, 65
Emory University, 259
Endangered Species Act, 348
Environmental Defense Fund, 347
Environmental Protection Agency, 354
Epstein, Rob, 243
Erdrich, Louise, 385
Escalante, Esteban V., 142, 148
  La pura verdad, 148
  Las mariposas de Hollywood, 148
Eshleman, Clayton, 277
Espina, Concha, 145
Esquire (magazine), 180
Esselen (tribe), 230
Executive Order 9066, 130, 134, 218
Everson, William (né Brother Antoninus), 248–9, 250, 345
  Archetype West, 248–9

FBI, 51, 193, 272, 318
Fabilli, Mary, 248
Fantasy heritage (genre), 46, 145, 146, 150
Fante, John, 385
Far, Sui Sin (Edith Maude Eaton), 125
  Mrs. Spring Fragrance, 125
Faulkner, William, 189, 388
Feiffer, Jules, 388
  Kill My Mother, 388

Ferlinghetti, Lawrence, 231, 232, 235–8, 242–3, 249
  A Coney Island of the Mind, 243
  "Note on Poetry in San Francisco," 249
  Pictures of the Gone World, 236
Field, Sara Bard, 194
Fierro de Bright, Josefina, 197
Fitch, Janet, 385
Fitzgerald, F. Scott, 9, 175, 179–80, 189, 200
  The Great Gatsby, 200
  The Love of the Last Tycoon, 180
Flanagan, Bob, 274, 276
Flanner, Hildegarde, 345
  A Vanishing Land, 345
Fleckenstein, Louis, 196
Flint, Timothy, 6, 78
Floyd, Pretty Boy, 199
Foote, Mary Hallock, 359
Forrest, Katherine V., 331, 333
  Kate Delafield mysteries, 331
Foster, Charles, 237, 267–8, 269
  "One Man's Society Island," 267–8
Foster, Sesshu, 374
  Atomik Aztex, 374
Fox, Hugh, 277
Fradkin, Philip, 353, 356
  A River No More, 353
  Magnitude 8, 356
  The Seven States of California, 353
Franco, James, 243
Frank, Waldo, 196
Frankfurt School, 264
Fraser, Kathleen, 258
  Each Next, 258
Frazier, James, 99
  The Golden Bough, 99
Frémont, John Charles, 67, 70–2
  Memoirs, 71
  Report of the Exploring Expedition to Oregon and North California, 70
French, Nora May, 261
Fresno State (see also California State University, Fresno)
Friedman, Jeffrey, 243
Friends of the Earth, 347
Friends of the Sea Otter, 347
Frontier, 3–7, 40, 48, 82, 92, 93, 105–20, 132, 157, 161, 163, 184, 196, 225, 247, 338, 386, 389
  Black frontier, 105–20
Frumkin, Gene, 264

Gabrielinos, 260 (see also, Tongva)
Galarza, Ernesto, 228, 298–9, 300
  Barrio Boy: The Story of a Boy's Acculturation, 298–9, 300

Merchants of Labor, 228
Galbraith, John Kenneth, 171
Garbo, Greta, 194
Garcés, Francisco, 6, 45, 54, 56
   Diary and Itinerary of Francisco Garcés, 54, 56
Garcia, (Jerry), 244
Gardner, Erle Stanley, 199
Garvey, Marcus, 114
Gathering of the Tribes, 231, 243 (see Human Be-in)
Gay liberation, 10, 11, 250, 255, 257, 328–9, 338
Gay Sunshine, 251–2, 259
Genet, Jean, 252
Genthe, Arnold, 190
George, Henry, 85
German expressionism, 223
Gershwin, Ira, 197
Gerstler, Amy, 274, 276
   The True Bride, 276
Gibbs, Mifflin Wistar, 106, 108
Gibson, William K., 373–4
   Burning Chrome, 373
   "The Gernsback Continuum," 373
   Neuromancer, 373
Gilb, Dagoberto, 297, 304
   The Magic of Blood, 297, 204
Gilliam, Harold, 347
   Between the Devil and the Deep Blue Bay, 347
Ginsberg, Allen, 231–44, 247, 249, 251, 252, 259, 263, 266, 267, 345, 372
   "The Green Automobile," 251
   "Howl," 232, 234–6, 238, 240, 241–43, 244, 247, 249, 251, 263–4
   Howl and Other Poems, 231, 244
   "Supermarket in California," 235
   Wichita Vortex Sutra, 259
Glaeser, Jim, 274
Gleason, Madeline, 244, 252
Glück, Robert, 258, 259
   Jack the Modernist, 258
   La Fontaine, 258
Goethe, Johann W. von, 145
Gold Rush (California), 3, 6, 13, 45, 46, 75–86, 90, 107, 108, 110, 120, 123, 124, 142, 172, 217, 336, 371, 388
Golden Era, 80, 85
Goldman, Emma, 196
Gómez, Adolfo León, 145
Gomez, Jewelle, 334, 336
   The Gilda Stories, 336
Gone with the Wind, 115, 179
Gonzales, Rodolfo "Corky," 296, 288
   I am Joaquin, 296
González, Adalberto Elías, 147
   La asesina del martillo o la mujer tigresa, 147

La muerte de Francisco Villa, 147
Los amores de Ramona, 147
Los expatriados, 147
Los misioneros, 147
Sangre Yaqui, 147
Gonzalez, Rigoberto, 364, 368, 368
   Mariposa Club, 368
   Mariposa Gown, 368
Gotanda, Philip Kan, 135
   A Song for a Nisei Fisherman, 135
   The Avocado Kid, 135
Grafton, Sue, 211
Grahn, Judy, 255, 258
   "The Psychoanalysis of Edward the Dyke," 255, 258
Grand Piano Reading Series, 257
Grateful Dead, the, 231, 243
Gray, Judd,, 203
Great Central Valley, The (Sierra Club Exhibit Format; Robert Dawson, Gerald Haslam, Stephen Johnson), 355
Great Depression, 8, 9, 129, 139, 168, 171, 173, 174, 176, 178, 179, 180, 190, 203, 204, 205, 206, 224, 327, 385, 387
Great Recession, 337
Greeley, Horace, 77, 90
Green, Julia Boynton, 261
Greene, Charles Sumner, 194
Greenpeace, 347
Grenier, Robert, 256
Griffith, D.W., 111
   Birth of Nation, 111
Griffith Park (Los Angeles, CA), 197

HD [Hilda Doolittle], 254
HIV, 11 (see also, AIDS)
Haake, Katherine, 363
   That Water, Those Rocks, 363
Hagedorn, Jessica, 135, 310
   Gangster of Love, 310
   Mango Tango, 135
Hair (musical), 348
Halberstam, Judith, 367–8
Hammett, Dashiell, 9, 199–204, 207, 209, 210, 211, 387
   "$106,000 Blood Money," 201
   "Bodies Piled Up," 201
   "Crooked Souls," 201
   Dain Curse, The, 201
   "Dead Yellow Women"
   Glass Key, The, 203
   "It," 201
   Maltese Falcon, The, 200, 202, 203, 387
   Red Harvest, 201
   "The Big Knockover," 201

Hammett, Dashiell (cont.)
  "The Gutting of Couffignal," 201
  "The Parthian Shot," 201
  "The Second-Story Angel," 201
  Thin Man, The, 203
Hanrahan, Captain William A., 242
Hansen, Joseph, 331–3
  Dave Brandsetter, 331
Harlem Renaissance, 7, 111, 114, 116, 193
Harlins, Latasha, 319
Harper's Weekly, 77, 90
Harryman, Carla, 256
Harte, Bret, 6, 69, 84–5, 86, 90, 92, 216, 219, 359, 385
  Luck of Roaring Camp and Other Sketches, The, 85
    "Miggles," 85
    "Plain Language and Truthful James," 85
    "Tennessee's Partner," 85
    "The Outcasts of Poker Flat," 85, 359
    "Notes by Flood and Field," 69
Harvard University, 62, 65, 92, 128, 160, 351
Haslam, Gerald, 355, 364–7, 369, 370
  California's Heartland: Writing from the Great Central Valley, 364
Hasting, Lansford, 67
  The Emigrant's Guide to Oregon and California, 67
Hawthorne, Nathaniel, 76
  The Scarlet Letter, 76
Hayes, Roland, 194
Hayworth, Rita, 197
Hearst, William Randolph, 386
Hedrick, Wally, 246
Heinlein, Robert, 375
  "The Year of the Jackpot," 375
Hejinian, Lyn, 256, 257
  My Life, 257
Hell's Angels, The, 243
Helper, Hinton Rowland, 61
  The Land of Gold: Reality Versus Fiction, 61
Hernandez, Tim Z., 364, 367, 369
  Breathing, in Dust, 369
    "The Eleventh Step," 369
  Mañana Means Heaven, 364
Hetch Hetchy, 7, 95, 97, 217
Heyday Press, 351, 370
Hickman, Lee, 277 (see also *Temblor*)
Hicks, Dr. Philip, 234
Hill, Julia Butterfly, 356
  The Legacy of Luna, 356
Himes, Chester, 106, 118–20, 180
  Cast the First Stone, 119
  If He Hollers Let Him Go, 118
  Lonely Crusade, 118, 119

Primitive, The, 119
Quality of Hurt, The, 118
Third Generation, The, 119
Hiroshima (Atomic Bomb site), 375
Hoffman, John, 234–5
  Tau & Journey to the End, 234
Hollywood, 3, 9, 115, 148, 171, 172, 174, 175–80, 186, 189, 196, 197, 198, 199, 203, 204, 207, 209, 210, 224, 225, 237–8, 269, 270, 273, 274, 285, 304, 311, 321, 337, 372, 373, 386, 388
Holmes, John Clellon, 232
Holmes, Oliver Wendell, 89, 360
Hongo, Garrett Kaoru, 136
Hoover, Herbert, 171
Hoovervilles, 216
Horkheimer, Max, 262
Horn, Judge Clayton W., 243
House, Freeman, 356
  Totem Salmon, 356
House Un-American Committee (HUAC), 193, 265, 273
Houston, James D., 364
  California's Heartland: Writing from the Great Central Valley, 364
Houston, Jeanne Wakatsuki, 134
  Farewell to Manzanar, 134
Howard University (Teacher's College), 111
Howard University Press, 135
Howl (film), 243
Hubbard, L. Ron/Scientology, 4, 376
  Dianetics: The Modern Science of Mental Health, 376
Hubble, Edwin, 99
Hughes, Langston, 106, 114–6, 192–4
  Big Sea, The, 115
  Fine Clothes to the Jew, 115
  Hollywood Mammy, 115–6
  I Wonder as I Wander
  Not Without Laughter, 115
  "The Negro Artist and the Racial Mountain," 115
  Ways of White Folks, The, 192
  Weary Blues, The, 115
Hughes, Ted, 271
Human Be-In, 231, 243 (See Gathering of the Tribes)
Humboldt State University, 228
Huncke, Herbert, 231
Hurricane Katrina, 354
Hurston, Zora Neale, 193
Huston, John, 203, 387
Hutchings, James M., 80, 89
  Hutchings' California Magazine, 80, 89
  "The Miner's Ten Commandments," 80

Huxley, Aldous, 189, 197, 240, 385
　The Doors of Perception, 240
Hwang, David Henry, 135
　FOB, 135
Hypnotic Eye, The (film), 239

Iberri, Alfonso, 145
Inada, Lawson Fusao, 135, 136
Immigration Act of 1965 (Hart-Cellar Act), 123
Immigration and Naturalization Service (INS), 132
Industrial Worker (magazine), 185
Inside the Actors Studio, 239
Isherwood, Christopher, 252
Islas, Arturo, 297
　Migrant Souls, 297
　Rain God, The, 297
issei, 127, 222, 367

Jackson, Helen Hunt, 2, 6, 44, 46, 147, 222, 389
　Ramona, 2, 6, 46, 147, 222
Jaffer, Frances, 258
Japanese American Internment camps
　Arizona: Gila River, 130;
　　Poston, 130, 131, 222, 318
　Arkansas: Jerome, 130;
　　Rohwer, 130
　California: Manzanar, 130;
　　Tule Lake, 130
　Colorado: Amache, 130
　Idaho: Minidoka, 130
　Wyoming: Heart Mountain, 130
Jeffers, Robinson, 7, 69, 88, 98–101, 168, 187–88, 191–3, 194, 226, 227, 247, 343
　Cawdor, 99
　Double Axe, The, 226
　"Granite and Cypress," 188
　"Hawk and Rock," 100
　Roan Stallion, 99
　Tamar and Other Poems, 99, 226
　"The Answer," 101
Jefferson Airplane, 231, 243
Jefferson, Thomas, 53–4
Jim Crow, 117, 283
John Reed Club (Carmel, CA), 174, 193
Johnson, Denis, 363
　Already Dread, 363
　Nobody Move, 363
Johnson, President Lyndon B., 347
Johnson, Shelton, 356
　Gloryland, 356
Jones, Leroi, 266
Joplin, (Janis), 244
Journey to the West (Chinese epic), 315

Julian, C.C., 206
Jung, Karl, 99, 194

Kadohata, Cynthia, 378
　In the Heart of the Valley of Love, 378
Kammerer, David, 233
Kandel, Lenore, 231, 243, 244, 248
　"First They Slaughtered the Angels," 244
　Love Book, The, 244, 248
Kang, Younghill, 128
　East Goes West, 128
　Grass Roof, The, 128
Kantorowicz, Ernst, 236, 252
　The King's Two Bodies, 252
Kashiwagi, Hiroshi, 130
　Laughter and False Teeth, 130
Kaskabel (Benjamín Padilla), 144
Kauffman, Michael, 356
　Conifer Country, 356
Kaufman, Bob, 241, 258
　Solitudes Crowded with Loneliness, 258
Kearny Street Workshop, 135, 316
Keith, William, 93
Kennedy, Bobby, 317
Kennedy, Mary Frances, 353
　An Alphabet for Gourmets, 353
　Art of Eating, The, 353
　Story of Wine in California, The, 353
　With Bold Knife and Fork, 353
Kent, Rockwell, 197
Kenyon Review, The, 254
Kerouac, Jack, 231–6, 238, 239, 240–3, 249, 345, 346, 359
　Dharma Bums, The, 235, 345
　"Jazz of the Beat Generation," 240, 250
　Mexico City Blues, 235
　On the Road, 231, 233, 238, 242, 250
　"The Mexican Girl," 249
Kill Your Darlings (film), 233
Killian, Kevin, 234, 259
Kim, Ronyoung, 129, 309
　Clay Walls, 129, 309
Kingston, Maxine Hong, 136, 315, 316, 321, 360
　China Men, 136
　Tripmaster Monkey, 315, 316
　Woman Warrior, The, 136
Kinsey, Alfred C., 250
Kip, Leonard, 78
　California Sketches, with Recollections of the Gold Mines, 78
King, Clarence, 6, 70, 88, 90–2, 385
　Mountaineering in the Sierra Nevada, 6, 90–2
King Jr., Dr. Martin Luther, 284, 317
King, Rodney, 318, 319
King, Thomas Starr, 89

King Ubu Gallery, 234, 238
Kiyama, Henry Yoshitaka, 126
   The Four Immigrants Manga, 126
Knopf, Alfred, 201
Kropotkin, Peter, 195
Kudaka, Geraldine, 136
   Numerous Avalanches at the Point of Intersection, 136
Kushner, Tony, 327, 333–6
   Angels in America, 327, 333–6
Kyger, Joanne, 244, 255, 256
   Joanne, 256
   Tapestry and the Web, The, 256

LA Noire (videogame), 388
Lam, Andrew, 313
   "Show and Tell," 313
Lamantia, Philip, 232, 233–5, 240, 247, 248, 345
Lamott, Anne, 364
   All New People, 364
Landacre, Paul, 197
Lange, Dorothea and Paul Taylor, 9, 172, 216, 387
   An American Exodus: A Record of Human Erosion, 9, 172, 174, 216
   "Migrant Mother" (photograph), 174
Language poets, 10, 253, 256–9
Lao, Alan Chong, 136
Larsen, Marthe, 240–1
LGBT, 10, 11, 12
League of Struggle for Negro Rights, 193
Leary, Timothy, 243
LeConte, Joseph, 92
   Ramblings in the High Sierra, 92
Lerdo de Tejada, Sebastián, 141
Lee, C.Y., 133
   The Flower Drum Song, 133
Lee, Gus, 314, 321
   China Boy, 314
Lee, Mary Paik, 129
   Quiet Odyssey: A Pioneer Korean Woman in America, 129
Lee, William Poy, 314–5
   The Eighth Promise: An American Son's Tribute to His Toisanese Mother, 314–5
LeGuin, Ursula K., 352
   Always Coming Home, 352
Leite, George, 233
Leonard, Zenas, 6, 66–8
   Narrative of the Adventures of Zenas Leonard, 67
Leong, Russell C., 319, 322
   "No Bruce Lee," 319
Lester, Peter, 108–10
Levertov, Denise, 253, 254, 256, 266
Levine, Philip, 228, 230, 364
   On the Edge, 228

Levis, Larry, 364
Lewis, Sinclair, 98, 190
Librado, Fernando, 41
Life (magazine), 172, 239, 242
Lincoln, President Abraham, 71, 90, 112, 113–4, 264
Lipton, James, 239
Lipton, Lawrence, 237, 239, 267 (see also Craig Rice)
   Holy Barbarians, The, 237, 239, 267
   Rainbow at Midnight, 237
Little Caesar (magazine), 274, 276
Loeb, David, 351
   Bay Nature (magazine), 351
London, Jack, 3, 8, 69, 98, 157, 162–5, 184–6, 190, 216, 359, 360, 386
   Call of the Wild, The, 162
   Iron Heel, The, 8, 163–5, 185
   Martin Eden, 185
   People of the Abyss, The, 163
   Revolution and Other Essays, 163
   "The Mexican," 186
   Valley of the Moon, The, 185, 190
   "War of the Classes," 162
   "What Life Means to Me," 162
Long, Philomene, 237, 239
Loos, Anita, 189
Lopez, Barry, 352
   Desert Notes, 352
López de Cummings, María del Sacramento, 146
   Claudio and Anita: A Historical Romance of San Gabriel's Early Mission Days, 146
Lorenzana, Apolinaria, 47
   Memorias, 47
Los Angeles County Museum of History, Science, and Art, 196
Los Angeles Daily Express, 206
Los Angeles International Workers of the World, 196
Los Angeles Police Department (LAPD), 331
Los Angeles Radical Club, 196
Los Angeles Saturday Night, 219
Los Angeles Star/La Estrella, 260
Los Angeles State College, 265
Los Angeles Times, 1, 114, 190, 195, 219
Los Angeles Tribune, 111, 318
Los Angeles Uprising, 10, 309, 318
Lowe, Pardee, 126
   Father and Glorious Descendent, 126
Lowell, Robert, 253, 263
   Life Studies, 263
Lowry, Judith Larner, 356
   Gardening with a Wild Heart, 356
Lowry, Lois, 389
   The Giver, 389

Loy, Mryna, 203
LSD, 231
Ludlow, Fitz Hugh, 89–90
Luhan, Mabel Dodge, 194
Luiseño tribe, 5, 30, 31–7, 40, 389
Lummis, Charles, 183, 261, 385
  Land of Sunshine, 385
Lukács, György, 258

Macdonald, Ross, 199, 210, 211
MacGowan, Alice, 194
MacPhee, Chester, 242
Macpherson, Aimee Semple, 194
Mademoiselle, 236
Madgic, Bob, 356
  Shattered Air, 356
Magical realism, 380, 387
Magnuson Act of 1943, 130
Magón, Enrique, 51, 144
Magón, Ricardo Flores, 51, 144–5, 153, 185, 195–6
  "El deber del revolucionario," 144
  "¡Fuera la propiedad individual!," 144
  "La revolución agraria," 144
  Regeneración, 51, 144, 195–6
  Revolución, 144
Maidu, 22
Mainwaring, Daniel, 224
  Build My Gallows High, 224
  Man Who Didn't Exist, The, 224
  Man Who Killed Goliath, The, 224
Malanga, Gerald, 252, 275
Mann, Thomas, 10, 262
Manroot (magazine), 255
Manzarek, Ray, 240, 243
Margolin, Malcolm, 351
  Bay Nature, 351
  East Bay Out, The, 351
  News from Native California, The, 351
  Ohlone Way, The, 351
  Way We Lived, The, 351
Margolis, William, 242, 268
  The Miscellaneous Man, 242
Mariah, Paul, 255
Marine Animal Protection Act (1972), 347
Markharm, Edwin, 161
  "The Man with a Hoe," 161
Marlowe, Christopher, 268
  "The Passionate Shepherd to his Love," 268–9
Marshall, James, 76
Marshall, Paule, 290
  Brown Girl, Brownstones, 290
Martí, José, 47
Martin, Peter, 236
Martínez Rendón, Miguel D., 145

Martinez, Victor, 300
  Parrot in the Oven: Mi Vida, 300
Marx Brothers, the, 178
Marx, Groucho, 239
  You Bet Your Life, 239
Marx, Karl, 178, 267
Marxism, 51, 258
Masumoto, David Mas, 353–4
  Epitaph for a Peach, 354
  Four Seasons in Five Senses, 354
  Harvest Son, 354
  Wisdoms of the Last Farmer, 354
Mather, Margarethe, 196
Mattachine Review, The, 250–2
Mattachine Society, 250, 253
Maupin, Armistead, 329–39, 386
  Babycakes, 331
  Days of Anna Madrigal, The, 339
  Michael Tolliver Lives, 338
  More Tales of the City, 329
  Sure of You, 331
  Tales of the City, 329, 331, 386
May, James Boyer, 264
Mayakovsky, Vladimir, 270
Maynard, John Arthur, 239, 267
  Venice West: The Beat Generation in Southern California, 239
McCarran-Walter Act of 1950, 132
McCarthy era, 10, 261–2, 331
McCarthy, Senator Joseph, 345
McCloskey, Representative Paul ("Pete"), 348
McClure, Joanna, 244
McClure, Michael, 231, 232, 234–6, 241, 243, 244, 247, 248, 249
  Beard, The, 244, 248
  "For the Death of 100 Whales," 235
  "Night Words: The Ravishing," 235
  "Poem," 235
  Poetry as a Muscular Principle, 248
  "Point Lobos: Animism," 235
McCoy, Horace, 9, 175–6, 179, 180, 199
  I Should Have Stayed Home, 175
  They Shoot Horses, Don't They?, 175
McDaniel, Hattie, 115
McDaniel, Wilma (Okie Poet Laureate), 177–8, 365, 367
  "No Girl Could Ever Be Young Again," 178
  "Picking Grapes 1937," 177–8
McGettigan, Francisca Vallejo, 149–51, 153
  Along the Highway of the King, 150
  Padres, Gringoes and Gold, 150
  San Francisco Souvenir, 150
McGrath, Thomas, 262–4
  "Fantastic Gentry Wakes Up Dead," 262
  Figures from a Double World, 262

McGrath, Thomas, (cont.)
    Letter to an Imaginary Friend, 263
    "Marsh Street Irregulars," 264
McGroarty, John S., 46, 146
    The Mission Play, 46
McIntosh, Ralph, 242
McKay, Claude, 193
McNichols, Charles L., 222
    Crazy Weather, 222
McWilliams, Carey, 9, 46, 53, 172, 187, 196–8, 215, 216, 218–9, 227–8
    Brothers Under the Skin, 219
    Factories in the Fields, 9, 172, 187, 215, 216, 219
    Ill Fares the Land, 219
    North from Mexico, 46
    Prejudice: Japanese Americans: Symbol of Racial Intolerance, 219
    Southern California: An Island on the Land, 215
    You Have Seen Their Faces, 172
Mead, Taylor, 252
Mencken, H.L., 201, 219
Messerli, Douglas, 227
MGM (Metro-Goldwyn-Mayer), 180, 203, 388
Mexican Revolution, 8, 51, 52, 139, 142, 144, 146, 148, 151, 185, 186, 196, 197, 300
Mexican-American War, 4, 6, 71, 83, 105
Meyers, Bert, 264
Mezzofanti, Cardinal Giuseppe, 33, 36
Miles, Josephine, 236, 244, 249, 345
Miller, Cincinnatus H. ("Joaquin"), 82, 92–3, 126, 385
    Songs of the Sierras, 93
    Songs of the Sun-Lands, 93
Miller, Henry, 233, 238, 345, 362
    Big Sur and the Oranges of Hieronymus Bosch, 345
Minh, Ho Chi, 132
Miranda, Deborah, 230
    Bad Indians, 230
Mirikitani, Janice, 136
    Awake in the River, 136
Mirror of the Times, 80, 109
Miwok, 25, 217
Miyakawa, Edward, 134
    Tule Lake, 134
Modernism (literary movement), 173, 182–98, 248
Modoc, 9, 218, 222
Mohr, Bill (*Momentum* Press), 277
Mojave (tribe), 222–3
Momaday, N. Scott, 385
Moncaleano, Blanca de, 145, 153
    Pluma Roja, 145
Monette, Paul, 331, 334
    Afterlife, 334
    Borrowed Time, 331

Mono, 26
Monterey Pop Festival, 243
Montoya, José, 299
    "El Louie," 299
    "La Jefita," 299
Moraff, Barbara, 244
Moraga, Cherríe, 332, 339
    A Xicana Codex of Changing Consciousness, 339
    This Bridge Called My Back, 332 (see also, Anzaldúa)
Morales, Alejandro, 297
    The Brick People, 297
More, Sir Thomas, 328
    Utopia, 328
Mori, Toshio, 130, 180
    Yokohama, CA, 130
    "Tomorrow is Coming, Children," 130
Morris, William, 99
Morrison, Jim, 240
Morrison, Toni, 106, 290
    The Bluest Eye, 290
Mosley, Walter, 287, 288, 382
    Devil in a Blue Dress, 287
    Futureland: Nine Stories of an Imminent World, 382
    "Little Brother," 382
Muir, John, 6, 85–6, 88, 92–7, 99, 101, 187, 343, 359
    A Thousand-Mile Walk to the Gulf, 95
    Mountains of California, The, 86, 93
    My First Summer in the Sierra, 94–5, 97, 359
    Our National Parks, 94
    Picturesque California, 93, 96
    Stickeen, 95
    Story of My Boyhood and Youth, The, 95
    Travels in Alaska, 95
Mukerji, Dhan Gopal, 127–8
    Caste and Outcast, 128
Muller, Marcia, 361
    Burn Out, 361
Muñoz, Gabriel Trujillo, 230
Muñoz, Jose, 328–9, 335, 339
Muñoz, Manuel, 364, 367, 368, 370
    Faith Healer of Olive Avenue, The, 367
    What You See in the Dark, 367
    Zigzagger, 367
Munson's Business College, 200
Murao, Shigeyoshi, 242
Murieta/Murrieta, Joaquín, 6, 82–3, 142, 359, 388
Murray, Yxta Maya, 305
    Locas, 305

NAFTA (North American Free Trade Agreement), 296, 380
NASA, 349

Index

Nagasaki (Atomic Bomb site), 375
Narco-corridos, 303
Nathan, George Jean, 201
Nation (magazine), 219, 253
National Association for the Advancement of Colored People (NAACP), 112, 114, 116
National Book Award, 136, 292, 300, 349
National Environmental Policy Act (1969), 347
National Resources Defense Council, 347
National Wild and Scenic Rivers Act (1968), 347
Native American Renaissance, 11
Naturalism (literary movement), 69, 164, 216
Nava, Domingo N., 145
Nava, Michael, 331
   Henry Rios, 331
Navarro, Gabriel, 148
   Alma Yaqui, 148
   Cuando entraron los dorados, 148
   El precio de Hollywood, 148
   Los emigrados, 148
Nelson, Senator Gaylord, 348
Nervo, Amado, 145
Neutra, Richard, 197
New Alchemy Institute, 347
New American Poets, 247, 271
New Deal, 117, 174, 187, 217–8, 223
   Federal Writers' Project, 187
New Narrative movement, 10, 258–9
New York Public Theater, 135
New York School (poetry), 274, 276
New York State Psychiatric Institute, 233
New York Times, The, 79, 205, 236, 250, 285
New York World, 203
New Yorker, The, 202, 353
New World Writing, 240
Newbery Award, 223
Nicoleño, 223
Niedecker, Lorine, 257
Nin, Anaïs, 233, 238
Nisei, 127, 221, 318, 367
Nisei Experimental Group, 130
Nissenan, 25
Nixon, Richard, 215, 223, 330
Noguchi, Yone, 126
Noir, 3, 4, 186, 189, 205, 215, 223–6, 229, 230, 273, 296, 388
Norris, Frank, 3, 8, 69, 157, 158, 159–62, 163, 165, 168, 184, 359, 372
   "The Epic of the Wheat," 160, 185
   McTeague, 160
   Moran of the Lady Letty, 160
   Octopus, The, 160–2, 185
   Pit, The, 160, 185
   Wolf, The, 185
Norse, Harold, 252

Northern Californian, 84
Northup, Henry, 277
Norton Anthology of American Literature, 55
Norton Anthology of Poetry, 258

O'Dell, Scott, 223
   Island of the Blue Dolphins, 223
O'Hara, Frank, 266
Obama, President Barack, 365
Oberlin College (Preparatory Academy), 110–1
Occidental College, 99, 196
Occupy Movement, 259
Ohio State University, 118
Ohlone tribe, 5, 351
Okada, John, 131
   No-No Boy, 131
Okubo, Miné, 130
   Citizen 13660, 130
Olmsted, Frederick Law, 90, 94
Olson, Charles, 65, 240, 243, 254, 266, 268
   "Projective Verse," 254
Olson, Governor Culbert, 218
Ordaz, Fray Blas, 31
Organization of Afro-American Unity, 134
Orientalism, 136, 141
Orlovsky, Peter, 234
Orwell, George, 382
   1984, 382
Overland Monthly, 85, 86, 92, 95, 219, 359, 385
Owens Valley/Owens Valley Water Project, 95, 97, 99
Owens, Wilfred, 262

Pacific Crest Trail, 347, 357
Pacific Electric, 198
Pacific Lumber Company, 223
Pacific Union College at Angwin, 116
Pagee, Thomas, 242
Paiute, 222
Pak, Ty, 318
   "The Court Interpreter," 318, 322
Palgrave, Sir Francis, 385
   The History of Normandy and of England, 385
Palomares, José Francisco, 47
Palóu, Francisco, 45, 56, 57
   Noticias de la Nueva California, 57
   Relación histórica de la vida y apostólicas tareas del venerable Fray Junípero Serra, 57
Pape, Greg, 364
Paris Review, 249
Parker, Charlie ("Bird"), 247
Parker, Dorothy, 189, 202
Parkman, Francis, 62
Partido Liberal Mexicano (PLM), 185
Parvin, Roy, 363

Parvin, Roy, (cont.)
  In the Snow Forest, 363
  The Loneliest Road in America, 363
Patchen, Kenneth, 233
Pattie, James Ohio, 6, 65–6
Penguin Poets series, 276
People v. Hall (1854 California Supreme Court case), 124
Perelman, Bob, 256–7
Perkoff, Stuart, 237–9, 266–7, 269
  "The Recluses," 266
  The Suicide Room, 237
Percival, Olive, 261
Pérez, Eulalia, 47
  Una vieja y sus recuerdos, 47
Pérez, Louis, 152
  The Girls of the Pink Feather, 152
Pérez, Luis, 151–2
  El Coyote, the Rebel, 151
Perry, Darthard, 272
Persky, Stan, 252
Picaresque Novel, 141, 151, 306, 311
Pico, María Inocenta, 47
  Cosas de California, 47
picturesque, 89–90, 359 (see also Sublime)
Pillin, William, 264
Pinkerton detective, 199–200, 201
Planet Drum Foundation, 347
Poe, Edgar Allan, 199
Poetics Journal, 257
Poetry Flash, 256, 259
Pollan, Michael, 354
  Botany of Desire, The, 354
  Cooked, 354
  In Defense of Food, 354
  Omnivore's Dilemma, The, 354
Pomo Indian, 351, 364
Ponce, Mary Helen, 298
  Hoyt Street: An Autobiography, 298
Pope, Marion Holden, 261
Popotillo, 145
Popular Culture, 3, 83, 147–9, 275, 356, 386
Porter, Bern, 248
  Berkeley: A Journal of Modern Culture, 248
Pound, Ezra, 173, 188, 193, 254, 268
Powell, John Wesley, 346
Powell, Lawrence Clark, 166, 197
Powell, William, 203
Prado, Holly, 277
Pre-Columbian society, 30
Preston, Richard, 356
  The Wild Trees, 356
Price, Jennifer, 356
  Flight Maps, 356
  "Thirteen Ways of Seeing Nature in LA," 356

Priestley, Eric, 272
Proletarian Culture, 8, 144, 147–9, 152, 164, 172
Proposition 8, 329, 337
Proposition 22, 338
Protest Fiction, 157–70, 389
Pulitzer Prize, 220, 255, 334, 347, 349
punk movement, 274
Pynchon, Thomas, 362, 363, 376, 387
  The Crying of Lot 49, 376–77, 387
  Vineland, 362

Quicksilver Messenger Service, 243
Quinn, Anthony, 197

Ramírez, Francisco F., 49–50
  El Clamor Público, 49–50
Ramiro, Mariano, 145
  "El Base Ball," 145
Ransom, John Crowe, 254
Rappe, Virginia, 200
Ray, Man, 248
Reagan, President Ronald, 11, 135, 259, 329, 331
Realis (genre), 46, 85, 160, 161, 164, 172–4, 180, 184, 215, 216, 229, 374
Rebolledo, Efrén, 145
Rechy, John, 329
  City of Night, 329
Reed College, 235
Reed, Ishmael, 11, 285–6, 288
  Flight to Canada, 286
  Free-Lance Pallbearers, The, 285
  Japanese by Spring, 286
  Last Days of Louisiana Red, The, 285
  Mumbo Jumbo, 285
  Reckless Eyeballing, 286
  Terrible Threes, The, 286
  Terrible Twos, The, 286
  Yellow Black Radio Broke-Down, 285
Reed, James, 67
Regionalist (vernacular dialect), 85, 218, 247, 358
Reisner, Marc, 353
  Cadillac Desert, 353
Replansky, Naomi, 264
Revoyr, Nina, 320, 322
  Southland, 320
Rexroth, Kenneth, 232–6, 238, 240–1, 243, 246, 247, 248, 249, 267, 345
  Dragon and the Unicorn, The, 345
  "Thou Shalt Not Kill," 240
Rice, Craig, 238 (see also Lawrence Lipton)
Ridge, John Rollin (Yellow Bird), 6, 13, 82, 388
  The Life and Adventures of Joaquín Murieta, the Celebrated California Bandit, 6, 82, 388
Rimbaud, Arthur, 276
Rios, Frank, 237, 268

Ritchie, Ward, 197
Rivera, Diego, 387
Rivera, Tomás, 296
  Y no se lo tragó la tierra, 296
Robertson, David, 355
  Real Matter, 355
Robin Hood of El Dorado, The (film), 388
Robinson, Edwin Arlington, 262
Robinson, Kim Stanley, 378
  Gold Coast, The, 378
  Pacific Edge, 378
  Wild Shore, The, 378
Robinson, Kit, 256
Rodgers, Richard and Oscar Hammerstein II, 133, 386
  Flower Drum Song, 133, 386
Rodriguez, Luis, 297, 304
  Always Running: La Vida Loca: Gang Days in L. A., 304
  Republic of East LA, 297, 304–5
    "Chicas Chuecas," 305
    "La Operación," 305
    "Pigeons," 304
    "Sometimes You Dance with a Watermelon," 304–5
Rodriguez, Richard, 65, 332, 333, 334, 338
  Brown, 338
  Days of Obligation, 334
  Hunger of Memory, 333
Roley, Brian Ascalon, 310–11
  American Son, 310–11
Rolfe, Edwin, 264
Rosenfield, Kim, 276
Roosevelt, Franklin Delano, 117, 171, 218
Roosevelt, Theodore, 7, 94, 159, 180
Roy, Camille, 259
Royce, Josiah, 69, 72, 198
Royce, Sarah, 69
  Across the Plains, 69
Ruiz de Burton, María Amparo, 6, 44, 45–7
  Squatter and the Don, The, 46–7
  Who Would Have Thought It?, 45–6
Rumaker, Michael, 249
Ruskin, John, 91
Russell, Bertrand, 193
Russo-Japanese War, 126, 128

Sagebrush School, 84
Salas, Floyd, 297, 298
  Buffalo Nickel, 298
  Tattoo the Wicked Cross, 297
Salt Dreams (Sierra Club Exhibit Format; William DeBuy and Joan Meyers), 355
Salton Sea (film), 230

Salvador Roldan v. Los Angeles County (1933 California Supreme Court case), 129
Samuels, Albert, 200, 201
San Francisco Chronicle, 79, 224, 231, 386
San Francisco Earthquake of 1906, 98, 127, 141
San Francisco Police Department, 379
  SFPD Juvenile Bureau, 242
San Francisco Renaissance, 227, 233, 236, 237, 240, 243, 244, 246 (see also Berkeley Renaissance)
San Francisco Riot of 1877, 124
San Francisco State College, 134
  Poetry Center, 234
San Francisco State University, 288
  Black Studies Program, 288
Sánchez, Rosaura and Beatrice Pita, 381
  Lunar Braceros, 2125–2148, 381
Sanders, Ed, 244
Saroyan, Aram, 359
Saroyan, William, 220–1, 227, 360, 370
  Human Comedy, The, 220
  My Name is Aram, 220
  Time of Your Life, The, 220
Sarris, Greg, 351, 364, 370
  Grand Avenue, 364
  Mabel McKay, 351
Sartre, Jean-Paul, 248
Saturday Evening Post, 79, 185
Save the Redwoods League, 347
Sawyer, John O., 356
  Northwest California, 356
Scalapino, Leslie, 255
Scheyer, Galka, 197
Schönberg, Arnold, 248
Schindler, Pauline, 206
Schindler, Rudolph, 197
Schulberg, Bud, 272 (see also Watts Writers Workshop)
Schuyler, James, 266
Schwarzenegger, Arnold, 284, 357
Scibella, Tony, 237, 268
Science fiction, 4, 11, 12, 285, 287, 291, 371–83, 388
Scott, Sir Walter, 99
Scott, Ridley, 379 (see also, *Blade Runner*)
Scottsboro Boys, 193, 194, 197
Screenwriters Guild, 203
Sea Shepherds, 350
Second Wave Feminism, 10, 250, 333
See, Carolyn, 375
  Golden Days, 375
Serra, Junípero, 6, 32, 45, 54, 56–7
Sessions, Roger, 248
Shasta, 23–4
Shaw, George Bernard, 193
Shaw, Jimmy, 230

Shepard, Sam, 386
  True West, 386
Sierra Club, 6, 94, 101, 346, 347, 350, 355
Sierra Club Exhibit Format (book series), 355
Silko, Leslie Marmon, 385
Silliman, Ron, 246, 255–7, 258
  The Alphabet, 257
Silverman, Aaron and Molly Maguire, 388
  The Raymond Chandler Mystery Map of Los Angeles, 388
Simon Fraser University, 255
Simon, Neil, 386
  California Suite, 386
Simon, Ted, 353
  The River Stops Here, 353
Simpson, Mona, 385
Sino-Japanese War, 128
Sinclair, Upton, 3, 8, 98, 157, 158, 165–7, 178, 186, 187, 218
  Cry for Justice (anthology), 158–9
  Depression Island, 178
  "I Candidate for Governor of California and How I Got Licked," 178
  "I Governor of California, and How I Ended Poverty – A True Story of the Future," 178
  Jungle, The, 165
  King Coal, 165
  Money Writes, 166
  Oil! A Novel, 166–7, 187
  "Shall We Murder Rockefeller"
  Singing Jailbirds, 166
Singin' in the Rain (film), 386
Sir Francis Drake Hotel, 234
Sister Spit, 337
Six Gallery, 232, 234, 238, 240, 246, 255
Skelley, Jack, 274, 276
  "Text," 276
Slavery (chattel), 105, 106, 108, 109, 113, 273, 292, 381, 382
Sleepy Lagoon Defense Committee, 197–8
Sleepy Lagoon Case, The (pamphlet), 198
Sleepy Lagoon Mystery, The (pamphlet), 198
Smith, Anna Deavere, 11
  Twilight: Los Angeles, 288
Smith, Jedediah, 65
Snyder, Gary, 70, 136, 227, 231, 232, 235, 247, 249, 255, 256, 266, 345, 349, 355
  "A Berry Feast," 235
  A Place in Space, 350
  "Above Pate Valley," 227
  Back Country, The, 349
  Back on the Fire, 350
  "Hay for the Horses," 227
  Mountains and Rivers Without End, 350

Myths and Texts, 349
"Night Highway 99," 136
Practice of the Wild, The, 350
Riprap, 349
Riprap and Cold Mountain Poems, 227, 349
"Smokey the Bear Sutra," 250
Turtle Island, 349
Snyder, Ruth, 203–4
Solnit, Rebecca, 187, 355–6
  Infinite City, 355
  River of Shadows, 356
  Savage Dreams, 356
  Yosemite in Time (with Mark Klett and Byron Wolfe), 356
Solomon, Carl, 233
Sone, Monica, 131
  Nisei Daughter, 131
Soto, Gary, 230, 297–301, 365
  A Summer Life, 298, 300
  Elements of San Joaquin, 230, 301
  Living up the Street, 298, 300
Spada, Sixto, 145
Spear, Roberta, 365
Speculative fiction, 336, 371–3, 375, 377
Spicer, Jack, 234, 235, 236, 237, 240, 241, 243, 249, 252, 253, 254, 255, 258, 266
  After Lorca, 253, 258
  Book of Magazine Verse, 253
  J, 253
  "The Unvert Manifesto and Other Papers Found in the rare Book Room of the Boston Public Library in the Handwriting of Oliver Charming. By. S.," 253
Spingarn, Lawrence, 264
Sputnik, 231
Stanford, Ann, 264
Stanford Asian American Theater Project, 135
Stanley, George, 237, 252
Steffens, Lincoln, 186, 194
Stegner, Wallace, 4, 346–7, 351
  Angle of Repose, 347
  Beyond the Hundredth Meridian, 346
  Conversations with Wallace Stegner on Western History and Literature, 346
  One Way to Spell Man, 346
  The Sound of Mountain Water, 346
  "The Wilderness Letter," 346
  Where the Bluebird Sings to the Lemonade Springs, 346–7
Stein, Gertrude, 247, 248, 327
  Everybody's Autobiography, 327
Steinbeck, John, 8, 65, 69, 157, 158, 159, 163, 168–74, 180, 194, 216, 220, 221, 227, 301, 359, 360, 370, 389
  Cup of Gold, 174

East of Eden, 168, 180
Grapes of Wrath, The, 8, 9, 163, 168–70, 171–2, 174, 216, 301
In Dubious Battle, 174
Sea of Cortez, 158
To a God Unknown, 168, 174
Sterling, George, 98, 190, 195, 261
Steve Allen Show, The, 239
Stewart, George R., 172
Ordeal by Hunger, 172
Stewart, Priscilla, 110
"A Voice from the Oppressed to the Friends of Humanity," 110
Stewart, Ramona, 224–5
Desert Town, 224–5
DOA, 225
High Sierra, 225
Out of the Past, 225
Stoddard, Charles Warren, 85, 93, 98
Stoddard, Elizabeth Drew, 75–6, 80, 359
Stonewall, 10, 329
Stowe, Harriet Beecher, 46, 76, 170
Uncle Tom's Cabin, 46, 76, 170, 216
Strayed, Cheryl, 356
Wild, 356–7
sublime, 89–90, 91, 187, 224, 343 (See also picturesque)
Sulfur (magazine), 277
Sullivan, Noel, 192, 194
Summer of Love, 231, 243
Sun & Moon Press, 277
Sunset (magazine), 187, 286
Surrealism/surrealists, 247, 249, 265, 267, 269, 276
Sycamore, Mattilda Bernstein, 338, 339
End of San Francisco, The, 339
So Many Ways to Sleep Badly, 338

Tac, Pablo, 5, 30, 31–7, 40, 42, 389
Indian Life and Customs at Mission San Luis Rey, 5
Prose Lingua Californeses, 33
Tagore, Rabindranath, 145
Takahashi, Mutsuo, 252
Takao Ozawa v. US, 128
Tamalpais Walking (Sierra Club Exhibit Format; Tom Killion and Gary Snyder), 355
Taylor, Paul, 9, 172–3, 216 (see also Dorothea Lange)
"Again the Covered Wagon," 173
An American Exodus: A Record of Human Erosion, 9, 172, 216
Tea, Michelle, 334, 337–8
Rent Girl, 337–8
Valencia, 337–8

Temblor, 277 (magazine; see also Hickman, Lee)
Tennyson, Alfred Lord, 330
"The Lotus-Eaters," 330
Tervalon, Jervey, 287–8
Dead Above Ground, 288
Understand This, 287
Teske, Edmund, 264
Testimony/testimonios, 44–5, 47–8, 54, 110, 173, 205, 243, 258, 306
Third World Liberation Front (TWLF), 134
Thomas, Dylan, 238, 240
Thomas, John, 268
"The Passionate Shepherd to his Love," 268–9
Story of the Eye, 268
Thomas, Joyce Carol, 288, 289–90
Bittersweet, 289
Blessing, 289
Bright Shadows, 289, 290
Crystal Breezes, 289
Inside the Rainbow: A Collection of Poems, 289
"To a Chicano," 289
"Where Is the Black Community?," 289
"Little Girl Born Black," 289
Marked by Fire, 289, 290
Thompson, Eloise Bibb, 110–12
A Reply to the Clansman, 111
Africans, 111
Caught, 111
Cooped Up, 111
"Mademoiselle Tate," "Masks," 111
Thompson, Hunter S., 10
Thoreau, Henry David, 76, 92, 94
Walden, 76
Thurman, Wallace, 106, 114–5
Fire!!, 114
The Blacker the Berry, 114
Thúy, Lê Thi Diem, 312
"The Gangster We are All Looking For," 312
Tijuana, Mexico, 210, 211, 264, 297, 305, 306
Tirado, Romualdo, 148
Los de abajo (play adaptation), 148
Tongva Tribe, 260 (see also Gabrielinos)
Tourism, 88, 187, 190, 222
Towne, Robert, 386 (see also, *Chinatown*)
Townsend, James ("Lying Jim"), 84
Trace (literary journal), 264
Travel Narrative, 52, 53, 54–55, 69, 93
Treaty of Guadalupe Hidalgo, 105, 139
Trinidad, David, 274, 276
Trocchi, Alexander, 237, 268
Cain's Book, 237, 268
Troupe, Quincy, 272, 286, 288
Autobiography of Miles Davis, The, 286
Avalanche, 286
Choruses, 286

Troupe, Quincy, (cont.)
  Embryo, 286
  Errancities, 286
  Skulls Among the River, 286
  Snake-Back Solos: Selected Poems 1969–1977, 286
  Trancircularities: New and Revised Poems, 286
    "Come Sing a Song," 286
    "For Malcolm, Who Walks in the Eyes of Children," 286
    "Ode to John Coltrane," 286
  Weather Reports, 286
Trujillo, Carla, 338
  What Night Brings, 338
Turner, Frederick Jackson, 3, 7
  "The Significance of the Frontier in American History," 3
Twain, Mark (Samuel Clemens), 6, 13, 84, 85, 90, 216, 359, 360, 385
  Adventures of Huckleberry Finn, The, 84
  "Jim Smiley and His Jumping Frog," 84
  Roughing It, 6, 84
  "The Celebrated Jumping Frog of Calaveras County," 359
  "Whittier's Birthday Speech," 360
Tydings-McDuffie Act, 129
Tyndall, John, 91

UNESCO World Heritage, 347
Ulica, Jorge (Julio G. Arce), 143–4, 153
  "Crónicas diabólicas," 143
  "Do You Speak Pocho," 143
  "La estenógrafa," 144
  "Los 'Parladores de Spanish,'" 144
Ulin, David, 356
  The Myth of Solid Ground, 356
Underground Railroad, 108
Union Oil, 348
United Farm Workers, 316
University of California
  UC-Berkeley, 44, 128, 134, 252, 289
  UCLA, 1, 132
  UC San Diego, 286, 292
University of Nebraska, 259
University of Nevada Press, 370
University of Southern California, 99, 115, 196
University of Washington, 99
University of Wisconsin, 92
Urrea, Luis Alberto, 295, 296, 297, 304–6
  Across the Wire: Life and Hard Times on the Mexican Border, 306
  By the Lake of Sleeping Children, 306
  Devil's Highway, The, 306
  Into the Beautiful North, 295, 306
  Nobody's Son, 305
US v. Bhagat Singh Thind (1923 US Supreme Court case), 128

Valdez, Luis, 296, 388
Vallejo, Mariano Guadalupe, 6, 44–8
  Recuerdos históricos personales tocante a la Alta California, 44–6
Vallejo, Platón, 47, 151
  Memoirs of the Vallejos, 47
Vallejo, Salvador, 47
  Notas históricas sobre California, 47
Van Der Veer, Judy, 226
  November Grass, 226
Van Gogh, Vincent, 271
  "Starry Night," 271
Vangelisti, Paul (*Invisible City* Press), 277
Venegas, Daniel, 51, 148, 153, 296
  El con-su-lado, 148
  El Malcriado, 148
  Las Aventuras de Don Chipote (*The Adventures of Don Chipote*), 51, 296
  El maldito jazz, 148
  Esclavos, 148
Vidal, Gore, 329
  Myra Breckinridge, 329
Vietnam War, 9, 10, 132, 134, 254, 296, 309, 315, 316, 317, 348
Villaespesa, Francisco, 145
Villarreal, José Antonio, 221, 295–7, 299, 304
  Pocho, 221, 295, 299, 304
Viramontes, Helena María, 230, 298, 301, 305
  Their Dogs Came with Them, 305
  Under the Feet of Jesus, 230, 298, 301
Vollman, William T., 364
  Imperial, 364

Waldman, Anne, 244
Walker, Alice, 290
  The Color Purple, 290
  The Third Life of Grange Copeland, 290
Walker, Franklin, 191
  Seacoast of Bohemia, 191
Wallace, David Rains, 352, 355
  Articulate Earth, 355
  Chuckwalla Land, 352
  Dark Range, 352
  Klamath Knot, The, 352
  Neptune's Ark, 352
  Turquoise Dragon, The, 352
  Vermilion Parrot, The, 352
  Wilder Shore, The, 355 (see also, Morley Baer)
Wambaugh, Joseph, 211
War Brides Act of 1945, 133

Index

Ward, Artemus (Charles Farrar Browne), 84
Warren, Earl, 218
Waters, Alice, 353
   40 Years of Chez Panisse, 353
Watkins, Carleton, 89, 91
Watkins, T.H., 351
   On the Shore of the Sundown Sea, 351
   Time's Island, 351
Watten, Barrett, 256
Watts Riot, 7, 10
Watts Writers Workshop, 11, 261, 272, 273, 286
   (see also Bud Schulberg)
Waugh, Evelyn, 385
Weed, Charles, 89
Weisburd, Mel, 264
weiss, ruth, 244
Welch, Lew, 345
Welles, Orson, 197, 306
   A Touch of Evil (film), 306
West, George, 174
   "Starving Pea Pickers," 174
West, Kanye and Kim Kardashian Wedding, 277
West, Nathanael, 2, 9, 178–80, 189
   The Day of the Locust, 2, 178–9
Weston, Edward, 98, 194, 196, 197
Whalen, Philip, 232, 235, 237, 241, 247, 249, 255, 266, 345
   "If You're So Smart, Why Ain't You Rich?," 235
   "*Plus Ça Change,*" 235
Whitfield, James Monroe, 112–3, 120
   "America," 113
   "How Long," 113
Whitman, Walt, 76, 236, 251, 263
   Leaves of Grass, 76
   "Whoever You Are Holding Me Now in Hand," 251
Whitney, Josiah D., 91, 92
   The Yosemite Book, 91
Whittier, John Greenleaf, 360
Wilderness (magazine), 351
Williams, Jonathan, 237
Williams, Shirley Anne, 292, 365
   Dessa Rose, 292
   Peacock Poems, The, 292–3
      "Any Woman's Blues," 292
      "This Is a Sad-Ass Poem for a Black Woman to Be Writing," 292
   Working Cotton, 292
Williams, William Carlos, 240, 271
   Paterson, 269
   "To Elsie," 271
Wilson, Darryl Babe, 230
   The Morning the Sun Went Down, 230

Wilson, Edmund, 157
   "The Boys in the Back Room," 157
Wilson, Harry Leon, 194
Winter, "Red" Ella, 193, 194
Winters, Yvor, 228
Witt-Diamant, Ruth, 234
Wizard of Oz, The (film), 179
Wong, Jade Snow, 126, 133, 180
   Fifth Chinese Daughter, 126
Wong, Shawn, 135, 136
   Homebase, 136–7
Wood, Charles Erskine Scott, 194
Woods, Daniel B., 78
   Sixteen Months at the Gold Diggings, 78
Woods, Russell, 242
Woodstock, 243
Working Class, 8, 51, 63, 134, 147, 166, 264, 315
World Wildlife Fund, 347
Wright, Frank Lloyd, 196, 197, 248
Wright, Harold Bell, 219

Yamamoto, Hisaye, 131–2, 318, 322
   "A Fire in Fontana," 318
   "Epithalamium," 131
   Seventeen Syllables, 131
   "The Brown House," 131
   "The High-Heeled Shoes," 131
   "Wilshire Bus," 131–2
   "Yoneko's Earthquake," 131
Yamashita, Karen Tei, 315–7, 321, 379–80, 387
   I Hotel, 315, 316–7
   Tropic of Orange, The, 379–80, 387
Yamauchi, Wakako, 135, 221–2
   And the Soul Shall Dance, 135, 221–2
   Music Lessons, The, 135
Yardbird Reader, 285
Yates, Peter, 264
Yeats, William Butler, 206, 254
Yerba Buena (California), 336
Yokut, 24–5, 40, 41
Yosemite Valley, Yosemite, 6, 7, 67, 86, 88–92, 94, 333, 353, 356
Young, Al, 284–5, 288
   Ask Me Now, 285
   Dancing, 284
   Snakes, 285
   Who Is Angelina?, 285
Young People's Socialist League, 197
Yuma, 36
Yurok, 18

Zahn, Curtis, 264
   "Tijuana," 264–5
Zeitlin, Jacob, 196–7
Zoot Suit Riots of 1943, 139